PENGUIN BOOKS

MAO AND CHINA

Stanley Karnow began his journalistic career in Paris in 1950 as a *Time* correspondent. After serving as chief correspondent in Asia for *Time* and *Life,* he reported from there for *The Washington Post.* He has been a correspondent for *The Observer* of London, *The Saturday Evening Post,* and NBC News as well as an editor of *The New Republic* and a syndicated columnist. He is the author of *Southeast Asia, Vietnam: A History,* and *In Our Image: America's Empire in the Philippines.* He was chief correspondent for the series "Vietnam: A Television History," and for "The U.S. and the Philippines: In Our Image." Born in New York City, he was educated at Harvard College, the Sorbonne, and the École des Sciences Politiques in Paris. He was a Nieman Fellow at Harvard, a Fellow of the John F. Kennedy School of Government at Harvard, a Fellow of the East Asia Research Center at Harvard, and a Poynter Fellow at Yale. He served in the U.S. Army in the China-Burma-India theater during World War II. A resident of Potomac, Maryland, he is married to Annette Karnow, a painter, and has three children and a grandchild.

D0094386

MAO AND CHINA

A Legacy of Turmoil

STANLEY KARNOW

Introduction by Nien Cheng

Third Edition

PENGUIN BOOKS

PENGUIN BOOKS
Published by the Penguin Group
Viking Penguin, a division of Penguin Books USA Inc.,
40 West 23rd Street, New York, New York 10010, U.S.A.
Penguin Books Ltd, 27 Wrights Lane,
London W8 5TZ, England
Penguin Books Australia Ltd, Ringwood,
Victoria, Australia
Penguin Books Canada Ltd, 2801 John Street,
Markham, Ontario, Canada L3R 1B4
Penguin Books (N.Z.) Ltd, 182–190 Wairau Road,
Auckland 10, New Zealand

Penguin Books Ltd, Registered Offices:
Harmondsworth, Middlesex, England

First published in the United States of America by
The Viking Press 1972
Published with a new introduction by
the author in Penguin Books 1984
This revised and updated edition with an introduction by
Nien Cheng published in Penguin Books 1990

1 3 5 7 9 10 8 6 4 2

Copyright © Stanley Karnow, 1972, 1984, 1990
Introduction copyright © Nien Cheng, 1990
All rights reserved

Acknowledgment is made to Praeger Publishers, Inc.,
for material quoted from *Shanghai Journal*,
by Neale Hunter. Copyright © Frederick A. Praeger, Inc., 1969,
reprinted by permission.

LIBRARY OF CONGRESS CATALOGING IN PUBLICATION DATA
Karnow, Stanley.
Mao and China: a legacy of turmoil / Stanley Karnow;
introduction by Nien Cheng.—Updated 3rd ed.
p.   cm.
Originally published: New York: Viking Press, 1972.
Includes bibliographical references.
ISBN 0 14 013.417 4
1. China—History—Cultural Revolution, 1966–1969.   2. Mao Tse-
tung, 1893–1976.   I. Title.
DS778.7.K37   1990
951.05'6—dc20   89-49315

Printed in the United States of America

Set in Caledonia
Designed by Wilma Jane Weichselbaum

To the memory of my father

INTRODUCTION

ANYONE who seeks to understand the Communist revolution in China should read this book. It is objective, factual, and lucid. One of the most distinguished journalists of our time and a gifted writer, Mr. Karnow "makes flowers bloom under his pen," as the Chinese say: *bi xia shen hua*. History comes to life with his perceptive analysis of events as well as the personalities of the leading players. Although a history of the Cultural Revolution and the background of events preceding the upheaval, it reads like a gripping political novel, absorbing and informative.

Mao and China was first published in 1972. It has stood the test of time. To have it reissued now is timely and relevant to the understanding of events in China today. The economic reform, the Open Door policy, and the people's demand for democracy all have their roots in the traumatic events of the ten years of the Cultural Revolution (1966–1976). Many of the Party leaders in power today were victims of the power struggle during those years and bear the scar of the psychological impact of their humiliation in the hands of the Red Guards. At the same time, the widespread suffering and general disillusion of the people have compelled them to reexamine the political system under which they live and emboldened them to seek alternatives. The Cultural Revolution irrevocably changed Communist China and irreparably damaged the relationship between the Chinese people and the government. This book gives us a clear account of the most serious power struggle within the Communist leadership and the greatest tragedy suffered by the Chinese people in modern history as a result of that struggle.

In the decades before President Richard Nixon so audaciously pushed open the door of Communist China, the country was closed to Americans. The only Americans living there were the few Communist sympathizers who took Chinese citizenship and worked in Beijing, mostly with Chinese government organizations engaged in publishing foreign-language propaganda journals, and a handful of Korean War ex-prisoners who opted to stay in China after falling victim to brainwashing. As a result, the tiny British colony of Hong Kong on China's doorstep became the logical place from which American journalists and experts could monitor China. They were aptly called "China watchers," a corps of highly qualified observers whose ranks Mr. Karnow joined in the late fifties. He arrived just in time to watch the disastrous aftermath of Mao Zedong's outlandish campaign to promote industrial and agricultural production by mobilizing the masses to organize rural communes and to operate urban factories in nonstop production. Productivity declined and machines broke down. China's economy was pushed to the brink of ruin. Mao lost power and had to relinquish his position as Chairman of the People's Republic to Liu Shaoqi. To recover his status as supreme leader of the Communist Party and the Chinese people, he launched the Cultural Revolution.

Perhaps nowhere else in the world were the Chinese Communist press and government documents so systematically translated and made available to journalists and writers for their interpretation as in Hong Kong. Its geographical proximity and Chinese population made it possible to include in this rich haul such items as provincial newspapers banned for export and internal government documents not intended for the eyes of foreigners. For interviews, there was always a stream of refugees, fleeing persecution or economic hardship, as well as European and Asian visitors to China passing through the British colony. *Mao and China* is outstanding because Mr. Karnow had the training, experience, and empathy to evaluate the wealth of information available to him.

No other book on the Cultural Revolution has a fuller account of the Red Guard movement. The young students brought up since 1949 knew nothing of either the outside world or China's history before the Communist takeover. Taught from infancy to worship Mao Zedong and to obey his commands, they were his natural choice to carry out the initial stage of the Cultural Revolution, when Mao wanted to catch his opponents in the Party leadership by surprise. The young people were organized by Mao's wife, who was assisted by the Army behind the scenes. They were told to destroy the Four Olds: old culture, old customs, old habits, and old ideas. Their slogan was: "If we do not destroy the poisonous weeds of capitalism, the scented flowers of socialism cannot flourish." As they went on a rampage of looting and destruction, they were praised and urged on by speeches of Maoist officials on the committee to conduct the Cultural Revolution and by editorials in the Party newspapers. And they were told to rout out the class enemies, including ex-capitalists, intellectuals, and people with foreign connections, as well as Party officials who were accused of betraying socialism by favoring the capitalist road. After they brought down the local governments and humiliated the Party bureaucrats, the Red Guards split into opposing groups and engaged in factional fighting. There was much bloodshed as they stole guns and ammunition from local garrisons. Mao had to impose military control. Then he sent the Red Guards to the countryside to "learn from the peasants." Many of the young people were banished for years, not allowed to return home until after Mao died. Never in China's long history has a whole generation of young people been so ruthlessly used and discarded. Undereducated and without skill, many of the ex–Red Guards allowed to return to the cities became manual laborers or were unemployed. Since the Communist government has officially denounced the Cultural Revolution as a "national catastrophe," the ex–Red Guards bear the stigma of having been the spearhead of the upheaval. The resentment of the ex–Red Guards against the Communist Party and their frustration with life in general constitute a dangerous destabilizing factor in Chinese society, rather like a time bomb waiting to explode.

While solidly informative, Mr. Karnow's book has its lighter moments. One of the most revelatory chapters includes an extensive interview with Albert Belhomme, an American soldier who had defected to the Chinese after the Korean War. He was settled as a factory worker by the Chinese government in Jinan, in the Shandong peninsula. He married a Chinese woman of peasant origin and lived the life of the working class, receiving none of the special treatment usually accorded an approved foreigner. Living in obscurity and accepted by his fellow workers as one of them, he shared their lives and activities without restraint and became eyewitness as well as participant in some of Mao Zedong's ill-conceived schemes to change China and to promote economic development by hysterical mass effort. In graphic language and with a sense of humor, he recounted such Maoist campaigns as "weeding out doubtful elements," "people's trials," "making steel in backyard furnaces," and "to kill the sparrows," and their effects on the lives and fortunes of those around him. Albert Belhomme's testimony was unique and significant because few foreigners would normally have the opportunity to mingle with the Chinese people as he did.

When Mao Zedong took over in China in 1949, he had a singular opportunity to lead the nation in peaceful economic development and recovery from the ravages of eight years of resistance against the Japanese invasion and three years of a civil war in which millions of

Chinese were killed or impoverished. But he was obsessed with the maintenance of his personal power and the theory of perpetual revolution. He dreamed of creating in China a model Communist society to be emulated by other Third World nations. And he wanted to go down in the history of the world Communist movement as the one leader who had successfully transformed an agrarian society into a modern industrial state by applying orthodox Marxist principles. To achieve his purpose, he had to ensure his position of supremacy and to mobilize the Chinese people. Periodically, he launched violent political campaigns to destroy potential enemies, real or imagined; and he removed from office those Communist leaders whom he considered a threat to his power and position. He used political means such as Party directives to regulate the economy and promote growth, and he tried to stimulate the people's enthusiasm by mobilizing them in mass campaigns. The result was erratic development, production increases alternating with stagnation or starvation. In all the twenty-seven years Mao ruled China (1949–1976), the Chinese people were never free from severe rationing of all daily necessities.

Mao Zedong habitually disregarded the individual rights and aspirations of the Chinese people. He saw them as divided into conflicting classes in a permanent state of antagonism. The workers and the poor peasants he considered his natural allies; and he used them to persecute the businessmen, the industrialists, the educated elite collectively referred to as "the capitalist class," his and the Party's potential enemies. The result was a fragmented society and mutual distrust among the population instead of unity and harmony. At the same time, perpetual revolution in the form of one political campaign after another kept everybody in a constant state of tension and insecurity. For self-preservation, people had to lie and spy on each other. Having had their dignity and self-respect repeatedly trampled and their honor compromised, many people became self-seeking and dishonest. And the inevitable executions, imprisonments, and exiles after each political campaign alienated millions of victims and their family members. When Mao Zedong took over the country, he was looked upon as a heroic revolutionary leader who was going to put China on her feet again. When he died in 1976, the Chinese people saw him as a symbol of cruelty and repression.

The present, aged leaders in Beijing were longtime comrades of Mao Zedong who had survived his turbulent years. In spite of personal ups and downs, they had shared Mao's power and helped him govern China. They are cast in Mao's image and limited by his thinking. As long as these old men are in charge, there is little hope for real progress in China. Since the hard-liners gained the upper hand after the Tiananmen Massacre, economic reform is stalled. Because China badly needs the infusion of foreign capital, the leadership pledged to keep the Open Door policy. What portends after Deng Xiaoping passes from the scene, no one can foresee. But the Communist world is changing. China cannot forever remain the odd man out. To follow whatever trend events take in the future, this book is indispensable.

Nien Cheng

PREFACE

THIS book, which largely concentrates on Mao Zedong's Great Proletarian Cultural Revolution, was published first in late 1972 and again in early 1984. Enormous changes occurred in China during that interval, and the years since have been equally dramatic. But these changes cannot be understood without looking back to the Cultural Revolution, a cataclysm whose consequences account for much of the strife that continues to roil China. Or, as Professor Roderick MacFarquhar of Harvard puts it, the Cultural Revolution is the "dark penumbra" that overshadows China's present and will certainly cloud its future. Hence the need for this new, revised edition.

Mao's last convulsive gasp, the Cultural Revolution was an extravagant vision that spiraled into almost incredible madness, a supposedly lofty dream that degenerated into a nightmare for millions, an experiment that was applauded by many as idealistic but which, in retrospect, ranks as one of the most horrendous episodes in human history. Mao died in 1976, yet his ghost still haunts China—as it will for decades, perhaps generations, to come.

Indeed, his presence was palpable in the huge portrait of himself that peered across Beijing's Tiananmen Square, where, early on the morning of June 4, 1989, Chinese troops slaughtered hundreds of students peacefully demonstrating for democracy. Deng Xiaoping, the octogenarian Chinese leader, approved the order to the soldiers rather than offer concessions that, he felt, would be construed as a sign of weakness and thus compromise his authority. He may have also feared a revival of the turmoil triggered by Mao, which had counted him among its victims. Foreign commentators described the suppression as the worst committed by the Communists since their takeover of China forty years before. The observation was woefully wrong. The massacre, and the arrests and the executions that followed, were not the harshest of the Communist regime's crackdowns—but, thanks to the Western television crews who filmed and broadcast the events, only the most ruthless the world had witnessed. By conservative estimate, scores of millions have died of brutality or famine during the Communist decades.

Mao was chiefly responsible, but for years his Party comrades supported him. With the establishment of their government in China in 1949, they assumed control over a people whose attitudes and behavior had been shaped by codes of conduct dating back thousands of years. These codes, derived from the Confucian ethic, placed a premium on harmony, with the family as the locus of political and social relations. So traditional Chinese society was essentially cellular and fragmented and, as such, unable to modernize. Mao's aim was to eradicate this archaic system, and to transfer the loyalties of the individual from the clan to the nation. In the process, he asserted, the energies of the "masses" could be released, mobilized, and chan-neled into the construction of a powerful China. Despite his rhetorical fidelity to Marxist doctrine, with its emphasis on materialism, he was really propelled by a spiritual impulse. His ultimate objective, he proclaimed, was to transform the "soul" of China.

Mao maintained from the outset that the Communist seizure of China was not the revolution he envisioned, but merely the oppor-tunity to promote a genuine revolution. Unlike the Soviet rulers, who celebrate their triumph in 1917 as the Russian Revolution, he called his victory in 1949 the "Liberation"—the term suggesting that he had only emancipated China from his enemies, Chiang Kai-shek's reactionary Nationalists and their American backers. True and total revolution, he pledged, still lay ahead. And he and his colleagues were prepared to exact a formidable price in lives to fulfill that goal.

They began shortly after 1949 by executing hundreds of thousands of landlords under the guise of introducing agrarian reform. In reality, their purpose was to replace the old rural structure with their own apparatus. The peasants, who had been promised land, were instead shunted into collective farms. Many resisted, production slumped, and food shortages ravaged several areas. Briefly eclipsed by his Party rivals, who blamed him for the setback, Mao retaliated by urging intellectuals and others to criticize them with a colorful aphorism borrowed from the Chinese classics: "Let a hundred flowers bloom, let a hundred schools of thought contend." But it was a ruse to expose the critics, thousands of whom were liquidated or, if they survived, stigmatized for life as "rightists." Deng Xiaoping, then the Party Secretary General, played a key role in the purge. Despite his rev-olutionary pretensions, Mao compared himself to Emperor Qin Shi Huang, the unifier of China in 221 B.C., who had imposed his rule by burying dissenting scholars. "Qin Shi Huang only killed several hundred intellectuals," Mao reportedly said. "We have killed four hundred thousand."

Mao's next move, in 1958, was to launch the Great Leap Forward, a scheme to develop China swiftly. The audacious concept, his propagandists asserted, was not only superior to Moscow's bureaucratic approach, but heralded a "new historical era" that would thrust China ahead of the Soviet Union on the road toward perfect communism. Thus, they declared, Mao's creative genius was elevating Marxism to glorious, hitherto unattained heights. In practice, however, the plan verged on insanity as Mao put ideology in command. Millions, deprived of their possessions and herded into "people's communes," were forced to work day and night, tilling the fields, digging irrigation ditches, forging crude steel in makeshift furnaces. Despite their primitive equipment, factories were compelled to operate around the clock. Local cadres, anxious to trumpet success lest they be accused of failure, faked production reports, thereby prompting Mao to set higher targets and demand faster results. The consequences were catastrophic. The economy collapsed. Starvation killed or crippled millions, and some military units nearly mutinied.

Appalled by the disaster, Mao's comrades concluded that he had lost touch with reality and could no longer be trusted to manage the country. But, reluctant to challenge his immense personal prestige directly, they resorted to a time-honored Chinese maneuver. Just as ancient courtiers kowtowed to the emperor while deviously circumventing his dictates, so the senior Communist Party figures genuflected to Mao as they gradually reduced his influence. As he later remarked: "They treated me with the respect they would have shown their dead father at his own funeral."

Mao struck back in 1966 with the Cultural Revolution, an offensive designed to crush his foes and retrieve his power. His chosen instruments were the Red Guards, young men and women frustrated by a stagnant society that had stifled their dynamism. Organized under the auspices of his Defense Minister, Lin Biao, and fueled by his exhortations to smash the Party structure along with vestiges of the "feudal" past, they exploded in a series of wild rampages. A kind of nationwide dementia swept across China as they wantonly terrorized, tortured, and murdered Mao's real or suspected enemies. Hundreds of high officials were jailed or banished to remote rural areas, among them Liu Shaoqi, the Chief of State, and Deng himself. The victims included technicians, teachers, writers, artists, musicians, and former members of the landlord and bourgeois classes. To have studied abroad or have relatives overseas sufficed to be branded a "foreign agent." Many, their heads fouled with excrement, were paraded through the streets, and often beaten to death. No family, at least in the cities, was untouched. Children denounced their parents, and married couples, desperate to survive, accused one another of imaginary crimes. The campaign soon slid into chaos as rival factions battled each other, frequently with weapons stolen from the Army. At least a million deaths, coupled with tens of millions humiliated or driven to suicide, left the Chinese people exhausted, traumatized, and cynical.

The Cultural Revolution also left China vulnerable to the Soviet Union at a time when the two Communist giants, after years of mounting differences, were steering toward armed conflict. Mao, sensing the danger, suddenly perceived security in a countervailing *rapprochement* with the United States. Accordingly, he invited President Richard Nixon to Beijing in February 1972. The sensational breakthrough generated the momentum that led President Jimmy Carter to cement formal diplomatic ties with China six years later.

Mao's death meanwhile brought in pragmatic leaders headed by Deng, who realized that China could recover only through drastic economic reforms based on a combination of incentives and heavy doses of outside capital. Hence they rejected Maoist doctrine in favor of free-market forces. And they turned to Japan and the West for investment and guidance. Soon foreign businessmen, technicians, teachers, students, and tourists were pouring into China to an extent unseen since the Communists took over. Simultaneously, unprecedented numbers of Chinese traveled abroad, largely to learn Western technology. The United States and China vaunted their friendship, and even entered into cooperative military and intelligence arrangements. For Americans, who had always yearned to convert China to Western ways, the Chinese finally seemed to have redeemed themselves.

Deng's reforms, initiated in 1978, yielded spectacular results during the next decade as the Chinese economy grew at an annual average rate of 10 per cent. His achievement became visible as peasants began to build brick houses and acquire electrical appliances. So astonishing was his success, in fact, that Soviet and East European leaders contemplated China as a model. Despite its accomplishments, however, the new permissiveness was disrupting the society. Inflation grew at an alarming pace. Nepotism proliferated as top officials, including

Deng, placed their children and other relatives in lucrative posts, and corruption spread as they accepted bribes and kickbacks. Numbers of professors and students, dismayed by the trend, started to clamor for democracy—by which they meant government accountability. Interestingly, many considered themselves to be dedicated Communists who felt that the rush into unbridled capitalism was betraying the proletarian principles of social equality.

But Deng, determined to proceed along separate tracks, recoiled from pursuing liberal political policies to match his liberal economic programs. For he, better than anyone, knew that the Communist Party, largely demolished during the Cultural Revolution, was still too feeble to face reforms that would unravel the tattered shreds of its authority. He could not even bring himself to negotiate with the young demonstrators in Tienanmen Square. So, as their protests intensified, he replied with guns. His decision had not been spontaneous. Weeks before the troops and tanks rumbled into Beijing, he privately said: "It is worth killing two hundred thousand if it assures twenty years of stability."

But instead of guaranteeing stability, the massacre widened the rifts that had divided China for decades. It further split the fragile Communist Party, many of whose senior members opposed the use of force. It distressed several top military officers, who have long held that the Army's role was to help rather than repress the people. It alienated the Chinese academic community, whose scientists, technicians, and other experts are vital to the country's development. And it troubled Western businessmen, dampening their enthusiasm to invest in a land that might be nagged by recurrent volatility. Exacerbating the uncertainties was the fact that Deng and his close associates were old men who had not appointed successors to provide for a smooth transition following their deaths. Thus their disappearance threatened to leave a vacuum that might ignite a bitter struggle for power, thereby aggravating China's turmoil.

Only China's unpredictability is predictable. So this book offers few forecasts. But its historical perspective may contribute to a clearer grasp of the future, however it unfolds. Perhaps, then, it will serve as a guide to events—as its editions have for the past seventeen years.

S.K.

Potomac, Maryland
November 1989

CONTENTS

PART FOUR

From Revolution to Reaction

PART FIVE

The Pendulum Swings

PART ONE

MAO AND
CHINA

❧

Marxism can be translated into reality only through a national form. . . . The need, therefore, is to Sinicize Marxism.
> —MAO ZEDONG, *1938*

CHAPTER 1

The Vision and the Challenge

✤

> *Classes struggle, some classes triumph, others are eliminated. Such is history, such is the history of civilization for thousands of years.*
>
> — MAO ZEDONG, *August 1949*

NO CONTEMPORARY LEADER displayed such determination over so many years in his struggle to achieve his goals as did Mao Zedong in his endeavors to permeate China with his unique concept of communism. Nor did any modern statesman impose such profound, pervasive, and traumatic change on so many millions of people within so short a span of time. But Mao failed to fulfill his extravagant dream. Thus his obsessive campaigns, instead of renovating China, confronted his successors, following his death, with the stupendous task of reconstructing a society disrupted by his ambitions. It was a challenge that would test them for decades—and which promised to daunt future Chinese generations.

Beginning as an obscure peasant agitator, Mao fought nearly thirty years of protracted warfare in order to gain control of the most populous nation on earth. Once in power, his regime gave China greater political cohesion, social stability, economic promise, military muscle, and international prestige than that vast, unwieldy land had known in centuries. But these accomplishments, in Mao's view, were not enough. After consolidating his authority, he attempted to set in motion a process of perpetual revolution that would purify the "soul" of the Chinese people, cleanse them of their individualistic and materialistic tendencies, and ultimately spawn a new species of "Communist man" capable of propelling China toward wealth and strength through self-sacrifice and dedication. Persuaded that his theories had universal validity, he believed that this spiritual revolution would eventually inspire the entire world to imitate the Chinese model.

Thus Mao's ideology, with its stress on human perfectibility, was largely moralistic, missionary zeal cloaked in his own version of Marxist-Leninist language. His famous "little red book" of *Quotations*, which was designed to vitalize his followers, seemed to combine Confucian proverbs and Biblical axioms with homilies of the kind popularized by Benjamin Franklin and Samuel Smiles.[1]* His sermons, usually preached to small groups of activists, also emphasized his fundamentalism. Addressing a rump session of the Communist Party Central Committee in October 1966, for instance, Mao decried those who "strive only for personal fame and profit, power and position," and called for the cultivation of "men of the new morality . . . Communist men wholeheartedly and completely devoted to the people." They, rather than investment capital, modern technology, and advanced weapons, were to be the "determining factor" in the construction of the nation. "Men are central," he asserted. "To overlook men is to overlook the greatest productive force."[2]

Mao's persistent, obsessive drive to create this new human species repeatedly brought him into collision with the very attitudes he sought to transform. He was opposed by large numbers of Chinese intellectuals, who would not conform to his rigorous doctrines despite their initial sympathy with his practical programs. He was challenged by important figures among his early military supporters, whose later sophistication led them to question his premise that guerrilla techniques should take precedence over contemporary strategies of war. He was defied by economic specialists, who favored caution and rationality rather than his visionary mobilization schemes. He was rejected by a significant segment of the Chinese Communist Party apparatus, for whom government meant bureaucratic continuity rather than episodic upheavals. Even his cherished "masses," the poor peasants and workers, subtly subverted his efforts to harness them into China's primary source of energy—though, in the traditional style of Chinese genuflecting to ancient imperial edicts, they went through the ritual of celebrating the cult of his personality. This widespread resistance to his ideological impulses finally prompted Mao to launch his last, most intensive campaign, the Great Proletarian Cultural Revolution. In February 1967, explaining his reasons for having instigated that traumatic upheaval, he said:

*Numbered reference notes begin on page 501.

In the past, we waged struggles in the rural areas, in factories, in the cultural field. . . . But all this failed to solve the problem because we did not find a form, a method, to arouse the broad masses to expose our dark aspect openly, in an all-round way and from below. The answer was the Great Proletarian Cultural Revolution.[3]

Yet even during the Cultural Revolution, Mao discovered that the two principal pillars of his program were themselves corroded by the self-seeking attitudes he was determined to eradicate. The Red Guards and other young radicals, urged by Mao to shatter the entrenched Party machine, quickly became as exclusive and autocratic as the *apparatchiks* they had ousted. The Army, instructed to direct the radicals in their mission, instead undertook to repress the youths in order to curb the tumult that threatened to weaken China—particularly at a time when the possibility of war with either the United States or the Soviet Union, or both, seemed to be growing.

A man of complex contradictions, Mao appeared to oscillate between doubt and confidence in his tactics during the Cultural Revolution. He was first encouraged by the dynamism of his acolytes as they assaulted the Party bureaucracy and smashed the symbols of past "feudalism." But when the turmoil reached gigantic proportions throughout China's cities, he sounded a note of regret at having uncorked forces that were spiraling beyond his control. Yet he never renounced his long-range aspiration. In one form or another, he forecast, the Cultural Revolution would continue for hundreds, perhaps thousands of years into the future. "The struggle in the ideological realm," he said, "will always exist."[4]

Pervading Mao's concepts and conduct, then, was his reluctance to concede to the reality that modern states, while ideally guided by lofty philosophies, actually operate on the basis of administrative routine and technical specialization rather than through exhortations, emulation movements, and mass enthusiasm. Though he did not wholly deny the value of scientific skills, his vision was essentially illuminated by the conviction that his brand of religious fervor constituted the prime ingredient in motivating man. In short, he held that "positive thinking" could be turned into material force. This belief found expression, for example, in his assertion that the "spiritual atom bomb" was more powerful than the real nuclear instrument, and in such parables as the tale of the Foolish Old Man whose sheer determination was sufficient to move mountains.[5]

Mao and his publicists proclaimed that this spiritual approach elevated Marxism-Leninism to a "higher and completely new stage." In many ways, however, Mao's thesis mirrored the extent to which the Marxist-Leninist dynamic had disintegrated. For his ideas were close to the romantic notions of Rousseau and the Jacobins that Marx had rejected in the mid-nineteenth century. As such, they represented the regression rather than the advancement of Marxist doctrine.

The genesis of utopian socialism in the nineteenth century had been part of the wider romantic revolt of the European intelligentsia against the beginnings of industrialization and its impact on human relations. Though he shared their hopes for an eventual utopia, Marx had rebuffed the romantics by affirming that salvation lay not in resisting modernization but in ruthlessly pushing through industrialization to the end and, at the same time, organizing the growing industrial proletariat. In other words, Marx contended, the climate for revolution would be ripe once a society had achieved abundance. And material progress could only be attained gradually through a historical process that evolved from well-defined economic and social conditions rather than from acts of will and displays of passion.[6] Accordingly, he predicted the triumph of communism in Germany, England, and France, the industrial nations of the time. In his view, the prospects for change in Russia were remote. He also minimized the importance of China and other undeveloped areas, arguing that disorders in those regions were significant only insofar as they deprived the imperialist powers of markets and resources, and thus would hasten the revolution in Western Europe.[7]

Lenin strayed from the Marxist orthodoxy. Seeing the opportunity to stage a *coup d'état* in Russia during World War I, he did not wait for the "objective" economic and social conditions in that backward country to mature. Yet he did retain certain Marxist precepts despite his violation of Marx's formula for revolution. His definition of communism as "Soviet power plus electrification" indicated, among other things, that he regarded industrialization and productivity as primordial. Moreover, he stressed the belief in a strong Communist Party organization that would serve as the vanguard of the industrial working class in its quest to establish the dictatorship of the proletariat.

While he inherited Marx's perception of class friction and Lenin's techniques for revolution, Mao effectively broke with both his precursors by tailoring their principles to fit what he called China's "concrete" situation. China lacked an industrial base from which Mao could hope to press toward the abundant society that Marx had envisaged as necessary for true communism. Therefore, just as Lenin seized power in 1917 before Russia's economic and social conditions for revolution were fulfilled, so Mao took advantage of the vacuum created by the prolonged Japanese invasion of China to topple Chiang Kai-shek's decrepit Nationalist regime. But in contrast to Lenin, who acknowledged the need for intensive industrialization, Mao focused on transforming the Chinese "soul" as a prerequisite to modernization. Hence he aligned himself less with Marx than with the romantic utopians who had interpreted history as a moral drama in which virtue rather than material progress was to be promoted.

One characteristic of the Maoist dynamic, especially in Mao's later years, was its shapelessness. Not once during the Cultural Revolution, for example, did Mao outline a clear-cut, practical program aimed at precise objectives. Instead, he exhorted his followers to destroy his opponents so that an undefined utopia might emerge at some unspecified point in the faraway future. In this respect, Mao held a good deal of appeal for New Left elements in the West and in Asia who were stimulated by the notion that disruptive action was an end in itself. Borrowing from Mao's *Quotations,* many American, European, and Japanese youths could declare that rebellion was justified even though they were unable to describe their ultimate aims. But if Mao's ambiguity seemed attractive outside China, it merely confused the Chinese themselves. Recalling the tumult of the Cultural Revolution, a Red Guard in Guangzhou explained, "All of the factionalism, fighting, the shifting alliances, and the different positions arose because the instructions from Chairman Mao just didn't work. He might say that all members of the 'left' should unite, but we were never told how to determine who was 'left' or 'right.' His statements were so general that everybody, even those who opposed him, could find something to justify his own position."

Mao's ideas, however, at least evolved from a blend of Chinese traditions and his own observations of China's "concrete" situation. For all his preoccupation with revolution, Mao never entirely departed from the traditions of statecraft that reached back in Chinese history over two thousand years. Like every dynastic founder since the rise of the Qin empire in 221 B.C., he relied upon military strength to gain as well as protect his authority; hence his dictum that "political power grows out of the barrel of a gun." Like every Chinese emperor since the plebeian Liu Bang ascended to the throne and founded the

Han dynasty, he consciously nurtured a personality cult designed to portray himself as a charismatic, infallible philosopher-king. And, like the "Sons of Heaven" who preceded him, he sought to govern without institutional checks and balances. Just as the emperors frequently circumvented their cabinets by appointing an Inner Court, so Mao bypassed the Communist Party structure during his most critical period by setting up a Cultural Revolution Directorate whose members included his wife, his secretary, his former bodyguard, and Lin Biao, then his trusted adjutant.[8]

Traditional Chinese attitudes and behavior also dictated Mao's external policies. Like their forebears, who viewed China as the "central kingdom" surrounded by predatory foreign "barbarians," Mao and his colleagues were always mindful of the danger of encirclement by the Soviet Union and the United States. Their alliance with Moscow, signed in 1950, was a temporary expedient that broke down within a decade, and not long afterward the two Communist giants were almost at the brink of war. At the same time, the Chinese felt themselves to be increasingly menaced by a growing American presence in Vietnam. Therefore, just as the early Ming rulers sought to assure China's security in the fifteenth century by dealing with rival Mongol princes, so Mao and his brilliant prime minister, Zhou Enlai, maneuvered to play their principal enemies off against each other. They countered the Soviet threat by seeming to edge closer to the United States—and, with dramatic flexibility, even invited President Nixon to visit Beijing. Meanwhile, they worked to "isolate" the United States diplomatically by reaching accommodations with America's allies in Western Europe and in the Western Hemisphere. Thus they demonstrated an extraordinary capacity for tractability, but without diluting their basic ideological belief in the inevitability of world revolution—a belief that corresponded to their conviction that they were the repository of absolute "virtue."

Despite his disavowal of Confucius, whose prescription for social harmony opposed his fixation on the need for protracted struggle, Mao nevertheless subscribed to the Confucian tenet of "virtue" as a key principle in public conduct. He owed to Confucius as well the notion that education was the only way to improve the human environment.[9] Mao's accent on education—broadened to embrace propaganda, indoctrination, and "thought reform"—was reflected in his portrayal of himself as the Great Teacher. For, as he saw it, one of his major roles was to remold the hearts and minds of China. This set him apart from his main Communist contemporary, Joseph Stalin, who paranoiacally slaughtered suspected foes by the millions. Mao's method was to persuade his enemies to rectify their alleged errors. Cautioning his cadres to exercise leniency in dealing with their opponents, he said: "So long as a person who has made mistakes . . . honestly and sincerely wishes to be cured and to mend his ways, we should welcome him and cure his sickness so that he can become a good comrade. We can never succeed if we just let ourselves go and lash out at him."[10]

While Stalin was a Westerner whose despotism was basically Oriental, Mao was an Oriental whose authoritarianism was tempered by Western influences. He no doubt absorbed these influences from reading Rousseau, John Stuart Mill, Darwin, Friedrich Paulsen, and other Western thinkers, whose works were belatedly scratching the minds of Chinese youth around the turn of the twentieth century. In addition, as he would later admit, the example of Stalin's failure in the Soviet Union served to confirm his view that brutality would not suffice to implant communism in man's marrow.

In the Soviet Union, Mao observed, the Bolsheviks had taken power, eliminated their enemies, extended their hold over the country, and placed the means of production under state control. Yet Stalin had neglected to transform the Russian "soul." Nor had he properly prepared his heirs to carry on the real revolution. After his death, consequently, his successors proceeded to "revise" the true faith. Mao explained this to André Malraux:

> You remember Kosygin at the Twenty-third Congress: "Communism means the raising of living standards." And swimming is a way of putting on a pair of trunks! . . . It isn't simply a question of replacing the Tsar with Khrushchev, one bourgeoisie with another, even if it's called Communist. . . . If we decided to make of it what the Russians are now doing . . . everything will fall apart. Our revolution cannot be simply the stabilization of victory.[11]

But of all the influences that shaped Mao's thinking, the most important were those that stemmed from his personal experiences during the decades before the Communist movement conquered China. And perhaps the most profound of these experiences were the years he spent in Yenan, where he and the ragged remnant of his troops arrived in 1936 after retreating six thousand miles under harassment from Chiang Kai-shek's Nationalists. Here, sheltered in caves dug out of the yellowish loess cliffs, the Communists were not only forced to fight for survival, but compelled to manufacture arms and ammunition, grow food, and, among other activities, proselytize among the peasants of the region in order to collect intelligence, assure their defense perimeters, and recruit soldiers. Organized into compact guerrilla bands imbued with an all-for-one-and-one-for-all *élan*, they accomplished their tasks without complicated equipment, formal institutions, or a complex command hierarchy. They were much like the sympathetic rebels in *All Men Are Brothers,** a Chinese equivalent of the Robin Hood story that Mao had read as a child.

This experience left Mao with the idea that many of the methods that had worked in the Yenan redoubt could be projected on a national scale. China, like Yenan, lacked capital, technology, and adequate areas of arable land. Like Yenan, however, it had one resource—people. Accordingly, he calculated, the attributes of altruism and selflessness that had unified and actuated his heroic guerrillas in Yenan could be infused into China's huge population with similar results. Just as first he had regarded Yenan as a microcosm of China, so Mao later came to consider China as a macrocosm of Yenan.

*Also known as *Water Margin*. The best-known English translation, entitled *All Men Are Brothers*, was done by Pearl Buck.

CHAPTER 2

The Ailing Giant

♣

Direct your eyes downward, do not hold your head high and gaze at the sky. Unless a person is interested in turning his eyes downward . . . he will never in his whole life really understand things in China.
— MAO ZEDONG, *March 1941*

MAO ZEDONG was confronted by a country whose problems would have posed an enormous challenge to any leader. For China since the late eighteenth century had been crumbling in a variety of ways. Its population had grown dramatically, causing severe economic and social strains that were partly responsible for widespread peasant restiveness and rebellion. At the same time, the imperial Chinese administrative system, which had shown remarkable stability for more than a century, began to deteriorate, undermined by its incapacity to respond to the burgeoning internal pressures. Exacerbating this decay was the impact of the West, which brought contemporary ideas to China yet humiliated many Chinese by revealing the weaknesses of the Middle Kingdom that they had so long revered as superior to all other nations on earth. By the first decades of the twentieth century, China was disrupted, fragmented, and confused—its decomposition serving to fertilize the soil in which a diversity of new movements, among them Mao's communism, could take root.

China's extraordinary population growth stemmed from a combination of factors that had been evolving for hundreds of years. As far back as the eleventh century, the introduction of new varieties of early-ripening and drought-resistant rice from Indochina had made double cropping feasible. The later introduction of such American crops as corn, sweet potatoes, and peanuts enabled the Chinese both to produce more crops in their valleys and plains and to improve cultivation of dry hills, mountains, and sandy loams. These innovations, which stimulated a substantial increase in food production, were paralleled after the Qing dynasty finally established its authority in 1683 by a century of domestic peace and order that further contributed to a rise in living standards. So attractive did China seem by the eighteenth century that Voltaire hailed its morality and organization as "the best the world has ever seen." The cumulative result of this relative prosperity was, however, an unprecedented and disastrous demographic explosion. The Chinese population, estimated to have been 100 million in the middle of the seventeenth century, tripled by 1800 and soared to more than 400 million by 1850.[1]

The effects of the population boom proved, almost in exaggerated fashion, the validity of the theories then being propounded by Thomas Malthus, who was familiar with China. As the number of Chinese multiplied geometrically, the means to sustain them could scarcely keep pace, since the country's technological shortcomings limited its ability to attain required levels of efficiency.

Over the centuries, the Chinese had worked their soil so assiduously that there were very few areas that had not been touched by human hands. They had built canals and irrigation channels, some with elaborate systems of foot treadles, buckets, and wheels for lifting water up to terraced paddy fields spectacularly carved out of hillsides. They had opened virgin regions, planting them with cotton, tea bushes, and mulberry trees for silkworm cultivation. These and other developments were mostly acomplished by manpower alone, since equipment and draft animals were in short supply. But as the population increased and the amount of available labor expanded, the pressures on the land grew to intolerable proportions, for several reasons.

First, the Confucian ideal of large families in which there was no primogeniture meant that the patrimony was divided among the sons in the form of progressively smaller and less productive farming units. Second, the disdain of intellectuals for practical matters inhibited men of learning from contributing their intelligence and knowledge to technological inventions that would have helped to boost agricultural output. Third, in contrast to Europe and America during the early phases of the industrial revolution, there were virtually no urban factories in China to siphon off the surplus rural labor force. And finally, the imperial Chinese government was unprepared and unwilling to cope with the new economic situation and its social consequences.

Government inertia mirrored the obsolescence of China's ancient bureaucracy both in the provinces and at the center. Officials delegated to govern huge regions according to rigid codes of behavior discovered that it was safer for their careers to remain passive than to risk initiatives that might fail and thus blemish their records. They learned to accommodate to difficulties rather than to resolve them, and their potential creativity was dampened by rituals so formal that their calligraphic style was deemed more important than the contents of their reports. At the top of the pyramid, the emperor himself was less and less able to assert his rule as the volume of state business proliferated. Instead of serving as the infallible autocrat capable of dictating wise and just decisions on all matters, he became the chief bottleneck in the increasingly clogged bureaucracy.[2]

In all Oriental societies, even to this day, a plausible measure of corruption has been acceptable as the oil that lubricates the administrative gears. Throughout Chinese history, in fact, civil servants were expected to subsidize both their public and private establishments from funds obtained through their official positions. But the disintegration of the Qing dynasty in the nineteenth century, like the decline of earlier and subsequent Chinese regimes, was characterized by excessive and oppressive graft and extortion.

Corruption was especially outrageous in the collection of the various levies exacted by the state. Government revenues, primarily derived from the land tax, grain tribute, salt tax, and customs duties, were collected through a system of "tax farming." Under this system, provincial officials were required to meet certain tax quotas, after which they could pocket further collections. This effectively mandated tax officials to bleed the people, which they generally did in collaboration with local landlords who acted as intermediaries in extracting payments from their tenant farmers. Posts in the provincial bureaucracy were obviously lucrative, and they became increasingly in demand. According to government records, the proportion of appointments acquired by purchase climbed from 29 per cent in 1840 to 49 per cent in 1895. During the same period, the percentage of officials who qualified on the basis of merit dropped sharply.[3]

Another major source of corruption was the ancient salt monopoly, which was operated by private merchants under state license. Salt was an indispensable item to the Chinese masses living on a diet composed mainly of cereals. The original concept behind licensing private merchants was to save the government the large investment involved in transporting salt over vast distances. In practice, the merchants managed to cling to their permits by paying enormous bribes to the officials who supervised the trade. The merchants at Yangzhou in northern Jiangsu province—where Marco Polo had served as a magistrate during his celebrated sojourn in China—are said to have paid the equivalent of $3 million a year to local functionaries in the late eighteenth century. These payments were often disguised as "donations" to public funds or "contributions" to military programs. The alliance between the merchants and officials was so mutually profitable that, on one occasion, an emissary detailed by the emperor to investigate the corruption was forced to abandon his effort because of obstructions thrown up by both the traders and the bureaucrats. Since the emperor himself received large gifts from the salt monopolists, it is unlikely that he was anxious to have their misconduct disclosed.

The tyranny of officials and landlords, combined with the privation caused by the growing population and diminishing opportunities, inevitably prompted banditry, riots, and other forms of dissidence. Revolt was nothing new in China. Striving to survive in a marginal economy, oppressed by feudal landowners and mandarins, plagued by floods, drought, and epidemic, disaffected peasants frequently turned into outlaws and, often joined by dissident officials, they sometimes mobilized sufficient strength to overthrow dynasties. The theme of insurrection was romanticized in classical Chinese poetry and in such novels as *All Men Are Brothers*.

Among the most persistent Chinese rebel institutions were secret societies that started as religious associations and gradually became subversive movements. Like groups of Freemasons, these societies had passwords, grand masters, and elaborate rituals that endowed them with a somewhat mystical flavor.

One of the oldest secret societies in China was the White Lotus Society, which was organized in the fourth century A.D. by eighteen acolytes of the Buddhist monk Hua Yin in the Lushan highlands, south of the Yangzi River. Their original purpose was to study the doctrines of Amitabha pietism, and they took the white lotus, a Buddhist symbol, as their emblem. In time, the cult lost its strictly religious cast. By the middle of the twelfth century, it had emerged as a powerful movement determined to oust the Song emperors, and not long afterward it opposed the Mongol legions that had swept into

China. One White Lotus leader at the head of the resistance against the Mongols was Zhu Yuanzhang, a poor peasant from Anhui province who had become a monk. By 1368, he had overthrown the Mongols and established himself as Emperor Hong Wu, the founder of the Ming dynasty. Knowing its capacities, he immediately banned the society.

The White Lotus Society played a less important role during the three hundred years of Ming rule. But it never disbanded and, as conditions in China deteriorated in the late eighteenth century, the movement rose again in opposition to the Qing dynasty. It staged its first large-scale outbreak in northern Shandong province in 1774, and the insurrection, fueled by popular discontent, spread quickly in the years that followed.

Though it justified its rebellion as a reaction against official despotism—"the people are forced by the officials to revolt," ran its slogan—the White Lotus Society did not raise a rival dynastic standard, set up an administration in the areas it conquered, or offer a positive alternative to Qing policies. Nor were its forces roving bands rather than organized troops, able to stand up against the government army. Yet even after the movement's defeat, its adherents continued their activities against the dynasty. In 1812, for example, one of them who worked as a cook in the imperial household unsuccessfully attempted to assassinate the emperor. Two years later, posing as persimmon peddlers, a White Lotus group infiltrated the palace but was fought off by the royal guards. In the years after that, the society went underground, splintering into factions with names like the White Clouds, the White Fans, and the White Eyebrows. Some elements surfaced again in 1900 as the Society of the Righteous and Harmonious Fists, better known in the West as the Boxers. The founder of the Chinese Republic in 1911, Dr. Sun Yat-sen, was said to have been associated with the White Lotus Society and other clandestine brotherhoods, as was his successor, Chiang Kai-shek.

The White Lotus Society was not the only movement to oppose the Qing dynasty. Muslim minorities in northern Gansu had risen up in the late eighteenth century against Han Chinese domination, and their revolt mushroomed to other Islamic regions of China in subsequent decades. By 1856, a Muslim leader called Du Weixiu succeeded in setting up a separate state in southwestern Yunnan province, with himself as its sultan. Not until 1873, after fierce fighting and appalling losses of life among the civilian population, was he finally crushed by the government.

Simultaneously, the imperial regime was engaged in an effort to subdue another dissident movement, known as the Nian, which had gathered momentum in north and central China in the early decades of the nineteenth century as a coalition of five outlaw bands, each identified by the color of its banners. Comprised mainly of cavalry units, the Nian rebels struck out from fortified sanctuaries in which, in Maoist style, they had secured the allegiance of the peasants. They were eventually defeated in 1868 after the enlightened General Zeng Guofan won over the villagers by employing many of the counterinsurgency techniques that would become fashionable a hundred years later.

Still another rebellion was triggered by the Triad, or Heaven and Earth Society. Created in 1647 as a Buddhist blood brotherhood devoted to the overthrow of the Qing dynasty, the Triad gradually became a loosely organized association of restive coolies, boatmen, petty officials, itinerant merchants, and others with grievances against the government, particularly in China's southern and coastal provinces. After sparking open revolts in the early nineteenth century, the Triad degenerated into a vehicle for racketeers, smugglers, and other assorted criminals, and it continued to operate a hundred years later among Chinese communities in Hong Kong, Singapore, and Malaysia. Mao Zedong and several of his Communist associates indirectly sought Triad support during the days when they were seeking to recruit followers.[4] Chiang Kai-shek similarly relied on the secret societies in his attempts to eradicate the Communists in Chinese coastal cities.[5]

The biggest upheaval to devastate nineteenth-century China, however, was the Taiping Rebellion. Ignited by a mystic curiously exalted by Christianity, the insurrection rapidly inflamed vast numbers of Chinese desperate to free themselves from corruption, oppression, and poverty. By the time it was over, the episode had cost as many as 20 million lives.

The founder of the Taiping cult, Hong Xiuquan, was born into a peasant family of the Hakka community, north Chinese who had migrated south centuries earlier but never fully assimilated into the local population. As a youth, Hong failed several times to pass the imperial examinations that would have given him an official position in the Qing administration. His frustrations undoubtedly aggravated his psychological instability, and in 1837, prostrated by a high fever, he had a vision in which he claimed that God and Jesus Christ bade him to save mankind from the devil. His acquaintance with the Bible,

Hong later recalled, came from religious pamphlets written by a Chinese Protestant missionary. These pamphlets inspired him with Old Testament zeal. For, as the story went, Hong awoke from his vision shouting: "Slay the demons! There is one and there is another. Many cannot withstand a single blow of my sword."[6]

The Orient has always been filled with mystics who wander from village to village, preaching their faith and hoping that propitious circumstances will win them followers. Hong fit this pattern. He drifted south into mountainous Guangxi province, then beset by famine, urging peasants to destroy Buddhist and Taoist idols as well as Confucian ancestral tablets on the grounds that only his monotheism promised salvation. Soon his God Worshippers Society, as he called his sect, was attracting not only poor peasants but assorted bandits, dispirited scholars, and even landlords motivated to oppose the government. The movement also joined forces in some areas with members of the White Lotus Society and the Triad. Hong's cousin Feng Yunshan, an unsuccessful scholar like himself, took over the military organization of the new cult. In one of his early public messages, Hong made it plain that his drive would be bloody. He wrote: "All who resist us are rebels and idolatrous demons, and we shall kill them without sparing. But whoever acknowledges the Heavenly King and exerts himself in our service shall have a full reward."[7]

Conferring upon himself the title of Heavenly King, Hong Xiuquan named his chief lieutenants Northern, Southern, Eastern, Western, and Assistant Kings. And, after proclaiming his intention to establish a new dynasty, he called his movement the "Heavenly Kingdom of Great Peace." The term "Great Peace," used by other dynastic challengers throughout history, is *Taiping* in Chinese.

At the outset of their ambitious campaign to conquer China, the Taiping forces probably comprised about three thousand men and women, most of them armed with spears and pitchforks and wearing red turbans. Like Muslim fanatics embarked on a holy war, they showed remarkable courage and discipline, and their puritanical aversion to looting and rape won them converts among villagers accustomed to plundering armies. Their ranks swelled, and by the spring of 1852 they had swept as far north as the Yangzi River and soon captured Nanjing, the second city of the empire, bringing most of central China under their domination. Though they threatened Beijing, their strength was inadequate to take the imperial capital.

In contrast to the other rebel movements of the period, the Taipings conceived a considerable array of programs based on a fascinating mixture of Christian and Chinese elements. Several of these programs, while never actually put into practice, were surprisingly similar to the reforms sponsored by later radicals, including Mao Zedong and his Communists.

Regulations in the Taiping army, like those promulgated by Mao for his soldiers, required that troops carry their own food and never enter private dwellings unless invited. Like the Communists, the Taipings also banned witchcraft, gambling, prostitution, and opium. In order to promote equality between the sexes, they abolished the old Chinese custom of foot-binding, mobilized women into military and labor units, and appointed them as officers and administrators. And borrowing from classical Chinese utopian thinkers, they worked out a system of primitive economic equality that included a blueprint to redistribute land among farming households, an agrarian scheme described in Christian rhetoric as a plan "to enable all under Heaven to enjoy the great blessings of the Lord God Almighty: land for all to till, food for all to eat, clothes for all to wear; money for all to spend. . . ."[8]

Despite its vigor and religious fervor, the Taiping movement began to weaken not long after reaching the peak of its power in the mid-1850s. Among other errors, its leaders failed to take advantage of the seizure of Amoy and Shanghai by their Triad allies and secure footholds in those important coastal cities. In addition, Hong Xiuquan and his lesser kings fell to squabbling among themselves, fragmenting the Taiping hierarchy into rival factions. Finally, the imperial army was expanded and reorganized under Zeng Guofan, the great Hunanese scholar-soldier whose skilled tactics later crushed the Nian insurgents. In the summer of 1864, Zeng's forces encircled the walls of Nanjing. Anticipating defeat and a cruel death, Hong Xiuquan committed suicide by poison. The city fell. All its defenders were slaughtered. The surviving Taiping leaders were executed, and the rebellion was effectively ended.

In the closing years of the Taiping insurrection, the imperial authorities adopted a policy unprecedented in Chinese history. They turned toward Western technology and, at the same time, sought the cooperation of the European powers in an effort to modernize and improve their defenses.

Dipping into tax and customs revenues, the Chinese Army purchased foreign weapons and built arsenals to manufacture Western-type guns and steamships. Early in 1862, when the Taiping rebels reached the outskirts of Shanghai, the British and French abandoned their neutral stance and began to help the Qing regime to protect the area in which Europeans had substantial commercial interests. An American adventurer from Massachusetts, Frederick Townsend Ward, was commissioned to recruit, train, and command a unit of four thousand Chinese known as the "Ever Victorious Army." Ward was succeeded after his death by a British officer, Major Charles George "Chinese" Gordon, whose mixed battalion of foreign and native troops saw action in the battle for Suzhou. A similar legion mustered by the French assisted the Chinese Army in the fight for Hangzhou.

Commenting on the Taiping episode nearly a century later, Mao Zedong called it a "peasant revolutionary war against feudal rule and national oppression" that collapsed under the "combined onslaught of the Qing government and the British, U.S., and French aggressors."[9] But the actual role of the foreign powers was less significant than the fact that the Qing government accepted outside aid at a time of crisis. For this indicated the degree to which the emperor was compelled to concede that China, the theoretical center of the universe, was no longer superior to all other nations on earth. Only seventy years earlier, rejecting Lord Macartney's proposal to increase trade between England and China, the Qian Long emperor had declared that "our Celestial Empire possesses all things in abundance . . . and therefore needs not import the manufactures of outside barbarians in exchange for our own produce."[10] Now, reluctantly admitting to China's weakness, a successor to the haughty Emperor Qian Long decreed in 1862 that "for the time being, we have to make use of foreigners to train our soldiers, as a scheme for self-strengthening."[11]

China's temptation to borrow Western methods in order to strengthen itself was an idea that began to tantalize Chinese intellectuals as far back as the 1840s, following the Opium War. That war started in late 1839, when the British retaliated against attempts by a conscientious Chinese official, Lin Zexu, to suppress Britain's efforts to bring Indian opium into Guangzhou and other coastal cities. In reality, the war represented the first drive by a European power to open China to "free trade," and it dramatically revealed to perceptive Chinese both their own backwardness and the dynamism of the West. The Qing government's so-called Army of the Green Standard, which

supposedly numbered six hundred thousand men deployed throughout the provinces, was actually a rabble. The prime talent of its officers
was to make money by doctoring their accounts. Like characters in
a Chinese opera, its soldiers could only posture with swords and
spears—except when given the chance to plunder hapless civilians.
Thus it was no match for British warships and troops, which easily
reduced the decrepit Chinese fortresses along the coast between
Guangzhou and Shanghai.

Their capitulation in the Opium War forced the Chinese to cede
Hong Kong to Britain as well as open the ports of Guangzhou, Amoy,
Fuzhou, Ningbo, and Shanghai to British residence and commerce.
In the ensuing years, through pressures of one kind or another, Britain, the United States, and the other Western powers imposed a
series of further "unequal treaties" on China that gave them considerable commercial and extraterritorial privileges. Under these ine-
quitable treaty arrangements, Tsarist Russia also took over huge tracts
of Chinese territory, thereby sowing the seeds of a bitter boundary
dispute that would erupt a century later.

One of the consequences of the foreign encroachments on China
was to incite strong xenophobic feelings among many Chinese. Despite Britain's victory in the Opium War, Guangzhou officials refused
to permit British merchants to trade freely until 1858. Elsewhere in
the country, officials encouraged the population to attack foreign missionaries and their converts, and this anti-Christian sentiment was
heightened during the Taiping troubles, which seemed to tradition-
alist Chinese to have been caused by Western influence.

But a small fraction of the Chinese intellectual community read
the European incursions as a warning that China had to remodel itself
by adopting at least some of the scientific knowledge and governmental institutions of the West. Among the early advocates of Westernization was Feng Guifen, a prominent scholar. Confessing his
shame that China could be defeated by small Western nations, he
urged the Chinese to resist the blind impulse to expel foreigners,
recommending instead that they "learn the superior technology of
the barbarians in order to control them." He proposed that government schools teach mathematics and science, and that the ancient
examination system for officials be revised to recruit more technicians
into the administration. He also stressed the need for China to make
better use of its people and economic resources within the framework
of its own institutions. Borrowing a phrase from the *Classic of
Changes*, he suggested that China strive to improve itself through

"self-strengthening."[12] It was this phrase that the emperor employed in his edict calling for the training of Chinese soldiers by foreign advisers. In later years, a group of reformers formalized the phrase by creating the *Qiang Xuehui*—the Self-Strengthening Society.

Another important figure among the reformist thinkers of the period was Yan Fu, who translated Darwin's *Origin of Species* into Chinese while serving as a naval cadet in England. Returning to China, he went on to translate Adam Smith's *Wealth of Nations*, Huxley's *Evolution and Ethics*, Herbert Spencer's *Principles of Sociology*, and other books, annotating many of them with commentaries. Other works on Western science, technology, and current affairs were translated and published by European and American missionaries and scholars then in China. Among the more influential journals were those edited by an American Methodist, Young J. Allen. Published in the Chinese language, they stressed the progressive characteristics of Western culture and criticized the Confucian ethic for its obsolescence.

Hong Kong and Shanghai, port cities that looked out to the world beyond China, were especially lively centers of foreign ideas. One of the keenest advocates of Westernization in Shanghai was Zheng Guanying, who divided his time between working for British commercial firms and writing essays on China's problems. Another was Wang Tao, who served as an assistant to Christian missionaries and later became an editorialist for Chinese newspapers in Hong Kong and Shanghai. After a three-year sojourn in Britain under missionary auspices, Wang favored the creation of a bicameral Chinese parliament "elected equitably and universally." Both he and Zheng also emphasized the necessity for a free press that would expose official abuses. Similar views were expressed by Liang Qichao, a scholar who became a Shanghai editor and gained a good deal of popularity among students in later years. These men were hardly radical by present-day standards. Loyal to the monarchy, they did not question the basic Confucian tenets. They believed, however, that Western techniques could profitably supplement traditional Chinese values. Or as one of their slogans held: "Chinese learning for the essential principles, Western learning for practical application."[13]

In about the middle of the nineteenth century, then, several Chinese officials began to attempt to put Western methods into practice. No less a personage than the emperor's brother, Prince Gung, outlined a program to establish a foreign affairs bureau, expand the use of Western advisers in a new Maritime Customs Service at all ports, and, among other things, educate functionaries in foreign languages. Enlightened officials such as Li Hongzhang and Zhang Zhidong started the construction of modern shipyards, arsenals, telegraph lines, and railways. One of Li's major efforts was the creation after 1885 of China's principal fighting force, the Beiyang naval fleet based in the north, which included two German-built battleships among its twenty-five vessels.

This trend toward Westernization was limited, however. For one thing, it was mainly restricted to China's Westernized coastal areas. For another, the Chinese government lacked both the drive and the resources to push the modernization schemes through effectively. Such projects as a Shanghai textile mill and the railway linking Beijing with the Manchurian border were completed only after long and costly delays. Li Hongzhang's northern fleet, though initially encouraged by the Qing court, soon fell victim to official corruption as palace eunuchs and other courtiers siphoned off naval funds for themselves. Li's ships were disastrously defeated in 1894, when China and Japan went to war for control of the Korean peninsula. This war marked the failure of the Chinese hope for "self-strengthening." After that, had it not been for the rival ambitions of the imperialist powers, China might have become a European colony. Instead, it was opened to a scramble for concessions that put several of its regions and cities under the virtual control of various European nations.

Attempts at "self-strengthening" through the adoption of Western techniques were also inhibited by the deeply ingrained habits and customs of the Chinese bureaucracy. Officials might voice praise for modern scientific methods, yet they could not shake off the legacy of their Confucian education, with its emphasis on sterile ritual and detail. Cultural pride, combined with the struggles involved in seeking and holding office, militated as well against their receptivity to innovations. Toward the end of the nineteenth century, as the power of the narrow-minded, domineering dowager empress grew, conservatism and xenophobia became increasingly fashionable in court circles. Usually known as Cixi, from the first two characters of her long title, the dowager empress had originally been a low-ranking concubine. She bore the emperor his only son, who died at the age of nineteen. After that, except during a brief challenge from her only nephew, whom she had placed on the throne after her son's death, her authority was absolute and reactionary—even though Western ladies who saw her, among them the wife of the American minister in Beijing, were impressed by her "womanly tenderness."

The defeat inflicted by the Japanese followed by the seizure of various areas by Germany, France, Britain, and Russia, seemed to augur the dismemberment of China. The atmosphere of crisis that gripped the court in 1898 prompted the Emperor Guang Xu, by now an ardent young man of twenty-seven, to defy the dowager empress. He sought advice from Kang Yuwei, a classical scholar from Guangzhou and one of the most daring iconoclasts of the time. To depend upon the conservatives to save China from catastrophe, Kang replied, would be "like climbing a tree in search of fish."[14] The emperor, whose tastes included a fondness for Western gadgets, thereupon commissioned Kang to submit a specific reform program. Thus, over a period of a hundred days from June through September of 1898, Kang and his progressive friends drew up a list of more than forty proposals recommending changes in nearly every realm, from agriculture, commerce, and education to military affairs and the postal system.

Kang's proposed reforms naturally threatened the entire Qing establishment, including the dowager empress, who was still vigorous at sixty-three. Theoretically in retirement, she nevertheless controlled the army and the powerful palace eunuchs, and she reacted predictably. Without displaying a trace of "womanly tenderness," she deposed the emperor in a *coup d'état* and had six of Kang's colleagues executed. Kang himself escaped to Japan. The attempt to alter China from above by moderate, gradual means had failed and, as the twentieth century dawned, the prospects for violent revolution in the future seemed almost inevitable.

While far from revolutionary in the modern sense of the term, a serious outbreak of violence immediately followed the failure of the reformers. It was the uprising of the Boxers, the secret society whose activists were supposed to practice an ancient form of military calisthenics along with Taoist sorcery and other magic rites. Founded as an affiliate of the White Lotus Society, which opposed the Qing dynasty, the Boxer movement was now encouraged by the dowager empress and the court reactionaries to exterminate the foreign influences spreading through China.

Like the rebellions that erupted earlier in the century, the Boxer rising gained its initial impetus from deteriorating economic and social conditions. The Yellow River—"China's sorrow"—had again flooded in 1898, causing extensive famine in Shandong province. Drought was also plaguing parts of north China. Aggravating these calamities were the dislocations created by the construction of new railways and the importation of foreign merchandise. The Boxers consequently attracted thousands of peasants, coolies, and other elements who could conveniently blame their poverty and frustrations on the "foreign devils."

The first alliance between the Qing government and the Boxers took place in stricken Shandong, where the governor enlisted members of the movement into his militia and exhorted them to attack local Christians. By the spring of 1900, mobs of Boxers were roaming through north China, slaughtering Chinese Christians and missionaries. In June, they entered Beijing and Tianjin, besieging the foreign legations and settlements in both cities. Inside the palace, meanwhile, the dowager empress was told by pro-Boxer courtiers that the foreign powers had demanded her abdication and were sending in troops to reinforce their demand. Her response was to declare war on the foreign powers.

Encircled by the Boxers, the eleven legations inside the Beijing diplomatic ghetto mobilized nearly a thousand foreign civilians and guards as well as three thousand Chinese Christians into a defense force that was able to hold out for almost two months. It was one of those midsummer adventures that thrilled the world—especially since the press, lacking credible information from Beijing, published fantastic tales of the event. After much bickering, an international contingent of some twenty thousand troops, about half of them Japanese, finally marched from Tianjin to the capital to rescue the beleaguered foreign community. Seventy-six foreigners had died during the siege of the legation quarter. Some two hundred fifty foreigners were killed in the surrounding provinces. The brutality was particularly severe in Shanxi, where the governor personally presided over the execution of forty-six missionaries and other foreigners. The number of Chinese Christians slaughtered ran into the thousands.

As the Western invaders began to plunder Beijing, the dowager empress and her closest courtiers fled the city in disguise. Li Hongzhang, once the exponent of "self-strengthening" and now governor of Guangzhou, was left to retrieve the situation. Under the Boxer Protocol, signed in September 1901, he acceded to the harsh demands imposed by the Western powers, including the payment of a staggering indemnity to the eleven nations whose legations had been assaulted. Despite her role in the episode, the dowager empress returned to Beijing with her court soon afterward, supported by foreign powers that considered her a symbol of "stability." Unable to regain her former authority, she nevertheless continued to act the monarch until her death in 1908.

Six decades later, at the height of his Cultural Revolution, Mao Zedong took a curious retrospective approach to the Boxer uprising. He praised the Boxers while condemning the enlightened officials who had tried to change the Qing government's reactionary policies. As one of his publicists put it, the Boxers were a "great anti-imperialist, anti-feudal revolutionary mass movement" that had waged a "heroic patriotic struggle" against the foreign conspiracy to partition China. The progressives of the period, in contrast, were depicted as "bourgeois reformers" who had "cherished the illusion that they could go completely to the side of imperialism and rely on its strength to realize their aims of constitutional reform and modernization."[15]

Mao's acclaim for the xenophobic Boxers was partly contrived to arouse Chinese nationalistic emotions at a time when he was attempting to isolate China from the outside world. Indeed, emulating the Boxers, his Red Guards stormed and burned a British legation building and harassed foreign diplomats in Beijing during the summer of 1967. But more significantly, Mao was using his own version of history to vilify contemporary rivals who, he believed, resembled the earlier reformers in advocating political gradualism in opposition to his doctrine of "armed struggle." Yet Mao in his formative years was swayed more by those early progressives than by the Boxers he later claimed to admire.

CHAPTER 3

The Making of a Rebel

In a very short time, in China's central, southern, and northern provinces, several hundred million peasants will rise like a mighty storm, like a hurricane, a force so swift and violent that no power, however great, will be able to hold it back.
— MAO ZEDONG, *March 1927*

HUNAN PROVINCE, where Mao Zedong was born, is an area of hills, lakes, and fertile farmland that had served for centuries as a corridor linking north and south China. Insurgent and imperial armies recurrently passed through this corridor in their drives to conquer or defend dynasties, leaving a trail of destruction in their wake. During peaceful interludes, the province was not only an artery for commercial traffic but an avenue along which new ideas flowed. Hence the Hunanese, insular yet exposed to outside influences, developed the skills of soldiering and scholarship as well as a familiarity with civil strife. And perhaps, as Mao himself once noted, the red peppers in their diet also contributed to their vigor.

In sharp contrast to other Chinese classicists whose approach was largely academic, the scholars of Hunan tended to accentuate the political, economic, and social aspects of Confucian texts. Wang Fuzhi, the seventeenth-century Hunanese philosopher, laid the foundations of this pragmatism by expounding the view that political systems, economic structures, social customs, and man himself were all subject to change. Foreshadowing one of Mao's basic dogmas, Wang argued that "there is not a single part of human nature already shaped that cannot be modified."[1]

The pragmatic tradition initiated by Wang inspired much of the advanced Chinese thinking in the nineteenth century, and many of

the most persuasive works of the period were produced by Hunanese
scholars such as He Zhangling, who compiled an anthology of political
and economic essays, and Wei Yuan, who wrote a treatise on world
history and geography. Local Hunanese officials, moreover, were
among the most enlightened in the country. In addition to encouraging educational reform and modern industries, they invited both
native and outside progressives to address students and other educated elements of the provincial population. The brilliant Hunanese
radical Tan Sitong, executed by the dowager empress in 1898 for his
role in the reform movement, based his patriotic Southern Study
Society in the province. The first girls' school in China was opened
in 1903 in Changsha, the provincial capital. One of the earliest American educational programs in China, sponsored by Yale, was established as well in Changsha.

Hunan was also the source from which the Qing government drew
many of its ablest civilian functionaries and military officers for posts
in other provinces throughout the empire. In 1865, for instance, five
of China's eight regional governors were Hunanese. The most effective Chinese general of his time was Zeng Guofan, the Hunanese
scholar who finally defeated the Taiping and Nian rebels. Another
eminent officer of the period, Zuo Zongtan, who consolidated Beijing's hold over Central Asia, was also from Hunan. This background
may account at least in part for the Hunanese predominance in the
twentieth-century Communist hierarchy. With its progressive intellectual ferment, the Hunan environment was certainly significant in
shaping Mao.

Located almost exactly in the geographical center of the province,
the village of Shaoshan is some thirty miles west of Xiangdan, a busy
market town on the Xiang River. It is an area of isolated farms lying
among hills and a few peaks, one of them the site of an ancient Taoist
hermitage in which, according to legend, a monk composed the *shao*
style of music that gave the village its name. Here Mao was born on
December 26, 1893, in a hillside farmhouse overlooking a lotus pond.
He was the eldest of three sons and a daughter. His brothers and
sister would later die violent deaths as political activists.

Mao's father, Mao Rensheng, had been a dispossessed peasant
who joined the army to escape heavy debts and returned to his native
village to become relatively rich. As Mao afterward recalled, his father
had gradually managed to acquire more than three acres of land, from
whose yield the family succeeded in saving one hundred forty bushels
of rice per year. Mao Rensheng converted this modest grain surplus

into cash, which he lent out at usurious rates of interest. He also began to expand into cereal trading, until he was a full-fledged merchant with a substantial amount of monetary capital.

From all accounts, including those of Mao himself, Mao Rensheng was a badly educated, bigoted, solitary man who demanded total obedience from his sons in conformity with the Confucian notion of filial piety. He compelled his children to work hard, beat them frequently, gave them no money, and often deprived them of food. Mao's mother, in contrast, was a devout Buddhist who exuded love, generosity, and gentleness, and she usually sided with her children against her husband. Relating his life to Edgar Snow in 1936, Mao humorously described the household as having been split into two "parties"—the Ruling Power personified by his father, and the Opposition "United Front" comprised of his mother, his brothers, and himself. "My mother advocated a policy of indirect attack," he recalled. "She criticized any overt display of emotion and attempts at open rebellion against the Ruling Power. She said it was not the Chinese way."[2]

Several Western writers using psychoanalytical techniques have sought to attribute Mao's revolutionary vocation to his avowed hatred for paternal authority. Mao himself has lent substance to this thesis. He told Snow that he learned in his disputes with his father that he could defend his rights only by "open rebellion."[3] But, as Jerome Ch'en has pointed out, the relationships in the Mao family were normal in China of that era. The father expected to be strict master of the house, and the children resisted or eluded his control in coalition with their mother.[4] But hints in the autobiographical account he gave to Snow suggest that Mao was not entirely lacking in sympathy for his father. Therefore, while his tender years were impressionable, Mao's longer-range outlook was undoubtedly molded by an assortment of other experiences.

Mao was only five years old when he started working on his father's land. Three years later, though continuing to lend a hand in the fields, he began to attend the local primary school in order to learn enough reading, writing, and arithmetic to keep the family ledgers. The school curriculum, unchanged for centuries, consisted of reciting incomprehensible Confucian classics. Despite Mao's later claim to have disliked this arid fare, the frequent references to the Chinese classics in his writing indicate that he absorbed a good deal of it. Like all Chinese schoolboys of his generation, he also devoured such traditional novels as *Romance of the Three Kingdoms*, *The Dream of the Red Chamber,* and *All Men Are Brothers,* with their tales of historical heroes and villains and daring bandits. Mao was especially captivated by *All Men Are Brothers,* which glorifies revolt, even though its rebels seek to rectify the abuses of the imperial system rather than alter the system itself.

Compelled by his father to quit primary school at the age of thirteen, Mao labored long hours in the fields by day and on the family ledgers at night. He grew into manhood and, in customary manner, acquiesced to an arranged marriage with a girl four years his senior. The marriage, later repudiated by Mao, was never consummated. During these years, meanwhile, Mao found time to continue reading. One of his favorite books was *Words of Warning to an Affluent Age,* by Zheng Guanying, a Shanghai merchant and scholar who pleaded for technical and economic modernization and a constitutional monarchy. According to Mao, the book inspired him to resume his education. He ran away from home, first to study with an unemployed law student in the village, and afterward to enroll against the wishes of his father at the Dongshan Primary School, a progressive establishment in nearby Xiangxiang, his mother's native district.

An incident occurred in Hunan about this time that, in Mao's later words, "influenced my whole life." There had been a severe famine in the province as a result of floods. When hungry peasants protested to government officials in Changsha, many were arrested and decapitated, and their heads were displayed on poles to discourage others. Though Mao heard the story from merchants returning from Changsha, the event scarred his mind. "I never forgot it," he told Edgar Snow thirty years afterward. "I felt that there with the rebels were ordinary people like my own family, and I deeply resented the injustice of the treatment given to them."[5]

Mao and his schoolmates were also fascinated in those days by an intermittent series of uprisings staged by a secret fraternity called the Society of Elder Brothers, which had many adherents among the peasants of Hunan. One of the leaders of the society, Huang Xing, must have seemed to Mao to resemble a character out of *All Men Are Brothers.* After several thrilling exploits, Huang plotted to assassinate local dignitaries assembled to celebrate the birthday of the dowager empress in November 1904. The plan misfired. Helped by an Anglican missionary, he escaped to Japan, returning to China nine years later as a general in Dr. Sun Yat-sen's Kuomintang. Mao's imagination was also stirred by another attempted revolt by the Society of Elder Brothers against landlords in his own birthplace, Shao-shan. After defending a nearby mountain stronghold, the rebels were suppressed and their leader, known as Pang the Millstone-Maker, was beheaded. Mao later recalled that he and his fellow students "all sympathized with the revolt" and regarded Pang as a hero.[6]

At that stage, however, Mao understandably took a cautious attitude toward unrest that directly affected his family. During one period of serious food shortages in Hunan, his father ignored the pleas of starving peasants for aid until, in desperation, they seized a rice shipment he was transporting to the city. Mao recollected that he had been displeased by his father's selfishness. But, he added with unusual candor, "I thought the villagers' method was wrong also."[7]

Yet if Mao's social ideas at that time were ambiguous, his nationalistic sentiments were coming into sharper focus. He was aware of China's humiliating defeats by Japan and the European powers throughout the nineteenth century. Years later, he remembered that he first acquired "a certain amount of political consciousness" from reading a pamphlet deploring China's loss of suzerainty over Korea, Taiwan, Indochina, Burma, and other territories and tributary states. "After I read this," he recalled, "I felt depressed about the future of my country and began to realize that it was the duty of all the people to help save it."[8]

By his own admission, Mao was then not opposed to the monarchy or the imperial bureaucratic system. Like many young, literate Chinese of the period, however, he gradually adopted the view that Western technology, institutions, and thought had much to offer China. The year he spent at the Dongshan Primary School, where he excelled as a student, was especially important in exposing him to contemporary Western trends. At the school he became acquainted with a teacher who had studied in Japan, deriving from that contact a vicarious pride in the Japanese defeat of Russia in 1905. There too he read about Kang Youwei and Liang Qichao, the Qing government reformers he was later to repudiate—though he admitted to having "worshiped" them in his youth. His voracious reading during that year undoubtedly included as well some of Yan Fu's translations of Darwin, Spencer, and Mill. Another book, also translated by Yan Fu, was enormously popular among young Chinese at the time. Entitled *Principles of Western Civilization*, it was by an obscure English sociologist named Benjamin Kidd who argued that the individual must sacrifice himself for the sake of society in the struggle for progress.

That belief would be echoed in Mao's credo more than a half-century afterward.

Another theme in Mao's thinking that had its origin in his school-boy-reading was his respect for martial strength and courage. He was impressed by George Washington and the American war for independence, about which he read in a now-forgotten volume called *Great Heroes of the World*. In 1964, he told a French delegation visiting China that he admired Napoleon the soldier more than Robespierre the revolutionary.[9] And his youthful imagination had been kindled by such ancient Chinese warriors as the legendary emperors Yao and Shun, and the king of Qin, who unified the empire in the third century B.C. In his first literary effort, published in 1917, Mao put forth a view that he continued to hold throughout his life: "The principal aim of physical education is military heroism."[10]

In the autumn of 1911, when he was nearly eighteen, Mao walked to Changsha in order to enroll in the secondary school there. He found the city bubbling with political excitement. Uprisings against the Qing government had erupted at Guangzhou to the south and in Wuhan to the north. The revolutionary effervescence spread to Changsha, where local radicals seized power. Mao was swept along in the ferment. Hardly had he arrived than he wrote a tract urging that Dr. Sun Yat-sen, the Kuomintang leader, return from Japan to head a new regime. Though he later described its thesis as having been "somewhat muddled," Mao remembered his tract as "my first expression of a political opinion." As a gesture of defiance against the Qing dynasty, Mao also cut off his pigtail. And, about the same time, he quit school to enlist as a private in the new revolutionary army. His uneventful military career, which lasted only six months, gave him the leisure to read progressive newspapers and journals in which, he recalled later, he initially became acquainted with the notion of socialism.[11]

After leaving the army, Mao drifted until he entered the Hunan First Normal School in the spring of 1913, when he was almost twenty years old. His five years in this school, an institution for training teachers, constituted one of the most fruitful periods in his early life. For it was here that he laid the groundwork of his scholarship, began to shape his political ideas, and acquired his initial experiences in social action.

The curriculum and *ambiance* of the Normal School exposed Mao to a wide range of literature, both traditional and contemporary,

Chinese and Western. One of his teachers, Yuan Liuqi, persuaded him to discard his journalistic style in favor of the classical phraseology that would put sinews into his writing. Another professor, Yang Changji, was even more influential. Educated in Japan and England, he not only introduced his students to modern currents in European thought but inspired their devotion to China's national heritage. He also put them in touch with youth movements elsewhere in the country by encouraging them to read *New Youth*, the iconoclastic review then being published in Beijing by Chen Duxiu, later to become the first Secretary General of the Chinese Communist Party. Mao's first printed article, his appeal for physical fitness and military courage, appeared in *New Youth* in April 1917.

Faithful to his belief in a Spartan existence, Mao adhered to the rugged physical schedule he would observe for years to come. He took cold baths daily, swam as often as possible, walked tirelessly in all kinds of weather, climbed mountains, and even toyed with theories on nudism. During one summer vacation, he and a schoolmate hiked through the Hunan countryside with no money in their pockets, surviving on food given to them by peasants for whom, in exchange, Mao wrote scrolls in his bold calligraphy.

Meanwhile, plunging deeper into political activities, Mao became secretary of the Students' Society at the Normal School and initiated measures designed to break down its old-fashioned institutional regulations. Among other moves, he freed a student about to be forced into an arranged marriage, organized resistance to a levy on students to meet additional school expenditures, and created the Association for Student Self-Government, aimed at mobilizing opposition to unreasonable demands by the school authorities. In April 1918, a month before his graduation, he set up the New People's Study Society, a student discussion group, most of whose members were destined to join the Communist Party. By this time, Mao's opinions had grown increasingly radical. He decried religion, capitalism, autocracy, and Confucian morality as the "four evil demons of the empire." When his schoolmates discussed strategies to save China, he advised them to imitate the heroic rebels in his favorite novel, *All Men Are Brothers*, by taking to the hills to fight for equality and social justice.[12] Exactly a decade later, Mao himself would ascend the misty heights of Jinggangshan to pursue a similar path.

The years at the Hunan Normal School gave Mao the solid erudition that he displayed throughout the rest of his life. His essays were adorned with learned footnotes and his poetry rivaled that of

T. S. Eliot for its classical references. During the Cultural Revolution, when students were being exhorted to smash traditional vestiges, he betrayed surprise that the campaign had gone so far as to proscribe the literature he had loved as a young man. When his niece, defending the ban, asserted that the students should have a "precautionary injection" before reading Tang dynasty poems and novels like *The Dream of the Red Chamber* in order to protect them against contamination by the classics, Mao replied impatiently: "You are being purely metaphysical."[13]

Later, however, Mao developed a strong bias against the excesses of formal education. He repeatedly cited such figures as Benjamin Franklin and Maxim Gorki as men who had succeeded without schooling. "One who goes to school for several years becomes more stupid as he reads more books," he said at a Communist Party conference in 1965.[14] About the same time, he addressed cadets at a military academy: "A little reading of books is all right, but a lot of it harms people—it really harms them. It is revolutionary war that rears cadres; the battlefield is the school."[15] Even his own education, Mao pretended, had been a waste of time. "I only learned something at the school for brigands," he told two of his closest comrades. "What I learned in thirteen years of study was not usable for making revolution. . . ."[16]

♣

For all their interest in Rousseau, Adam Smith, Darwin, Huxley, and other Western thinkers, Chinese intellectuals around the turn of the twentieth century paid virtually no attention to Karl Marx. The reason was simple: the Marxist concept of communism emerging in a highly developed industrial state bore no relevance to a society like China. Even so basic a document as the Communist Manifesto, issued by Marx and Engels in 1848, was not published in full translation in China until April 1920. By then, a cataclysmic event had occurred that gave communism a large measure of credibility. The event was the Russian Revolution. It struck many educated Chinese as a model to emulate in their own efforts to rise out of the dismal conditions that had overtaken China at the time.

The first Chinese Republic proclaimed by Dr. Sun Yat-sen in 1911 had disintegrated. The recognized Chinese ruler in Beijing, Yuan Shikai, had died in 1916, leaving a vacuum that was quickly filled by warlords who fragmented the country as they built up their regional bases. Meanwhile, despite their rhetorical loyalty to President Wilson's principles of national self-determination enunciated at the close of World War I, the Western powers continued to carve up China. In particular, they secretly agreed to give Japan the special rights formerly held by Germany in the northern province of Shandong. This move ignited a student demonstration in Beijing on May 4, 1919, that rapidly turned into a nationwide protest. Known as the May 4th Movement, it became the vehicle for a wide variety of political, economic, social, and nationalistic grievances that had been irritating Chinese intellectuals for years.

Within this context of discontent, ferment, and hope, then, the Russian Revolution had undeniable appeal. It was a welcome blow to the capitalist nations that were the cause of China's degradation. In addition, Lenin's seizure of power in Russia offered a lesson in the technique of staging a revolution that might serve progressive Chinese activists in their own attempts to bring about change in China. For those Chinese who still clung to the conviction that the methods of the West would save China, here was a Western "scientific" approach that could be imitated. Therefore, for many Chinese, the Bolshevik take-over in Russia was less the triumph of an alien and incomprehensible doctrine called Marxism than the victory of a system that could be employed to unify nationalism and eradicate imperialism in China. Indeed, the strategies that the Russians pursued in China were essentially aimed at eliminating the influence of their Western and Japanese rivals even more than establishing a Chinese brand of communism.

Significantly, the earliest enthusiasts for the Russian Revolution in China were two Beijing University scholars who frankly admitted their ignorance of Marxism. One was Li Dazhao, the university librarian and later history professor, who had evolved an abstract theory of man's relations with historic forces and the role of "the people" in society. The other was Chen Duxiu, head of the University Literature Department and editor of *New Youth*, who had long believed that Western democracy and science could create a new order in China. In the spring of 1918, though not entirely convinced by communism despite their admiration for the Bolsheviks, they set up a Society for the Study of Marxism. It was the forerunner of the Chinese Communist Party, to be founded three years later. Among its members was Mao Zedong, who had just arrived in Beijing and was employed as an assistant in Li's library.

Mao may have found the Marxist study sessions too tame. Perhaps he was troubled by his lowly status as a library assistant, which earned him rather humiliating treatment from the haughty university scholars. Sharing a bedroom with seven friends and trying to subsist on a monthly wage of eight dollars, he may have wanted to escape his miserable living conditions. Whatever the motive, he was restless. At one point, he considered going to France on a so-called "work and study" program—as did later Communist luminaries like Zhou Enlai, Chen Yi, and Li Fuchun—but evidently decided that he lacked the talent to learn foreign languages. Instead, he chose to return to Changsha as a primary-school teacher. There he began to read the translations of Marxist texts, then being circulated in China for the first time. There, too, he formed youth groups and even mobilized a student strike against a brutal provincial warlord. Defying the warlord's ban on his writing, Mao also contributed articles to local publications, including a magazine sponsored by the Yale University educational mission to China. One of these articles, hailing the Russian Revolution, stressed that the organization of people according to their social class was the key to unity and ultimate success.[17] That thesis, clearly inspired by Marx, lent substance to Mao's later disclosure that he had come to consider himself a Marxist "in theory and to some extent in action" by the summer of 1920.[18] Soon afterward, he claimed to head a Communist faction in Hunan—even though a national Communist Party had not yet been founded.

In Changsha, having repudiated the marriage arranged by his parents when he was fourteen, Mao wed Yang Kaihui, the daughter of the Hunanese professor who had befriended him during his first year at the Normal School. A decade later, Yang Kaihui and Mao's sister, Zehong, were arrested by the pro-Nationalist governor of Hunan and executed. In 1957, sending condolences to the wife of a comrade who had also died, Mao recalled Yang Kaihui in a sentimental poem:

> My proud poplar is lost to me,
>   and to you your willow;
> Poplar and willow
>   soar to the highest heaven.[19]

If Chinese radicals and reformers were infected by the messianic message of the Russian Revolution, the Bolsheviks were beginning to be fascinated by the possibilities of political action in China and elsewhere in the Far East. In a heated strategy debate at the Second

Comintern Congress in July 1920, it was determined largely on Lenin's insistence that the International and local Communist groups should collaborate with "national revolutionary" movements in colonial areas, regardless of their ideological coloration. This decision was to have far-reaching consequences in China, for it laid the basis from which the Kremlin could, in the name of a "united front," subordinate the Chinese Communists to Chiang Kai-shek's Kuomintang whenever Soviet interests so demanded. Even at the outset, Comintern agents sent to the Orient seemed to play a deceptive game with their potential protégés as they sought to muster a wide spectrum of "nationalist" sympathy for the Soviet Union.

The first of these Comintern operatives, Gregory Voitinsky, reached China in the summer of 1920. He went straight to Li Dazhao and Chen Duxiu, the founders of the Society for the Study of Marxism, and proceeded to guide them in the establishment of a Chinese Communist Party. It was by no means an easy task. Among other things, an organization was difficult to shape since so many candidates for Party membership were undisciplined radicals with only the vaguest notions of Marxist-Leninist doctrine. Finally, in July 1921, the first Chinese Communist Party Congress assembled at a girls' school inside Shanghai's French Concession. Among those present were two delegates from each of the six self-styled Communist factions in China, with Mao representing the Hunan contingent. Also attending were Voitinsky and a recently arrived Dutch agent, Henrik Sneevliet, alias Maring. The whole affair had a faintly comic character. Sniffed out by the police, the delegates fled the city and eventually, pretending to be taking a holiday excursion, completed their sessions on a boat in the middle of the famous lake near Hangzhou, in nearby Zhejiang province. The Congress announced the Party's intention to "overthrow the capitalist classes" while showing an "attitude of independence, aggression, and exclusion" that would "allow no relationship with other parties or groups."[20]

While the Comintern operatives had encouraged the Chinese Communist notion of exclusivity, they themselves had no such idea in mind for Soviet strategy. On the contrary, the Russian objective was to accept support wherever it could be found. Earlier, the Soviet Foreign Minister, G. V. Chicherin, had attempted a dual approach by simultaneously indicating a desire for normal diplomatic relations both with the recognized Chinese regime in Beijing and with Sun Yat-sen's opposition Kuomintang based in Guangzhou. Now, after the Congress of the new Chinese Communist Party had ended, Maring embarked upon a similar zigzag. Traveling south, he sounded out such figures as Wu Peifu, the British-backed warlord of central China, and the governor of Hunan, Zhao Hengdi, later to become Mao's principal foe in the province. Eventually Maring met with Sun Yat-sen. The result of his mission, after lengthy negotiations, was an arrangement under which the Soviet Union would assist Sun's government with military aid and advisers, the most notable of whom would be Michael Borodin. In May 1924, the Kremlin broadened its options in China by establishing formal diplomatic ties with the very Beijing regime that Sun was seeking to overthrow.

As for the Communists, they were directed by Moscow to cooperate by becoming a "bloc within" the Kuomintang—or, in effect, diluting their identity as a Party. When some Chinese Communists protested at a Comintern meeting held in Moscow in 1922, Karl Radek put them down with a blistering report: "Comrades, do not indulge in too rosy expectations, do not overestimate your strength. . . . You must understand, comrades, that neither the question of socialism nor of the Soviet Republic [in China] are the order of the day."[21] The Russians communicated virtually the same message in a different context to Sun Yat-sen when, seeking to allay his fears of Kremlin domination, they assured him that they did not regard China as suitable terrain for "the communist order or even the soviet system."[22]

Several of the Chinese Communists who would prove to be most durable over the years were those who collaborated wholeheartedly with the Kuomintang during that period. The suave, skillful Zhou Enlai, who had recently returned to China from four years in Paris, became chief of the Political Department of the Kuomintang's military academy at Whampoa, outside Guangzhou, serving under Chiang Kai-shek. Mao also cooperated energetically with the Kuomintang, displaying such organizational talent that he was elevated to the movement's Executive Central Committee as an alternate member. This promotion brought him under attack from Communists who deplored the loss of their independence, and for a time, he was accused of having shifted to the right. Yet Mao evidently believed, as did the Kremlin, that the Chinese Communists would ultimately take over the Kuomintang from within through patient, prudent infiltration. The failure of that strategy later made him suspicious of "united front" arrangements he could not control. And, along with other experiences, it led him to doubt the wisdom of Soviet prescriptions for China.

It was in the mid-1920s that Mao, now operating as a professional political activist, began to perceive that tremendous revolutionary dynamism could be unleashed through the mobilization of China's vast, impoverished peasant population. The notion was neither so heretical as some students of communism have contended, nor so original as Mao's personal publicists have claimed. Both Lenin and Stalin had recognized that peasants could play a revolutionary role in underdeveloped areas. So had many early Chinese Communists, among them a landlord's son by the name of Peng Pai, who had created associations of discontented peasants in his native Guangdong province in 1923. But in contrast and even in opposition to the Russians and many of his own comrades, who clung to the classical Marxist dogma that the urban proletariat must constitute the revolutionary vanguard, Mao introduced the proposition that the peasantry was potentially the backbone of the Chinese revolution. True to his dictum that theory is derived from direct observation, he first began to evolve this thesis from an examination of conditions in Hunan, his home province.

During the course of several visits to Hunan, Mao was impressed by the extent to which Hunanese peasants were rising in protest against local landlords and officials. This ferment accelerated in the autumn of 1926, when Chiang Kai-shek's Kuomintang legions, moving north from Guangzhou in their expedition to eradicate warlords and unify China, inspired peasants in Hunan with the idea that a revolution had started that licensed them to overthrow their oppressive masters. Early in 1927, after a month spent investigating five counties in the province, Mao wrote a passionate report that laid the foundation for his lifelong conviction that rural rather than urban regions were the key centers of revolution not only in China but throughout the world. Predicting that the force of the peasants would "bury imperialism and militarism," he asserted that the value of any revolutionary party would be judged by its willingness to lead them. Further deviating from orthodox Marxism-Leninism, he neglected to affirm in his report that the peasants must be guided by the proletariat. Mao's report justified the "excesses" of peasant agitation in a celebrated passage expressing his doctrine that only "armed struggle" can bring about real change:

A revolution is not a dinner party, or writing an essay, or painting a picture, or doing embroidery; it cannot be so refined, so leisurely and gentle, so temperate, kind, courteous, restrained and magnanimous. A revolution is an insurrection, an act of violence by which one class overthrows another.[23]

Though the Kuomintang had initially encouraged peasant revolution in the southern province of Guangdong, where destroying the propertied classes served its purposes, Chiang Kai-shek soon discovered as his armies moved northward that his officers were linked to local landlords. Thus he began to back away from the radical agrarian policies favored by the Communists. At the same time, he maneuvered adroitly through a period of confused political rivalries to unite both the right and left wings of his party against the Communists. He was helped in this by Stalin, who was persuaded that the Kuomintang had to be preserved for the sake of Soviet national interests as well as to reply to Trotsky's criticisms of his strategies. Increasingly isolated, the Chinese Communists were therefore easy prey for Chiang in April 1927, when he decided to suppress them completely. He delivered his most devastating blow in Shanghai. There, having secretly enlisted support beforehand from the foreign community and the city's underworld, he ruthlessly massacred the Communists, many of whom naïvely believed that he was still counting on their cooperation. Despite this debacle, Stalin continued to urge the remnant Communists to collaborate with the Kuomintang. Somewhat later, however, the Kremlin issued an ambiguous directive authorizing the remaining Communists to initiate military activities designed to set up "soviet" areas in the Chinese hinterlands.

In the summer of 1927, obedient to that directive, Mao mobilized four regiments of peasants, miners, and Kuomintang deserters, calling them the First Division of the First Peasants and Workers Army. Confident that the rural population would rally to his side at harvest time, he led these ragtag units into Hunan. Like the operation organized by Zhou Enlai, He Long, and Zhu De a couple of months earlier against Nanchang, the capital of Jiangxi province, Mao's thrust ended in disaster. Expected assistance from workers in Changsha never materialized. Two of his regiments fell to fighting against each other, while two others were decimated by Kuomintang troops. Barely escaping capture himself, Mao managed to guide a thousand survivors up into Jinggangshan, a remote, precipitous mountain area that straddles the border between Hunan and Jiangxi provinces. There, in an impregnable fastness that recalled the rebel redoubt in *All Men Are Brothers*, Mao established a base. He was joined shortly afterward by other Communists seeking refuge. They included Zhu De, the Sichuanese who had studied in Germany, as well as Chen Yi, who would become China's Foreign Minister in 1958, and Lin

Biao, the brilliant soldier whom Mao in his closing years designated as his official successor.

The failure of the Autumn Harvest Uprising, as it became known, earned Mao a rebuke from the Communist Central Committee and dismissal from the Party's supreme Politburo. Undoubtedly reflecting Moscow's wishes, the Party also conferred the mantle of leadership on Li Lisan, one of Mao's former schoolmates from Hunan, who hewed to the Soviet line that the future of the revolution required the urban proletariat in the vanguard. For years after this, Mao's activities were so obscure that in March 1930, the Comintern published a long obituary reporting his death from consumption. During these years, however, Mao was using his enforced exile in the Jinggangshan wilderness to become familiar with the techniques of guerrilla warfare that would eventually give him the power to capture control of the Party. Lacking food and means of intelligence, he sought help from villagers in the mountain region. Accordingly, he devised his famous "three rules and six injunctions," which warned his soldiers against such infractions as confiscating food and stealing "even a needle or a piece of thread from the people." Recognizing that he could not overcome the superiority of his adversaries by frontal assault, he devised the hit-and-run tactics summed up in his slogan: "The enemy advances, we retreat; the enemy halts, we harass; the enemy tires, we attack; the enemy retreats, we pursue."

Early in 1929, having decided that Jinggangshan was no longer suitable, Mao and Zhu De led their force, now grown to about eleven thousand men, down to a new base area in southern Jiangxi province. There they proclaimed the formation of their "soviet." Meanwhile, other Communist groups were setting up bases elsewhere around the country. He Long, who had been a bandit chieftain before becoming a Communist, organized his base along the border between Hupeh and Hunan provinces. A base under Fang Zhimin, another guerrilla leader, was created at the juncture of Zhejiang and Anhui provinces. By setting up these sanctuaries in provincial frontier regions, the Communists were able to slip into different jurisdictional areas in much the same way that American gangsters in the days before strong federal laws sought immunity by crossing state boundaries. The strategy of flexible, autonomous territorial bases proved to be effective. Between 1928 and 1933, Communist Party membership in China climbed from forty thousand to three hundred thousand. During the same period, the Communist Army's strength increased from roughly a thousand to about a hundred thousand rifles.

The growth of the Communist forces did not elude Chiang Kai-shek, who by then had jettisoned his Soviet advisers in favor of a German advisory mission headed by General Ludwig von Falken-hausen. Starting at the end of 1930, he launched a series of five so-called "bandit extermination campaigns" aimed at smashing Mao's Jiangxi sanctuary. The fifth and most intensive campaign was more than the Communists could endure. At least 2 million peasants in their region were killed or starved to death as the Kuomintang armies burned everything in sight. The Communists lacked a plausible strat-egy to counter this drive. Like Chiang Kai-shek, they were being counseled by a German—a Comintern agent named Otto Braun, who went under the Chinese *nom-de-guerre* of Li De. But unlike Chiang's adviser, Braun was a former schoolteacher with little military expe-rience. He mistakenly convinced the Communists to defend every inch of their territory. As a result, Mao himself later conceded, they fought "stupidly" until they had no choice but to break through Kuo-mintang encirclement and embark without specific plans upon what would be hailed as their epic Long March.

The Long March has been compared to Hannibal's trek over the Alps and Napoleon's retreat from Moscow. It was probably more difficult than either. Lasting slightly more than a year, from October 1934 to October 1935, it propelled Mao and his followers six thousand miles from Jiangxi to northern Shaanxi province, where they estab-lished a temporary headquarters at Bao An before creating a per-manent base at Yenan fourteen months later. During that year, the Communist force of ninety thousand men that had started out was reduced to about twenty thousand. For the journey was a series of running battles fought as the Communists crossed rivers, mountain ranges, and arid areas. "There were so very many battles," the vet-eran Communist General Peng Dehuai told Robert Payne. "Now, when I look back, it seems to be one enormous battle going on forever."[24]

Strenuous as it was, the Long March served Mao in several ways. It tested his senior officers, most of whom survived its ordeals to become the toughened elite of the Chinese Communist Party. It provided him with a truly heroic legend with which he could inspire later generations. It taught him valuable lessons in mobile warfare against a superior enemy. And it afforded him the opportunity to assert his unqualified leadership of the Chinese revolutionary move-ment. At Zunyi, a captured town in the southern province of Guizhou, he convened a conference in January 1935 at which he finally subdued those who still favored urban revolution, and took over the Communist Party as Chairman of its Politburo.

In the closing years of his life, Mao would be depicted in millions of official posters, badges, and busts as an aging Adonis who combined the godlike attributes of infallible wisdom and unshakable strength. But at forty-three, when Edgar Snow encountered him at his northern Shaanxi base, Mao seemed "quite free from symptoms of megalomania." He was, as Snow described him, a "gaunt, rather Lincolnesque figure, above average height for a Chinese, somewhat stooping, with a head of thick black hair grown very long." He laughed easily at earthy jokes as he chain-smoked cigarettes, and he enjoyed nothing so much as Hunan's almost inedibly hot red peppers. Yet, in Snow's view, something about Mao suggested a "power of ruthless decision" when he deemed it necessary. Another American writer, Agnes Smedley, who saw Mao in Yenan, was similarly impressed. Initially repelled by Mao's inscrutable, faintly feminine characteristics, she found that "the sinister quality I had at first felt so strongly in him proved to be a spiritual isolation." Mao was respected rather than loved, Miss Smedley wrote, "as stubborn as a mule, and a steel rod of pride and determination ran through his nature. I had the impression he would wait and watch for years, but eventually have his way."[25]

Though he often gave an appearance of studied inactivity, Mao did more than wait and watch, especially after he shifted his base to Yenan in late 1936. Setting the example himself by tending a garden, he organized a system under which his soldiers farmed, raised livestock, sewed clothing, operated modest industrial workshops, and fulfilled other tasks. This drive for economic self-sufficiency was necessitated by the fact that the Yenan base was encircled and blockaded by Chiang Kai-shek's Nationalists. As they had in the Jinggangshan region, the Communists also expanded the area under their control by mobilizing peasant support. One of their methods for attracting peasants was an agrarian reform scheme designed to distribute land to tenants and to reduce rents. These and other such programs, carried out without the benefit of elaborate bureaucratic structures, confirmed in Mao the notion that spirit and will power could be more effective than institutions—and that notion remained with him through his later life.

Mao also read and wrote obsessively during the Yenan years.

Edgar Snow reported that he would disappear for three or four nights of intensive reading whenever a visitor brought him new books. According to one of his aides, Mao worked almost steadily for nine days and nights in 1938 to complete his famous essay, *On Protracted War.* Virtually all his writing dealt with two broad subjects—military affairs and political questions. In the military realm, he emphasized many of his old principles of irregular warfare: that guerrillas must be fearless in their disdain for enemy weapons, yet cautious enough to avoid annihilation when confronted by a superior foe. In his political essays, Mao seemed to be groping to shape an ideological framework for the China he envisaged. Starting from Lenin's premise that revolution required a "bourgeois-democratic" stage before reaching socialism, he conceived of an initial phase called "new democracy." During this phase (which theoretically continued for at least two decades after Mao marched into Beijing in 1949), the Kuomintang and other "bourgeois" movements were represented in the Chinese People's Political Consultative Conference even though that body was nothing more than an instrument of the Communists.

As the legend of Mao spread, more and more teachers, students, artists, and other educated Chinese streamed into Yenan. Their pilgrimage had one important effect on Mao's personal life—and, three decades later, on the life of all China. It brought into the region a minor movie actress from Shanghai by the name of Lan Ping, who evidently believed that she could improve her career under Communist auspices. While not beautiful, she was tall, graceful, and infinitely more appealing than the unkempt female guerrillas in the area. Mao, then in his mid-forties, was roughly twice Lan Ping's age. Their flirtation encountered complications, however. He was then married to He Zizheng, his third wife, a former schoolteacher and Communist organizer who had borne him five children, one of them while making the Long March. Her rugged life had ruined her health. Whether Mao sent her to the Soviet Union for medical treatment before or after meeting Lan Ping has never been clear. In any case, he eventually divorced He to wed Lan Ping, to whom he gave the alias Jiang Qing, or "green river," from a couplet in one of his favorite T'ang poems. It was under that name that she would become celebrated as the termagant of the Cultural Revolution.

The flow into Yenan of "intellectuals"—meaning, by Chinese measure, anyone with at least secondary schooling—also had important ideological consequences. These educated, urban Chinese contrasted sharply with the rugged, often illiterate peasants who had risen to posts of authority in the Communist ranks. Moreover, many of them were equipped with an academic knowledge of Marxism-Leninism that was largely alien to the "concrete" Chinese situation of the time.

Despite his revolt against Confucian tradition, Mao respected the role that intellectuals had played in reforming Chinese society over the centuries. But he recognized that one of China's ancient plagues was the wide gap that separated the educated classes of the cities from the majority of peasants. He therefore urged, as he would repeatedly in the years to come, that the intellectuals who had rallied to his side be indoctrinated so that "they gradually overcome their weaknesses, revolutionize their outlook, identify themselves with the masses, and merge with the older Party members and cadres, and the worker and peasant members of the Party."[26] He also began to stress the need for the "Sinification of Marxism" in order to provide his Communist Party with an independent philosophy derived from the "concrete conditions and struggles of China" rather than Soviet doctrine. Criticizing comrades who "can only repeat quotes from Marx, Engels, Lenin, and Stalin from memory but . . . understand very little or nothing about their own history," he asserted that Marxism could only function in a "national form." He said: "We must discard our dogmatism and replace it by a new and vital Chinese style and manner, pleasing to the eye and to the ear of the Chinese common people."[27]

This effort to persuade his educated recruits to discard foreign models in favor of Chinese realities prompted Mao to launch a "rectification campaign" in February 1942, which, seen in retrospect, was an early forerunner of the Cultural Revolution. Its aim was "thought reform"—a therapeutic process through which, as Benjamin Schwartz has explained, the Chinese intelligentsia could undergo moral cultivation and thereby acquire what Mao considered to be proper "proletarian" attitudes.[28] For, unlike Marx and Lenin, whose ideas were basically materialistic, Mao came to regard "proletarian" as denoting a spiritual state of mind rather than an economic class. He had already begun to formulate his thesis that the mechanics of the Communist Party organization were far less vital than the quality of its members.

The attempt to give his concept of communism a distinctly national—and implicitly superior—flavor also induced Mao to promote himself as a new species of Chinese hero. He therefore initiated a cult of his own personality that was to build up to fantastic proportions in his final years. Though Edgar Snow had observed no hero-worship of Mao in 1936 in Yenan, Communist Army publicists a few years later began to extol him as "our brilliant great leader, our teacher and our savior." This adoration was apparently not shared by the Communist Party apparatus, however. Central Committee resolutions omitted Mao's name, and the first edition of his *Selected Works* was issued in the period after 1944 by a regional branch rather than by the Party headquarters in Yenan. [29] Even in those days, there may have been incipient divisions between Mao and the Party stalwarts headed by Liu Shaoqi, as the Red Guards would allege during the Cultural Revolution. [30] Subtle differences also separated Liu from Mao at the Party's Seventh Congress in April 1945. The Party officially enshrined Mao's "theory of revolution" in its new Constitution, and Liu praised him as "not only the greatest revolutionary and statesman in Chinese history but also its greatest theoretician and scientist." [31] Yet Liu, the quintessential organization man, also affirmed in his report to the Congress that it was "impossible" that the Party could stray from the "correct political line"; the interests of the Party and the people were identical. In short, Liu adhered to Lenin's belief in the inviolable Party vanguard—and this would eventually bring him into collision with Mao's conviction that only the masses, with himself as their spokesman, were infallible.

On the battlefield, meanwhile, the Communists made phenomenal progress from the mid-1930s until 1945 as a result of three factors—their own strategies, Chiang Kai-shek's failures, and the devastation caused by the Japanese invasion of China. A combination of circumstances rather than Mao's purported infallibility propelled the Communists forward. Still, Mao was able to consolidate his gains by shrewdly taking advantage of those circumstances as they emerged.

A triangular conflict menaced China in late 1936, as Mao was moving his north Shaanxi base from Bao An to Yenan. The Japanese, having occupied the northeastern region of Manchuria five years earlier, were threatening to descend into China to challenge both Mao's Communists and Chiang's Nationalists, who were fighting each other. Mao, evidently expecting their initial attack to strike his territory, was anxious to respond to the Japanese in coalition with Chiang. The Comintern, then favoring "united-front" tactics throughout the world, also advocated this approach. But Chiang still gave priority to his "bandit-suppression campaign," as he labeled his effort to liquidate the Communists. Finally, a dramatic incident intervened to force Chiang's hand.

Marshal Zhang Xueliang, a Manchurian warlord saddened by the loss of his homeland and captivated by Mao's pleas for unity against the Japanese, kidnaped Chiang at Xi'an, the ancient capital not far from Yenan. Planning to prosecute Chiang, the Marshal invited the Communists to take part in the "people's trial." But Zhou Enlai, then chief political commissar for the Communist Army, took a different tack. Possibly acting on Kremlin orders,[32] he offered to spare Chiang on condition that the Nationalists halt the civil war and concentrate instead on a joint defense against the Japanese. In exchange, Zhou pledged that the Communists would cease their attempts to overthrow the Nationalist regime and place their army, henceforth to be designated as the Eighth Route Army, under Chiang's command. Chiang accepted, and was freed. Later, though he remained loyal to the principle of an anti-Japanese alliance, Mao apparently recalled Chiang's betrayal of the Communists a decade earlier and refused to subordinate the leadership of his troops to the Nationalists. The wrangling over that point later blocked the formation of a coalition government and brought down the "united front."

If the deal between the Communists and the Nationalists seemed to favor Chiang in the short run, it proved to be a boon to Mao over the longer term. For, by operating in the countryside, he could use the patriotic and nationalistic appeal of the struggle against the alien Japanese to win the support of peasants who might otherwise have been unmoved by the Communist ideology or its promises of social and economic justice. And the Japanese unwittingly assisted Mao by focusing on him as their primary enemy, as well as by pursuing a scorched-earth strategy that drove peasants into the Communist ranks. As a consequence, the strength of the regular Communist army grew tenfold in eight years—from some fifty thousand in 1937 to about a half-million by 1945.[33] During the same period, the Communists spread out from Yenan and a few other small base areas to extend their control over 100 million people, or more than one-fifth of the Chinese population. Years later, when a Japanese visitor to Beijing expressed regrets to him for Japan's aggression, Mao replied that, on the contrary, the invasion had helped rather than hindered his cause. "So instead of your apologizing to me," he told the Japanese, "perhaps I should thank you."[34]

From its outbreak in July 1937 until the American atomic blow against Japan ended it eight years later, the Sino-Japanese war was largely a *drôle de guerre*. Both Chiang and Mao had envisaged a "protracted resistance" divided into three stages: first, the Chinese would inflict heavy casualties on the advancing enemy from defensive positions; second, after stabilizing the front lines, they would open flanking attacks against the Japanese; and third, having weakened the enemy, they would launch a general counteroffensive. But in reality, the war consisted of an initial push by the Japanese, in which they captured China's key coastal cities, followed by a long stalemate.

The Nationalists, though receiving the bulk of American and Soviet aid, failed to undertake a single major action against the Japanese during the entire conflict. Their officers and men became soft and corrupt. When the Japanese staged a final offensive in the summer of 1944, the Nationalists lost seven hundred thousand troops, one hundred forty-six towns, and about a hundred thousand square miles of territory containing 60 million people in a matter of seven months.[35] By the end of that year, Chiang's army was described by one observer as "a pulp, a tired, dispirited, unorganized mass, despised by the enemy, alien to its own people, neglected by its government, ridiculed by its allies.[36]

The Communists, meanwhile, not only expanded in numbers but improved their military capabilities and structure. In September 1937, at the outset of the war, they gained an enormous psychological boost and immense prestige by routing a long Japanese column at Bingxinguan, a mountain pass in northern Shanxi province. Three years later, they made an equally dramatic impact with their famous Hundred Regiments Offensive, which foiled Japanese plans to seize the 1940 autumn harvest in north China. For the most part, however, the Communists fought behind the lines, harassing the Japanese from increasingly widespread guerrilla sanctuaries. In contrast to the demoralized Nationalist troops, Communist soldiers were disciplined, highly motivated, and extraordinarily rugged. While organized into regular divisions, their army had as its core small squads, headed by Communist Party members, which facilitated constant political indoctrination. This indoctrination was so intensive that Evans Carlson, a United States Marine colonel and the first foreign military observer to reach the Communist zones, noted that soldiers often wore tracts pinned to the back of their caps so that the man behind could study political lessons during marches.[37] Another American military expert has pointed out that from the early 1930s onward the Communist Army gradually shifted from a collection of guerrilla bands to a centralized, specialized, conventional, professional army.[38] This trend, which accelerated during the civil war and especially during the Korean War, was to bring Mao into conflict with several senior Chinese officers who gradually adopted the view that guerrilla techniques had become obsolete.

Just before and immediately after the Japanese surrender in late 1945, the United States sought to prevent a Chinese civil war by encouraging the Communists and Nationalists to reconcile their differences. Stalin, apprehensive lest an internal conflagration in China provoke American intervention and thereby involve the Soviet Union, was reported to have gone even further by urging Mao to dissolve his army and join Chiang Kai-shek's government. It may be, as Mao's supporters charged during the Cultural Revolution, that Liu Shaoqi and other high-level Chinese Communist Party figures were also in favor of a settlement. But neither the American Ambassador, Patrick Hurley, who was miscast for the assignment, nor General George C. Marshall, whose talents were keener, nor Stalin, Liu, and others could persuade the two Chinese adversaries to agree. Playing for time in the hope that the corrupt Nationalist regime would collapse, Mao seemed moderate in contrast to Chiang, whose awareness that the Communists could only grow in strength prompted him to behave more aggressively. The Nationalists in fact sparked the formal outbreak of the inevitable civil war in July 1946 when, fearing that the Communists were seeking to reinforce their units in Manchuria, they blocked their attempt to withdraw from central China to north of the Yangzi River.

Like the conflict against the Japanese, the civil war demonstrated the Communists' military skill and Nationalist incompetence. It also showed the extraordinary ability of the Communists to expand from numerical inferiority to superiority over the Nationalists. With about a half-million regular troops under arms at the outset of the war, the Communist force was one-fourth the size of the Nationalist army. By the middle of 1947, the Communists had nearly half as many men as the Nationalists. A year later, the two sides were almost equal in numbers—though the Communists, with their higher morale and better generalship, were plainly stronger.[39] Only Chiang Kai-shek, with his blind faith in his own invincibility, was unable to see that the Communists had virtually won the war by the end of 1948.

The respective strategies adopted by Mao and Chiang in the civil war were dictated by essentially the same geographical considerations that had guided the military policies of ambitious Chinese factions from ancient times. Just as the kingdoms based in western China followed a "horizontal" design in their conquests by pushing across the Yellow River plain to the sea, so the Communists sought to drive to the coast from their sanctuaries in Shaanxi and other interior provinces. And just as the southern states traditionally pursued a "vertical" pattern aimed at stretching their command over the north, so the Nationalists tried to extend their control from Guangzhou upward into Manchuria.

The Communists, in their retrospective analysis of what they called the "third revolutionary war," viewed the conflict as having passed through three successive stages. This analysis fit Mao's theory that an inferior force could defeat a bigger enemy only through a gradual process calculated to shift the balance of power in its favor. Largely because of Nationalist blunders, the process went faster in the civil war than Mao had anticipated. In November 1948, he noted that "the war will be much shorter than we originally estimated."[40]

The first stage, beginning with the eruption of hostilities in July 1946, was a "defensive" interlude for the Communists. Instead of striving to acquire territory, they worked to consolidate their own positions while reducing Chiang's numerical superiority by nibbling at his weakest points. Accordingly, they deliberately withdrew from several areas, including their celebrated Yenan headquarters—a tactic that the deluded Nationalists erroneously hailed as a sign of imminent victory. During this period, too, Chiang undertook a move that provided the Communists with a decisive advantage later. Defying American advice, he sent his best troops deep into Manchuria, thereby putting an enormous strain on his supply lines.

In the summer of 1947, the Communists entered their second stage by launching a limited counteroffensive against the provinces of central China and the principal railways used by Chiang to supply his forces in the north. This maneuver was prompted by the accurate assumption that Chiang had seriously overtaxed his communications capabilities by moving his troops into Manchuria, and consequently had increased the vulnerability of his rear areas. At the end of the year, though still engaged in mobile rather than positional warfare, the Communists captured the key railway juncture of Shijiazhuang, in Hebei province south of Beijing. Chiang could no longer move equipment or reinforcements northward except by air, an inadequate means of transportation in those days.

By mid-1948 the Nationalists were clearly on the defensive, their most effective units helplessly tied up in Manchuria and northern China, their troops weary and demoralized. While rampant infiltration and corruption ravaged his regime, Chiang committed such irreparable political mistakes as outlawing innocuous liberal movements and thereby driving their members into the Communist ranks. At this point, the Communists initiated their final strategic stage with a series of campaigns that carried them through central and eastern China. By this time, Chiang had fled to Taiwan, and Mao, disregarding the advice of Stalin as well as some of his own comrades, ordered the capture of Nanjing, the Nationalist capital. A few months afterward, he would be in Beijing, his own capital, as chief of state of the People's Republic of China.[41] Now, as he stood on the brink of triumph after nearly a whole life devoted to struggle, he paused to compose a poem in which a line would depict his future as it did his past:

> The true way that governs the world of men is that of radical change.[42]

CHAPTER 4

Cracks in the Monolith

♣

> *There is no such thing as a perfect leader,*
> *either in the past or present, in China or*
> *elsewhere. If there is one, he is only pre-*
> *tending, like a pig inserting scallions into its*
> *nose in an effort to look like an elephant.*
> —LIU SHAOQI, *July 13,* 1947

ON A HOT EVENING in September 1964, a delegation of French officials was ushered into the *salon* of an unpretentious bungalow near Hangzhou, a scenic resort in central China. The room was modestly furnished with overstuffed armchairs, small tea tables, and a sprinkling of strategically located enamel cuspidors. In contrast to nearly every dwelling in China, no portrait of Mao Zedong gazed down from the wall. For this was Mao's summer residence adjoining the same lake where, more than four decades earlier, his embryonic Communist Party had held its first meeting disguised as a holiday excursion. Soon Mao himself, the living legend, shuffled stiffly in to welcome his guests.

Mao was approaching the age of seventy-one at the time, and one of the guests, observing him carefully, speculated that there must have been a grain of truth in the rumors then circulating that he had suffered a mild stroke or heart attack not long before. He was much thinner than his photographs depicted him, his baggy brown tunic and trousers reinforcing the impression that he had lately lost a good deal of weight. Presumably defying doctor's orders, he chain-smoked a Chinese brand of Virginia cigarette, his right hand trembling as he lighted one after another. He walked with difficulty, guided by a male nurse who tactfully held his elbow when he first entered the *salon* and again as the group later moved to an adjacent dining room.

If Mao looked unhealthy, the conversation that evening also suggested he felt disappointed, perhaps even frustrated, as he sensed his life drawing to a close. For at dinner, slurping his soup, belching unabashedly, and picking his broken black teeth, he repeatedly focused on a subject that appeared to obsess him—the danger that China, growing soft and complacent in the absence of hardship, might betray his hopes following his death. He seemed to be worried that the Communist Party, after fourteen years in power, was degenerating into a bureaucracy as rigid and ritualistic as the ancient Chinese mandarinate. He seemed apprehensive as well that the People's Liberation Army, its very name now an anachronism, was becoming flabby for lack of combat experience. Above all, Mao made no secret of his fear that China's younger generation might fail to uphold his concept of perpetual revolution and turn instead to the Soviet type of revisionism that, he believed, would inevitably lead back to feudalism and capitalism.

When one of the Frenchmen described the "ardor and spirit" he had found among the Beijing University professors and students with whom he had talked, Mao brushed aside the comment with unusual rudeness. "What they told you isn't necessarily the truth," he remarked. "It's not a good university." Another guest, who praised the students he had visited at the Xi'an Polytechnical Institute, provoked an equally skeptical reply. "Of course they sounded fine to you, but don't believe everything you hear," Mao grumbled. Then, his high-pitched nasal voice tinged with melancholy, he went on to catalogue the shortcomings of China's youth, "They know nothing of war and revolution, landlords and rich peasants," he said. "They must learn to struggle. Maybe they will learn. . . ."[1]

A smiliar note of uncertainty echoed through Mao's interviews with other foreign visitors to China during that period. Speaking with Edgar Snow in late 1964, for example, he deplored the fact that Chinese youth had never fought a war or been oppresed by imperialism and capitalism, and were only acquainted with the "old society" from history books. Thus it was possible, Mao said, that China's younger generation might negate the revolution after his disappearance.[2] He also complained to André Malraux that his adversaries inside China—"the bourgeois-nationalists, the intellectuals and so on"—were indoctrinating their children to oppose his policies. The "youth problem" had yet to be solved, he asserted, adding ominously, "Youth must be put to the test."[3] But perhaps Mao's feeling that he had to act quickly to reverse China's revisionist drift was reflected most clearly in a poem he wrote in early 1963:

So many deeds cry out to be done,
And always urgently;
The world rolls on,
Time passes.
Ten thousand years are too long,
Seize the day, seize the hour! . . .
Away with all pests!
Our force is irresistible.[4]

Though the pressures of advanced age and probable illness had undoubtedly exacerbated Mao's mood, his impatience was not merely a symptom of an old man's crankiness. For, it was later evident, he had ample reason to believe that his dreams for China were being subverted by many of his veteran comrades as well as by large segments of the Chinese people. In a sense, he had become a victim of his own success.

🜩

The Communist victory had given China in the years after 1949 greater domestic strength and international stature than that land had known since the zenith of the Qing dynasty in the eighteenth century. In Mao's view, however, these accomplishments were insufficient. Hoping to shape a new human species cleansed of individualistic and materialistic tendencies, he sought to perpetuate his kind of spiritual revolution. But this aim soon met with passive and sometimes active resistance from numbers of Chinese peasants, workers, and particularly intellectuals who had supported the Communists less for Mao's ideological theories than for their ability to bring peace and order to China after decades of war and civil strife. More significantly, important factions in China's Communist Party, government, and Army also came to question and even reject Mao's principles, contending that the management of a country demanded organization, specialization, and bureaucratic routine rather than his mass-mobilization schemes, indoctrination campaigns, and moral exhortations. Still, Mao refused to alter his vision. The more he perceived real or imagined opposition to his ideas, the more he was confirmed in his conviction that the Chinese mentality needed a thorough transformation. Nothing less than a complete change in China's psyche—a "cultural revolution" that would "touch people to their very souls," as he put it—was imperative.

No ruling group, however monolithic it may seem, is without tensions capable of reaching the tolerable proportions that cause overt conflict. In the case of China, the Communist leaders succeeded in tolerating internal stresses and strains for years, even to the extent of appearing to the world to be an extraordinary model of unity. In fact, political, military, and economic strategy disputes had divided Mao and his associates more than once during the decades before they rose to power. And these disputes continued after the establishment of their regime in Beijing.

In contrast to the Bolsheviks, who had no real political, economic, social, or administrative experience before seizing the Kremlin, the Chinese Communists had commanded territory and people ever since their retreat into their mountainous Jinggangshan redoubt in 1927. After officially proclaiming the Chinese People's Republic on October 1, 1949, they were able to extend to a national scale many of the control methods they had employed for two decades.

With Mao as its Chairman, the Communist Party was the locus of power, exercising authority through its own apparatus as well as through the government and Army. Party representatives operated within state agencies, factories, and schools and, as commissars, inside every Chinese military unit. By liquidating a million or more land-lords in the early 1950s, the Communists destroyed the rural gentry, thereby permitting the Party hierarchy to reach from the supreme Politburo in Beijing down to the lowest village cadre. The Party also directed a formidable array of labor, youth, artistic, and other na-tionwide federations, each with millions of members, designed to manipulate public opinion every time a new policy was set in motion. The entire population was consequently exposed to continual study sessions, meetings, demonstrations, and rallies. Combined with "thought-reform" programs and vast mobilization movements, these exercises were essentially calculated to create a new environment in which, theoretically at least, the individual could not escape absorp-tion into the "masses."

This complicated system initially appeared to be highly effective, for two main reasons. First, the new Chinese leaders had been forged in the same furnace. Almost all had served as soldiers, surviving the Long March and fighting the Japanese before finally conquering Chiang Kai-shek's Nationalists. As a result, they seemed to be an exceptionally solid group. Second, their functions overlapped and intertwined so intimately that it was difficult to discern possible splits among them. Most key Army officers and government figures were also Party dignitaries, while most Party members held Army or government positions. This was particularly true in the provinces, where Party, government, and Army organizations were closely related. Mao himself personified this multiplicity of roles, serving simultaneously until 1959 as Chief of State and Party Chairman.

But this structure was less homogeneous than it seemed to be. A good deal of friction troubled the Communist movement prior to 1949 as the Party gradually acquired the bureaucratic trappings of a large, compartmentalized institution. As a consequence, it no longer fit Mao's Yenan ideal of a flexible guerrilla-style force adept at handling political, economic, and social as well as military tasks. In short, as he saw and deplored it, the romantic rebels of *All Men Are Brothers* had turned into prosaic functionaries.

The bureaucratic trend was especially pronounced in the Communists' Red Army, whose officers had grown inclined over the years to adopt what Mao persistently criticized as a "bourgeois military mentality." In the beginning, when they lacked manpower and matériel, Communist officers could make a virtue of necessity by accepting Mao's strategy of small-unit, hit-and-run guerrilla warfare. But as their legions expanded in the early 1930s, they began to question Mao's emphasis on the importance of ideology and the primacy of men over weapons. Comintern advisers like Otto Braun, alias Li De, taught them conventional Soviet military tactics. They were also influenced by the idea prevalent among soldiers everywhere that rank, regulations, modern equipment, and professional status are desirable. Moreover, they learned from battlefield experience against both the Nationalists and the Japanese that large-scale deployments of trained, disciplined regulars were more effective than ragtag guerrilla actions. Even a general like He Long, the prototype of the Maoist peasant soldier, had lost respect for guerrilla techniques by the time he was able to lead regular Eighth Route Army troops against the Japanese in Hebei province in 1938.[5]

Disagreements over military strategy produced some of the earliest rifts between Mao and his comrades. In the late 1920s, for example, the prestigious Zhu De disregarded his guerrillas, preferring instead to fight conventionally against the Nationalists, then attempting to dislodge the Communists from their Jiangzi base area. This "bourgeois" approach earned Zhu a rebuke from Mao.[6] Questions of military policy were again involved in the early 1930s, when rival Party and Army figures, including Zhou Enlai, temporarily stripped Mao of his authority.[7]

Professionalized officers also challenged Mao by rejecting or reducing whenever possible the power of political representatives attached to their units. The introduction of commissars into the Army, originally conceived in the mid-1920s by both the Communists and the Nationalists, reflected an ingrained Chinese suspicion that soldiers were men whose loyalties were only to themselves. Like the Catholic priests who accompanied the Spanish conquistadores in their conquest of America, the commissars were charged with guaranteeing fidelity to the cause—or, in Mao's imagery, with assuring that the Party "commands the gun." In practice, however, their presence in units frequently led to internal clashes of authority. During periods when Mao's line prevailed, commissars often nagged officers and even tried to direct their strictly military operations. At other times, when Army professionals had the upper hand, the commissars were relegated to minor assignments. Rarely did the two groups manage to work out a durable relationship, perhaps because their roles were basically incompatible.

Before 1949, meanwhile, there were other esoteric forewarnings of the cataclysmic dispute that would erupt later between Mao and the Communist Party *apparatchiks* headed by Liu Shaoqi. Their rivalry was scarcely a simple contest for authority, though that was certainly part of the quarrel. It was largely rooted in divergent concepts of the function of the Party, and, consequently, the controversy had extremely broad implications. For the crucial question of which direction China would take fundamentally depended upon whether Mao or the Party predominated.

As Stuart Schram has written, Mao never really perceived the Party in the full Leninist sense to be a strong, self-sustaining central organization, a kind of Mother Church. Nor did he, like Lenin, view the Party's vocation to be the essentially political task of mobilizing and guiding the proletariat. Mao's belief, based on his experience, was that only "armed struggle" could achieve victory—or, as he put it, "political power grows out of the barrel of a gun."[8] Thus he attached enormous importance to the Army, without which, in his words, "the people have nothing."[9] If the Party "commands the gun," it was a Party that he considered to be his personal instrument. The Party line was his line. Allegiance to the Party signified obedience to him as the author of the correct ideology.[10]

In short, Mao was persuaded, pre-eminence belonged to the leader rather than to the Party machine. Just as in later years he obliquely attacked his Chinese adversaries for revisionism by criticizing Khrushchev, so Mao indirectly promoted the cult of his own personality by praising Stalin. He had no reason to revere Stalin, who had repeatedly tried to subvert his policies, yet, celebrating the Soviet dictator's sixtieth birthday in December 1939, Mao referred to him as the "commander of the revolutionary front," and "leader of the world revolution," adding, "Marx is dead, and Engels and Lenin too are dead. If we did not have a Stalin, who would give the orders?"[11]

Mao would demonstrate that concept of leadership most dramatically in 1959 when, facing censure by prominent Party and military comrades following the collapse of his ambitious "Great Leap Forward," he threatened to quit Beijing, return to his Jinggangshan redoubt, raise a new peasant force, and fight his way back to power.[12] Though that tactic may have been a bluff, Mao still thought of himself as a unique figure towering above the Party apparatus. Perhaps it was no accident that, sounding like General de Gaulle, he said to André Malraux: "I am alone with the masses."[13]

Such a posture was plainly more than any bureaucracy could abide. Hence there was a certain plausibility to the documents issued during the Cultural Revolution indicting Liu Shaoqi and his Party colleagues for having persistently betrayed Mao. But these differences, to whatever degree they existed, were latent for years. Mao plainly would not have hailed Liu's contributions to the movement in his "revised" history of the Party had he suspected him of treason. Nor would he have left Liu in charge of the Yenan headquarters when he descended to Chongqing in August 1945 to negotiate with Chiang Kai-shek. Moreover, Mao implicitly designated Liu as his successor in early 1950 by delegating him to serve as acting Chief of State when he went to Moscow to sign a treaty with the Soviet Union. Yet there is no doubt that Liu did disagree with several of Mao's basic tenets at certain critical stages in their relationship. It seems clear that key figures within the Communist movement could develop sharply contrasting ideas despite similarities in background and experience.

Five years Mao's junior, Liu was also born of well-to-do peasant parents in Hunan province, just across a mountain range from the Mao family farm. Like Mao, he attended the Normal School at Changsha, the provincial capital, though there is no evidence that they knew each other there. In all probability, they did not become acquainted until 1922, when Liu was assigned to organize coal miners in the region of Hunan, where Mao was then secretary of the embryonic Party's district committee. Before that, Liu's activities in the

Communist movement had been limited. He had helped to set up workers' schools in the suburbs of Beijing, and, selected by the Kremlin agent in China, Gregory Voitinsky, he had spent less than a year in Moscow studying economics and labor questions at the so-called University of the Toilers of the East, a Soviet school for prospective Communist cadres from Asia. From all accounts, Liu was disappointed by his sojourn in Russia. He was there during a winter of severe famine, with little more than potatoes and black bread to eat. He could not speak the language, and found the Russians too preoccupied with their own dire problems to befriend a shy, awkward, lonely Chinese. In addition, the university courses created for Asians were mainly propaganda meetings in which nothing of real substance was taught. Nevertheless, Liu's visit to Moscow was significant. For it introduced him to Leninist ideology, from which he derived a lifelong conviction in the primacy of the Party as the dominant force in the struggle to achieve revolution.

In contrast to Mao, who concentrated on mobilizing peasant support from the start of his revolutionary career, Liu devoted most of the fifteen years after returning to China from the Soviet Union in 1922 to organizing urban workers. He lived a furtive underground existence under an assortment of aliases, darting from one city to another to elude either Nationalist agents or European police, and occasionally going to jail. In 1928, he was elected to the Party's Central Committee and, four years later, to the Politburo. By the late 1930s, having repaired to Yenan, he appeared to be Mao's second-in-command.

Definite temperamental differences separated the two men. Mao's charismatic character exuded magnetism, but Liu was introverted, taciturn, and, as an old comrade recalled from their early days together, "a bit too glum and devoid of youthfulness."[14] Counterpointing Mao's dazzling creativity, Liu was a plodder who depended on sheer hard work rather than brilliance. For a long time, however, these differences complemented rather than contradicted each other. If Mao was the yogi, Liu was the commissar and, on the surface at least, they seemed to operate in harmony.

But this harmony, like the apparent cohesion of the Chinese Communist movement itself, was deceptive—or, at best, transient. According to Zhang Guotao, one of the founders of the Party and the only prominent Communist official to defect to the West, Liu was critical of Mao's strategies as far back as 1937, when he first reached

Yenan. In a still unpublished report reviewing the Communist movement's conduct over the previous sixteen years, Liu indirectly blamed Mao for encouraging peasant uprisings and creating rural bases on the grounds that these moves represented "leftist adventurism." Zhang also disclosed that Mao, unwilling to risk further trouble at a time when his own authority was shaky, sought to win Liu over to his side rather than dispute with him openly. He accepted Liu's criticism and guaranteed his Politburo position. In turn, Liu agreed to an accommodation.[15] However, in a series of lectures delivered in Yenan in July 1939, Liu made it plain that he still did not fully subscribe to Mao's notions of leadership or his populist principles.

Published as a book entitled *How to Be a Good Communist*, the lectures repeatedly referred to Marx, Engels, Lenin, and Stalin, and they even quoted lavishly from Confucius and Mencius. Yet mention of Mao's role in the Communist movement or his theories of "class struggle" was conspicuously absent. Instead, Liu stressed the Leninist orthodoxy that the Party must be upheld as a disciplined organization that demands obedience from all its members. "Every Party member must place himself within the party in order to lead and urge forward the Party as a whole, and not outside the Party in order to lead it." In what would later be regarded as a shocking display of *lèse-majesté*, Liu did not hesitate to apply these rules to Mao himself:

> In our Party, there are no special privileges for individuals; any leadership which is not exercised in the name of the organization cannot be tolerated. Comrade Mao Zedong is the leader of the whole Party, but he too obeys the Party. . . .
>
> We obey the Party, we obey the Central Committee, we obey the truth; we do not obey individuals. No individual merits our obedience. Marx, Lenin, and Mao Zedong have done their work well; they represent the truth, and it is only for this reason that we obey them.[16]

In another passage, equally damaging to Mao's later claim to have inherited the mantle of Marx and Lenin and even to have surpassed them in creative originality, Liu singled out "some people" within the Communist movement who

> attempted to imitate in a superficial way certain styles of Marx and Lenin, picked up at random some Marxist-Leninist terminology, regarded themselves as the Marx and Lenin of China, posed as Marx and Lenin within the Party, and had the impudence to ask our Party members to respect

them as we do Marx and Lenin, to support them as "leaders" and to offer them loyalty and devotion. They also made bold to appoint themselves as "leaders," climbed into responsible positions without waiting to be nominated by others, issued orders like patriarchs within the Party, attempted to teach our Party, abused everything within the Party and wilfully attacked, punished and rode roughshod over Party members. . . . It is beyond doubt that this kind of people within the Party should be opposed, exposed and buried in oblivion by our Party members.[17]

Liu continued these veiled assaults against Mao in another series of lectures delivered in July 1941 and published later under the title *On Inner-Party Struggle*. Again, he made no mention of Mao's ideological contributions but inveighed against "some comrades" who regarded themselves as "revolutionary as revolutionary could be" and held that "the more bitter the inner-Party struggle, the better."

To them, the more seriously the problem is brought up, the better; the more fault-finding, the better; the more high-sounding terms, the better; the more name-calling, the better; the more severe and the more rude the manner and the attitude, the better; the louder the voice, the better; the longer the fact, the better; the oftener the teeth are bared, the better.[18]

Within the next few years, however, Liu underwent a marked change. Evidently accommmodating to new realities, he began to pay public tribute to Mao, who was then starting to glorify himself as he sought to endow his Communist movement with a distinctly national flavor. For the first time, in an essay written in 1943, Liu described Mao as a "resolute and great revolutionist" and urged Communists to "arm themselves" with his ideas in order to eradicate divisive "Menshevik" tendencies within the Party.[19] And at the Seventh Party Congress, held in April 1945, he extolled Mao in the loftiest language yet, calling him "not only the greatest revolutionary and statesman in Chinese history, but also its greatest theoretician and scientist."[20] His extravagant rhetoric notwithstanding, Liu subtly held back from total submission to Mao at the Congress by asserting the Party's infallibility as the vanguard of the masses and by scoffing at the Mao cult in colorfully pungent terms. On one occasion, he remarked, "There is no such thing as a perfect leader, either in the past or present, in China or elsewhere. If there is one, he is only pretending, like a pig inserting scallions in his nose in an effort to look like an elephant."[21]

When they proclaimed their People's Republic in 1949 in Beijing, the traditional "northern capital," the Communists inherited a country in shambles. Since the turn of the century, China had been ravaged by revolution and internecine conflict, warlordism, foreign invasion, and chronic calamities like drought, flood, and famine. Unbridled inflation during the last days of Nationalist rule had paralyzed commerce and destroyed confidence in the money system. Such as it was, the Manchurian industrial base built up by the Japanese had been looted by the Soviet army of more than $2 billion worth of equipment. Dams, irrigation works, and canals had fallen into disrepair, and railroad lines had been cut and recut by contending armies. And the population, having suffered enormous casualties as a result of war and natural disasters, was dispirited, hungry, and exhausted. Still, the new Communist regime had important assets to bring to the immediate task of reconstruction.

First, large regions of rural China had escaped the turmoil, remaining relatively stable as they pursued their age-old patterns of agriculture, handicrafts, and internal trade. Second, because of its localized, cellular nature, Chinese society had a remarkably resilient capacity to rebuild itself after cyclical periods of turmoil. And finally, after years of governing the territories under their control, the Communists had experience as well as discipline, organization, and a sense of purpose. Thus they were able to meet the urgent challenge of rehabilitating China with extraordinary speed. It was during this phase of reconstruction, however, that Mao and his comrades began to revive many of the controversies that had troubled their earlier years and would later spiral into even more acerbic disputes.

The Communists scored impressive accomplishments soon after taking power. They stabilized the currency, repaired the railways, started an extensive public health and sanitation program, replaced corrupt local bureaucrats with relatively honest officials, and initiated a system for distributing available food and clothing equitably. Their hold on the nation consolidated, they embarked in 1952 upon a dynamic drive to develop heavy industry. Helped by the Soviet Union with loans, technical assistance, and blueprints, they went forth in dazzling style. Factory centers in Manchuria were restored and expanded, and new industrial areas were opened in Inner Mongolia and the remote regions of the barren west. A town like Luoyang, the ancient Han dynasty capital on the Yellow River, was transformed from a sleepy market place into a big city eight times its former size, its suburbs smoky with tractor, ball-bearing, and steel plants, its population a babel of Cantonese, Sichuanese, Mongolians, Hunanese—deliberately mixed up, as a European visitor observed, "like chemicals in a test tube."[22] So rapid was the industrial pace that coal could not be dug fast enough for the steel mills, and electric power was insufficient to satisfy the demands of textile plants and machine-tool factories. A British traveler to one booming town found workers at lathes while carpenters were still putting a roof over their heads.

This tremendous effort, announced in midstream to be China's First Five-Year Plan, yielded phenomenal industrial results. By 1957, when the Plan ended, iron and steel production had increased more than fourfold, while coal and cement output had doubled. According to the estimates of Western economists, the annual growth rate had averaged about 7 per cent—a performance so successful that India was inspired to shift the emphasis in its then forthcoming Five-Year Plan from agriculture to heavy industry. But despite the brilliance of their achievement, the Chinese leaders were locked at the time in serious policy disagreements that would ravage them in later years.

While not easily discernible as the Communists established their regime, one of the underlying problems in China from 1949 onward was the increasing authority of the People's Liberation Army in the provinces. The Army had fought the civil war against Chiang Kai-shek's Nationalists as a flexible conglomerate of disparate and autonomous "field" forces rather than as a monolith responsive to centralized orders. Each of these forces eventually conquered a particular area of the country, in which it created is own power base. Local officers developed vested interests in the regions under their command, and they were often able to exert decisive influence in the shifting disputes between Mao and the Party. In short, they became what Colonel William Whitson has called "Communist warlords"— even though, in contrast to China's earlier warlords, they were basically devoted to national unity.[23]

In some instances, the regional units of the People's Liberation Army were shaped by sophisticated figures like Chen Yi, the son of a wealthy Sichuanese landlord, who had studied in France before returning to China to join the Communist Party and acquire military experience. In other cases, disgruntled peasants, bandits, and others either anxious to right grievances or simply seeking adventure threw in their lot with leaders who in turn pledged allegiance to the Com-

munist cause, frqequently for expedient rather than ideological motives. Such a leader was He Long, later to become a Politburo member
and one of China's ten Marshals. The son of a poor Hunanese peasant,
he was only sixteen when he killed a government official in a fight
and fled into the mountains to begin years of wandering as a fugitive.
By 1915, at the age of twenty-one, he had rallied a private army of
twenty thousand men and was prominent in the Society of Elder
Brothers, a secret fraternity active in Hunanese reformist movements.
A decade later, with a short lifetime of rudderless rebellion behind
him, He bequeathed himself and his troops to the Communists, assuming in the deal the title of commander of the Twentieth Corps of
the Fourth Army Group. That this pretentious-sounding military unit
was really He's private army under a formal designation was reflected
in the fact that its officers included his older sister, the Annie Oakley
of Hunan province.

After World War II, when the Communist struggle against the
Nationalists intensified, the guerrilla bands of the type mobilized by
He Long had swelled into the five conventional Field Armies that
comprised the Communist armed forces then demolishing Chiang
Kai-shek's Nationalists. These Field Army formations were unique
in two respects. First, virtually every senior Communist officer had
spent his entire career in units that over a span of two decades had
originated, expanded, and finally evolved into a single Field Army.
A soldier like Wang Shangrong, to cite an example, started out as
one of He Long's subordinates in 1927. More than twenty years later
he was still associated with He as a Corps commander in the Third
Field Army, a unit that traced its beginnings to He's private guerrilla
band. Second, each Field Army remained attached to the regions in
which it had first fought the Japanese and later the Nationalists.
Having battled mostly in northwest and southwest China, members
of the First Field Army were entrenched in those areas until the mid-
1960s and even after. Similarly, Second Field Army officers were
heavily represented in north-central China as well as in the border
regions of Yunnan and Tibet, while Chen Yi's Third Field Army
predominated in the coastal provinces it had conquered. The Fourth
Field Army, headed by Lin Biao, had occupied Manchuria and the
southern provinces. Nie Rongzhen's Fifth Field Army, also known
as the North China Field Army, was strong in the sector around
Beijing, where its precursor units had operated as far back as the
1930s.

One of the few veterans whose affiliations ranged well beyond a single Field Army formation was the tough, irascible Peng Dehuai. Like He Long, with whom he was close, Peng was a Hunanese peasant forced by poverty into banditry and later into soldiering. In 1928, with his own guerrilla band behind him, he joined Mao in the Jinggangshan redoubt, and though he quarreled with nearly everyone, his ability earned him promotion to deputy commander in chief of the Communist Army in the 1930s. As a result, Peng was instrumental in organizing both the First and Second Field Armies, taking over as commander of the former. He later headed the Chinese "volunteers" sent into the Korean War, emerging in 1954 to become China's Defense Minister. But his devotion to the Army as a separate institution carried him into a fierce clash with Mao and, in 1959, Peng was purged in the most critical shake-up to rock the regime until then. However, his relationships within the Army were so extensive that he remained a formidable adversary for Mao even after his dismissal.

Clearly, then, the Field Armies that constituted the main body of the Communist military force not only were composed of officers with tightly knit personal and professional ties built up over a generation, but were firmly implanted in the regions in which they had fought. The different regional commanders and their comrades represented potential "independent kingdoms," as Mao's propagandists later labeled those who opposed his authority. In most areas, moreover, local officers were intimately associated with the provincial Party apparatus, and their bonds were reinforced in the period after 1957 when, for a variety of reasons, political, economic, and military decentralization was accelerated. The intricate web that linked the Party and the Army was not revealed until early 1967, however, when both resisted Mao and his Cultural Revolution from the regions in which their strength was so deeply rooted.

Some Western analysts have speculated that the Chinese decision to intervene in the Korean War in 1950 was partly prompted by Mao's determination to redeploy the Field Armies in order to dislodge them from their regional sources of power. If so, his elaborate effort was futile, since most of the Chinese officers and men who returned from Korea were reassigned to the areas they had left. In addition, all but one of the commanders appointed to head the thirteen Chinese military regions set up at the end of the Korean War in 1954 were still in office a decade later, and, in one way or another, most survived the turbulence of the Cultural Revolution.[24]

If the Korean War did little to uproot the Army units from their provincial spheres of influence inside China, it did have a sharp impact on Chinese military thinking. After colliding with the dynamic American military colossus, professional Chinese soldiers emerged from Korea more doubtful than ever that the Maoist model of the invincible guerrilla armed primarily with proletarian *élan* could be effective. In the following years, senior Chinese officers treated Mao's precepts with increasingly open disdain as they turned to what he would later criticize as a "bourgeois military line."

Until October 1950, when their "volunteers" streamed across the Yalu River, the Communists had never engaged in contemporary warfare. Their conflict with the Japanese had been largely a stalemate interrupted by sporadic battles, while their war against the Nationalists was essentially against an enemy that was crumbling faster than it could be defeated. But in Korea, the Communists ran into American troops equipped with the latest weapons and backed up by an industrial machine able to give them enormous logistical support. Lacking tanks, artillery, and transport facilities, the Communists could only sacrifice huge numbers of men in "human-wave" tactics that, as one Chinese prisoner put it, were "indescribably miserable."[25] Even flying out of sanctuaries in Manchuria, which gave them the choice of both time and place of combat, the Chinese Air Force suffered losses at the rate of ten-to-one against American pilots. In short, the Communists were unable to match the superior firepower, technical skill, and supply system of the United States, and the outcome was devastating. Though they held the United Nations coalition to a standstill, largely as a result of American restraint and eleventh-hour Soviet aid, the Chinese sustained more than a million casualties. Among the dead was one of Mao's sons, Mao Anying, killed while piloting a fighter airplane. And in the end, what had been a relatively limited operation for the United States in twentieth-century terms was, as Frank Armbruster has observed, a "maximum, but obviously inadequate, effort" by the Beijing regime.[26]

The Korean debacle prompted Chinese military leaders to reassess their strength and their strategies. No longer did they seriously credit Mao's thesis that American imperialism was a "paper tiger." Instead, urging "responsible officers" to give their men a "correct understanding of the American army," their directives began to stress more heavily the need for China to construct a "strong, modernized national defense."[27]

It would be a crude oversimplification to say that Mao totally disparaged the value of military expertise and that Chinese Army professionals rejected his focus on ideology. As early as 1949, Mao had underlined the necessity for China to develop a "completely modernized armed force,"[28] approving programs to build nuclear bombs, missiles, and other sophisticated as well as conventional weapons. Meanwhile, even Chinese officers like Peng Dehuai accepted Mao's notion that political indoctrination was imperative for molding a soldier's spirit. Therefore, many of the differences between them were mainly a matter of emphasis. Yet these differences, exacerbated by related doctrinal, economic, and international problems, gradually polarized to the point at which Mao and a significant faction within the Chinese military establishment found themselves in bitter, irrevocable disagreement.[29]

One of Mao's fundamental ideas, based on his guerrilla-warfare concepts, was that the individual soldier could only understand "why he fights and why he must obey" if his discipline were self-imposed. Accordingly, the Communist Army throughout its insurgent days functioned without an official distinction between officers and men and, in principle at least, troops were encouraged to recommend tactics and even criticize their superiors. But if this symbolically egalitarian practice had actually died years before as the Army grew in size and specialization, it was formally buried in February 1955 when, following the Korean War, Communist military leaders set up a far more elaborate system of officers' ranks, pay-scales, and promotion schedules than they had ever had. They also expanded the number of China's military academies, lengthened training courses, and created a complex command structure—all of these innovations indicating that the Chinese Army bore only a scant resemblance to the rebel band of Mao's dreams. The Maoist ideal of the self-motivated soldier was further eroded that year when the Army ceased recruiting men by appealing for "volunteers" and began calling up conscripts under a new Military Service Law. Now, more than ever, the gap between amateur and career troops was sharply defined. As one of China's senior military specialists, Marshal Nie Rongzhen, pointed out with approval, conscription "draws a distinction between privates . . . and professional officers."

Though Chinese officers themselves had long been moving toward military conventionality, Soviet influence during the first half of the 1950s propelled them faster in that direction. The Kremlin had rescued the Chinese from a disastrous defeat in Korea, mainly by providing them with MIG-15 jet fighter aircraft. After that, Chinese military leaders turned increasingly toward Moscow for the modern matériel that they could not manufacture at home or acquire else-where. The Russians were hardly generous. Their military aid, valued at some $2 billion until 1957, had to be reimbursed—and was, in fact, repaid by the Chinese by 1965. Moreover, they carefully avoided supplying Beijing with any offensive equipment, such as medium- or long-range bomber aircraft, that might later threaten the Soviet Union. Nevertheless, Soviet assistance to China was extensive and decisive. It outfitted the Chinese infantry with its basic weapons, contributed to the development of a Chinese Navy and Air Force, and, in extremely cautious fashion, helped Beijing to start its program to construct a nuclear arsenal. Several thousand Soviet military ad-visers were also assigned to China and their effect, while difficult to measure, undoubtedly was to reinforce the bureaucratic and profes-sional tendencies of Chinese officers. It is likely, too, that these Rus-sian advisers insisted on the primacy of weapons over ideology, thereby contravening one of Mao's basic theses. The degree to which this trend pleased Chinese career officers was reflected in a statement by General Su Yu, the Chief of General Staff, urging the Army to "strengthen our study in modern military science" by learning from the "advanced experience of the Soviet forces." But Mao was worried by this "blind faith in foreigners" that must have reminded him of the attitudes of Westernized Chinese earlier in the century. In his view, the Russians had little to teach China. "After defeating Chiang Kai-shek, Japanese imperialism and American imperialism," he said, "our experience is much richer than that of the Soviet Union, and it is wrong to regard it as worthless." He also complained that the Soviet military advisers in China were instructing the Chinese Army in offensive warfare, which violated his belief that a "defense-in-depth" was his country's best strategy. Soviet advice, he said, "does not conform to practical circumstances."[30]

Still, by the mid-1950s the Chinese military hierarchy showed signs of becoming a professional caste that emphasized technology, downgraded ideology, and paid only lip service to Mao's dictum that it must "cherish the people." Inevitably, Maoist spokesmen began to raise a cry of alarm that military modernization would be futile if not dangerous unless anchored in firm political foundations. This reaction mirrored Mao's fear, later justified by events, that the "gun" was slipping out of his grasp. A campaign of official newspaper articles, radio broadcasts, and oratory was unleashed against officers who "ex-aggerate the role of weapons . . . as the decisive factor in the outcome of war" while minimizing the importance of men properly motivated through political indoctrination. Underlining this thesis, a Chinese Army journal compared a modernized military organization to a "tiger growing wings," explaining that the wings of technology were merely an external appendage grafted onto a beast whose ferocity depended upon its revolutionary spirit. Professional officers failed to comprehend this, the journal complained: they rhetorically praised ideology but really believed that "modernization has no class character. . . . This is a fundamental point on which we differ from the bourgeoisie and the mono-military outlook."[31]

About the same time, political commissars responsible for maintaining ideological standards in the Army began to deplore the widening gulf between officers and men created by conscription and the new system of ranks. Marshal Luo Ronghuan, then the senior commissar as head of the General Political Department, criticized officers who exercised their powers "indiscriminately," thereby weakening the unity "between the upper and lower levels in our Army." Because they now wore braid and insignia, Luo went on, many officers "do not mix freely with the men, no longer show concern for their living conditions . . . and do not care for their ailments and individual difficulties." Longing for the all-for-one-and-one-for-all *élan* that inspired Communist guerrillas a generation earlier, Luo bemoaned the "bureaucratism and documentarianism, conceit and self-complacency" that infected Chinese officers as they sat in offices, neglecting their troops, and devoting "an excessive amount of their time to attending meetings, writing documents, directives, reports and plans. . . ." The remedy for this situation, Luo proposed, was increased "political consciousness." Otherwise, he affirmed, the "solidarity of our Army will be undermined, and its combat strength sapped."[32]

Similar commentaries published during that period aired additional shortcomings in the behavior of professional officers. One of these pointed out that officers declined to submit to criticism by their men, arguing that this would tarnish their prestige. Another asserted that Army specialists refused to educate troops, contending that modern science and technology were "very mysterious" and that "enlisted men must carry out orders much like a machine, since the era of military democracy is out of date."[33] Still another attack against the Army professionals accused them of one of the most heinous crimes that could be leveled against a Chinese soldier—"warlordism."[34]

If they were blamed for betraying the egalitarian principles of the Communist Army, career officers were also charged with adopting an aloof attitude toward the population, thus violating the Maoist catechism that revolutionary soldiers must immerse themselves among the people like "fish in water." In his indictment, Marshal Luo Ronghuan alleged that professional officers had misconstrued "modernization" of the Army to signify that their own living standards deserved to be elevated. He criticized them for turning their offices, barracks, and clubs into "places of splendor," and for displaying a taste for "extravagance . . . that divorces them from the masses."[35] Backing up this charge, Luo's General Political Department accused officers of such specific misdeeds as awarding themselves extra food rations, providing their families with luxuries, and seducing school-girls and married women.[36] This question of the Army's relations with the population was especially relevant to the tensions then developing between Mao and China's military leaders.

Mao's concept of the Army as a force available for economic, political, and social as well as purely military tasks meant that troops could be committed to everything from agricultural and industrial projects to educational assignments and police duties. In other words, recollecting his Yenan experience, Mao saw the modern Chinese soldier as a latter-day version of the all-purpose guerrilla. But his vision was not shared by China's professional officers, who maintained that the diversion of troops to nonmilitary activities would dissipate their energies and interfere with the full-time training schedules indispensable to the modernization of the Army. The debate between Mao and the Chinese military hierarchy over this issue escalated throughout 1958, when the Army was badly demoralized by the orders given out to pursue economic "human-wave" tactics in the ambitious Great Leap Forward. That dismal experience contributed to the clash between Mao and Defense Minister Peng Dehuai that led to Peng's dismissal yet failed to erase fully the Army's suspicions of Maoist doctrine.[37]

Similarly, the Army was expected to commit itself to the population in order to fulfill Mao's notion that, under military tutelage, every Chinese could be made a soldier. Underlying this belief was Mao's conviction that China could best be defended by a "passive" strategy in which an aggressor invading the country would be drowned in an "ocean of people"—hence his repeated appeals for the formation of a vast citizen militia. But here again, professional officers balked for various reasons. First, persuaded that modern war had become a complex exercise to be waged by specialists, they no longer put much faith in the idea of the peasant fighter. Second, they were reluctant to enter into a program to organize a milita in which political commissars and other ideologues would play a key role. And finally, just as they felt that Army participation in economic construction detracted from their real vocation, so the mobilization of the militia struck them as a burden that would interfere with the training of regular soldiers. This dispute, which remained unresolved for years, gradually aggravated the discord within the Beijing leadership. Indeed, one of the "crimes" attributed by Mao to General Luo Rui-qing, the Chief of General Staff purged early in the Cultural Revolution, was his purported opposition to the militia.

Tensions between Mao and the upper echelons of the Army were also heightened in the late 1950s by the complicated issue of nuclear strategy. As far back as August 1945, after Hiroshima was obliterated by the American atomic bomb, Mao had reiterated his dictum that men rather than weapons counted in war. His statement, as he made clear at the time, was directed at Chinese Communist military men who "erroneously" held that atomic bombs could be decisive in a conflict.[38] A decade later, the subject of nuclear policy had expanded into a complex debate that touched on such larger questions as economic development priorities and Sino-Soviet relations.

At the core of the debate were divergent assessments of the significance of atomic weapons. Chinese career officers, like professional soldiers everywhere, were essentially concerned with tangible, practical, short-term tactics. Their opinion was expressed in 1957 by General Su Yu, when he worried aloud that the "tremendous destructive power" of nuclear arms, particularly in a first strike by the enemy, would cripple China.[39] While under no illusions about the devastation that atomic bombs could wreak, Mao contrastingly took the view that the longer-range effects of nuclear war might actually be beneficial. He explained this position to the Indian Prime Minister, Jawaharlal Nehru. According to one version, he said:

> If half of humanity is destroyed, the other half will still remain but imperialism will have been destroyed entirely and there will be only socialism in the world. Within a half-century, or a whole century, the population will again increase by more than half. . . .[40]

Mao's view of nuclear war coincided with a tough American posture that then alarmed Chinese officers. In March 1955, Secretary of State John Foster Dulles spelled out the Eisenhower Administration's "massive retaliation" doctrine as it applied to Asia by announcing that the United States would not hesitate to employ atomic weapons in the event of "open armed aggression" by the Chinese Communists in the region.[41] Interpreting this and similar warnings as evidence of an American nuclear threat, China's professional officers recommended a new defense posture. They proposed that China divert resources away from economic development in order to provide its armed forces with the most modern equipment. They also advocated closer ties with the Kremlin as a way of gaining the protection of the Soviet nuclear umbrella.

But neither of these suggestions appealed to Mao. Though he tried to convince Soviet Premier Nikita Khrushchev to harden the Communist bloc's line against the United States after the Russians launched their first earth satellite in 1957, Mao must have anticipated that China could not rely on the Kremlin. His forecast proved to be correct when Moscow reneged on an agreement to give Beijing a "sample" atomic bomb and other assistance in building a nuclear arsenal. Second, both Mao and the Party bureaucracy were in accord in their opposition to attempts by career officers to have more of China's resources allocated to the modernization of the Army. By 1958, the Chinese Army brass had plainly lost the first round of its fight to place "expertise" over "Redness." Yet the clash between the proponents of professionalism and the advocates of ideological purity, by no means confined to military matters, would plague the Communist hierarchy for years to come.

During the mid-1950s, Mao and the Party leaders were rapidly moving apart over a wide variety of other questions that mirrored their essential disagreement on one central issue—the path that China should pursue in its economic development. If Mao believed that only the transformation of human consciousness could bring about material progress, the Party leaders believed that only material progress could transform human consciousness.

As they faced the challenge of elevating China from poverty and backwardness, the Party leaders contended that modernization could only be achieved through rational economic planning and practices based on organization, discipline, and technical proficiency. Above all, they argued, ruthless, industrialization was the avenue to growth. Focusing their attention on the cities, they stressed the need to rely on urban workers as well as on the cooperation of scientists, engineers, managers, and other experts irrespective of their ideological credentials. Consistent with this "elitist" approach, they also insisted that the Party apparatus was best qualified to formulate and carry out economic policy. In other words, as Stuart Schram has suggested, the Chinese Party stalwarts were following in the footsteps of Lenin and Stalin in their affirmation that a "technocratic bias" was indispensable for the advance toward socialism.[42]

Mao favored a diametrically different strategy. Starting from the premise that change was impossible as long as "old ideas reflecting the old system remain in people's heads,"[43] he maintained that priority be given to political and ideological programs calculated to purge men of their inherently conservative tendencies, "Revolutionaries are made, not born," he argued. Thus he asserted, in violation of the Party's principles, that the main emphasis be put on moral rather than material incentives, ideology rather than expertise, popular spontaneity rather than organizational discipline, will power rather than rules and regulations. He also held that industrialization would falter unless agricultural production were boosted but, in his view, the only way to increase farm output was by harnessing peasants in large collectives in order to guide and intensify their labor. And in promoting the "mass line," as he labeled his brand of populism, Mao sought to subordinate the Party bureaucracy to his own charismatic authority. In short, he regarded himself rather than the Communist Party as the source of wisdom capable of inspiring, motivating, and generating the energies of the masses.

Seen in perspective, there was remarkable continuity in the attitudes of Mao and his Party adversaries before and after the Communists took over China in 1949. Just as he had predicated his struggle to gain power on the mobilization of peasants, so Mao persisted in his conviction that the rural sector was the key to China's progress as a Communist state. Just as the Party, like the Army, had acquired respect for technical skills as it grew in size and complexity, so its leaders reinforced their belief that development could only be handled through specialization, industrialization, and modern management. This difference was expressed neatly in a pair of contrasting slogans. "Collectivization must precede mechanization," claimed Mao. On the contrary, replied Liu, "mechanization before collectivization."

One of the earliest controversies between Mao and the Party after the establishment of their regime focused on the role that scientists, engineers, and other intellectuals as well as "bourgeois" industrialists and managers should play in the Communist state. The industrial success of the First Five-Year Plan had been due in large measure to the ability of the Beijing regime to enlist the collaboration of thousands of Chinese technical specialists, most of whom were uncommitted to communism. As a survey of the membership of the Chinese Academy of Sciences indicated, many of these experts had returned to China from the United States, Western Europe, and Japan.[44] In part, they were attracted by the integrity, patriotism, and efficiency of the Communists, especially after years of Nationalist corruption and ineptitude. In addition, they were reassured by the fact that the Communists, seeking a broad base of support, had initially set up a so-called "democratic coalition" government in which ideology was subdued. The new administration, with the durable Zhou Enlai as its Premier, counted twenty-five representatives of minor non-Communist political groups among its fifty-six ministers and senior department heads. Serving under Mao in his capacity of chief of state were three non-Communist Vice-Chairmen of the Republic—among them Mme. Song Qingling, the sophisticated, American-educated widow of Dr. Sun Yat-sen. Besides personifying the bridge between the two Republics, her prestigious participation was obviously contrived to present the Communists in a favorable light to the middle-class Chinese of the coastal cities.

This "united front" arrangement, officially entitled a "people's democratic dictatorship," seemed to be a liberal variation of Lenin's more exclusively proletarian "democratic dictatorship of workers and peasants." But soon disagreements arose over whether the relatively conservative experts and intellectuals posed a threat to the revolution.

Nearly two decades later, attempting to stress Mao's unswerving fidelity to the revolution, radical publicists in Beijing asserted that he had terminated the "new democratic" phase and initiated the "transition to socialism" in 1949. This revision of events was designed to suggest, in simpler language, that Mao had opposed cooperation with bourgeois elements but had been betrayed by Liu Shaoqi and the Party bureaucrats, who had favored moderation toward "right-wing" intellectuals and capitalists. Documents dredged up from the early 1950s cited Liu as saying that "socialism is something for the future," and that "the bourgeoisie in China has a progressive part to play."[45] Liu was also alleged to have encouraged Chinese industrialists to build more private factories, advising them they would therefore help to stimulate the economy. Visiting the north China city of Tianjin, the home of his wife's wealthy family, he was reported to have told the owner of a local textile mill: "Your mill employs a thousand workers, so it would be much better if you had ten such mills employing ten thousand workers."[46] He was also quoted as having explained to a group of businessmen in the same city: "The government is calling for greater production efforts. To respond to the government's appeal, you must practice exploitation. This is not a question of who exploits whom. When you run factories, increase your production and pay taxes to the State, the State is thus exploiting you in turn."[47]

Though these and similar statements were unearthed in order to slander Liu as a long-standing "pro-capitalist," they were actually not so different from the theories voiced by Mao during that period. In his essay "On the People's Democratic Dictatorship," published in June 1949, Mao demonstrated far more flexibility than he would display in later years. He declared that the Communists merely intended to "regulate" rather than destroy capitalism, and he generously promised the "progressive" bourgeoisie the same rights that workers and peasants would enjoy under the "democratic dictatorship." Only when "the time comes to realize socialism," he went on, would the bourgeoisie be "educated and remolded."[48] But this matter of timing, never made clear, became a pivotal point in the quarrel between Mao and the Party. For Liu and his comrades, in their stress on industrialization, evidently felt that the "new democratic" phase should last a considerable length of time so that the technocrats could be encouraged to contribute to the economy. Mao, on the other hand, began to have qualms about what he considered to be an unholy alliance between his unique style of communism and the ideologically dubious intellectuals.

These qualms stemmed in part from Mao's ingrained distrust of the intelligentsia. Looking back across the centuries of Chinese history, he was appalled by the gulf that divided the vast majority of the people from the educated minority. Even though their literary, artistic, and administrative accomplishments warmed his aesthetic feelings and national pride, he saw evil in the traditional mandarins, whose long fingernails symbolized their disdain for manual labor. Scorning the value of formal education, he pointed out that the two most successful Ming dynasty emperors had been illiterate while their incompetent successors had been men of learning.[49] Perhaps Mao's hatred for scholars mirrored his humiliating experience serving them as a menial assistant in the Beijing University library. He had certainly observed in Yenan that they had little in common with his guerrilla ideal. He had also discovered that they tended to be most resistant to his "spiritual" brand of communism, with its accent on moral rearmament. After all, high school and university graduates even in China have not been easy candidates for conversion to religious fundamentalism. Hence he held intellectuals in low esteem—unless, of course, they submitted to "thought reform," prostrated themselves before the "masses," and acquired a genuine "proletarian" outlook. Even so, he doubted their ability to undergo this process sincerely.

In 1955, Mao had personally conducted a campaign against Hu Feng, an undistinguished Communist writer who had objected to the political controls imposed by the regime on Chinese literature. Not long afterward, clearly concerned that China was drifting away from his revolutionary dream toward Soviet-style "revisionism," Mao began to caution against "rightist trends" while calling for fresh drives to intensify "class struggle." Singling out educated Chinese in one speech, he asserted that most were only tepid in their support of Marxism since they came from bourgeois backgrounds. Therefore, he said, they required "rectification" and, predicting future efforts to cleanse intellectuals and other dubious elements, he warned: "In the ideological field, the question of who will win in the struggle between the proletariat and the bourgeoisie has not been really settled yet. We still have to wage a protracted struggle against bourgeois and petty bourgeois ideology."[50]

The Party leaders flatly rejected this call for continued "struggle," however. "The question of who will win in the struggle between socialism and capitalism in our country has now been decided," proclaimed Liu Shaoqi in September 1956,[51] adding that bourgeois intellectuals and specialists who had helped the nation deserved to be praised rather than censured. And, without mentioning Mao by name, he attacked "some members of our Party who hold that everything should absolutely be of 'one color,' " describing their attitude as a "sectarian viewpoint."[52] This theme was echoed by Deng Xiaoping, the new Party Secretary General, in a statement criticizing the Maoist notion of "classifying . . . social strata into two different categories."[53] The official Party newspaper, the *People's Daily,* also berated "doctrinairism," while the chief of the Party's Propaganda Department, Lu Dingyi, refuted one of Mao's basic tenets in a conciliatory appeal to intellectuals. "As everyone knows," Lu said, "the natural sciences, including medicine, have no class character."[54]

To a large extent, the simmering quarrel between Mao and the Party boiled up because of shortcomings in China's economic development drive. The First Five-Year Plan of 1953–1957 was performing brilliantly in the field of heavy industry. But the records broken in iron, steel, coal, and other industrial production were not being matched in the agricultural realm. Between 1953 and 1955, the production of grains like rice and wheat repeatedly failed to meet the targets set up by the government, while cotton output actually declined.[55]

This situation was critical, for the simple reason that Chinese industrialization depended upon agriculture. Under a series of agreements, the Soviet Union had contracted to provide China with the blueprints, advisers, and low-interest loans to construct more than two hundred major factories. However, the main burden of financing and meeting the other requirements of industrialization fell on the shoulders of the Chinese peasants. They were expected to grow food for an expanding urban population; produce 90 per cent of the fibers, cotton, and other raw materials needed for light industry and, at the same time, yield the additional surpluses for export to cover the cost of importing the capital equipment for heavy industry. By the spring of 1955, though, it was plain that the Chinese peasantry was not accomplishing this superhuman task. A Beijing pronouncement issued in March warned that "if growth of agricultural production does not catch up, it is bound to affect . . . the speed of industrialization."[56]

Several factors conspired to hamper agriculture. Concentrating on heavy industry, the government had allocated only a tiny fraction of its development budget to the rural sector, leaving peasants without adequate draft animals, farm tools, chemical fertilizers, seed, and credit. These scarcities, coupled with the fact that the earlier agrarian reform had multiplied the number of privately owned farms, contributed to a rise in capitalistic tendencies in the countryside. Poor peasants, unable to settle their debts, were being compelled to sell their land and become laborers, with the result that distinct classes were re-emerging in the villages. Later, when the government moved to correct this trend by introducing measures to curb private activities, wealthier peasants reacted by cutting back production or even selling their property in order to elude controls. All this, exacerbated by the assorted pressures exerted on the rural population by zealous Party officials, combined to depress the Chinese agricultural scene.[57]

A possible solution to the problem might have been to scale down industrialization into line with agricultural production. But such a retreat was more than the Chinese leaders could have accepted. Mao therefore offered a remedy consistent with his theories—mobilize the people, China's primary resource. In July 1955, he proposed that the loose cooperatives then in operation be rapidly enlarged into big farm collectives in which peasants would be turned into an agricultural proletariat. That this recommendation met stiff resistance from the Party apparatus was evidenced in Mao's blast at the time against "some of our comrades who are tottering along like a woman with bound feet, always complaining that others are going too fast."[58]

These "women with bound feet," as later information would disclose, were Liu Shaoqi and other senior Party figures, and their resistance to Mao's idea was based on various apprehensions. Looking back at the dislocations caused by tamer collectivist efforts only a year or two before, they were concerned that peasant opposition to the new campaign would inhibit agricultural output even more. Recalling events in the Soviet Union in the early 1930s, they also feared a similar upheaval in China so soon after having established their regime. Moreover, faithful to orthodox Marxism, they contended that it was senseless to accelerate collectivization before China's industrial capacity had been raised, since large farms could only be operated efficiently with tractors and other machinery, chemical fertilizers, electrification, and such skilled personnel as engineers, agronomists, and economists. Liu had stressed this point as early as 1951 when, scorning "utopian" agricultural schemes, he had asserted that "the realization of socialism in the rural areas requires the development of industry."[59] Now, reiterating the same theme differently, he claimed that agriculture could only be collectivized "step by step . . . within a relatively long period."[60]

This debate intruded directly into the dispute between Mao and the Party over the role of intellectuals under communism. For Mao, with his view of collectivization as a fundamentally political and ideological process, was persuaded that the effort to socialize the countryside must be paralleled by a broader drive against "rightist conservatism . . . still causing trouble in many fields."[61] Hence he believed that his collectivization should not only convert the peasantry but simultaneously cleanse the bourgeois "technocrats" whose cooperation was needed by the Party bureaucracy in its thrust toward industrialization.

Despite the Party's resistance, Mao's collectivization policy prevailed and, by the end of 1956, roughly 100 million peasant families were incorporated into Agricultural Producers' Cooperatives, as the big collective farms were labeled. But the ambitious plan soon proved to be a failure. Facing the prospect of again becoming tenants, this time of the state, many peasants destroyed their farm implements, neglected their confiscated fields, and slaughtered their draft animals and livestock rather than surrender them to the collective. Food hoarding became widespread, and attempts by the government to attract produce to "controlled free markets" quickly led to unbridled speculation. Bad weather in many parts of the country aggravated these difficulties, and the upshot was an alarming decrease in the agricultural harvests, which in 1956–1957 dropped far below the natural rate of population increase.[62] Famine, later reported in areas of Guangxi province, probably occurred elsewhere as well. Many collectives were disbanded, and peasants in some regions fled to the cities, thereby imposing further strains on urban housing and food supply systems.[63]

Foreshadowing the dismal aftermath of the Great Leap Forward three years later, the failure of this major experiment in collectivization was conveniently blamed on local Communist cadres. They were accused of having committed such "errors" as beguiling peasants with false promises of improved income, inflating production targets in order to curry favor with their superiors, and displaying "blind optimism" in claiming that those targets could be fulfilled.[64] But the real culprit in the eyes of the Party leadership was Mao.

Though they knew that Mao was no Stalin, the Party leaders were undoubtedly inspired by Khrushchev's denunciation of the late Soviet dictator's "crimes" in February 1956 to launch a similar assault against the personality who had encouraged a cult of himself in their own country. At their long overdue Eighth National Congress held in Beijing in September 1956, Liu Shaoqi and his colleagues not only revamped the upper echelons of the Party hierarchy as a way of diluting Mao's authority, but subjected him to a thinly veiled and humiliating attack.

Under the Party Constitution promulgated in 1945, Mao had been given extraordinary power by being named to serve concurrently as Chairman of the Party Central Committee, Chairman of the Politburo, and Chairman of the Central Secretariat. At the 1956 Congress, however, he was deprived of the Central Secretariat, which controlled the Party's day-to-day operations. Henceforth, that vital Party organ would be under the supervision of a new Secretary General, Deng Xiaoping, a veteran *apparatchik* whose arrogance eventually earned him Mao's intense hatred. Formerly there had been no Vice-Chairman of the Central Committee. Now the Party created four Vice-Chairmanships for men who had never fully subscribed to Mao's theories—Zhou Enlai, the suave, flexible Premier; Marshal Zhu De, the old Army commander; Chen Yun, a pragmatic economic planner; and Liu Shaoqi. As First Vice-Chairman, Liu was delegated to share part of Mao's power to conduct "certain important conferences." The Party also established a Standing Committee of the Politburo, comprised of the Chairman, the four Vice-Chairmen, and the Secretary General. This meant, in effect, that China would be governed by a collegium in which Mao no longer ruled supreme.

Early in the Cultural Revolution, Mao sought to explain this reorganization of the Party hierarchy as having been undertaken at his own initiative. He had observed, he said, that the successors to Stalin were unprepared to rule following the Soviet dictator's death because they lacked experience. He therefore decided to divide the leadership into "first and second lines," placing Liu and Deng Xiaoping in the forefront while withdrawing himself to the background. "When I retreated into the second line by letting others handle the daily work," he said, "my purpose was to cultivate their prestige so that when I went to see God, the country would be spared great chaos. But I didn't expect that the situation would turn out differently."[65]

Mao's version of his downgrading seemed to have been an attempt on his part to "save face." For it was plain from Liu Shaoqi's Political Report at the 1956 Congress that the Party outvoted Mao on several key issues. Refuting Mao's notion of "protracted class struggle," Liu affirmed the Party's view that "the struggle between socialism and capitalism in our country has now been settled." Rejecting Mao's calls for campaigns to purify the conservative intelligentsia, he asserted that "we must enlist the services of bourgeois and petty bourgeois intellectuals in building socialism, and learn from them." Liu also criticized Mao's plan for rapid collectivization as typical of "leftists" who deviate from the Party line "in demanding that socialism be achieved overnight." And, most significantly, he obliquely impugned Mao for having "tried to weaken the leading role of the Party" while authorizing himself to "go on taking arbitrary action." Conspicuously failing to extol Mao, as he had at the Seventh Congress in 1945, Liu insisted instead that the Party must respect the principle of "collective leadership."[66]

The Party Secretary General, Deng Xiaoping, echoed this theme even more strongly. Stressing that they stand "not above the Party but within it," he said that Party leaders should set an example "in obeying the Party organizations and observing Party discipline." Khrushchev's revelations of Stalin's misconduct, Deng pointed out, "showed us that serious consequences can follow from the deification of the individual." Obviously with Mao in mind, he went on to emphasize that the Chinese Party "abhors" the cult of the personality because "no individuals are free from flaws and mistakes in their activities."[67]

If this vigorous assault against Mao's belief in his own infallibility were not enough, the new version of the Party Constitution promulgated at the 1956 Congress deleted the reference to his "Thought" as the guide for all Communists, substituting in its place the assertion that the Party was "the vanguard of the Chinese working class, the highest form of its class organization." Years later, it was alleged by Mao's supporters that Marshal Peng Dehuai, then Defense Minister and a Politburo member, had plotted with Lui and Deng Xiaoping to make the blasphemous amendment to the Constitution.[68]

This was not the first or the last time that Mao suffered a setback. In the early 1930s he had been stripped of power by Zhou Enlai and others, and, as the American Communist writer Anna Louise Strong put it, he would be placed "nicely on a shelf like a Buddha" by Liu and the Party leaders during the mid-1960s.[69] After the 1956 Party Congress, however, Mao's eclipse was brief. Within less than two years, he was well on his way toward launching the Great Leap Forward. What gave him the opportunity to revive his revolutionary momentum was a short but intensive interlude known as the "Hundred Flowers" campaign. This interlude, which turned the spotlight on the "bourgeois" intellectuals, owed its initial impulse to the reverberations reaching China from the Soviet Union and Eastern Europe following Khrushchev's posthumous denunciation of Stalin.

"Let a hundred flowers bloom" and "Let a hundred schools of thought contend" had been slogans designed to inspire independent philosophical discussion in ancient China. Mao resurrected these slogans in the spring of 1957 as an invitation to China's academic, artistic, and managerial intelligentsia to criticize the Communist regime freely. Most Western analysts have suggested that Mao, sensitive to Khrushchev's de-Stalinization statement, felt the need to provide Chinese intellectuals with a safety valve through which to voice their complaints against Communist policies and practices. In a carefully documented study based on fresh information, however, Richard Solomon has concluded that Mao's real intention was to encourage the intellectuals to attack the Party. Mao's purpose in this tactic, according to Solomon, was to drive a wedge between the Party and the "technocrats" in order to rupture their alliance and undermine the economic development strategy they were pursuing in opposition to his own attempts to promote the "mass line."[70] Whatever his precise motives, the maneuver did in fact give Mao the chance to regain the revolutionary momentum he had temporarily lost.

In late 1956, ignited by Khrushchev's anti-Stalin speech at the Twentieth Congress of the Soviet Communist Party, the flames of dissent spread through Poland and erupted in a rebellion in Hungary. One of the first reactions in Beijing was concern for the cohesion of the Communist bloc. Attempting to preserve bloc unity, Zhou Enlai went to Warsaw in an effort to help the Poles gain a degree of autonomy from the Kremlin without impairing Moscow's hegemony in Eastern Europe. Essentially, however, the Chinese interpreted the cracks in the Communist monolith in terms of their own domestic tensions.

As they observed the post-mortem effects of Stalin's excesses, the Chinese Party leaders seemed to believe that China might be similarly nagged by internal ferment unless Mao's rigorous doctrines were checked and more temperate policies prevailed. So, through the medium of reproaching Stalin, they indirectly denounced Mao's attempts to perpetuate revolution.[71] Mao, in contrast, saw the Hungarian upheaval as proof of his view that tolerance of bourgeois intellectuals by the Party only fostered conservative trends that eventually eroded Communist ideology. His solution was increased tension rather than moderation.

Mao outlined this approach in a major address entitled "On the Correct Handling of Contradictions Among the People." It was, characteristically, a sweet-and-sour pronouncement. He hailed China's unity, minimized the danger that "counterrevolutionaries" menaced the regime, and even allowed that differences between the proletariat and the bourgeoisie could be resolved. At the same time, he repeated that "class struggle is not yet over," implying that "antagonistic" conflicts between the "people" and their enemies still existed within a socialist society.[72] His declaration, which would later provide him with the theoretical foundation to define his Party opponents as "enemies" during the Cultural Revolution, set the stage for the "Hundred Flowers" drama.

The appeal by Mao for free speech immediately uncorked a torrent of critical commentaries. The non-Communist Minister of Education,

Zhang Xiruo, accused the Party of "doctrinairism," charging that its members relied on rigid dogma as "their sole blueprint, their sole dictionary, all their capital, and their only support." Zhu Anping, the editor-in-chief of the non-Party newspaper *Guangming Daily*, blamed Party officials for having "bungled their jobs to the detriment of the State," while other writers, artists, scholars, doctors, and even workers and peasants also expressed their dissatisfaction.[73] One of the angriest diatribes came from Ge Beiji, a young lecturer in economics at Beijing University who indicted Party officials for granting themselves privileges while the people suffered from shortages of food and other commodities:

> China belongs to 600 million people, including the counterrevolutionaries. It does not belong to the Communist Party alone. . . . If you carry on satisfactorily, well and good. If not, the masses may knock you down, kill the Communists, overthrow you. This cannot be described as unpatriotic, for the Communists no longer serve the people. The downfall of the Communist Party does not mean the downfall of China. . . .[74]

In the light of allegations he himself would direct against them years afterward, Mao was apparently delighted by this bitter assault on the Party *apparatchiks*. Indeed, some of the criticisms which iconoclasts leveled at the Party during the "Hundred Flowers" era were identical with those uttered by Mao a decade later. In June 1957, for example, a leader of the fellow-traveling Democratic League named Deng Zhumin indicted Communist functionaries for their self-righteousness, complacency and arrogance, hypocrisy, ostentation and extravagance, debauchery, vindictiveness and "subjective presumption," adding that their inability to appreciate the "sorrows of the masses" was incompatible with Marxism-Leninism.[75] In January 1967, in a speech entitled "Twenty Manifestations of Bureaucracy," Mao described the Party *apparatchiks* as truculent, arbitrary, brainless, corrupt, deceitful, egotistical, feudalistic, irresponsible, and "as slippery as eels," adding that "they are divorced from reality, from the masses. . . ."[76]

Another curious feature of the crescendo of criticism unleashed during the "Hundred Flowers" period was its focus against the Party rather than against Mao personally. Therefore, if Mao did not entirely orchestrate the attacks, he deliberately used them against the Party in a strategy that, in the jargon of the Cultural Revolution, was known as "right in form but left in essence."

Less than three weeks after announcing its start, Mao began to call a halt to the free-speech movement, asserting that "all words and actions that deviate from socialism are completely mistaken."[77] A month after, the Beijing press officially signaled the end of liberalism and the beginning of an "anti-rightist" offensive. This "rectification" drive not only suppressed the unfortunate intellectuals who had been beguiled into venting their feelings publicly, but, more significantly, Mao channeled it into a campaign to purge the Party organization that, not long before, had humiliated him. In May 1957, in a statement that remained unpublished until the Cultural Revolution, Mao issued a broadside against "bourgeois" and "revisionist" elements within the Party who "echo the rightist intellectuals in society, and are united with them as closely as elder and younger brothers."[78] In addition to the arrest and imprisonment of dissident writers, artists, technicians, and other such types, a wholesale crackdown initiated inside the Communist apparatus also claimed as victims four alternate members of the Central Committee and some sixty other high officials, including the head of a Provincial Party Committee and four provincial governors.[79]

Thus, as Solomon has explained, Mao largely succeeded in breaking the relationship between the Communist bureaucrats and the "technocrats" by demonstrating that the Party could not rely on intellectuals. Implicit in this maneuver was the message that an economic-development strategy which depends upon experts rather than the "masses" presents great dangers for the Party. By extending his purge of the Party into rural regions of China, Mao's further purpose was to rid the countryside of officials who might interfere with his forthcoming program—the frenetic collectivization campaign called the Great Leap Forward.

CHAPTER 5

The Leap That Failed

⚓

*I have witnessed the tremendous energy of
the masses. On this foundation it is possible
to accomplish any task whatsoever.*
— MAO ZEDONG, *September 1958*

THE GREAT LEAP FORWARD was the biggest and most ambitious
experiment in human mobilization in history. Though it lasted
less than a year, it had deployed by its peak in the fall of 1958 more
than a half-billion peasants into twenty-four thousand "people's communes" in which all private property was confiscated. Everything
from food and clothing to child care and haircuts was guaranteed by
the commune as peasants, formed into military brigades, were shifted
from fields to dam sites and from makeshift factories to "backyard"
steel furnaces amid a frenzy of slogans and exhortations urging them
to work around the clock in order to perform economic miracles. "The
achievements of a single night surpass those of several millennia,"
announced Chinese publicists, while the ideologues asserted that the
Great Leap Forward had opened a "new historical era" signifying
that China was outstripping the Soviet Union in the "transition to
Communism."[1]

Beijing propagandists, reflecting Maoist tenets, explained that the
Great Leap had been "spontaneously started by the mass of the peasants on the basis of great socialist consciousness."[2] But the fantastic
phenomenon flowed logically from Mao's implacable conviction that
the only way to develop China was through the mobilization of its
sole resource—people. As early as mid-1957, he had abruptly halted
a birth-control campaign on the grounds that China's huge population
"is an objective . . . asset." Soon afterward, he put forth the ques-
tionable thesis that the Chinese people, being "poor and blank," could

therefore be easily guided into intensive revolutionary efforts.[3] Undoubtedly impelling Mao, too, was a personal feeling of urgency. He was then nearly sixty-five, with not many years left to live, and he apparently felt that he had accomplished little to make China the powerful nation of his dreams. In short, he was impatient, and, speaking to a government conference in January 1958, Mao candidly expressed his restless mood.

"As much as we may brag about our large population and our thousands of years of history and culture, our country is no better than Belgium," Mao said, explaining that China's industry was embryonic, its agriculture primitive, and its people largely illiterate. His objective, then, was to raise China to the level of Great Britain within the next fifteen years. During that period, Mao forecast, Chinese steel production could be increased to 40 million from its present 5 million tons, and coal output to 500 from its present 100 million tons. Electric-power capacity could be boosted more than tenfold, he predicted, while the agricultural progress necessary to match these industrial advances could be attained in eight years. All this could be achieved, Mao asserted, through sheer determination and human energy. "Our nation is imbued with enthusiasm," he said. "It is like an atom, capable of releasing tremendous force." And, refuting critics who claimed that his ambitions were too lofty, he added:

There is nothing wrong with the craving for greatness and success. There is also nothing wrong with yearning for quick success and instant benefits. . . . It is better to strike while the iron is hot. It is better to achieve something at one stroke than procrastinate. . . . One revolution must be followed by another, and the revolution must advance without interruption.[4]

Foremost among those who had criticized Mao's desire for "quick success and instant benefits" were the Party bureaucrats. To translate his beliefs into action, Mao had to override their objections, which were mirrored in a variety of cautious commentaries published in the Beijing press in the latter part of 1957. "The power to change the objective world is limited," declared Feng Ding, a Party philosopher, in an obvious rebuttal to Mao. Vice-Premier Chen Yun, the most prominent of the moderate economic planners, warned that "one cannot reach heaven in a single step." Even Premier Zhou Enlai favored temperance in opposition to Mao's "mass movements," voicing his views to an Indian agricultural mission then visiting Beijing. As the Indians recorded the conversation, Zhou was cited as saying that

> . . . from the organizational point of view, a big cooperative farm that tried to control a large number of workers perhaps could not really be so much more efficient than the small cooperative farm. . . . In fact, there was a possibility that this might lead to a lack of initiative on the part of individual workers and working teams, and hence be detrimental to efficiency. . . . There were some enthusiasts who wanted bigger and bigger cooperative farms but he had, indeed, serious doubts about large and complex farm cooperatives.[5]

The doubts voiced by Zhou and others were officially reflected in a Party statement issued on September 14, 1957. Observing that the large collectives were "generally not adaptable to present production conditions," the Party leaders recommended reducing them in size to comprise about a hundred families—or about the dimensions of the "mutual-aid teams" organized five years before. They also proposed, in another step backward, that these smaller agricultural production units should "remain unchanged for the next ten years."[6] These suggestions, plainly designed to appease the weary peasants and give the regime a chance to consolidate its position in the rural areas, would have turned back the clock on collectivization had they been accepted. But within a month, two additional directives published in the name of the Party Central Committee took an entirely different tack.

Bearing Mao's imprimatur, these new directives referred to the impending Great Leap Forward for the first time in proclaiming a nationwide movement to channel the farming population into the construction and repair of irrigation systems, dams, dikes, and roads as well as the collection of organic fertilizers in various regions. Tens of millions of peasants were shunted around the countryside to the assorted projects from late 1957 through early 1958 and, as a European visitor to China then described one scene,

> Monumental ant heaps were busy on the sites of future reservoirs. Endless lines of blue-clad men and women were filing up mountainsides like some unnatural stream changing its course. In the background, scattered all over the fields, multitudes of people were moving around with two buckets hanging from their shoulder poles. All together, they recalled the rhythmic breathing of some mythological colossus, suddenly awakened and flexing its milliard muscles in a supreme effort to change the face of the earth.[7]

In the midst of these convulsions, an unusual paradox for China suddenly occurred—a manpower shortage. The weather in early 1958 looked fine, promising good summer and fall harvests. But with multitudes of peasants engaged in construction tasks, labor was required to begin the spring planting. To meet this need, contingents of office employees, factory workers, students, and others were transferred from China's overcrowded cities to the villages. Peasant women had been recruited for farming tasks, and their enlistment necessitated the establishment of communal mess halls, nurseries, and other services formerly handled within the family household. At the same time, the deployment of tremendous labor brigades demanded the control and discipline that only a military-type system could assure.[8] Thus "a new social organization appeared fresh as the morning sun above the broad horizon of East Asia"—the "people's commune." In Mao's words, the commune would amalgamate "industry, agriculture, commerce, education, and the army," thereby becoming the "basic unit of society."

Though they had initially fought against the creation of big collectives, the Party leaders evidently went along with the new scheme. In part, they seemed to have no alternative solution to the baffling problem of maintaining agricultural production without curbing industrialization. As later documents indicated, the Party machine may have also come to believe that it could fortify itself through the Great Leap Forward by exercising control over the "people's communes." Whatever the reason, Liu Shaoqi publicly endorsed the campaign in the spring of 1958 in terms that differed totally from his statements of a year earlier. Repeating one of the slogans contrived to stimulate the peasants, he intoned: "Hard work for a few years, happiness for a thousand."[9]

Like most Communist innovations, the "people's communes" were first tested on a small scale before given ideological approval. The pilot area was a county of Henan province, the cradle of Chinese civilization, where experiments in rural cooperation had been carried on since the 1930s. Here, twenty-seven collective farms covering 53,500 acres and comprising 43,885 people were merged into a single unit in April 1958. By way of showing the Kremlin that China had a new weapon as powerful as the Soviet satellite, this pioneer commune was entitled the Sputnik Federated Cooperative. Other pilot communes were soon set up in the Liaoning, Sichuan, and Guangdong provinces. In August, the decision was made to extend the communes to the entire nation and within forty-five days it was officially reported that virtually the whole peasant population—121,936,350 families—had been brought into the new collectives. Mao returned from an inspection tour of the countryside, convinced that his utopian vision was being realized. "I have witnessed the tremendous energy of the masses," he announced. "On this foundation it is possible to accomplish any task whatsoever."[10]

Coercion alone could not have conceivably marshaled a half-billion people. Large numbers of peasants were undoubtedly attracted to the collectives by the promise of equal food, clothing, and shelter or, as the Communist slogan put it, "to each according to his needs." Others were swept along by a fresh excitement that at least represented a change in their drab lives. For the most part, however, the enormous development was testimony to the ability of Party cadres at manipulating people. Local officials in many communes consciously created an intoxicating atmosphere by beating drums, clashing cymbals, and blowing horns as they called peasants out to work, and the movement in several places was organized along military lines. At the Zhaoying commune in Henan province, as a correspondent for Beijing's New China News Agency described it, the work day began at dawn with the ringing of bells and the shrill of whistles.

> In about a quarter of an hour, the peasants line up. At the command of company and squad leaders, the teams move up to the fields, holding flags. Here one no longer sees peasants in groups of two or three, smoking or going leisurely to the fields. What one hears is the sound of measured steps and marching songs. The desultory living habits that have been with peasants for hundreds of years are gone forever. . . .[11]

But for all its dynamism, the Great Leap Forward seriously lacked management. Among other things, peasants were instructed to plow furrows as deep as six feet and to plant rice seedlings one or two inches apart as prescribed by Mao in his "eight principles" of agriculture. But these procedures were meaningless unless implemented under ideal conditions and so, in many instances, they led to crop failures. Misguided irrigation and dam projects also ruined the soil in several areas, while attempts to compel peasants to work day and night resulted in their exhaustion. Meanwhile, commune officials anxious to overwhelm their superiors and gain merit for themselves inflated production statistics, prompting the central government to raise output quotas which, in turn, actuated the further falsification of statistics. This focus on the overfulfillment of quotas was reduced to the absurd in June 1958 when, in a burst of zeal, the Association of Chinese Paleontologists pledged to cut thirteen years off its twenty-year program in order to overtake "capitalist" research in fossils.[12]

Though the Great Leap Forward was primarily concentrated in the countryside, it also reached into China's urban areas. How the episode affected the life of an individual in a city was recalled afterward by Albert Belhomme, who lived and worked in China during the Great Leap Forward and its aftermath.[13] Belhomme was one of twenty-one American soldiers who defected to the Chinese during the Korean War. Sent to the Shandong province capital of Jinan, a city of more than a million people on the Yellow River, he was provided with a Chinese wife, whose peasant parents resided in the nearby countryside. After training, he was employed as an electrician in a local paper mill constructed by the Japanese during their occupation of the region in the 1930s. As a consequence, Belhomme had the extraordinary experience for a Westerner of sharing the existence of a Chinese worker.

Belhomme recounted that a mood of tension was deliberately created in Jinan even before the Great Leap Forward officially began. Party cadres stepped up the frequency of meetings and rallies, festooning factory walls with posters and banners demanding accelerated production. At the same time, they inaugurated a campaign to "weed out doubtful elements" suspected of "bourgeois" or "capitalist" inclinations. This drive touched off a wave of suicides by people who presumably feared prosecution. In one week alone, Belhomme said, he saw three people throw themselves off a railway bridge in front of approaching trains. A schoolteacher of his acquaintance jumped from the upper story of a high building. A doctor, a Communist Party member, had been having a love affair with a nurse. Perhaps anticipating discovery, he killed himself by taking an overdose of sleeping pills.

As the campaign against "doubtful elements" became better organized, suspects were brought before "people's trials." Belhomme described the way these trials were conducted:

We were all required to attend the proceedings, which were held in the factory auditorium. We sat on benches facing the stage. On the stage sat the judge, flanked by the prosecutor and the defense attorney. The defense attorney, appointed by the authorities, apparently considered the defendant guilty but would mention some of his good points in hopes of lightening the sentence. Every time I went to a trial I was certain the defendant would be found guilty, because there was always a large van with barred windows waiting outside to take the convicted person away.

As Belhomme recounted, the trials were invariably attuned to the current campaign. When "rightists" were under attack in early 1958, for example, those arraigned were accused of ambiguous political "crimes" like having belonged to pro-Nationalist or anti-Communist associations before 1949. One defendant at that time was formally indicted for theft but, Belhomme recalled, the principal charge raised against him was that he had served as an interpreter for the Japanese "Fascist aggressors" twenty years before. Later, as the emphasis changed to boosting production, the main "crimes" tended to be economic. Cheating on an output quota would be labeled "corruption," and "sabotaging production through deliberate neglect" might mean anything from mishandling a machine to indolence.

As the defendant faced the judge, witnesses mounted the stage to speak out against him. The testimony against the defendant was generally vague. "He doesn't work well," or "he is lazy," or "he shows capitalistic tendencies," the witnesses would say. I never saw a witness speak in favor of a defendant.

We in the audience were encouraged by the Party cadres among us to comment aloud during hearings. If a defendant tried to deny the charges against himself—which was rare—we would shout: "See how he lacks humility, refusing to acknowledge his mistakes." Sometimes, if the judge allowed the defendant to sit down, which was also rare, the audience would protest: "Make him stand up." Of course, nobody in the audience really cared whether the defendant was guilty or innocent. We were shouting in order to show the Party officials that we were on the Party line. The people who shouted the loudest were probably those who were most afraid of being hauled up themselves on some phony charge or another.

A variation of the full-scale "people's trial," Belhomme related, were "criticism" sessions attended by roughly a hundred workers assembled by Party officials. These meetings were held to judge lesser offenses. A worker heard to complain that Communist Party members were "golden boys" who accorded themselves special treatment was brought before such a "criticism" session. He wisely confessed, and was sent out as a laborer on a road gang for three months. Another worker, a lathe operator in the mill's machine shop, was confronted at one of these sessions by a contradictory set of charges. After breaking a production record by turning out one hundred seventy-six bolts in a single day, he had been accused by Party officials of displaying "capitalistic" inclinations in striving to earn an increased wage under the piece-work system. He thereupon restrained his output but soon found himself under fire for failing to produce his capacity. Simultaneously damned for zeal and slackness, he sagely accepted blame on both counts and, amid much confusion, was let off with a reprimand.

As the Great Leap Forward gathered momentum, one of its most peculiar exercises was the revival of an earlier offensive against flies, sparrows, mosquitoes, and rats, the "four pests." Mao himself had blessed this offensive, viewing it as consistent with his concept that the masses could accomplish "anything whatsoever" under his guidance. "Not even Confucius called for wiping out the four pests," he said, "but now Hangzhou is planning to eradicate them in four years, and other places plan to do so in two, three, or five years. Thus there is great hope for developing this nation of ours. It is groundless and wrong to be pessimistic, and we must criticize and repudiate the pessimists."[14]

In the drive against flies, Belhomme recounted, families were issued swatters and required to appear every Sunday morning to fill large collection sacks with the insects they had killed during the week. The amount of time consumed in this operation was considerable as Party cadres, mindful of targets, counted each dead fly as it was transferred with a pair of bamboo tweezers from the matchbox in which it had been saved to the large sack. But if the drive against flies was time-consuming, the anti-sparrow campaign proved to be an ecological boomerang. As Belhomme recalled:

The strategy against the sparrows was to keep them flying until they dropped from exhaustion and could be killed. But then we began to notice something strange. The trees were covered with whitish webs made by some sort of worm or caterpillar. And soon there were millions of these goddam bugs about a half-inch long falling into your hair and down your neck. At the mill you had to carry your food across a courtyard from the kitchen to the mess hall. When you reached your table, you'd find these caterpillars floating around in your soup and mixed up with the mushrooms in your noodles. The Chinese aren't squeamish, but everyone was disgusted. It was a big loss of face for the Party.

A year later, a Ministry of Agriculture statement conceded that the war against sparrows had been a mistake. Henceforth, the Ministry statement said, the "four evils" marked for extermination would be flies, mosquitoes, rats, and—replacing sparrows—bedbugs.

The Great Leap Forward was rolling ahead at breakneck pace by the summer of 1958. Now, only production counted. Like Chinese "human-wave" tactics in warfare, machines and men were thrown into the battle to attain or surpass output quotas regardless of cost. As Belhomme related it,

> We worked day and night for a week in our shop to build seven 64 kilowatt generators. I must have slept standing up, because I never laid down once during that week. But our generators needed more power than the city could provide, so they got hold of a Polish-made 300-horsepower diesel engine to run the seven generators. A single 300-horsepower engine isn't powerful enough to run seven generators. The Party cadres refused to listen to reason. After all, didn't Mao say we could perform miracles? Well, the engine ate up too much oil under the strain, and finally its bearings wore out. They got another engine and wore that one out, and then found still another and ruined it too. In the end, we went back to using municipal power, which meant that the whole mill would frequently stop because the city couldn't produce enough.
>
> The paper-manufacturing machines were designed to turn out between seventy-five and ninety meters of paper per minute along a woolen conveyor belt. When the big production push started, the Party cadres said we could increase output by speeding up the belt. They cranked up the machine to one hundred-twenty per minute. No vibrations? One-fifty. No noise. Why not try two hundred? Up it went. Then the machine started rattling and shaking—even the building was rocking—and that was it. It wasn't built to take that kind of punishment. Its bearings were made of copper or babbitt metal instead of steel, and they couldn't stand the friction. Also, the conveyor belt wasn't designed to revolve at such high speeds. It slid off its track, getting tangled and torn. We had to stop the machine to order a new belt about every week. Not only were belts expensive, but deliveries were slow. The machine was idle while we waited and, of course, production dropped.

Toward the end of the autumn harvest in 1958, the Beijing authorities sought to keep the labor force fully occupied without additional investments. Thus they launched the "backyard furnace" program, exhorting millions of peasants, workers, students, teachers, office employees, and others to produce pig iron and steel in makeshift ovens constructed in villages, factories, schoolyards, and other available sites throughout the nation. As Belhomme noted in Jinan, its frenzy brought the Great Leap Forward to a climax.

We were told at a meeting in our factory in September 1958 that a country without steel was like a man without bones. So, to become strong, we must produce more steel. With that, we were ordered to build small ovens in which we would make iron that would be sent to bigger plants to be refined into steel.

This not only meant that we had to cut back on manufacturing paper at our mill, but as far as I could see, it put a terrible strain on the whole economy. Trains, trucks, and even hand-drawn carts were diverted to transporting bricks, coal, and iron ore for the campaign. People were taken off their jobs and put to work at the ovens. My wife and other women were given the task of cracking coal and ore with a cast-iron hammer, working twelve hours a day. About five hundred peasants were brought into our factory to help handle the furnaces. Many burned themselves badly. Besides, they should have been repairing dikes and irrigation ditches out in the country, as peasants do between harvests. I think that the floods that came later could have been avoided if the dikes hadn't been neglected.

Most Chinese found, moreover, that the metal produced by these primitive ovens was of such poor quality that it could not be used. Nevertheless, having decided to manufacture iron and steel in this fashion, the Communists refused to admit defeat. Rather than halt the campaign, they blindly urged people to intensify their efforts. In Jinan, the sky glowed red in the night from the fires of the furnaces, and inevitably a shortage of iron ore developed. At this stage, futility was compounded by destructiveness.

Members of the Party street committees went from house to house confiscating pots and pans, ripping up iron fences, and even tearing locks off doors. When people complained, they were told that their utensils were unnecessary, since they would soon be eating in communal mess halls. After some people were caught trying to steal back their own utensils, Party cadres smashed up the pots and pans. They tore the radiators out of our shop at the paper mill and melted them down.

By now, Party officials could no longer deny that the "backyard furnace" drive was uneconomical. And though it was not formally ended before the spring of 1959, the campaign gradually faded away. Until then, Communist cadres would only concede privately that something had gone wrong. "You can expect a person who eats a lot to shit a lot," one of them observed to Belhomme," but those ovens— we fed them and fed them, and nothing came out."

Years later, people had denuded the abandoned furnaces of their bricks and wooden scaffolds, leaving huge, cold, immovable chunks of iron incongruously adorning the landscape like grotesque pieces of sculpture. The Chinese wryly referred to these reminders of the Great Leap Forward as "monuments." They were, indeed, monuments to a demoniac dissipation of human energy.

If the Great Leap Forward had been reckless, its aftermath was costly, painful, and tragic. Not only had the episode arrested the formidable economic momentum generated by the Communists in their first eight years in power, but between 1959 and 1961 it plunged the Chinese people back into the kind of poverty they had begun to forget, making them increasingly cynical and apathetic. The abortive experiment also exacerbated conflicts within the Communist leadership that were to have severe political consequences.

The irrationality that had paralyzed Albert Belhomme's paper mill in Jinan was only an example of the traumas that dislocated industry throughout China. Large quantities of coal and iron had been wasted in the "backyard furnaces." As a result, locomotive, machine-tool, and other plants were forced to burn wood scraps and sawdust for fuel, while campaigns were inaugurated to collect scrap metal for industrial purposes. In Liaoning province, the Machine Industry Bureau found in a survey of thirty-one key enterprises that forty thousand tons of equipment could not be finished for lack of parts. An electric generator plant in Shenyang, the Manchurian industrial city formerly called Mukden, was discovered to have some seven thousand motors unable to function because of sloppy workmanship. A Japanese engineer who had worked in a cement-manufacturing complex in north China revealed that the eight plants that comprised the complex completely ceased operations in March 1961, putting six thousand men out of work. A dearth of raw materials as well as widespread sickness among the workers due to food scarcities contributed to the stoppage. "The old spirit is gone," the engineer said at the time. "The Chinese are now engaged in a struggle for daily survival."[15]

Chinese industry suffered another crippling blow in the summer of 1960, when the Soviet Union abruptly terminated its aid and assistance programs to the Beijing regime. Exasperated by its growing dispute with the Chinese, the Kremlin withdrew its entire contingent of 1390 Russian technicians from China, thereby suspending completion of about 200 modern industrial, scientific, and military projects scheduled to have been built with Soviet help. Though this action by Moscow eventually prompted the Chinese to become more self-reliant, Beijing admitted that it "disrupted China's original national economic plan and inflicted enormous losses upon China's socialist construction."[16]

The industrial setback caused by the Great Leap Forward was reflected in a 25-per-cent drop in China's exports to Hong Kong from 1958 to 1959. More dramatically, the Communists were compelled to "revise" both their production claims and new output goals. In a report to a Party conference in August 1959, Premier Zhou Enlai reduced the original steel production claim for the previous year from 11 to 8 million tons and scaled down the claim for iron output by 4 million tons. For the coming year, he said, "we are . . . adjusting economic targets in the light of realities."[17]

The havoc wrought in agriculture by the Great Leap Forward was even more critical. In many areas, spurious new farming techniques had ruined the soil. Dikes, irrigation systems, and other crucial water-control facilities were neglected. Mass mobilization campaigns upset traditional cultivation patterns and drove the peasants to exhaustion. These blunders, exacerbated by bad weather for three successive years, predictably led to a sharp drop in agricultural production. Lord Montgomery, visiting China during that period, learned from official sources that grain output in 1960 had been only 150 million tons— less than in 1952, when there had been 100 million fewer mouths to feed—and that the prospects for 1961 were not bright.[18] At the same time, Foreign Minister Chen Yi told another British visitor to Beijing that living standards were "a little tight. We must," he added, "find substitutes for food grains."[19]

Through their strong, pervasive control network, however, the Communists were able to equalize the food shortages by maintaining a strict rationing system. Widespread famine, which had so often afflicted China in the past, when the death toll during lean years ran into the millions, did not occur. Still, in the wake of the Great Leap Forward, as many as seventy thousand people were reported to have died of starvation in areas of Gansu province, a marginal region even in the best of times. Belhomme also told of deaths among peasants in the villages across the Yellow River, north of Jinan, where poverty was endemic. The casualties from food scarcities probably stemmed for the most part from diseases caused or aggravated by malnutrition.

Refugees reaching Hong Kong from Guangdong recounted that hospitals in Guangzhou and other provincial cities were crowded with cases of tuberculosis, hepatitis, and edema.

In a country with the continental dimensions of China, conditions vary from region to region. Therefore, if the food crisis was severe in fertile areas, it was fair to surmise that poorer parts of the country were worse hit. During the winter of 1960-1961, according to refugees arriving in Hong Kong, there was no meat, no fish, scarcely any vegetables, and only meager portions of rice in Guangdong, one of China's richest provinces. Statistical evidence of the gravity of the crisis in Guangdong was apparent when the number of food parcels sent by Hong Kong Chinese to their families in the province soared from fewer than 1 million in 1959 to nearly 12 million in 1961.[20] In the spring of 1962, when the Communist authorities temporarily relaxed controls on emigration, more than two hundred thousand people, almost exclusively motivated by hunger, fled from Guangdong across the border into Hong Kong in the space of a few weeks. Reports from other parts of China told of similar food shortages. Even though the regime tried to put on a good face in Beijing, the nation's capital, a French correspondent there at the time described the atmosphere as sadly reminiscent of "the darkest days of the German occupation in Paris," as people lined up for hours to receive only scanty rations.[21]

In their search for "substitutes for food grains," Chinese throughout the country attempted to nourish themselves on grass, corn stalks, and other flora. A girl from Hubei province reported that peasants were eating cakes made from cotton seeds, a form of fodder normally reserved for pigs.[22] A common dish in north China in those days was a dumpling made from sorghum and sweet-potato flour and stuffed with a mixture of tree leaves and turnip tops.[23] In Jinan, according to Belhomme, the police put on special patrols to prevent people from stripping leaves from the acacia and birch trees that lined the city streets. Meanwhile, the regime encouraged the population to experiment with strange edibles. The authoritative People's Daily featured an article on chlorella, a single-cell hydrophyte found in sewers, that was said to be rich in albumin. The Botanical Research Institute of the Chinese Academy of Sciences favored "a large variety of perennial wild plants," including the cinnamon rose and the monkey oleander, while other scientists advertised a "nonpoisonous, highly nutritious plankton" called "red worm" as a source of protein. And there were, of course, some gruesome food substitutes. During the worst period of scarcities, a nurse from Beijing disclosed, her hospital canteen served placenta from the maternity ward disguised as beef.

Crime proliferated as the struggle for survival became acute. In several places, hungry peasants pilfered fields and even staged raids against state granaries. Many peasants fled from their communes, either wandering into the cities as beggars or roaming the countryside as outlaws, ambushing trucks and robbing travelers. For the first time since the Communists eliminated prostitution in the early 1950s, there were reports of girls selling themselves for food-ration coupons. In Jinan, Belhomme related, the rate of petty theft and robbery rose as desperate townsfolk deliberately sought arrest in hopes of being fed in jail. But little evidence suggests any significant political opposition to the Communist regime. Instead, a mood of disillusionment set in, betrayed in some places by instances of sarcastic humor. In Guangdong province, cynical peasants distorted slogans to describe diligent workers as those "who still expect a thousand years of happiness in the future," and the sneering response to a complaint was: "Keep quiet, you're in paradise."[24]

One serious kind of resistance to the regime took the form of "spontaneous capitalistic tendencies," as it was officially termed. Neglecting the "collective" crops cultivated for the state, such as rice, wheat, and other grains as well as cotton and fibers, peasants devoted themselves to raising and marketing vegetables and livestock privately. The government later sanctioned limited private enterprise when it found that only material incentives could spur food production. But the lapse into profit-making activities was in fact a natural impulse that started as early as 1959, when the food shortages were initially felt. The way it evolved in most Chinese cities was probably similar to its emergence in Jinan as described by Belhomme:

At first, peasants with grain, vegetables, or meat to sell were very timid. They came to the outskirts of the city at two or three o'clock in the morning, and transactions were carried on by the light of a match. People bought all kinds of things they didn't usually eat, like carrot and turnip tops, and the prices were high.

As conditions worsened, the peasants became bolder, coming right into the city in daylight. The police gave up trying to stop them, and soon parts of the city were so crowded with peddlers and customers that you couldn't ride a bicycle through certain streets.

Everyone who could raise some money patronized the black market. Families sold heirlooms to buy food. I heard that very poor people even sold their children. My wife's parents dismantled part of their house to sell the beams as firewood so they could buy sweet potatoes.

The peasants who sold black-market food became rich. They bought bicycles and even radios in spite of the fact that their villages had no electricity. They also spent huge amounts eating in the "free" restaurants, where you could order good meals without ration coupons at high prices. Once, in one of these restaurants, I saw a peasant in patched, homespun clothes reach into his pocket and pull out a wad of cash that would have choked a horse.

Gradually, shrewd middlemen gravitated toward the thriving black market, improving and expanding its operations. Due to its proximity to Hong Kong, the Guangdong province capital of Guangzhou became a key black-market center. Among other phenomena, a big business developed in cigarette-lighter flints, which became a parallel currency in much the same way that cigarettes had been a medium of exchange in Europe after World War II. Unrestricted in their travels, operators would buy flints in the south China city of Guangzhou for about two cents apiece, returning to sell them in Jinan for fifty cents each. Chinese who had resettled in China from abroad reaped profits by selling the food, clothing, and other merchandise sent to them by relatives in Hong Kong, Singapore, and other places. Inevitably, too, clerks at state stores passed on extra rations to their families and friends, prompting the regime to inaugurate a campaign to "close the back door" in the distribution system.

It is no surprise, then, that the disruptions caused by the Great Leap Forward led to demoralization, corruption, and an erosion of Communist principles and practices at the lowest village level. An insight into the extent of this erosion was provided in a collection of official Communist documents captured by Chinese Nationalist guerrillas in a raid on Lian Jiang, a county of some three hundred thousand people located in coastal Fujian province.[25] From February 1962 through April 1963, the documents disclosed, peasants reverted to capitalistic activities as well as to such old customs and superstitions as arranged marriages, fortune-telling, and idol worship. Warning that "exploitation of man by man has again appeared in the villages," one document revealed that peasants in some communes were cultivating as much as half of the collective land for private purposes. One peasant was reported to have acquired considerable wealth by speculation, profiteering, and contracting labor for construction projects. A certain Li Zhaofang, who had become affluent by lending money at usurious rates, was said to have built a new house and bought a wristwatch, silk, and gold bars. "Why should we go out to work when the weather is hot?" he was alleged to have asked his wife. "We wouldn't have to worry even if there should be three years of drought."[26]

Even more alarming, the documents said, Party officials in Lian Jiang county had slid into such "bad tendencies" as embezzlement, misappropriation of funds, and excessive consumption. Many had built new homes by stealing bricks, tiles, timber, and other building materials from state warehouses and commandeering peasants to perform the work. The documents also charged officials with staging elaborate parties at state expense to celebrate births, weddings, and other occasions. At one of these parties, a Party cadre made a profit by demanding "gifts" from the guests in time-honored Chinese fashion. The food for the party was taken from the commune. Commenting on this and other cases of extravagance, a Party investigator concluded that "a considerable number of persons do not have a clear understanding of the direction of socialism."[27]

The aftermath of the Great Leap Forward also touched off troubles within the People's Liberation Army. Appalled by reports of their peasant families suffering from famine, troops openly criticized the regime they were pledged to defend. Accounts of disaffection in the Army were disclosed in secret military documents distributed and published in the early 1960s. One of the documents revealed that four hundred eighty of the six hundred men in an engineering battalion, stationed in Wuhan, a city on the Yangzi River, had families in "disaster areas" of Henan, Shandong, and Gansu provinces.[28] According to another, sixteen relatives of sixty soldiers from Sichuan province, one of the wealthiest agricultural regions in China, had died between May and December 1960 as a result of food shortages. Recording the reactions of troops to the economic situation, the document said:

They expressed a great variety of opinions, made guesses, and showed suspicions. A few of them blamed their superiors and found fault with the local authorities. Last winter, the problem of food became the outstanding and most acute ideological issue of the company. Some soldiers, having read letters from home, complained bitterly, asking: "Where did the food go?" "Why did they not have enought to eat?" "Is it true that the State has held back food from the people? . . ."

Lei Dianzhong, deputy leader of the Fourth Squad, asked: "After the communes were established, why have the crops become worse than be-fore? . . ." Other individuals expresed grave discontent. Some soldiers whose relatives died because of the disasters wept, became depressed, and refused to talk.[29]

At the same time, hunger among the troops themselves badly impaired the physical fitness, efficiency, and morale of the Army. Soldiers grumbled that they had only joined the Army to be better fed, but were now suffering along with the rest of the population. The number of instances of edema and hepatitis among troops rose alarmingly, and an entire unit was even afflicted with parasitic dis-eases of the blood. The lack of food in one armored unit was such that "when a man has driven a tank for more than an hour, he becomes dizzy and nauseated." In many companies, poor conditions drove men to suicide. One unit reported eleven suicides in 1960.[30]

The breakdown in discipline led to what one document called a "deterioration in the will to fight."[31] "The idea of revisionism" was spreading in the Army, some documents warned, suggesting that officers and men were losing respect for Maoist ideology. In several instances, soldiers hard hit by the food shortages spoke out acrimo-niously against the regime. A deputy squad leader named Liu Shenghua, whose two sisters had died of edema, was one of those who could not restrain his bitterness. "During target practice last September, he said: 'At the time of my discharge, I shall not want anything but a rifle.' Someone asked him: 'Why a rifle?' He replied: 'To fight the Party!' "[32]

CHAPTER 6

The Marshal vs. Mao

*In the view of some comrades, putting pol-
itics in command was a substitute for everything. . . . But putting politics in command
is no substitute for economic principles,
much less for concrete economic measures.*
— PENG DEHUAI, *August 1959*

*If you don't follow me, I'll recruit a new Red
Army and begin over again. I think, how-
ever, that you will follow me.*
— MAO ZEDONG, *August 1959*

THE GREAT LEAP FORWARD left China with an economy in shambles, a disaffected army, a famished population, and widespread
apathy and cynicism. Yet Mao Zedong stubbornly refused to concede
that his concept had been at fault. Instead he claimed, as he had on
earlier occasions, that the bureaucracy had failed to carry out his
orders properly. In a memorandum issued in November 1959, for
example, he criticized rural officials for having "misunderstood" his
directives. Among other errors, Mao said, they had bungled his instructions for planting crops, and he accused them of "trumpet blowing" in having set unattainable output targets and then falsifying
production statistics.[1] The causes of the failure, Mao explained later
to Lord Montgomery, had been "inexperience, waste, and bad organization at the lower echelons" of the Communist Party.[2]

These explanations lacked credibility. For the Great Leap Forward, as everyone in China was told from its inception, had burst
forth from Mao's creative genius. His tours around the countryside
to give the campaign its initial push had been punctuated by official

press and radio announcements affirming that he was "like the sun giving light wherever it shines." His radiance, these pronouncements claimed, had generated the "great material force" that was propelling the program at its phenomenal pace.[3] "Heaven is here on earth" as a result of Mao's prophetic vision, said the *People's Daily*, and other newspaper articles extolled his bravery, selflessness, stamina, foresight, and love for the masses in their attempts to depict him as a godlike model for all Chinese to emulate. Indeed, as part of the effort to promote physical vigor, Mao's publicists reported that he swam the mighty Yangzi River on no fewer than seven separate occasions in September 1958—when he was approaching the age of sixty-five.[4] In the face of this extravagant propaganda, then, Mao's disavowal of responsibility for the devastation rang hollow.

At the end of 1958, therefore, the Party leaders who had curbed his authority in the past again moved to reduce his power. Meeting in December at Wuzhang, part of the sprawling Wuhan industrial complex that spans the Yangzi River in Hubei province, the Party leaders effectively halted the Great Leap Forward. Backtracking from the pledge to remove the "last vestiges of private ownership" in the communes, they permitted peasants to retain their houses, fruit trees, tools, livestock, and gardens. They also replaced the piecework system with regular wages supplemented by incentive pay. And, among other things, they dropped the ambitious ideological contention that China was hurtling into that nirvana known as communism.[5] At the same meeting, Mao handed in his resignation as Chairman of the Republic—though he would remain Chairman of the Party Central Committee. An official communiqué issued at the time declared that, having sought to resign on several previous occasions, he had retired voluntarily. Describing him in almost obituary language as the "sincerely beloved and long-tested leader of the people," the communiqué added that Mao would henceforth "concentrate his energies on dealing with questions of the direction, policy, and line of the Party and the state" as well as devote "more time to Marxist-Leninist theoretical work."[6]

The Party leaders had apparently persuaded—perhaps even compelled—Mao to relinquish his position as head of state. Years later, when the growing tensions between him and the Party had erupted into the open, Mao was quoted as recalling his dismissal bitterly: "I was most dissatisfied with the decision, but there was nothing I could do about it." Referring to the accolade that had accompanied his ouster, he was reported to have said wryly that his Party adversaries "treated me with the respect they would have shown their dead father at his own funeral."[7] But, then still concerned with protecting Mao's public image, the Party leaders directed rank-and-file officials to explain his demotion carefully to the people "so that the reasons for this may be understood by all, and that there may be no misunderstanding."[8]

A variety of considerations dictated this cautious approach. In contrast to the Russians, whose brutal methods reached insane proportions under Stalin, the Chinese Communists have been relatively humane in their internecine quarrels. Thus the Party leaders may have been genuinely deferential to their old chief. They were also, in the wake of the devastating Great Leap Forward, reluctant to trigger an internal squabble that would further weaken the country. In addition, they seemed to have believed that they could manipulate Mao's immense prestige in the pursuit of their own policies. This tactic, which they did in fact use for years afterward, was later described by Mao's publicists as "waving the Red Flag in order to oppose the Red Flag." At the same time, however, the Party leaders knew that Mao had substantial power to wield against them in a showdown. Indeed, Mao demonstrated this power in the summer of 1959 in a sharp and significant clash with a faction of opponents headed by Marshal Peng Dehuai, the Defense Minister.

A crusty old officer with the body of a bull and the face of a bulldog, Peng was essentially a peasant. His ideological knowledge was limited—even though, as an old comrade recalled, his pockets were usually stuffed with political pamphlets that he read haltingly whenever he could spare the time. His military talent was also debatable. During the war against the Japanese and again in the Korean War, his impulsive, aggressive nature propelled him into several strategic errors. Moreover, he was a difficult, churlish individual who had squabbled with nearly every senior Communist, including Mao, at one time or another. One of his ambitions in the 1930s had been to replace Zhu De as commander in chief of the Army, and, according to those who knew him, his disappointment at being passed over added to his surliness. Mixed with these shortcomings, however, was a quality that gave Peng enormous influence in the Communist movement. He was, as one of his ex-comrades called him, a "soldier's soldier"—a stubborn, rugged fighter capable of enduring the worst kind of battlefield hardships along with his troops.[9] He was hugely popular with his men, and his cool courage even inspired Mao to compose a rather banal poem in his praise:

Mountains are high, trails are long, valleys are deep;
Large formations of troops rush in all directions.
Who can calmly rein in his horse and sheathe his
sword?
Who else but our valiant great General Peng![10]

But Peng's devotion to the Army, combined with his peasant instincts, were among the very traits that induced him to challenge Mao in the period following the Great Leap Forward. He had several grievances against Mao. As a professional soldier, he blamed the Great Leap Forward for setting back military modernization as well as aggravating Beijing's dispute with the Soviet Union, the only source of China's sophisticated weapons. He was also troubled by the extent to which schemes to employ troops as farm laborers had hampered military training and eroded Army morale. And, remembering his peasant origins, he was shocked by the disruptions caused to the countryside by Mao's wild drive.

Personal vanity and ambition also aggravated the quarrels within the Chinese Communist leadership. Like many of his comrades, Peng apparently resented the personality cult that Mao had built around himself and on one occasion, decrying the traditional slogan wishing Mao ten thousand years of life, was heard to grumble: "He won't even live a hundred years."[11] According to another report, Peng vetoed the erection of busts of Mao in military installations on the grounds that "we will only have to remove them in the future."[12] Peng was said to have complained as well that, as Defense Minister, he had to submit to the Military Affairs Commission of the Central Committee headed by Mao. "What kind of Defense Minister am I?" he was quoted as saying. "I'm neither like the Soviet Defense Minister, who has the power to command, nor like the American Secretary of Defense, who controls the budget. I just welcome and bid farewell to people."[13]

In late 1958 or early 1959, therefore, Peng put himself at the forefront of a group determined to defy if not overthrow Mao. Among his known allies were General Huang Kecheng, Chief of General Staff; Zhou Xiauzhou, the Party boss of Hunan province; and Lin Bogu, a seasoned and highly respected member of the Politburo. Like Peng and Mao, these men were all Hunanese. Oddly enough for a barely literate soldier, Peng counted among his other associates one of China's most cosmopolitan intellectuals, Deputy Foreign Minister Zhang Wentian. A Politburo member and former ambassador to Moscow, Zhang had worked in the United States and studied in the Soviet Union and had, among other sidelines, translated D'Annunzio, Oscar Wilde, Tolstoi, and Henri Bergson into Chinese. As later evidence made plain, the Peng faction also had the sympathy if not the active support of the pivotal Beijing Committee of the Communist Party headed by another Politburo member, Peng Chen. If they were not actually part of the Peng "clique," as subsequent allegations against them claimed, Liu Shaoqi, Deng Xiaoping, and other senior Party *apparatchiks* must have known of the plot against Mao and conceivably gave it their tacit blessing. Years afterward, assessing the assorted internal enemies he had faced, Mao described their different styles. Liu Shaoqi and Deng Xiaoping were "open and not secret," but Peng, he said, had been a "double-dealer."[14] Given his chauvinism and profound ideological self-righteousness, Mao may have been offended less by Peng's intrigue than by the old Marshal's connivance with the Soviet "revisionists."

Relations between Beijing and Moscow were deteriorating rapidly at that stage, for a variety of reasons. Not the least among them was Soviet hostility to Mao's assertion, issued during the Great Leap Forward, that he was outstripping the Russians on the road to pure communism. On a visit to the Chinese capital in the summer of 1958, Khrushchev bluntly told Mao that such "innovations" as the "people's communes" were nonsense.[15] Soon after that, the Kremlin leader abandoned all sense of fraternal propriety by telling an American politician, Senator Hubert Humphrey, that Mao's "communes" were an "old-fashioned and reactionary" experiment that had failed in the Soviet Union a generation before.[16] Increasingly worried by what they considered to be Beijing's growing truculence in international affairs, the Soviet rulers also signaled their intention to abrogate an earlier promise to give the Chinese a "sample" atomic bomb and technical data for manufacturing nuclear weapons.[17] These moves apparently prompted Peng Dehuai to take the Russians into his confidence.

Both Peng and Zhang Wentian had been relatively close to the Soviet leaders for years. In addition to having studied and later served as ambassador in Moscow, Zhang had been intimately linked to the Russians as Chinese representative to the Comintern. As late as November 1957, when Mao was urging the Communist bloc to stiffen its position against the "imperialists," Zhang had contrastingly endorsed Moscow's plea for "peaceful coexistence."[18] Peng, meanwhile, had been a frequent visitor to the Soviet Union to oversee the Kremlin's program of military assistance to the Chinese Army. In fact, it was Peng who had negotiated the 1957 nuclear accord that now, less than two years later, the Russians were threatening to break.

In April 1959, Peng embarked on a "military good-will" tour of Eastern Europe. While in Tirana, the capital of Albania, he met another traveler, Nikita Khrushchev. The encounter was deliberate. One of Peng's objectives, if not his principal aim, was to dissuade Khrushchev from retracting his pledge to assist China in developing a nuclear arsenal. In the course of their conversation, much of which undoubtedly concerned conditions inside China at that time, Peng showed Khrushchev the draft of a letter he planned to hand to Mao, criticizing the Great Leap Forward and its aftermath. Perhaps Peng hoped to convince Khrushchev that the Chinese Army was opposed to Mao's adventurism and deserved to receive nuclear aid from Moscow. Though he had no intention of giving the Chinese an atomic bomb—and, indeed, broke the Sino-Soviet nuclear agreement a month later—Khrushchev presumably encouraged Peng to proceed with his plan to challenge Mao.[19] When he heard of the talks between Khrushchev and Peng not long afterward, Mao must have been reminded of the days, decades before, when Stalin had tried to replace him with Chinese rivals more receptive to Soviet dictates. Understandably furious, Mao later accused Khrushchev of having conducted "behind-the-scenes factional activity against a fraternal Party,"[20] and charged the Peng group with "betrayal of the fatherland" by having "sown discord at the bidding of a foreign country."[21]

Apparently anticipating Peng's challenge on the eve of their clash, Mao was in an unyielding mood. A month earlier, he had returned to his birthplace of Shaoshan for the first time in thirty-two years, and there he composed a poem in which his remembrance of things past reinforced his present self-confidence:

> Red flags fly from the spears of the enslaved peasants,
> Black hands raise high the last of the tyrannical landowners.
> Only because so many sacrificed themselves did our wills
> 　　become strong,
> So that we dared command the sun and moon to bring a new day.

Soon after that, Mao wrote another, more esoteric verse in which he alluded to the celebrated fifth-century poet Tao Yuanming, who had dreamed of a utopia that could not have matched the earthly paradise of the "people's communes" during the Great Leap Forward:

Where has Magistrate Tao gone now?
Can one cultivate the land in the Peach-blossom Spring?[22]

The scene of the showdown between Peng and Mao was, incongruously, the exquisite mountain resort of Guling, in the Lushan highlands of central Jiangxi province. With its vista of gardens, lakes, and ancient temples perched atop craggy rocks, Guling had long been an appealing spot for scholars and poets, who left inscriptions in steles that still dotted the landscape. The area was later a vacation retreat for Europeans from nearby Shanghai and there, too, Chiang Kai-shek had built a splendid summer residence. Now the Communist Party dignitaries were assembled at Guling for meetings that would last through July and August of 1959. Among those present, along with the nearly two hundred full and alternate members of the Party's Central Committee, was a senior Soviet diplomat, F. N. Antonov. Officially billed as an "observer," Antonov was certainly aware of Peng Dehuai's intentions and, from his conveniently located pavilion, he may have even imparted advice to Mao's enemies.[23]

For six successive mornings in early July, probably before most of the delegates had arrived, Peng put forth his views to a small conclave of comrades. Over the two previous years, he said, the Party had become so "highly elevated" by its purported "victories" that it currently had "fever on the brain." During the Great Leap Forward, he had personally inspected the rural areas, among them Mao's native village in Hunan not far from his own birthplace, and found their production reports to be false. Each region should have told the truth without waiting for its lies to be exposed, Peng emphasized. "You must take off your own pants, rather than let others pull them down." The heads of one province, Jiangxi, were still claiming to have boosted output by 67 per cent the previous year. "They should be stripped once and for all to save others the trouble," Peng said. As for the failure of the Great Leap as a whole, he stressed, "everybody had a share of the responsibility, including Comrade Mao Zedong."[24]

Deploying themselves for a more formal assault against Mao, Peng and his colleagues printed and distributed a polished version of the letter criticizing Mao that Peng had shown to Khrushchev in Tirana nearly two months before. Written in the characteristically sweet-and-pungent style of a bold memorial to a bygone emperor, the memorandum was too clever for Peng's primitive brush, and must have been the work of Zhang Wentian and others in the conspiracy. But it was a salvo that would echo and re-echo for years to come.

In traditional fashion, the so-called "Letter of Opinion" opened on a note of fulsome praise for Mao's policies. Economic growth attained in China during the Great Leap Forward "has never been achieved in other parts of the world," it affirmed. Then, subtly criticizing Mao, the message went on to contrast the shortcomings of his experiment with its claims of success. Though capital construction projects "will gradually yield results," the memorandum said, they had been "too hasty and excessive" and had therefore created "imbalances and new temporary difficulties." Despite their "great significance," the "people's communes" had experienced "a period of confusion regarding the question of ownership." As for the "backyard-furnace" drive, it had served to "temper and improve" rural officials even though "material and financial resources were squandered" and the "tuition fee" of some 2 billion *yuan* for such an educational effort was rather exorbitant. Turning to the causes of these blunders, Peng's letter directed its fire against Mao and his supporters.

They had encouraged the frenetic race to concoct phony statistics, the memorandum said, deluding everyone into believing that "the problem of food had been solved and that our hands would be freed to engage in industry." But even then, "there was serious superficiality in our understanding of the development of the iron and steel industry," with nobody properly able to cope with steel refining, transport, labor needs, and other such matters. Because no attempt was made to "seek truth from the facts," the letter asserted, "it seemed that communism was just around the corner, and more than a few comrades became dizzy." Extravagance, waste, and inefficiency proliferated because "we considered ourselves rich while actually we were still poor."

Accordingly, the Peng faction complained, "it was not easy to get a true picture of conditions," and even as late as January 1959, Provincial and Municipal Party Committees were "still unable to find out the realities of the over-all situation." The trouble was that "there were only tasks and targets, but no concrete measures"—and this, as the memorandum put it in convoluted Communist jargon, prompted "petty-bourgeois fanaticism" that led to "leftist" mistakes. "Bewitched by the achievements of the Great Leap Forward and the passion of the mass movement," said the statement, "some leftist tendencies emerged, since we had always wanted to enter communism in a single step."

As a result of this "fanaticism," programs were not pursued on a "positive, steady, and reliable basis." Goals that required a decade to fulfill were supposed to be accomplished in a year "or even several months." In areas where bumper harvests were announced, quantities of food were wasted as "everyone was encouraged to eat as much as he could." New and untested techniques were adopted "without evaluation," and certain "economic and scientific laws were negated lightly." All these and other blunders, the Peng letter made clear, stemmed from Mao's blithe assertion that his brand of ideology could perform miracles.

In the view of some comrades, putting politics in command could be a substitute for everything. . . . But putting politics in command is no substitute for economic principles, much less for concrete economic measures.[25]

Mao was overwhelmed by the ferocity of a bombardment that, as he later put it, "nearly leveled half of Lushan." He was also stunned by the attacks of other comrades, who accused him of being "despotic and dictatorial" and compared him to the paranoiac Stalin "in his declining years."[26] His initial instinct was to defend himself. At one meeting, therefore, he denied that there had been anything wrong with seeking "greater, faster, better, and more economical results," as one of the inspirational slogans of the Great Leap had proclaimed. The "shortcomings and mistakes" of the Great Leap had been minor, he contended, describing them in Peng's phrase as the "tuition fee that must be paid to gain experience." Moreover, the setbacks had been transient, Mao said: "Come back in ten years to see whether we were correct."[27]

During the next week, Mao was apparently silent as he tried to measure the strength of his foes. As a youth, he later explained, he angered quickly at "bad remarks" against himself, but since then he had learned to listen before responding. Finally, on July 23, he counterattacked. At a plenary session of the Central Committee he delivered a long, rambling, disjointed reply to the Peng group that was alternately humorous and solemn, apologetic and self-righteous, academic and earthy, sentimental and tough, persuasive and menacing. It was, with these contradictions, the real, elusive Mao, and it was climaxed by the typical gesture of the charismatic leader—the threat to reject the bureaucrats and return to the masses in whose wisdom he would find support.

Opening on an ironic note, Mao reminded his audience that right-wing critics of his policies had likened him to the Qin emperor Shi

Huangdi, who fell because of his vast expenditures on the Great Wall of China. "Now we are about to collapse because of what we have done," Mao said. But such complaints were inconsequential, exaggerated.

> China is not going to sink into the sea and the sky won't tumble down simply because there are shortages of vegetables and hairpins and soap. Imbalances and market problems have made everybody tense so that the people as a whole have become tense. But this tension is not justified, even though I'm tense myself. No, it wouldn't be honest to say I'm not tense. I'm tense before midnight, but I take some sleeping pills and then I feel better. You ought to try sleeping pills if you're tense.

He had urged speed during the Great Leap Forward, but now Mao admonished lower-ranking officials for having tried to set a rapid pace. "There can be no room for rashness," he said. "When you eat pork, you can only consume mouthful by mouthful, and you can't expect to get fat in a single day. Both the commander in chief [Zhu De] and I are fat, but we didn't get that way overnight."

Mao then addressed himself to Peng Dehuai's charge that the Great Leap Forward had been a case of "petty-bourgeois fanaticism." Estimating the ideological coloration of the population, he calculated that 30 per cent of the people were revolutionary activists, 30 per cent opposed change, and 40 per cent "follow the tide." The one-third who actively favored the revolution, he said,

> . . . comprise 150 million people. They want to run communes and mess halls and undertake large-scale collectives. They are very enthusiastic. Can you call this "petty-bourgeois fanaticism"? They are not the petty bourgeoisie, but poor peasants, lower-middle peasants, proletariat, and semi-proletariat. . . . The "neutral" 40 per cent went along with them for a time and then 350 million people had the passion.

Mao urged that the communal mess halls be retained since, according to his estimate, 150 million "activists" wanted them. Indeed, he went on, communal eating arrangements should be extended rather than curbed, since they were "not invented by us, but by the masses." Those who criticized the mess halls and other innovations of the Great Leap Forward were only inflating its errors and neglecting its accomplishments. Errors were inevitable, Mao argued, pointing to the giants of history who, presumably like himself, had not been perfect.

Everybody has shortcomings. Even Confucius made mistakes. So did Marx. He thought that the revolution would take place in Europe during his lifetime. I have seen Lenin's manuscripts, which are filled with changes. He, too, made mistakes. . . . Have we failed? No, our failure has been only partial. We have paid too high a price, but a gust of Communist wind has been whipped up and the country has learned a lesson.

His own mistake, Mao explained, was his failure to perceive the errors being committed by the State Planning Commission and the government ministries, which abandoned attempts to manage the economy rationally during the Great Leap.

I am not trying to make excuses—even though this is still an excuse—but Premier Zhou Enlai and I knew little about this business of planning. I am not Chairman of the State Planning Commission. Before August of last year, I devoted myself mainly to revolution. I am absolutely no good at construction, and I don't understand industrial planning. So don't write about my wise leadership, since I had not even taken charge of these matters. However, Comrades, I should take the primary responsibility for 1958 and 1959. It is I who am to blame.

Dramatizing his confession of guilt, Mao cited the ancient Confucian dictum that "he who first made clay idols to bury with the dead should have no posterity." This apothegm, originally intended to discourage a ritual associated with human sacrifice, had come to mean that evil deeds would be punished. Recalling that one of his sons had been killed in the Korean War and another was insane, Mao asked poignantly: "Am I, therefore, to have no posterity?"

Rank-and-file Communist officials were also guilty when they deprived peasants of their belongings at the height of the Great Leap Forward campaign to set up "people's communes," Mao emphasized. The "egalitarianism" of the communes had been wrong: "Nobody should say, what's yours is mine, take it and walk away. That is the law of underworld gangsters who steal and rob and exploit labor." Mao approved of the bandits in *All Men Are Brothers* who had "robbed the rich and helped the poor." But, he added, "what was taken from the peasants must be returned to them. We cannot confiscate the property of working people."

These failings proved once again, Mao continued, that insufficient attention had been paid to educating both local officials and peasants. "An illiterate person can be a Prime Minister, so why can't our commune cadres and peasants learn something about political economy?"

he said. "Everybody can learn. Those who cannot read may also discuss economics and, through discussion, they will understand the subject more easily than the intellectual. I myself have never read textbooks!"

Thus, Mao conceded to Peng, he shared the responsibility with the Party for the troubles caused by the Great Leap Forward. But if he admitted to his mistakes, so must the Party officials. "Comrades, you must also analyze your errors, and you will feel better after you have broken wind and emptied your bowels."

The real danger now, Mao stressed, was the rise of his enemies who, in their opposition to "adventurism," were becoming rightists under the influence of the imperialists and bourgeoisie. The "people's communes" and other features of the Great Leap Forward "will never collapse" despite Peng Dehuai's desire to abolish them, he affirmed. Indicting Peng as an "ambitionist" and a "hypocrite," he accused him of working to "sabotage the dictatorship of the proletariat, split the Communist Party, organize factions in the Party, spread their influence, demoralize the vanguards of the proletariat, and build another opportunist party of their own." Therefore, Mao asserted, their conflict at the Lushan meeting was a "class struggle"—a continuation of the "life-and-death struggle between the two antagonistic classes of the bourgeoisie and the proletariat in the revolution."

Apparently in response to warnings that the purge of Peng would ignite a military revolt against him, Mao felt compelled to carry the quarrel to a showdown. He turned to the senior officers present. If outvoted, he said defiantly, he would go back to the countryside to recruit a new peasant army and return to overthrow the government. "If you don't follow me, I'll recruit a new Red Army and begin over again," he challenged them. "I think, however, that you will follow me."[28]

At that point the Chinese generals reportedly stood up in turn and pledged their allegiance to Mao.[29]

Still, Peng stubbornly declined to yield. He warned that conditions in China were deteriorating so rapidly that a "Hungarian rebellion" was bound to erupt and that the Soviet Army would have to be summoned to restore order. As Mao sought to cut short the debate by adjourning the meeting, Peng reminded him of a dispute between them in the wilderness two decades earlier. "In Yenan you fucked my mother for forty days," Peng barked. "Now I've only fucked your mother for eighteen days and you're trying to stop me, but you won't."[30]

Peng was correct—at least for the moment. Even though the generals lined up behind him, Mao seemed unable to rally the Central Committee to condemn Peng and his group rapidly. He therefore turned to an assortment of persuasive tactics in an effort to dislodge his adversaries. Early in August, he addressed a firm yet conciliatory letter to Zhang Wentian, Peng's closest supporter, warning him of the implications of their conspiracy. Mao charitably attributed Zhang's "error" to chronic malaria, but suggested that the illness might be beneficial if it sweated the wickedness out of him. Mao concluded: "Comrade, take my advice: rectify yourself thoroughly."[31]

Mao also wrote to another adversary, Liu Zhongyun, a senior official in the State Planning Commission. Liu was wrong to have underlined only the blunders of the Great Leap Forward, said Mao. But he commended Liu for having "laid bare" his mind, saying: "Over the past ten years, we have not come across a comrade who dares to expose cogently, analytically, and systematically the shortcomings in our plans. . . . I have not come across such a person. I know that such persons exist, but they are afraid to go over the heads of their superiors."[32]

In short, Mao was striving to demonstrate, it was inaccurate to label him a despot who would not brook criticism. On the contrary, he welcomed criticism—provided, of course, that it did not represent an attack by the "rightists" and other bourgeois foes whose aim was to wreck the Communist movement. But the problem was how to distinguish between acceptable and hostile criticism. An equally difficult problem was how to recognize when prominent Party luminaries like Peng Dehuai and his associates had deviated from the official orthodoxy to become "enemies of the people." Mao assembled the conference delegates at a series of meetings in an attempt to give them the answers.

At one of these meetings, he reiterated his fundamental thesis that "class struggle" within the Party as well as in society would continue for a long time before pure communism was attained. Since this struggle was "full of twists and turns," Mao said, it was understandable for comrades to wonder why "the chief culprits of today were the meritorious statesmen of yesterday." The answer was that they had strayed from the "correct" line, refused to confess to their sins and mend their ways, and, as a result, became transformed from tolerable critics to adversaries beyond redemption.[33]

In the case of Peng Dehuai and his faction, Mao went on to elaborate, they had never been true Marxists but were "bourgeois and opoprtunist elements" who had managed to "sneak into our Party" disguised as "fellow travelers of Marxism." This was obvious from their behavior, Mao asserted. They had "employed conspiratorial means to split the Party," thereby violating discipline in their effort to destroy Communist unity. More important, they had consulted Khrushchev, which proved that they were "working hand-in-glove with a foreign country" in their plot to sow discord.[34]

Mao then carried his case back to the Central Committee with another speech. Unlike his discursive address of the previous month, this talk was short and sharp. A year before, he said, "there was no clear sign of a split" in the Communist Party, but now "such a sign" did exist. The task, then, was to separate the "mistaken" comrades whose errors could be corrected from those who adamantly refused to repent. The dizziness of the Great Leap Forward was over and there would be "no more pompous exaggeration," said Mao. The main thrust at the moment, he emphasized, was to "oppose the right"—as personified by Peng Dehuai and his cohorts.[35]

Just as his impetuosity had led him to commit battlefield blunders, so Peng's impulsiveness compromised his challenge to Mao. He had struck too soon. Two years later, when the cumulative effect of the Great Leap Forward had plunged China into a deeper social and economic abyss, he might have succeeded. But in 1959, Peng could not muster the support he needed to sustain his offensive against Mao. Compelled to retreat, he went through the ritual of confessing his alleged sins and appealing for absolution.

In his recantation, Peng described his utterances as having been "a series of rightist absurdities" that had dealt a "blow to the activism of the broad masses and cadres, and damaged the prestige of the Party Central Committee and Comrade Mao Zedong." His "crime," he added, was all the more heinous for having been "prepared and organized" rather than "casual."[36]

On August 16, the Central Committee issued a verdict against Peng and his associates in a lengthy document condemning them for their present deviation as well as for "divisive activities" purportedly committed more than two decades earlier. Their "mistakes," the verdict read, were not "isolated" or "accidental," but represented a "right opportunist line" they had pursued for years. They were officially dismissed from their respective government posts—but, pending admission of all their "errors," they could retain their places in the Party, and "we shall see how they behave in the future."[37]

Peng's reaction to his ouster was a letter to Mao so passionately abject in style and substance that it constitutes almost a caricature of ceremonial self-abnegation. His dismissal was a "great victory" for the Party, he wrote, since it revealed "how horrible would be the danger if I were not exposed and criticized so thoroughly in time." "Bourgeois attitudes" had permeated him to such depths that for the past thirty years "I have been unworthy of your education and patience, so much so that I cannot express in words my regret and gratitude." Asserting that he had "failed the Party, failed the people, and also failed you," Peng requested Mao's authorization to labor in the countryside in oder to "steel myself and reform my ideology."[38] On September 17, he was officially replaced as Minister of Defense by Marshal Lin Biao, the brilliant Korean War commander. The Chief of General Staff, General Huang Kecheng, also dismissed, was replaced by General Luo Ruiqing, who until then had been Minister of Public Security.[39] Zhang Wentian was relegated to obscurity.

"Now that I'm out of office I feel free," Peng was reported to have exclaimed, and, consistent with Mao's treatment of his foes, he was accorded an unusual degree of independence. Permitted to retain his nominal membership in the Politburo, Peng was assigned first to serve as superintendent of a state farm in the northern province of Heilongjiang and later allowed to travel throughout China investigating agricultural conditions. These trips apparently confirmed his feeling that he had been justified in criticizing Mao's policies. In November 1961, Peng prepared five separate studies on the situation in Hunan, all deploring the food shortages that persisted in that region. A year later, he produced an eighty-thousand-word memorandum detailing the accuracy of his observations on the Great Leap Forward and demanding his "rehabilitation." Though never reinstated in the government, Peng's Party position remained equivocal and even as late as December 1966, after a group of Red Guards arrested him in Chengdu, he defiantly defended himself. "I was no executioner of the masses," he said. "I was half right and half wrong. I made mistakes, but I rendered meritorious service as well."[40]

If Mao ostensibly emerged triumphant from his clash with Peng, his victory was limited. First, Peng had overtly voiced what most of the Party apparatus really thought of the Great Leap Forward and its blunders. Hence his disclosures marked a turning point that would be followed by a considerable Party effort to reverse Mao's past economic policies in favor of a more moderate approach to development. Second, as the official indictment against him had affirmed, Peng's challenge did indeed damage Mao's prestige by shattering the Chairman's carefully cultivated mystique of omniscience, and this provided the Party leaders with a fresh opportunity to curb Mao's power. Finally, Peng's daring assault against Mao had a striking impact on senior Chinese military officers, and it touched off a conflict between Mao and his adversaries for control of the Army that was never entirely resolved. Far from restoring Chinese Communist unity, the purge of Peng and his "clique" was the beginning of a new phase in a struggle that would reach even more traumatic heights in the Cultural Revolution.

CHAPTER 7

The Party Takes Command

> *Liu Shaoqi and his confederates tried to put Mao nicely on a shelf like a Buddha so that people would blindly kow-tow to him while their clique managed the affairs of State in their own way.*
>
> —ANNA LOUISE STRONG, *1969*

> *They treated me with the respect they would have shown their dead father at his own funeral.*
>
> —MAO ZEDONG, *1967*

IN THE SPRING of 1961, accompanied by his wife, Liu Shaoqi traveled south from Beijing into Hunan province. There he spent forty-four days investigating economic conditions in several areas, including the village of Huaminglou, his birthplace in Ningxiang county. A cold, aloof man hardened by years as a ruthless Communist organizer, Liu usually kept his emotions in check. But he was appalled by what he saw in Hunan. In one village, the population had decreased as a result of deaths from malnutrition, and food shortages still persisted. Irrigation systems, dikes, and water conservancy projects had fallen into disrepair, and peasants almost everywhere he visited were bitter, weary, and apathetic at having been compelled to labor like animals during the Great Leap Forward. Though government propaganda was officially attributing China's difficulties at that time to floods, droughts, and other natural calamities, Liu privately offered a different explanation. "The problems were not caused by natural calamities," he said. "They were man-made."[1]

The man was Mao and, in the early 1960s, the Party leaders headed by Liu moved quickly to reshape the strategies that had caused such damage to China. Henceforth, they announced, "all possible material, technical, and financial aid" would be funneled into agriculture in a crash program to boost farm production.[2] In contrast to the First Five-Year Plan, which bled the peasants to pay for heavy industry, factories would now serve the rural sector. Farm output would no longer be spurred through Maoist mobilization schemes but with technical investments. Urban capital construction was suspended, and factories were ordered to concentrate on turning out tractors, farm implements, insecticides, and irrigation equipment. Instructions went out to build small- and medium-sized chemical-fertilizer plants, and imports of chemical fertilizer from Japan and Belgium soared. Swallowing their Chinese pride and their belief in the superiority of communism, the Party leaders also took the unprecedented step of contracting to purchase 5 to 6 million tons of grain, principally wheat, from Australia, Canada, and other capitalist nations at an annual cost of $300 to $400 million. These grain purchases were partly intended to feed China's coastal cities and thereby to relieve the pressure on China's primitive railway system.

Fundamental in this new approach was an attempt to introduce rationality into Chinese economic operations. "We want to keep our two feet on the ground," advised the Beijing directives stressing the need for pragmatism. For one thing, mechanization would no longer mean the serial production of heavy-duty tractors, but the manufacture of modest machinery suited to particular topographical conditions and job requirements. Efforts would be made to supplant human manpower with threshers, huskers, tillers, harrows, multi-share plows, and other simple tools that could be repaired on the spot. To help in this task, some twenty-five thousand small workshops were established under the auspices of the Second Ministry of Light Industry. Similarly, local Party cadres were told to stop setting ludicrous targets and to face realities. "We still cannot control nature completely," declared one Beijing pronouncement. "Traditions that have come down to us from our ancestors all contain some truth. . . . What crops to plan, when to sow, how to cultivate, when to harvest—these cannot be changed by man's will." Another article, urging cadres to heed the wisdom of "sage old peasants," stated: "We must oppose that kind of leadership in production that does not start from real conditions, that claims to know and give orders without knowing. . . . If you do not know, do not pretend that you do."

An equally important shift in this new policy of "retrenchment," as it was euphemistically labeled, was a drastic alteration in the structures imposed on the countryside during the Great Leap Forward. Though the people's communes were theoretically left intact, they were radically modified to place power in the hands of "production teams," each comprising twenty to thirty families. These units, which resembled the "mutual-aid" groups set up six years before, were authorized to determine their own utilization of manpower, land, draft animals, and implements. Moreover, they were permitted to decide on expenditures and income distribution without interference from commune, provincial, and central government officials—provided, of course, that they produced negotiated quantities of grain, cotton, fibers, and other "cash" crops for the state.

Perhaps the most significant switch in agriculture, however, was to a liberal policy given the typical numerological slogan of "three privates and one guarantee." Now, peasants could legally cultivate limited private gardens, pursue their own handicrafts, and sell their produce at free markets so long as they fulfilled the grain and raw material output quotas recommended by the state. This was less an innovation than the legitimization of private farming and black-market activity that had sprung up spontaneously during the hungry days after the Great Leap Forward. To the Maoists it represented a great leap back to the capitalist laws of supply and demand, but the Party leaders, desperate to stimulate production, felt that any workable method was acceptable. "We must employ every possible means that contributes to the productive enthusiasm of the peasants," said Liu Shaoqi, adding that the prospect of capitalist tendencies appearing "is not so horrible."[3] Secretary General Deng Xiaoping expressed the pragmatic approach more colorfully: "Private farming is all right as long as it raises production, just as it doesn't matter whether a cat is black or white as long as it catches mice."[4]

These various calls for liberalism were echoed by economic specialists within the Party apparatus. Vice-Premier Chen Yun, a consistent advocate of moderation, asserted that only by "beating a retreat" to some sort of *laissez-faire* practice could the regime hope to improve peasant morale and thereby revive production."[5] And the Vice-Chairman of the State Planning Commission, Bo Ibo, reporting that "the situation in the countryside is worse than it was before the war," proposed that one way to raise their output was through "more income, more food, and more consumer goods for those who perform more work."[6] He said:

It is wrong to think merely of production and not of the life of the people, to neglect harmony between work and rest, to disregard safety in production, to look simply at present-day production and ignore the next step, to eat up reserves in the warehouses, to use equipment and manpower to excess, and thus fail to maintain a steady productive rhythm. These things are bad for management.[7]

In parallel with this focus on temperance and practicality, the Party leaders emphasized the need for specialized skills, suggesting that bourgeois "technocrats" would be not only tolerated again but encouraged to join in the effort to pull the country out of its economic mess. "Questions of right and wrong in science are not decided by subjective 'convincing arguments,' but by their conformity . . . to reality," said a *Red Flag* article in January 1961.[8] Speaking to graduates of Beijing University a few months after that, Foreign Minister Chen Yi stressed the importance of professional knowledge to meet the challenge of "building up our country as a great socialist power with modern industry, modern agriculture, and modern science and culture." In a direct slap at one of Mao's tenets, Chen said that it was a "mistake" to judge people by their political leanings as long as "they are successful in their studies and contribute to socialist construction."[9] And, he added, "who wants to fly with a pilot who is ideologically pure but cannot manage the controls?"

Chen Yi's speech was welcomed by the Beijing University students as a "liberation." Moreover, it was followed by real changes. Professors who had been purged for political faults were "rehabilitated," and the educational curriculum was broadened. Closed fields of research, such as psychoanalysis, were reopened. Translations of Western authors began to reappear, and there was a marked relaxation in the control of Chinese poets, playwrights, and novelists.[10]

Apparently striving to consolidate their own position, the Party *apparatchiks* also began a thinly disguised literary onslaught against Mao and his policies. The authors and journalists employed in this effort were associated with either the Party's Propaganda Department or its Beijing Committee—and were plainly, therefore, acting on behalf of Liu Shaoqi and his colleagues as well as for Peng Chen, Party boss of the capital. Most of these literary broadsides were aimed at three different targets. First, though accepting the idea of Mao as China's leader, they assailed the cult of his personality. Second, they underscored the devastation caused by the Great Leap Forward and demanded an end to such experiments. And finally, they contended that Marshal Peng Dehuai had been unjustly purged for having dared to say openly what numbers of Party officials personally believed. Liu Shaoqi probably favored a reversal of the verdict against the old Marshal, for he was quoted as having said that "some comrades also made speeches that more or less resembled those made by Peng Dehuai."[11]

Paradoxically, several of Mao's most vigorous literary opponents were the very men who had stifled intellectual freedom within the Chinese Communist movement since the early 1940s. Foremost among them was Zhou Yang, a Hunanese whose experience as a left-wing writer and editor reached back thirty years. In August 1962, under the auspices of the Party's Propaganda Department, Zhou organized a two-week conference of literary bureaucrats at Dairen, at which one speaker after another lashed out at Mao and the privations caused by the Great Leap Forward. The Vice-President of the Hunan branch of the Chinese Writers' Union, Kang Zhuo, stressed the "contradiction between socialist ideological leadership and the actual needs of the peasants," urging authors to dramatize the pressures imposed by Mao on the rural population. In an assault against Mao's thesis that the proletariat be portrayed as flawless heroes, Shao Zhuanlin, Secretary of the Writers' Union, criticized "oversimplification, doctrinairism, and mechanical theories" in Chinese literature. Instead of depicting heroic and villainous extremes, Shao said, writers should describe the vast majority of the population as "people in the middle," as yet uncommitted to the revolution.[12]

At the same time, an even more withering if subtle fusillade against Mao came from the pen of the prominent historian and deputy mayor of Beijing, Wu Han. In June 1959, obviously writing with the approval of his immediate superior, Peng Chen, Wu had produced an essay on Hai Rui, a high official of the Ming dynasty who had served in the region of Suzhou in the sixteenth century. Entitled "Hai Rui Scolds the Emperor," the analogy was transparently contrived to criticize Mao through the words of the ancient mandarin. In one passage, he quoted Hai Rui as bravely telling the emperor almost precisely what Peng Dehuai was preparing to say to Mao about the time the essay was published.

In earlier times you did quite a few good things, but how about now?. . . Your mind is deluded, and you are too dogmatic and prejudiced.

You think you are always right and refuse criticism. Your faults are too numerous. . . . The whole country has been dissatisfied with you for a long time, and the inner and outer ministers and officers all know it.[13]

After Peng Dehuai's purge, Wu Han went a step further. In February 1961, he staged a drama in the form of a Beijing opera entitled *The Dismissal of Hai Rui*. In it, Hai Rui demanded that peasants be returned their illegally confiscated land, and was banished for his audacity. Though he certainly recognized the allegorical assault against him at the time, Mao did not respond until late 1965, when he mounted a campaign against Wu Han as his opening salvo in the Cultural Revolution. Only then did the *People's Daily*, under Mao's control for the first time in years, quote the Chairman's pronouncement: "Emperor Jia Jing dismissed Hai Rui. In 1959, we dismissed Peng Dehuai. Peng Dehuai *is* a Hai Rui."[14]

Mao's most acerbic literary critic, however, was the former editor of the *People's Daily*, Deng Tuo, who in 1959 had been appointed chief of ideological and cultural activities in the Beijing Party Committee. For almost a year and a half, Deng wrote a column called "Evening Talks at Yanshan," attacking Mao's policies in a language so Aesopian that only a restrained circle of Beijing "insiders" could decipher his message. In one essay, Deng denounced the Great Leap Forward with the parable of a merchant who dreamed of amassing riches from a single egg and was therefore "just speculating" rather than pursuing the "proper and usual way of production in order to increase his wealth." Like Mao, Deng implied, the merchant "substituted illusion for reality." In collaboration with Wu Han and Liao Muosha, another Beijing Party official, Deng went so far as to suggest that Mao was suffering from a psychosis that accounted for his irrational conduct. "A person afflicted with this disease must promptly take a complete rest," their article advised. "If he insists on talking or doing anything, he will make a lot of trouble."[15]

Deng Tuo went beyond his other literary colleagues in assailing Mao's foreign policies. In an essay favoring a *rapprochement* with the United States, he put forth the dubious argument that the Chinese had actually discovered America and, consequently, the "long tradition of Sino-American friendship is an important historical fact." Deng also criticized Mao's alienation of the Soviet Union and the loss to China of Russian aid by warning that "if a man with a swelled head thinks he can learn a subject easily and then kicks out his teacher, he will never learn anything." In another essay, he ridiculed Mao's assertion that "the East Wind will prevail over the West Wind," an allusion to potential Communist superiority, calling the slogan "just hackneyed phrases without much meaning." His advice to Mao and other "friends who are fond of big talk," Deng wrote, was to "read more, think more, and talk less."[16] In September 1962, Mao moved to halt this criticism, and Deng terminated his series of articles with a final piece entitled "The Thirty-six Strategies." It recalled the old Chinese military saying that the best of the thirty-six strategies was retreat. Deng's retreat spared him for only four years, and he was bitterly denounced during the Cultural Revolution.

Meanwhile, Mao had plenty of other evidence to remind him that strenuous efforts were being made to weaken his authority. In 1960 the Party created six regional bureaus responsible directly to the Secretariat and clearly designed to reinforce the power of the Central Committee. Accompanying this structural change, numerous directives emphasized the virtues of order, routine, discipline, and other rules calculated to stiffen the Party bureaucracy and undermine Mao's concept of "mass" enthusiasm.[17] Not long afterward, the Central Committee convened a "work conference" at which Liu Shaoqi, Deng Xiaoping, Peng Chen, and many others among the seven thousand delegates present spent nine days criticizing Mao's policies as having brought the Chinese economy "to the brink of collapse."[18] In August 1962, consistent with this trend, Liu Shaoqi published a new edition of his 1939 series of lectures, now entitled *On the Self-Cultivation of Communists*, which studiously omitted any reference to the "Thought" of Mao and even denounced him indirectly under the guise of criticizing "some comrades" who wanted "to have people sing their praises and flatter them . . . try to dress themselves up as 'great men' and 'heroes' in the Communist movement and . . . stop at nothing to gratify their desire."[19]

Mao must have been troubled as well about this time by various attempts to absolve Peng Dehuai of his "crimes." Peng, then striving to vindicate himself, was apparently supported by several senior Party and Army figures, perhaps including Liu Shaoqi. These men had no particular affection for Peng. But they may have felt that his "rehabilitation" would usefully serve to strengthen the Army during a period when China was approaching three simultaneous external security crises.

Information reaching Beijing from Communist spies on Taiwan indicated that Chiang Kai-shek's Nationalists were planning to cross the hundred-mile strait in an invasion of the mainland. This intelligence was faulty. Still, sensitive to China's vulnerability, the Communist leaders deployed troops throughout the coastal provinces, and it was only after receiving assurances from American diplomats in Warsaw that the United States had no intention of backing Chiang that the Communists relaxed on the eastern front. But the illusion of a threat had been enough to unnerve them. Moreover, the crises in other areas in 1962 were quite real.

As the Sino-Soviet schism widened, Kremlin agents in Xinjiang, where the Russians had long been influential, began to stir up resistance to Chinese rule among Uighurs, Kazakhs, and other Muslim minorities resentful of Beijing's political and cultural domination. In the spring of 1962, some sixty thousand of these Muslims, encouraged by Soviet propaganda, fled over the frontier into the Soveit Republic of Kazakhstan while others, unable to escape, staged abortive revolts in two or three Xinjiang cities.[20] This appeared to Beijing, with much justification, to be a case of Soviet subversion, and it augured worse to come. Meanwhile, the Chinese were becoming embroiled in a border dispute with India, the international repercussions of which might be serious. Thus the Chinese leaders sought to assure the reliability of their Army.

None of these considerations swayed Mao into reversing his decision against Peng Dehuai. He could not take the risk of reinstating a known adversary in the Chinese military establishment. Faithful to his dictum that "political power grows out of the barrel of a gun," he had consistently concentrated through the years on winning military support. That had been his strategy in the 1930s and now, as he faced the challenge of regaining his authority, one of his principal objectives was to entrust the Army to officers of unequivocal loyalty to himself and to his concepts. But he was in no position to dictate terms. He was therefore compelled to compromise with his Party foes. After Peng Dehuai's dismissal, the Party leaders had accepted his choice for Defense Minister, Marshal Lin Biao. And Mao, in exchange, conceded to the Party's candidate for Chief of General Staff, General Luo Ruiqing.

A tall, slightly stooped native of Sichuan province, then in his mid-fifties, General Luo was a secret police and espionage expert rather than a soldier. He had trained at a special Moscow academy run by the Cheka, the Soviet State security apparatus, and he later attended a similar Comintern school in France. On his return to China in the late 1920s, he was appointed an Army political commissar, and a severe wound he suffered in battle against Chiang Kai-shek's Nationalists left him with a face twitch befitting his sinister secret police role. As an undercover operative, Luo was careful in the course of his career to keep both his political and personal associations ambiguous. A former Chinese Communist official who knew Luo in the 1930s remembered him as a friendless, distrusted man, a "necessary evil" in the system.[21] Logically, Luo was appointed Minister of Public Security when the Communists established their regime. After 1959 his main function as Chief of General Staff was to protect the interests of the Party and its affiliated military professionals inside the Army—in short, to counterbalance Lin Biao.

In contrast, Lin Biao was a distinguished soldier whose military talents had repeatedly earned him praise from enemies and comrades alike. Born about 1908 as Lin Yourong—he later assumed the *nom de guerre* "Biao," meaning "tiger cat"—Lin was the son of a bankrupt textile manufacturer who had been forced to find employment as a purser on a Yangzi River steamer. Lin's birthplace, a village near the northern border of Hubei province, was a center of peasant unrest in the early decades of the twentieth century. Inspired by the political ferment of the period, Lin went to Shanghai to join the Communist Youth League, and afterward moved to Guangzhou to enroll at Whampoa, the military academy then operating under the Nationalists with Communist participation. Lin specialized in infantry training, received his commission in 1926, and promptly enlisted in the Communist Party as a full-fledged member.

During the following years, Lin was involved in nearly every major event in the evolution of the Communist movement. He participated in the abortive attempt in 1927 to seize Nanchang, the capital of Jiangxi province, and soon after that he accompanied Zhu De's Army when it linked up with Mao Zedong in the misty heights of Jinggangshan. He later led the advance guard of the celebrated Long March and by 1936, at the age of twenty-eight, he was commander of the 115th Division of the Eighth Route Army.

Daring and courageous, Lin was seriously wounded while commanding his division against the Japanese in Shanxi province in 1938. He was sent to Moscow for medical care and, according to some accounts, joined in the defense of Leningrad during its siege by the Germans in the winter of 1941–1942. In the civil war against the Nationalists, Lin suffered a series of setbacks until, devising a bold new strategy, his Fourth Field Army swept from Manchuria down to Hainan Island, China's southernmost territory. Not long after, he reportedly returned to the Soviet Union, either to recover from another wound or to be treated for tuberculosis. Long absences from view during subsequent years fueled speculation that his health was chronically poor. His occasional public appearances, in which he looked frail and spoke in a thin voice, further contributed to his image as a sick man.

Lin's political record over the years zigzagged within the labyrinth of Communist power rivalries, his chief opponent in bids for prominence apparently having been Peng Dehuai. Aware of their conflicting ambitions, Mao seemed to set Lin and Peng against one another in order to secure his own authority. In 1937, for instance, Mao was reported to have deliberately slighted Lin by giving Peng command of the First Front Army. In 1954, linking Lin to an alleged plot to carve out a semiautonomous Manchurian Communist state under Soviet tutelage, Mao again punished Lin by suspending him from the Politburo and naming Peng to be Defense Minister. At the Lushan conference five years later, however, Mao cleverly turned the tables by using Lin as his spearhead against Peng. Following that maneuver, Mao employed Lin to bring the Army under his control.

The political scene in China was in such disarray in the wake of the Great Leap Forward that Lin warned soon after taking over as Defense Minister, "We must ensure that the armed forces do not get out of hand,"[22] and he quickly embarked on an intensive campaign to guarantee the Army's fidelity to Mao. He made an effort to appease officers and men by according them promotions and special food rations, and he laid particular stress on investigating the causes of their dissatisfaction. He also made some concessions to the military professionals by emphasizing his concern for modern weapons and techniques. But far more important was his drive to indoctrinate the Army along Mao's ideological lines.

On one hand, striving to deflect responsibility for the disasters of the Great Leap away from Mao, Army propagandists blamed the debacle on "confused" rural cadres. In addition, Lin Biao initiated a dynamic program to "rectify" the attitudes of officers and men. Introducing more than two hundred thousand new political commissars into Army units, he ordered that the ideological leanings and class backgrounds of troops be scrutinized and that their thinking be strictly supervised. Model heroes and units were either discovered or invented, and widely publicized as examples to be imitated not only by troops but by all Chinese. One of these ideal units was the "Good Eighth Company of Nanjing Road," which had patrolled the main street of Shanghai without falling prey to prostitutes, black marketeers, and other bourgeois temptations that continued to flourish even after the Communists took the city. The most outstanding of the individuals offered for emulation was a soldier called Lei Feng, who had purportedly been a diligent student of Mao's works before being killed by, of all things, a falling telephone pole. The banality of Lei Feng's death was deliberately stressed. For, as the propaganda stated, heroes were expected to display their "revolutionary spirit" in "ordinary routine work" rather than in flamboyant exploits.[23]

In early 1964, Lin Biao escalated his campaign by launching a nationwide appeal to "learn from the People's Liberation Army." The purpose of this fresh effort was to portray the Army, in contrast to the Party apparatus, as the organization that truly fit Mao's ideals. Like the Army, Maoist spokesmen asserted, all Chinese must "resolutely oppose the bureaucratic working style that is divorced from reality and the masses," and rely on ideology rather than technocracy.[24] In February 1965, demonstrating the "extremely high proletarian character" of the Army even further, Lin erased the differences between officers and men by abolishing rank insignia and titles. This decision, with its stress on the egalitarian spirit that had inspired Mao's guerrillas in the Yenan days, was plainly calculated to undermine the Chinese career officers who had only a decade earlier transformed the Army into a formal, stratified structure.

Lin's campaign to shape the Army into a Maoist instrument marked the entry onto the public scene of a redoubtable personage— Mao's wife, Jiang Qing, the former movie actress. She emerged from obscurity to make her political debut in the summer of 1961 with an article praising a "certain" Army company that years before had "shouldered the most honorable task of safeguarding our great leader, Chairman Mao." Though barely noticed outside China when it was published, the article was important both for its content and for its authorship. Using the technique of recalling the past to serve the present, the article implied that Mao again needed the Army to protect him against internal adversaries. And the fact that his wife was now playing a political role indicated that Mao distrusted the Party to such a degree that he felt compelled to turn to supporters whose loyalty was unquestioned. Indeed, Jiang Qing later revealed, she had acted as a "roving sentinel" for Mao during this period, observing developments in culture, education, and even international affairs.

Jiang Qing's appearance was paralleled by the emergence into Chinese political life of another woman—Wang Guangmei, the wife of Liu Shaoqi. Totally unlike Jiang Qing, with her slightly disreputable background as a Shanghai movie actress, Wang Guangmei was a handsome, sophisticated lady whose father had been a Westernized industrialist in north China. Thus there was almost a "class struggle" between the two women, and their quarrel eventually degenerated into a bitterly feminine dispute.[25]

Lin Biao encountered substantial resistance from professional Chinese officers associated with the Party apparatus in his efforts to bring the Army into the Maoist orbit. Chief of General Staff Luo Ruiqing often disregarded Mao's "Thought" in his statements, emphasizing instead the Army's purely military vocation. He organized weapons competitions in order to improve military skills while minimizing the importance of indoctrination sessions designed to raise the ideological "consciousness" of troops. And if Lin Biao's propagandists publicized models like Lei Feng as exemplary soldiers imbued with Maoist doctrine, Luo Ruiqing and the Party glorified such "heroes" as An Yemin and Guo Xingfu, who had excelled as fighters because of their technical talents.[26] Similarly, Mao and Lin ran into stiff opposition from the Party in early 1964, when they shifted former Army political commissars into trade, finance, and other government bureaus in Beijing as well as in the provinces. Once again, the *apparatchiks* rejected Mao's attempt to put his ideology over expertise, and *Red Flag*, the Party's authoritative theoretical journal, explained: "Politics cannot take first place over economics, because the main task . . . is economic construction and, therefore, politics must serve the existing economic base."[27]

In the years that followed, as both men struggled to undermine the Party bureaucracy, Mao would promote Lin Biao to the prestigious position of his official successor. But in late 1971, Lin was purged in a mysterious episode that eliminated several key members of the Chinese high command.

⚓

By the early 1960s, Mao had perceived that he was making little headway in his revitalization of a revolutionary China. On the contrary, "spontaneous" capitalism was spreading throughout the country as a result of the liberal economic policies inaugurated by the Party. And, as economic conditions improved, peasants, workers, students, and other Chinese as well as Party officials were more reluctant than ever to subscribe to the principles that had led to the Great Leap Forward. Villagers and local cadres ignored central Party directives as they focused on earning money, eating better, building houses, and ameliorating their living standards. In Beijing, writers like Wu Han and Deng Tuo were airing their critical views with unusual freedom, and even senior Party and government leaders were lapsing into bourgeois if not corrupt practices. The mayor of Guangzhou, Zeng Sheng, was reliably reported to have imported everything from cameras and tape recorders to prostitutes and American films from nearby Hong Kong, and he regularly indulged himself in banquets that featured such Guangdong province gastronomic delicacies as stewed seal, braised turtle, and chicken steamed in chrysanthemum petals.[28] According to charges later leveled against him, Party Secretary General Deng Xiaoping was so enamored of bridge that he commandeered private railway cars and special aircraft to transport his card-playing cronies to different parts of the country for foursomes.[29]

In September 1962, Mao made his first major move since the Great Leap Forward to arrest the erosion of his ideals. At a Party Plenum in Beijing, he launched what he termed a Socialist Education Campaign with the ambitious objective of "educating man anew and reorganizing our revolutionary ranks." Plainly referring to the Beijing literary set then sniping at him, Mao warned that a number of writers were "creating a climate of public opinion for the restoration of capitalism." He also focused on the problem of cultivating youths, asserting that their "class education . . . must be strengthened to ensure that our nation will remain revolutionary and incorruptible for generations and forever." Finally, he affirmed his intention to resurrect collectivist controls in order to repudiate the liberal economic trends that had been "incited by the bourgeoisie and its exponents within the Party."[30] In this program, then, Mao was already beginning to formulate the ideas that would later prompt him to unleash the more ambitious Cultural Revolution.

The first phase of Mao's counterattack against the liberals began with an effort to eliminate "harmful bourgeois influences" in the fields of art and literature. He complained that "socialist transformation had by now achieved very little effect," calling it "absurd" that "many Communists are enthusiastic in promoting feudalist and capitalist art but are not enthusiastic in promoting socialist art."[31] Intellectuals were approaching the "brink of revisionism" and, unless halted, "would inevitably become like the Petofi Club of Hungary," the group of intelligentsia that had been instrumental in sparking the uprising against the Communist regime in Budapest in 1956.[32]

Mao's problem, however, was to find loyal activists to assist him in carrying out a purge of literary dissidents. He could count on his wife, Jiang Qing, to serve as a cultural tsarina, but her authority was limited. When he looked to Liu Shaoqi and the *apparatchiks* for help, as he did in 1964, Mao must have known that it would be difficult to rely on them to strike down the writers and journalists who were actually operating on their behalf against him. The best he could do under the circumstances was to build up a case against the Party that he would unveil when he launched his Cultural Revolution a few years later.

Mao was confronted by a similar dilemma in the next phase of his projected counterattack, when he sought to reverse the "capitalistic" trends that were rapidly overtaking the countryside as the Party introduced liberal economic measures in order to repair the damage caused by the Great Leap Forward. To Mao, these trends were alarming. In some places, he noted in a document published in May 1963, "landlords and rich peasants" had regained power by manipulating local officials, and were putting out anti-Communist propaganda as well as "developing counterrevolutionary organizations." Elsewhere, the document said, "speculation and profiteering have reached serious proportions" as wealthier peasants "exploited" labor, engaged in moneylending, and made private land deals. Perhaps most distressing, lower-level Party committees in cooperation with village "capitalists" were subverting communism:

> In organizations and the collective economy, there have emerged a group of corrupt elements, thieves, speculators and degenerates who have ganged up with landlords and rich peasants to commit evil deeds. These elements are a part of the new bourgeoisie, or their ally.[33]

The Party leaders, considering themselves to be good Communists, were as determined as Mao to stop the slide toward capitalism and corruption in the countryside. But their methods for correcting the deteriorating rural situation opposed his approach in much the same way that their respective policy lines had diverged for years.

Consistent with his lifelong principles, Mao proposed that the "masses be set in motion" by permitting the poorer peasants to criticize local Party cadres and the re-emerging rural gentry. Wayward cadres would in turn be forced to confess their "errors" to peasant associations formed for that purpose. In short, just as he had provoked a conflict between intellectuals and the Party during the "Hundred Flowers" interlude nearly a decade before, so Mao was now trying to set dispossessed peasants against rural officials in order to weaken the Party *apparatchiks*.

But Liu Shaoqi and his comrades perceived that this strategy threatened the power of the rural Party organization. They also feared that fresh tensions in the countryside would undermine agricultural production, then beginning to recover after three lean years. Thus they countered Mao with a directive asserting that the effort to curb capitalism in the countryside be a slow, gradual process managed by Party investigation teams.[34] Liu also challenged Mao's tactic of using his wife for political activities by employing his own spouse, Wang Guangmei, to help draw up that directive. Disguised as a peasant woman, Wang Guangmei went to work with the Peach Garden Main Brigade at the Lu Wang Zhuang Commune in Hebei province, not far from Beijing. Over a period of a year there, she gathered the experience to advise the Party on rural conditions.[35]

In early 1965, aware that his attempts to purify the rural Party structure were being blocked, Mao came back with a new edict. Directing his fire against "those people in authority within the Party who take the capitalist road"—the formula he would later use over and over again to designate Liu Shaoqi and his colleagues—he reiterated his demand for a release of mass criticism "from below." Party officials must submit to supervision by the "masses," he insisted, evoking again the familiar image that "we must not be like women with bound feet" who prefer caution.[36] Here again, he was opposed by the Party bureaucrats even though they paid lip service to his appeals for mobilization of the masses. Compelled to confess his "crimes" during the Cultural Revolution two years afterward, Liu Shaoqi conceded that he had only played a charade in having appeared to support Mao, saying: "I committed the mistake of 'actually leaning to the right though seeming to lean to the left.' "[37] In Mao's view, even that confession was a charade.

If he was frustrated by his inability to impose his ideology on the countryside, Mao was equally disappointed by his failure to revamp the Chinese educational system, which in his opinion was increasingly losing touch with "proletarian" reality. The question of education obsessed him more than any other issue at that time. For Chinese youth represented the country's future leaders and, Mao feared, his brand of communism would be drastically altered if not entirely scrapped after his death unless he could mold a new generation of "revolutionary successors."

Mao's fears were largely justified. Many young Chinese were disillusioned in the wake of the Great Leap Forward, when educational and job opportunities were sharply curtailed. Unable to find employment after graduation, youths were becoming "delinquent," or so it seemed to Mao. The Army press, reflecting the Maoist view, repeatedly excoriated young "playboys and hooligans who do not want to hold decent jobs" and whose "extravagant clothing fits in nicely with their decadent and lustful style of living and their desire for sensual excitement."[38] As examples of "extravagant" dress, the radical journals singled out colorful, open-neck blouses worn by girls, and tight trousers and pointed-toe "rocket" or "peppercorn" shoes favored by young men.[39] Maoist publications criticized such "bourgeois" phenomena then in vogue as "beehive" coiffures for young ladies and "ducktail" haircuts for youths. One newspaper complained that the People's Park in Shanghai, which in pre-Communist days had been barred to Chinese and dogs, was now being "polluted" by "men wearing woollen jackets . . . and women with powdered faces and tinted lips" who discussed food, pleasure trips, and exchanged "reactionary stories."[40]

Mao's concern that young Chinese were becoming soft and complacent was also mirrored about this time in a series of scathing attacks in the Army press against Feng Ding, the prominent Party philosopher, who in lectures to youth groups had defined "happiness" as a "normal life in which there is peace without war . . . good food, good clothing, and spacious living quarters, and harmonious relations among members of the family." This definition of happiness "is almost identical with that of the Soviet modern revisionist," replied an Army journal, warning that "revolutionary youth should absolutely not be taken in by him" but must "severely condemn him and completely rid their minds of his erroneous influence."[41] Yet Feng Ding's materialistic view of happiness was undoubtedly shared by numbers of even the most radical Chinese youth. Interviewed in Hong Kong during this period, a former schoolteacher from Beijing affirmed that all her students had been "revolutionary." But, she explained, they believed that the revolution would bring them higher incomes, better apartments, more food, a bicycle, and "maybe even an automobile some day."[42] In short, as Mao would put it, they were waving his Red Flag in order to oppose his Red Flag.

In universities and other institutions of higher learning, meanwhile, tensions were growing between the children of Party and government officials, who believed in "elitist" education, and students of worker and peasant origin, whose presence in classes lowered educational standards. Concerned with producing skilled technocrats, the Party favored a formal system of education. But this was anathema to Mao. In speech after speech, he inveighed against long schooling periods, heavy curricula, and examinations in which students were "ambushed by strange, remote questions" that resembled the "eight-legged essays" required of candidates for the mandarinate during the Ming dynasty. Such students, Mao said, were unable to distinguish between rice and wheat, or pigs and horses. In particular, he grumbled, it was criminal to force youths to sit through long, tedious lectures by boring professors. "Students should be permitted to doze off when a lecturer is teaching. Instead of listening to nonsense, they do much better taking a nap to freshen themselves up. Why listen to gibberish anyway?"[43]

Mao's obsession with the failure of Chinese youth to live up to his expectations was dramatically reflected in his talks with foreign visitors to China during that period. In an interview with Edgar Snow, he even went so far as to suggest that China's younger generation might "make peace with imperialism" after his death and conspire to "bring the remnants of the Chiang Kai-shek clique back to the mainland."[44] In July 1964, Mao boldly voiced his apprehensions in a significant essay entitled "On Khrushchev's Phoney Communism and Its Historical Lessons for the World." Written in his brilliant polemical style, the essay illustrated the degree to which Mao considered the dilution of "orthodox" communism in the Soviet Union since the demise of Stalin to portend the path China might take following his own death. His statement was a clear warning that the time was at hand for a major thrust to stop the slide toward "revisionism" in China.

In the Soviet Union, Mao wrote, Khrushchev had betrayed true Marxism-Leninism by promoting "material incentives," encouraging "free competition," "undermining the social collective economy," sponsoring "bourgeois liberty, equality, fraternity and humanity . . . and debasing socialist morality," and colluding with American "imperialism" in an attempt to place "the vested interests of a handful of people" above the interests of the Communist bloc. This had "opened the floodgates for the revisionist deluge" in the Soviet Union. The "historical lesson" for China was obvious.

> Let us look at the facts. Is our society today thoroughly clean? No, it is not. Classes and class struggle still remain, the activities of the overthrown reactionary classes plotting a comeback still continue, and we still have speculative activities by old and new bourgeois elements and desperate forays by embezzlers, grafters, and degenerates.[45]

Accordingly, Mao asserted, urgent efforts had to be initiated in China to defeat "spontaneous capitalist tendencies" and reinforce the collective economy, destroy the "bourgeois" attitudes of intellectuals, break down the power of the bureaucracy, and eliminate professionalism in the Army. Moreover, the Party apparatus required purification—or else "it would not take long, perhaps only several years or a decade, or several decades at most, before a counterrevolutionary restoration on a national scale inevitably occurred . . . and the whole of China would change its color." This was precisely what had happened in the Soviet Union, where Khrushchev's "goulash communism" had become "simply another name for capitalism." This was the dream of the "imperialist prophets" who, basing their predictions on the changes that had taken place in the Soviet Union, were hoping for a "peaceful evolution" in subsequent Chinese generations.[46]

To prevent this disaster in China, Mao affirmed, the Party must not only hew to his "correct line and correct policies," but it was imperative to "train and bring up millions of successors who will carry on the cause of proletarian revolution." Or, as he put it:

> In the final analysis, the question of training successors for the revolutionary cause of the proletariat is one of whether or not there will be people who can carry on the Marxist-Leninist revolutionary cause started by the older generation of proletarian revolutionaries, whether or not our descendants will continue to march along the correct road laid down by Marxism-Leninism or, in other words, whether or not we can successfully prevent the emergence of Khrushchevite revisionism in China.
>
> In short, it is an extremely important question, a matter of life and death for our Party and our country. It is a question of fundamental importance to the proletarian revolutionary cause for a hundred, a thousand, nay ten thousand years.[47]

Shortly afterward, when the Cultural Revolution erupted, Liu Shaoqi would be dubbed "China's Khrushchev" by the Maoists, and the millions of "revolutionary successors" would be known as Red

Guards. So, as early as the middle of 1964, Mao had undoubtedly anticipated the storm that he himself would unleash. But the tempest was preceded by an intricate internal crisis which paralleled China's rapidly deteriorating relations with the Soviet Union and the rapidly growing potentiality of a threat from the United States.

***

Though the dispute between the Chinese and Russians until the mid-1960s was primarily over ideology, international strategy, and economic aid, other tensions were building up between the two Communist neighbors along a border region that stretched more than six thousand miles from the Pacific Ocean through Mongolia to the barren wastes of Central Asia. In the spring of 1962, the Russians were maneuvering to undermine Beijing's influence in Xinjiang. In the years before and after that, other sectors of the frontier had been the scene of friction. According to Foreign Minister Chen Yi, the Soviet Union provoked more than five thousand incidents along the border between July 1960 and the end of 1965, and had deployed increasing numbers of troops in the frontier region in a manner that "presupposes China as the enemy."[48] At about the same time, attempts by China and the Soviet Union to settle their boundary differences through negotiations had collapsed. Clearly, the Chinese had reason to fear that their quarrel with Moscow could spiral into a shooting war. This fear was exacerbated, meanwhile, by events to their south.

In early 1965, Mao was rather sanguine about the situation in Vietnam. Speaking with Edgar Snow, he predicted with confidence that the United States would lose interest in the war there and withdraw its troops in a year or two.[49] But soon afterward, American bombardments of North Vietnam and the landing of combat troops in the South made it plain that the United States intended to escalate rather than reduce its commitment in Vietnam. Now, Mao realized, he was being flanked by the world's two most powerful nations—and the pressures they exerted on China were having a profound impact on his internal troubles.

As Mao perceived one part of this complicated dilemma, the expansion of the Vietnam war into a direct challenge to China's national security would require the use of Chinese troops for strictly military purposes. In that event, he could no longer count on the Army as an instrument in his political quarrel with the Party bureaucrats. In addition, a conflict with the United States would bring to the fore the Chinese Army professionals affiliated with the Party apparatus he was seeking to subdue. Confronted by the prospect of an enlarged Vietnam war, Mao's task was to avoid Chinese involvement at almost any cost.

A war with the Soviet Union, though it appeared to be less plausible at the time, would have also deprived Mao of the Army's services as a political weapon to wield against the Party. This too had to be averted. Yet Mao would not repair China's breach with the Kremlin without diluting his implacable hostility to the despicable "revisionists." Nor could he compromise with the Russians without courting the risk of having them again intrude into China's affairs in support of his rivals, as Khrushchev had done in the case of Peng Dehuai. While Mao eventually complied with a Russian request for transit facilities to ship Soviet supplies to Hanoi, he could not accept Moscow's repeated proposal for a Sino-Soviet agreement to act jointly against the United States in Vietnam. For he sensed that such an arrangement, which would have accorded airfield rights and other privileges inside China to the Russians, was also an invitation to the Soviet Union to exercise its influence among receptive Chinese Army officers.

Ideally, therefore, Mao had to maintain tensions with both the United States and the Soviet Union—but without allowing those tensions to carry China into full-scale conflict with either. This foreign policy was essential to his fundamental goal of eliminating his domestic foes and putting China on the track toward permanent revolution. To play his tricky and dangerous game successfully, however, Mao had to overcome the fierce resistance of his Party and Army adversaries.

The debate over strategy that raged in Beijing through most of 1965 gradually polarized into two fairly clear-cut postures. On one side stood Mao and Marshal Lin Biao—"doves" in the sense that their aim was to side-step war in order to devote their energies to purging China of its alleged "revisionists." On the other side was General Luo Ruiqing, representing Liu Shaoqi and the Party bureaucracy as well as the military professionals. Determined to wrest the Army from Mao's hands, they offered the "hawkish" proposal that China intervene in Vietnam—having first taken the precaution of resolving its dispute with the Kremlin in order to gain Soviet nuclear protection to deter an American atomic counterattack.

As early as February 1965, Luo Ruiqing put forth the line that China must do its "utmost" to aid Hanoi, while a typical Party bureaucrat, the trade union boss Liu Ningyi, went even further in asserting that Beijing "will definitely not stand by idly without lending a helping hand" if the Americans extended the war into North Vietnam.[50] In contrast, the Maoists exuded extreme caution, saying that China would fight only if the United States "forces a war on us [and] we have no choice but to take it on to the end."[51] One of Mao's supporters prudently warned against "taking the enemy lightly and advancing in a reckless way," explaining that good soldiers "avoid battle" when they cannot be sure of victory.[52] That enunciation of Mao's guerrilla-warfare theories drew scorn from General Luo. Passive defense of the sort advocated by Mao was "a spurious kind of defense," he said, adding that "the only real defense is active defense."[53]

By the spring, as the American presence in Vietnam grew, the policy debate in Beijing sharpened. In a speech commemorating the Soviet defeat of Nazi Germany in World War II, Luo Ruiqing insisted that the United States was "playing a role more ferocious than that of Hitler" and suggested that the Americans could be beaten through concerted Sino-Soviet action. Pointing out that the American atomic monopoly had been "broken many years ago" by the Russians, Luo implied that the Soviet nuclear umbrella would serve to discourage the United States from counterattacking. His oration concluded on an emotional note that must have shocked Mao. Expressing his "full confidence in the great Soviet people and the great Soviet Army," Luo vowed that Beijing and Moscow would be reunited to "fight shoulder to shoulder against our common enemy."[54] In reply, the Maoists made it clear that there could be no *rapprochement* with the Soviet Union, now headed by Leonid Brezhnev and Alexei Kosygin since the dismissal of Khrushchev in late 1964. According to the Maoist thesis, "revisionism" must be thoroughly eliminated "in order to promote the revolutionary struggles."[55]

An important feature in this debate was the arguments over the significance of nuclear warfare. Reflecting the professional military view, Luo Ruiqing scoffed at Mao's old dictum that nuclear weapons were a "paper tiger" far less devastating than the "spiritual atom bomb" of the revolutionary masses. "We are materialists . . . who will continue to master the material atom bomb," said General Luo, implicitly rejecting Mao's guerrilla concepts as outmoded.[56] The

Maoists responded that nuclear weapons had been rendered useless, since they could not be employed in revolutionary struggles in which targets were elusive. As evidence for this contention Mao disclosed to Edgar Snow that he had read General Maxwell Taylor's book, *The Uncertain Trumpet*, in which the prominent American opponent of "massive retaliation" had argued against the effectiveness of nuclear war.[57]

The strategy debate reached a climax in early September 1965, when the twentieth anniversary of Japan's surrender in World War II was celebrated in Beijing. Addressing a rally in the presence of Liu Shaoqi and the other Party *apparatchiks*, Luo Ruiqing reaffirmed his thesis that China could afford to take risks in Vietnam if the dispute with Russia were patched up because "the united front against United States imperialism today is much broader than the anti-fascist front in the past." He consequently urged immediate military preparations to "give more effective support" to the Vietnamese Communists, insisting that America's "much-vaunted 'air and naval superiority' is no longer of any avail."[58] At this stage, Mao unsheathed a monumental document. Appearing under the signature of Marshal Lin Biao, it was entitled "Long Live the Victory of People's War!" and it spelled out Mao's attitudes not only toward his domestic adversaries and his Soviet rivals, but toward the wider question of international strategy.

The Maoist essay flatly rejected General Luo's suggestion that any compromise could be reached with the Soviet Union. The Kremlin had "demoralized . . . revolutionary people everywhere" and had "greatly encouraged U.S. imperialism in its war adventures," the document declared. Therefore, it stated, Soviet "revisionism" must be opposed before the struggle against "imperialism" could be won. Expanding the attack against Russian "revisionism" to include Mao's internal foes, it emphasized that nothing could be done in the fight against bourgeois and capitalist trends at home and abroad until the Maoist ideology had emerged triumphant. Thus the top priority belonged to the domestic purges that Mao was about to inaugurate.

Lin Biao's essay also assailed the proposal by General Luo and the Chinese Army professionals that Beijing turn to Moscow for nuclear protection. "Certain people," Lin Biao said, attributed the Communists' success against Japan and Chiang Kai-shek to "foreign assistance." But this assertion was "absurd," since the Communists had fought mainly with captured enemy weapons and foreign aid therefore could have played "only a supplementary role." In addition to rejecting the idea of a *rapprochement* with the Kremlin, this argument was contrived to refute Luo Ruiqing's appeal for "more effective support" for Hanoi, as well as to advise the Vietnamese Communists and other guerrilla movements elsewhere not to expect much help from China. For Mao's whole theory of "people's war" was predicated on the notion, Lin affirmed, that such conflicts must be waged by peoples themselves, without external intervention.

> Revolution or people's war in any country is the business of the masses in that country and should be carried out primarily by their own efforts. . . . If one does not operate by one's own efforts . . . but leans wholly on foreign aid . . . even though this be aid from socialist countries which persist in revolution—no victory can be won, or consolidated even if it is won.

In response to Luo Ruiqing's willingness to incur the risk of a clash with the United States, Lin Biao evoked Mao's principle that the wise guerrilla retreats in the face of overwhelming odds. Success was impossible, Lin explained, "without taking full account of the enemy tactically . . . and without being prudent." And, apparently addressing himself to the Chinese career officers who regarded Mao's concepts as obsolete, Lin said: "You rely on modern weapons and we rely on highly conscious revolutionary people. . . . It is adventurism if one insists on fighting when one cannot win."[59]

A hint that the debate was ending in favor of Mao was dropped in early September by that perennial weathervane, Foreign Minister Chen Yi, when he told a group of Japanese visiting Beijing: "To tell the truth, America is afraid of China and China is somewhat afraid of America. I do not believe that the United States would invade present-day China."[60] Not long afterward, Luo Ruiqing dropped out of sight, the first prominent victim of the Cultural Revolution. The charges issued against him later, even if partially accurate, made it clear that he had indeed sought to heighten the possibility of a collision with the United States. Between January and October 1964, according to these allegations, Luo had unilaterally ordered an increase in weapons production and traveled "at least thirteen times" to various regions "to supervise battle preparations." The indictment also disclosed that Luo provoked two clashes between Communist and Chinese Nationalist patrol craft in the Taiwan Strait in August and November 1965 in an attempt to escalate tensions. As the charge put it, Luo authorized the Fuzhou Military District headquarters commanding the central China coast to "attack the enemy on its own initiative" so that the Communists would "not lose the initiative in battle."[61]

Though they had backed up Luo Ruiqing to varying degrees, the other Party leaders were apparently implicated in the Vietnam issue to a lesser extent. The mayor of Beijing, Peng Chen, had started out supporting Mao but, perhaps as his own position weakened afterward, he switched to the side of those who favored *rapprochement* with the Soviet Union. Liu Shaoqi displayed caution throughout the dispute. Yet his last public statement, a speech delivered in July 1966 advocating deeper Chinese involvement in Vietnam, revealed him to have been among the "hawks."

The entire episode was evidently a reflection more of China's domestic political troubles at the time than of its strategy toward Vietnam or even the Soviet Union. And the key issue at stake was the role that the Army would play. Party bureaucrats and professional officers were eager to spark a crisis in order to divert the Army toward purely military functions and thereby pull it out of Mao's grasp. Mao, on the other hand, needed peace in order to use the Army for his political purposes—and, most probably, would not have dared to launch the Cultural Revolution had he doubted the Army's loyalty.

But what guarantee did Mao have that the United States would not disrupt his plans by pushing the Vietnam war into China? It seems likely that, among other communications, the American ambassador advised Chinese representatives at the Sino-American talks in Warsaw in June 1965 that Washington had no intention of escalating the conflict beyond the borders of Vietnam. Mao apparently accepted that assurance—just as, in the spring of 1962, he believed President Kennedy's pledge, communicated through Warsaw, that the United States would not support a Nationalist invasion of mainland China.

One of the ironies in this tacit understanding between China and the United States was that by lowering the menace of Chinese intervention, Mao obliquely served as an American accomplice in the Vietnam war. At the same time, by minimizing the American threat to China, President Lyndon Johnson unwittingly provided Mao with the respite he required to trigger the Cultural Revolution. Even more ironically, propagandists in both Beijing and Washington were striving during this period to portray the conflict in Vietnam as a struggle between Maoist revolution and American-style democracy.

By the fall of 1965, Mao was ready to launch a more ambitious campaign to impose his unique ideology on China than he had ever before attempted. The moment had arrived to translate into action the nervous lines of the poem he had written three years earlier:

> Seize the day, seize the hour! . . .
> Away with all pests!
> Our force is irresistible.

PART TWO

REVOLUTION
WITHIN
REVOLUTION

The Great Proletarian Cultural Revolution now unfolding is a great revolution that touches people to their very souls. . . .
— *Central Committee Decision,*
August 8, 1966

CHAPTER 8

The Opening Salvos

♟

Who are our enemies? Who are our friends?
This is a question of the first importance for
the revolution.
　　　　　　—MAO ZEDONG, *March 1926*

M OMENTOUS HISTORICAL EVENTS do not begin according to schedules. Mao Zedong's Great Proletarian Cultural Revolution was no exception. It took shape gradually—even though, with their passion for precision, Chinese Communist publicists would later date its origin at September 1965.

After spending the summer at his Hangzhou retreat, Mao returned to Beijing at that time to convene the Politburo Standing Committee, technically the most powerful body in China. As he surveyed the six other members of the Committee, Mao could distinguish his enemies from his friends. Liu Shaoqi and Deng Xiaoping represented the entrenched Party apparatus that had long opposed his personal rule, while Vice-Premier Chen Yun, the liberal economist, had consistently resisted his collectivist schemes. On the other hand, Mao could depend upon Defense Minister Lin Biao, who had been working strenuously for six years to bring the Army under his aegis. And he could probably trust Premier Zhou Enlai, though his past allegiance had been variable. The sixth Committee member, Marshal Zhu De, then nearly eighty, was an honorific figure now nearly senile.

Mao's essential motive in convening the Standing Committee was to reiterate his alarm at the "revisionist" trends that had been growing since the aftermath of the Great Leap Forward. But he realized that he could not launch a full-scale, frontal assault against the Party leaders whom he believed to be promoting these trends. For the Party stalwarts were strong enough to resist him—and might even, in a premature showdown, defeat him. Their authority was deeply rooted in their provincial and district committees and through Peng Chen, the Party boss in Beijing, they dominated the Chinese capital. They were intimately linked to senior officers in China's central military establishment, and were closely allied with Army commanders in various regions of the country. They also controlled a formidable and pervasive array of affiliated youth, labor, and other national federations as well as newspapers, radio stations, and other propaganda media. Indeed, as Mao himself later put it, "some departments and areas of our country were dominated to such an extent by revisionists that they . . . could not be penetrated even with a needle."[1] Thus Mao was isolated, despite his enormous prestige. And, consequently, he saw himself and his followers as "rebels" in a new revolution aimed at overthrowing the "power-holders" of the Party bureaucracy.

At the outset, the confrontation between Mao and his foes was not sharply defined. Respectful of his towering stature, Mao's rivals hesitated to challenge him directly but tried instead to subvert his plans. At the same time, aware of the heavy odds against him, Mao proceeded slowly and prudently, using deception rather than bluntness. The Cultural Revolution therefore opened with a series of elusive, cautious, and often confusing maneuvers.

Mao's first shot, fired at the Politburo Standing Committee meeting, was a surprisingly mild plea for renewed efforts to "criticize bourgeois reactionary thinking," particularly in art and literature. The target he offered for criticism was Wu Han, whose play, *The Dismissal of Hai Rui,* written four years before, had appeared to Mao to be an allegorical attack against his purge in 1959 of Marshal Peng Dehuai, then Defense Minister.

To Western observers of China, Mao's gesture seemed at the time to be merely another attempt to revive the faltering "socialist education" exercise he had inaugurated in 1962. In part, their inability to perceive the potential scope of Mao's objective stemmed from the failure of most foreign analysts—and probably most educated Chinese as well—to fathom the depths of the divisions within the ruling Communist hierarchy. Many outside specialists, with their tendency to interpret Chinese political dynamics in their own terms, were also unable to appreciate the extent to which Mao considered art and literature as crucial ideological instruments in his "spiritual" approach to revolution. Suggesting as it did that Mao was concerned only with artistic and literary dissent, the phrase "Great Proletarian Cultural Revolution" was a misleading English label for his movement, even though it was invented by official Chinese translators in Beijing. For the literal meaning of the Chinese *Wu Chan Jieji Wenhua Da Geming* is "a full-scale revolution to establish a working-class culture."[2] Hence the word "culture" more closely approximated the German *"Kultur"* or the French *"civilisation"* in signifying that Mao's broader ambition was to alter China's whole way of life.

None of this was lost on the Chinese Communist Party "insiders." They quickly discerned that in singling out Wu Han, Mao was actually focusing his fire against Peng Chen and the Beijing Party apparatus. For Wu Han, a deputy mayor of the capital city as well as a historian, was one of Peng's protégés. Hence it was plain to the Party bureaucrats, familiar as they were with the classical Chinese device of humiliating a subordinate in order to undermine his superior, that Mao's sights were leveled at a far more prominent foe. They sensed, too, that Mao's offensive would not stop with Peng Chen.

The Party *apparatchiks* mobilized to voice their hostility to Mao at the strained meetings of the Politburo Standing Committee, which dragged on into October. Deng Xiaoping, the obstinate Party Secretary General, was reported to have expressed his opposition to Mao's call for changes in the Chinese educational system, and he was backed up by Liu Shaoqi. At another Party conference in Beijing at the time, Peng Chen also asserted that Mao had no right to claim infallibility. Lu Dingyi, chief of the Party's Propaganda Department, obliquely added to the reaction against Mao with a diatribe against Stalin's "personality cult."[3] The Party press echoed this challenge to Mao by stressing the need for balance in the planned Cultural Revolution. In an obvious calculation to counter Mao's concepts of a protracted "life-and-death" conflict, in which his "proletarian" disciples would eventually eliminate the "revisionists" who had gained the upper hand in the Party, *Red Flag* urged that the campaign be carried out with "maximum reasoning," while the *People's Daily* warned against "exaggerating" the "class struggle."[4]

Time and again in the past, Mao had welcomed the emergence of an opposition as a "negative example" he could use to rally support for his cause. In late 1965 he may not have been entirely chagrined to see disaffection that would serve him as evidence that a thorough purge of the Party was imperative. But now, perhaps more than ever before in his career, his leverage was so limited that he could not even use the principal journals in Beijing as a launching pad for his intended campaign. Indeed, there was scarcely anyone of stature he could trust. Thus he delegated his wife, Jiang Qing, to go to Shanghai to enlist the help of sympathizers in that city. Later, explaining his motives for this extraordinary move, Mao candidly admitted that he had reason to doubt that Peng Chen's Party organization in Beijing would obey his instructions. As he put it, "My suggestions could not be implemented in Beijing."[5]

Shanghai, China's largest metropolis, was a study in contradictions. As the former center of European imperialism in China and now the country's major port, it was rife with alien "capitalist" influences. Several Western banks and other firms continued to retain offices there, employing Chinese compradors who still functioned as they did in the days before the Communist take-over. As late as 1965, foreign visitors noted that many of the city's young people displayed "bourgeois" tastes in their dress and manners and were even acquainted with contemporary trends in Western music and movies. The Shanghai leadership also contained men like Cao Diqiu, the mayor and the city's First Secretary, who sided with the Party bureaucrats in Beijing and elsewhere in the resistance to Mao's policies. But there were also strong radical elements in Shanghai that fervently subscribed to the Maoist canon. One of these was Zhang Chunqiao, a veteran journalist who had risen to the post of Director of Propaganda in the local Party Committee. Defying his superiors in the municipal apparatus, Zhang had been active within recent years in assisting Jiang Qing to promote revolutionary operas, films, and other artistic endeavors in Shanghai. Quite naturally, she turned to him when she arrived.

Jiang Qing's specific assignment in Shanghai was to find a writer capable of producing an article criticizing Wu Han in such a way that it would be understood by the Communist cognoscenti to be an attack against Peng Chen. With the help of Zhang Chunqiao, she discovered Yao Wenyuan, a young publicist who had earned himself a minor reputation as an ultraradical literary critic. If Maoist accounts of the episode are accurate, Jiang Qing and her two cohorts went to work on the article in secrecy for fear that the Shanghai Party *apparatchiks* would obstruct them. There were even hints later that the trio had been in danger of assassination.[6] According to other accounts, the Party bureaucracy discovered the plot but could not decide how to handle it. In a document that appeared later, the Party First Secretary, Cao Diqiu, was quoted as having explained his dilemma:

> What was mostly on our minds at the time was our relationship with
> Beijing, with Peng Chen in fact. Should we alert him? If we did not, he
> would be caught unawares. If we did, it would be against the wishes of

Chairman Mao. What were we to do? Our Secretariat puzzled over the problem again and again.[7]

In the end, illustrating its real loyalties, the Shanghai Party signaled Peng Chen that the disguised attack against him was imminent. And Peng Chen, in turn, telephoned Zhang Chunqiao, complaining: "Why haven't you notified us? Where is your Party spirit?"

Whatever Zhang Chunqiao replied, the article denouncing Wu Han was published on November 10 under Yao Wenyuan's signature in the Shanghai newspaper *Wen Hui Bao*. A long, tedious piece that went through at least six drafts before completion, the article argued that since Wu Han had glorified a Ming dynasty official for having distributed land to impoverished peasants, his drama deviously disseminated the view of those who sought to "demolish the people's communes and to restore the criminal rule of the landlords and the rich peasants" by favoring liberal economic programs in the wake of the Great Leap Forward. The play was therefore a "poisonous weed" that had been promoted by the "bourgeois opposition to the dictatorship of the proletariat and the socialist revolutionary struggle."[8] Implicit in this assertion was the charge that Peng Chen, Wu Han's superior, was a leader of "bourgeois" opponents to the Maoist line.

Like the other senior figures in the Chinese Communist Party, Peng Chen had undoubtedly been appalled by the damage caused by the Great Leap Forward. According to a later indictment against him, he was alleged to have described the hectic collectivization scheme as a "romantic" vision that violated the "objective laws" of economic development.[9] And he had been cool to efforts by Mao and Jiang Qing to introduce "proletarian" themes into classical Chinese art and literature. In July 1964, for example, he had cautioned against attempts to purge the theater of its traditions quickly, saying that "reforming Beijing opera is not like cooking chestnuts, which can be sold while they are still roasting."[10] He had also argued, in contrast to Mao's appeals for abrasive "class struggle," that China's political atmosphere should foster "discipline and freedom, unity of will and liveliness and ease of mind."[11] Now, however, Peng Chen's primary concern was to protect his Beijing apparatus against Mao's purges. For he recognized that the attacks being mounted against his underlings were really a threat to his own authority.

The conflict then developing in China was not a simple confrontation between Mao and his Party rivals. Factional disputes and personal feuds within the Communist movement made it difficult for individuals and groups to attack each other directly. Peng Chen was therefore compelled to resort to a variety of dodges as he sought to cope with Mao's equally complicated assaults against him.

Peng Chen's first move was to issue a directive to the editors of the *People's Daily* enjoining them from reprinting the article by Yao Wenyuan. Soon afterward, however, Peng was pressured by Premier Zhou Enlai to reverse that directive. Realizing that Zhou was speaking for Mao, whose desires could not easily be disregarded, Peng switched to a different tactic. He instructed the *People's Daily* to print the Yao Wenyuan article, but he personally wrote an "editor's note" depicting the polemic surrounding Wu Han's play as academic rather than political. Mao had always advocated free discussion as a "means of exposing and resolving contradictions," he emphasized, thereby implying that Yao Wenyuan's assault against Wu Han would not be the final word on the subject.[12]

Following that gambit, Peng Chen prompted the Party's stable of literary critics in Beijing to defend Wu Han. He also encouraged the historian himself to explain his position in a ritualistic "self-criticism." Wu Han complied, conceding that his error had been his failure to understand that "proletarian literature and art must serve contemporary politics." In producing his drama, he said, he had "merely portrayed an ancient event for its own sake, and wrote a play only in order to write a play."[13]

By this time, evidently uncomfortable in the political climate of Beijing, Mao had retreated from the capital. One of his last public acts before he left was to attend a banquet to celebrate the eightieth birthday of Anna Louise Strong, the American writer who served until her death in 1970 as a publicist for the Chinese Communists. Also present at the banquet were a number of other leftist Americans resident in Beijing, among them Frank Coe, Sol Adler, and Sydney Rittenberg.

Mao's movements went unmentioned in the Chinese press for more than five months after his departure from Beijing in late November. It was the longest period he had dropped out of public sight since 1949, and his absence naturally touched off speculation about the state of his health. A French visitor to China, who had observed Mao's trembling hands at a dinner a year earlier, unwittingly encouraged the notion that he was suffering from Parkinson's disease. Many Chinese were persuaded that he had died, and they continued to claim, even after his re-emergence, that he had been replaced by a "double." But Mao, very much alive, was strenuously maneuvering against his adversaries. In late December, assembling a group of disciples at a meeting in Shanghai, he rejected Wu Han's contention that the play about Hai Rui had been politically innocuous. Despite the historian's denial, Mao asserted, the drama had been a deliberate slander.

At the same time, turning to his faithful military supporters for assistance, Mao commanded Lin Biao to mobilize the Army for an intensive campaign designed to test the loyalty of cadres in low-level county committees as well as in the Party's powerful regional bureaus. Claiming that many Party functionaries were neglecting Mao's principles in favor of a more "professional" approach to their problems, a directive issued by Lin Biao prescribed that officials must henceforth take the Chairman as their sole guide—or else face "disqualification from leadership duties."[14] This message was reinforced by editorials in the *Liberation Army Daily*, the newspaper published in Shanghai under Lin Biao's aegis, extolling Mao's "Thought" as the "peak of contemporary Marxism-Leninism" and "our invincible banner."[15] In addition, acting under military auspices, Jiang Qing stepped further into the limelight as head of a forum convened in Shanghai to publicize the Maoist dogma in art and literature. These moves were part of an escalating challenge to Peng Chen and a warning to other Party figures that they still had time to swing over to Mao's camp. Now, more clearly than ever, the growing dispute between Mao and his enemies was being polarized.

Meanwhile, with Mao operating from Shanghai and his residence at nearby Hangzhou, Peng Chen began to reinforce his position in Beijing. He reactivated a so-called Group of Five, composed of himself and four other senior Communist officials, that had been organized in the fall of 1964 to supervise an earlier Party program to purify art and literature. His apparent aim in reviving this body, which had never actually functioned, was to create the impression that he was implementing the Cultural Revolution in accordance with Mao's instructions. This stratagem of "waving the Red Flag in order to oppose the Red Flag," as the Maoists later described it, would repeatedly be pursued by Mao's adversaries as a means of muddling the conflict.

A Maoist sympathizer inside Peng Chen's Group of Five was Kang Sheng, a Politburo member who specialized in security and intelligence affairs. A myopic man in his late sixties whose thick spectacles enhanced his sinister reputation, Kang was a dogmatic and stubborn Communist veteran. At a meeting held in early February, he argued that the group should recruit known radicals to draw up an indictment of Wu Han for his veiled attack against Mao. But Peng Chen rejected that proposal, reiterating that the historian's play should not be treated as "a political question."[16] Then, evidently without consulting Kang Sheng, he directed his staff to prepare a lengthy study covering the events of the previous months and offering recommendations for the reform of art and literature. The announced purpose of the study, the "Outline Report on the Current Academic Discussion Made by the Group of Five in Charge of the Cultural Revolution," was to guide Party Committees throughout the country in the reform effort.

The "February Outline Report," as it was abbreviated, was later vilified by Maoists as an attempt to exonerate Wu Han and other critics of Mao's policies, and this assessment was not incorrect. For the report suggested that Wu Han and others be given the same latitude to express their views as intellectuals had been accorded during the "Hundred Flowers" period. In an obvious swipe at Mao's cultural judges, it criticized "scholar-tyrants who are always acting arbitrarily and trying to overwhelm people with their power."

On the afternoon of February 5, Peng Chen carried a draft of the "Outline Report" to Liu Shaoqi's home in the verdant Zhongnanhai sector of Beijing, where the Chinese leaders lived in suburban comfort. Liu advised Peng Chen to clear the report with Mao personally. Two days later, Peng Chen flew to Hangzhou to see Mao, accompanied by three prominent Party propagandists, one of them being Wu Lengxi, who was then serving simultaneously as editor-in-chief of *People's Daily* and director of the New China News Agency. According to a Maoist version of the encounter, Peng Chen sought to ingratiate himself with the Chairman by conceding that Wu Han was "not on the side of socialism." He also withheld the "Outline Report" from Mao but released it in Beijing four days later, claiming that it bore the Chairman's seal of approval.[17]

Time and again throughout the history of the Chinese Communist movement, even the fiercest of Mao's foes refrained from attacking him openly, but instead attempted to appear loyal to the Chairman while shaping his writ to their own purposes. This was now Peng Chen's ruse. His immediate aim was to demonstrate his fidelity to the Chairman while shielding his colleagues who had run afoul of Mao's line. In taking this approach, Peng Chen may have estimated that he might eventually reach some kind of compromise with Mao. He may have also believed that the national Party apparatus would support his scheme to achieve such a compromise. If so, Peng Chen erred in two respects. First, he failed to appreciate the extent to which Mao was determined to push through his campaign. And second, he failed to perceive that the other Party leaders were not above sacrificing him in order to consolidate their own positions as their confrontations with Mao grew in intensity. Indeed, one of the perplexing aspects of the Cultural Revolution in its later development was the way the powerful Party machine crumbled as the *apparatchiks* betrayed one another in apparent efforts to save themselves and their particular cliques. Whatever help he may have expected from the Party bureaucracy, Peng Chen himself behaved no differently toward his own comrades in Beijing as Mao's offensive against him escalated.

In late February, after Peng Chen had released his "Outline Report" to the Party Committees, Mao countered with a withering riposte. The final communiqué of the forum on art and literature that had been held in Shanghai by his wife, Jiang Qing, plainly announced that there would be no conciliation with his adversaries. Instead, the communiqué spelled out Mao's intention to launch the Great Proletarian Cultural Revolution as a dynamic campaign conducted under military auspices against the "revisionist" Party apparatus. The statement declared that China was headed toward an "arduous, complex, and long-term struggle" designed to eliminate the "dictatorship of the black line" that had "diametrically opposed" Mao since the establishment of the Chinese People's Republic nearly sixteen years before. This struggle "has a vital bearing on the future of the Chinese revolution and the future of the world revolution." It would "take decades, or even centuries" to achieve success. More ominously, the communiqué asserted that Mao's drive would be carried out by the Army—the "chief instrument of the dicatatorship of the proletariat in China" and the "mainstay and hope of the Chinese people and the revolutionary people of the world."[18]

The Shanghai communiqué, then, was Mao's blueprint for action. Now on the defensive, Peng Chen sent the controversial Wu Han out of Beijing on a trip to inspect provincial agricultural projects, an assignment for which the historian was totally unqualified. Not long after, Peng divested himself of another liability, Lu Dingyi, the chief of the Party's Propaganda Department, by granting him a leave to "convalesce" in south China. A few weeks later, he also dropped Deng Tuo, the Beijing editor and writer who had cleverly assailed Mao in a series of articles in 1961. But if Peng believed that he could escape repudiation by disassociating himself from these and other suspicious subordinates, he failed to realize that senior Party leaders were taking the same approach toward him. Late in March, for example, Liu Shaoqi, his wife, and Chen Yi left Beijing without any official fanfare for a three-week state visit to Pakistan, Afghanistan, and Burma. Their only plausible motive for quitting China at that crucial juncture was to avoid involvement in the purge they surely anticipated.

Several other signs clearly indicated to Liu Shaoqi and other Party insiders that Mao was bracing for a major offensive. On March 11, Lin Biao had circulated a letter to China's industrial and communications departments stressing that the country could only "maintain vigorous revolutionary enthusiasm and a firm and correct political orientation" through "unified thinking, revolutionary thinking, correct thinking—that is, Mao Zedong's thinking."[19] The letter was significant. As the first message addressed by the Minister of Defense to a strictly civilian audience, it was consciously calculated to dramatize that Lin Biao was now playing a decisive political role. The letter was contrived to emphasize as well that Mao had the support of the Army in his campaign against his enemies. By identifying Mao's "thinking" as the only "unified, revolutionary, and correct" line, Lin Biao was also affirming that the Party no longer mattered. Almost pleased by the prospect of a bitter fight ahead, Mao said at the time: "The deeper the socialist revolution goes, the greater will be the resistance offered by the exponents of capitalism, and the better they will reveal their countenance."[20]

Taking advantage of Liu Shaoqi's absence from China, Mao triggered the attack against Peng Chen. On March 28, two days after Liu's departure, Mao denounced the Beijing Party machine and its boss by name for the first time. Characteristically adorning his statement with classical allusions, Mao told a group of his followers that the moment had arrived for Sun Wugong, the legendary "monkey king," to raise his "golden cudgel" against Peng Chen's "imperial court." Then, speaking more bluntly, Mao called for Peng Chen's dismissal, the dissolution of the Beijing Committee, and the dismantling of the Party's entire Propaganda Department based in the capital.[21] Two days after that, abandoned by his senior comrades just as he had expended several of his own associates, Peng Chen made his last public appearance in his capacity as Beijing Party chief at an airport function. His downfall, though not officially announced for two months, marked the end of the first phase in Mao's preparations for the Cultural Revolution.

Nearly a year later, looking bloated and bedraggled after months of imprisonment and possibly torture, Peng Chen and his wife, along with other key members of his apparatus, were dragged into a Beijing stadium by soldiers and Red Guards and, their hands trussed behind their backs, forced to kneel in disgrace before the "masses." In accordance with Mao's techniques, however, their lives were spared. For they were more valuable as "negative examples" than as dead trophies.

By the early spring of 1966, the acute struggle between Mao and his rivals was intensifying in different ways. The various participants were publishing esoteric commentaries and making symbolic gestures or secretly maneuvering against one another. In the universities and secondary schools, students—guided by local leaders or acting spontaneously—were beginning to perceive the approaching disarray as an opportunity to make a broad range of demands. Not until later, when Red Guard journals, wall posters, and other documents poured forth in unprecedented profusion, was it possible to discern some pattern in the events of those hectic days.

Mao's strategy was, as it had been from the start, to create an atmosphere in which his enemies would become bold enough to reveal themselves. As his publicists put it, "a poisonous snake comes out of its hole under certain weather conditions." Thus Mao had waited for the propitious moment to "capture" the Beijing boss and his cohorts.[22] Now he proclaimed Peng Chen's deposition in an internal directive sent out in the middle of May to every echelon of the Party and government across China. This directive, the "May 16 Circular," formally revoked the "Outline Report" concocted by Peng Chen in February. The circular also disbanded Peng Chen's Group of Five, which had been trying to temporize the Cultural Revolution in order to defend the Party apparatus. And it clearly indicated that Mao intended to initiate fresh purges. "People of the Khrushchev brand" were still "nestling in our midst" in the Party, government, and Army, and the circular urged that these "counterrevolutionary revisionists" be repudiated, dismissed, or transferred to less sensitive assignments.[23]

To carry out this ambitious program, Mao appointed a new Cultural Revolution Directorate, composed of disciples whose primary qualification was fidelity to his cause. The head of the new directorate,

Chen Boda, a native of Fujian province, then in his early sixties, typified these disciples. Chen's only claim to importance stemmed from his many years' service as Mao's private secretary, speechwriter, and ideological adviser. In short, he was Mao's mouthpiece, without authority of his own. Similarly, his chief deputy was Mao's wife, Jiang Qing. Along with several other radicals who had held only minor posts until then, the new group also included an obscure soldier by the name of Wang Dongxing, who had once been Mao's bodyguard. The new Cultural Revolution Directorate, then, was essentially a modern replica of the Inner Court relied upon by ancient Chinese emperors during troubled periods when they could no longer trust their official subordinates.

Mao mapped out an assortment of different tactics as he escalated his campaign. One of these, calculated to induce the Chinese intelligentsia to rally to his side, was particularly dramatic. He persuaded the aged *doyen* of China's writers, Guo Morou, to make a self-abasing "confession" that would provide intellectuals with a model they could emulate.

Guo Morou, who is only barely known in the West except to scholars, was as towering an eminence in twentieth-century revolutionary Chinese literature as Voltaire had been in the European Enlightenment. Trained as a medical doctor in Japan, where he later lived in exile for long periods, Guo became a prolific poet, translator, novelist, playwright, essayist, and propagandist for the Communists. In the middle of April, he demonstrated his loyalty to Mao in spectacular fashion. Addressing a session of the National People's Congress, the rubber-stamp Chinese legislature, Guo declared that all he had written in the past should be "burned to ashes, for it has not the slightest value." He had not studied Mao's works sufficiently, he explained, protesting that his ideological outlook was "muddled." The moment had therefore come to prostrate himself before the proletariat, Guo said:

> Though I am over seventy, I still have a bit of ambition left. If I am asked to wallow in mud, I am willing to do so. If I am asked to cover myself with grease, I am willing. Even if I am asked to stain myself with blood and to throw hand grenades at the American imperialists should they dare to attack us, I shall be willing to do so.
>
> I really mean what I have said. I should now properly learn from the workers, peasants and soldiers, and if possible I will do my best to serve them.[24]

This emotional apologia was matched by sharper assaults against cultural figures linked to the Party machine. Premier Zhou Enlai called for a fierce onslaught against "bourgeois ideology in the academic, educational, and journalistic fields" as well as in art and literature. And Yao Wenyuan, the rising young Maoist critic who had earlier attacked the historian Wu Han, now published a devastating diatribe against Deng Tuo, who had mocked Mao a few years before. Alleging that Deng Tuo was being protected by prominent Party figures, Yao appealed for broader and more daring revolutionary thrusts that would "show up all monsters and goblins in their true colors."[25]

Consistent with this line, Mao began in the late spring to focus his fire at Chinese educational institutions, which he considered to be centers of dissidence that required drastic change if they were to produce the "revolutionary successors" capable of shaping the future of China in accordance with his vision. Among other moves, he sent a directive to Lin Biao declaring that "the domination of our schools by bourgeois intellectuals should by no means be allowed to continue."[26] This directive was an order to his military followers to start organizing the young activists who would afterward emerge as the Red Guards. Dissatisfied teachers and students were also encouraged to agitate against the system, and their willingness to protest reflected both their own traditions and a variety of tensions then nagging them.

Students have always been a significant force in China. In ancient times, they were the potential scholars whose mastery of the classics entitled them to the highest places in the imperial administration. By the turn of the century, the external pressures imposed by Western imperialism and the internal decay of the Chinese government combined to provoke youths into a search for new systems. They became an explosive element, spearheading the May 4th Movement, which erupted in 1919 as a patriotic demonstration and quickly expanded into a demand for wide reforms. But the students who agitated for China's modernization were betrayed by the leaders they helped to lift into power. Those who supported Chiang Kai-shek soon found his regime to be inept and corrupt. After Mao's victory, many also discovered that the Communists did not live up to their ideals.

One of the first outbursts of student unrest under the Communists appeared only eight years after the establishment of the Chinese People's Republic, when Mao inaugurated the "Hundred Flowers" experiment. Prompted not only by a desire to rectify abuses in education but to curb the injustices of the Party dictatorship as well, students took advantage of the temporary breath of freedom to manifest their feelings vociferously and often violently. As a later student generation would during the Cultural Revolution, they plastered the walls of universities and schools with crude, hand-painted posters demanding more liberalism in their curricula and denouncing such iniquities as favoritism for the children of Party members. Students in several cities staged strikes and fought with police. Three youths were publicly executed for engineering a riot in a suburb of Wuhan, the industrial city on the Yangzi River, and thousands of students were shipped off to labor in rural villages and remote border regions. The party further tightened its control by introducing dependable Communist officials into the educational system as university presidents and vice-presidents, school principals, and political instructors.[27]

Other problems continued to plague the students. The economic recession caused by the failure of the Great Leap Forward, for example, left large numbers of graduates without jobs to match their educational experience. Unemployed or underemployed young people crowded into China's cities, despite repeated campaigns by the authorities to transfer young people to the countryside to work with peasants. For those who found jobs, advancement was blocked as older employees clogged government, industrial, and academic positions. The Party apparatus was also top-heavy with aging Communist veterans unwilling to make room for the younger generation. At the same time, recurrent programs to infuse politically reliable "proletarian" youths into the educational system resembled the painful effort in the United States to open Ivy League universities to black students. Like the blacks from America's urban ghettos and southern towns, the Chinese students of poor worker and peasant origin were unprepared to compete against the children of Party and government officials, whose training had been superior. Attempts to lower the prevailing academic standards in order to accommodate the "proletarian" youths aroused the opposition of brighter students and their teachers. The poor youths, in turn, resented the privileges accorded "elite" students, many of whom attended special boarding schools, enjoyed preferential employment after graduation, and were even treated leniently when they misbehaved. By any measure, there were potentially explosive "class" tensions in China's educational institutions.

Thus Mao's Cultural Revolution seemed attractive to frustrated students regardless of their particular grievances. His call to oust the "bourgeois" administrations from the universities and schools could be interpreted by students of all political persuasions as a license to rebel. Therefore, though turbulence was deliberately encouraged, it spread rapidly because students were receptive to the need for change. Their conduct, however, was largely a confused reaction against authority that gathered momentum but lacked specific, clear-cut objectives.

The first clashes of the Cultural Revolution inside the academic community broke out at Beijing University, familiarly known as Beida, the oldest and most prestigious institution of higher learning in China. Established in 1898 as Imperial University, Beida has been closely associated with China's political developments throughout the twentieth century. It was here that Mao had worked as a library assistant under Li Dazhao, one of the founders of the Chinese Communist Party. The university had also been the scene of patriotic student demonstrations in the 1920s and 1930s. After the Communist victory in 1949, Beida remained relatively free from political pressures. Its president in the 1950s was Ma Yinchu, an American-educated non-Communist and one of China's most famous economists. A stubborn advocate of such liberal notions as birth control, Ma was dismissed in 1960. His replacement was Lu Ping, a robust and energetic man then about fifty, who had been a Communist youth leader for years. In addition to managing the university administration, he was also First Secretary of its Party Committee. If Lu was a dogmatist compared to Mao Yinchu, he was still too pragmatic for Mao Zedong's radical disciples. For, like the Party *apparatchiks*, he believed in the primacy of technocracy over ideology. He emphasized the importance of academic excellence, selected his faculty on the basis of their professional ability, and even stressed that China had much to learn from Soviet, British, and American education.[28]

This line, with its accent on expertise rather than "Redness," ran into resistance from a faction of ultraleftists, among them a woman cadre in the philosophy department, Nie Yuanzi, who had been admonished by Lu Ping for her extremist views as early as 1961. How she survived in the years after that has never been made clear. By the spring of 1966, however, she and her comrades at Beida came into contact with Mao's wife, who was then recruiting radicals in the drive to intensify the Cultural Revolution on the campuses. Nie, with her long record of opposition to the Party machine, was an obvious candidate to head the revolt at Beijing University.

Mao's attack on Peng Chen and the Beijing Party Committee,

going on at that time, had prompted a predictable response from other Communist officials in the capital and elsewhere across the country. Many went through the motions of assailing Mao's alleged foes while striving to maintain control over the campaign as a way of protecting themselves. Lu Ping took essentially the same approach at Beijing University. He voiced his support for the purge of Mao's adversaries but insisted that the "struggle must be conducted in a very careful manner," ruling out, for example, the use of wall posters and mass meetings. In the view of the radicals, this tactic was contrary to Mao's order to unleash the "masses." Early in the afternoon of May 25, Nie Yuanzi and her comrades put up a poster on a wall outside the university dining hall addressed to Lu Ping and his colleagues:

> To hold meetings and to post big-character posters are mass militant methods of the best kind. But you "lead" the masses by preventing them from holding meetings and putting up posters. You have manufactured various taboos and regulations. By so doing, have you not suppressed, forbidden, and opposed the mass revolution? We bsolutely will not allow you to do so!
>
> You shout about "strengthening the leadership and standing fast at one's post. . . ." You still want to "stand fast" at your "posts" in order to sabotage the Cultural Revolution. We warn you that a mantis cannot stop the wheels of a cart and mayflies cannot topple a giant tree. You are daydreaming!
>
> Now is the time for all revolutionary intellectuals to go into battle! Let us unite and hold high the great red banner of Mao Zedong's thought . . . resolutely, thoroughly, totally and completely wipe out all monsters and demons and all counterrevolutionary revisionists of the Khrushchev type, and carry the socialist revolution through to the end.[29]

This passionate diatribe against Lu Ping and his associates stupefied the Beijing University students. Groups of them gathered around the poster, questioning its validity and wondering what would happen next. Their attitude for the most part was cautious. But a few hours later, when he learned of the attack against him, Lu Ping mobilized members of the Communist Youth League to respond with posters excoriating Nie Yuanzi and her faction as "renegades," asserting that their resistance to the Party in the university represented "opposition to the Central Committee of the Party." The same evening, Nie was hauled before a meeting in the university dining hall. She was interrogated and accused of seeking to undermine the Party. When one of her comrades tried to come to her aid, according to his version of the incident, he was dragged out and manhandled.[30]

During the following week, fearing reprisals from the Party rather than acting out of real conviction, most of the students appeared to side with Lu Ping and the university authorities. They besieged Nie Yuanzi in her room, calling her a "rightist." At that stage, Mao brought his weight to bear with a gesture that was to give a fresh and decisive impetus to the Cultural Revolution.

Ensconced in his Hangzhou retreat, Mao had kept abreast of developments through his agents in the university. Indeed, his wife was in contact with Nie Yuanzi while elements of the Army, obeying his instructions to Lin Biao, were helping to mobilize student activists. He therefore welcomed Nie's poster, hailing it as "China's first Marxist-Leninist big-character poster," presumably because it represented a radical outburst rather than a recurrence of the liberal protests that had churned up the university during the "Hundred Flowers" episode.[31] A version of the "Paris Commune" could be created in China, he suggested, stressing that the significance of such an experiment would even "surpass" the brief and abortive power seizure by French workers in 1871.[32]

Mao's reference to the Paris Commune pointed in the direction he hoped to take. He believed that the Chinese "masses" could, through sheer energy, grasp the authority of the state and establish true "proletarian democracy," as the Communards had unsuccessfully tried to do. In this approach, however, Mao deviated from both Marx and Lenin. Though Marx supported their uprising after it started, he had warned the rebellious French workers beforehand that their planned insurrection was a "desperate act of folly," and Lenin, implicitly criticizing the "adventurism" of the Commune, condemned the notion of destroying all administration immediately as an "anarchist" dream.[33] Months later, after an attempt to emulate the Paris Commune in Shanghai had floundered, Mao would quietly abandon the idea as unworkable. But now the vision seemed captivating. He ordered that the text of the explosive poster written by Nie Yuanzi and her comrades be broadcast to the nation and published in the press on June 1, 1966.[34]

Mao's endorsement of the poster electrified Beijing University. Even though many students had read and discussed the text a week earlier, they crowded into the university dining hall on the evening of June 1 to hear it broadcast. One university official tried to prevent the assembly, advising the students against "listening blindly," while another threatened to have the Beijing radio station "suppressed." But the students ignored them. According to a Reuters dispatch from Beijing, the atmosphere at the university "seemed festive rather than tense."[35] The students sang revolutionary songs, chanted slogans, and, beating gongs, cymbals, and drums, paraded around a campus festooned with colored paper streamers. Numbers of students from other universities and schools as well as mobs of inquisitive citizens joined the throng, and the excitement rose when an official from the revamped Beijing Party Committee arrived to announce that Peng Chen, the Communist boss of the capital, had been dismissed along with Lu Ping and other members of the university directorate.[36]

The university campus soon began to resemble a fairground. Mounted on makeshift rostrums erected in Hyde Park fashion, student speakers poured out emotional tales of intimidation by the deposed Party apparatus. The oratory warmed to a feverish pitch when nearly six thousand students and teachers who had been sent to work in the countryside the previous autumn returned with accounts of the hardships they had suffered in the villages.[37] More than a hundred thousand posters went up on the university walls assailing not only Lu Ping and other prominent figures but obscure professors and even fellow students. Inspired by personal feuds or sheer exuberance, many of the posters featured puerile attacks against officials and teachers for such alleged "counterrevolutionary" activities as "luxurious living" or displaying "lordly airs." As their appetite for denouncing the authorities sharpened, some students broke into the homes of professors, smashing their furniture and destroying their "bourgeois" books. Several faculty members were forced to march through the campus wearing dunce's caps and placards proclaiming their "crimes." A jocular note crept into the turbulence when a group of young people singled out an elderly American Communist sympathizer by the name of Robert Winter, who had taught English for years at the university and was then living in retirement on the campus. The youths pasted a poster on his door written in English: "Bob Winter stinks."*[38]

Many students, swept along in the general melee, must have simply seen the situation as an opportunity to raise hell. But many shared a genuine sense of elation at having been liberated from the oppressive controls of the Party machine, with its network of cadres

---

*Winter was afterward arrested and sent to a "labor reform" camp. He was released in 1970.

and informers. Their surge of rebellion also reflected a release from assorted social tensions, not the least of which were the sexual prohibitions imposed by the puritanism of China's revolutionary society. At the same time, the new freedom seemed to offer an escape from concerns about studies and jobs and the other frustrating uncertainties of an unpredictable system. Students appeared to be attracted less by the positive substance of Mao's dogma, if they understood it at all, than by his sanction of their right to kick over the traces. To a European journalist then visiting China, a Chinese girl explained the effervescence as a phenomenon that students anywhere in the world would have envied.

We, the young, who will inherit this country, can go to our chief of government and tell him what bothers us and why. And in the wall posters we can now write about things that have been forbidden for twenty years. Do you really want to know what the Cultural Revolution is? It is a *feast of criticism*.[39]

The excitement at Beijing University inspired students elsewhere in the capital and throughout the country to agitate for the removal of unpopular political and academic figures. Mao came forth with the new slogan, "Rebellion Is Justified," which encouraged them to assault officials and institutions indiscriminately. And the Beijing press, now expressing the Maoist line, published daily exhortations to "sweep away all freaks and monsters," all "bourgeois 'specialists,' 'scholars,' 'authorities,' and 'venerable masters.' " As a *People's Daily* editorial put it:

The fact that the Khrushchev revisionist clique has usurped the leadership of the Party, Army and state in the Soviet Union is an extremely serious lesson for the proletariat throughout the world. At present, the representatives of the bourgeoisie—the bourgeois scholars and authorities in China—are similarly dreaming of restoring capitalism.[40]

Despite these strident appeals to clean out adversaries of Mao's doctrines, very few important Party *apparatchiks* were actually dismissed from provincial posts that spring. Those who were purged included a handful of newspaper editors and a scattering of cultural figures, such as the composer He Lüting, whose anthem "The East Is Red" continued to be played long after his disappearance—and was even used as the signal emitted by the first Chinese earth satellite,

launched three years later. Though the provincial university campuses appeared to be stormy, the peals of thunder far exceeded the
strikes of lightning. Some prominent educational officials, like the
president and upper echelon at Wuhan University, lost their posts.
But the general ferment more typically resembled the commotion in
the northern coastal city of Tianjin, where thousands of students from
six universities and institutes staged a series of noisy demonstrations—only to dismiss one assistant professor of history.[41]

In short, much of the apparent animation at this point in the
Cultural Revolution was a charade being enacted by the Party. Seeking to defend itself, the Party apparatus simulated agitation, even
sacrificing some of its more expendable members in order to appease
Mao. In the universities, the Party also revived so-called Work Teams
in an ostensible effort to uproot "counterrevolutionary" professors
and academic officials, but in reality to shield itself. At least as cunning
as his adversaries, Mao was well aware of their duplicity—and probably encouraged them in order to trap the Party.

The Party Work Teams had been organized on a limited scale as
far back as late 1962 as instruments to carry out the Socialist Education
Campaign, a movement inaugurated by Mao to curb the trend toward
liberalization then growing in the universities in reaction to the rigors
of the Great Leap Forward.[42] Functioning as they did under Party
auspices, however, the Teams carefully refrained from shaking the
apparatchiks from their positions of control. Indeed, according to
Maoist documents published later, the conflict at Beijing University
in the spring of 1966 had its origins two years earlier, when Nie
Yuanzi and her radical comrades sought to gain control of a Team
investigating the alleged "revisionist" tendencies of Lu Ping and his
colleagues. At that time, the Maoists claimed afterward, the university
leadership was protected by Secretary General Deng Xiaoping, who
neutralized the leftists on the grounds that they were "carrying the
struggle to excess." Though he then lacked the power to take action
against them, Mao must have known that the Party was blocking his
radical disciples. In a significant article written during that period,
he underlined the importance of training China's youth to become
"successors of the revolutionary cause" and cautioned against "conspirators and careerists like Khrushchev" who were trying to "usurp
the leadership of the Party and the state." It was "essential to test
and judge cadres . . . in the long course of mass struggle."[43]

In early 1966, Mao had "tested" his adversaries by delegating
Peng Chen and members of the Beijing Party Committee to run the

Cultural Revolution, and then purging them when they betrayed his aims. Now, in early June, Mao adopted the same strategy against Liu Shaoqi, Deng Xiaoping, and the other senior Party leaders by giving their Work Teams the responsibility for managing the Cultural Revolution in the universities. Mao was certain that he could discredit them, for he was confronting them with an impossible set of alternatives. If they permitted the radicals to speak out freely, they would face radical attacks for having opposed Mao in the past, and they would be compelled to recant ignominiously. If they attempted to prevent the radicals from criticizing them, they would be accused of repressing the "masses" and, like Peng Chen, be subjected to further denunciations and possible dismissal as "revisionists."[44] Later, when he was sure that his strategy was succeeding, Mao would reveal that his maneuver had been deliberate. Speaking to Liu, Deng, and his other Party foes at a meeting in mid-July, Mao explained that the test of a true revolutionary leader was his willingness to "transform" himself under the tutelage of the "masses," the repository of ultimate wisdom. There was a tone of theological fundamentalism in his warning to his rivals that they had deviated from his truth:

> We should trust the masses and be their pupils before we can be their teachers. . . .
>
> Some comrades are very ferocious when they struggle against other people, but they are unable to wage the struggle against themselves. They will never be able to pass the test in this way.
>
> When you are told to kindle a fire to burn yourselves, will you do it— even in the knowledge that you will yourselves be consumed by the flames?
>
> Be prepared for the revolution to come down on your heads. Party and government leaders and responsible Party comrades must all be prepared.[45]

The Party leaders had courted this fate, as Mao calculated they would, by having used the Work Teams to stifle the radicals in the universities. They had therefore strayed from the "direction and line" of the Cultural Revolution.[46] But Liu Shaoqi and his Party colleagues originally believed that they could restrict the scope and focus of Mao's campaign, and shape it to their own advantage. Months later, under pressure to make a ritual confession of his "crimes," Liu Shaoqi admitted that the Teams under his guidance had "adopted various methods to suppress the masses, such as prohibiting demonstrations and parades in the streets, and wall posters."[47] From the beginning of June into late July, Liu conceded, the Teams had operated to hinder rather than to stimulate the Cultural Revolution.

The majority of the responsible members of the work teams neither understood the Great Proletarian Cultural Revolution nor properly learned from
the masses. At the very outset, they asked the broad masses who had been
aroused to act according to plans and steps which we and the work teams
conceived on the basis of our subjective wishes.

This ran counter to the law governing the development of the revolutionary mass movement, and many serious incidents occurred. In fact,
we took a reactionary bourgeois stand, practiced bourgeois dictatorship,
suppressed the great Cultural Revolution which was then vigorously developing, confused right and wrong, white and black, thereby inflating the
arrogance of the bourgeoisie and demoralizing the proletariat.[48]

Stripped of its jargon—and allowing for the exaggerated contrition
of an old Party veteran seeking to absolve himself of guilt—Liu Shaoqi's description of the role of the Work Teams was plausible. The
Teams were fighting to preserve the Party's authority in that crucial
period, and their rough tactics reflected the seriousness with which
the Communist bureaucracy viewed the issues at stake.

Headed by Zhang Chengxian, an experienced Party official from
Hebei province, the Team that entered Beijing University in early
June was at first welcomed by the student radicals. Since the Team
was functioning under the aegis of the new Beijing Party Committee
that had replaced Peng Chen and dismissed Lu Ping and the old
university administration, the leftist teachers and students believed
that their protests would be encouraged. Within a week, however,
they perceived that the Team had different designs. Instead of promoting continued ferment, it halted demonstrations, banned student
speeches, and assigned radical youths to such chores as scraping
posters off the walls. The gates of the university were locked to anyone
unable to show identification. About two weeks later, when the radicals tried to organize a meeting to denounce Lu Ping and the other
purged members of the university leadership, they were refused
permission. When they defiantly held an unauthorized meeting,
many were labeled "counterrevolutionary" by the Team and forced
to confess to their "sins."[49]

At the same time, Team members tried to channel student energies by arbitrarily selecting victims whom the youths could attack.
The Beijing University Team singled out a woman professor in the
Foreign Languages Department, and instructed one of her students,
a young girl, to criticize her. When the young girl refused, she herself
was brought before a board of political examiners and denounced as
a "rightist."[50]

On July 12, five students in the university's Department of Geophysics, supported by Nie Yuanzi, finally revolted by putting up a poster protesting against the Work Team.[51] The Team retaliated by assailing her and the other radicals. By now, in a chaos of rhetoric that would soon become even more confusing, the two camps were both pledging allegiance to Mao and indicting each other as "bourgeois," "reactionary," and "counterrevolutionary revisionist." Most of the students, baffled by this verbiage, were cautious. Recalling his inability to sort out the rival groups, one student later explained that his main concerns were his application for Party membership, his postgraduate job assignment, and his personal future. Consequently, he said, he was hesitant to take sides.[52] Many other students were equally prudent. Unable to remain neutral, the most dangerous position, they shouted slogans without conviction while watching carefully to judge which way the political winds were blowing. They were, in effect, the reluctantly vocal majority.

In another part of Beijing, a similar tempest was brewing at Qinghua University, China's foremost polytechnic institution. Founded in 1911 as a preparatory college for students planning to study in the United States, Qinghua was raised to university status in 1925 as an important center of Sino-American educational cooperation. Under the Communists, it concentrated mainly on science and engineering and, by 1960, the university had some twelve thousand students and nearly two thousand faculty members.[53] The president, several department heads, and numbers of teachers and students at Qinghua also served among the five hundred cadres on the university's panoply of Party committees.[54] In contrast to Beijing University, however, Qinghua had been relatively calm during the spring of 1966. For one thing, its scientific and technological focus made it a more conservative institution. And for another, the Qinghua student body included many children of distinguished notables. When it erupted, therefore, the revolt at Qinghua was apparently orchestrated by Mao's operatives for a specific purpose—to assail Liu Shaoqi's wife, Wang Guangmei, who had arrived at Qinghua as a leader of the Work Team formed to bolster the Party machine there.

With Jiang Qing a key figure in charge of the Cultural Revolution and Wang Guangmei a Party troubleshooter, the two women were clearly engaged in a private vendetta. But in the ideological climate of the period, Wang Guangmei was at a disadvantage. Elegant, well-educated, and, above all, born into luxury, she could scarcely claim to stand for austere proletarian virtues in a system that measured the attitudes of people by the acreage of their grandfathers' farms. Even her name, Guangmei, was against her. Chosen by her father, who was traveling in the United States at the time of her birth in 1922, it signified "beautiful America."[55]

One of eleven children, Wang Guangmei was born and raised in Tianjin, the thriving cosmopolitan port city for Beijing and northern China in those days. Her family—by Communist standards of the "bureaucratic capitalist" class—was wealthy, worldly, and powerful. Her father, after serving in lucrative official posts for the local warlord government in northern China of the early 1920s, parlayed his capital and contacts into a fortune by acquiring vast tracts of real estate, factories, and other holdings. One of her uncles managed the largest textile mill in the region. Another relative, Wang Shuming, became commander in chief of Chiang Kai-shek's air force and Chief of General Staff of the Nationalist armed forces. Her brother Guangying— his name, reflecting her father's admiration for Great Britain, meant "beautiful England"—continued to run one of the family factories after the Communist victory and was hailed as a "Red capitalist" in those more tolerant days.

Wang Guangmei received an education befitting her family's status and Western leanings and her own modern inclinations. She entered Furen University, a Catholic-sponsored institution in Beijing, and went on to Yanjing, an American-subsidized university in the same city and the leading Christian college in China. Her English therefore was excellent and she had no trouble finding employment as an interpreter. Like many other idealistic young Chinese, she went to work for the Communists. Her first job was with their military procurement office in Beijing. In 1946, she switched to the Communist mission then trying to negotiate a reconciliation with the Nationalists under the auspices of General George C. Marshall. Her cultivated style appealed to two senior members of the Communist group: Luo Ruiqing, later Chief of General Staff and an early victim of the Cultural Revolution, and Ye Jianying, the top figure in the group, who would survive the purges to become one of China's highest-ranking officers. When the negotiations collapsed, Wang Guangmei considered pursuing her studies in the United States, but Ye Jianying persuaded her to go instead to Yenan. There, assigned to the Foreign Affairs Department of the Party Central Committee, she met Liu Shaoqi. At twenty-four, she was roughly half his age.

Having just discarded his fifth wife, Liu Shaoqi had an uneven marital record. One of his wives had been executed by the Nationalists in the early 1930s, and he had divorced four others. Now he fell in love with the "bourgeois" Wang Guangmei, and they married in 1948. She bore him two daughters in addition to serving as stepmother to several of his numerous children by previous marriages. With her grace and sophistication, she became a suitable "first lady" of China, a function she performed when Liu was elevated to chief of state in 1959. They traveled together to Pakistan, Afghanistan, and Burma, and she particularly impressed Indonesia's President Sukarno, a man easily charmed by pretty women. She was also effective as hostess to the many foreign delegations that streamed into Beijing in the early 1960s. As a Party agent at Qinghua University during the stormy summer of 1966, then, she was clearly miscast.

The Party Work Team, with Wang Guangmei prominent on its staff, arrived at Qinghua on June 9 proclaiming in the rhetoric of the Cultural Revolution that the university administration required a complete overhaul. The Team thereupon dismissed the university's entire Party apparatus without examining the ideological credentials of individual cadres or giving those at fault the chance to "remold" themselves in accordance with Mao's teaching that all except "antagonistic" enemies can win redemption through self-criticism. One of the Team's motives for this maneuver, the Maoists alleged, was to promote its favorites into positions of authority. Thus Liu Tao, Liu Shaoqi's daughter and a student of automation control, was made a deputy secretary of the Party branch in her department even though she was still only a candidate for Party membership. Similarly, He Pengfei, Marshal He Long's son and a mechanical-engineering student, was appointed to the Party committee in his section. Other children of high officials were also given posts in the new Party bureaucracy.[56]

The chief radical to rise in opposition to this operation was an obscure young student of chemical engineering, Kuai Dafu. Probably encouraged by Mao's operatives, Kuai tried to mobilize a student group behind him. But the Qinghua students were either too apathetic or prudent to support his cause. With extraordinary courage, Kuai acted virtually alone. He opened an offensive against the Party Team at the university by raising doubts about its claim to revolutionary competence. In a poster expressing these doubts, he said:

Power is in the hands of the Work Team, and this must prompt every revolutionary leftist to ask: Does this power represent us? If it does, we must support the Team. If not, we must seize its power.[57]

Wang Guangmei apparently remained indifferent to this challenge, but the Party Team reacted immediately. At first its members tried to reason with Kuai. He could not decently accuse the majority of the Party of "revisionism," they said. But Kuai stubbornly refused to concede, sticking to his charge that the Party was a "gang of bourgeois royalists" resisting the Cultural Revolution.[58] At an ensuing series of meetings, he continued to hold his ground. Alleging that the Party bosses had fabricated evidence against him, he vowed, "I would still declare that I am a revolutionary even if I were dragged to the gallows."[59] Arrested in July, he staged a hunger strike punctuated by histrionic communiqués warning that his imminent death would be a curse forever on the Party "reactionaries." One of these communiqués, addressed to a senior member of the Party Team, reached melodramatic heights:

> I have fasted for more than fifty hours. I feel exhausted, disintegrated. I fear that I may not live through tomorrow. I therefore request that you talk with me while I can still speak. I have many things to say to the Party Central Committee, to Chairman Mao, to my parents, and to you people. If you are too busy, send a representative and a stenographer that I may dictate my last will and testament.[60]

Kuai Dafu did not die, of course. Released on condition that he admit his "errors," he confessed to having been "ultraleftist" in displaying "sectarian tendencies" and "revolutionary rashness" in his "political oscillations." His "petty-bourgeois world outlook" had led him to dramatize his "individual and personal heroism" in order to "put myself in the limelight."[61]

The confession was only a dodge, however. Not long afterward, when the Maoists had gained the ascendancy, Kuai resumed his radical stance and accused the Party Team of having "spread poison" among the Qinghua students.[62] His charges were subsequently used as the basis for an indictment against Wang Guangmei. And, in a ritual confession, she was compelled to concede that the Party Team at Qinghua had "suppressed democracy and differing opinions, creating a reign of white terror" in the university. By restricting the "enthusiasm, creativity, and initiative of the masses," she had been guilty of "right-wing opportunism."[63] Despite this *mea culpa*, which was apparently contrived to deflect a growing Maoist assault against her husband later in 1966, she was betrayed by her own children and subjected to a humiliating inquisition.

During the early weeks of the summer, events in the provincial cities echoed the pattern set in Beijing as Party Work Teams penetrated regional universities in order to control the Cultural Revolution. This revealed, in part, that the Party was able to coordinate its defenses to a remarkable degree on a nationwide basis. But the extent of the activity also reflected the contagious ferment infecting young people in vastly different areas of the huge country.

In the ancient city of Xi'an, the capital of Shaanxi province, student restiveness became manifest as early as May in reaction to the campaign then developing against Peng Chen and his allegedly "bourgeois" literary protégés. Students ceased attending afternoon classes, stopped doing homework, and dropped their extracurricular activities, devoting most of their time instead to political meetings. On June 1, when Mao ordered that the text of the radical poster put up by Nie Yuanzi at Beijing University be broadcast, the ferment intensified. Throughout the night, students in Xi'an painted wall posters and wrote statements in a disorganized "feast of criticism" against teachers, comrades, officials, and almost anyone else who came to mind.

The initial agitation in Xi'an lacked direction. But one group of young radicals at Jiao Tong Da Xue, the Transport and Communications University—known familiarly as Jiao Da—was disciplined and purposeful. These students mounted a rhetorical assault against the university officials, charging them with promoting a "black line" against the Cultural Revolution. Their ambiguous accusations evoked an equally murky response from the university authorities, who quickly called a meeting to counterattack, branding the radicals "rightists" and denouncing their "wild actions." Within a few hours, fresh posters went up on the walls labeling the leftists "counterrevolutionaries." The next day, a Party Work Team arrived on the scene to take charge of the situation.

Headed by a senior member of the provincial Party apparatus, the Team moved rapidly to restore order. Students were prohibited from staging parades, putting up posters, and delivering speeches, and most of the youths, apparently respectful of the Party's power, observed the bans. The Team also sought to appease the radicals by mildly reproving one of the university officials and persuading him to confess to his "mistakes" at a public meeting. The episode might have ended there had not the radicals, either fired up by internal combustion or inflamed by outside fuel, escalated their protests against the Party Team. They telegraphed Mao, asking him to send a representative to Xi'an. They also defied the Party by plastering posters throughout the city complaining of "repression." In addition, they sent spokesmen to Beijing to plead their case before the Central Committee and dispatched representatives to contact other student groups as far away as Sichuan.

Tensions in Xi'an were so acute by the first week of June that no less a personage than Huo Shilian, the First Secretary of the Shaanxi Party Committee and boss of the province, intervened. Calling on workers, peasants, and local officials as well as Party youth organizations to criticize the radical students, he even threatened to employ regional Army units, then passively standing on the sidelines, to maintain peace. Huo also mobilized a special squad to "investigate" the young radicals who were creating trouble.

The fate of one student activist singled out by the Party squad in the university has been described by an Englishman, Andrew Watson, who was teaching at the Foreign Languages Institute in Xi'an during the period.[64] A girl named Wang Yongding had imprudently signed twenty posters attacking the university's Party committee. Soon afterward, she was herself described in posters put up by Party members as a "witch" and "drowning dog," while the university radio station labeled her "an enemy of the people." Arrested by the Party squad, she was interrogated for the names of her comrades and forced to write thirty-two separate statements acknowledging her "crimes." Despite her "confessions," the harassment continued. On June 8, she was put on public display in what was called an "animal exhibition." Her letters and private papers were confiscated, and seven students were assigned to guard her, presumably until she was brought to trial. But on July 9, she committed suicide by jumping from the window of the room where she as being held. According to Watson, hers was not the only suicide in those days.

In the southern city of Guangzhou, meanwhile, local Party bureaucrats were similarly attempting to protect themselves by controlling the course of the Cultural Revolution. How their maneuvers appeared in microcosm was described by Dai Xiaoai, a student activist in a Guangzhou secondary school prior to his defection to Hong Kong.[65]

As Dai recalled, the Cultural Revolution was first announced in his school by the principal, who also served as Party boss in the institution. At a meeting in late April, he instructed the students to paint posters, write articles, and mobilize discussions criticizing Wu Han, Deng Tuo, and the other literary figures in Beijing who were then being repudiated in the national press. The students knew nothing about these writers, but they followed orders. They copied phrases from the newspapers and invented trite slogans such as "Wu Han, you are a son of a bitch" and "Deng Tuo, surrender or be destroyed." This activity was initially amusing as a change from school work, but after ten days, even the most active students in the school began to lose interest in the repetitious exercise.

Wu Han was to suffer an ignominious fate, however. Imprisoned for three years, he was repeatedly beaten by his jailers until, in October 1969, he was taken to a hospital, vomiting blood. He died shortly afterward, as did his wife, who had also been incarcerated. Their daughter, a child at the time of her parents' deaths, later committed suicide by swallowing poison.

But in the middle of May, when Mao moved openly against Peng Chen and the Beijing Party Committee, the principal in Dai's school felt constrained to revive the campaign. He selected two teachers to be criticized by the students. One had temporarily been in trouble during a drive against "rightists" in 1957, while another was reputed to have a "bad" family background. The students were now aroused, since the accused were real people rather than remote villains in Beijing. Flimsy accusations against the two teachers were repeated for several days until the principal, anxious to keep the agitation going, urged the students to compel them to undergo a more cruel series of indignities.

We forced the teachers to wear caps and collars which stated things like "I am a monster." Each class confronted and reviled them in turn with slogans, accusations, and injunctions to reform their ways. We made them clean out the toilets, smeared them with black paint, and organized "Control Monster Teams" to see that it was properly done. We would charge them with specific mistakes and not relent until they admitted that they were true. It took nearly a week of constant struggle to make the man admit he had said "Mao was wrong" in conversation with one of his fellow teachers. They had little rest and were forced to sleep apart from their fellow teachers. We would join into informal groups, raid their quarters, and begin to work on them again. They could not escape us.

After about two weeks, we were afraid that the literature teacher would kill herself. We kept her under constant surveillance, and even wrote a poster and attached it to the mosquito net over her bed reminding her that she was being watched and could not succeed in committing suicide.

One of the peculiar features in this gratuitous terror was that Dai and the other students had actually respected the two teachers they were so brutally persecuting. However, as Dai recalled, their guilt was never doubted—the students could not possibly conceive that the sacrosanct Party might be wrong. As a consequence, even though he originally had compunctions about assailing the teachers, Dai quickly developed a genuine hatred for them. To attack them, he later said, "was our duty, and we showed no mercy."

In early June, as the rhetoric of the Cultural Revolution intensified with appeals to uproot "representatives of bourgeoisie" in the Party, government, and Army, Dai's school principal took a further step to insulate himself. He exhorted the students to repudiate seven more teachers, three as "rightists" and four as "bad elements" who had committed serious errors in the past. These teachers were all competent, popular, and dedicated, and Dai and his comrades were puzzled that they should have been chosen for criticism. They began to question the principal's motives, gradually perceiving that he and his associates were trying to defend themselves by victimizing subordinates. After discussing possible moves, the students sent delegates to the offices of the Provincial Party Committee to voice their suspicions. An official there politely listened to their story and promised to send a Work Team to investigate the school. In early July, therefore, a Team composed of sixteen cadres arrived to assume "all authority" over the school management. Within three days, the direction of the Cultural Revolution in the school was shifted.

Students were ordered to halt their attacks against teachers. Now their target was to be the school administration, including the principal, who was forced to wear a cardboard replica of a cow's head as he faced criticism. The fiercest assailants of the administration were naturally the teachers who had been persecuted earlier. They vilified the principal, who sought to ease the pressure by confessing lavishly to his mistakes. Amid this ferment, Dai noticed one phenomenon. Just as the principal had previously sacrificed his underlings in order to protect himself and his associates, so the members of the Work Team seemed to be denouncing the school administration in order to display the Party's zeal. The big fish, Dai observed, were merely eating the smaller fish. But in no way had the Team unleashed the "masses," in accordance with Mao's dictates. On the contrary, Dai concluded, the students' controlled activities bore little resemblance to Mao's vision of the Cultural Revolution as a dynamic upheaval that would reach into the "souls" of the Chinese people.

Even though Mao's base of power in mid-1966 was Shanghai, the Cultural Revolution in that metropolis was also phony. For here, too, the local Party bureaucracy went through the motions of carrying on the campaign while actually working to keep it within bounds. According to Neale Hunter, a young Australian teacher who lived in Shanghai during that period, the most avid spokesman for the Cultural Revolution in the city seemed to be the mayor and First Secretary of the Party's Municipal Committee, a chubby little Sichuanese by the name of Cao Diqiu. A quiet, unimaginative *apparatchik* concerned primarily with the management of a complex industrial center, Cao had been the epitome of Party orthodoxy. Now, to shield himself against the radicals, he took the initiative in sponsoring Mao's drive. "The people who will be most criticized in this movement are those who hang up lamb but sell dog meat," he announced in a speech on June 4, warning that he would uproot Party members who "wave Red Flags as a cover for an attack on the Red Flag." But the student radicals believed that Cao and his Party comrades were themselves waving the Red Flag to oppose it. They accused him of planning to "deceive the people" by attempting to "confuse the issue," and their charge was valid.[66]

Though Mao had decreed that students be given free rein, the Work Teams that went into Shanghai's universities under the auspices of Cao Diqiu and the Party frequently behaved in dictatorial fashion. One of the most repressive of these Teams in Shanghai, according to Maoist accounts, was led by the Chief of the Security Police, Huang Chibo. an impatient, volatile man, Huang was reported to have lost his temper in several encounters with young leftists. Angered by one radical,

Huang, without letting him finish, sprang off the couch so fast that he left his shoes behind. Arrogantly placing his hands on his hips, he said: "Do you still want to argue the point, you stupid young punk? You've forgotten all about Party leadership! You don't give a damn about the Work Team! You say you want the Party to lead, but you really think we're not revolutionary enough. You're the only revolutionaries around here, I suppose. Do you think that just because you've fooled the workers you can pull the wool over *our* eyes too?

"You're not supporting Chairman Mao, you're supporting Chairman Chiang Kai-shek! . . . You haven't listened to advice from anyone—not even from your own wives! . . . You've tried to create chaos. You've made things so difficult for the Party cadres that their work has been paralyzed. What kind of people are you? If you thought about your position, you'd break out in a cold sweat!"[67]

On another occasion, sounding very much like the stereotype Party *apparatchik* in a bad movie, Huang was quoted as telling unruly students that "if you don't do as we say, then we have other methods, not such nice ones." In still another riposte to the radicals, he said:

You *still* insist on disobeying the Party! Chiang Kai-shek had eight million men, and he could not defeat us. . . . What chance have you got? . . . The Work Team *is* the Party. If you try to take power here, we will see that you lose power. . . . Has the Communist Party become an object of hatred in your eyes? If so, you are in grave danger.[68]

The Shanghai Foreign Languages Institute, where Neale Hunter taught, was considered too unimportant to warrant a Work Team, but it went through much the same experience as the city's larger colleges and universities. On June 3, just as the Cultural Revolution was beginning to escalate in Beijing and elsewhere, a group of five young teachers at the Institute put up the first wall poster attacking its Party Committee for "lagging behind" in the movement. The Party Secretary responded quickly. Parrying the radical thrust, he called for a war against "bourgeois academics": "We must don the armor of Mao Zedong's ideas and root them out to the last man." Then, to appease the leftists, he quietly inspired the Institute's Communist Youth League to inaugurate a campaign against the Dean of English, a typical "bourgeois academic" who was said to have translated the complete works of Chaucer into Chinese. The choice of this obvious scapegoat seemed to satisfy most of the students, whose faith in the Party leadership was solid. But the radicals were unmoved. They raised the ante with an attack against the Vice-Secretary of the League, whom they accused of being the son of a landlord and a degenerate.[69]

Once again, instead of meeting the challenge head-on, the Party Secretary selected another "bourgeois academic," one of the Institute's vice-presidents, a jolly old Communist veteran with crew-cut gray hair and a passion for tennis and swimming. The indictment against him was a collection of ludicrous and petty complaints. But most of the students believed the charges, and their energies were for a time diverted. The leftists continued to press their offensive, however. They blamed the Institute for recruiting only a small percentage of students from "proletarian" backgrounds, and vilified the school officials themselves for having "landlord" and "capitalist" families. They even held the Institute's Party Committee responsible for the fact that one graduate, assigned to the Chinese diplomatic service, defected to the United States Embassy in Burundi in 1964.[70]

In Shanghai, as in other Chinese cities, though, the Party apparatus remained strongly entrenched despite the rising turbulence. As he observed this situation from his Hangzhou retreat, Mao must have sensed that the real thrust of his Cultural Revolution was being blunted. After eight months of absence from the capital, he decided to return to Beijing. And on the way, he staged a dramatic performance. On July 16, he dived into the Yangzi River near the city of Wuhan and broke all Olympic records by swimming nearly fifteen kilometers in sixty-five minutes.

This heroic exploit, if it actually took place as claimed, was no doubt contrived to quell speculation that Mao was ill and dying. Official press accounts insisted on his "wonderful health," reporting that "he was vigorous and showed no signs of fatigue" after his marathon swim.[71] His plunge also announced symbolically that he had emerged from the shadows to take personal charge of the Cultural Revolution. Press dispatches made this clear by quoting lines from a poem he had written on the occasion of an earlier swim: "I care not that the wind blows and the waves beat; it is better than idly strolling in a courtyard."[72] Moreover, the exercise was plainly designed to communicate to the "masses" that no obstacle, be it the tricky current of the Yangzi River or the powerful Chinese Communist Party bureaucracy, was too formidable to be overcome by those armed with Mao's doctrines. His defeat of the Yangzi, intoned an official Chinese commentator, proved "the splendor of Mao Zedong's thought."[73]

One of the many mysteries of that murky period was why Mao remained in Shanghai for so long when it was apparent that Liu Shaoqi and the Party machine were betraying his concept of the Cultural Revolution. Some analysts have contended that Mao lacked the strength to confront the Party *apparatchiks* before then, and chose to return to Beijing in a desperate bid to retrieve his authority. Others have argued that he waited to return to Beijing until the Party, having been delegated to manage the Cultural Revolution, could be criticized for the "errors" he was certain they would commit.

Mao reached Beijing on July 18 to attend an improvised Party session. Judging from all the evidence, he dominated the meeting. He criticized the Party *apparatchiks* for their supposed supervision of the Cultural Revolution. They were "afraid of revolution," he said, and sat in their offices rather than going "to places where there are disturbances to take a look." Consistent with this theme, he decried the size of the Party bureaucracy, with its numerous clerks and secretaries, saying: "I am alone here and am doing quite well. . . . We did not have such mammoth offices in the past." Mao accused the Party Work Teams of obstructing the Cultural Revolution by restraining the free expression of students. Even the "rightists" should be allowed to speak out, he asserted. "Let them air their views! Why should we be afraid of a few big-character posters and reactionary slogans?" There was nothing wrong with conflict, he said, for "it tempers the leftists when they are beaten up." Above all, Mao told the Party bureaucrats, they must kindle the fires of revolution even though "you will yourselves be consumed by the flames."[74]

In the weeks following that session, Mao ordered the dissolution of the Work Teams in the universities, hoping to erode the Party's power. But the Party *apparatchiks* refused to surrender, and so, supported by Army elements, Mao mobilized a new weapon—the Red Guards.

CHAPTER 9

The Children's Revolt

> *A revolution is not a dinner party, or writing an essay, or painting a picture, or doing embroidery; it cannot be so refined, so leisurely and gentle, so temperate, kind, courteous, restrained, and magnanimous. A revolution is an insurrection, an act of violence by which one class overthrows another.*
>
> —MAO ZEDONG, *1927*

BY DAWN ON August 18, 1966, Beijing's vast Tiananmen Square—the Plaza of the Gate of Heavenly Peace—was packed with more than a million young Chinese. Most were dressed in khaki, their crimson arm bands bearing the inscription *Hong Wei Bing*—"Red Guard." Shivering as they waited in the morning cold, they sang songs and chanted catechisms from a small breviary bound in bright red plastic entitled *Quotations from Chairman Mao*. Finally, timing his appearance with theatrical precision to the rising sun in the east, Mao Zedong emerged onto an upper gallery of the Tiananmen Gate. He wore the olive-green uniform of a simple soldier, a muffin-shaped military cap on his head. A thunderous roar rolled through the hundred-acre square to welcome him—and a new phase of the Cultural Revolution had begun.

Though he had not charted the course of his campaign precisely from the outset, Mao's essential aim at this stage of the Cultural Revolution was to unleash the Red Guards against his rivals in the Communist Party apparatus. Simply "dismissing people from office" and other "pure organizational steps" would not suffice to uproot "bourgeois" ideas, his spokesmen had asserted. Only by "boldly mobilizing the masses" could a real revolution be set in motion.[1] Thus, in his drive to overthrow the Party bureaucrats, Mao was also striving to inculcate his disciples with the proletarian *élan* that he feared the Chinese had lost. For that reason, he saw the Cultural Revolution as a crucial educational exercise as well as a decisive power struggle.

Since his return to Beijing, Mao had been maneuvering to isolate and weaken the Party machine so that it might be swept away by the Red Guards, who supposedly represented the most activist elements among the "masses." Relying on loyal military units and Army political commissars under the command of Lin Biao to organize them, Mao encouraged young leftists to intensify their agitation. On August 1, he blessed two different Red Guard groups in Beijing for their announced intention to "rebel against all reactionaries."[2] A few days later, further whipping up the spirit of revolt, Mao published his own "big-character poster"—the first and only time in the Cultural Revolution that he would issue so open a pronouncement. It was entitled "Bombard the Headquarters," and its contents left no doubt that his design was to smash the Party leadership. Praising the radicals who had initially shaken Beijing University in the late spring, Mao's proclamation indicted "some comrades from the central down to the local levels" who had "diametrically" opposed his Cultural Revolution in the "last fifty days or so." These comrades were obviously Liu Shaoqi and his associates, and Mao's tirade against them was extraordinarily passionate.

They have enforced a bourgeois dictatorship and struck down the surging movement of the great Cultural Revolution of the proletariat. They have stood facts on their head and juggled black and white, encircled and suppressed revolutionaries, stifled opinions different from their own, imposed a white terror, and felt very pleased with themselves. They have puffed up the arrogance of the bourgeoisie and deflated the morale of the proletariat. How vicious they are![3]

Once again, Mao's enormous prestige prevented his opponents from replying squarely to his attack. In a series of private talks delivered in early August, Liu Shaoqi resorted to other tactics. He echoed Mao's criticism of the Party Work Teams for their heavy-handed treatment of young radicals. But he emphasized that the Teams had been appointed with Central Committee approval, thus implying that Mao, as Chairman, shared responsibility for their "crimes." In addition, Liu blamed the Team members themselves for their excesses. He even conceded that the creation of the Teams had been a "mistake," and proposed that they be disbanded.[4] At the same time, however, Liu underlined the need for moderation. "Landlords, rich peasants, bad elements, counterrevolutionaries, and rightists" were "men and not animals," and to kill them was senseless, since their children and grandchildren would only "avenge their deaths" in the future.[5]

The whole thrust of Liu's strategy at this point, then, was to narrow the scope of the Cultural Revolution in the hope that, like so many past "rectification" drives, it would gradually lose momentum. And, contravening Mao's exhortations, he also stressed the sanctity of the Party. "At present we have a proletarian dictatorship," he said. "The Chinese Communist Party is Marxist. It is not justified to rebel against the Communist Party."[6]

Despite his disdain for formal measures, Mao evidently decided to lend a certain legitimacy to his assault against the Party bureaucracy. On August 1, he convened a Plenary Session of the Party's Eighth Central Committee in Beijing. The Plenum was the first to be held since 1962, even though the Party Constitution required such meetings every two years.

It was the most momentous Party conclave since the founding of the Chinese People's Republic. Mao had undoubtedly hoped to swing most of the Central Committee behind him, thereby isolating Liu Shaoqi and the other senior Party figures. But, though he packed the hall with radical students and other sympathizers, he barely managed to rally a majority of those present to his colors. As he candidly admitted later, "Many people could not be converted to my view." Perceiving that his policies would have to be "tested in practice" rather than dictated officially, he therefore used the Plenum to lay down guidelines that his disciples could follow as they propelled the Cultural Revolution forward in the months ahead.[7] As usual, he welcomed resistance as further evidence that only the "masses" could purge the Party of its "revisionist" tendencies while simultaneously forging their own revolutionary character.

Lin Biao, soon to be revealed as Mao's heir apparent, delivered the keynote address at the Party conference, and his message was unequivocal.[8] Loyalty to Mao and his ideology was the only yardstick by which a true Communist could be measured, he asserted. Speaking in his thin, reedy voice, he combined protestations of humility with stern warnings:

I am not equal to my task, and may fail in my duties. I may make mistakes. But to do the best I can to avoid mistakes, I shall rely on the Chairman. . . .

With the Chairman as the axle, we are the milling stones and must do everything according to the thought of Mao Zedong. There is no other way. There cannot be two policies or two command headquarters. No wishful thinking should replace the thinking of the Chairman, and we cannot stage a rival drama in competition with that staged by the Chairman. We want monism, and closely follow the Chairman. . . .

There are many ideas we do not understand. We must firmly execute the Chairman's directives. I have no special talent, but I rely on the wisdom of the masses, ask the Chairman for instruction when doing everything, and do everything according to his orders. I do not interfere with him on major matters, nor do I trouble him on minor matters. . . . The Chairman is the genius of the world revolution.

In the wake of the Cultural Revolution, five years later, as the decimated Communist Party machine was being rebuilt, Lin Biao would be excoriated for having thus portrayed Mao as a "genius." The argument used against Lin was that as Mao's heir he had attempted to promote his own personality cult at the expense of the Party. But now, as the Cultural Revolution accelerated, Lin sought to affirm Mao's infallibility—implying that only the Chairman and his close courtiers were in true communion with the "masses."

In explaining the necessity for the Cultural Revolution, Lin Biao did not deny the need for "developing production and raising the technological level" of China. But to "promote material incentives as the revisionist countries do," he claimed, would surely mean "retrogression and reversion to the old rule." Thus he reiterated the Maoist canon that "the important factor in productivity is man": "we must change ideas and concepts and heighten our sense of responsibility to society" in an effort to alter human nature. "When we win on the spiritual front, we shall also win on the material front." Hence the Cultural Revolution—the "large-scale struggle to transform men"—was imperative.

This ideological drive would not be easy, Lin Biao conceded, for "reversals, numerous struggles, and criticisms" lay ahead. Had Mao failed to intervene when he did, "the bourgeoisie would have gained the upper hand, and we would have lost the battle." Equally arduous would be the problem of educating the worker and peasant "masses" to understand the campaign, he said, since "they may have difficulty distinguishing fish eyes from pearls and must be taught that the thoughts of Mao Zedong are the pearls." Thus the urgent task at the moment was to launch a "general examination, a general alignment, and a general reorganization of the ranks of cadres" in order to overhaul the Party completely. Those who eagerly studied Mao, attached importance to ideology, and displayed revolutionary passion would be "promoted." Those who committeed errors but "accept education and resolutely repent" might be "given a chance . . . to be tested in future work." As for the "incorrigibles"—those "who oppose the thought of Mao Zedong," those who "are impetuous by nature" and "upset" ideological policies, and those who lacked "revolutionary zeal"—they would be ousted. For unless they were purged, they would "carry out subversive activities once trouble flares up" and the Cultural Revolution would be threatened by a "stalemate" that would signify Mao's failure.

Ignoring the Party Constitution, which authorized structural changes only at Party Congresses, Mao used the August Plenum to revamp the Communist leadership. He demoted Liu Shaoqi, Zhou Enlai, Zhu De, and Chen Yun from their posts of Vice-Chairmen and elevated Lin Biao to be his sole deputy. He also downgraded Liu to eighth place in the hierarchy while the relatively new face of Tao Zhu, who had risen meteorically from regional boss in south China to become chief of the Propaganda Department in Beijing, now appeared in the Party's number four spot—where, however, it would remain only briefly. But these reshuffles were not really Mao's style, especially at this juncture in the Cultural Revolution. Rearrangements of the Party "from above" were only expedients, and Mao's aims went further. His mobilization of the Red Guards, then, was aimed at launching a purge "from below."

Though Red Guard groups had formed in Beijing and elsewhere as far back as May, the massive movement of youths that emerged in the capital in mid-August was plainly the result of precise and unusually efficient organization in which the Army played a major role—at least at the beginning. Only the Army had the means to transport thousands of young Chinese into the city as well as lodge, feed, and outfit them in khaki uniforms for their first demonstration. Only the Army could plan so monumental a demonstration and execute it down to such details as providing outdoor latrines to accommodate youths who would participate from dawn to midnight in the delirious pageant. Another clue to the Army's involvement was reflected in the fact that the "little red book" of Mao's *Quotations* distributed to the young radicals had been originally published in May 1964 under military auspices for the indoctrination of soldiers.[9]

Without specifically mentioning them by name, a Sixteen Point Decision issued by the Plenum on August 8 clearly indicated that the Red Guards would serve as Mao's principal weapon in the Cultural Revolution. The Decision, in which Mao outlined his hopes for the campaign, vowed to accomplish nothing less than a "great revolution that touches people to their very souls." This ambitious dream demanded the eradication of "old ideas, old culture, old customs, and old habits of the exploiting classes," and their replacement by "new ideas, new culture, new customs, and new habits to transform the spiritual aspect of the whole society." The "brave vanguards" in this offensive would be "large numbers of revolutionary youngsters" who had been "hitherto unknown," the Decision stated, adding:

> They have energy and wisdom. Using big-character posters and debates, they are airing their views and opinions in a big way, exposing and criticizing in a big way, firmly launching an attack against the open and covert representatives of the bourgeoisie.

But just as the delegates at the Party Plenum had been sharply divided, so the Sixteen Point Decision was scarcely a cohesive blueprint for the Cultural Revolution. For it contained such clouded and contradictory directives that it could only have been a compromise document patched together by an assortment of leaders with widely divergent views.

Premier Zhou Enlai may have extracted concessions from the Maoists in exchange for swinging his invaluable support behind their cause,[10] since the Decision reflected his concern for insulating certain sectors of China from the rising storm. It stressed, for example, that the Cultural Revolution should not "impede" industrial and agricultural production. Similarly, with China's nuclear- and advanced-weapons' development in mind, it decreed that scientists and technicians be exempted from the struggles as long as they "love their country, work actively, are not against the Party and socialism, and do not secretly collaborate with any foreign power." Promising to protect the Chinese military establishment from disruption, the Decision also instructed the Army to conduct its own "socialist education movement" without external interference.

Mao must have pledged to certain senior Party figures that the Communist apparatus would not be totally disrupted. The Decision drew a distinction between "good" Party members who "encourage the masses" and those who "do their best to confuse the boundary line between revolution and counterrevolution" and therefore deserve dismissal. Moreover, it qualified the "majority" of Party cadres as "good and relatively good" while quantifying those who were beyond redemption as only a "small number." In addition, the document asserted that no campaigns of criticism against alleged "reactionaries" could be undertaken without prior discussion and approval by Party committees "at the corresponding levels."

At the same time, however, the Decision was vague enough to permit the radicals to employ force. Though it urged the Red Guards to use persuasion rather than coercion, the document also asserted that "anti-socialist rightists must be fully exposed and knocked down" and "their influence must be eliminated." Warning that the Cultural Revolution would "unavoidably meet with resistance," it also affirmed that "if only the masses are fully aroused to action, such resistance will break down quickly."[11] This fiery rhetoric was paralleled by Maoist exhortations to the Red Guards to run rampant. Even in late July they had been told by Chen Boda to "be ready to fight,"[12] and Kang Sheng, another prominent Maoist, had advised: "Do not fear chaos."[13] And, of course, there was Mao's personal dictum: "Destruction before construction."

Fogged by ambivalence from the start, then, the Cultural Revolution would seesaw between periods of turmoil when the radicals were in the ascendancy, and periods in which more conservative elements arose to impose law, order, and discipline. The weeks following the Party Plenum were a period of violence that had its beginning with Mao's huge reception for the Red Guards on August 18 in Beijing. It was the first of eight such rallies in which, through November, a total of more than 11 million young people entered the capital.

Aware that a potentially volcanic force was bottled up in the frustrations of China's younger generation, Mao's aides consciously worked to build their emotions up to a fever pitch in the days before the rally. In a speech to Red Guards who had been brought to Beijing for the demonstration from other regions of the country, Chen Boda spoke in the highly charged terms that were to become the common idiom of the Cultural Revolution for months to come. He reminded the provincial youths that they had been chosen as "successors to the cause of the proletarian revolution," urging them to "grow up braving storm and stress."

Comrades, you must be absolutely fearless, you must steel and temper yourselves over and over again, and you must be able to withstand all trials and tribulations and all possible unforeseen setbacks. You must be able to bear all kinds of ordeals and the sharp conflicts between individualism and collectivism, between individualism and Communism. [14]

Exhortations of this kind were matched by less formal pep talks in which radical cadres, among them Army political commissars, cued Red Guards on how to behave during the scheduled rally. The youths were rehearsed in marching, advised which of Mao's aphorisms to read and what slogans to shout, and taught the lyrics of a stirring new song entitled "Sailing the Seas Depends on the Helmsman."

The décor for the mammoth rally resembled the settings for similar demonstrations staged in the Tiananmen Square in the sixteen years since the Communists took power. A huge image of Mao adorned the fifteenth-century Gate of the Heavenly Peace, while portraits of Marx, Engels, and Sun Yat-sen flanked the other sides of the immense enclosure. The Square was festooned with red flags and balloons and banners bearing such slogans as "Long Live the Chinese People's Republic" and "Hail to the Unity of the Workers of the World." And the multitude that filled the Square testified to the enormity of China's population.

Yet the August 18 rally differed significantly from the sort of demonstration choreographed in twentieth-century totalitarian states. It was not, in Nazi or Fascist style, an exercise in which the Führer or Duce harangued the mob, nor was it characterized by the cold solemnity of a May Day parade in Moscow. On the contrary, it seemed to be an almost religious ritual as Mao the god communed with the devotees of his cult.

From the moment he emerged onto the gallery of the Tiananmen Gate in the early morning sunlight until he retured after the evening's fireworks display, Mao played the part of a benign, paternal deity. He delivered no rousing address but left the oratory to his subordinates. Steered by a young nurse, he shuffled stiffly to and fro on the gallery, sometimes waving mechanically to the blur of faces below and, twice or three times during the day, descending into the "masses" to puff at his cigar and chat with selected Red Guards. Wearing a military uniform for the first time in public in order to symbolize his reliance on the Army, he designated Lin Biao to speak to the assemblage. As Mao peered over his shoulder like a faintly nervous parent watching his child perform, Lin stumbled through his speech in a manner scarcely calculated to inspire confidence in him as the Chairman's heir:

> Chairman Mao is the most outstanding leader of the proletariat in the present era and the greatest genius in the present era. . . . Mao Zedong's thought marks a completely new stage in the development of Marxism-Leninism. It is Marxism-Leninism at the highest level in the present era. It is Marxism-Leninism for remolding the souls of the people. It is the most powerful ideological weapon of the proletariat.[15]

Lin Biao's accent on "remolding souls" lent a theological tone to the Beijing rally that must have mystified many of the young people present. But whatever they understood of the rhetoric, the Red Guards reacted as if intoxicated. They broke into rhythmic chanting of Mao's name, some weeping unabashedly as they waved their little red books like magic talismans at the object of their reverence. They screamed slogans, leaped into the air with excitement, and, when Mao descended into the Square like Zeus stepping down from Olympus, pressed forward against a cordon of soldiers for a glimpse of him. Much of this hysteria was genuine, but several scenes were carefully enacted for the benefit of official cameramen. In one episode, obviously contrived to portray his human qualities, Mao paused to sit among a group of Red Guards and discuss their problems. In another scene, recorded in a film of the rally shown throughout China and abroad, a pretty girl student from Qinghua University came forth from the crowd to encircle his arm with a brassard reading "Red Guard." Then and there, a propaganda account of their dialogue related, Mao persuaded her to change her name from Pingping, meaning "refined gentleness," to Yaowu, signifying "will to do battle."[16]

Thus Mao identified himself with the Red Guards as his cry to them to "spread disorder" was given authoritative encouragement in *Red Flag:*

> The revolutionary youngsters are using Mao Zedong's thought to condemn and reform the old world, and to wipe out completely the old ideologies, culture, customs, and habits accumulated over thousands of years. They want to turn the old world upside down and to build a new world based on Mao Zedong's thought. Is this fanaticism? No it is not. It is earth-shaking revolutionary ambition.[17]

Similar rallies resonated throughout China in the days that followed. Thousands of students braved a driving rainstorm to parade
in Shanghai, and a half-million people were reported to have held
outdoor meetings in Guangzhou. Huge crowds streamed out in cities
as diverse as Fuzhou on the coast, Harbin in the industrial north,
and Lhasa, the capital of remote Tibet. Repeating the rhetoric broadcast from Beijing, speakers at these demonstrations vowed to "answer
the call of Chairman Mao" by promoting the Cultural Revolution.
This nationwide convulsion, though it initially seemed simply to be
orchestrated from Beijing, was an extremely complex and often puz-
zling phenomenon.

Stimulated by appeals to rise up in revolt against Chinese traditions, Red Guard groups mushroomed around the country, and they
assumed a baffling assortment of titles. Some, like the Chingkangshan
Red Guards, named their units for landmarks in Chinese Communist
history. Others commemorated important dates in the Cultural Revolution, like the May 16th Detachment, so-called to honor the circular
issued by Mao on that day, or the August 18th Red Guards, whose
title celebrated the Beijing rally. There were multitudes of Red Flag
and Red Banner factions, and groups with militant slogans for names,
like the Mao Zedong Thought August First Fighting Regiment, the
Scarlet Guards for the Defense of Mao Zedong's Thought, and the
Struggle-Until-Death to Defend Chairman Mao Combat Corps.

The titles of only a few of the Red Guard units that sprang up in
Guangzhou at the time illustrated the confusion that prevailed in that
city. They included the Guangzhou District General Headquarters
of the Red Workers Militia Detachment, which had its offices at the
Dawn Restaurant on Beijing Road; the Students Joint Revolutionary
Committee, with its headquarters at the First Workers' Cultural Palace, which included an assortment of primary- and secondary-school
Red Guard factions; and the Card-Carrying Workers Revolutionary
Rebels Headquarters, composed mainly of young men who had
drifted into the city from outlying villages. Later, when many of these
factions became clustered in rival coalitions, the Guangzhou scene
grew even more complex. As part of the East Wind coalition, for
example, the Guangzhou Red Workers Revolutionary Rebels Headquarters opposed the Guangzhou Red Workers Joint Revolutionary
Committee, which belonged to the Red Flag coalition, while the
Government Organs Great Alliance Revolutionary Committee
clashed with the Government Organs Red Headquarters.[18] Understandably, one of the major difficulties encountered by the Beijing

leaders as they tried to conduct the Cultural Revolution was their inability to sort out the crazy quilt of Red Guard factions.

Some Red Guard groups contained thousands of adherents, while others had only ten or twelve members who had pledged allegiance to a single energetic chief. Many youths belonged to several units simultaneously or shifted from one faction to another, depending on circumstances. A young Cantonese worker, who estimated that there had been eighty-five separate Red Guard organizations in his factory, disclosed that he had switched affiliations in order to travel outside the city.[19] Operating through "liaison stations" in colleges and universities in different cities, a few Red Guard fraternities appeared to be national in scope. As the Cultural Revolution accelerated during the summer, thousands of radical activists left Beijing to tour the country, dispensing advice to aspiring Red Guards in the provinces. At the same time, millions of youths were pouring into the capital.

Throughout August, most of the provincial Party leaders resorted to various devices to control the Red Guards. One was to suppress directives issued by Mao's subordinates in charge of the Cultural Revolution. The mayor of Shanghai, Cao Diqiu, destroyed a document cataloguing the "crimes" of his Director of Education in order to prevent an upheaval in the city's schools and universities. The Red Guards later alleged that Mayor Cao had acted on instructions from the Secretary General of the Party, Deng Xiaoping, who was then seeking to dampen the radical offensive.[20]

The *apparatchiks* also resisted the Cultural Revolution by placing self-protective interpretations on the Sixteen Point Decision issued by the Party Plenum in Beijing on August 8. They emphasized its ban on violence and invoked passages describing the "majority" of Party cadres as "good" or "relatively good"—hence loyal to the Maoist line. The local Party leaders also tried to manage the Cultural Revolution by focusing the indignation of young leftists against helpless scapegoats.

At the Shanghai Foreign Languages Institute, for instance, eighty-one teachers and other officials were singled out by the Party for criticism in mid-August. Among them was an elderly woman who had been educated in the United States, an instructor whose father had been associated with Chiang Kai-shek, and a former Catholic nun who had quit the Church. As a teacher at the Institute recalled, these people made "perfect victims" because they were "no threat to anyone, and the Party authorities knew this very well."[21] At the same time, to create the impression that it was not above purging itself, the Party Committee at the Institute also chose to sacrifice ten from among its two hundred members. When a handful of radicals perceived this tactic for what it was, they tried to protest, but the Party machine succeeded in turning a majority of students against them.

As the Cultural Revolution intensified, youth groups splintered into smaller units that frequently fought each other less for ideological motives than simply to assert themselves. With rival factions all proclaiming their undying allegiance to Mao and his ideals, the situation appeared as confusing to Chinese as it did to the outside world.

Reminiscing on those days in August, a former Red Guard who had fled from Guangzhou to Hong Kong said: "The whole business was too complicated for words. I didn't understand it then, and I don't understand it now."[22] He recalled that the students at his secondary school had been "excited beyond belief" by the news of the August 18 rally in Beijing. Particularly inspiring to them was a photograph of Mao wearing a Red Guard arm band. The picture, far more effective than words, made it plain to the youths that they were authorized to create a Red Guard unit in their school. They immediately convoked a meeting, but discovered that they had no guidelines. They could not determine who would be eligible for membership, how to select leaders, or the nature of their relationship to the Party cadres in the school. Finally, after a night of discussion, they decided to form a group called the Mao Zedong Doctrine Red Guards, which would be open to all students whose political conduct had been "good" irrespective of their class background. This decision was reversed a day later, however, with the arrival of a student from Qinghua University who had been sent south along with hundreds of other Beijing youths to instruct provincial students in the organization of Red Guard units. Only truly "revolutionary" elements should be enrolled as Red Guards, he advised. He then defined these elements according to family lineage as the "Five Kinds of Red"— children of workers, poor peasants, revolutionary martyrs, revolutionary cadres, and revolutionary soldiers.

This formula, dictated as it was by a "veteran" Red Guard from Beijing, was accepted by the Guangzhou students. But it was to have a divisive effect on the Red Guard movement in the southern city. Not only did it alienate many students who could not qualify as authentic revolutionaries, prompt them to organize their own factions, and fragment the Red Guard movement further. It also disappointed many young radicals to observe that revolutionary Red Guards, by rejecting members of other classes, were becoming as "elitist" as the Party bureaucrats they were supposed to overthrow. For these among other reasons, the Red Guards never shaped a solid national or even regional organization, but continued to dispute among themselves.

Many of the early Red Guard groups in Beijing, Shanghai, Guangzhou, and other Chinese cities were being formed under the auspices of municipal Party committees intent on shielding themselves from attack. The *apparatchiks* worked to divert and dissipate the energies of youths by encouraging them to assault trivial symbols of the past. Issuing a "declaration of war on the old world," Red Guards in Beijing poured forth to change the names of avenues, shops, restaurants, and other establishments. They urged that Legation Street, the thoroughfare that formerly housed foreign embassies, be called Anti-Imperialist Street, and they altered the name of the Eastern Peace Bazaar, a Beijing department store, to East Wind Bazaar.[23] In Guangzhou, youth groups compelled dress manufacturers to stop copying Western fashions, and they ordered barbers to cease cutting hair in what they referred to as "cowboy" and "airplane" styles. They broke into eating places, decorating one called the Peace Restaurant with posters denouncing it as a "nest of pleasure for depraved young men and ladies" and a "rendezvous for the drunken and daydreaming bourgeoisie."[24] One Red Guard faction in a Beijing secondary school published a pamphlet entitled "A Hundred Rules for Destroying the Old and Establishing the New," proposing that regulations be promulgated to outlaw jewelry, prohibit folk songs, and authorize children to criticize their parents, a daring suggestion in a land where the Confucian concept of filial piety was still strong.[25] Amid this ferment, another group of young rebels demanded that traffic lights be "revolutionized" so that red would signal "go" and green "stop."[26]

One of the most vivid accounts of this destructive period has been provided by Dai Xiaoai, a Red Guard mentioned earlier who defected to Hong Kong from Guangzhou.[27] He and his comrades sallied forth on August 23 to exterminate "old ideas, old culture, old customs, and old habits" by invading the homes of the "Seven Kinds of Black"— "landlords, rich peasants, counterrevolutionaries, bad elements, rightists, monsters and freaks, and pro-capitalists." Singing revolutionary hymns and shouting slogans, the students went first to the nearest police station, where the residences of their intended victims were indicated on a map of the precinct. Using police records to guide them, the youths worked their way up and down the streets of the neighborhood, hanging signs on designated houses. Then they returned for their search-and-destroy mission.

In practice, we confiscated things like vases and furniture decorated in the traditional way. If there were revolutionary objects, like pictures of Mao Zedong, we left them alone. Usually we would smash something just for effect and confiscate everything else. . . . We took all foreign-made items, like blankets and quilts from Hong Kong as well as jewelry, scrolls, and even books that had been published before 1949.

Because we were afraid that people would hide things, we searched their houses very thoroughly. Some of us would tear down the walls and look behind the plaster while others seized shovels and picks and tore up the cellars looking for hidden items. . . .

While we searched each house, we made the occupants stand to one side while a few members of the group shouted that they must confess their counterrevolutionary crimes. If the women had long hair, we cut it. Sometimes we would shave half of the hair on a man's head and defy him to shave the rest. Our object was to humiliate these people as much as we could.

After two or three days, there was hardly an area of Guangzhou that had not been combed by Red Guards. Seeking to immunize themselves, people covered their gates with Mao's quotations, painted their furniture red, and themselves destroyed objects of value. When private targets became difficult to find, however, the students smashed other relics.

Statues, paintings, and other such objects in public parks, temples, and cemeteries were quickly destroyed. We had no plan on these occasions, but simply roamed the streets looking for things. Someone would shout, "Let's go to such-and-such temple," and we would all follow. Very often, some other group would have been there first and left nothing but a pile of ashes or a group of statues smeared with paint. At least once a day, we would cart a statue to a large intersection and ceremoniously smash it to pieces. Passersby would stop and watch us. Some would congratulate us, but most lowered their heads and hurried by. . . .

In truth, this part of the movement was, in some ways, the most fun of all. We were free to do as we pleased, nobody checked on us, and we controlled ourselves. We felt like adults, really for the first time. I thought that what we were doing was important. Therefore, I enjoyed myself fully. It was a great deal of fun.

The Guangzhou leaders were relieved to see the Red Guards direct their fury against innocent citizens rather than against the municipal authorities. No less a personage than Zhao Ziyang, the First Secretary of the Guangdong Province Party Committee, congratulated the youths for their vandalism. Less than four months later, Zhao himself would face the wrath of the Red Guards, accused of having deceptively maneuvered to salvage his own power.

An authoritative clue to the number of persons rounded up by the Red Guards in the early stage of the Cultural Revolution was provided on October 2 by Xie Fuzhi, Minister of Public Security, when he disclosed that a total of 21,779 landowners, rich peasants, counterrevolutionaries, and other "evil" elements had been "arrested" by the radical youths. Xie claimed that the Red Guards had confiscated among other items more than 25,000 rifles, nearly 14,000 portraits of Chiang Kai-shek, close to 38 tons of gold, approximately 10 million silver coins, and a couple of million American dollars.[28] He also estimated that some 400,000 "reactionaries" had been subjected to some form of harassment by the Red Guards.[29] The validity of Xie's statistics has never been established, since neither Chinese nor Western sources inside China were able to observe more than individual instances of Red Guard brutality. Judging from the number of these instances reported during the later summer of 1966, however, the extent of violence must have been considerable. But it was probably far less than the turbulence that was to erupt in the summer of 1967 and again in the spring of 1968, when rival factions fought pitched battles in many parts of China.

Red Guards like Dai Xiaoai in Guangzhou may have regarded their destructive activities as a "great deal of fun," but victims of the Cultural Revolution in its opening phase were humiliated, terrorized, and even killed or driven to suicide by the fanatical youths. In late August, diplomats in Beijing witnessed Red Guards beat a man with ropes while a large crowd, many of them children, cheered and shouted approval.[30] Youth activists broke into the Sacred Heart Convent, a Catholic school in Beijing for foreign children, smashing its religious relics and forcing eight aged European nuns to run a gantlet of bamboo sticks. The nuns were subsequently deported to Hong Kong, where one of them, a woman in her seventies, died a day after their arrival.[31] Much later, when the tide had turned against the Red Guards, numbers of Chinese summoned up the courage to protest against the August holocaust. One man divulged in a wall poster pasted up in the capital that his wife, a woman of fifty, had been stabbed to death by Red Guards at a meeting in which she had presumably been accused of "capitalist" tendencies. Naming the Red Guard leader allegedly responsible for the killing, the man claimed that his appeals for justice had gone unheeded. In a similar poster, a youth charged that both his parents had been murdered by pupils of Beijing's Guang Street Primary School, where his mother had served as principal. A Chinese truck driver who worked in Beijing that summer afterward reported that he had spent night after night carting away the corpses of citizens who had run afoul of Red Guard gangs.[32]

In several places Red Guard groups physically assaulted prestigious Chinese figures suspected of "bourgeois" or "revisionist" leanings. Early in November, for instance, radicals in Anhui province arrested the region's Party boss, Li Baohua, whose father, Li Dazhao, had been one of Mao's early patrons and an original organizer of the Chinese Communist movement in 1921. According to a report from the area, Li Baohua was flogged and tortured by the youths as they sought to force him to confess to his "sins."[33] Shanghai Red Guards even broke into the home of Madame Sun Yat-sen. Deploring this incident in a private speech somewhat later, Premier Zhou Enlai admonished the radicals for attacking people solely on the basis of their "class" origin. "Some youngsters have acted like hooligans," he said.[34]

Among the many accounts related by Chinese refugees during those days were the personal experiences of two young people who escaped by swimming throughout the night across the bay that separates the coast of Guangdong province from Macao, the quaint little Portuguese enclave on the edge of China. The woman, Lihan, had been a painter and stage designer in Guangzhou. The man, Ling, was a cellist with a fondness for Western music.

A frail, shy man in his early thirties, Ling had two strikes against him. As the son of a French-educated economist, Ling had long been under suspicion because of his dubious "class background." And as a member of the Guangzhou Symphony Orchestra, he was vulnerable to criticism for having performed the works of Western "bourgeois" composers like Mozart and Beethoven.

Until the early 1960s, Ling recalled, the Guangzhou Symphony Orchestra had been relatively unmolested by politics. But after the inauguration of Mao's Socialist Education Campaign in 1962, ideological pressures gradually mounted. A Communist Party Committee was formed in the orchestra to pass judgment on the purity of its musicians. Several conductors and instrumentalists, dismissed for "bourgeois" proclivities, were sent out to the countryside to work as farm laborers. Nearly every night, after their performance, members of the orchestra were required to meet under the auspices of the Party Committee to criticize themselves and each other. The musicians were also called upon to debate the ideological significance of the orchestra's repertory, with Party cadres usually steering the discussion toward denunciations of Western composers. By the end of 1965, Western classics had been banned as "imperialist," Soviet compositions were prohibited as "revisionist," and even folk music was outlawed as "feudal." The last concert held under the aegis of the orchestra took place in April 1966. A visiting East German string quartet played Mozart, Dvořák, and Ravel. To prevent the public from being "contaminated," Ling related, attendance was by invitation only. Soon after that, the orchestra was disbanded.

Ling tried to earn a livelihood by giving violin and piano lessons. But as the Cultural Revolution intensified during the spring, Western musical instruments were declared to be "bourgeois," and his few pupils apprehensively peeled away. Frightened, he destroyed his violin, smashed his record collection, and burned his scores. His fears heightened as the ferment in Guangzhou escalated sharply after Mao uncorked the Red Guards at the August 18 rally in Beijing. On one occasion, Ling observed Red Guards taunting a schoolteacher whose face had been painted with chalk and ink to portray him as a "demon." The man stood silently, his head lowered and eyes closed, as the youths shouted and spat at him. On another day, Ling recounted, he watched a gang of adolescents terrorize the celebrated Guangzhou opera star Hong Xiannu, who was charged with "opposing Mao" by having performed traditional dramas. It was rumored that her own daughter was among the youths tormenting her.

Unable to swallow the shame of denunciation, or perhaps anticipating worse, numbers of Chinese committed suicide. Ling testified to having witnessed four suicides during a two-week period. One afternoon he saw a middle-aged man dressed in the tunic of a Communist Party cadre fling himself from the fourth-floor window of a downtown building. Not long afterward, he saw another man leap from the roof above the Dai Dong Restaurant facing the Pearl River. And the same day, he watched as two bodies were dragged out of the river.

Strolling the streets one morning, Ling recalled, he was stopped by Red Guards. Finally, he thought, his moment had come. But the youths were mild, and they merely demanded that he get rid of his "peppercorns," as they called his "bourgeois" pointed shoes. Without hesitation, Ling walked into the nearest shoe store and bought a round-toed "proletarian" pair. But the incident served as a warning. His only salvation, he persuaded himself, lay in flight from China.

Guangzhou, because of its proximity to capitalist Hong Kong, was filled with shady characters who managed to elude Communist controls. Through an acquaintance, Ling was introduced to a smuggler by the name of Tam who was willing for a fee to guide him to the coast opposite Macao. After arranging the escape plan, Ling contacted Lihan, the young woman painter and stage designer. He was certain, knowing her experience, that she would accompany him.

At twenty-nine, Lihan was an unusually beautiful young woman who had endured many tribulations in China. These tribulations, she frankly admitted, had been due to two errors in judgment. As a Catholic, she had made the mistake of believing the Communist claim that religious tolerance existed in China. And she had trusted friends without realizing that under duress they might have no choice but to betray her.

Born in Guangzhou, the daughter of a merchant seaman, Lihan had been a child when her family emigrated to Hong Kong. Like thousands of Chinese residing in the British colony, she had frequently returned to Guangzhou to visit relatives. But on one of these trips—it was during the hectic Great Leap Forward—she was suddenly arrested and charged with "espionage under the cloak of religion." Tried without benefit of counsel, she was sentenced to five years of "labor reform" to be served on a prison farm in the northern part of Guangdong province. In retrospect, she attributed her arrest to a conversation with four Catholic friends in Guangzhou to whom she had mentioned the names of priests she knew in Hong Kong. Their talk, however innocuous, had undoubtedly been reported to the authorities.

Presuming that "labor reform" had "remolded" her, the Religious Affairs Bureau in Guangzhou asked Lihan to serve the Party by informing on her Catholic friends. In short, her assignment to "spy under the cloak of religion" exactly matched her own indictment five years earlier. Fearing a new imprisonment if she refused, Lihan agreed. But her reports lacked substance because, she claimed, her friends were too wary to speak candidly. In the view of the Party officials, however, she was being uncooperative, and they branded her a "bad element," imposing restrictions on her activities. She could not leave home for more than four hours without police authorization, her mail was censored, she was compelled to attend special political meetings, and she could be mobilized at any time for "voluntary" manual labor. She was therefore a natural target for the Red Guards as they swept through Guangzhou in August 1966.

Unlike many of those classified as "Seven Kinds of Black," Lihan was somehow spared the indignity of being paraded through the streets wearing a dunce's cap. Instead, the Red Guards ordered her to print a sign with her name, address, and classification as a "counterrevolutionary," which she would have to hang from her neck if she left her house, and display on her door when she was at home. She was being watched, the youths told her, warning that she would be severely punished if she disobeyed them. "The first time I went out with that sign," Lihan recalled, "children surrounded me, spitting and jeering. I ran back home and stayed there. I refused to go out again, it was so terrifying."

Actually, it had been pointless for her to go into the city, since people designated as "Seven Kinds of Black" were banned from riding buses, entering restaurants, attending cinemas, and even strolling through parks. They were prohibited from making bank withdrawals—an academic rule, since their deposits had been confiscated—nor could they continue working. Lihan managed to earn some money, however, by designing toys at home. A few brave friends, Ling among them, took her designs to the toy factory and brought her food from time to time.

Day and night, Lihan recalled, her neighborhood resounded to the din of drums, gongs, and the shouts of Red Guards as they roamed the streets. She lay awake in the expectation that, any moment, the young vigilantes would break through her door. The nearest they came was an adjoining house, where they removed all the furniture except the bed, and burned every Chinese book published before 1949 as well as translations of "bourgeois" authors like Pushkin and Goethe. That close call coincided with Ling's proposal that they attempt to escape from China. Lihan accepted.

The smuggler, Tam, planned the escape carefully. He persuaded Ling and Lihan to join forces with two men, Chen and Liao, who were also seeking to flee the country. Itinerant patent-medicine peddlers who were being persecuted as "petty capitalists," Chen and Liao were familiar with the region between Guangzhou and the coast.

While Tam procured false documents to enable the party to travel beyond the Guangzhou suburbs, he sent Liao ahead to wait with food, clothes, and plastic swimming tubes at a village on their way.

At five o'clock on the morning of September 9, Tam, Chen, Ling, and Lihan boarded a bus in Guangzhou that took them to a village not far from the outskirts of the city. There they changed buses, rode to another village, again changed buses, descended at still another village—and continued in that zigzag fashion for four days, sleeping at country inns. Their object was to avoid main roads, where their papers might be examined by the authorities.

On the fifth day, they reached the rendezvous with Liao. From there they set off on foot across the terrain of barren hills toward the coast. After three days, their food ran out. Tam volunteered to find supplies in a nearby village. He never rejoined them. Whether he was captured by the police or soldiers or simply decided to abandon the group was never known. The others plodded on, surviving on sugar cane and sweet potatoes stolen at night from the fields of the few farms that dotted the desolate area. Finally, on the evening of September 19, they came within sight of the coast. It had taken them ten days to cover nearly a hundred miles. From the rocky shore they looked across to the lights of Macao, three thousand yards away. They could not risk waiting despite their fatigue. They slid into the water, clung to their plastic tubes, and paddled quietly, passing the shadows of sampans and junks riding at anchor in the bay. By morning, after eight or nine hours afloat, they had washed up onto a Macao beach. They were free. Yet their sense of accomplishment was mixed with faint abashment when they learned that more than two hundred Chinese had achieved the same feat in the preceding weeks.[35]

Those who fled were fortunate. As the Cultural Revolution intensified, the Red Guards and other radicals often resorted to brutal and primitive kinds of terror—torturing, mutilating, even crucifying Mao's real or suspected enemies, and displaying their dismembered corpses in public as a warning to alleged "reactionaries." They committed their worst atrocities in Tibet, a fervently Buddhist region they disdained as "feudal," where among other outrages they castrated monks and raped nuns. Many, youths of peasant or worker origin consumed with hatred for the educated elite, derived a perverse pleasure from venting their frustrations on the Chinese academic community. At Hunan Medical College, for example, they drove several eminent professors to suicide after denouncing their "bourgeois" tendencies. They murdered the entire senior faculty of

Zhongshan University's history department by hanging them from trees lining the campus entrance. Cadavers, victims of battles between competing Red Guard factions, often littered the grounds of Beijing University. In 1967, as the violence in Beijing reached a peak, trucks cruised the capital, collecting the dead. An American scholar who interviewed the survivors of the period quoted one as recalling: "They didn't want people to see too many bodies lying around, so they tried to pick them up as soon as possible. The crematorium was so busy they had to stack the bodies like bricks, all around outside the crematorium, waiting to be burned."[36]

Persecuted, ostracized, and desperately lonely, men and women often found solace in illicit love, which caused the birthrate to rise sharply during the Cultural Revolution. Furtive affairs could be conducted with relative ease in rural areas, where intellectuals accused of "counterrevolutionary" activities were compelled to perform humiliating peasant jobs, such as cleaning pigpens or accumulating night soil. They avoided detection by slipping into the woods, and cadres frequently showed indulgence toward those who were caught. By contrast, it was difficult to disappear in the crowded cities, as evidenced by the case of Yang Yiren and Lin Xiaohe, teachers who had incurred the wrath of the radicals and were assigned to weed the school grounds as penance. Their respective spouses, also under suspicion, had been sent to the countryside, and Yang and Lin comforted each other as they worked side by side. Soon they were in love, which they consummated in Yang's apartment. They were discovered there one night by the Red Guards and charged with adultery. Their punishment was medieval. They were paraded stark naked through the streets as jeering crowds spit at them, then released. Lin went home and promptly hanged herself. The Red Guards, as an admonition to others, exhibited her body for four days in front of her house.[37]

Special targets of the Red Guards during the early days of the upheaval were Chinese who had been educated in the West. Many were apolitical technocrats who, out of loyalty to China, had cooperated with the Communists, and some had risen to key positions before the Cultural Revolution. In the eyes of the radical Maoists, however, they represented the remnants of the bourgeoisie and, as such, were beyond redemption. The case of Nien Cheng illustrated the plight of thousands who belonged to a world that Mao hoped to destroy. She survived to write *Life and Death in Shanghai*, an account of her experience—and probably the most poignant personal chronicle to emerge from the Cultural Revolution.

Brilliant and sensitive, Cheng was born into a sophisticated family that believed in the education of women—a rare attitude in China at the time. She was sent to school in England, where, in 1935, she met her future husband, who was also studying there. Devoted to his country, he elected to serve Chiang Kai-shek's Nationalist government during China's war against Japan. He was working for the regime in Shanghai in 1949, when the Communists marched into the city, and the same sense of patriotism inspired him to offer them his services. They made him an adviser to Chen Yi, the new Communist mayor, a skilled military commander whose Third Field Army had captured the city. One of Zhou Enlai's protégés, Chen later became China's Foreign Minister.

Then eager to cement trade relations with the West, the Communists urged selected foreign firms to remain in China. They encouraged Cheng's husband to accept an appointment as manager of the Shell Oil Company's Shanghai office. The first Chinese ever elevated to that rank in a Western company in China, he mainly acted as intermediary between the Communist government and Shell's directors in London. The Chengs, classified as "national capitalists," were permitted to live in comfort. Their house in Shanghai, staffed by a legion of servants, featured among its furnishings a priceless collection of antique porcelains, and they were also allowed to maintain bank deposits and other investments abroad. They were not alone in their enjoyment of such privileges. Some ninety thousand "national capitalists" resided in Shanghai in relative luxury, drawing 5 per cent a year tax-exempt interest from bonds given them in compensation for confiscated factories and other enterprises. Many held official jobs that employed their special talents. One, Rong Yiren, received an annual income of more than 2 million *yuan*, the rough equivalent of $1 million, as an indemnity for six textile mills that the Communists had nationalized. He contributed his skills to the regime, serving as Vice-Minister of Textile Industry and as deputy mayor of Shanghai, a largely honorary position designed by the Communists to reassure others of his class that they were secure.[38] Like the Chengs, he felt that he could count on the Communist hierarchy for protection—at least until the Cultural Revolution.

In 1957, Nien Cheng's husband died of cancer, and a British manager replaced him. Shell invited her to become his assistant, a job that involved settling the thorny problems that faced a foreign firm functioning in a Communist state. She was shrewd and dynamic, and her contacts within the Party bureaucracy also made her invaluable. Besides, as she later wrote, she "enjoyed the distinction of being the only woman in Shanghai occupying a senior position in a company of world renown." As the Cultural Revolution began to gather momentum in early 1966, however, the Communists ordered Shell to close its Shanghai office. Cheng, now unemployed, contemplated going to Hong Kong to escape the turmoil. But she was reluctant to leave her daughter, Meiping, a young movie actress. So she stayed in Shanghai—confident, as she subsequently put it, that the Cultural Revolution "would last no longer than a year, the usual length of time for a political campaign."[39] It was a grievous miscalculation.

No sooner did Mao launch the Cultural Revolution than local Communist officials sought under questioning to make Cheng reveal that the Shell office in Shanghai had been a nest of British spies. She resisted. In August 1966, Red Guards broke into her house and, screaming revolutionary slogans, smashed her antiques. They finally threw her into solitary confinement, where she was to suffer for more than six years from heat, cold, disease, isolation, and beatings as interrogators relentlessly pressed her to confess. Then in her fifties, she was not physically strong, but still she refused to accommodate them. For she perceived that she was an expendable pawn in a larger game, and that her inquisitors were merely obeying orders. They hoped to wrench from her an admission of Shell's alleged espionage activities that their bosses in Beijing could turn against Zhou Enlai, Chen Yi, and their moderate associates, who had originally authorized Western companies to operate in China. Once they had extracted that evidence, her life would be worthless. In short, they were pursuing a classic Chinese tactic: "Kill the chicken to get the monkey." So, Cheng realized, her only salvation lay in refuting the charge, which she repeatedly did, despite her agony.

Ultimately, she endured and was "rehabilitated" by the Chinese leaders who, following Mao's death, were attempting to atone for the excesses of the Cultural Revolution. They allowed her to leave China and, in 1980, she emigrated to the United States, where the account of her torment became an immediate bestseller, winning her widespread acclaim from an American public that, by then, was just beginning to grasp the extent of the upheaval that had devastated China. Indeed, not since Pearl Buck's novels depicting the ordeals of Chinese peasants during the 1930s had any book on China captured such attention. But Cheng continued to be haunted by the death of her daughter, who had either been murdered or compelled to commit suicide under circumstances that were never fully clarified. And, in that regard, her experience matched that of millions of Chinese, for whom the Cultural Revolution was a holocaust.

Squandering their passions in facile assaults against symbols of the past, the Red Guards were missing the primary objective of the Cultural Revolution—to topple Mao's adversaries in the entrenched Communist Party bureaucracy. In a series of fresh exhortations at the end of August, therefore, Maoist spokesmen urged the youths to direct their attacks squarely against the Party *apparatchiks*. Speaking to a half-million young activists at Mao's second rally in Beijing on August 31, Lin Biao congratulated them for "washing away all the sludge and filth left over from the old society." But, he reminded them, their principal target should be the "bourgeois" and "revisionist" leaders who "have wormed their way into the Party. . . . It is essential to hold fast to this main orientation."[40] In another Beijing demonstration, two weeks later, Lin again stressed the need to strike at the Party. Mao's call issued in early August to "bombard the headquarters," Lin explained, meant: "Bombard the handful of persons in power who are taking the capitalist road."[41]

These appeals served to animate radicals in the provinces who were beginning to realize that their Party leaders had grabbed control of the Cultural Revolution in order to protect their own authority. Fire was now focused against regional Party machines that had hitherto managed to elude attack. In the meantime, the Maoist message to intensify the drive against the Party was being carried across the country by thousands of Red Guards from Beijing, who streamed into China's cities with instructions to organize and direct local youth movements.

Party organs in different parts of China reacted in various ways to deflect the Maoist offensive. In several places they again resorted to their old tactic of sacrificing expendable officials. In the Manchurian industrial city of Changchun, for example, the Party Committee dismissed Song Zhenting, its Director of Propaganda, staging an elaborate meeting to vilify him as a "counterrevolutionary opportunist" who had "opposed the red flag while pretending to hold it aloft."[42] Another official thrown to the radicals by his Party comrades was Peng Xiaoqian, vice-governor of Henan province, who was described as an "out-and-out reactionary landlord-class element."[43] Party operatives engaged in similar maneuvers in other provinces, but in still other areas, Party bosses openly resisted the Maoists by forming rival Red Guard contingents and by mobilizing workers, peasants, and even soldiers to fight the radicals.

One of the most formidable foes of Mao's campaign at the time was the Party boss of southwestern Sichuan and its surrounding provinces, Li Jingquan, who derived his considerable political strength from connections in Beijing as well as from the singularity of the area under his supervision. A bald, bespectacled man who looked as benign as a middle-class merchant, Li traced his revolutionary experience back to the 1920s, when he joined the Communist movement as a student at the Peasant Training Institute run by Mao in Guangzhou. Years later, after surviving the celebrated Long March, he emerged as a political commissar in General He Long's 120th Division of the Eighth Route Army. In addition to cementing a solid professional relationship, the two Communist veterans became brothers-in-law through marriage to sisters, and He Long's rise as a dynamic military figure in Beijing gave Li vital protection in the capital. Meanwhile, another of Li's important patrons was Deng Xiaoping, the Party Secretary General. Deng, who wielded enormous influence in his native Sichuan, had been instrumental in appointing Li to the post of the provincial Communist chief. By the early 1960s, then, Li was a powerful wheel in the Party machinery. As potentate of Sichuan, he ruled a province that was rich, populous, isolated, and particular enough to have existed as a separate nation. And he not only belonged to the Politburo in Beijing, but directed the Party's Southwest Regional Bureau, which controlled Guizhou, Yunnan, and Tibet along with Sichuan.

With nearly 80 million people in the mid-1960s, Sichuan was exceeded in population by only seven nations in the world. It had long been China's leading grain producer, normally exporting some 2 million tons of rice to poorer provinces. Not only was Sichuan self-sufficient, but its defensive wall of mountains had traditionally made it an almost impregnable fortress. Rebels against imperial authority in ancient times frequently built their bases in Sichuan, and the province had been the site of Chiang Kai-shek's capital during World War II. Under Li Jingquan, the Maoists now claimed, Sichuan had become an "independent kingdom"—and that allegation was not wholly inaccurate.

But despite his power and autonomy, Li Jingquan was still an integral part of the national system. The days of the warlords were finished, and he could not secede from the People's Republic when he perceived the Cultural Revolution threatening his position. Like other Party *apparatchiks* elsewhere, moreover, he could not predict the scope and intensity of Mao's campaign. To defend himself and his comrades, Li resorted to the same subtle, complicated maneuvers being used by other regional Party figures at this juncture.

As early as the spring of 1966, when the Cultural Revolution was gathering steam, Li Jingquan had jettisoned a few subordinates in an effort to create the illusion that he dutifully subscribed to Mao's drive. Newspapers in Sichuan assailed obscure literary and propaganda functionaries in order to deflect radical attacks against more prominent Party officials. Li also sent some two thousand Party Work Team cadres into the universities, colleges, and high schools to keep students under control. In late July, when Mao decreed that the Teams be withdrawn from educational institutions, Li ignored his directive on the grounds that the situation in Sichuan was unique.[44]

Late in August, when Red Guards from Beijing arrived in the cities of southwestern China to urge local youths to challenge the Party's authority, Li reportedly condemned their activities as "another Hungarian uprising." He instructed Party committees throughout the region to counter the Beijing youths and their provincial allies by forming their own movements. One such movement, composed mainly of workers, was called the Industrial Workers Combat Corps. Another, made up of students at Chongqing University, gave itself the romantic label of Spring Thunder.[45] Li allegedly financed these movements with Party funds, arguing that "it is impossible not to spend some money for such a great campaign."[46] He also infiltrated his own agents in the leftist Red Guard organizations. And, as the Army's senior political commissar in the region, he enlisted the aid of the area commander, General Huang Xingding, to restrain the radicals. Huang and other military spokesmen addressed a meeting of more than three thousand Red Guards in the middle of September, exhorting them to "defend the interests of the Party and the state" by displaying a "high sense of discipline."[47] Meanwhile, sensitive to charges that he was suppressing the Maoist drive, Li ordered local officials to make ambiguous public confessions calculated to appease the radicals. He even appeared himself at a rally in the Sichuan capital of Chengdu, admitting to the crowd that he intended to repent his "errors."

Though Li had managed to navigate skillfully, the radical pressures gradually rose against him. While the Cultural Revolution was far from being a simple conflict among personalities, individuals often played important roles in the shaping of major events, and to a large extent this was true in Sichuan. The thrust against Li was propelled by a pair of relentless radicals called Liu Jieting and his wife, Zhang Xiting. Former district Party officials in Ibin, a city in the southern part of the province, Liu and Zhang claimed to have been suspended from their posts and later jailed for trying to criticize Li Jingquan's "revisionist" policies in the early 1960s. When they persisted, the couple alleged, Li had them expelled from the Party.

Like many minor officials with grievances against their superiors, Liu and his wife saw the Cultural Revolution as the chance to take revenge. Amassing a pile of documents indicting Li, they went to Beijing to present their case to the Maoist leaders. After a month of fruitless lobbying, they finally gained access to Wang Li, a member of the Cultural Revolution Directorate. The material against Li Jingquan, he apparently perceived, could be used in the struggle against the Party bureaucracy.[48] But the effort to oust Li would not be easy.

The strife in Sichuan ultimately reached such proportions that, after much deliberation by the Maoist leadership, a military commander was assigned to the province to restore law and order. In the fall, however, Li Jingquan's tactic of turning the workers against intruding Red Guards was being used by Party *apparatchiks* all over China. This maneuver, known to Maoists as "hoodwinking the masses," led to widespread clashes that took a serious toll on China's economic production.

In the Shandong province city of Qingdao, for instance, at least two large skirmishes between Red Guards and Party-backed workers erupted within a week. The first occurred on August 16, when some four thousand workers battled students who had gathered to denounce a local Party cadre. Some days later, forty thousand workers and government employees were deployed in a demonstration in which more than a hundred Red Guards were reportedly injured. Another fight broke out in early September in the northern city of Shenyang, at the Anshan Iron and Steel Works, one of China's biggest industrial complexes, when Red Guards attempted to enter the plant to proselytize among workers. According to several accounts, troops were finally brought into the factory to quell the disturbance. About the same time, Red Guard and worker factions rioted in Guangzhou when radical youths from Beijing tried to pull down a bronze statue of Sun Yat-sen, celebrated in Guangzhou not only as the founder of the first

Chinese Republic but as a native of Guangdong province.[49] Red Guards from Beijing also met resistance in Xinjiang, where General Wang Enmao, who served as both Party boss and military commander, mobilized workers and troops to oppose them. One of General Wang's organizations, the August First Field Army Dedicated to Defend the Thought of Mao Zedong to the Death, was believed to harbor former Nationalist soldiers taken prisoner during the civil war and exiled as laborers to the remote frontier zone.[50]

In mid-September, recalling that the Sixteen Point Decision issued on August 8 had proscribed attempts to "incite the masses to struggle against each other," the *People's Daily* pointed out that the directive was being "openly defied" by "responsible persons in some localities and units" who had "created various pretexts to suppress the mass movement . . . and even provoked a number of workers and peasants . . . to oppose and antagonize the revolutionary students."[51] But all these incidents, though unprecedented in China since the Communists had established their regime, were mild compared to what would grip the country in the months ahead.

Amid the ferment, however, there were signs that the Beijing leaders then propelling the Cultural Revolution were at odds over how far and how fast to push the campaign. On one hand, Mao and his inner circle—including Lin Biao, Chen Boda, Jiang Qing, and others—realized that the Cultural Revolution would lose momentum unless they persisted in stimulating the Red Guards. Thus they continued to bring young people to massive rallies in the capital. But Zhou Enlai and his government associates as well as some military professionals seemed to fear that unrestrained turbulence would weaken China's economic and social stability and tried to keep the drive under control.

Heralded as the "great exchange of revolutionary experiences," Mao's reiterated call to Red Guards to visit Beijing and other parts of China was eagerly greeted by young Chinese as a chance to travel beyond the narrow confines of their homes for the first time in their lives. Millions of young people therefore shunted around all over China from the middle of August through the end of November in one of the greatest human movements in history. The sheer weight of numbers placed an enormous burden on the fragile Chinese railway system, yet the regime's capacity to handle these multitudes was testimony to its organizational ability—at least within a short span of time.

The former Red Guard Dai Xiaoai later recalled that he and his comrades felt, as they embarked for Beijing in late September, that they were escaping into an exhilarating "atmosphere of freedom." As they jammed into the train for the journey to Beijing, none of the members of his Red Guard unit viewed the trip as a political exercise. One boy hoped that they might see snow in the north, another looked forward to eating Pekinese food, and a third remarked exultantly that he never imagined that he would travel across the country "without spending a cent."[52]

Arriving in the capital after forty-eight hours in a crowded train compartment, Dai and his comrades were taken by bus to a room in the First Ministry of Machine Building. There, they were shown their sleeping quarters—bamboo mats spread on a layer of straw. There, too, a Ministry employee was assigned to rehearse them for their performance in the parade to be staged on October 1, the anniversary of the founding of the Chinese People's Republic. The boys were instructed to march in columns of fifteen, some carrying Mao's *Quotations* and others displaying placards emblazoned with the Chairman's sayings. The rehearsals went on until the afternoon before the rally. The youths then slept for five or six hours, awakening at eleven o'clock that night. Each was given a small string bag with a couple of slices of steamed bread, a few pieces of fruit, and three hard-boiled eggs for the next day. Some boys ate the eggs immediately. At midnight, they started out to walk across the city to take their assigned places for the morrow's demonstration.

Soldiers were everywhere, directing Red Guards to their spots in the parade, which was scheduled to move from west to east through Tiananmen Square. As his unit marched to its position, Dai recalled, thousands of young people were in the streets, many of them running about and shouting hysterically. Some had accidentally strayed from their groups. Others, having slipped away in the darkness to relieve themselves at makeshift latrines, were desperately searching for their units. Those who had reached their places after hours of walking were so tired that they spread out newspapers and slept on the cold pavement, awakening to find their clothes damp with dew. As southern rice eaters, Dai and his comrades were unable to swallow their bread, which had hardened into inedible lumps. Hungry, thirsty, and exhausted, they waited, some singing songs to keep up their spirits. Finally, at ten o'clock, the revolutionary anthem "The East Is Red" blared through the loudspeakers, followed by rhythmic chants of "Long Live Chairman Mao." The rally had begun.

For an hour before the procession got under way, the speeches of the Communist leaders boomed through loudspeakers located around the city. Dai observed that most of his comrades as well as other Red Guards were inattentive to the oratory. Some caught up on their sleep, others played games, and a few wandered around chatting with friends. Dai was impressed by Zhou Enlai's eloquence, but neither he nor his comrades could understand Lin Biao. His voice was weak and hesitant, and his accent incomprehensible to them. "If his speech had not been published in the newspaper the next day, we never would have known what he said. We wondered why the Great Commander had chosen this kind of successor. Could Lin Biao really lead the Chinese revolution and the world revolution?"

Despite these misgivings, the Guangzhou Red Guards were impassioned as they paraded quickly past the array of Chinese leaders reviewing them from the gallery of the Tiananmen Gate. Many of them wept at seeing Mao and, Dai recalled, they later recorded in their "little red books" the exact time that they had sighted him— 12:45 P.M.

Like millions of other Chinese youths, Dai and his comrades had been thrilled by the excitement of travel across China, and not long after returning to Guangzhou, they embarked again on a trip to "exchange revolutionary experiences." By this time, however, hordes of Red Guards were wandering around the country. Railway stations were shaking with turbulence as different groups fought for trains, and departures were postponed for hours as the authorities tried to control the mobs. One night, a Japanese visitor boarded a northbound train at Guangzhou's East Station, took a comfortable berth reserved for foreigners, and went to sleep. When he awoke next morning, the train was still in the station—delayed by the turmoil.[53]

The chaos on the railroads often left Red Guards stranded in faraway places that lacked the facilities to lodge and feed them. En route home after revisiting Beijing in early November, for example, Dai and his comrades stopped for a few days at the northern port city of Tianjin. They and hundreds of other Red Guards there discovered as they decided to leave, however, that no passenger trains originated in Tianjin. They would have to find places on trains, already packed, passing through from Beijing. Many of the people crowded into the Tianjin station had been waiting there for days—tired, hungry, dispirited. Dai and his friends eventually managed to board a train by smashing the glass of a coach door. Inside the coach, youths battled for space, cursing each other in a babel of dialects.

As they crisscrossed the country, the Red Guards rapidly learned how to survive without funds. They ate in restaurants, confessing to the manager afterward that they could not pay and offering to sign the bill. They applied to the authorities for "cost-of-living supplements," padding the rosters of their units with fictitious names in order to collect extra sums. In some cities, the Red Guards extorted money from officals by threatening to denounce them as "reactionaries" or "counterrevolutionaries," or even menacing them with physical violence.[54] Years later, when discipline had largely been restored to China, many Red Guards were held accountable for the debts they had incurred on these "exchanges of revolutionary experiences." Many were also tried and convicted for robbery, extortion, and other crimes committed at the time. The later crackdowns, mainly carried out by the Army, served to indicate that the Chinese bureaucracy must have continued to function at least partially despite the widespread confusion in the land during the autumn of 1966.[55]

It had already been evident, of course, that the Cultural Revolution threatened severe strains for the Chinese economy. In particular the movements of millions of Red Guards around the country was plainly bogging down China's feeble rail network. As early as mid-September, before the Red Guard tourists were out in full flourish, Zhou Enlai disclosed that domestic transport of freight had declined by 10 per cent and that this was having a "tremendous impact" on China's foreign trade. Communications among various provinces had been impaired, and construction projects were being adversely affected, he also revealed.[56] The mobilization of state employees as guides for the Red Guards was also interfering with normal government functions. Industrial operations were being hampered by the skirmishes between radical youths and workers, and there was a danger that the Red Guards might carry the Cultural Revolution into the villages and disrupt agriculture as well.

No leader in Beijing labored so strenuously during that period to keep the Cultural Revolution on an even keel as Zhou Enlai. Despite his age—he was then approaching seventy—his energy was prodigious. In addition to formulating economic and foreign policy, directing the country's bureaucracy, and attending banquets and other ceremonies, he spent several nights a week with Red Guard groups, frequently staying up until dawn in efforts to convince them to restrain themselves.

Zhou was not an opponent of the Cultural Revolution. On the contrary, he fully favored Mao's offensive. But he believed that a victory for the Maoist cause would be hollow if China's basic stability were undermined in the process. Thus he endeavored to keep the drive sane and rational, and in his directives, speeches, and talks with Red Guards he repeatedly stressed the same themes. He advised the youths to organize their units along tighter lines, largely in order to make them easier to control. He urged them to rely on persuasion rather than force, pointing out that coercion would alienate segments of the population who could otherwise be won over. And he constantly emphasized the need to maintain industrial and agricultural production, without which China would face famine and a weakened defense establishment.[57]

On the subject of organization, for example, Zhou admonished the Red Guards for having "sprung up like dandelions on a spring lawn." The units were not "compact" enough, he said, and required "strict" cohesion if they were to function as a "reserve" of the Army. It was essential that the wild assortment of Red Guard factions be shaped into a entity that could be managed. Accordingly, he called on the youths to "amalgamate" their different groups in order to achieve unity.[58] "We cannot suppress the student movement," he said, "but it must definitely be centralized."[59]

Zhou also criticized the Red Guards for judging people according to "family lineage" and explained that "class analysis" was a complicated and difficult business. His own background was "feudal," and his father had been a minor magistrate who had certainly indulged in corruption. But redemption was possible, Zhou asserted, if "one's objective acts are good and one has rebelled against his original class."[60] He also counseled the youths to exercise caution in their assaults against alleged "class enemies," pointing out that "bourgeois" revolutionaries like Madame Sun Yat-sen deserved "respect" for having collaborated with the Communists against Chiang Kai-shek, her brother-in-law. And it was important, Zhou insisted, to distinguish between those "bourgeois elements" who were "making trouble" and those who were "law-abiding." Peaceable citizens should not be molested, irrespective of their political coloration. "Civilized" criticism in wall posters was acceptable, but "we need not pull [these people] down and confiscate their property."[61] Activities such as those of the Shanghai radicals who forced ten thousand "capitalists" to face their critics in a public demonstration were tarnishing China's image in the eyes of "world opinion," Zhou argued, adding:

Our country is strong enough to render such conduct unnecessary. Capitalists should not be dragged out to be paraded around. If we do that, the foreign news media will clamor that Chairman Mao has changed his policy, and that capitalists are to be liquidated physically. Classes are to be eliminated, but people are not to be killed.[62]

Upbraiding young "hooligans" among the Red Guards who were committing murder in the name of the revolution, Zhou repeatedly emphasized that violence was not only illegal but ineffective as a weapon for transforming ideological attitudes.

We all know that it is not difficult to kill a man with a gun—all that is necessary is to aim accurately. It is also not difficult to bruise a man with fists—all that is needed is brute strength. . . . But struggle by violent means merely touches people's flesh. Only struggle through reason can reach their souls.[63]

Above all, Zhou tried to prevent the disruption of the economy. He instructed the Red Guards to refrain from attacking government ministries, for they had "work to do."[64] He also issued several directives ordering the young people to cease their nationwide train trips, exhorting them instead to emulate the Communists' celebrated Long March of the mid-1930s by traveling on foot.[65] And he repeatedly denounced the Red Guards for intruding into factories and farm villages. "The Cultural Revolution should be conducted only in middle-sized and large cities. . . . Industry and agriculture cannot take a vacation in order to stage revolution. . . . Production and the service trades cannot be suspended. Otherwise, what shall we eat?"[66]

These admonitions were echoed by Zhou's government associates as well as in the official Chinese press and even in certain Red Guard newspapers. For example, Foreign Minister Chen Yi advised the Red Guards to behave "carefully" at the National Day celebrations on October 1, lest they trouble foreign guests and discredit China.[67] About the same time, a Beijing directive disclosed that unruly youths were stealing "codes, files, and secret materials" from government and Party bureaus and warned that such felonies would be punished by law.[68] Newspapers were filled with appeals to the Red Guards to temper their excesses. *Red Flag* called on the "revolutionary young fighters" to restrain their "conceit and rashness" by adopting as their code the "three-eight" credo of the Chinese Army, conceived by Mao during the 1930s to discipline his peasant soldiers.[69] In a similar effort, a New China News Agency feature article described "model" youths who, like boy scouts, courteously helped old ladies to cross the street.[70] One Red Guard newspaper, possibly representing a conservative faction, published an unusual exclamation: "Insist on moderation."[71]

But for all his enormous energy and diplomatic skill, Zhou Enlai was unable to hold back the storm. The Red Guards continued to invade government offices, break into factories, injure and sometimes kill their adversaries, and fight among themselves. They even launched verbal attacks against Zhou himself, criticizing his "family lineage," assailing his speeches as "poisonous weeds," and forcing him on more than one occasion to deny charges that he was "counterrevolutionary."[72] In order to survive, Zhou was compelled to shift to the left. By late November, he had surrendered to the radicals— at least for the moment. This was reflected in almost obsequious praise for Mao's wife, Jiang Qing, whose power was then rising sharply, and in a remarkable admission he made to a group of Japanese visitors to Beijing at the time. An individual's personal opinions should "advance or retreat" according to the will of the majority, Zhou explained, making it plain that he had no choice but to accommodate to the Maoist view.[73] In addition, Zhou like everyone else sought to protect himself and his more important colleagues by sacrificing lesser subordinates. Early in December, he authorized a rally to denounce Liao Chengzhi, a key figure in Sino-Japanese relations, who had angered the Red Guards. Zhou also allowed the Red Guards to stage a demonstration against Rong Gaotang, a Vice-Chairman of the State Physical Culture Commission.[74] It became apparent afterward, however, that Zhou's main motive in maneuvering as he did was to preserve his authority for a more propitious period. Faithful to Mao's guerrilla tactics, he was retreating in the hope of improving his position for a counteroffensive.

The decision to accelerate the Cultural Revolution during the autumn of 1966 was essentially inspired by Mao. He was not blind to the turmoil he had created. Yet he seemed to believe, even though he regretted the damage, that there was no turning back from the course he had charted. At a private meeting of the Party's Central Committee in Beijing late in October, he reviewed the situation with extraordinary candor.[75]

"Something disastrously wrong was done by me," Mao confessed: he had blundered in the early stages of the Cultural Revolution by approving the radical attacks against the Beijing University authorities in May and by publicizing his own exhortation to the Red Guards to "bombard" the Party apparatus two months later. After that, Mao said, the upheaval erupted so rapidly "as to surprise me." He had thus miscalculated in failing to anticipate that the "violent impact" of his gestures would "stir up the whole country" to such an extent. "I myself caused this trouble," he told the senior Communist officials at the meeting, "and I cannot blame you if you have complaints against me."

But errors were inevitable, Mao went on. "Many mistakes were made and many people died" during the twenty-eight years it took for the Communist Party to come to power. The Cultural Revolution was then only in its fifth month. "Experience can be gained only after at least five years," he explained.

In part, Mao said, the present difficulties were the result of his decision years earlier to relinquish authority to his comrades. His health had been poor, and he had learned a lesson from events in the Soviet Union, where Stalin had not properly prepared for his succession. So, Mao explained, he had retreated to the "second line" in order to permit his potential heirs to gain experience. "I wanted to have their prestige established before I died," he said. "But I didn't expect that things would turn out the other way."

What happened, Mao contended, was that his subordinates split into factions, setting up "independent kingdoms" and never discussing problems within the Central Committee. Even worse, they neglected him. The most independent of them all, Mao alleged, was Deng Xiaoping, the Party Secretary General. "He is deaf, but at meetings he would sit far away from me," Mao claimed. "He has not reported to me about his work since 1959."

Now the time had come to put the Cultural Revolution back on the track—meaning that the Party *apparatchiks* could save themselves by criticizing their errors, correcting their mistakes, and transforming their attitudes to conform to the Maoist canon. In short, Mao would give them the chance to capitulate peacefully. In that way, he promised, "all will go well again." But there was the hint of a threat. "Who wants to strike you down?" he said. "I, for one, do not want to strike you down, and I don't think the Red Guards want to strike you down either."

Liu Shaoqi appeared to accept Mao's offer by making a ritualistic confession of his mistakes.[76] He blamed other Party figures for having led him astray and tried to define his own blunders as faults that could be "rectified" rather than as hostile acts against Mao that would earn him condemnation as a heretic. It was an abject—and, as it turned out, futile—performance.

Reaching back to 1946, Liu allowed that he had believed in the "illusion of peace" between the Communists and Nationalists. He also conceded to charges that he had protected "bourgeois industries and commerce" as well as "urban feudal leaders" in the days after the Communist victory. In addition, Liu said, he had wrongly resisted Mao's agricultural collectivization programs in the mid-1950s. Following the collapse of the Great Leap Forward, he went on, he had erroneously favored moderate economic policies. In these and other deviations from the Maoist truth, he had made the mistake of having placed "too much confidence" in Chen Yun, the liberal economic planner, and had been misguided by Deng Xiaoping.

During the opening phases of the Cultural Revolution, Liu also confessed, he had "sanctioned the wrong decisions of others and made erroneous decisions myself" in having permitted the Party Work Teams in the universities to "suppress the masses." This mistake, he said, was shared by his wife, Wang Guangmei, who had belonged to the Team at Qinghua University in Beijing. He had failed to appreciate that the Cultural Revolution "marked a new stage of more intensive and extensive development in the socialist revolution" and, consequently, he had "distrusted the masses." He had erred because he had not learned to "grasp Chairman Mao's thought."

Liu therefore bowed to Mao's decision to downgrade him in favor of Lin Biao, whom he described as "better than I in every respect." Henceforth, he vowed, he would assiduously study Mao's "thought" and work "in the interest of the Party and the people."

If Liu had expected this self-abasing effort to gain him redemption, he miscalculated. For Mao's conciliatory invitation to his Party foes to air their errors had been a maneuver designed to achieve a triple purpose. First, it was aimed at isolating the "handful" of important Party leaders who had "put forward the wrong line," like Liu and Deng, from the larger number of cadres who could be "rehabilitated" if they corrected their mistakes. Second, it was contrived to stimulate internecine squabbling among the senior Party figures as they sought to salvage their positions. Finally, by inducing Liu and others to confess, Mao was able to expose them to further attack. Far from winning acquittal for his admissions, Liu soon found himself assailed more stridently than ever.

Lin Biao delivered the first major broadside against Liu. At the same Party meeting, Lin depicted the Cultural Revolution as a "fierce struggle between the proletariat and the bourgeoisie," in which Liu and Deng Xiaoping represented the "policy that suppresses the masses and opposes revolution." As far back as 1959, Lin alleged, Liu and Deng had plotted to "shelve" Mao and take control of the Party, and now they sought to "sabotage" the Cultural Revolution. The success of Mao's campaign, Lin indicated, depended upon their elimination.[77]

The indictment of the two senior Party leaders was endorsed by Chen Boda, Mao's ideological adviser and the head of the Cultural Revolution Directorate. He charged Liu and Deng with having attempted to "revise" the Maoist canon, asserting that they had "terrorized" Red Guards and other radical activists dedicated to the Chairman's cause. Chen reserved his angriest invective for Deng, denouncing him as an arrogant individual who "relied on his brilliance and considered himself a born encyclopedia." Discussing a question with Deng was "more difficult than climbing a mountain," Chen said. And, he declared, nothing less than the ouster of Liu and Deng would prevent China from sinking into "revisionism." "There will be a settling of accounts," he warned. "We are old, and it is important that we do this while we are still alive."[78]

These attacks against Liu Shaoqi and Deng Xiaoping were quickly publicized in Beijing and elsewhere around China through the medium of the Red Guard press, and they served to signal to the radicals that Mao was as determined as ever to propel the Cultural Revolution forward. Maoist rhetoric took on a renewed tone of brutality. At a rally in Beijing, for example, the radical Shanghai literary critic Yao Wenyuan called for the ouster of all suspected adversaries of the Cultural Revolution. Borrowing a harsh image from Lu Xun, a celebrated leftist Chinese writer of the 1930s, Yao urged Mao's followers to "beat the wild dog to death," for there could be no compromise in the drive to "overthrow the reactionary state power of the landlords and the bourgeoisie."[79] In a similar vein, a Red Guard faction in Beijing vowed to "make the air thick with the pungent smell of gunpowder . . . turn the old world upside down, smash it to pieces, create chaos, and make a tremendous mess—and the bigger the better!"[80] Exhortations of this kind were matched by the increasing prominence of Mao's wife, Jiang Qing. Besides appearing more frequently to whip up radical enthusiasm, she was promoted in late November to the post of "cultural adviser" to the Army, thus indicating that the Maoists were seeking to dominate the Chinese military establishment more fully.[81]

At the same time, in an address to Red Guards in the capital, Lin Biao put forth a new and explosive phrase that augured further tremors. Reviving the "principles" of the Paris Commune of 1871, which Mao had often cited as a model of proletarian egalitarianism, Lin announced the inauguration of "extensive democracy." From now on, the "broad masses" would be unleashed to "criticize and supervise the Party and government, leading institutions, and leaders at all levels." Nobody, with the presumed exception of Mao and his inner circle, would be immune to assault.[82] In effect, "extensive democracy" signified potential anarchy.

Throughout November and December, Red Guard and other activist groups ran rampant in their offensives against the authorities— and against each other. On November 10, more than two thousand Shanghai industrial workers, dissatisfied with the municipal administration, descended on the city's railway station, hijacked a train, and set off for Beijing to present their case to Mao, thereby snarling up traffic along the China coast.[83] In Guangzhou, resentful at having been deprived of opportunities to go around the country "exchanging revolutionary experiences," workers rioted against the factory management.[84] Paradoxically, the Maoist decision to encourage the "broad masses" to attack Party and government leaders had infuriated many radicals who had wanted the Red Guard movement restricted to youths whose origins were "truly" proletarian. In several places, the ultraleftists formed their own factions. Some radical units in Guangzhou felt so betrayed by what they considered to be a dilution of the ranks of the "revolutionary rebels" that, in one demonstration, they even threw stones at portraits of Chen Boda and Jiang Qing.[85] At least one major Red Guard group later turned against Mao himself on the grounds that he "sold out" the revolution.

Meanwhile, the open season on criticism announced by Lin Biao produced unbridled denunciations of the highest central government officials. A partial list of Beijing officials to incur the Red Guards' wrath, compiled by Western analysts in Hong Kong in late November, included five Vice-Premiers, seven Ministers, eleven Deputy Ministers, the Chief Justice of the Supreme Court, and four senior military members of the National Defense Council in addition to hundreds of lesser functionaries.[86] Not all those who drew fire were dismissed. Even though Zhou Enlai was compelled to oust some of his associates, he managed to defend colleagues like Li Xiannian, Minister of Finance; Li Fuchun, Chairman of the State Planning Commission; and Foreign Minister Chen Yi.

But one figure who did not survive was Tao Zhu. He had soared meteorically from Communist boss of south China to become the Party's propaganda chief—and then fell as rapidly.

Born in Hunan, like so many other Chinese leaders, Tao Zhu had served prior to 1949 as an Army political commissar in south China, gradually building up his authority and prestige in that area after the Communist victory. In 1961, when the Party reorganized its regional structure, he was appointed to head the Central-South Bureau, which controlled the vital corridor reaching from Henan province down through Hubei and Hunan to Guangdong and Guangxi. This appointment made him, along with such figures as Li Jingquan of the Southwest Bureau, one of the most powerful Communists outside Beijing. From all accounts, Tao Zhu was a vigorous, intelligent man, fundamentally faithful to the Party machine rather than to the cult of Mao's personality. He had undoubtedly shared the Party's disenchantment with the Chairman's economic policies following the Great Leap Forward, possibly feeling as well that the glorification of Mao had reached ridiculous proportions. He was later alleged to have slandered Mao by remarking that "the sun also has black spots."[87]

Therefore, though his phenomenal elevation in early 1966 seemed to observers at the time to mark him as one of Mao's loyal disciples, Tao Zhu probably owed his promotion more to his fidelity to the Party. For Liu Shaoqi and Deng Xiaoping were then very much in command of Party affairs. By the end of the year, however, Tao Zhu could no longer stand by Liu and Deng without drawing fire against himself. Thus he ostensibly sided with the Maoists, joined in the chorus denouncing the two Party leaders for having "distorted Chairman Mao's policies," and pursued a "bourgeois reactionary line."[88]

Tao Zhu's main aim was, it seemed, to defend his own Party subordinates in the south, upon whom he relied for his power. But that tactic proved to be his undoing. In late December, he was accused of having "stretched out his protective wings" to prevent the radicals from undermining his regional apparatus.[89] Soon afterward, according to reports from Beijing, he was paraded through the streets of the capital by Red Guards cursing his name.[90]

The downfall of Tao Zhu and the regional leaders he had tried to defend meant that the Maoists, having been largely repulsed in their earlier attempts to topple the provincial Party bureaucracy, were trying another thrust into the Chinese cities and even into the countryside. On December 15, reversing the previous decision to prevent the Cultural Revolution from interfering with agriculture, the Maoist leadership issued a ten-point directive urging the Red Guards to invade villages in order to "revolutionize" peasants and "expedite" farm output. Henceforth, the directive stated, the "power structure" in the villages would be in the hands of local Cultural Revolution committees composed of poor peasants.[91]

Ten days later, similarly striving to destroy the Party leaders in charge of China's industries, the Maoists ordered the Cultural Revolution carried into mines and factories. Rejecting the argument that this would slow down industrial operations, radical publicists denounced Party officials who "seek to suppress the revolution under the pretext of taking a firm hold on production."[92] Matching these moves, Jiang Qing and Chen Boda exhorted the Red Guards and other activists to seize control of the All-China Federation of Trade Unions, the Party's principal labor organization.[93]

These measures clearly augured an expansion of the Cultural Revolution. The *Red Flag* promised that the Maoist offensive would be pushed forward on a mammoth scale in 1967. "Hundreds of millons of people under the command of Mao Zedong's thought [must] launch a general attack on the enemies of socialism," the journal said, adding that "the leading organs and leading cadres at all levels" in the Party and government should expect to be targets of the "masses."[94] With that appeal, the stage was set for the "January Revolution"—and the months of widespread disorder and violence that followed would make the turbulence in China until then seem mild by comparison.

PART THREE

THE ERUPTION

We are paying a very high price in the great Cultural Revolution.
—MAO ZEDONG, *August 1967*

CHAPTER 10

The January Tempest

♟

*There are casualties in all revolutions, so let
us not exaggerate the seriousness of this situation. Many people have committed suicide
or been killed. But these deaths are fewer
than those incurred during the Japanese war
and the Civil War, or in natural disasters.
Thus our gains are greater than our losses.*
— LIN BIAO, *March 1967*

ALTHOUGH HE HAD not initially plotted a precise timetable for his
campaign, Mao Zedong instinctively conducted the Cultural
Revolution like a guerrilla commander fighting a superior enemy. He
was, after all, the "rebel" striving to overthrow the powerful Party
leaders who had usurped his authority. Like a guerrilla, therefore,
he attacked, retreated, retrenched, and attacked again as he sought
to isolate his adversaries while building up his own strength. Describing his strategy to a group of foreign visitors to Beijing, he later
explained that the first phase of the Cultural Revolution had opened
with assaults against literary dissenters in the fall of 1965 and lasted
through the Eleventh Party Plenum in August 1966. This, Mao said,
had been "primarily a mobilization stage" designed to rally support
for his cause. From August until the end of the year, he went on,
the second phase had singled out the targets of the Cultural Revolution and was, consequently, the "orientation" stage. Starting in
January 1967 were the "crucial" stages in which his followers launched
their offensive to topple the "bourgeois revisionist" Party bureaucrats.[1]

Throughout the first half of 1967, however, Mao would observe
that his drive was running aground. On one occasion, he condemned
Red Guard actions as "bordering on anarchy."[2] Later, deploring dis-

unity of the radicals, he confessed that his hopes for their cohesion had been a "subjective wish that did not conform to the objective law of class struggle," since he had miscalculated the extent to which "different factions would still stubbornly seek self-expression."[3] The factional squabbling, Mao said, finally convinced him that his effort to shape the Red Guards and other student activists into "revolutionary successors" was a "fruitless task." Underlying this failure was the fact that China's educational system had been "dominated by revisionism" since the founding of the Communist regime. Hence students were infected with "bourgeois ideas" which were manifested in the "individualistic" tendencies that prompted radical organizations to divide into rival factions. In short, Mao asserted, his acolytes had demonstrated that they were "leftist in form but rightist in essence."

This did not mean, though, that the concept of the Cultural Revolution had been mistaken. On the contrary, Mao stressed, it merely confirmed his conviction that the route to real change lay in permanent revolution. Only a perpetual process of purification could cleanse human nature of egotism, the worst of the "bourgeois" tendencies, and make possible the emergence of a new species of "Communist man" dedicated to society. It was imperative, Mao said, that "two or three Cultural Revolutions be carried out every hundred years."

But if Mao regarded the Cultural Revolution as a recurrent necessity, many of his prominent comrades adopted a vastly divergent view as they witnessed the tumult that swept across China during 1967. During that year, the upheaval shattered civilian authority, paralyzed key sectors of the economy, provoked an Army mutiny, frayed the social texture of several regions, and nearly plunged some areas of China into civil war. Alarmed that China's very survival was in jeopardy, senior government and military leaders eventually insisted on measures to subdue the turmoil. After that, its forward momentum blunted, the Cultural Revolution gradually faded into a movement characterized more by rhetoric than reality. From January until early September of 1967, therefore, Mao's campaign went through its decisive stage.

Having set the direction of the Cultural Revolution in late 1966, Mao inaugurated 1967 with an impassioned call to the Chinese people to assault his foes across a wide front. His New Year's Day proclamation was military in both style and substance, and this feature revealed the extent to which he saw the drive against his adversaries as a form of revolutionary war.

The hour had come, Mao announced, for a "general attack" not only against the Party apparatus but against "monsters and demons anywhere in society." The Cultural Revolution, he said, should be pushed beyond "offices, schools, and cultural circles to the factories and mines and the rural areas" so that his followers could "capture all positions." Rejecting the warnings of Zhou Enlai and others that Chinese industry and agriculture be protected against disruption, he denounced "some muddle-headed people" who feared that the Cultural Revolution would "impede production." These misguided "comrades," he explained, failed to appreciate a basic "truth" of the Maoist canon—that "revolution can only promote the development of the social productive forces." Those who argued for moderation sought "a pretext to repress the revolution" and they, along with other opponents of this "irresistible historical trend," would be dumped "onto the rubbish heap by the revolutionary masses."

Now, Mao also made plain, he expected workers and peasants to join with the Red Guards and other activists in a "mighty force" that would "storm the positions" held by the Party. "Extensive democracy," the phrase employed earlier by Lin Biao, was the new ideological slogan. It meant that there were no longer limits on either the participants or the targets in the Cultural Revolution. "Hundreds of millions of people" were authorized to assault the "enemies of socialism and, at the same time, criticize and supervise the leading organs and leading cadres at all levels."[4]

Mao's proclamation, like every Communist directive, was embroidered with caveats. It prohibited the radicals from resorting to "coercive measures," insisting instead that "different opinions among the masses should be debated" in a reasonable manner. It suggested, too, that the majority of Party cadres could be won over by carefully drawing a "strict distinction" between those who admitted their "errors" and the "few diehards who stick to the bourgeois reactionary line." But these nuances were lost as radical activists, interpreting Mao's call as a license to release their energies, rose up throughout the country with unprecedented dynamism.

In Beijing, eager to demonstrate their zeal, radical youths immediately responded to Mao's exhortation by staging a public rally to disgrace the senior Communist Party officials already purged as "counterrevolutionaries." The most prominent figure hauled before the rally was Peng Chen, formerly the city's Party boss. Also arraigned were Lu Dingyi, who had headed the Party's Propaganda Department; Yang Shangkun, a key member of the Central Committee

Secretariat before his dismissal; and General Luo Ruiqing, the ousted Chief of General Staff. Though he had lost his post in the spring, Peng Chen had apparently been unmolested until the night of December 4, when eighty Red Guards broke into his Beijing home, roused him out of bed, and drove him off in a truck. Perhaps underestimating their seriousness, Peng Chen reportedly submitted to the youths as meekly as a "paper tiger."[5] Luo Ruiqing, in contrast, had been under arrest for months. Evidently confined to a room in a Beijing building, he had unsuccessfully attempted to commit suicide the previous spring by jumping from a window.[6] His leg broken, General Luo was dragged to the Red Guard rally in a cast.

The rally opened on the afternoon of January 4 at the Beijing Workers Gymnasium, decorated for the occasion with a huge portrait of Mao and banners bearing his aphorisms. As they waited for the proceedings to start, the crowd chanted Mao's quotations and sang a stirring new song entitled: "We Crush Those Who Oppose Chairman Mao." The Red Guards led their victims onto a platform. The group of "reactionaries" included the wives of Luo Ruiqing and Lu Dingyi. All presumably had their hands bound behind them. According to a Maoist account,[7] the Red Guards forced the "sons of bitches" to turn their "canine heads" toward the "masses." And despite Mao's injunction against "coercive measures," the youths "knocked down" their victims and "put their feet on them" as the crowd applauded, cheered, and shouted slogans against the "despicable swine." The rally continued throughout the night into the next day as more than twenty orators read lengthy indictments against the former officials. Most of the speakers denounced Peng Chen and the other victims as members of Liu Shaoqi's "clique," indicating that the Red Guards were priming themselves for an assault against the Chief of State himself.

At that stage, however, the group surrounding Mao seemed to be divided in its attitude toward Liu Shaoqi and Deng Xiaoping. Extremists like Mao's wife appeared to favor a direct personal attack against them, but Zhou Enlai was anxious to avoid violence. The purpose of the Cultural Revolution, he argued, was to attack mistaken policies rather than individuals. "We should thoroughly criticize the bourgeois reactionary line represented by Liu and Deng, and we should smash it," he told a Red Guard audience, but "these two men still belong to the Standing Committee of the Party Central Committee" and deserved to be treated with the respect due their rank.[8]

While Zhou Enlai tried to restrain the Red Guards, radicals in the Jiang Qing camp were apparently stimulating the youths to harass Liu Shaoqi. Late in December, young activists at Qinghua University had seized one of Liu's daughters, Liu Tao, and compelled her to denounce her father. Herself a Qinghua student, aged twenty-two, Liu Tao had evidently had no choice but to comply with the Red Guard demand. She asserted that Liu Shaoqi had "opposed and resisted Chariman Mao for more than twenty years" and also called Liu's wife and her stepmother, Wang Guangmei, a "royalist."[9] Shortly thereafter, Red Guards captured Liu's second son, Liu Yunruo, and put him through the same ordeal. A Soviet-educated aircraft technician in his mid-thirties, Liu Yunruo was forced at a Beijing rally to demand that his "dog's head" of a father "surrender unconditionally to Chairman Mao" and "bow to the people and admit his guilt"—or else face "extinction."[10]

About the same time, according to a Red Guard account, a group of forty Red Guards set a trap using another of Liu's daughers as bait to snare his wife, Wang Guangmei.[11] The Red Guards separated into two squads. One drove to the high school where Liu's teen-age daughter, Pingping, was attending a political meeting. From there, they telephoned Wang Guangmei to inform her that Pingping had been hit by an automobile and was in a Beijing hospital with "serious injuries." Meanwhile, the other Red Guard team drove to the hospital, took over its switchboard, and telephoned Wang Guangmei with the same story. Youths were posted at the hospital entrances to grab the woman who was, officially at least, still the First Lady of China.

To the Red Guards' dismay, however, the first of Pingping's relatives to rush into the hospital was not her mother but her younger sister Tingting, a girl of fourteen or fifteen, accompanied by one of her father's bodyguards. Quickly perceiving the trick, the bodyguard tried to telephone Wang Guangmei. But the Red Guards blocked him. They then "persuaded" Tingting to call her mother to confirm that her sister's left leg had been injured and would require an operation. When Wang Guangmei asked to speak to a physician, a Red Guard took the telephone and, posing as the surgeon, described Pingping's condition: "She is in bad shape. Her joint is broken. We are all set to take her to the operating room. Hospital regulations require the parent to sign approval. . . ."

Roughly an hour later, a small car pulled up at the hospital entrance. Out of it emerged not only Wang Guangmei, but Liu Shaoqi himself. Liu immediately realized that he and his wife had been deceived. The Red Guard version of what followed, though it is contrived to tarnish Wang Guangmei's image, unwittingly serves to bring her into focus as a lady of great pride, courage, and sensitivity. Assuring Liu Shaoqi that she could handle the youths herself, she sent him home and drove with Red Guards to Qinghua University to confront a rally of radicals. On the way, she disclosed to one of them that she had suspected a trap from the beginning.

"Then why did you show up?" he asked.

"As soon as I got word that Pingping had been injured," she replied, "I couldn't have cared less about this business."

Wang Guangmei stood before a kangaroo court of radicals of Qinghua University from ten o'clock at night until five in the morning. In the end, she signed a statement praising the Red Guards for their "revolutionary action," vowing to submit herself to further "self-examination," and promising to send the students a regular report "exposing Liu Shaoqi's "bourgeois reactionary line" as well as "things pertaining to his daily life and moral character."[12] There was no evidence, however, that Wang Guangmei ever fulfilled this pledge, and she would face a far more rigorous test at the hands of the Red Guards in April. Except for Pingping, who was reportedly arrested in the spring of 1968, the fate of Liu's children has remained a mystery.[13]

Nowhere in China did Mao's call to the Red Guards to "storm the positions" of the Party apparatus "at all levels" have a more disorderly effect than in the sprawling metropolis of Shanghai.

In the fall of 1966, the city's mayor and Party boss, Cao Diqiu, had shrewdly maneuvered to preserve his authority by sacrificing a few minor officials and thereby creating the impression that he was obeying Mao's exhortations. He had also mobilized his own Red Guard factions to defend himself and his colleagues against the radicals. By October, therefore, a fragile stalemate prevailed in Shanghai—and, for similar reasons, in most other parts of China.

But, inspired by the Maoist criticisms of Liu Shaoqi, the Shanghai radicals gradually intensified their pressure against the city's Party Committee. They were, in fact, directed by Maoist emissaries from Beijing bearing specific instructions.

In mid-November, Zhang Chunqiao, one of the city's few Party officials to have initially sided with Mao, returned to Shanghai after more than four months in Beijing. As a member of the Cultural

Revolution Directorate, he was now a national figure. His mission was to organize the radical challenge to the Shanghai Party Committee. He gave his blessing to a coalition of radical students and workers, the Shanghai Workers Revolutionary Rebel Headquarters.[14] A week later, the Shanghai Maoists were further boosted by the arrival of Nie Yuanzi, the woman who had sparked student protests at Beijing University the previous May. Claiming to be Mao's personal representative—more probably she was operating on behalf of Jiang Qing—Nie Yuanzi denounced the Shanghai *apparatchiks* as supporters of Liu Shaoqi and Deng Xiaoping. On November 25, determined to escalate the offensive against the Shanghai mayor and his associates, she mobilized a demonstration whose militant tone was reflected in its main slogan: "We Swear to Rain Down Ten Thousand Bombs on the Bourgeois Reactionary Line of Cao Diqiu and His Municipal Committee!"[15]

Such was the atmosphere in Shanghai—and elsewhere in China at the time—that the Party authorities could not overtly stifle the radicals without inviting the charge that they were "repressing the masses." Thus unfettered, the Shanghai radicals went into action. On December 2, strengthened by suburban students and workers, they occupied the offices of the *Liberation Daily*, the Shanghai Party's official newspaper. In reprisal, the Party formed a coalition of its own students and workers, the Scarlet Guards for the Defense of Mao Zedong's Thought. After two weeks of inconclusive skirmishing between the two groups, Mayor Cao decided to appease the radicals, apparently in the belief that he would deflate their ardor. He publicly conceded that the *Liberation Daily* had indeed been guilty as charged of pursuing a "reactionary line." But the radicals, interpreting the Mayor's gesture as a sign of weakness, were emboldened rather than calmed. They intensified their verbal fusillades against him, finally compelling him to denounce the Scarlet Guards. Learning of Cao's betrayal, the Scarlet Guards turned against him. Fighting broke out among rival factions in the city and suburbs and, amid the confusion, the Municipal Party Committee buckled. The Maoist troubleshooter Zhang Chunqiao, who had been shuttling back and forth to Beijing, again returned to the city. Shanghai was now open to a take-over by the radicals under his command.

Peng Chen's Beijing apparatus had been removed in the spring of 1966 as a result of high-level machinations. In Shanghai, contrastingly, radicals appeared for the first time in the Cultural Revolution to have overthrown a local Party machine "from below." This achievement seemed to lend reality to Mao's vision of the "masses" rising to topple the "bourgeois revisionist" Party bureaucrats, and his publicists greeted the Shanghai episode with extravagant fanfare. Afterward, they would be compelled to recognize that their victory had been empty—but not before the Shanghai upheaval provoked a series of violent tremors throughout the Chinese provinces.

On January 4, acting with the approval of Mao's Cultural Revolution Directorate in Beijing, eleven radical Shanghai groups coalesced under the leadership of the Workers Revolutionary Rebel Headquarters to assert control over the city. They seized the city's principal newspapers and its radio and television stations and, to publicize their supremacy, they arraigned Mayor Cao and the defeated Shanghai Party bureaucrats at a public rally—held, appropriately, in a snowstorm. Also put on display was Chen Beixian, the head of the Party's powerful East China Bureau, who until then had escaped direct criticism. Typically indiscriminate, the radicals vilified the Party officials for "crimes" ranging from "opposing the masses" to importing "pornographic films" from Hong Kong. Two deputy mayors, adorned with dunce's caps and placards identifying them as "reactionaries," were driven through the city streets in an open truck.[16] The senior Party *apparatchiks* were ordered to confess to their links with the "revisionist" conspiracy purportedly organized by Liu Shaoqi and Deng Xiaoping.[17]

The Maoist high command in Beijing seemed delighted by this apparent triumph, for they hailed the Shanghai episode as a "brilliant example" for all of China to emulate.[18] "Internal rebellion is a good thing," Mao remarked. "The rise of the revolutionary forces in Shanghai . . . is bound to be felt throughout east China and in all the country's provinces and municipalities."[19] The *People's Daily* echoed this theme, calling on radicals to "seize power, seize power, seize power. . . . The mass of workers and peasants, revolutionary intellectuals and revolutionary cadres together should act as masters of their own affairs and establish a new proletarian order."[20]

But the Shanghai episode did not produce the effect that Mao wished. Though they successfully crippled Party organizations in a few places, the radicals were strongly rebuffed in most areas. The resulting eruption of complicated and confused clashes seemed to be propelling China toward an assortment of local civil wars.

In the southwest, the Party boss of Yunnan province, Yan Hongyan, committed suicide by poison after coming under attack by Red Guards who had streamed into the region from Beijing.[21] On January

25, the Great Alliance of Proletarian Revolutionaries claimed to have taken control of Guizhou, another province in southwestern China.[22] Radicals seized the Party newspapers and radio stations in Anhui, Zhejiang, Fujian, Hubei, and Shandong provinces.[23]

The January upheaval also brought down Liu Landao, the head of the Party's Northwest Bureau, whose headquarters were located in the Shaanxi province capital of Xi'an. According to Andrew Watson, a young English teacher who was resident there at the time, the downfall of Liu and his colleagues stemmed from an erosion of the Party bureaucracy in the area which had gone on steadily during the preceding months. In the fall, as Watson has described it,[24] the regional Party machine had managed to survive by relying on industrial workers to fight off rebellious youth contingents. Like "hard-hats" in the United States and Western Europe, the Chinese workers had no compunctions about beating up unruly students who threatened the Party apparatus to which labor owed its loyalty. But by mid-December, with increasingly shrill appeals for revolt emanating from Beijing, many workers, government employees, and even policemen in Xi'an began to turn against the Party—even though they remained hostile to the student radicals. Thus the Party bureaucracy buckled for lack of support while students, workers, and others splintered into assorted factions that skirmished against each other. Amid this turmoil, the senior Party officials in Xi'an were detained in a special compound and forced to perform manual labor and write confessions of their "sins." The once prestigious Liu Landao among them, they were also, in the usual fashion, paraded through the streets of the city wearing dunce's caps and compelled to face huge crowds at denunciation rallies. With the Party's controls broken, however, Xi'an slid toward anarchy. Not until the Army intervened later was a semblance of order restored. But the military move in Xi'an, as elsewhere in China, contributed to new problems that persisted throughout the spring.

In many other provinces, meanwhile, regional Party machines managed to mobilize continued support among workers, peasants, demobilized soldiers, and students to resist the onslaught of the radicals. The military authorities in several sensitive border areas, fearful that China's defense might be enfeebled by the turbulence, deployed troops to quell the disturbances. In some instances, this created tensions within the ranks of the Army.

Beginning in early January, fighting broke out between Party and Maoist factions in the Jiangxi province capital of Nanchang. This was the city where Communists headed by Zhou Enlai and Zhu De had staged an uprising against Chiang Kai-shek's Nationalists on August 1, 1927—a date since commemorated by the Communists as Army Day. Now, in Nanchang, the local Party bureaucracy organized six groups to oppose the radicals. The largest, known as the Workers Red Defense Corps, spearheaded an offensive against the radicals by storming their different headquarters throughout the city. Starting at three o'clock in the morning of January 9, the Workers Red Defense Corps raided colleges and high schools, confiscating loudspeakers, mimeograph machines, bicycles, and miscellaneous property belonging to radical students. During the raids, which continued for more than a week, some four hundred young people were reportedly hospitalized with serious injuries. Just as Red Guards of every coloration strove to portray themselves as Mao's true disciples, so now the Party *apparatchiks* in Nanchang did the same, and branded the radicals as "reactionaries." Army units afterward intervened, ousting the city's Party bosses—but without favoring the radicals.[25] Later the radicals would vent their wrath against the Army in a series of desperate assaults that reached a crescendo of violence in the summer.

In early January, factional clashes were even bloodier in Nanjing, the former Nationalist capital lying on the south bank of the Yangzi River, in Jiangsu province. On January 3, the Party, evidently hoping to prevent Red Guards from coming into the city from Beijing, ordered its supporters to block the railway at Zhuxian, a town north of Nanjing. At the same time, the Nanjing Party bureaucrats appealed to workers from nearby Shanghai and Wuxi for assistance. An estimated hundred thousand workers took the offensive against the main radical group, the Red Rebel General Headquarters, primarily composed of students.

A leftist youth who escaped from the city during the turmoil reported that the workers started by attacking a radical stronghold at Zhouyang, a suburb fifteen miles southeast of Nanjing on the rail line to Shanghai. The workers captured twenty-three young radicals, he said, and confined them to the Jiangsu Hotel in Nanjing. The battle was joined a day later, according to his account, when two thousand radicals streamed into the city to rescue their comrades. Both sides wielded bricks, clubs, and knives, and a Maoist version of the episode claimed that the workers met the counterattack by flinging some of their hostages from the upper floors of the hotel. By the end of the first week of January, casualties in Nanjing were said to be forty-three dead and more than five hundred seriously injured.[26] Subsequent evidence indicated that the Party sympathizers in Nanjing were initially aided by the local Army garrison, under General Xu Shiyou, the commander of the region covering east China. Two years later, General Xu was to emerge as a member of the new Politburo and one of China's most powerful military figures.

Violence also flared up in the remote region of Xinjiang. The turbulence there especially worried the Beijing leaders, who had several reasons for considering the region to be extremely sensitive. First, China's nuclear and missile test sites were located in the vicinity of Lop Nor, a large lake in southeastern Xinjiang. Second, the majority of the population of 8 million consisted of Uighurs, Kazakhs, and other Muslims who had resisted Han Chinese domination. Finally, bordering as it did on the Soviet Union, the area was regarded by the Beijing leaders as the "front line in the struggle against revisionism."

As early as September 1966, four hundred Red Guards from Beijing had arrived in the Xinjiang capital of Urumchi in order to "exchange revolutionary experiences" with local students. The Party *apparatchiks* in Urumchi went through the motions of welcoming the Beijing youths, who proceeded to recruit university and high-school students into an organization entitled the Red Guard Revolutionary Rebel Headquarters.[27] But the Party bureaucrats were mistaken in believing that they could keep the students in line. The Red Guards soon began to criticize the "feudal" religious practices of Xinjiang Muslims. They also denounced "those in power . . . who had sneaked into the Party and are taking the capitalist road."[28] That broadside was plainly aimed at General Wang Enmao, a veteran Army political commissar whose control over both the Party and military apparatus in Xinjiang since 1952 had made him virtual warlord of the area.

Originally a peasant from Jiangxi province, Wang had joined the Communists in the mid-1920s as a guerrilla and later became attached to a unit in He Long's 120th Division of the Eighth Route Army. He accompanied the Communist legions that pushed into Xinjiang in 1949, and he remained there to carve out his career like a powerful proconsul on the fringe of an empire. By his own admission, Wang governed the area with an iron fist, dealing "severe blows" to Party dissenters as well as against Muslims resisting integration into Chinese society.[29] In the spring of 1962, revolting against Wang's rule, some sixty thousand Uighurs and other Muslims had responded to Russian inducements to flee to Soviet Kazakhstan. That Wang escaped public censure for that episode may have been due to his connections with He Long, who had risen to the rank of Marshal and membership in the Politburo. He Long also had interests in Xinjiang as indirect boss of the Production and Construction Corps, a paramilitary force of nearly four hundred thousand men engaged in economic development in the territory. But now, as He Long came under Maoist attack in January 1967, so did many of his old comrades, Wang Enmao among them.[30] Wang rushed to Beijing to discuss the threat to his authority in Xinjiang. During his absence the region erupted.

The first large-scale clash in Xinjiang occurred on January 26 at Shihezi, a military outpost of eighty thousand inhabitants lying in the shadow of the massive Tian Shan range that separates China from the Soviet Union. There, members of the Production and Construction Corps as well as active and demobilized soldiers had been incorporated into a region-wide organization elaborately called the August 1 Field Army Sworn to Defend the Thought of Mao Zedong to the Death. Wang Enmao had created this organization, known as the August 1 Field Army, in order to counter the Red Guards. Accordingly, when radical youths in Shihezi made a foolhardy bid to seize power, the August 1 Field Army reacted brutally.

As a Red Guard account described it, the August 1 Field Army had earlier warned against creating disorder. But the youths persisted in calling for the overthrow of the Party "power-holders," and General Wang's supporters deployed ten truckloads of men armed with rifles and hand grenades. They encircled the Red Guards, who were staging a street rally, and opened fire. After that, the Red Guards claimed, members of the August 1 Field Army fanned out through the town in pursuit of suspected radicals. They stopped a bus, forced ten youths to descend, and shot them on the spot. Other youths were arrested and tortured. One Red Guard version of the event claimed that captured leaders had their eyes gouged out before being executed.[31] More than a hundred young activists were said to have been killed in the incident and hundreds more imprisoned in nearby labor camps.[32]

A Red Guard who escaped after seven months in detention later related that he and his comrades had been taken to a state farm run by the Production and Construction Corps. There, according to his account, several among them were tortured by Army officers trying to make them confess that their opposition to General Wang represented opposition to Mao. Students were flung from moving trucks with their hands tied behind their backs, as part of their punishment, he said, and officers stripped one girl and seared her breasts with a burning joss stick. The Red Guards were compelled to work sixteen hours a day and jammed into a vegetable bin at night. They were also subjected to "self-criticism" sessions at which, the youth said, they were told that they could only gain release by "transforming" their ideological attitudes.[33]

The Shihezi incident reverberated in Urumchi and other parts of Xinjiang. In Beijing, seeking to avenge their comrades in the border region, Red Guards raided the Ministry of State Farms and Land Reclamation, which was linked to the Xinjiang Party administration. They arrested Wang Zhen, the Minister, an old associate of Wang Enmao.[34] Premier Zhou Enlai ordered General Wang Enmao to return immediately to Xinjiang to impose a cease-fire in the region. Zhou also advised General Wang that a special investigation team would be sent to the area.[35] Soon afterward, Beijing issued a directive instructing the Red Guards to refrain from attacking either the political or the military apparatus in Xinjiang.[36] As elsewhere in China, however, the contending factions could not be pacified by mere decrees, and tensions continued to plague Xinjiang for months to come.

In the southern province of Guangdong, meanwhile, radicals stimulated by Mao's call for rebellion succeeded in upsetting the local Party machine—but failed to gain power for themselves. The Guangdong apparatus, based in Guangzhou, was seriously weakened in early January by the purge of Tao Zhu. Without his support, the Guangdong Party bureaucrats maneuvered deviously to protect their authority. But they rapidly succumbed to the radicals. Yet the radical triumph in Guangdong was only a brief prelude to a period of turmoil.

The Guangzhou leftists were encouraged to escalate their activities in early January by both the Maoist exhortation to revolt and the apparent success of the radicals in Shanghai. Their cohesion was also cemented by the emergence of a dynamic young leader, Wu Zhuanbin, a Hunanese student of physics at Guangzhou's Sun Yat-sen University. A tall, articulate youth who always wore a neat khaki uniform, Wu had displayed unusual courage in the spring, when he openly attacked the Party chief at his university. In the fall, after returning from a pilgrimage to Beijing, he formed two Red Guard units. One of them, the Sun Yat-sen University Red Flag Commune, was open to a large number of students. The other, a tightly knit platoon called the August 31 Combat Detachment to commemorate the date Wu had passed in review before Mao, had only about two hundred members, most of them orphans—unconcerned that their unruly conduct might bring retribution against their families. These Red Guards were not only talented polemicists but skilled hand-to-hand fighters, and their elitist character contrasted ideologically with the Maoist concept of revolution by the masses. Nevertheless, Wu maintained close contacts with the Cultural Revolution Directorate through a liaison office he had established in the capital. On January 19, he received a long-distance telephone call from his Beijing agent informing him that the Cultural Revolution Directorate now authorized the Guangdong radicals to overthrow the Provincial Party Committee.[37]

Until then, Guangzhou had been the scene of only sporadic, disorganized skirmishing. On January 11, for example, a radical group had taken control of the *Nan Fang Daily*, one of the city's Party journals.[38] In some neighborhoods, Red Guards had also clashed with workers defending their factories.[39] But when he received approval from Beijing to assault the Guangdong Party bureaucracy, Wu Zhuanbin moved to meld the various cliques then active in Guangzhou. With remarkable speed, he created a coalition of eight worker and student associations known as the Guangdong Province Revolutionary Rebel Joint Committee—or, more simply, the Provincial Revolutionary Alliance. Included in the coalition were students and young workers from Beijing, Harbin, and Wuhan who had come to Guangzhou as delegates from their own Red Guard units.[40]

Soon, however, the Provincial Revolutionary Alliance was denounced by other Guangzhou Red Guards who complained that the coalition was "monopolized" by northerners and therefore not truly representative of Guangzhou. The Provincial Revolutionary Alliance, they alleged, had excluded many local organizations, thereby displaying "small-group" tendencies that violated Mao's appeal to "trust the masses."[41] This controversy, already acute in mid-January, foreshadowed the confused tensions that later gripped Guangzhou as dozens of divergent factions asserted themselves. To a large extent, though, the dissension stemmed from the fact that the thrust by Wu's Red Guards to take power in Guangzhou was outwitted by the local Party boss, Zhao Ziyang.

The Guangzhou radicals launched their *coup d'état* in classical style on January 22 by occupying the city's radio and television stations. They also took over the bureaus of both the municipal and provincial Public Security apparatus, which controlled the police, and they then proceeded to dismiss Zhao Ziyang and his associates from office. But Zhao, an experienced operative, maneuvered to deflate them. Instead of resisting their assault, he cheerfully capitulated by handing the Red Guards the symbolic seals of his authority.[42] He then issued a statement conceding that his Party machine had committed a "grave error of orientation and line" by following the orders of Liu Shaoqi and Deng Xiaoping. Henceforth, he vowed, he and his colleagues would strive for redemption by acceding to the "supervision of the . . . broad revolutionary masses."[43] Zhao even offered to face criticism at a public rally.

Wu Zhuanbin's Provincial Revolutionary Alliance was prepared to accept this surrender, but rival radicals considered it to be a charade, a "sham seizure of power" staged by "out-and-out royalists" and "servile tools" of Zhao Ziyang.[44] Within a matter of weeks, the rhetorical quarrels among competitive Guangzhou factions had escalated into serious physical conflicts, and the Army stepped in to restore order. The violence intensified into a long period of civil strife.

***

Nor was Beijing spared the rebellious ferment. Hardly a day passed during January without its Red Guards assailing Party, government, and Army figures, clashing among themselves, or splitting into rival factions. For nearly a week, Red Guards demonstrated against the Soviet Embassy compound, hanging effigies of Leonid Brezhnev and Aleksei Kosygin from trees in front of its gates and denouncing the "revisionist renegades of the international Communist movement."[45] A Red Guard unit affiliated with the College of Geology closed the Beijing zoo as well as the celebrated Summer Palace, northwest of the city, while youths from Shanghai desecrated the famous tombs of the Ming dynasty emperors, causing "incalculable losses."[46] One of the most extraordinary incidents to occur during this stormy period was an uprising staged by a Muslim group resident in Beijing. Though claiming fidelity to Mao, these Muslims protested against national and religious persecution by the Han Chinese, and their agitation was symptomatic of the extent to which the Cultural Revolution provided a pretext for different segments of China's population to express their grievances.

Indigenous to Xinjiang and Gansu, where they numbered about 5 million in the mid-1960s, the Muslim Huis are a Turkic people ethnically akin to the Uighurs and Kazakhs. Many had emigrated over the years to Beijing, clustering in the Xuanwu district, where they lived amid their own small shops, their restaurants and coffee houses, and their mosques. But in the fall of 1966, infected by the dissident mood of the Cultural Revolution, some of them formed an organization called the General Headquarters of the Beijing Hui Nationality

Rebel Regiment for the Thought of Mao Zedong. Despite this revolutionary title, the real purpose of the movement was to agitate for the religious and cultural rights of Muslims. Hui activists plastered up wall posters in their neighborhood irreverently proclaiming their faith in Allah along with their devotion to Mao. They also skirmished frequently with Red Guards who intruded into their ghetto in forays aimed at eradicating Islamic "feudalism."

On January 18, some four hundred Huis stormed a police station in the Xuanwu district, injuring several policemen in the scuffle. The police arrested three of their leaders, and a large Muslim crowd returned to attack the police station again. "Crush the dogs' heads of the police," they shouted as they broke windows and smashed furniture. The police repulsed them, and the Muslims retreated to one of their mosques. Besieged there by the police for nearly two weeks, they were finally subdued. But, minor as it was, the Muslim resistance served to confirm radical allegations that anti-Maoist "dark forces" were "still powerful."[47]

The general turbulence in Beijing by this time had spiraled to such proportions that, with the exception of Mao and Lin Biao, no Chinese leader was immune to Red Guard attack. Radicals forced the closure of several offices of the Public Security Bureau, the repository of police authority, and denounced Xie Fuzhi, the Minister of Public Security.[48] Jiang Qing had earlier inspired this assault by asserting that the Public Security Bureau was "riddled with bad characters." Now, in late January she came to Xie's defense, calling him a "good comrade" who had earned his revolutionary chevrons in the initial offensive against Liu Shaoqi, Deng Xiaoping, and the other senior Party bureaucrats.[49] She also admonished the radicals for assailing such figures as Xiao Hua, chief of the Army's political department, and Foreign Minister Chen Yi, who was then in the process of confessing his "mistakes."

Yet even as she sought to protect these leaders, Jian Qing and her colleagues on the Cultural Revolution Directorate were themselves being decried by certain Red Guard factions. She and her associates had been "slandered," she said, in wall posters throughout Beijing. While conceding that she might have "short-comings," she lashed out at her critics, claiming that they were trying to "isolate" Mao by attacking his disciples.

Much of the criticism against Jiang Qing and her comrades came from Maoist radicals who, given license to revolt, apparently felt that nobody except Mao was sacred. Attempting to describe their ideological error, Jiang Qing tortuously argued that these factions had swung so far to the left that they had become "reactionary." In other words, as she put it, they were showing "manifestations of extreme democracy and liberalism" that reflected an alarming trend toward anarchy.[50]

The turbulence shaking China was now aggravated by the emergence of a nationwide coalition of student groups dedicated to defending the Party against the Red Guards and Maoists. Known as the *Lian Dong*, or United Action Committee, this coalition differed from the many youth and worker factions set up by local Party machines in that it was mainly composed of the children of officials. As such, it heightened the element of authentic "class struggle" in the conflicts between the upper and lower echelons of Chinese society.

First mobilized under the auspices of the Party Work Team that entered Beijing's Qinghua University in the spring of 1966, the United Action Committee had initially included such members as Liu Tao, the daugher of Liu Shaoqi, and He Pengfei, the son of Marshal He Long.[51] As the Cultural Revolution gained momentum, the organization attracted other groups and individuals with similar aims. In Beijing, for example, it became associated with a faction of high-school students called the Xizheng Picket Team, whose leaders included Chen Xiaowu, the son of the Foreign Minister, and Dong Liangge, the son of Dong Biwu, one of China's two deputy chiefs of state.[52] An affiliated group in Guangzhou, the Doctrine Red Guards, counted among its leaders Huang Zhunming, the son of General Huang Yongsheng, the regional Army commander.[53] Other factions in the United Action Committee came from a number of secondary schools especially created for the children of high-ranking Party, government, and military figures. One such institution, the October 1 School in Beijing, catered to fifteen hundred privileged youths in a gardenlike atmosphere. Unlike ordinary Chinese schools, where one teacher handled thirty-five or forty pupils, the ratio of students to faculty at the October 1 School was seven to one. Its staff included gardeners, drivers, and other servants, and its state subsidy was reportedly ten times larger than the allocation provided to regular schools.[54] At a similar Beijing institution called the August 1 School, students were told: "You will be generals, ministers or premiers in the future. . . . You are not meant to peddle bean sauce or vinegar in the streets."[55]

The fight between the United Action Committee and the radicals, as it began to take shape in late 1966, was symptomatic of the struggle that had pitted the Party elite and Mao against each other for decades. Maoist strategy was designed, of course, to topple the Party apparatus. The Party, on the other hand, intended to prevent an upheaval that might shatter its organization throughout the country, and the United Action Committee was conceived as an instrument to defend that cause. Its fundamental conservatism, however, was clouded by the leftist rhetoric of its spokesmen as they "waved the Red Flag in order to oppose the Red Flag."

The policy of the United Action Committee was publicized in the fall of 1966 by Tan Lifu, the head of a Red Guard faction at Beijing Technical University. The son of a senior official in the Chinese judicial establishment, Tan had been associated since the summer with the children of Liu Shaoqi and He Long in founding the organization. Speaking in Beijing in October, he put forth the proposal that Red Guard membership be limited to "Five Kinds of Red"—the children of workers, peasants, revolutionary martyrs, revolutionary cadres, and revolutionary soldiers. Youths with other family backgrounds were to form separate units to be led and trained by the Red Guards. This proposal, though seemingly radical, was denounced by the Maoists. They saw it as a violation of Mao's design to uncork the "broad masses." In their view, Tan would have turned the Red Guards into an exclusive organization kept under close Party supervision. Although Tan disappeared not long afterward, and the Red Guard units were opened to youths of all persuasions, the United Action Committee maintained its cohesion as a movement composed of "elitist" students.[56]

After a period of quiescence, the Beijing branch of the United Action Committee surfaced again in early December. In all likelihood, the Party machine had revived the Committee for defensive purposes as the Maoist attacks against Liu Shaoqi and Deng Xiaoping grew in intensity. Employing wall posters, tracts, and flimsy newspapers, the Committee protested against the persecution of the Party leaders, contending that it was criminal to derogate prestigious Communist veterans.[57]

On the evening of January 6, several hundred of the Committee's members marched into the headquarters of the Beijing Municipal Party Committee, then under Maoist control. They boldly denounced the Cultural Revolution Directorate and shouted "Long Live Liu Shaoqi."[58] United Action Committee posters went up around the city accusing the Directorate of pursuing a "left opportunist" line and claiming that Jiang Qing, the most illustrious of the Maoists, was "going crazy."[59] This rhetoric was matched by increasing violence as United Action Committee squads clashed with Red Guard units.

An indication of the brutality shown by conflicting factions to each other was described in one document that charged the Xizheng Picket Team with having "inhumanly" maltreated its rivals.[60] A nineteen-year-old student, Wang Guanghua, the document said, had been kidnaped by the Xizheng Team. Taken to the Team's headquarters at the No. 6 Middle School in Beijing, Wang was tortured by his captors as they tried to make him sign a statement denouncing his Red Guard unit. They clubbed him with rifle butts until his face was a pulp, his ribs were broken, and he was urinating blood. According to the document, Wang finally died, and his corpse was secretly cremated. Another victim of the Xizheng Picket Team, the same document disclosed, was a retired worker by the name of Xu Beilin who had been tortured and then hanged, the Team claiming that he had committed suicide. Other documents revealed similar instances of savagery, and the violence spiraled in the months ahead.

Speaking to Edgar Snow in late 1970, Mao himself confirmed that these factional battles had been fierce. Conveniently forgetting that he had originally encouraged the ferment, Mao deplored the Red Guards' lack of discipline.[61] It was implicit in his disclosure, however, that he had simply lost control of the Cultural Revolution by early 1967. Certainly the Maoist leaders recognized that the situation had become desperate. In several talks with Red Guards during January, Premier Zhou Enlai criticized their "seizure and control of everything," and warned that their continued unruliness would "wreck the social order and production, and thereby make us a laughing stock." He recommended what he called a "much better and more practical" policy—the "supervision formula," under which Party and government cadres would not be ousted by radicals but, rather, would perform their functions under the Red Guards' nominal aegis.[62] Even Jiang Qing now also tried to halt the turmoil, telling the Red Guards that "'blowing the wind and sparking the fire . . . is no longer effective."[63] In contrast to Zhou, however, she did not caution the Red Guards against purging the administration, but merely urged them to pursue the campaign in a more orderly fashion.

By this time, though, the Red Guards had acquired a momentum of their own that could not be stopped or slowed down by oratory. They had gone to extremes—and only extreme measures would halt them.

CHAPTER 11

The Revolt of the Proletariat

> To sabotage the Great Proletarian Cultural
> Revolution and shift the target of the strug-
> gle, a small handful of power-holders in the
> Party . . . try to lead some of the masses
> onto the evil road of economism, where they
> would pursue exclusively personal and tem-
> porary interests in disregard of the interests
> of the State and the collective.
> —*Central Committee Circular,*
> *January 1967*

I N EARLY 1967, the Maoist leaders were deeply troubled by a new
phenomenon potentially more critical than clashes among rival
Red Guard factions. Workers in nearly every major city and province
of China had begun to express their dissatisfaction with economic and
social conditions. In many areas, they were being joined by discontented peasants and a wide assortment of other elements in China's
labor force. Maoist propaganda condemned these revolts as an ideological deviation labeled "economism," asserting that the rebellious
workers, peasants, and others had been "hoodwinked" by "reactionary" Party officials into agitating to satisfy their "personal and short-
term interests."[1] There was a measure of truth to this allegation, for
Party cadres in several places did in fact attempt to win the support
of workers by giving them bonuses. But many workers and peasants
were prompted to agitate for reforms by genuine grievances that
stemmed from serious labor problems.

One of these problems was unemployment. Though precise statistics were never made available, hundreds of thousands of urban
workers probably lost their jobs in the early 1960s, when the failure
of the Great Leap Forward had forced the government to cut back

on industrial production and capital construction. The slowdown in industry and construction also contributed to unemployment among school graduates trying to enter the labor force. In Guangzhou, for example, it was estimated in the mid-1960s that the majority of secondary-school students remained idle from three to five years after graduation—unless they were sent to do manual labor in provincial villages or in Xinjiang and Inner Mongolia.[2]

The practice of sending superfluous graduates to rural regions—a movement known as Xiafang, or "down to the countryside"—was supposed to fulfill Mao's dream of closing the traditional Chinese gap between intellectuals and peasants. But the movement created other kinds of labor problems. Accustomed to urban comforts, the city youths adapted badly to the rigors of primitive village life.

Several of these rusticated students, who later fled home to Guangzhou, recorded their experiences in a report descriptively entitled "Three Years of Blood and Tears."[3] They related that many of their comrades, too weak to put in long hours of heavy manual labor, had collapsed from exhaustion, fallen sick, and even died. Their inability to work hard, they recounted, inevitably provoked the resentment of the peasants, who had little use for "city slickers" under any circumstances. The peasants deprived them of food rations and, in some instances, beat them. An account of conditions in another village said that educated youths assigned to a labor brigade were deliberately accorded low wages under a complicated "work point" system, with the consequence that they ended each month in debt. When they complained, according to the report, the students were told to ask their families for money. Eight of these students ended by committing suicide. Others clashed constantly with peasants and rural cadres. As the account commented; "Could life be duller, more monotonous, more uninteresting?"[4]

With the breakdown of controls during the Cultural Revolution, thousands of young people who had been sent to the countryside grasped the opportunity to escape, and they poured back into the cities on the pretext of participating in Mao's revolutionary drive. If they had been troublesome in the villages, they now became even more disorderly as they swelled the ranks of protesting workers in the cities.

Industrial apprentices were another source of labor discontent. These youths, usually adolescents with only primary-school educations, were recruited to serve three-year terms on half wages, at the end of which they were theoretically scheduled to be elevated to full worker status, with commensurate salary increases. But in the mid-1960s, they began to show signs of disappointment. They were generally able to master their simple jobs within five or six months, yet they could not expect promotion before the completion of their training. This meant that they were committed to thirty months of regular labor at half pay until they reached the lowest rung of the wage scale. One of their demands, therefore, was a reduction in the apprenticeship period.

The industrial apprentices who finished their terms in late 1966 were irritated by what they considered to be an even bigger injustice. At that time the authorities, apparently for budgetary reasons, decided to postpone promotions. Instead, apprentices faced two alternative prospects. They could be ordered to continue working at half pay. Or, under an industrial decentralization scheme then taking shape, they could be transferred to the countryside as employees in rural factories. These equally unattractive choices understandably put the apprentices in a rebellious mood, and their dissidence contributed significantly to the outbreaks in China's cities in the new year.[5]

Still another—and more volatile—source of labor unrest lay in the legions of underprivileged, insecure contract workers who had been shunted into Chinese cities throughout the previous decade. In an effort to recover from the disastrous Great Leap Forward, the Beijing regime had cut wage and welfare expenditures by contriving a so-called "worker-peasant" system under which unskilled urban jobs could be filled by labor imported from rural regions on a seasonal or rotational basis. This system, the reverse of the Xiafang movement, was also purported to conform to Mao's doctrine of erasing differences between the cities and the countryside. In fact, it was largely designed to exploit cheap manpower as well as to save state funds in a variety of other ways.

For one thing, peasants could be substituted in urban industries for higher-paid workers, who were then sent to rural areas at lower salaries. During the 1965-1966 winter season, for example, nearly eight thousand permanent workers were dismissed from the country's sugar refineries and replaced by peasant laborers, thus reducing wage costs by 2.5 million *yuan*. Peasants accustomed to hard physical labor could also be employed as railway and dock coolies—jobs shunned by more sophisticated urban workers. Moreover, peasants assigned to temporary work were usually required to provide their own food and lodgings. They received neither medical benefits nor family allowances, and they could be returned to their villages before they became eligible for retirement pensions.[6] In short, then, the temporary contract workers were the "niggers" of China. And their rebellion, when it first erupted in late 1966, came as a revelation that the Chinese Communist regime had clung to a system that would have shocked the most egregious capitalist.

Even though they would later berate them for having chosen the "evil road of economism," the Maoists gave the workers the initial impetus to revolt. On December 26, Jiang Qing and her comrades hailed the formation of a new revolutionary labor organization called the All-China Red Workers General Rebellion Corps, which had taken over the Ministry of Labor and planned to dissolve the National Federation of Trade Unions, an instrument of the Party bureaucracy. At the same time, asserting that they had "suffered the most" and therefore had the "greatest spirit of revolt," she exhorted the contract workers to rebel against the "political oppression and economic exploitation" to which they had been subjected under the system allegedly created by Liu Shaoqi, Deng Xiaoping, and the Party machine.[7]

This appeal to the most alienated elements of the Chinese labor force to participate in the Cultural Revolution was purposely timed to coincide with Mao's decision to push his campaign into the farms and factories. But it was a decision that backfired badly.

The rebellious workers at first seemed to be joining the Red Guards in the drive to topple the Party apparatus. Appropriating the language of the Cultural Revolution, they extolled Mao while denouncing his "counterrevolutionary" adversaries. But soon it became apparent that these militant phrases were only rhetorical cosmetics to camouflage a basically economic labor revolt. Most of the workers wanted higher wages, lower working hours, better housing, improved medical care, and other benefits. The contract workers in particular sought the abolition of the onerous system under which their status was, at best, second-class.

By no accident did one of the earliest outbursts of labor unrest occur in the Shanghai port, where many stevedores were peasants brought from the countryside. The labor force in the harbor also included many apprenticed youths, salaried at eighteen *yuan* per month, half the pay of a permanent worker.

At the end of December, these dock workers began to mobilize. In one area of wharfs and warehouses, where the labor force numbered fewer than three thousand, workers formed fifty-seven separate groups to agitate for improved wages and working conditions. The harbor officials, fearful of being branded as "revisionist counter-revolutionaries," promised to satisfy every demand. But the more the authorities sought to placate them, the higher the workers escalated their claims. At one point, according to an eyewitness description of the scene, harbor officials appeared to be playing hide-and-seek as irate workers pursued them around the docks.[8] Amid this upheaval, operations in the port of Shanghai slowed down and eventually ceased.

The Shanghai dock strike, the first overt labor protest to occur in China since the Communists took power, had a contagious effect. Similar disturbances spread to the northern Chinese ports of Qingdao, Tianjin and Dairen. Foreign ships scheduled to unload chemical fertilizers, machinery, and other merchandise and pick up such Chinese export commodities as rice, coal, and soybeans were condemned to long and costly delays. The captain of a Japanese vessel stranded in Shanghai telegraphed an angry complaint to Beijing, while a European ship held up in that port signaled its impatience by flying the Chinese flag upside down.[9] Local Chinese, interpreting these gestures as insults, squabbled with foreign seamen on several occasions. Foreign firms, worried by the ferment, instructed their ships to divert course, and China's external commerce began to slide. Tokyo businessmen, especially alarmed by the tumult, decided to send a delegation to Beijing to discuss the problem with Nan Hanzhen, head of the Committee for the Promotion of International Trade. A distinguished banker and commercial specialist, Nan had long enjoyed the confidence of Japan's financial community. But before the Japanese delegation could embark on its mission to consult him, it received startling news. Indicted by Red Guards as a "bourgeois revisionist," Nan had committed suicide. He was seventy-five years old at the time.[10]

The storms whipping through China's ports also dealt a blow to the *amour-propre* of the Beijing regime. Until this point, the Chinese Communist regime had been proud of the correctness of its commercial relations with the outside world. Underlying the Communists' sense of propriety was an intensely nationalistic impulse to live up to China's claim to be equal to other nations. Though they bargained hard, they had consistently endeavored to honor their commitments. But now, with their ports is disarray, they could not meet their obligations. Once again, it seemed to them, China presented a spectacle of disorder and unreliability, as it had in the past. Sensitive to this image, the Chinese leaders strenuously attempted to revive normal port activity, and dispatched truckloads of sailors and soldiers to break the harbor strikes in Shanghai and elsewhere. Unfamiliar with the ports, however, the troops were ineffective, and the restoration of order was difficult. The strike in Qingdao, for example, dragged on for six weeks.[11] Afterward, when the tumult had begun to subside, harbor officials were singled out as having been responsible for the episode. Significantly, they were charged with "damaging the international prestige of China."[12]

Apparently inspired by the port upheavals, railway workers throughout east China also struck for better working conditions. China's railway network was vital for the transport of people, food, and raw materials as well as for troops and military supplies. Thus the railway disturbances, when they broke out, crippled the country far more severely than the port upheavals.

The first of the railway strikes, evidently timed to follow the harbor disorders, was planned for the final days of December by the Scarlet Guards for the Defense of Mao Zedong's Thought, the workers' faction that had been organized in Shanghai by the Municipal Party Committee. On the morning of December 30, employees in the Shanghai Railway Control Office pulled the switches that halted all rail traffic in the vicinity of the city. Service abruptly stopped on the main rail lines running northwest to Nanjing and southwest to Hangzhou, leaving more than fifty passenger and freight trains stranded along the route.[13] An official account, published to celebrate the heroism of two engineers who managed to steer the No. 14 Express from Shanghai to Beijing, inadvertently provided a glimpse of the turmoil on the tracks. Strikers had blocked the tracks and smashed signals along the line in an effort to stop the train, according to this account. At one stage, the two thousand passengers packed in the train were near panic when the lights went out—sabotaged, presumably, by strikers who had somehow climbed aboard. Farther along the way, passengers fainted as the crowded train encountered fresh difficulties. But despite adversity, the No. 14 Express chugged forward until it finally reached the capital several days after leaving Shanghai. Normally, the trip should have taken twenty-three hours.[14]

The railway strikes did more than inconvenience passengers. Coal shipments were delayed throughout China, for example, and at one period the Yangshubu thermal power plant in Shanghai was down to a two-day supply.[15] Coming as it did in the middle of winter, the coal shortage imposed serious hardships. Steel, textile, and other industries were affected as well when rail deliveries of raw materials failed to reach factories. Food supplies carried by train from Guangdong province to Hong Kong—China's principal source of foreign exchange earnings—dropped sharply. Other commodities, due to be transported from the interior to ports for export abroad, were also held up. In early January, for example, Japanese freighters arriving in the northern port of Qinhuangdao were advised that scheduled shipments of soybeans had been diverted to Dairen. The ships steamed back across the Gulf of Liaodong to Dairen—only to discover that the soybean cargoes had been delayed somewhere along the railway down from Manchuria and might not reach the port before February.[16]

The trains that were functioning, in the meantime, were strained to the limit as hundreds of thousands of workers poured into Beijing from provincial cities. Their ostensible objective was to present their grievances to the central government. In reality, most were simply taking advantage of the confusion to enjoy more trips to the capital— just as Red Guards had freely roamed the country months earlier under the guise of "exchanging revolutionary experiences." Factories, mines, and other enterprises were badly disrupted as workers quit their jobs. At the Bingdingshan colliery in Henan province, for example, when more than seven thousand miners left for Beijing, the output of coal declined.[17] Production stopped from late December through mid-January at the Gingdao Si Fang Locomotive Works in Shandong for the same reason.[18] Even the Dajing Oil Field in northern China, long celebrated as a model Maoist enterprise, was hit as its managers sent some ten thousand young workers to Beijing on the pretext that they deserved to participate in the Cultural Revolution. Zhou Enlai called this gesture, which he said had partially paralyzed oil-drilling operations, "counterfeit revolution." The vast migration of workers to Beijing, he further charged, was a form of sabotage by "bourgeois reactionary" elements striving to subvert the Maoist leadership.[19]

Zhou Enlai's allegation was not entirely unfounded. Local officials in several areas had indeed advanced considerable sums of money to protesting workers in hopes of appeasing them, and the workers promptly left their jobs for tours of the country. In Shanghai, the Municipal Party Committee instructed the city's banks to disburse millions of *yuan* in state funds to agitating labor groups in an attempt to satisfy their demands.[20] Party bureaucrats and factory managers also raised salaries, dispensed bonuses, and even handed out free merchandise. One Shanghai workshop distributed bicycles to its thirty employees, while another small plant gave each of its workers three dozen bath towels. Other enterprises in Shanghai sought to placate workers with such items as leather shoes and winter overcoats, and one factory allocated 4 million *yuan* in "premiums" to its staff.[21] In Harbin, the authorities paid every employee in the transport department "back wages" of a thousand *yuan*—the equivalent of two years' salary.[22] Using the excuse that they had not been paid for supplementary labor performed in 1958, the directors of a Beijing marketing agency accorded themselves and their staff some forty thousand *yuan* in "retroactive" overtime pay.[23]

Mao's publicists referred to these material inducements as "sugar-coated bullets" that threatened to kill the true proletarian spirit of austerity. Their attacks against Communist officials alleged to have fostered "economism" not only provided an insight into the extent to which government money was squandered, but offered a glimpse of the way pilgrims to Beijing passed their sojourns in the capital.

Among those accused of wasting state funds was Xiao Wangdong, Vice-Minister of Culture. According to an indictment against him, he spent nearly 4 million *yuan* to subsidize visits to Beijing by assorted art, literary, film, and other groups that did little to promote the Cultural Revolution once they reached the capital. The indictment charged, for instance, that he footed the bill for a troupe of actors that whiled away its time in Beijing in typical Thespian style by eating, drinking, and playing poker. On one occasion, Xiao mobilized the actors to stage a phony demonstration against him so that he could go through the motions of "self-criticism" and thereby display his revolutionary ardor. After the demonstration, the indictment claimed, he served tea and cakes to his "critics."[24]

Another Beijing dignitary accused of riddling workers with "sugar-coated bullets" was Lü Zhengcao, the quiet, respected Minister of Railways and one of China's foremost communications specialists. A lengthy diatribe issued by one Maoist faction charged him with having "incited a great multitude of workers to leave their production posts" by offering them free train trips to Beijing. Railway traffic had been hampered by delays, accidents, and other "tremendous difficulties" as a result. The attack against Lü also alleged that he had provided cheap food and lodgings for workers coming into the capital, encouraging their disruptive movement.[25]

Assaults of this kind against Lü Zhengcao and other Chinese administrators placed Zhou Enlai in an awkward position. The Premier was loath to lose these skilled technicians, without whom the nation's essential services might well be endangered. Yet he could not risk his credibility with the radicals. Thus he sought to appease the Maoists while simultaneously protecting his subordinates by urging men like Lü Zhengcao to confess their shortcomings. The Railway Minister accordingly admitted his "mistakes," pledging that he would henceforth carry out his functions in a "responsible manner."[26] But the Red Guards were not satisfied. Late in January, forcing him to wear a white dunce's cap as a sign of his humiliation, they paraded Lü through the streets of Beijing.[27] After that, he disappeared from public view, presumably to do penance in a labor camp.

Though the Maoist allegations accusing Party officials of bribing labor were frequently exaggerated, workers did in fact explode in a frantic spending spree with huge sums acquired from the government treasury. Until they were closed by Red Guards in mid-January, department stores in Beijing were jammed with workers purchasing almost everything in sight. According to a Japanese dispatch, daily sales of wristwatches tripled and sales of woolen yarn soared twenty-fold above the previous month. A worker who had come into the city from north China was observed buying a dozen shirts for the equivalent of his annual wage. Other workers were seen carrying away bicycles, sewing machines, and radios.[28] And the drive for commodities was not confined to Beijing. A report from the Yunnan provincial capital of Kunming described the hectic scenes there as workers, their pockets bulging with cash, indulged in shopping orgies.[29] This rush for consumer goods was short-lived—primarily because the supply of merchandise was soon exhausted. But, if he was aware of it, the episode may well have confirmed Mao in his conviction that China would require several Cultural Revolutions before "spontaneous tendencies toward capitalism" could be eliminated from its people.

Nor were workers the only Chinese to show "capitalistic tendencies." Peasants in several regions plundered government grain stocks, pilfered commune funds, refused to deliver cereals to state purchasing agents, slaughtered livestock, and, among other things, abandoned collective rice and wheat fields in order to cultivate private crops.[30] Those living in suburban areas streamed into the cities to sell their produce illicitly at high prices and to join in the revolutionary ferment. Though the Maoists predictably accused the "bourgeois revisionist" Party bureaucrats of encouraging them to agitate, the peasants themselves had sufficient cause to revolt. The kind of dissatisfaction troubling them was mirrored in a list of grievances set down in mid-January by villagers from Nanhui, a county south of Shanghai. To some degree, their complaints were probably shared by peasants throughout China.

"We are second-class citizens," the Nanhui peasants complained. They grumbled that the countryside was considered a "general rubbish heap" to which reactionaries, criminals, and "anyone else in need of reform is sent." Rural areas lacked schools, cultural facilities, newspapers, medical services, and competent officials, they protested. It was difficult for young men to find wives, as country girls preferred urban workers—and with good reason, since city workers lived in apartments and earned high salaries while badly paid peasants lived in thatch-roofed huts "exposed to wind and rain, and often about to collapse." Factory workers received meat, bean curd, and other special rations, but peasants were not even allowed to retain the very food they had cultivated. Above all, the protesters argued, the rural population was unable to express itself. "Workers, soldiers, and Party members have associations to represent their interests," they pleaded, "but the peasants have no voice."[31]

Meanwhile, the workers, students, office employees, and others whom the regime had transferred to rural areas took advantage of the turmoil and confusion to drift back to the cities. Several factories that had been shifted to the interior of the country for defense purposes were abandoned as workers returned to their homes.[32] By far the biggest movement to the cities, however, was undertaken by young people who had been sent to the far-off reaches of Gansu, Inner Mongolia, and Xinjiang to work on state farms or construction sites.

During the mid-1960s, more than a hundred thousand youths had gone from Shanghai to Xinjiang, either as volunteers or as forced exiles. Many had been appalled by their experiences in that vast, arid border region, where, instead of being assigned to modern agricultural projects equipped with tractors and other machinery, as advertised, they were herded into barbed-wire compounds and compelled to work like coolies under military supervision.[33] Now, seizing the chance to escape, they streamed back to Shanghai. Some claimed that they had been unjustly banished by Liu Shaoqi's Party "revisionists," while others asserted that they had come back to participate in the Cultural Revolution. But whatever their justification, they created a new problem in Shanghai. Not only were they swelling the city's population, already bursting with hundreds of thousands of displaced Red Guards, peasants, and other outsiders. As volatile rebels, they also contributed to its instability. Moreover, having returned illegally, they lacked residence permits, ration coupons, and all the other documents required as Chinese citizens. They could only survive by stealing, black marketeering, and engaging in other shady activities. In the Shanghai tradition, they gradually banded together into outlaw gangs and, for many years afterward, one of the main tasks of the city authorities was their arrest and deportation.

⚵

Throughout January, the Maoist leaders in Beijing and the provinces made repeated attempts to restore order to the Cultural Revolution. On January 5, the eleven radical organizations in Shanghai that had attempted to seize control of the city from the Municipal Party Committee published a declaration calling for discipline. It charged "reactionaries" in the Muncipal Party Committee with having provoked the labor revolt, conspired to paralyze Shanghai's water and electricity supply, and plotted to bring public transport to a standstill. Faithful disciples of Mao, the declaration said, should "serve as the vanguard and backbone not only in grasping revolution, but also in stimulating production." Workers should therefore "make a clear distinction between right and wrong, avoid delusion, quickly wake up, return to your production posts, and rejoin the proletarian revolutionary line."[34] Four days later, thirty-two Shanghai organizations issued a ten-point "Urgent Notice" that was even stronger in tone. The notice warned workers that they could be prosecuted for "sabotaging production" if they stayed out on strike. It also warned all agitators, whatever their political coloration, that they could face punishment for seizing public buildings, committing acts of violence, or "undermining social order."[35] At the same time, in an effort to put teeth into these directives, the Shanghai radicals announced that the metropolitan police would henceforth suppress unruly elements, even to the extent of inflicting the death penalty for certain crimes.[36] In an effort to reactivate the city's municipal services, some youth groups occupied the Railway Control Office and other Shanghai administrative bureaus.

But the Maoist strategy in Shanghai rapidly proved to be ineffective—if not actually disruptive. In the first place, the threat to unleash the police was largely bluff. For the city's Public Security Bureau was just as divided as every other municipal department and could not be considered reliable.[37] There were also growing indications that the Shanghai radical movement itself was fragmenting into a multiplicity of factions despite the propaganda proclaiming its unity. Several of the thirty-two groups that signed the "Urgent Notice" on January 9, for example, were offshoots of the eleven organizations that had published the similar message only four days earlier.[38] In addition, even though the radicals blamed the local Party apparatus for "economism," it was plain that the real targets of their attack were the workers, peasants, and others who had gone out on strike in December to seek redress for genuine economic and social grievances. This approach, ironically, served to alienate the Maoists from a significant segment of the proletariat.

The potential dangers in the Shanghai situation were not immediately visible to the Maoist leaders in Beijing. On the contrary, as earlier described, they initially praised the city's radicals for their "forceful counteroffensive" against the "bourgeois reactionaries." Underlying this unusually rapid endorsement was Mao's apparent conviction that, as his vision held, the "masses" were really capable of assuming and exercising power in a responsible manner. He saw the radical take-over of Shanghai as a resurrection, Chinese-style, of the Paris Commune of 1871. But it soon became clear that the notion of a Shanghai Commune was chimeric. As disorders persisted in the city throughout January, it also became obvious that Shanghai could not be held up as a model of revolutionary stability. The leaders in Beijing now turned to less imaginative measures to curb the turmoil that was now overrunning nearly every city as well as many rural areas of China.

Judging by the series of almost daily decrees they issued in January, the Maoist leaders were desperate. They directed that stores be closed in an effort to halt the sale of consumer goods, and they instructed the Army and police to prevent the public from withdrawing money from banks.[39] They declared a moratorium on the payment of back wages, bonuses, welfare benefits, and other special allowances, promising workers that their complaints would be reviewed.[40] They ordered a stop to the movement of rusticated students and laborers from the countryside to the cities, urged peasants to cease their protests, and put out numerous pleas to youths to return to Xinjiang and other border regions.[41] They commanded radicals to withdraw from radio stations they had seized, ordaining that stations would henceforth only broadcast programs initiated in Beijing.[42] And, among other edicts, they canceled the traditional Lunar New Year holiday in order to reduce the strain on the country's disrupted financial and transport systems.[43]

Premier Zhou Enlai was characteristically in the forefront of this strenuous effort to stabilize the nation. No subject was too trivial to command his attention and, despite the enormous pressure on him, he apparently handled himself with almost superhuman equanimity. He listened to complaints from parents whose children had been banished to Xinjiang, promising to investigate their grievances.[44] He frequently stayed awake until dawn as he talked night after night with students, workers, provincial representatives, government officials, and Army officers. He passed judgment on the ideological purity of Red Guard units and their leaders.[45] At five o'clock on the morning of January 10, he addressed an assembly of transport workers, informing them that free train travel was being suspended and appealing for their cooperation in restoring normal railway traffic.[46] At another meeting, he asked radical youths to stop squabbling, explaining that the Cultural Revolution was "not an individualistic power struggle nor the power struggle of small cliques."[47] Zhou repeatedly stressed in his speeches that there was no need to overthrow China's entire political and economic structure. Instead, he emphasized the importance of carrying out a selective, surgical purge by eliminating a few "reactionaries" while encouraging others to reform. Consonant with that approach, he protected his close subordinates against Red Guard harassment—even though, in the process, he exposed himself to criticism.

From time to time, Zhou's admonitions were echoed by the senior radicals, among them Chen Boda and Jiang Qing, even though their motives differed from his. They were aware of the dangers of prolonged turmoil to the Chinese economy and, too, they knew that the fragmentation of the Red Guard organizations would subvert the Cultural Revolution. But they realized that moderation would blunt the forward thrust of Mao's drive. They therefore adopted an ambivalent position. They appealed for radical unity, but pressed the Red Guards to take stronger action against suspected Party "revisionists." They urged their followers to "struggle through reason," but also authorized them to defend themselves "with force." Reiterating the Maoist slogans publicized at the outset of the Cultural Revolution, they continued to assert that "rebellion is justified" and that "destruction must precede construction." The ambiguity of these directives effectively gave local radicals the freedom to pursue their own campaigns.

By the end of January, then, China resembled a spastic whose limbs were unresponsive to its brain. Central authority in Beijing was largely intact. But the provinces writhed in chaos as Red Guards, having shattered the regional Party structures, were unable to erect new political mechanisms. Only one institution had the capacity to fill the power vacuum—the Army. Thus the next attempt to impose order began under military auspices. Yet it brought on a period of further conflicts.

CHAPTER 12

Out of the Barrel of a Gun

> *The Chinese Red Army is an armed body for carrying out the political tasks of the revolution.*
>
> —MAO ZEDONG, *December 1929*

> *The attitude toward the People's Liberation Army is in fact the attitude toward the dictatorship of the proletariat, and an important criterion for determining whether or not a person is a genuine revolutionary.*
>
> —Red Flag, *May 1967*

MAO ZEDONG had unleashed the Red Guards at the start of 1967 with instructions to "storm the positions" held by the Communist Party in China's political, economic, and social institutions. But now, only a few weeks later, the "irresistible historical trend" destined to defeat the "enemies of socialism" was faltering. The Maoist radicals were meeting stiff resistance in many areas as local officials counterattacked with their own legions of students, workers, and peasants, or staged confusingly deceptive demonstrations of fidelity to the Maoist cause. Even in the places where they had managed to topple the Party bureaucracy, like Shanghai, the Red Guard groups were fragmenting into rival factions. Despite Mao's inspirational appeals, the radicals could neither seize power nor wield it effectively. Instead of forging a new revolutionary order, they were creating chaos.

At this critical juncture, Mao might conceivably have conceded that his campaign had miscarried and abandoned its more ambitious objectives, as he did when the Great Leap Forward stumbled. But such a policy would have been extremely hazardous. For if his adversaries had cut down his authority after the collapse of the Great Leap, they would now retaliate even more fiercely against him. Retreat meant not only the defeat of his dream but, quite possibly, his very downfall. His only plausible alternative, then, was to turn to the sole force that had the sinew, the prestige, the discipline, and the organization to swing the balance in his favor—the People's Liberation Army. On January 23, he publicly instructed China's military commanders to go to the aid of his radical followers.

Until then, though instrumental in mobilizing the Red Guards, China's troops had been under orders to remain neutral in the drive against the Party machine. Those orders were now rescinded. Mao directed the Army to give "active support" to "genuine" radicals in need of assistance. "Counterrevolutionaries" must be "resolutely suppressed," and he authorized the Army to "strike back with force" against them should they resort to violence. In addition, he warned that the Army itself might be subjected to a purge if it shielded "diehards who persist in the bourgeois reactionary line."[1]

Much later, in justifying his call for Army support, Mao explained that the radical students had proved themselves unreliable. They were "intellectuals"—a species he had long disdained—who suffered from "wavering character" and the lack of will to pursue "thorough revolution." For that reason, Mao claimed, he had entrusted the most crucial stage of the Cultural Revolution to soldiers who were "merely workers and peasants in military uniforms" and therefore constituted the true proletariat.[2]

Whatever the validity of this rationale, Mao's decision to rely on the Army scarcely brought the results he had anticipated. Chinese soldiers, like soldiers everywhere in the world, were essentially dedicated to the preservation of stability. Their basic impulse was to impose law and order, the very antithesis of revolution, and hence their intervention served mainly to frustrate the Maoist radical movement. The upheavals that ensued, moreover, further prompted the Army to strengthen its political authority, notably in the composition of the so-called Revolutionary Committees that were gradually created to govern the Chinese provinces. After April 1969, when a new national Communist Party structure was established, the Army plainly emerged in a predominant position—at least for a time.

For all his purported omniscience, Mao could not have predicted these consequences. Yet his move to enlist the Army in the Cultural Revolution was made with apparent reluctance. Signaling his plan to a group of senior Chinese officers beforehand, he seemed to communicate a feeling of desperation. He had opted to commit troops to the side of the floundering radicals, he explained, because he saw "no other recourse." The struggle against his Party enemies had grown so "extraordinarily acute," that it was too late for "compromise." It was also too late to discuss the pros and cons and whys and wherefores of military intervention. The situation demanded drastic measures, he asserted, suggesting in effect that troops should act first and ask questions later. "Power must be seized before anything else is done. We can no longer continue to deal in abstractions. Otherwise, our hands will be tied."[3]

Mao had undoubtedly been contemplating the notion of positive military involvement in the Cultural Revolution for some time. During the previous months, he appeared to be developing increased concern for the ideological purity of the Army. In early October, his Defense Minister and heir-apparent, Lin Biao, had emphasized at a rally of soldiers the necessity for the Army to reinforce itself with Mao's "Thought."[4] At Lin Biao's orders, teams of Army political activists were sent to Beijing for special training. Mao soon afterward hinted symbolically that troops needed stronger ideological guidance by appointing Jiang Qing to be the Army's "adviser" on artistic and literary matters. The possibility of military intervention was also mirrored in the fact that both Party and Army elements began to betray their hostility to the idea.

The Party feared military participation in the Maoist campaign for the obvious reason that its apparatus was no match for the Army if regional commanders undertook to dismantle it. A prominent official who probably voiced opposition to the scheme was Tao Zhu, who had become the Party's propaganda chief in 1966. The exact nature of his resistance to the new Maoist line has never been clear. But one esoteric sign that his prestige was waning in late 1966 was perceptible when in November a Beijing opera company and three other artistic troupes that had functioned under his supervision were shifted to the control of Jing Qing in her new capacity as cultural "adviser" to the Army.[5] A few weeks later, Tao Zhu was purged amid Red Guard denunciations accusing him of almost every imaginable crime.

Several senior Chinese military figures were equally reluctant to sanction the Army's involvement in the Cultural Revolution. These veteran Communist officers were closely linked to central and provincial Party *apparatchiks* who were being singled out for attack by the radicals, and they were naturally inclined to stand by their old comrades. The professional soldiers among them were also worried that a deeper Army commitment to the Maoist campaign would weaken China's national security, particularly as Soviet and American pressures seemed to be mounting.

Resistance to involving the Army in the Cultural Revolution—or thrusting the Cultural Revolution into the Army—was apparently led by officers like Marshal He Long. He was intimately connected with many key Party officials, especially in southwest China, where his First Field Army had operated for years. As a professional soldier, he was also sensitive to China's defense priorities, and he was wary of engaging the Army in an ideological drive that might divide its leadership and reduce its effectiveness in the event of war. He Long's views seemed to have been shared in varying degrees by other members of the Beijing military hierarchy, including Marshal Zhu De, the aged and illustrious "father" of the Chinese Communist Army.

But the Army chiefs, like the Party bureaucrats, could not openly oppose Mao without seeming to be guilty of heresy. Their strategy was thus to contrive an impression of enthusiasm for the Cultural Revolution while taking steps to restrict the Army's real role in the drive. Typical of these steps was an "urgent directive" issued on October 5 by the Military Affairs Commission and the Army's General Political Department and couched in the fashionably fierce rhetoric of the period. The directive urged cadets and young officers to join in the Maoist offensive to uncover "counterrevolutionaries." More significantly, however, it specified that this agitation should be strictly limited to military schools and academies—in which, quite clearly, it could be controlled.[6] To prevent the turmoil from disrupting its ranks, moreover, the Army set up its own Cultural Revolution Directorate, separate from the civilian group headed by Chen Boda and Jiang Qing. Predictably, the officer appointed to manage this Army directorate was General Liu Zhijian, a senior military commissar who had long been associated with Marshal He Long.[7]

Throughout the autumn of 1966, top Chinese military men went through the motions of genuflecting to Mao while cautioning troops against involvement in his campaign. He Long himself exemplified this dual approach in a speech he delivered in mid-November to Army instructors and cadets then visiting Beijing. He lavishly praised Mao as the Army's "greatest inspiration" and the "reddest sun in the heart of each and every revolutionary fighter," recommending that all soldiers arm themselves with the Chairman's portrait as a symbol of their "infinite love and adoration" for him. Switching from hyperbole to reality, however, He then told the troops that they should "neither take part in nor interfere with local Cultural Revolution activities, and shall not participate in such pursuits as bombarding [Party] headquarters, making rebellion, confiscating private property, and holding parades."[8]

Early in October, to take another instance, Marshal Ye Jianying, a Vice-Chairman of the Military Affairs Commission, had warned troops against "interfering" in the Cultural Revolution. "We must confine ourselves to our own campaign," he said, adding that soldiers should "not carry out Red Guard activities." Minimizing the need for a purge within the Army, Ye estimated that only 3 per cent of military cadres could be classified as "bad elements."[9] This plea for moderation was echoed by Marshal Xu Xiangqian, another Vice-Chairman of the Military Affairs Commission. Chinese defenses might be damaged if the Army was shaken by internal discord, he observed in November. American escalation in Vietnam and the Soviet build-up in Siberia were combining "to menace the security of China." So the Army "must be certain that there is no threat to its command structure," since "we would be in a plight if the enemies took us by surprise." Thus Xu urged young soldiers to refrain from harassing their superiors:

> Give consideration to the very arduous administrative tasks shouldered by the leading cadres. You must give them time to direct their troops and to handle routine work. . . . Many are old men between the ages of fifty and sixty. Many are sick, yet they must make preparations for war at any time. You must have regard for their work and their health. This is not meant to impede your revolutionary action, but you should show concern for them whenever you can.[10]

But by the turn of the year, Mao was maneuvering to overcome the Army's recalcitrance by dividing its senior officers. On one hand, he encouraged the radicals to assail He Long and the generals whom he considered to be his most implacable adversaries, while at the same time he undertook to reassure Ye Jianying, Xu Xiangqian, and the professional soldiers that an Army commitment to the Cultural Revolution would not impair China's defense capabilities. In short, his design was to isolate a minority of his military opponents while appeasing a majority of the Army's leadership. This design was disclosed early in January in an editorial in the *Liberation Army Daily*, the military journal published under Lin Biao's guidance. The editorial announced that a "handful" of purported "reactionaries" who had "wormed their way into the Army" would be ousted. But because the Army "has the important responsibility of defending the motherland," the editorial cautioned, its "arrangements" for conducting the Cultural Revolution "should be different from those of other units."[11]

A Red Guard offensive against He Long initiated in late December quickly attained large and somewhat ludicrous proportions. In Beijing, wall posters, pamphlets, and other literature denounced He for everything from slandering Mao to indulging in sexual perversions. One brochure claimed that he had described Mao's doctrines as "no better than dogshit" and had forbidden his subordinates to study them. Another recalled that his older sister had been an opium-smoking bandit and, consequently, an "exponent of pure feudalism." He was also accused of such "bourgeois" tastes as keeping pet monkeys and feasting on fat puppies. One Red Guard attack even asserted that He frequently slept with several prostitutes simultaneously.[12]

Though most of this vilification was distorted, there was probably some truth to the charge that He protected numerous relatives whom he had placed in influential positions. One of his sons had been instrumental in organizing the United Action Committee at Qinghua University early in the Cultural Revolution. Two of his nephews were high-ranking Army political commissars in Beijing, and his brother-in-law, Li Jingquan, controlled the Communist Party apparatus in southwest China.[13] Trying to blacken He's image even further, Red Guards alleged that he had plotted a *coup d'état* against Mao in February 1966. The Maoist leaders knew this accusation to be false, yet it served their purpose to let it spread for several months before issuing a denial.[14]

He Long was finished by the middle of January. Whether he was actually arrested has never been made clear. In early May, however, Red Guards arraigned him before a kangaroo court and, after briefly admitting his "errors" in customary style, he disappeared from public view.[15]

A similar assault was staged against Marshal Zhu De, then eighty years old and the most venerated officer in the Communist movement. Zhu De had been exalted in the past almost as highly as Mao— and even by Mao himself. But now he had apparently voiced misgivings about committing the Army to the Cultural Revolution, and this resistance exposed him to a spate of denunciations. The Red Guards labeled him a "swine" and a "big warlord," addicted to such "feudalistic hobbies" as raising orchids.[16] These Red Guard attacks also revealed, undoubtedly with some measure of accuracy, that Zhu De had criticized the excesses of the Great Leap Forward in 1958. It was also likely, as the radicals claimed, that he had advocated increased reliance on military specialization in opposition to Mao's theories of guerrilla warfare.[17] The extent to which this assault could go was limited, however, since Zhu De's prestige in the Army was enormous. Hence the campaign against him gradually faded, and he continued to appear at ceremonial occasions, mainly as a symbol of unity. In April 1969, when the Communist Party structure was revamped, he remained in the Politburo—though no longer on that body's powerful Standing Committee.

The campaigns against He Long and Zhu De were matched, meanwhile, by a sweeping purge of senior officers presumed to have opposed Army intervention in the Cultural Revolution. Among those dismissed were Xu Guangda, commander of the Armored Forces; Li Shouxuan, head of the Army's Railway Corps, and Wang Shangrong, Director of Operations on the General Staff. These along with an impressive array of other officers had been associated with He Long. One of them, Liao Hansheng, a Vice-Minister of National Defense and First Commissar of the Beijing Military Region, was He's nephew.[18] Paralleling this move, Mao fired the entire membership of the Army's own Cultural Revolution Directorate, including its head, Liu Zhijian, who was specifically accused of having resisted the Chairman's plan for military intervention in his campaign.[19] In its place, Mao named a new group with Marshal Xu Xiangqian as its boss. The appointment of Marshal Xu, who had been cool to the idea of Army involvement in the Cultural Revolution, was plainly aimed at placating the military professionals. Beyond that, Mao packed the group with his loyal disciples, among them Xiao Hua, chief of the Army's General Political Department and a protégé of Lin Biao; Guan Feng, a radical theoretician; and You Lijin, political commissar of the Air Force. Another member of the group was Lin Biao's wife, Ye Zhun, who was then emerging as a dynamic leftist. And of course, there was Mao's wife, Jiang Qing, an "adviser" to the new body.[20]

Mao was able to eliminate such a panoply of powerful foes because he had carefully taken measures beforehand to win the acquiescence of officers who were uneasy about the effects of the Cultural Revolution on China's defenses. He assured them that the Army's political role would not extend to sensitive frontier regions, and, to allay their fears of prolonged disruptions elsewhere in the nation, he apparently promised to put the Cultural Revolution on a more orderly course.

Moreover, he issued written guarantees to back up these promises.

On January 28, five days after directing the Army to intervene in his drive, Mao decreed that the Cultural Revolution "should be postponed for the time being" in the coastal provinces facing Taiwan, in the southern areas adjacent to Vietnam, and along the northern border sector contiguous to the Soviet Union.[21] Though public Chinese propaganda was then still focused primarily against American "imperialism," Mao divulged in a private message to the Army leaders that he believed Soviet pressures on China were growing. Soviet air as well as ground operations in the vicinity of Xinjiang were increasing, he pointed out, and Chinese troops in that neighborhood "must be on guard and in a state of preparedness."[22]

Also in late January, Mao approved an eight-point directive prohibiting the Red Guards from ransacking homes, compelling people to wear dunce's caps and placards, parading them through the streets, forcing them to kneel, and submitting them to other indignities.[23] The Red Guards were once again told to stop traveling around China, and were given deadlines to return to their native towns.[24] These orders had been issued before, but now the Army was authorized to enforce them. In addition, it was authorized to take control of provincial radio stations and the nation's civil airlines.[25]

While Mao saw military intervention in the Cultural Revolution as a positive boost to his radical followers, Zhou Enlai apparently viewed the Army's involvement as a chance to restore order. But Zhou had to exercise the same kind of delicate tact and diplomacy during this period that he had frequently displayed in earlier crises. He could not openly advocate military repression of the Red Guards without exposing himself to radical attacks, yet he could not encourage the radicals without intensifying the tumult he sought to avoid. His task, then, was to appear to stand on every side on all questions. He met this challenge with consummate skill, by making himself indispensable to Mao's inner circle as well as to the senior Army officers who were eager to keep the Cultural Revolution in check.

Judging from available evidence, both Mao and Lin Biao repeatedly relied on Zhou to negotiate complicated problems with local military commanders. It was Zhou, for example, who worked out a temporary settlement in late January among rival Army elements in Xinjiang.[26] He also played an important role in resolving similar disputes in Henan, Sichuan, and Guangdong, and he was to serve as the key intermediary in the dramatic Army mutiny that erupted in July in the Yangzi River industrial complex of Wuhan. Mao may partly have depended upon Zhou to deal with the Army because Lin Biao, who should have been supervising his military subordinates, lacked the Premier's diplomatic talents. Lin Biao was also a chronically sick man, often absent, and scarcely able even when available to devote long hours to tortuous talks with diverse factions. Lin's disappearance from public sight during the crucial months between November 1966 and April 1967 was apparently due to an illness that, according to his own disclosure, left his nerves badly frazzled.[27]

Mao could also count on Zhou as a go-between with the Army because the Premier had many long-standing associations with the upper echelons of the Chinese military establishment. He had been head of the Political Department at Chiang Kai-shek's Whampoa Military Academy in the mid-1920s, at a time when the school's staff and student body included such future Communist military leaders as Marshals Ye Jianying, Nie Rongzhen, and Lin Biao. Zhou had also been a major figure in the famous Nanchang Uprising on August 1, 1927, the first Communist attempt to seize and hold a Chinese city. His ties with China's senior officers were further cemented during the 1930s, when he served as the Red Army's chief political commissar. And, probably more important than these common experiences, Zhou and the military high command tended to share a concern for maintaining China's stability in the face of recurrent Maoist adventures.

Although Mao issued his call to the Army to help the radicals on January 23, troops had actually begun to go into action weeks earlier— and, contrary to the Chairman's hopes, they did little to advance his cause. In fact, they either suppressed unruly Red Guards or tried to arrange compromises between rival factions. So, well before Mao's order was proclaimed, the Army had already started to contravene his wishes by restoring discipline to troubled areas. From the beginning, therefore, the Army's intervention significantly altered the direction of the Maoist campaign.

In early January, as clashes between radicals and Party *apparatchiks* spread, the Army had mobilized to protect various government installations and enterprises against the growing violence. On January 11, for instance, troops took over the banks in order to prevent workers, office employees, and others from withdrawing their deposits.[28] They also moved to guard local roads, bridges, factory warehouses, and, particularly, rural granaries, which were then being stormed by peasants in quest of rice, wheat, and other cereal stocks.[29] Soldiers assigned to these missions were assaulted by disorderly factions despite directives from Beijing insisting that "no person or organization may attack" the Army.[30] Their patience worn thin, military units in several places reacted by cracking down on their assailants without regard for ideological nuances.

One of the first military thrusts aimed at disciplining unruly youths occurred in mid-January in the Hunan province capital of Changsha, where Mao himself had been a radical student more than a half-century earlier. Soldiers there arrested Red Guards who had broken into the city's Party headquarters and were trying to besiege the local Army garrison.[31] A similar episode took place in the town of Fangshan, thirty miles southwest of Beijing, where leftist youths were confronting the local Party machine. On instructions from Xie Fuzhi, the Minister of Public Security, truckloads of troops based in the capital drove into the town, halted the skirmish, and assumed police duties.[32] In both instances, Maoist spokesmen announced that the Army had intervened to suppress "counterrevolutionaries." In reality, the troops had moved mainly to stop the turmoil.

Far more crucial at the time, meanwhile, was the Army's involvement in two other regions—Heilongjiang province, in the heart of industrial Manchuria, and the northern province of Shanxi. Military intervention in these areas had a drastic impact on the future shape of the Cultural Revolution.

Mao saw the Army's commitment to his radical disciples as a means rather than an end. His ultimate hope was that the radicals would overthrow the Party apparatus with Army support, and would then proceed to establish a Chinese equivalent of the Paris Commune—a system which in his view would make the state bureaucracy constantly responsive to the "masses," enfranchised as they were to revoke the mandates of their elected delegates at any moment. In short, he saw it as the perfect vehicle for perpetual revolution. Mao had welcomed the uprising at Beijing University in the spring of 1966 as a portent that a new Commune was in the making. He had referred to the Commune again when he outlined the objectives of the Cultural Revolution. Now he observed developments in Shanghai, where the radicals were currently preparing to inaugurate their version of the Paris Commune.

But the Shanghai People's Commune, as its name would be, was having serious birth pains that would eventually make it stillborn.

The vast number of radical factions were unable to unite as each group demanded representation in the Commune's potential ruling committee. Clamoring for power, each faction fought against the other and also against Zhang Chunqiao, the local Maoist leader, who was saddled with the unenviable task of putting the Commune together.[33] In the midst of this confusion, the creation of the new body was postponed day after day until February 5, when its formation was finally announced at a noisy rally.[34] By this time, though, the Commune concept was dead. For it was clear to everyone, including Mao, that the radicals were hopelessly inept unless firmly guided. Soon afterward Mao described the Shanghai situation as "bordering on anarchy," explaining that "we cannot manage without cadres and specialists." The Paris Commune was no longer his ideal—except, perhaps, for the remote future. Instead, he now advocated the establishment of so-called "triple alliances," formations that had initially been imposed by the Army in Shanxi and Heilongjiang provinces to supplant the collapsing Party apparatuses.[35]

These coalitions were intended to comprise veteran officials, young radicals, and Army officers. The officials would provide indispensable administrative experience. The radicals would add revolutionary coloration. And, since power grows out of the barrel of a gun, the officers would be responsible for setting up the new coalitions and preventing them from falling apart.

Formalized as Revolutionary Committees, the "triple alliances" were quickly endorsed in Beijing as the model to be emulated everywhere, and, with great difficulty, they were gradually erected across China in the years that followed.

If the impulse for establishing the "triple alliances" plainly came from the Army, precisely how the formula was contrived has never been clear. The effort to create the new bodies was too swift, too uniform, and too coordinated to support the notion, widely publicized in the Maoist press, that local military units acted spontaneously. More likely, the regional commanders who set up the "triple alliances" in January were responding to directives from the highest echelons of the Chinese military establishment in Beijing. According to one thesis, senior officers in the capital as well as moderate leaders like Zhou Enlai conceded to Mao's call for Army intervention on condition that troops be used primarily to enforce discipline. If so, then Mao must have agreed to allow the Army to curb the radicals—even though his appeal for military involvement exhorted soldiers to support them.[36] And his agreement could have been contingent upon the Army's conduct in handling the situation in Shanxi province.

Lying on a mountainous plateau more than four thousand feet above sea level, the Shanxi provincial capital of Taiyuan had been the scene of intermittent clashes between Red Guard and Party groups for months. As elsewhere in China, the conflict there began to polarize more sharply in early January. The Party mobilized workers, students, peasants, and others against the Red Guards, reportedly strengthening them with money and, in some cases, weapons. The radicals, in turn, welded together twenty-five different factions. Fighting between the two sides escalated. The Party organizations encircled radical strongholds, routing out and beating their foes. In reaction, the Red Guards streamed through the city streets, breaking into the homes of suspected enemies and, according to their version of events, confiscating arms and ammunition.[37]

Local Army units had remained neutral throughout this turbulence. Finally, on January 12, some two thousand troops wheeled into action across the city. As a team of German engineers working in Taiyuan at the time later recalled, these troops bore automatic weapons and others carried rifles with fixed bayonets as they rode on trucks mounted with machine guns. Artillery and antiaircraft pieces were set up at strategic street corners. But not a shot was fired.[38] The provincial Party bureaucracy crumbled. And the radicals proclaimed that they had seized power.[39]

Oddly enough, this instance of military intervention went unpublicized until January 25, when Beijing hailed it as an example of the Army's response to Mao's call. The delay suggests that the Shanxi operation had been a test case, initiated to measure the Army's effectiveness in helping to topple a Party apparatus.

But despite claims by the radicals that they now wielded authority, it soon became apparent that real power in Shanxi was invested in its military force. When the region's Revolutionary Committee was officially inaugurated in the middle of March, its chairman was not a newly emergent radical imbued with Maoist fervor but a veteran Party figure, Liu Geping, a Muslim who had been the province vice-governor and chief political commissar of its military garrison. His deputies on the Committee included other Army commissars and local Party officials.[40] In short, though it purged certain Party *apparatchiks*, the Cultural Revolution in Shanxi was less an overthrow of the old bureaucracy than a reshuffle of its members. And, while they would squabble among themselves for months to come, these leaders made it plain from the beginning that they had no intention of tolerating radical effervescence. Or, as a military spokesman described the Army's role in the province, troops had "strengthened the proletarian dictatorship and insured the establishment of revolutionary order."[41]

Even more decisive than Shanxi was the birth of the Revolutionary Committee in Harbin, a key industrial and communications center in Manchuria. Developments there were important in two respects. The provincial Revolutionary Committee, set up on February 1, was the first "triple alliance" publicly endorsed by Beijing, and it consequently superseded the abortive Shanghai Commune as the model formula for the nation. Moreover, its composition was unusual. The Committee's chairman, Pan Fusheng, not only was the former Party boss of the area, but years before had been purged as a "right-wing opportunist." Thus he hardly personified the Marxist orthodoxy. Yet his appointment to head the new Committee was deliberate—and it reflected an attempt to resolve a serious problem troubling the more moderate military and civilian leaders then coming to the fore in Beijing in the wake of the destructive January upheaval.

Though the Army was moving to restore order in different regions, there was a pressing need for experienced officials to help to revive China's paralyzed administration. But officials who had faced Red Guard attacks were understandably afraid to expose themselves again to humiliating assaults. Like turtles sensing danger, they hesitated to stick their necks out. In addition, the young Maoist radicals were reluctant to relinquish their newly acquired authority to bureaucrats they had overthrown. And they, too, were in no mood to see the old officials stage a comeback. On one hand, therefore, the choice of a man like Pan Fusheng was calculated to demonstrate to wary officials that they were welcome to return to their posts. At the same time, his elevation served to remind the Red Guards that nobody was beyond redemption. This fresh policy of leniency for officials was spelled out in an authoritative *Red Flag* editorial. "It must be soberly recognized that most cadres are good," the editorial declared, explaining that even those who had committed "serious mistakes" could "make amends" through education by the "masses." Moreover, the editorial went on, experienced officials were "more mature politically," had "greater organizational skill," and displayed "the ability to exercise power and administer work for the State." Without their guidance, the radicals resembled a leaderless "herd of dragons, each going his own way." Hence the moment had come for the Red Guards and other activists to cooperate with former officials.[42]

Pan Fusheng, then in his early sixties, did indeed exemplify the "renovated" Party *apparatchik*. As a senior official in Henan province, where Mao initially tested the Great Leap Forward in 1958, Pan had run into difficulties for resisting the Chairman's intensive collectivization program. According to an indictment published at the time, he had argued that the province was too poor and its population too apathetic to support accelerated collectivization. He reportedly complained that peasants were being turned into "beasts of burden," that "oxen are tied up while human beings are harnessed in the fields." As a result, Pan disappeared from sight until late 1962, when he emerged as head of the nation's Federation of Supply and Marketing Cooperatives.[43] By May 1966, he had regained stature as First Secretary of the Heilongjiang Communist Party Committee.

As elsewhere in China during the late summer and fall of 1966, Red Guards in Heilongjiang held mammoth rallies to denounce the local Party machine. And, as in other Chinese cities, the Party leaders in Harbin went through the motions of demonstrating their zeal for the Cultural Revolution. According to his own account, Pan Fusheng allowed himself to be criticized by the Red Guards and even went without food or sleep for four days as he submitted to the "remolding" of his ideological attitudes.[44]

By the turn of the year, the situation in the province had gotten out of hand. Student groups had been agitating for months. Demobilized soldiers, unreconciled to the rigors of farming and land reclamation in the northern parts of the region, now mobilized a so-called Glorious Veterans Army to demand improved conditions. Similarly, rusticated youths returned to Harbin to form a War Preparedness Army. Industrial and transport workers created other movements, and soon Harbin was plunged into chaos.

Inevitably, the Army stepped in to halt the strife. As an official report made clear, it was the Army that put up Pan Fusheng as the head of the new Revolutionary Committee.[45] The Army's presence was also apparent not only in the person of the Vice-Chairman of the Committee, General Wang Jiadao, military commander of the province, but in the keynote speaker at the ceremony inaugurating the Committee, Song Renqiong, the Army's chief political commissar in the sector.[46]

Hailing the creation of the Heilongjiang triple alliance, Beijing publicists emphasized that law, order, and discipline had triumphed.

The *People's Daily* explained that it represented the "consolidation of the proletarian dictatorship" and, in a distinct switch from the days when Red Guards were being told that "rebellion is justified," the newspaper warned radicals to behave themselves. "It is entirely wrong," said the *People's Daily*, "to oppose everything, cast out everything, and strike down everything."[47]

Illustrating the advantages of stability, a document issued in Beijing described the improvement that took place in the Harbin railway system after order was restored. Inadvertently, the document also disclosed the extent of the damage that had been inflicted on that same rail system by the riots that had roiled the city before the Army take-over. Prior to January 25, the document revealed, passenger train service between Harbin and the Shandong province city of Jinan had been suspended for two months. Strikes by engineers and other workers put fifteen locomotives out of action for periods up to eighteen days, with the result that eight hundred freight cars were inoperative. More than six thousand tons of merchandise had piled up in one of Harbin's stations during the month of January. The disturbances also caused more than half of the freight and passenger traffic to run late, sometimes by a whole day. The Army presumably exerted considerable pressure on the Harbin transport workers to return to work and make up for the losses. For after the founding of the Heilongjiang Revolutionary Committee, the document claimed, railway operations in Harbin broke "the highest level in history."[48]

Matching its intervention in Shanxi and Heilongjiang, the Army moved swiftly to impose order in Beijing and elsewhere in China. On the night of February 11, for example, troops in the capital marched in formation to the headquarters of the Municipal Public Security Bureau, the city's central police authority, and occupied it amid the beating of drums and clashing of cymbals. The Beijing military garrison then issued a communiqué announcing that police and public security personnel would henceforth function under Army auspices.[49] On the same day, the Army set up its first Military Control Commission in Beijing, and similar bodies were quickly established in Shanghai, Guangzhou, and other cities, where they effectively authorized local commanders to exercise police powers.[50] About the same time, the Army initiated military and ideological training programs in universities and schools.[51] Army control stretched out into the countryside as well, as soldiers obeyed instructions to supervise peasants and rural cadres in the spring plantings.[52] Not long afterward, troops moved into factories, mines, and other enterprises in order to enforce "labor discipline" and assure the rhythm of production.[53]

As a former employee of a paper mill in Guangzhou has described the Army's involvement, soldiers succeeded in halting the turbulence that had inhibited industrial activity. But they also troubled the workers and interfered with management.[54] The East River Paper Mill, with nearly two thousand workers, was one of the largest and most modern in Guangzhou, and its operations had been frequently interrupted in December and January for many reasons. Once, the mill stopped for three days for lack of electricity when a local power complex was reportedly sabotaged. It also slowed down from time to time as young workers, who had organized several Red Guard factions inside the factory, left to "exchange revolutionary experiences around the country." Production often ceased as workers staged demonstrations, attended rallies, or squabbled among themselves. Finally, in late February, a so-called Military Work Team arrived, composed of two hundred unarmed soldiers. Their chief was an Army political commissar, and he rapidly asserted his command over the plant. One of his initial acts was to demote both the factory's Party boss and its personnel director to common workers on the vague grounds that they had "abused their authority." He then established a plant committee along the lines of a "triple alliance," with twelve soldiers among its thirty members. He also dispersed troops throughout the mill, assigning two or three men to every dormitory and putting two noncommissioned officers in each of the plant's five workshops as monitors.

But if this military presence in the East River Paper Mill served to maintain order, it failed to inspire the workers. Most of the soldiers were from Hunan and other provinces north of Guangzhou and, speaking an alien dialect, could not communciate with the plant employees. In addition, though they were not harsh, the troops behaved like overseers. The commander of the Military Work Team also interfered with the management of the mill. Eager to increase the plant's production in order to dramatize the virtues of Army control, he instructed the mill superintendent at one point to turn out an inferior grade of paper more quickly. The superintendent initially refused but under pressure finally complied. Still, there had seemed to be no plausible alternative to Army supervision of the mill. "Conditions were so confused," the former employee said, "that the place would have fallen apart if the soldiers had not come in."

The Army's intervention elsewhere was bolstered by a series of admonitions from Beijing telling the radicals to restrain themselves. In early February, Zhou Enlai openly castigated an assembly of Red Guards for their chaotic and "arrogant" conduct. He said that their violence had alienated a "great many people" who might have otherwise been won over to the Maoist cause. It was better to "conquer the hearts" of adversaries than to "scratch their skins," Zhou explained, and warned against tormenting officials whose "errors" could be "reformed."[55] Somewhat later, Zhou criticized a group of young radicals even more forcefully when he disclosed that Red Guards had killed Zhan Linzhi, Minister of Coal Industry, after submitting him to forty days of public criticism and torture.[56]

Similar expressions of concern were echoed by Maoist zealots in Beijing. Even the most dogmatic members of the Cultural Revolution Directorate, like Wang Li, cautioned that "anarchy is the biggest danger at the moment."[57] Mao himself voiced disappointment in the "little red generals," as he had originally called the Red Guards. Among other things, he remarked in one talk, they were being corrupted by "money" and "cars," wasting their time at "too many rallies," and displaying "sectarian" tendencies as they squabbled among themselves for power.[58] On another occasion, urging the radicals to show "more dignity and justice" toward their foes, Mao said:

> Slogans put up in Beijing are of low quality. They refer repeatedly to "smashing the heads of dogs." There surely cannot be so many dogs' heads. They are all human heads. Posters of this sort are difficult for the masses to understand. Pictures of people being pilloried, with their arms twisted behind their backs like jet airplanes, have been published and transmitted abroad by foreign correspondents.
>
> The level of the struggle is too low. We must educate the next generation. If not, it will resort to the same low tactics. What is important is to fight on the political level.[59]

Expressing the Beijing hierarchy's disenchantment with the Red Guards, an article published jointly in the *People's Daily* and the *Liberation Army Daily* diagnosed the radicals' principal shortcomings. They suffered from "ultra-democracy and liberalism," which were "corrosives" that "eat away unity, subvert organization, cause apathy, and create dissension," as well as damage "strict discipline and alienate the leadership from the masses." Another affliction of the Red Guards was their "pursuit of the limelight," which drove factions and individuals to assert themselves rather than work "anonymously." The Red Guards also displayed symptoms of a "mountain-stronghold mentality," defined as the obsession of certain radicals to "control a small unit and proclaim themselves the rulers" as they strove for "hegemony and power." In addition, the article said, there was the "sectarianism" of radicals who "tend only to see the things under their noses and concern themselves only with their own small groups" while disregarding the interests of the entire nation. These propensities could be summed up in a single word—"ego." And, the article warned, "they cause the revolutionary ranks to disintegrate, to waver, to lose their fighting power, and to fail to unite, and they may eventually lead the revolution to doom."[60]

The authorities in Beijing did more than merely speak out against the more virulent young activists. They also decreed the dissolution of several Red Guard organizations, and their switch to moderation was punctuated by a baffling change in ideological labels. Groups like the Red Worker Rebels and the National Construction Army Rebels were now disbanded for such allegedly "reactionary" activities as intruding into government offices, plundering state property, and raiding private homes.[61] Directives also commanded the radical young people not only to return to their universities and schools but, once there, to undergo a "painful process of protracted ideological struggle" in order to overcome their "egotistical" inclinations.[62] In late February, moreover, Beijing instructed the panoply of diverse factions in the capital to merge in a single Red Guard Congress.[63] Publicized as a move to cement and strengthen the radicals, the formation of the Congress was obviously contrived to facilitate control over the disparate Red Guard splinter groups then resisting efforts to restrict their freedom. In short, having uncorked the Red Guards, the Chinese leaders were now trying to force them back into the bottle.

A stream of fresh decrees also poured forth from Beijing urging forgiveness for most Party officials, whose services were desperately needed to stabilize the country. Effectively reversing the earlier exhortations to youths to "bombard" the Party bureaucracy, Mao and his associates now stressed that seasoned officials must be respected and even obeyed. In a major policy declaration published in late February, for example, *Red Flag* unequivocally laid down this line. Extremists were laboring under the "misconception" that "all those in authority are not good . . . and should therefore be overthrown," the journal said. The tendency was to assault an official for a "single fault" without considering his merits, "to seize only his mistakes, willfully exaggerate them, and carelessly brand him with unwarranted labels." But this approach was "completely wrong. . . . It would be very dangerous if the scope of attack were erroneously expanded and the spearhead of the struggle were directed against the broad sections of cadres." *Red Flag* demanded, consequently, that the Red Guards accept the guidance of the Party *apparatchiks* they had formerly been cited to denounce. "If the masses alone are active without a strong leading group to organize their activity properly, such activity cannot be sustained for long, or carried forward in the right direction, or raised to a high level."[64]

Variations on this theme were repeated throughout China's provinces. In the city of Qingdao, for instance, radicals were derided for spreading the "fallacious view" that all officials were opposed to Mao.[65] A directive issued in the southern province of Guizhou condemned the Red Guards for indiscriminately assailing local functionaries, claiming that most officials had "good backgrounds" even though they may have "made some mistakes" early in the Cultural Revolution.[66] The new line was also publicized in Shanghai, where the radicals now conceded that they had aborted their attempt in January to create a Commune. The purpose of the Cultural Revolution, they now said, was "not merely to dismiss people from office."[67] Somewhat reluctantly, they echoed the exhortation to welcome selected officials into a "triple alliance" to govern the city.[68]

Though they had recognized the necessity for disciplining unruly Red Guards, the Maoist leaders in Beijing were certainly not in favor of eliminating the radicals from positions of power. Yet, by early March, it was becoming apparent that military commanders in many areas were taking advantage of their new authority to ostracize and even suppress the Red Guards and other radical activists. Noting this trend, the Maoists warned that even though some radicals displayed "shortcomings or errors," it was "imperative" to give them "full weight," heed their "opinions," and "never regard them as simply the supporting cast" in the drama of the Cultural Revolution.[69] But the Army had extended its domination across the country and showed no signs of placating the radicals.

CHAPTER 13

The Army Attempts to Rule

The situation in China today resembles the situation in 1949, when the country was under military control.
— ZHOU ENLAI, *February 1967*

"THE PROLETARIAN POLITICAL POWER was seized by us with rifles, and it will be defended by us with rifles," a military unit in Shandong province had announced on January 28, and that proud proclamation summed up the Army's attitude throughout China.[1]

Troops had moved into factories and rural communes to supervise industrial and agricultural production. Since February 11, when they took over the Public Security Bureau in Beijing, soldiers had assumed police duties in several cities. Military Control Commissions, designed to formalize the Army's influence, were also being set up in almost every provincial capital. Troops were running radio stations in Beijing and other places and, in late February, they were reported to be in control of four provincial newspapers as well as the *Beijing Daily*, the organ of the Party's municipal apparatus in the national capital. They were managing airports and railway stations, guarding warehouses, and even handling freight in the port of Shanghai.[2] On March 30, Lin Biao estimated in a private speech that more than thirty Army divisions—nearly four hundred thousand men—were being deployed to run China's essential services. "Nothing like this has happened in the past seventeen years," he remarked.[3]

In addition, the five tripartite Revolutionary Committees which had been established by early spring were basically dominated by Army officers with veteran Party officials as their main subordinates. The Shandong Committee, founded on February 3, was headed by Wang Xiaoyou, the local Army political commissar, with the regional military commander as his deputy. The chairman of the Guizhou Committee established ten days later, Li Zaihan, was also the Army political commissar in his area—as was Liu Geping, the boss of the Shanxi province "triple alliance" set up on March 18. Created on February 24, the Shanghai Revolutionary Committee was led by a prominent Maoist civilian, Zhang Chungiao, who had been instrumental in ousting the city's old Party apparatus. But seven of the Shanghai Committee's thirteen "leading members," as they were called, were infantry, Air Force, and Navy officers.[4] There was nothing illusory in the Army's contention that it constituted "the pillar of the proletarian dictatorship."[5]

Plainly an illusion, however, was the propaganda that sought to disseminate the myth that the Army was boosting the Red Guards into positions of authority, as Mao had hoped. For in fact, local commanders in several regions were cracking down on disorderly youths in most vigorous fashion. In many provinces, the casualties inflicted by the Army on Red Guards and other radicals ran into the thousands. The brutality created the impression, particularly among observers in the West, that Chinese Army troops were no different from, say, the Indonesian soldiers who had slaughtered an estimated half-million suspected Communists in Java and Bali in 1965 and 1966. But the Chinese military establishment was different, and its participation in the Cultural Revolution was complicated.

The Chinese Army was far from a police force. Decades of indoctrination, combined with their unique experience, had endowed its officers with a sense of dedication to revolution. At the same time, however, Army commanders believed in the necessity of a strong China. Only to a certain degree would they tolerate disruption. As they strove to organize the tripartite Revolutionary Committees, therefore, Army officers found themselves caught in a dilemma. By and large they welcomed the compromise arrangements, yet they could not overcome a whole array of problems that made truly authentic "triple alliances" almost impossible to achieve.

Innumerable radical factions were still as undisciplined as a "herd of dragons." Despite the many efforts to unite them, they could not agree on acceptable representatives to sit on the Revolutionary Committees. Meanwhile, Beijing's appeals to the Red Guards and to Party officials to cooperate on the Committees were predictably falling flat. Confronted by this fragmentation of Red Guard and Party factions, the Army was unable to form more than six Revolutionary Committees in China's twenty-nine provinces and municipalities from the formation of the Heilongjiang Committee on January 31 to the birth of a triple tripartite body in Beijing on April 20, and these were essentially façades concocted to camouflage military control. Regional Army commanders in most other parts of the country could not even erect such façades. For their efforts to appear devoted to the revolution were basically incompatible with their determination to impose order. Hence they aggravated the chaos they were seeking to curb.

In several areas, the Army backed relatively conservative factions, often offshoots of groups that local Party machines had mobilized months earlier, when they were going through the motions of subscribing to the Cultural Revolution. Sometimes, Army commanders deliberately chose to support these factions because of their own close ties with the Party apparatus. But this tactic inevitably intensified friction at the provincial levels. For one thing, rival factions assailed the military-supported groups and even attacked the Army itself. On occasions, too, the Army was itself divided about which faction to back, and clashes would erupt among military units loyal to competing groups. Elsewhere, the turbulence was exacerbated by the Army's sincere inability to distinguish between "true" and "false" radicals, since everyone spouted the Maoist litany with equal fervor. Commanders who favored one faction courted the risk of drawing fire from other groups, while officers who tried to remain neutral were accused of opposing the Cultural Revolution.[6] In Guangzhou, the military garrison conceived a simple solution to this problem. It set itself up as the sole arbiter of ideological purity, declaring that "the difference between a genuine and a fake revolutionary lies in his attitude toward the Army."[7] And, on the basis of that tenet, the Guangzhou commander proceeded to suppress any element that seemed to resist his dictates.

Years later, Mao would concede that it was difficult even for him to "sort out" his foes from his followers during the zigzags of the Cultural Revolution.[8] In the spring of 1967, however, he must have perceived that his dream of spawning a new species of "Communist man" was as far from attainment as it had ever been. Many Party officials remained unresponsive to his efforts to win their allegiance out of fear that they might be subjected to renewed denunciation. The Red Guards were no longer model "revolutionary successors" but a collection of mobs struggling to fulfill individual ambitions. The Army, against its own principles, had been largely reduced to a constabulary. In a talk to a Red Guard assembly in late March, Lin Biao said:

There are casualties in all revolutions, so let us not exaggerate the seriousness of this situation. Many people have committed suicide or been
killed. But these deaths are fewer than those incurred during the Japanese
war and the Civil War, or in natural disasters. Thus our gains are greater
than our losses.[9]

Much of the original fighting between radicals and military units
during the late winter and early spring of 1967 had been concentrated
in China's coastal and border provinces. In deference to the Army's
professional officers, who were concerned by the threat of external
attack, Mao had decreed that the Cultural Revolution "should be
postponed for the time being" in these vulnerable areas. But just as
Mao's words were insufficient to deter extremist Red Guards aflame
with the fires of rebellion, so it offered a convenient pretext to the
Army to repulse the radicals ruthlessly.

One of the most prolonged of the provincial civil wars to rage
during the Cultural Revolution started about this time in the Guangxi-
Zhuang Autonomous Region, an area of southern China adjacent to
Vietnam. The Guangxi region is a poor, mountainous subtropical
province partly populated by the Zhuangs, a people ethnically akin
to the Thais, and it had long been noted for its instability, its dissident
secret societies, and its bandit sects. It was from Guangxi, for example, that the Taiping rebels launched their devastating insurgency
in the middle of the nineteenth century. Later in the nineteenth
century, the province was a cockpit for European imperialist competition as the British moved down from Hong Kong to set up river
trading stations at Wuzhou and Nanning while the French, their
missionaries in the vanguard, pushed up from Indochina. The rebellious Zhuang spirit surfaced again in January 1967, when local Red
Guards attempted to wrest power from the region's Party apparatus.
But they met a formidable adversary in Wei Guojing, an ethnic
Zhuang who, as both Party boss and the Army's political commissar
there, had ruled the region virtually single-handedly. Apparently
anxious to avoid trouble in a province adjoining Vietnam, the Maoist
leaders in Beijing endorsed Wei Guojing's decision to suppress the
radicals. But in his crackdown on the Red Guards, Wei Guojing
unwittingly solidified widespread radical opposition to his military
establishment. A conflict thus began in Guangxi between the Red
Guards and the Army that, among its other effects, disrupted the
flow of Chinese Communist supplies to North Vietnam. A year later,

the conflict would reach a dramatic climax in a battle which destroyed half of the city of Wuzhou and took thousands of lives.[10]

A similar sequence of events took place during the same period in Yunnan, another province bordering on Vietnam. Here the Party boss, Yan Hongyan, had committed suicide in January 1967 after unsuccessfully trying to resist Red Guard harassment. His death spelled the collapse of the provincial Party apparatus, and local radical factions coalesced quickly to fill the power vacuum. But like the Army in Guangxi, the Yunnan military garrison moved swiftly to curb the radicals while claiming that it was "supporting the left" in conformity with Mao's instructions. Under the command of General Jin Jiwei, Army officers dissolved or reorganized local Red Guard factions, and dispatched the most incorrigible radicals to remote rural villages to work as laborers.[11] But the Red Guard groups were strong enough to respond, and, according to some evidence, they were supported by troops that had broken away from the garrison. Armed clashes involving youths, workers, peasants, and soldiers gradually grew in intensity through the spring until, in late May, a major battle erupted in the province capital of Kunming. By early 1968 as many as eighty thousand lives were said to have been lost throughout the province.[12]

In Fujian province, long considered by the Communists to be the logical beachhead for an invasion by Chiang Kai-shek's Nationalists, local Army units were evidently sanctioned by Beijing to repel the Red Guards with comparable ferocity. As elsewhere in China, the Fujian radicals had gone into action around the turn of the year, seizing the Party newspaper and the main radio station as well as government offices, factories, and other enterprises. Emboldened by their success, they had gone on to assault the region's Army installations. On two occasions in late January, radical youths stormed the military headquarters in Fuzhou, the province capital, kidnaping and beating up soldiers. The Army counterattacked in early February, compelling various Red Guard factions to lay down their weapons and unite under military control. This brief restoration of order was initially welcomed by the Maoist leaders in Beijing, in the mistaken belief that the diverse Fujian groups had formed a "triple alliance." But the temporary truce between the Army and the radicals in the area soon crumbled, and chronic strife continued to nag the region.[13]

Meanwhile, three especially worrisome frontier areas were Xinjiang, Inner Mongolia, and Tibet. These areas were not only vulnerable to foreign threats, but each had a background of internal instability stemming from the resistance of its ethnic minorities to Han Chinese rule. To a degree that seriously troubled the Beijing leaders, moreover, this ethnic resistance was related to the external threats. In northwestern Xinjiang, the Uighurs, Kazakhs, and other Muslim minorities had long been encouraged by the Soviet Union to oppose Chinese cultural assimilation and political domination. Similarly, the inhabitants of Inner Mongolia were constantly exposed to propaganda from the People's Republic of Mongolia, a Soviet satellite, evoking the glories of Genghis Khan and the heritage of Mongol nationalism. Recurrent insurgencies had plagued Tibet ever since the Communist conquest in 1951, and in more recent years, the Beijing government had reason to suspect, Tibetan rebels were being inspired by India and perhaps armed and financed by the United States Central Intelligence Agency. As they saw it, in short, national interest took precedence over ideology where China's security was concerned. Thus they tolerated the Army's repression of Red Guards and other young extremists.

In an effort to stop the violence that had erupted in Xinjiang in January, the Beijing leaders had issued a directive on February 11 calling a halt to the Cultural Revolution there. Red Guards and other student radicals were told to return to school and prohibited from political proselytizing outside their own institutions of learning. They were also forbidden from attacking Army units, such as the Production and Construction Corps. The directive flatly declared that "elements that have seized power and stolen weapons and ammunition shall be treated as counterrevolutionaries and arrested."[14] The ordinance prescribed as well that military units cease their political activity, contending that this would interfere with "war preparations," presumably to defend China against the Soviet Union.

This edict effectively lent support to General Wang Enmao, the Xinjiang Party boss and Army commander. With Beijing's obvious approval, Wang proceeded to crack down on the radicals. Troops took over the region's newspapers, radio stations, and railways and the Army staged a rally in Urumchi, the Xinjiang capital, at which seven alleged "counterrevolutionaries" were paraded before a crowd of forty thousand.[15]

But the Xinjiang situation did not remain stable for long. Frustrated by the curbs imposed upon them, the radical Red Guards continued to assail Wang Enmao and his supporters. Clashes between rival factions broke out, and, aggravating the tension, the regional military establishment split as General Zuo Ji, the Army's First Deputy Political Commissar, sided with the radicals against Wang. Thousands of young people who had been exiled to Xinjiang fled back to their native cities. In the meantime, as it had in the spring of 1962, the Soviet Union accelerated its attempts to incite the Muslim minorities to rise up against their Chinese rulers. Beamed across the border from Tashkent and Alma Ata, where there were large Muslim communities, Uighur-language radio broadcasts denounced Mao's "Han chauvinism" and urged the Xinjiang minorities to escape to the "happy life" in the Soviet Union.[16] According to some evidence, the Soviet authorities secretly began to infiltrate weapons, portable radios, and other equipment to Muslim guerrilla bands operating in the Tian Shan range of Xinjiang.[17]

Inner Mongolia, like Xinjiang, had long been beset by problems arising from the fears of its indigenous Mongols that they would lose their ethnic identity. These fears had a basis in reality. Since 1958, Beijing had been carrying on a program of assimilation aimed at eradicating what was called the "local nationalism" of the Mongols. Instruction in the Chinese language was made mandatory in the area's primary schools. Mongol officials were replaced by Chinese functionaries. And, through an intensive immigration policy, Chinese were moved into the province until, by the late 1960s, they outnumbered the Mongols by an estimated ratio of twelve to one. As an incentive to emigrate into the region, Chinese farmers were given land confiscated from Mongol shepherds. This added to Mongol resentment and contributed to the potential volatility of the province.[18]

One local leader who sensed these dangers was Inner Mongolia's Party boss, Ulanfu, a veteran Mongol Communist who had been educated in Moscow and Beijing. As early as 1951, he had urged the Han Chinese to "respect the equal rights and opinions of national minorities," and he worked strenuously throughout the mid-1960s to protect the rights of Mongols.[19] His nationalistic attitudes inevitably made him the target of Maoist attacks when the Cultural Revolution gathered momentum in the fall of 1966. But supported by the Army in Huhehot, the regional capital, Ulanfu fought back.

In the middle of January, inspired by Red Guard actions in other parts of China, Maoist radicals in Huhehot occupied the telegraph office, the railway station, the principal newspaper office, and several government buildings, proclaiming that they had "seized power." Faced with this threat to his authority, Ulanfu instructed the Army to react. Bristling with machine guns and artillery, troops from the city garrison surrounded the local Red Guard headquarters and forced the youths to surrender.[20] In the days after that, soldiers and radicals clashed frequently. On February 5, when the Red Guards staged a rally to protest against Army repression, soldiers fired into their ranks, killing several students. This ignited new Red Guard riots, and again the Army responded with force. Fresh military units wheeled into Huhehot, arresting both local leaders and agitators who had come into the city from Beijing. The troops also smashed the Red Guards' propaganda equipment and decreed a ban on their activities.

Alarmed by this situation, Zhou Enlai instructed representatives of the different Inner Mongolian factions to meet with him in Beijing. In contrast to General Wang Enmao, the Xinjiang commander who had confidently gone to the capital, Ulanfu suspected a trap. He refused to attend Zhou's meeting, but instead sent a delegate. The result of the parley, held on February 16, was a truce that lasted only two weeks. Calculating that Zhou's intervention had merely been a ruse designed to gain time, Ulanfu again ordered his troops to arrest the radicals who had been released following the truce. His next step was to establish an Inner Mongolia Revolutionary Committee under his own leadership—and without Beijing's approval.

In the view of the Beijing Maoists, there was only one answer to this challenge—military force. General Teng Haiqing, Deputy Commander of the Beijing garrison, was directed to lead the Twenty-first Army from neighboring Shaanxi province into Inner Mongolia. Other Army units were deployed in the area. The operation now had all the aspects of a civil war. By April 7, apparently having encountered little resistance, Teng Haiqing had taken control of Huhehot. Martial law was declared and a curfew imposed. A week later, the government in Beijing removed Ulanfu from office and placed General Teng in command of the province. Thus Inner Mongolia came under the supervision of military men apparently loyal to the Maoist leadership.[21] For months, these officers coped with the dual problem of repressing radicals who refused to submit to discipline and of fighting off supporters of Ulanfu, many of whom were stimulated by a spirit of Mongol nationalism to continue the struggle against Han Chinese domination. This spirit was well expressed in the name that Ulanfu's sympathizers gave to their resistance organization. They called it the Genghis Khan Combat Corps.[22]

In Tibet, meanwhile, the Army headed by General Zhang Guohua worked consistently to restrain both local radicals and Red Guards who had come there from Beijing. Having commanded the first Chinese Communist troops to conquer Tibet in 1951, General Zhang had been there ever since—and he may well have regarded the area as his personal domain. During the summer of 1966, he had permitted Red Guards to release their revolutionary energies by invading ancient Tibetan temples and monasteries, destroying religious paintings, books, printing blocks, statues, and treasures that the Communists considered to be "feudal relics." But drawing the line at any challenge to his own authority, he kept the radicals on a tight political leash, warning them against "making trouble" and, rephrasing Mao's earlier slogan, told them that "it is forbidden to bombard our proletarian revolutionary headquarters."[23] Like entrenched Party officials and Army officers elsewhere in China, he also mobilized his own student organizations to counter his radical adversaries.

Despite the distance between Lhasa and Beijing, there were leaders in the capital who appreciated Zhang Guohua's attempts to keep peace in Tibet. One was Premier Zhou Enlai. In October 1966, Zhou had decreed that young radicals from Beijing and other parts of the country were not to enter Tibet to "exchange revolutionary experiences." But Mao's wife, Jiang Qing, quietly countermanded Zhou's decree by authorizing five Beijing youth groups to go to Tibet, where they formed a coalition called the Metropolitan Revolutionary Rebels. Apparently at Zhang Guohua's behest, Zhou issued another directive ordering the Beijing radicals to return home. The young people appealed to Jiang Qing for permission to stay, and once again undermining Zhou, she granted their request.[24] By early 1967, claiming that he was trying to turn Tibet into a "watertight independent kingdom," the radicals were clamoring for Zhang Guohua's dismissal.[25] With the same idea in mind, Jiang Qing and her comrades on the Cultural Revolution Directorate summoned Zhang to Beijing for "consultations." No doubt because he sensed a maneuver to purge him, he refused.[26]

Throughout the fall of 1966, the war between Zhang Guohua and the Red Guards in Tibet had been primarily verbal. In late January 1967, however, Mao's edict to the Army to intervene in the Cultural Revolution provided Zhang with the pretext to direct his troops against the obstreperous Red Guards. On February 7, he brought the Army's 155th Division into Lhasa and proceeded to arrest four hundred youths, killing one and wounding a number of others in the roundup. He also imposed martial law, set up military checkpoints at the city gates, and closed traffic on the roads leading east to Sichuan and north to Qinghai.[27] When the Red Guards attempted to counterattack, Zhang deployed Chinese and Tibetan troops against them, killing scores of youths in several days of street fighting.[28] One witness to the repression, though biased in favor of the radicals, described the treatment meted out by soldiers to a captive Red Guard. His hands pinioned behind his back, the youth was brought into the Lhasa military headquarters and then, according to the witness,

> Ten men surrounded him, and began to beat him savagely. Some pulled his hair, others grabbed him by the neck and still others struck his head with their pistols. They punched his face, his chest, and his back. Soon his face was a mass of blood and flesh swollen out of shape. They tore his clothes and kicked him in the groin until he fell to the floor, and then they trampled on his stomach and chest. After that, they carried him away to his cell.[29]

During the ensuing month, according to reports from Lhasa, Zhang Guohua's troops systematically cracked down on the Red Guards, seizing their documents, cameras, and printing presses, and arresting their leaders.[30] On February 26, the Beijing leadership confirmed that Zhang was really a faithful Maoist, and instructed all Red Guards in the region to give him their cooperation.[31] A week later, the Army command in Lhasa staged a victory celebration at which one speaker, in a skillful demonstration of Communist mirror-language, denounced the radicals for having "colluded with landlords, rich peasants, bad elements, counterrevolutionaries, rightists, and American and Chiang Kai-shek agents . . . in their vain attempt to rebel against the proletariat."[32] On March 8, complying with a Beijing order, the Metropolitan Revolutionary Rebels who had invaded the area finally embarked for home as Army-supported factions shouted at their send-off: "Farewell to the god of plague."[33] Two months later, General Zhang Guohua was transferred to a more important and far tougher assignment—as political and military boss of turbulent Sichuan.

Sichuan was also experiencing an extraordinary upheaval during the early months of 1967, and the self-sufficient nature of the province made its disorder crucial. For Sichuan had all the attributes of a separate state. To the Maoist leaders in Beijing, the specter of an autonomous Sichuan serving as an enemy base of operations was real and frightening. Moreover, the power of the Sichuan Party machine seemed to lend plausibility to this prospect. The Sichuan Party chief, Li Jingquan, was Marshal He Long's brother-in-law, and he was also close to Deng Xiaoping, the Party Secretary General, who had formerly served in Sichuan. The Maoists therefore made a special effort to topple Li's apparatus.

But Li was a formidable foe. In November, he had gone to Beijing to pledge his loyalty to Mao, obtaining the Chairman's blessing in exchange for the vow that he would "obey the masses."[34] With that endorsement, Li had mobilized his own worker and student factions as a defensive force, claiming that they were the real Maoists. He also went through the motions of submitting to the rituals of the Cultural Revolution, explaining to his associates that the key to survival was "unlimited patience and sham confessions."[35] Demonstrating this stratagem on one occasion, he played out a scene that might have come from a Chinese opera. He allowed himself to be marched through the streets of the province capital to a meeting at which he abjectly admitted his "sins." That the performance was a subterfuge was clear from the fact that it was held under the auspices of one of Li's own organizations.[36]

By late January, however, Li Jingquan no longer felt it necessary to rely on such subtle maneuvers. Mao's edict to the Army gave him the authorization he needed to direct troops against his opponents. Beginning in early February, the Army in Sichuan inaugurated a series of forays against the Red Guards that gradually escalated into a crescendo of violence by the middle of spring. Most of the initial action occurred in Chengdu and Chongqing, the former Nationalist headquarters on the Yangzi River. Troops set up checkpoints at the gates of both cities, arresting Red Guards as they tried to leave or enter. In some instances, they strafed vehicles filled with youths attempting to break the cordon, and they reacted strongly against counterattacks on police and military installations. When a contingent of Red Guards stormed the Public Security Bureau office in Chengdu, soldiers quickly quelled the assault and went on to punish a number of youths publicly in order to discourage others. They stripped them naked, bound their hands behind their backs, paraded them through the city, and, as an added touch, compelled the captive youths to wear their Red Guard arm bands.[37]

On February 8, Li Jingquan staged another charade by prompting his faithful factions to proclaim that they had "seized power" in the province in accordance with Mao's dictates.[38] A week later, skillfully employing Maoist phrases to justify its repressive measures, the Sichuan military command declared that anyone attempting to "turn the spearhead of the struggle against the Army" would be subjected to "all the serious consequences arising therefrom."[39] Though the

Beijing leaders later denounced the declaration as a forgery—Jiang Qing burned it publicly—they probably approved it at the time. For, in all likelihood, they believed that Li Jingquan and the Army were carrying out their instructions. The rare references to Sichuan in the official Beijing press during February noted with satisfaction that provincial troops had organized so-called Mao Zedong Thought Propaganda Teams to help the "masses" understand the need for discipline.[40] Beijing also appeared to be pleased with an Army program to assist peasants in the spring planting. Early in March, indeed, one of the members of the Cultural Revolution Directorate was even reported to have praised Li Jingquan and his comrades as "comparatively good people and able men."[41]

During this period, however, Li Jingquan and his Army colleagues in Sichuan were strenuously consolidating their position. They rounded up thousands of Red Guards, compiled dossiers on them, and staged rallies against their leaders. Provincial soldiers made a special effort to arrest Liu Jieting and his wife, Zhang Xiting, who had been squabbling with the local Party apparatus for years. Troops ransacked their home and lavishly labeled Liu "the greatest counterrevolutionary in the southwest." But, as he had before, Liu managed to elude capture by fleeing to Beijing, where he later succeeded in persuading the Maoist leaders to alter their benign attitude toward the Sichuan situation.[42] By the end of March, though, more than twenty thousand Red Guards had been jailed in Chengdu, and an estimated hundred thousand were imprisoned throughout the province. According to radical accounts, so many young people were under arrest that the Army kept them confined in old temples or corralled in city parks.[43]

An extremely complex tangle developed at about the same time in Henan province, the rich wheat-growing province straddling the Yellow River in central China. Here, as elsewhere in the country, Red Guards and other young radicals had harassed the local Party bureaucracy throughout the fall of 1966, but with little success. The Henan Party had been largely able to withstand the assaults because its former boss, Liu Jianxun, had been appointed Secretary of the Beijing Municipal Party Committee in September and he presumably used his influence in the capital to protect his provincial comrades.[44] But in early 1967, the political situation in Henan became almost indescribably complicated. A wide array of youth factions formed two rival alliances. One of them, the Henan Provincial Revolutionary

Rebels Command, was evidently backed by the local Army garrison. The other was apparently created by the provincial Party.

On February 7, the Party-supported coalition grabbed control of the newspaper as well as government bureaus in Zhengzhou, the province capital, claiming to be the new authority in the province. To commemorate its purported *coup d'état*, the coalition baptized itself the February 7 Commune. The leaders of the Cultural Revolution in Beijing, possibly recalling the miscarriage of the highly publicized Shanghai Commune, greeted the event with silence. But in Henan, the Revolutionary Rebels Command charged immediately that this was a hoax staged by entrenched Party *apparatchiks* anxious to preserve their positions. They also alleged that Liu Jianxun had deviously manipulated the coup in an effort to defend his own predominance.[45] At that, the rival groups began skirmishing. In the first fight, which broke out at the office of the *Henan Daily* as members of the February 7 Commune seized the newspaper, more than three hundred people were injured.[46] During the following weeks, the February 7 Commune went on to assail the region's senior Army officers, calling them a "handful of swine" for suppressing students. Even more daringly, its activists attacked military installations at an Air Force base outside Zhengzhou and attempted to infiltrate an artillery school located in the city.[47] The violence continued to escalate.

As viewed by Mao's inner circle in Beijing, the Henan predicament was difficult to resolve. On one hand, the provincial military commanders could not be censured, since they had carried out the current Maoist line of imposing law and order. Some of the Beijing leaders may have also believed that condemning the Army might provoke a military mutiny—as would indeed occur in the city of Wuhan only a few months later. But at the same time, they could not indict the February 7 Commune, since it was closely linked to Liu Jianxun, who stood in favor in Beijing. Finally, Zhou Enlai undertook to mediate the dispute—and his effort was a dismal failure.

On February 17, Zhou telegraphed an order to Zhengzhou instructing the Army to separate the rival factions in the city, take over the *Henan Daily* and suspend publication, and select delegates from the competing groups to be sent to Beijing to meet with him.[48] When they assembled in the capital ten days later, however, spokesmen for the squabbling Henan organization could not reconcile their differences even under Zhou Enlai's diplomatic auspices. Instead, they accused each other of "bourgeois" and "counterrevolutionary" heresies, and they all chanted Maoist catechisms to prove their ideological purity.[49] Despite its failure, though, the meeting in Beijing worked in favor of the Army in two respects. First, it punctured the February 7 Commune's claim to have secured authority in Henan. And second, it gave the Army commanders the time to reinforce their hold over the region. By mid-April, therefore, the Army had effectively assumed the responsibilities of the Henan Party Committee, and it proceeded to arrest thousands of youths on such ambiguous charges as "attempting to subvert the Cultural Revolution."

If the Henan military commanders had been actively involved in their region's dispute from the start, the Army in the southern province of Guangdong did not apparently intervene in the local situation until early February. In the weeks before their move, senior officers in Guangzhou had watched provincial authority dissolve as rival Red Guard factions fought against local Party bureaucrats and among themselves. At first the confusion had baffled and paralyzed them. They could not follow Mao's directive to assist the radicals, for the simple reason that they were unable to discern which among the vast variety of groups then swirling around Guangzhou deserved their support. Their safest course was to remain neutral—unless, of course, young agitators attacked military installations. Mao's edict had clearly forbidden assaults against the Army, and this meant that troops could retaliate against assailants regardless of their ideological complexion. But activists in the Provincial Revolutionary Alliance, headed by the student leader Wu Zhuanbin, made the mistake of violating the injunction, and their blunder ultimately weakened the whole radical cause in Guangzhou.

The Alliance contended that it represented the true Maoist gospel and, in accordance with the Chairman's decree, deserved Army support. On February 8, seeking to accentuate their contention, a number of Alliance activists therefore invaded the Army headquarters in Guangzhou, cut its telegraph lines, and occupied the premises until ordered out by the Military Commission in Beijing.[50] The Red Guards also criticized General Huang Yongsheng, the military chief of south China, and accused him of neglecting them.[51]

This diatribe against General Huang was imprudent, for he was not only the most powerful individual in Guangdong at the time but, with his later appointment as Chief of the General Staff, he would become one of the most influential figures in the country—until, along with Lin Biao, he fell in disgrace in mid-1971.

Then in his early sixties, Huang Yongsheng was a career officer with nearly forty years' experience as a soldier. As a young peasant in Jiangxi province, he had enlisted in a Nationalist unit that defected to the Communists, and he eventually joined Mao at his Jinggangshan redoubt. Huang made the celebrated Long March—which act established him as a member of the Communist elite—and he later saw action against the Japanese in north China. Afterward, as a corps commander in Lin Biao's Fourth Field Army, he fought against the Nationalists from Manchuria down to Guangxi. He remained in south China following the victory in 1949, becoming boss of the Guangzhou Military Region, which controlled more than two hundred thousand troops stationed in Guangxi, Guangdong, and Hunan. Huang was elected to the Communist Party's Central Committee as an alternate member in 1956.[52] As a soldier, however, his major preoccupation was the maintenance of law and order, especially in a city like Guangzhou, whose proximity to Hong Kong made it easily corruptible.

High Party officials in Guangzhou, as elsewhere, defended themselves by encourging their own children to form loyal Red Guard groups. One such group—possibly affiliated with the United Action Committee in Beijing—was the Doctrine Guards. Among its members was Huang Yongsheng's son, Huang Zhunming, a secondary-school student. According to Maoist accounts, the Doctrine Guards served to protect local functionaries by breaking up radical demonstrations, and these plainly "counterrevolutionary" activities were undoubtedly sanctioned by General Huang.[53] In February, after the Provincial Revolutionary Alliance raided the Guangzhou military headquarters, Huang extended the Army's support to a wider array of relatively conservative factions which came to be known as the East Wind coalition. Meanwhile, the Provincial Revolutionary Alliance expanded into a broader movement under the name of the Red Flag.[54] Huang's task, as he saw it, was to tame the Alliance—but in such a way that he would not be vulnerable to charges of suppressing the "masses."

On March 15, in conformity with a nationwide trend, Huang Yongsheng set up a Military Control Committee as the instrument of Army authority in Guangdong province. But that gesture was merely the official expression of an accomplished fact. For Army units labeled Military Training Platoons had been rapidly moving into factories, offices, schools, and other enterprises throughout the latter half of February.[55]

One student from Guangzhou has described the platoon assigned to his secondary school. It comprised twenty soldiers headed by an officer and a political commissar, and their main duties were to hold meetings and write wall posters. The troops were clearly briefed to denigrate the Red Guards, for they selected passages for study from Mao's writings that implied criticism of the Provincial Revolutionary Alliance and they often convened sessions to denounce radical teachers. The radicals felt crushed. The student, himself a radical sympathizer, put it this way: "After nearly a year of making revolution, we were to receive no reward at all, only 're-education.' " Protest was futile, since it was "counterrevolutionary" to assail the Army.[56]

Huang Yongsheng further sought to emasculate the Provincial Revolutionary Alliance by keeping its leader, Wu Zhuanbin, under surveillance by the Military Training Platoon assigned to Sun Yat-sen University. Even so, Wu was free to receive his disciples and, according to one visitor, he vowed that he would continue fighting against the Army at the risk of imprisonment.[57] The young radical agitator kept his word—and met the fate he predicted. Backed by extremist members of the Cultural Revolution Directorate in Beijing, he mobilized several assaults against the Army throughout 1967 and into the spring of 1968.[58] After that, Wu disappeared from public view, perhaps to undergo "labor reform" in some remote camp.

In February, as he accelerated his campaign to restore order in Guangdong, Huang Yongsheng took the daring step of flatly outlawing the more turbulent Red Guard movements. One of these was the August 1st Combat Corps, an affiliate of the Provincial Revolutionary Alliance. But Huang's decision to ban the August 1st Combat Corps backfired, for the group was shortly to be vindicated by Zhou Enlai. The perplexing problems that faced the Maoist leaders in Beijing as they tried to judge the ideological leanings of various factions were reflected in two documents concerning the controversial organization. One, the Army's opinion of the movement, was published by the Guangzhou military garrison on March 1, the day the August 1st Combat Corps was proscribed. The other, the Corps's view of itself, was issued later, following its vindication.

To the Army, the August 1st Combat Corps was a "counter-revolutionary" organization whose members included former labor camp inmates, escaped convicts, speculators and market manipulators, landlords, rich peasants and their children, all of them having "committed towering crimes against the people" under the "cloak" of revolution. Among their alleged crimes, members of the faction kidnaped officials in the Haizhu and Liwan districts of Guangzhou, and stole their seals of office. In one neighborhood, the document went on, they smashed open the safe belonging to a Party street council and took eighty thousand *yuan* as well as the official records. On more than one occasion, members of the August 1st Combat Corps were supposed to have stormed police stations and attempted to release prisoners, whom they described as "victims" of the police. The Army also charged that they wantonly arrested people and ransacked their homes, set up kangaroo courts, conducted illegal trials, and incarcerated their enemies in underground cells. These "reactionaries" also disguised themselves as soldiers in order to provoke hostility against the Guangzhou military garrison. And in addition to furnishing "intelligence information" to espionage agents in Hong Kong, members of the August 1st Combat Corps "insulted females and even raped young girls." In short, said the Army denunciation, "they were born rascals."[59]

The Corps's self-portrayal was predictably different. Its hundred thousand members were factory workers whose "revolutionary character was relatively firm." The "democratically elected" leaders of the Corps were demobilized soldiers employed in industry and government departments. Far from sowing discord as the Army alleged, the Corps pointed out that its members had intervened on three occasions to halt labor unrest and, on February 24, had joined in putting out a fire at a Guangzhou oil depot. On the day the Corps was banned, the document went on, troops arrested thousands of its adherents, jailing many of them for months without trial. Those imprisoned were beaten and compelled to confess to "crimes" and their families were deprived of welfare benefits, the document asserted. The document also claimed that several members of the August 1st Combat Corps, crippled Army veterans among them, were forced to face denunciation rallies wearing placards identifying them as "counterrevolutionaries." The Guangzhou military garrison's refusal to rehabilitate the Corps proved that the local Army commander "stubbornly clung to the bourgeois reactionary line."[60]

General Huang Yongsheng eventually changed his attitude toward the August 1st Combat Corps, conceding that his garrison's understanding of the Cultural Revolution had been "inadequate."[61] But that switch did not come until the following October, when the Guangdong radicals no longer seemed to represent a threat.

During the spring, however, the confusion in Guangdong province became so great that China's semi-annual International Trade Fair, scheduled to open in Guangzhou to thousands of foreign businessmen on April 15, appeared to be in jeopardy. To adjourn the

Fair—as Beijing was forced to do under extreme pressure a year later—would have constituted an acute "loss of face." But ugly Red Guard incidents in Guangzhou once the Fair opened would be equally humiliating. Thus urgent action was necessary to calm the city, and inevitably, Zhou Enlai stepped onto the scene.

Whether Zhou was acting on his own initiative or in response to a request from General Huang Yongsheng has never been clear. In either case, he flew to Guangzhou on April 14, accompanied by ten aides who promptly investigated the situation throughout the city. Zhou convened representatives of the diverse Guangzhou factions to a meeting at the Sun Yat-sen Memorial Hall. Though his objective was mediation, his talk tended to favor the radicals. He had a few kind words for the Army, but he bluntly criticized the military garrison for having committed "errors" in manhandling student activists. He also exonerated several radical organizations, the August 1st Combat Corps among them, that had been outlawed by General Huang. And he went out of his way to praise Wu Zhuanbin, then under military surveillance, lauding his "political prescience" and devotion to "revolutionary truth."[62] The net effect of Zhou's speech was to arouse the radicals, and they erupted soon afterward in a fresh burst of violence that would again plunge Guangzhou into chaos. He may have also alienated Huang, and their conflict might well have contributed to a later dispute that ended with the general's dismissal in 1971.

For Zhou Enlai to have deliberately stimulated the radicals was uncharacteristic, since he had consistently labored to prevent the Cultural Revolution from destroying all vestiges of China's social and economic stability. During February, he had maneuvered assiduously to protect his own cabinet of ministers, upon which the management of the country depended. And he had persuaded key technicians to stay at their jobs and restored those who had been ousted, arguing tirelessly that the nation could not afford to lose its skilled officials. He had even gone so far as to revive the old Party structures that had existed within such vital government agencies as the National Commodity Price Commission, the Central Administrative Industry and Commerce Bureau, and the Ministry of Finance. But toward the end of March, there were signs that Zhou was under pressure to shift to a more radical posture.

This shift was hardly capricious. It must surely have reflected Mao's view that the Army had swung the pendulum too far and, as a result, the dynamism of the Cultural Revolution was flickering and might even fade out completely. Voicing just such an apprehension, *Red Flag* asked rhetorically whether Mao's campaign would be "carried through to the end or abandoned halfway." For Mao, the answer to that question was predictable. Like a guerrilla fighter, he had retreated temporarily. Now the time had arrived to counterattack.

PART FOUR

FROM REVOLUTION TO REACTION

Fight, fail, fight again, fail again . . . till their victory; that is the logic of the people.
— MAO ZEDONG, *August 1949*

CHAPTER 14

The Radical Resurgence

⚓

> *The enemy still has strength and will not concede defeat. Whether we can mobilize the force to defend Chairman Mao to the death is the challenge that we revolutionary rebels now face. Thus we must cast away illusions and prepare for battle.*
>
> —KUAI DAFU, *March 1967*

ON MARCH 16, 1967, a perceptive Japanese correspondent in Beijing filed a long dispatch to his newspaper that differed sharply from his reports of only a few weeks earlier. Though political posters still adorned walls everywhere and theaters remained closed, he observed, calm had largely returned to the capital. Days passed without noisy demonstrations, and mobs of youths no longer blocked traffic and harangued pedestrians. Buses once crammed with Red Guards now had space for ordinary citizens and were running on schedule. Tiantan Park, where hordes of provincial Red Guards had camped during their pilgrimages to glimpse Mao Zedong, was again open to the public, and the Temple of Heaven was intact—except that a sign that formerly identified it as a "house of worship" had been removed. Shops and markets, plundered by briefly affluent workers in January and then shut, were doing business as usual. Restaurants functioned as they had before. In one of Beijing's narrow lanes, the journalist paused at an old gray house, the sun gilding its tiled roof. An ancient woman with bound feet stood in the doorway, chatting with her grandchild. Drying laundry draped the cobblestone courtyard, where another woman sat on a stool mending the sole of a cloth shoe. Down the lane came a peddler, his cart laden with cabbages and radishes and potatoes, singing a song of vegetables. Quite suddenly, the Japanese correspondent felt himself back in the city he once knew. Beijing, he speculated, would soon regain its past tranquillity.[1]

Though the journalist's description was vivid, the prediction could not have been more inaccurate. For a revival of normality was precisely what troubled Mao and his comrades—and that possibility prompted them to rekindle a fresh conflagration.

The Maoists had staked all on a cataclysmic upheaval that would shake every Chinese "soul." Yet now not only had Mao's dream of inspiring a Chinese version of the Commune evaporated in Shanghai but, by the beginning of April, Revolutionary Committees had been established in only four provinces and one city. Even in these places, power was primarily in the hands of the Army and veteran Party cadres, with tamed radicals serving mainly as revolutionary window dressing. Army officers and their Party associates also dominated most other regions of China. Central governmental authority had declined to such an extent that spokesmen in Beijing referred to several dissident areas as "independent kingdoms" ruled by local "emperors" and "warlords." In a private meeting in late April, Zhou Enlai revealed that the Beijing hierarchy was striving to "negotiate" settlements with military and civilian officials in twelve provinces and was totally out of contact with seven other regions.[2] In Maoist rhetoric, this trend represented an "adverse current of counterrevolutionary restoration" that had to be halted lest the Cultural Revolution collapse.

Probably still at his Hangzhou retreat, where he annually spent the winter, Mao appeared to have little to say during this period. Actually, there was little he could say. After all, it was he who had ordered the Army into action and had called for leniency toward Party officials, and he could not openly concede that these policies had backfired. Thus he turned to one of his time-honored tactics. Operating through intimate aides like Chen Boda and Jiang Qing, he authorized his more radical disciples to express alarm at the conservative drift that seemed to be overtaking the country. In that way, the impression could be created that the "masses" were clamoring to regenerate the Cultural Revolution.

One of the earliest cries of alarm came in mid-March from Nie Yuanzi, the radical woman cadre who had initially triggered the revolt at Beijing University a year before. At a conference at the university, she claimed that Party "reactionaries" were creeping back into their old positions. This augured a "capitalist" resurgence that could only be stopped by a radical counteroffensive.[3] Qi Benyou, a left-wing extremist in the Cultural Revolution Directorate, sounded a similar theme two days later in a speech warning that efforts to subvert Mao's campaign were being encouraged at the very highest levels in Beijing.[4] The same line resonated even more strongly in a gloomy article by Kuai Dafu, the first Red Guard leader at Beijing's Qinghua University. Liu Shaoqi "refuses to accept defeat," and his wife, Wang Guangmei, "is active everywhere," Kuai wrote, adding that "reactionary slogans" were again proliferating, and "the political wave against Chairman Mao is running high." Unless this tide was stemmed, he forecast apocalyptically, "the enemy will launch political, economic, and military attacks, and imperialism, revisionism, Chiang Kai-shek, natural calamities, and human disasters will befall us simultaneously." Therefore, radicals "must cast away illusions and prepare for battle." And, Kuai made plain, the battle should be fought with guns.[5]

This interpretation of events was echoed in the official Chinese press. In early March, *Red Flag* declared that "a big question now confronting the people of the whole country" was whether the Cultural Revolution would be "carried through to the end, or abandoned halfway." Shortly afterward, it contended that Mao's drive should be propelled forward regardless of its cost to industry, agriculture, and other sectors of the economy, "revolution must be put in command of production."[6] While admonishing the Red Guards to cease their internecine squabbling, other editorials also warned against the Army's attempts to quell the young radicals. "We will absolutely not tolerate slinging mud at the Red Guards, and must resolutely hit back," announced the Shanghai newspaper *Wen Hui Bao*. One radical publicist exhorted young activists to prime themselves for renewed turbulence. "The enemies will never lay down their butcher knives and become Buddhas," he asserted, and called on the Red Guards to "launch resolute attacks against the open and hidden representatives of the bourgeoisie."[7]

A revolutionary upsurge began to take shape at the end of March as the Maoists opened a three-pronged offensive destined to unfold with extraordinary speed and fervor. On one flank, they would escalate their assault against Liu Shaoqi, his wife, and his colleagues. On another, they planned to denounce Party and government officials who had clung to their old positions or had returned to them. And most significantly, they intended to push through measures to curb the authority of the Army, then the biggest single obstacle to radical ambitions.

In verbal intensity, Mao's onslaught against Liu Shaoqi makes Stalin's campaign against Trotsky seem mild. Yet nowhere is the difference betwen Mao and Stalin illustrated so dramatically as in their drives against their respective rivals. Stalin simply marked Trotsky for liquidation and, in 1940, finally had him assassinated. To Mao, in contrast, it was imperative that Liu Shaoqi be kept alive. For Mao's far-reaching objective was not merely to eliminate his adversaries but to convert the Chinese people to his brand of spiritual Communism. Mao needed Liu as the "negative example" that personified "bourgeois revisionist counterrevolutionary" evil. Had Liu not existed, Mao would have been compelled to invent him. As a tactical maneuver, moreover, Mao hoped that his focus on Liu would encourage the majority of Party cadres whom he considered to be "good or comparatively good" to join with the radicals in supporting his cause. As he saw it, most Party officials would abandon Liu rather than face dismissal for his sake, and could therefore be won over. As he issued orders for the fresh assault against Liu in the spring of 1967, Mao said: "Isolate and attack the smallest minority."[8]

Mao's earlier efforts against Liu and his closest colleagues had run aground after January. In the first place, the attempt to portray Liu as a villain for having advocated private gardens, free markets, and other material incentives had not only failed to tarnish his image but, on the contrary, suddenly made him popular. For the first time, peasants could identify the gray, faceless figure they had hardly known as the man who had eased their suffering after the Great Leap Forward.[9] In addition, though he had made a ritual confession, Liu stubbornly refused to capitulate to the Maoists and demanded his right to arraignment before the Party Central Committee.[10] This shrewd argument won him a respite, for it reminded the other Beijing leaders, some of Mao's stanchest acolytes among them, that they too might be vulnerable to summary dismissal unless legal formalities were observed. Zhou Enlai underscored this point in a heated dispute with a group of Red Guards in early January, when he told them that it was permissible to criticize the "bourgeois reactionary line" symbolized by Liu and Deng Xiaoping, but that they could not personally indict the two men since "they are still members of the Politburo Standing Committee."[11]

Mao, in further contrast to Stalin, was also concerned with legitimacy. But to convene the nearly two hundred members of the Party Central Committee to impeach Liu Shaoqi was too risky a venture. Mao had barely scraped through the Eleventh Central Committee

Plenum held in August 1966, and resistance to the Cultural Revolution within the Party since had clearly increased. Toward the end of March, he contrived another device. Returning to Beijing from Hangzhou, he convoked a meeting of the Politburo Standing Committee to censure Liu and Deng Xiaoping informally. He had enlarged the Committee from its original complement of seven to eleven members, three of the four additional faces being his supporters. As the Committee assembled, crowds of Red Guards somehow appeared in the streets outside, denouncing Liu and Deng as "counterrevolutionary revisionists."

Even so, Mao managed after much persuasion to mobilize a majority of only one vote in favor of his motion against Liu and Deng. Those who voted with him, besides Lin Biao and Zhou Enlai, were Chen Boda and Kang Sheng, both in the Cultural Revolution Directorate, and Li Fuchun, a Vice-Premier and one of Zhou's protégés. Backing Liu and Deng were the old Marshal Zhu De, the liberal economist Chen Yun, and Tao Zhu, who was still functioning despite the fierce attacks against him two months earlier.[12] Only a Plenary Session of the Central Committee could legally remove Liu and Deng from their Party positions, and such a meeting would not be held until two years later. But the narrow vote gave Mao the support he needed for a public campaign against them.

As early as March 26, twenty Red Guard factions in Beijing formed a "preparatory committee" to organize the offensive against Liu Shaoqi.[13] Within a week, the committee had mobilized a massive demonstration in the capital. At dawn on April 2, hundreds of thousands of Red Guards, schoolchildren, soldiers, and others converged on Tiananmen Square carrying huge portraits of Mao and chanting his slogans. Beating drums and clashing cymbals, they marched toward the ornate red and gold gate to the Zhongnanhai compound inside the ancient imperial city, where the official residences of Liu and the other Chinese leaders stood behind high gray walls. With loudspeaker trucks guiding their movements and cueing their slogans, the marchers passed in procession for six hours—and they repeated the demonstration day after day for nearly a week while similar parades were staged in Shanghai, Harbin, and other provincial cities.

Beijing's walls were plastered with hostile posters assailing Liu and his wife, Wang Guangmei. Some demanded that Liu be executed for alleged "collusion" with the Soviet "revisionists," while others caricatured him as a monstrous oppressor of the "masses." One caricature depicted him as a cannibal devouring virtuous workers and peasants, and cartoons invariably portrayed his wife wearing Western clothes and high-heeled shoes to denote her "bourgeois" tastes.[14] At the same time, the official Beijing press began to publish a series of critical commentaries on "the top Party person in authority taking the capitalist road," or "China's Khrushchev."

The opening shot in this barrage was a lengthy *Red Flag* article published on April 1, which, though signed by Qi Benyou, the radical historian and publicist, bore the imprint of Mao's brilliant polemical brush. It offered a revealing analogy between the present time and the closing years of the Qing dynasty, when the abortive attempt by Westernized Chinese reformers to modernize China's crumbling imperial institutions had given way to the xenophobic Boxer uprising against the foreign community in Beijing. Mao's aim in reaching back to that historical episode was plainly to draw a parallel between his Red Guards and the Boxers, both of whom the article glorified as "heroic revolutionaries." Just as the Boxers had been correct in having attacked "bourgeois reformers," Mao argued, so the Red Guards were justified in denouncing Liu Shaoqi and his "revisionist" comrades. And just as the "bourgeois reformers" had believed in constitutional change and "modernization from above," so Liu had tried to subvert the Maoist revolution by introducing liberal economic measures following the Great Leap Forward. Therefore, the article declared, Liu had exposed his "ugly bourgeois soul" by having advocated "the development of capitalism and the safeguarding of the bloody system of exploitation of man by man." Challenging Liu's claim to being a "veteran revolutionary," the article indicted him on eight charges, ranging from the allegation that he had favored a compromise with Chiang Kai-shek's Nationalists after World War II to the assertion that he had resisted the Cultural Revolution two decades later.[15]

Liu refuted these charges not long afterward. The entire Chinese Communist Party, including Mao himself, he pointed out, had decided to sign a "cease-fire agreement" with Chiang's Nationalists in January 1946. He also denied the charge that he had attempted to cripple the Cultural Revolution. But he would study Mao's works, Liu promised, since "only then shall I be able to reply as to why I committed errors."[16] This "confession" amounted to a rejection of the Maoist indictment, and as a consequence, the drive to defame Liu escalated to extravagant proportions. Beginning in April, a proliferation of newspaper articles and radio discussions focused on *How to Be a Good Communist*, the lectures that Liu had originally delivered to Communist cadres in Yenan in July 1939 and had reprinted in revised book form in mid-1962. Typical of the diatribe against the book was a *People's Daily* editorial that condemned it as a "pernicious influence" not only in China but "also throughout the world."[17] The criticism was valid from a Maoist angle. Liu's basic approach, consistent with Leninist orthodoxy, held that every Communist subordinate himself to the Party organization, which was by definition infallible. This thesis not only undermined Mao's dogma that each individual could perfect himself, but defied the Chairman's claim to be the sole spokesman for the "masses." Moreover, republished at a time when Mao's authority was waning, the revised edition of Liu's book had seemed to be an attempt to demean Mao. One passage, for instance, spoke of "some comrades" who "regarded themselves as the Marx and Lenin of China . . . and had the impudence to ask our Party members to respect them as we do Marx and Lenin. [They sought] to appoint themselves as 'leaders' . . . abused everything within the Party and wilfully attacked, punished, and rode roughshod over Party members." Such comrades, Liu urged, must "be opposed, exposed and buried in oblivion"—which was precisely what Mao, now seeking revenge, was trying to do to him.[18]

The Red Guards now resorted to every imaginable device to blacken Liu's reputation. A radical Beijing faction called the Jinggangshan Fighting Corps alleged that Liu's grandfather had been a landlord, his father a "rich peasant," and his eldest brother in the employ of a warlord. Liu, they said, had "sneaked into the Party" in 1921. The document then went on with a list of Liu's purported crimes so devastating that it unwittingly reflected on Mao's blindness to the culprit at his side. When the Party underwent a reshuffle in 1935, it asserted, Liu managed to hang on to his position in the Central Committee by "opportunistic means." During a famine in the early 1940s, he had feasted daily on chicken and even demanded oranges while his hungry comrades survived on corn pudding. The Red Guards also charged Liu with having brutally mistreated his numerous wives. And they heaped scorn on his present wife, Wang Guangmei.[19] She had been subjected to humiliating Red Guard interrogation in January. Now, she was forced to submit to even worse abuse.

On April 10, Red Guards affiliated with Qinghua University set up a kangaroo court to judge Wang Guangmei. With two brief interruptions, the proceedings rambled on from six-thirty in the morning until ten o'clock at night. Apparently expecting to be jailed immediately, Wang Guangmei had brought a towel, a toothbrush, and other toilet articles to the "courtroom," a hall on the seventh floor of one of the university buildings. From time to time during the interrogation, she was given tranquilizers by a soldier, presumably one of Liu Shaoqi's military aides. Despite her admitted nervousness, however, she tenaciously fought back against her young inquisitors.

The weather was still cool in Beijing in early April, and Wang Guangmei arrived at the trial in a fur coat, a gift she had been given when she went on a state visit to Afghanistan with Liu Shaoqi in the spring of 1966. The Red Guards, anxious to dramatize her "bourgeois" tastes, had brought as evidence a thin silk dress and the high-heeled shoes she had worn while on official trips to Indonesia and Pakistan. They demanded that she change her clothes. She refused, and the dialogue between the Red Guard prosecutor and herself reflected the absurdity of the entire episode:

PROSECUTOR: You must put on that dress!

WANG GUANGMEI: I will not!

PROSECUTOR: You have no choice in this matter!

WANG GUANGMEI (of the dress she is wearing): This is good enough for receiving guests.

PROSECUTOR: Receiving guests? You are under attack here today!

WANG GUANGMEI: I am not going to put on that dress. It is not presentable.

PROSECUTOR: Then why did you wear it in Indonesia?

WANG GUANGMEI: It was summer at that time, and I wore it in Djakarta.

PROSECUTOR: Why did you wear it in Lahore?

WANG GUANGMEI: I am not going to put it on, whatever you may say.

PROSECUTOR: Let me repeat. You are under attack here today. If you are not honest with us, take care!

WANG GUANGMEI: Even if I must die, it does not matter.

PROSECUTOR: Death? We want to keep you alive. Put on the dress!

WANG GUANGMEI: Shouldn't we be discussing serious subjects?

PROSECUTOR: Who wants to discuss things with you? Let me tell you again that you are under attack!

WANG GUANGMEI (angrily): On no account can you encroach upon my personal freedom.

PROSECUTOR (amid the sound of laughter): You are a member of the reactionary bourgeoisie and a class dissident. You will not be given an iota of minimum democracy, let alone extensive democracy! Dictatorship is being exercised over you today, and you are not free.

WANG GUANGMEI: I will not put on that dress, come what may. If I have committed mistakes, I am open to criticism.

PROSECUTOR: You are guilty! You are under attack today, and you will face further attacks in the future. Put on the dress!

WANG GUANGMEI (evasively, pointing to the fur coat she was wearing): This was a gift from Afghanistan. They said I was fashion-minded.

PROSECUTOR: We want you to put on that dress you wore in Indonesia.

WANG GUANGMEI: That was summer. There is winter clothing for winter, summer clothing for summer, and spring clothing for spring. I cannot put on a summer dress now.

PROSECUTOR: Skip that nonsense. We know nothing about such bourgeois stuff as what is good for summer, winter, or spring or for receiving guests or for travel.

WANG GUANGMEI: Chairman Mao has said that we must pay attention to climate, and change our clothing accordingly.

PROSECUTOR (amid laughter): What Chairman Mao said refers to the political climate. And the way you stand in that respect, you will freeze to death even though you're wearing a fur coat. Now, are you going to put on that dress?

WANG GUANGMEI: No.

PROSECUTOR: All right! We'll give you ten minutes. See what will happen at a quarter to seven. Try to defy us by not wearing that dress. We mean what we say. (Changing subject.) What do you think of the unhorsing of Liu Shaoqi?

WANG GUANGMEI: That is fine. Then there will be no revisionism in China.

PROSECUTOR: We still want to drag him out for attack. That will take place some day, don't you think?

WANG GUANGMEI: You are at liberty to attack him if you wish. (After a pause.) Your methods of attack are not really very good. You ought to do better at criticism and repudiation.

PROSECUTOR: Ignore her! In ten minutes you will see.

WANG GUANGMEI: You . . . I can ring someone up and ask for a spring dress.

PROSECUTOR: That won't do.

WANG GUANGMEI: This dress is made of silk. It's too cold.

PROSECUTOR: Put it on and wear your fur coat over it.

WANG GUANGMEI: If I were really opposed to Chairman Mao, I would deserve to freeze to death.

PROSECUTOR: You are opposed to Chairman Mao.

WANG GUANGMEI: I am not against him now, and I will not oppose him in the future.

PROSECUTOR: No more nonsense with her. Well, there are seven minutes left.

WANG GUANGMEI (after a pause, pointing to the pair of high-heeled shoes they had brought): How about my just putting on the shoes?

PROSECUTOR: That isn't enough. You must wear everything.

WANG GUANGMEI: You have no right.

PROSECUTOR: We do have the right! You are under attack today. We are at liberty to attack you however we wish, and you have no freedom. We are of the revolutionary masses, while you are a notorious and counterrevolutionary woman. You cannot confuse the class line![20]

When the ten minutes ended, according to a Red Guard account, a group of students pushed Wang Guangmei to the floor and tried to change her clothes. She struggled against them, alternately evoking Mao's injunction against force and complaining that the silk dress was too small. But the youths continued awkwardly to disrobe her as the audience chanted such slogans as "A revolution is an act of violence," and "Die-hards will eventually turn into dogshit spurned by mankind." Exhausted, Wang Guangmei finally surrendered. She donned the silk dress and the high-heeled shoes and the Red Guards mockingly added a necklace of Ping-Pong balls around her throat. As they photographed her humiliation, she repeated her warning that they had violated Mao's rule against coercion. "Nonsense!" replied the Red Guard prosecutor. "Coercion is justified when dealing with such a reactionary bourgeois element as you." The audience supported his remark by chanting another of Mao's aphorisms: "Everything reactionary is the same. If you do not hit it, it will not fall."

During the marathon inquisition that followed, the Red Guards faced a tough and resilient adversary. When they accused Wang Guangmei of having "disgraced" the Chinese people by lighting President Sukarno's cigarette during her visit to Djakarta, for instance, she was quick to remind them that the Indonesian leader had been one of Beijing's close allies at the time. When they charged her with "sneaking" into the Communist movement, she recalled that one of her first jobs for the Party had been as a translator for Premier Zhou Enlai. She also denied that she had persecuted Red Guards at Qinghua University during the early days of the Cultural Revolution. And when her Red Guard interrogators called her work as a rural investigator in 1964 "scandalous," Wang Guangmei snapped back at them: "Where do you get your information? You've spent no more than five days at the grass-roots level, while I stayed there for almost a year. I understand things better than you do."

Knowing that her interrogation was calculated to discredit her husband, Wang Guangmei defended Liu Shaoqi with rare valor and unusual skill. She allowed that he had committed errors, quoting Lenin to the effect that "it is impossible to work without making mistakes." But she rebuffed charges that Liu's career had been a series of "crimes." When he had proposed marriage to her in 1947, she reminisced somewhat sentimentally, he "honestly" told her about his former wives and several children. She denied that Liu had favored capitalism, asserting that his primary concern during the initial phase of the Communist regime had been to boost the "prosperity of the country" through the development of private industry. She brushed aside the tale that Liu alone had urged a compromise with Chiang Kai-shek following World War II, pointing out that Mao and others had also advocated a truce with the Nationalists. Similarly, she recalled, though Liu was blamed for sending Work Teams into the universities to control the Cultural Revolution during its opening phase, the entire Politburo Standing Committee had approved that decision. "Liu Shaoqi is not Chiang Kai-shek," she insisted. "He is not in any way a counterrevolutionary."

As her trial droned on into the evening, Wang Guangmei's endurance and polemical talent plainly frustrated her young assailants. They repeatedly lost their tempers as she evaded their questions or threw back quotations from Mao to prove her case. During one hot exchange, she silenced her interrogators by referring to Mao's dictum that good revolutionaries "must listen to the views of others whether or not they are favorable." When the Red Guard prosecutor impatiently demanded that she "hurry up and make a clean breast of Liu Shaoqi's misdeeds," she replied coolly: "How can I tell you his misdeeds if he has none?" But when the youth claimed that she was unworthy of membership in the Communist Party, she flew into a rage, barking at him: "Don't you bully me!" Still, at the end, Wang Guangmei conceded that the attacks against Liu and herself had driven her to tears. Their fall from grace meant, she suggested, that they would be disowned by their children. Thus her extraordinary sixteen-hour ordeal curiously ended on a Confucian note of concern for filial relations.

The Red Guards directed Wang Guangmei to submit a written "self-examination" within ten days after her trial. But she sidestepped this order by requesting a verbatim transcript of the testimony so that, she claimed, she could study the record and gain "a deeper understanding of the seriousness and wickedness" of her alleged mistakes. She continued to circumvent Red Guard pressures until late June, when she finally produced a "confession." Once again, however, it was an evasive document. She admitted to personal "errors" but declined to provide the radicals with what they really wanted—evidence against Liu Shaoqi.[21]

In early April, paralleling their revived campaign against Liu Shaoqi, the Maoists renewed their drive to denounce senior Party and government officials. The most prominent of those to come under fire were Foreign Minister Chen Yi, Finance Minister Li Xiannian, and Li Fuchun, Chairman of the State Planning Commission. They also directed an especially virulent attack against Tan Zhenlin, the country's foremost agriculture specialist.[22] These men were all Politburo members as well as Vice-Premiers under Zhou Enlai, and the assault against them had one essential purpose—to oust officials who had taken advantage of Mao's earlier appeal for leniency toward veteran cadres to suppress radical elements in their departments. The real target of the offensive, however, was Zhou Enlai.

Confronted by the new challenge to his authority, Zhou Enlai resorted to three tactics. He tried to protect deputies like Li Fuchun, an old comrade from his Paris days, whose technical skill as an economic planner was indispensable and whose ideological credentials were beyond reproach. He permitted limited though sometimes severe criticism of other associates, notably Chen Yi, whose cooperation he appreciated but whose outspoken scorn for the Red Guards made him difficult to defend. And he agreed to sacrifice Tan Zhenlin, whose utility he apparently considered marginal.

· In short, by providing the Maoists with victims, Zhou hoped that he could salvage enough power to keep China's administration operating with a measure of efficiency. But this approach worked unevenly. For the radicals voraciously chewed up officials, and the more they were fed the hungrier they became. Within half a year, Zhou would lose eight of his fifteen Vice-Premiers, three out of six chairmen of the vital Staff Offices, seventeen of the government's thirty-two ministers, and other important functionaries.[23] Many of these figures returned three or four years later, however, when the Cultural Revolution had become a memory.

The most surprising feature of the campaign against Chen Yi was that he succeeded in surviving it—just as he had weathered a series of previous assaults and would endure future attacks. For Chen, despite his hedonistic propensities, was a rugged Communist veteran quite capable of handling his adversaries. The son of a well-to-do magistrate, Chen had acquired—both in China and abroad—tastes that scarcely fit the Maoist ideal of proletarian austerity. As a Sichuanese accustomed to one of the finest provincial cuisines in China, he indulged in exquisite Chinese banquets and, on one occasion, agreed to dine at a foreign embassy in Beijing only on condition that he be served French pastry and Napoleon brandy.[24] He delighted in traditional opera and dancing, played excellent chess, and composed poems in praise of flowers.[25]

Beneath this elegant and refined manner, however, Chen Yi was an experienced and able soldier. In the spring of 1949, as commander of the Third Field Army, he was responsible for the capture of Shanghai, and he later forged a powerful political base in east China. Afterward, as Foreign Minister, Politburo member, and one of China's nine living Marshals, he raised his voice for rationality in the midst of some of Mao's more visionary episodes. In one of his most celebrated pronouncements, later to be used against him, Chen had cautioned Beijing University students in 1961 that it was a "mistake" to judge people solely on the basis of their political orientation.

In the spring of 1966, Chen Yi had sought to restrain the ferment in the Foreign Ministry by organizing fifteen Work Teams similar to those sent by Liu Shaoqi into the universities.[26] Not long afterward, when the Red Guards denounced him for preventing them from purging "bourgeois reactionaries" under him, Chen slapped back. "I'll give you some cold towels to cool your hot heads," he told one radical faction and, resisting another Red Guard group, he said: "If you attack me for forty-eight days, I'll attack you for forty-nine, and if you use ten abusive words, I'll use eleven."[27]

Later, however, Chen Yi was compelled to retreat—at least temporarily. On January 24, 1967, addressing a large Beijing audience in the presence of Zhou Enlai, Chen Boda, Jiang Qing, and other leaders, he confessed that he had misunderstood the Cultural Revolution because he "seldom went deep among the masses to learn humbly from them" and had consequently "lost sight of their revolutionary enthusiasm." Henceforth, Chen Yi vowed, he would throw himself "into the furnace of this great mass movement and burn away my mistakes."[28] The confession won him redemption. Chen Boda declared him "vindicated," and Zhou Enlai praised him for the "painful recognition" of his errors.[29] But in the weeks that followed, as the Red Guards persisted in their efforts to oust Foreign Ministry officials, Chen Yi again exploded. He retracted his confession and now claimed that it had been "forced" on him, asserting that he was innocent of any misconduct.[30] And he resumed his counterattacks against unruly radicals. On February 12, he scolded Red Guards who had intimidated a returning Chinese ambassador: "If you want to fight so badly, why don't you to to Vietnam and fight the Americans?"[31]

Early in April, Chen Yi joked about the Red Guard campaign against him. He cheerfully told an Australian delegation that if he weren't so busy he would publicly respond to his critics. "I can put up posters, too," he said. In a similarly jocular vein, he told a group of Japanese, "If the foreign ministers of other countries were criticized like me, the world would be a more peaceful place."[32]

But the war between Chen Yi and the Red Guards was no laughing matter. The radicals repeatedly staged demonstrations against him until, in the middle of April, the Maoist leaders felt compelled to support them at least partially. Chen Boda now approved the denunciations of Chen Yi but argued against his dismissal, while Zhou Enlai announced that he would personally assume the supervision of the Foreign Ministry. The radicals interpreted these concessions as signs of weakness, however. They continued their offensive against Chen Yi until, on May 13, mobs of rampaging youths armed with knives and crowbars broke into a Foreign Ministry building. The mob, led by a student faction from the Foreign Languages Institute, the training school for Chinese diplomats and interpreters, occupied the building for six hours, beating up officials and soldiers who stood in their way and stealing classified documents. One youth was reported to have shouted: "What's so terrific about secrets? To hell with them."[33]

This unprecedented outburst of violence against the Foreign Ministry partly reflected the Red Guards' impatience with the restraints imposed on them by Zhou Enlai. Indeed, at a meeting following the assault against the Ministry, they handed Zhou an ultimatum bluntly demanding that Chen Yi and two Vice-Ministers of Foreign Affairs,

Ji Bengfei and Qiao Guanhua, be dismissed and arraigned before a Red Guard tribunal.* When Zhou rejected this ultimatum, posters went up around Beijing criticizing him. And a Red Guard contingent staged a return raid against the Foreign Ministry on May 29, again removing confidential documents.[34]

The Foreign Ministry radicals were inspired as well by a dynamic and ambitious new chief, Yao Dengshan. A middle-ranking diplomat who had served in Finland and Ceylon, Yao was stationed in Djakarta during the abortive attempt by Indonesian Communists to take power in the fall of 1965. Beijing's alleged involvement in this attempted coup—combined with the Indonesian Army's slaughter of thousands of Chinese resident in the archipelago—led to a deterioration in relations between Indonesia and China, and the Chinese diplomatic mission was eventually expelled from Djakarta. Yao, by then its *chargé d'affaires,* was given a hero's welcome on his return home on April 30. He was greeted at the airport by the entire Beijing hierarchy except for Mao and Lin Biao, and they accorded him an audience the next day.[35]

Perhaps as a result of these experiences, Yao had delusions of grandeur. He spearheaded the Red Guard raids against the Foreign Ministry, and in the summer he tried to elevate himself to the position of Foreign Minister. He failed and, by September, would be denounced as a "thug" and a "political gambler."[36] But before his downfall, Yao and his comrades almost totally disrupted the Chinese Foreign Ministry and certainly aggravated the heart condition that later brought Chen Yi's career to an end. Chen died of cancer in January 1972. The publicity accorded his funeral obliquely symbolized his complete "rehabilitation" and also served as an indirect criticism of the radicals.

If Zhou Enlai had tried to protect Chen Yi, he found it expedient to make Tan Zhenlin a sacrificial offering to the Red Guards. Indeed, Tan's symbolic value as a scapegoat for the Red Guards lifted him into a position of importance that far exceeded any authority he had actually exercised. In early spring, therefore, he was publicized as the ringleader of the "counterrevolutionary current" that had undermined the Maoist cause during the two previous months.

One of the few authentic "proletarians" in the upper echelons of the Communist movement, Tan Zhenlin was born around the turn

*Ji was appointed Foreign Minister after Chen Yi's death in January 1972. Qiao led the Chinese delegation to the United Nations in the autumn of 1971.

of the century into an extremely poor peasant family in Hunan, Mao's native province. Having learned to read while working as a printer's apprentice, he enrolled in the young Communist Party in the mid-1920s. Tan participated in peasant uprisings in Hunan and then retreated to Mao's Jinggangshan redoubt, where he rose rapidly as a political commissar in the Communist armed forces. He fought almost everywhere in the country during the wars against the Japanese and the Nationalists, serving at the time of the Communist victory as deputy political commissar in Chen Yi's Third Field Army, which conquered east China. Ironically, in light of his subsequent fate, Tan had been a foremost advocate of the Great Leap Forward. His support for Mao's intensive collectivization program in 1958 in fact earned him membership in the Politburo and a Vice-Premiership. He later became Director of the Agriculture and Forestry Office, and it was in that job that he ran afoul of the Red Guards. For Tan apparently resisted attempts by the young radicals to take over his organizations. In short, despite his past fidelity to the Maoist line, Tan evidently felt compelled to defend himself against Red Guard interference. In the early summer of 1966, for example, he had created Work Teams to supervise the Red Guard units then mushrooming in the Agriculture and Forestry Office and its ancillary agencies. He also persisted in voicing his allegiance to Liu Shaoqi and the Party machine, declaring on more than one occasion that it was wrong to "dispense with Party leadership and rely on the masses for everything."[37] Later, he mobilized his own Red Guard factions, reinforcing them with Mao Zedong Thought Propaganda Teams. But the radicals were undeceived by these maneuvers. And they were encouraged by Mao's wife, Jiang Qing, who had bluntly accused Tan of plotting to "erase the achievements" of the Cultural Revolution.[38]

In January 1967, Tan Zhenlin resorted to the same tactic being used by other Chinese officials. He directed his own Red Guard groups to "seize power" in his agencies.[39] This tactic bought him time. For soon afterward, when Mao called for a "lenient" policy toward government officials, Tan not only was able to claim that his efforts to shield his subordinates had been justified, but proceeded to suppress his leftist enemies. From early February until late in March, his supporters arrested, beat up, and arraigned radicals in the Ministry of Agriculture, the Central Meteorological Bureau, and other departments under his control. At mass rallies the young radicals, bound and trussed, were forced to bow their heads and confess to being "counterrevolutionaries."[40] Tan also dissolved leftist movements within his apparatus, exiling their members to "labor reform" camps or construction gangs in remote rural areas.

The facility with which Tan carried out these crackdowns indicated that he must have enjoyed the tacit support or at least tolerance of the Army, then engaged in imposing law and order in Beijing and the provinces. And, judging from his silence at the time, Mao himself probably approved of his drive. In any case it did not contradict his disapproval of unruly extremists.

But when Mao's tactic on the Cultural Revolution shifted, Tan Zhenlin's position changed quickly. On March 14, acting on instructions from the Cultural Revolution Directorate, thousands of university and secondary-school students flooded the streets of Beijing, denouncing Tan and demanding that the Maoist cause be rescued from "reactionaries." Mao's personal imprimatur on these demonstrations was assured by Qi Benyou, then emerging as the leading spokesman for the Maoist hierarchy. Qi described Tan as a "representative figure" in the "anti-revolutionary" wave that had taken hold in February, and that "all statements made in his defense must be retracted."[41] In other words, Qi plainly suggested, Tan Zhenlin had been singled out as the symbol of a trend that was subverting the Cultural Revolution. The new indictment of Tan was also a veiled warning to Zhou Enlai, who had pleaded that his senior associates be spared.

Zhou now switched his stand. He labeled Tan a "traitor" and endorsed the campaign to dismiss him. From then on, the vilification of Tan Zhenlin surged ahead in its monotonously typical manner. Red Guards dredged up "evidence" disclosing that Tan's father-in-law had been an "industrial-commercial capitalist," that his brother-in-law had served Chiang Kai-shek and that, among his other sins, he had sheltered landlords, rich peasants, and other "bourgeois parasites."[42] But along with these familiar bromides, the radicals presented a valid case against Tan in their contention that he had maneuvered to immunize his government bureaus against the Maoist purge.

Tan managed to survive through the month of April, and even appeared atop the Tiananmen Gate with Mao and the other Chinese leaders at the annual May Day celebration. Then he faded from public view, undoubtedly to one of the "labor reform" camps to which he had exiled his Red Guard foes. Yet his name became synonymous for the duration of the Cultural Revolution with any adversary of the radicals. Red Guards throughout China referred to their Party, government, and Army enemies as "local Tan Zhenlins."

CHAPTER 15

The Troubled Spring

*There cannot be peaceful coexistence in the
ideological realm. Peaceful coexistence cor-
rupts.*

——JIANG QING, *April 1967*

IN THEIR THREE-PRONGED EFFORT to regenerate the Cultural Revolution early in the spring, the Maoists had been relatively successful in their offensive against Liu Shaoqi and their stepped-up
assaults against Party and government officials. Now they were confronted by the far more complicated and sensitive problem of the
Army.

Late in January, after committing the Army to the Cultural Revolution, Mao had quickly observed that local commanders were concentrating on maintaining stability rather than helping the radicals
to overthrow local Party machines. Military crackdowns against
Maoist agitators were reported to be so severe that the Chairman
dispatched investigative missions to several areas to find out what
precisely the situation was.

In Anhui province, which straddles the Yangzi River in central
China, one such mission concluded that the region's Military Control
Committee had banned Maoist factions, "indiscriminately" arrested
radicals, and was "monopolizing" authority to the exclusion of the
"masses." Representatives of Anhui's Army command were summoned to Beijing and ordered to release "without exception" all radicals who had been jailed and to exonerate those who had been labeled
"counterrevolutionaries." A mission sent to Inner Mongolia revealed
a similar case of Army repression after General Teng Haiqing, Deputy
Commander of the Beijing garrison, had led the Twenty-first Army's
three divisions into Inner Mongolia in February and taken control of

Huhehot, its capital. Since then, the mission found, troops had erad-
icated "large numbers of revolutionary masses" while backing "conservative" groups linked to the "revisionist" provincial Party
organization. Still another mission returned with an even more damaging account of the Army's activities in Qinghai, the large, mountainous, sparsely populated province lying between Tibet and
Xinjiang in western China. On February 23, the mission reported,
the deputy Army commander in Xining had "usurped military power"
in a "counterrevolutionary coup" and then, claiming that Red Guards
had opened fire on his men, killed and wounded numbers of them,
including many teen-age girls. The Beijing authorities ordered the
Qinghai officer and two of his subordinates placed in solitary confinement pending trial, and absolved the Red Guards from any guilt
for the incident.[1]

Mao knew that to permit the Army to continue quelling his young
Red Guard supporters meant the end of the Cultural Revolution, a
prospect he abhorred. Yet it was also clear that, with virtually all of
China's government and political system in shambles, any move to
restrain the Army would license fresh outbursts of violence, an alternative that was equally undesirable. Mao contemplated this dilemma throughout the month of March—and then came up with a
solution that was almost fanciful. On April 1, he renewed his instructions to the Army to assume responsibility for controlling the country
and assisting in the establishment of tripartite provincial Revolutionary Committees. But, in order to prevent military commanders from
quashing the radicals, he curtailed their real authority. As a consequence, presuming that they now had Mao's sanction to behave as
they pleased, the radicals went on rampages, while the Army, confused by contradictory directives, acted according to its own dictates.
The result was unparalleled chaos.

The first of these directives admonished the Army for having
judged the ideological complexion of diverse Red Guard movements.
Henceforth, no faction could be branded "counterrevolutionary"
without Beijing's prior assent. The directive also instructed local officers to liberate "without exception" not only youths arrested for
criticizing the Army, but even those activists who had been jailed for
raiding military installations. Many officers had overreacted to Red
Guard attacks against the Army, the directive said, and had taken
these assaults "too seriously." Finally, the Army was prohibited from
further crackdowns and commanders were urged to give the Red

Guards free rein in the future. Plainly reflecting Mao's deeply rooted belief that the "masses" by their very nature cannot err, the directive declared:

> Chairman Mao has more than once taught us that "it is not a crime to make revolution," "it is not a crime to speak out," and "it is not a crime to practice extensive democracy." To force the masses to admit guilt is extremely wrong. Suppression of the revolutionary masses under the pretext of "suppressing counterrevolution" is strictly forbidden.[2]

Less than a week later, the leaders circulated an even more stringent directive that circumscribed the Army's power in two more ways. First, it forbade the Army from shooting at unruly elements—even in instances in which troops themselves were under fire. Second, asserting that a "small handful" of officers were pursuing the "bourgeois reactionary line," it warned that a purge might be carried out within the ranks of the Army. In order to emphasize its importance— and perhaps to dispel doubts as to its authoritativeness—the directive bore this rare annotation: "Comrade Lin Biao. This document is very good. Mao Zedong. April 6."[3]

These decrees temporarily emasculated the Army. By depriving commanders of the right to judge the ideological leanings of Red Guard factions, for example, Mao withdrew his confidence in the Army's ability to serve as a political arbiter. By compelling officers to release Red Guards imprisoned for acts of violence, he undermined the Army's prerogative to enforce law and order. And by preventing soldiers from using their weapons even in self-defense, he was indirectly encouraging armed mobs to run riot. Lastly, by hinting that the Army was tainted with "bourgeois reactionary" tendencies, he was implicitly encouraging his followers to assail China's military establishment with the same zeal that they had assaulted the Party bureaucracy.

If these directives were not sufficient, Mao took additional steps to weaken the Army's position. In early April, he removed Marshal Ye Jianying as Vice-Chairman of the powerful Military Affairs Commission, replacing him with General Xie Fuzhi, Minister of Security and apparently more sympathetic to the radical line.[4] He also dismissed Marshal Xu Xiangqian, who had been appointed in January to manage a modified version of the Cultural Revolution inside the Army. An old professional soldier primarily concerned with national security, Marshal Xu had evidently maneuvered to keep Mao's campaign from disrupting the armed forces at a time when the danger of war with the United States or the Soviet Union, or both, was believed to be growing. That effort now cost him his position—at least for the present. He was supplanted by General Xiao Hua, one of Lin Biao's closest subordinates and head of the Army's General Political Department, who quickly brought intensive ideological pressures to bear on military commanders and their troops.[5]

These pressures took the shape of a political indoctrination program endorsed by Mao and personally inaugurated by Lin Biao, designed to rid the Army of its "malignant elements" and "correct mistakes" made by officers who had cracked down on radical extremists.[6] Starting in April and continuing through May, a series of newspaper articles and radio broadcasts exhorted the Army to support the Red Guards even though, as one journal put it, "they have some shortcomings."[7] The Army should not "exaggerate" offenses by the Red Guards, another journal said, explaining that the "errors" of the young radicals "must be condoned" and the youths themselves be "trusted to rectify" their own faults.[8] The indoctrination program also required that military commanders atone for their alleged misconduct by openly admitting their failings and asking the radicals whom they had wronged for forgiveness.[9]

This procedure, again predicated on Mao's tenet that the "masses" were the fountain of virtue, caused serious dissension within the Army. In Shandong province, according to one official document, several officers hotly argued against conducting public self-criticism sessions on the grounds that such demonstrations would "dampen" military morale, "upset" troops, provoke "splits" within the regional command, and make the Army vulnerable to attack.[10]

Meanwhile, a spate of Maoist pronouncements reproved the Army for its failure to advance the radical cause. Predictably, the most prolific of the Army's critics was Jiang Qing, whose prominence if not survival depended upon a continuation of revolutionary ferment. Like any politician, Jiang Qing tailored her style to fit her audience. Speaking to student activists in Beijing on April 4, she whipped up their enthusiasm by reproaching the Army for suppressing Red Guards and other young militants, stressing that it was the "duty" of military commanders to back radical factions.[11] Ten days later, she delivered essentially the same message to the Military Affairs Commission, the nation's highest Army council—but in a long, rambling discourse that, with its digressions and historical analogies and protestations of humility, seemed to typify classical Chinese persuasive oratory.

She opened her speech to the Military Commission by commenting that she and Mao "live together" and therefore, "though there are many things I do not know," her credentials as his most intimate associate lent weight to her remarks. Lest the senior officers misconstrue her address, however, she emphasized her devotion to the Army. She had always loved the Army, she insisted—even if the Army had not always loved her. She recalled the commanders in Yenan who had refused to permit her to wear the Army's red star insignia on her cap. Nevertheless, she went on, she had persisted in trying to gain acceptance by China's officers, and even now, whatever they thought of her, "my heart still belongs to the Army." Jiang Qing then meandered through an ancient parable and emerged with the real point of her speech—it was not enough for the Army to have fought the Japanese, defeated the Nationalists, and resisted the United States in Korea. Commanders could not rest on their laurels. "They must come out of their barracks and their offices, and return to our old tradition of mingling with the masses," she said. They must respect the Red Guards and other representatives of the "masses," and join with them in the construction of new revolutionary power structures to replace the shattered Party administration.[12]

⚓

The new restraints on the Army, combined with exhortations to the radicals to resume their momentum, had immediate, widespread, and devastating repercussions throughout China. Multitudes of rival Red Guard groups again fell to squabbling, either in renewed drives to seize local power or in attempts to settle old scores. At the same time, regional Army commanders were exposed to fresh attacks from factions they had suppressed earlier. Military garrisons in many areas fought back in self-defense, disregarding Mao's directive. In several places, Army units swept up in the ferment squared off against each other. As a consequence, the country was quickly in what the Maoist press later labeled "unprincipled civil wars"—meaning, according to the official definition, sheer anarchy.[13] In an alarmed editorial, the authoritative *People's Daily* warned that the nation was being devoured by flames fanned by "a sinister gust of wind." The conflagration was "wrecking production, destroying State property, and threatening the lives of people," the paper cautioned, and unless the violence was checked it would "upset the orderly process of revolution"—a curious phrase in light of Mao's original concept of the Cultural Revolution as a cataclysmic episode that would reach into the "very souls" of the Chinese population.[14]

Mao and his associates had hoped that, beginning in February, this "orderly process of revolution" would rapidly spawn tripartite Revolutionary Committees in all of China's provinces and special municipalities. General Xie Fuzhi, Minister of Security, disclosed that the Maoists had expected the "triple alliances" to have been established everywhere in the nation before the end of May. But, Xie remarked gloomily in early May, "the deadline may need to be extended."[15] In Beijing alone during the first ten days of the month, he revealed, there had been one hundred thirty-three bloody incidents involving sixty-three thousand people, a "two-figure" number of whom were killed. He also divulged that industrial output in the capital had fallen 7 per cent in April as a result of labor protests and "armed struggles" among rival worker and student factions.[16] At a private conference in the capital on May 7, Xie said candidly: "The situation here at the moment is not good. There are fights and splits . . . and the tendency is toward anarchy."[17]

Reports of turbulence emanated from Beijing almost daily through the spring. On May 3, for example, three workers were killed and sixty seriously hurt in scuffles between labor groups at the Beijing Watch Factory, located in a northern suburb. The factory was forced to suspend operations for two days until troops could restore order.[18] Soon afterward, more than two hundred Red Guards stormed Beijing's main government building in an attempt to kidnap high officials, injuring seven soldiers who tried to block their way.[19] Meanwhile, at Beijing University students broke into two hostile coalitions. An organization led by Nie Yuanzi, the university's veteran radical activist, mobilized some seven thousand students to combat a rival movement of five thousand students and teachers directed by Zhou Peiyuan, a vice-president of the institution, who had received his Ph.D. at the California Institute of Technology. In one skirmish, following a memorial service for a young girl who had been driven to suicide by repeated denunciations, four young people were reported killed and three hundred wounded as partisans on both sides wielded clubs, knives, and meat cleavers, a popular amateur weapon among Chinese. The fighting escalated to such proportions that Chen Boda had to be rescued by police when he ventured into the university in an attempt to reconcile the competing factions.[20]

Similar clashes among student organizations also broke out in Tianjin. There, on April 27, thousands of Red Guards ended a demonstration protesting against the mistreatment of Chinese in Indonesia by fighting for three hours among themselves. Troops and workers finally quelled the riot—but not before more than two hundred young people had been injured. When the Red Guards in Tianjin again started skirmishing almost immediately afterward, Zhou Enlai rejected requests from the city's authorities for help, saying in effect that he was too busy coping with far more tumultuous situations elsewhere.[21]

Much more serious than intramural Red Guard disputes were the increasingly frequent and fierce collisions between youth factions and military units. In the Gansu province capital of Lanzhou, the site of China's main nuclear research laboratories, the Army garrison went into action against radical groups attempting to grab control of the regional Party apparatus. On April 18, eight truckloads of soldiers encircled the offices of the *Lanzhou Daily* and proceeded to shoot at young activists occupying the newspaper building, reportedly killing and wounding "several hundred" of them.[22] Troops also struck at Red Guards in Jixi, a city in the Manchurian province of Heilongjiang. As related in Beijing wall posters, soldiers armed with grenades, rifles, and machine guns surrounded a rally being held there by sixty thousand Red Guards on the morning of May 14. Presumably determined to punish the youths for having raided factories, coal mines, and other enterprises in the heavily industrialized area, the soldiers fired into the crowd, continuing their repression in the days that followed by rounding up more than a thousand young agitators. The Army's intervention against the radicals had plainly been authorized by the Heilongjiang Revolutionary Committee— a significant indication that the first provincial "triple alliance" formed in China scarcely qualified any longer as a model of fidelity to the Maoist cause.[23]

In a number of places Red Guard factions appeared to be taking the initiative in attacking military units and installations. In some instances, radical youth groups represented Army political commissars whose Maoist leanings pitted them against regional commanders striving to maintain law and order. Such was the case at Shijiazhuang, a pivotal railway junction in Hubei province, south of Beijing. Evidently mobilized by Army political commissars in the district, a Red Guard movement known as the May 1st Rebel Corps assailed the local garrison on eight separate occasions in May, climaxing its offensive with a raid on June 3 against a military hospital situated in the city. Some three hundred young activists flung bricks, tiles, and medicine bottles at the patients, sprayed them with high-pressure water hoses, and smashed the laboratory. More than two hundred patients and participants were said to have been injured.[24] A similar skirmish between Red Guards acting on behalf of contending Army factions also occurred in late May in Jinhua, another important railway center in Zhejiang.[25]

Battles flared up with growing intensity as summer approached. A particularly savage episode occurred in early June in the Hunan province capital of Changsha, where Mao had been a student. There, incensed that old Party and government officials were still exercising authority with military protection, radical factions had staged a series of protest demonstrations beginning in late April. Operating under Army auspices, labor groups had moved against the young radicals. Skirmishing between the two sides gradually intensified. On June 6, when a coalition of radical students planned to hold a rally at the Sino-Albanian Friendship Hall, workers ambushed them as they arrived for the meeting. What followed makes the student–hard-hat conflict in America seem pale by comparison. Armed with clubs, knives, bayonets, crowbars, and chains, the workers first destroyed three loudspeaker trucks belonging to the students and, in their initial assault, killed five youths. When the students retreated into the hall, the workers besieged the building, then set it afire and slaughtered the young people who fled the flames. According to one account, they killed fourteen or fifteen students trying to escape through the west wing of the hall. The same account claimed that they grabbed one girl, stripped off her clothes, gouged out her eyes, and clubbed her to death. Other students died as they leaped from the burning building. Employing a ruse used in confrontations elsewhere, workers posed as doctors and nurses and helped the injured students into ambulances, drove them outside the city, and murdered them in cold blood.[26] Altogether, sixty students were slain during that day in Changsha, and many more were listed as missing.[27] One student described the corpse of a comrade of twenty-two whose "face had been beaten to such a pulp that he could not be recognized." In his pocket, along with his identity card, was half a cucumber that the boy had carried to quench his thirst during the conflict.[28]

Shortly afterward, the Hunan Red Guards published a long indictment of the Army for having violated Mao's instructions by suppressing "true revolutionaries."[29] But despite this complaint, the man who emerged as boss of the area was General Li Yuan, commander of the Forty-seventh Army.

Frustrated by what they considered a betrayal of their cause, the

Hunan radicals subsequently formed a coalition called the Provincial Proletarian Revolutionary Great Alliance Committee—abbreviated in Chinese as *Sheng Wu Lian*—and published one of the most remarkable documents of the Cultural Revolution. Entitled "Whither China?" the document audaciously excoriated Mao on the grounds that his failure to fulfill his promise to support the seizure of power by the "masses" permitted old Party officials and Army officers to retain their authority—and therefore encouraged the rise of a "red capitalist class" of whom Zhou Enlai was "the chief representative."[30] A year later, desperate efforts by these and similarly disappointed Red Guards elsewhere in China to assert themselves were to lead to the last major gasp of the Cultural Revolution.

Another area where the chaotic conditions of the spring were particularly marked was Henan, in central China. There, earlier in the year, despite attempts by Zhou Enlai to reconcile the Army and its Red Guard adversaries, the provincial military garrison had suppressed the largest local radical movement, the February 7 Commune. Though dismayed by this blow to their disciples, the Maoist leaders in Beijing feared antagonizing the region's commanders—or as Xie Fuzhi, the Minister of Public Security, put it: "The Henan problem involves the Army, and it cannot be solved quickly."[31] Indeed, faced with a *fait accompli*, the Beijing authorities issued an edict on April 12 giving full authority to the military command to rule Henan and to arrest Red Guards regardless of ideological persuasion who violated "public security rules and regulations." The edict also endorsed the past conduct of Henan's senior officers who, it said, had "consistently backed true revolutionaries" and were "correct in the general orientation of the struggle." The Beijing leaders pledged not to interfere in the Army's decisions concerning the February 7 Commune, declaring euphemistically that the "broad masses" of Henan would determine its fate.[32]

Early in May, however, Mao reversed that edict. He had reportedly examined the Henan question personally and concluded that the February 7 Commune represented his line and deserved total support.[33] Accordingly, he dispatched a squad of agents to the Henan capital of Zhengzhou with instructions to direct the Red Guards to wrest authority from the provincial military command. Mao apparently did not expect trouble. He probably estimated that the sheer weight of his supreme judgment would suffice to prompt the Henan Army officers to surrender or, at least, to concede to some kind of face-saving compromise. But he miscalculated. Bluntly disobeying his order, the provincial military establishment inflicted a severe setback to the radicals in one of the bloodier clashes of a bloody period.

This challenge to Mao in Henan was unprecedented—and far-reaching in its consequences. Until now, regional commanders had rarely defied the Chairman directly but would, in the traditional style of Chinese officials responding to the emperor, genuflect to his decrees while maneuvering to evade them. But the Henan garrison had established a new pattern for insubordination, and it would be imitated during the weeks ahead elsewhere in China—and most dramatically, in late July, in Wuhan. The Army's virtual act of sedition in Henan was both a cause and an effect. It inspired other military units throughout China to rebel openly against Mao, and it reflected the degree to which the turmoil of the Cultural Revolution had already eroded his prestige and power.

Given a new lease on life by Mao, the Henan radicals sought to personalize their opposition to the provincial garrison by focusing their fire against General He Yunhong, the deputy political commissar of the regional command. They claimed with considerable justification that "the hangman of Henan's Cultural Revolution" had imprisoned, tortured, and killed numerous members of the February 7 Commune.[34] In response to these charges, the Henan garrison blamed the Red Guards for "sowing social chaos" by having "pointed the spearhead of the struggle" against the Army, thereby undermining its endeavors to impose the "dictatorship of the proletariat." As tensions grew, General He himself convened a "political work conference" in Zhengzhou at which he accused the radical activists of trying to "hoodwink the masses" by staging "bogus shows of power" designed to display their strength.[35] These exchanges of rhetoric ultimately led to a showdown on May 26, when the February 7 Commune and its affiliated factions assembled twenty thousand followers at a rally in the Zhengzhou stadium to denounce General He for his "crimes."

The Army could have plausibly banned the demonstration. But the local commanders devised other plans. They alerted their own "mass" organization, the Provincial Revolutionary Rebels, whose ranks included an estimated ten thousand tough industrial workers only too eager to vent their wrath on students. In preparation for close combat in city streets, the workers pasted identifying strips of white adhesive tape on their wrists, and divided themselves into flexible six-man teams outfitted with clubs, crowbars, chains, belts, and other improvised weapons as well as rattan helmets. Uniformed soldiers, presumably acting as "advisers," were dispersed among them. Apprised in advance that the radicals intended to parade through the factory district of Zhengzhou following their rally, the workers waited.[36]

Night had fallen as the thousands of February 7 Commune members and sympathizers spilled out of the stadium. With Mao's special envoys at their head, they marched across the bridge spanning the Jinshui River, past the remains of earth ramparts that once enclosed the ancient city, over railway tracks, and into Zhengzhou's industrial suburbs. Chanting Maoist slogans, singing revolutionary hymns, and shouting epithets gainst General He Yunhong, they turned into Mianfang Lu—Cotton-Spinning Road—the site of the city's numerous textile plants. Suddenly the whistle of the Zhengzhou Cotton Textile Mill No. 6 screamed "like the wail of a ghost" in the eerie darkness, as a Red Guard later recalled. It was the signal for the Army-supported workers to spring their ambush.

Strategically poised on the upper floors of factories overlooking the road, the workers bombarded the paraders with bricks, tiles, stones, and other missiles, then poured out onto the street swinging their weapons. The youths, caught by surprise in the narrow street, panicked. Many pleaded for mercy. Others, unable to distinguish friend from foe in the darkness, hit back at their own comrades. Still others tried to resist. Some four hundred young people took refuge in a nearby mill, but workers laid siege to the building and finally forced them out by launching tear-gas bombs and grenades provided, presumably, by the Army. At one point, a survivor related afterward, a six-wheeled truck roared at full speed into the fray, mowing down people in its path. No match for the well-organized labor platoons, the young radicals were decimated. By dawn, according to their own rough count, "scores" had been killed, more than a thousand were wounded or missing, and the macadam surface of Mianfang Lu was "smeared with blood."[37]

The turmoil in Zhengzhou was far from finished. During the following days, riots continued to lash the city. Students, workers, and soldiers as well as peasants from rural suburbs ran amuck—looting shops, invading factories, smashing schools, and fighting among themselves in skirmishes undoubtedly motivated more by personal than political quarrels.[38] Breaking discipline, a few military units fragmented into rival factions, and clashed.[39] Hospitals issued desperate appeals for medicine and plasma.[40] Corpses piled up at the local crematorium.[41] On May 27, the outbreaks disrupted China's two main railway lines traversing Zhengzhou, halting vital east-west traffic between the coast and the interior, and north-south traffic between Beijing and Guangzhou.[42] Amid this turbulence, the city garrison made plain its intention to tame leftist elements by force. Military spokesmen proclaimed that the "counterrevolutionaries" would be shown "no kindness," warning: "It is necessary to depend upon guns . . . to maintain and consolidate political power."[43]

Meanwhile, fighting erupted in other parts of Henan province. In the town of Luoyang, the military garrison mobilized local industrial workers and suburban peasants in an offensive similar to the thrust against radical students in Zhengzhou. One of the strongest labor contingents formed under Army auspices was recruited from among the twenty thousand employees of the Luoyang Tractor Plant, one of China's showcase factories.

On June 5, for example, some four thousand Luoyang workers assaulted students at a vocational-training institute attached to the Luoyang Glass Factory, setting fire to the building and rounding up the youths as they emerged. Next day, with the late spring temperature in the inland city registering nearly a hundred degrees, the students counterattacked at the Luoyang Ball-Bearing Plant, another one of China's industrial showpieces.[44] The almost daily fighting apparently reached a high point of violence on the afternooon of June 19, when a battle broke out between Tractor Factory workers and students enrolled in a technical school run by the plant. Unable to dislodge the students who were holed up inside the school, the workers brought in local construction experts armed with a five-ton demolition ball, and simply proceeded to wreck the building, leaving dozens of youths buried in the debris.[45] About that time, macabre testimony to the carnage in Henan appeared in Beijing, where Red Guards who had escaped to the capital displayed the blood-stained shirts of comrades killed in the provincial strife on a truck parked outside the city's main department store.[46]

More than six months later, after further outbreaks of violence, the tensions in Henan would be eased by a tenuous compromise between the region's old Party officials and the Army. But like other such accommodations elsewhere in China at that stage, the Henan arrangement frustrated the radicals, and they continued to clamor for the power that they claimed to be their due. As late as spring of

1968, the Henan military garrison was still suppressing Red Guards under the guise of eradicating "wicked elements" and "counter-revolutionaries."[47]

♣

Probably no region troubled the Beijing leaders more acutely during the first half of 1967 than did Sichuan, the immense granary lying in remote splendor beyond the gorges of the Yangzi. In February and March, the Maoist leaders had apparently approved the crack-down on unruly radicals conducted by Li Jingquan, the provincial Party boss, and his local military associates. Though Li and his colleagues had imprisoned an estimated hundred thousand Red Guards and other leftist militants, they were hailed as "comparatively good people and able men," and that endorsement encouraged them to continue their repression.[48] But in April, as Mao and his subordinates moved to reverse the trend toward stability, they took special steps to promote a radical resurgence in Sichuan.

The zigzagging fortunes of the Sichuan radicals could be traced in the adventures of Liu Jieting, a Party official from Ipin. Liu Jieting and his wife, Zhang Xiting, had been purged by Li Jingquan for having opposed his liberal economic policies after the Great Leap Forward. Viewing the Cultural Revolution as an opportunity to avenge themselves, Liu and his wife went to Beijing to present their grievances to Mao's inner circle. From then on, their ups and down and ins and outs were like a veritable barometer of the changing political climate in Sichuan. The Maoists would neglect Liu during the calmer interludes of the Cultural Revolution, even to the extent of raising no objections to his imprisonments by the Sichuan Party apparatus. When they needed a symbol of radical dynamism, however, they would restore him to favor. In early April, therefore, they turned to him as a convenient lever to revive the Sichuan radical movement.

Having again escaped from Li Jingquan's clutches, a feat he seemed to perform with almost magical dexterity, Liu Jieting had reached Beijing in late March and presented the Maoist leaders with a catalogue of "crimes" committed by the Sichuan Party machine and its military cohorts against the region's "true revolutionaries."[49] Had they not been planning to regenerate the radical drive in Sichuan, the Maoists would have probably ignored him. But Liu's appearance was now expedient—if not contrived.

On April 1, Zhou Enlai, Jiang Qing, Chen Boda, and other members of the Beijing hierarchy convened a meeting to assess the Sichuan issue. Present, besides Liu Jieting and his wife, were two senior officers representing the Sichuan Army command. After a good deal of heated discussion the Beijing leaders criticized the two officers for having oppressed the radicals and instructed them to confess their faults.[50] The conference then exonerated Liu Jieting, his wife, and a number of other Sichuan radicals, and directed that the Red Guards who had been jailed by the provincial Party apparatus be released. The decree also retracted the earlier Maoist commendation for Li Jingquan and, branding him a "pro-capitalist," called for his dismissal.[51]

These widely publicized decisions had an electrifying impact in Sichuan. Interpreting the exoneration of Liu Jieting to signify their own vindication, Red Guards throughout the province rose up with renewed vigor. Moreover, the judgments rendered against Li Jingquan and the Sichuan Army command had licensed them to focus their fire on the region's political and military establishment.

Starting in early April, leftist factions unleashed a series of forays against Party-backed organizations in Chengdu, Sichuan's capital and one of China's loveliest cities. In the first of these attacks on April 5, four radical groups disrupted an outdoor rally being held by the Industrial Workers Combat Corps, the labor movement that had been mobilized under Li Jingquan's auspices. During the following week, the rival sides fought five more skirmishes, leaving some four hundred participants injured.[52] After that, the violence rapidly spread to other parts of the province. On May 1, in one of the rare naval encounters of the Cultural Revolution, two hundred youths were drowned in the Yangzi near Chongqing when their boat was rammed and sunk by a vessel steered by their foes.[53] Fighting also erupted in Ibin, a town upriver from Chongqing that is the uppermost point accessible to Yangzi steamers. There, more than a hundred people were reported to have been killed during the first four days of May.[54] But the biggest battles in Sichuan during that period were centered in Chengdu, and they spiraled to a scale that was virtual civil war.

In the heart of the fertile Sichuan basin, Chengdu had been transformed by the Communists from a charming provincial city into a thriving industrial complex of more than a million inhabitants, its suburbs humming with textile mills, iron and steel works, and several sensitive armaments plants, among them factories producing tanks and frames for jet fighter aircraft. In early May, the fiercest conflicts to roil Chengdu occurred in the city's industrial district. The Sichuan

Cotton Mill served as a stronghold of the main radical faction, the Red Flag Combat Division, while the Industrial Workers Combat Corps had its bastion in a weapons plant cryptically designated for security purposes as Factory No. 132.

Starting on the afternoon of May 1, the Industrial Workers staged probing attacks against the radical groups in the Sichuan Cotton Mill, abducting a number of youths and putting them through the ritual of torture and confession. The radicals mobilized squads to rescue their comrades, and soon thousands of Chengdu workers, students, and masses of suburban peasants had joined in the melee. On May 5, contingents of the Industrial Workers stormed the radical positions in the textile factory. The fighting dragged on through the day, abating inconclusively at dark with some two hundred participants seriously injured.[55] Mobs continued to roam around the city throughout the night, clashing sporadically.

The Industrial Workers Combat Corps had held several wounded Red Flag youths as hostages in their headquarters at Factory No. 132. The next morning, eight nurses drove to the plant in an ambulance to retrieve the injured. Though seven of the nurses were women clad in white uniforms, the Industrial Workers regarded them as the enemy. According to one account, they pulled them into the factory and, stripping off their clothes, beat them. News of this brutality spread quickly, bringing Red Guards to the plant from all corners of Chengdu. They encircled the buildings and, wheeling loudspeaker trucks into place, appealed to the Industrial Workers to capitulate. By noon, Factory No. 132 was under siege. But the plant was a weapons factory—and that made the difference. At 2:45 P.M., workers in a factory workshop squeezed off two bursts of gunfire, probably from AK-47 automatic rifles being manufactured for delivery to Vietnam. A few minutes later, two more bursts echoed from another part of the plant. Nobody was hit. Yet the shots gave the skirmish a new and fatal dimension.

The weapons in their hands seemed to endow the workers with a fresh sense of power. When a Red Flag loudspeaker truck called on them to lay down their arms, the workers responded by firing at the vehicle. Two young people in the truck, one of them a schoolgirl, were killed instantly. All restraints gone, armed workers in other sections of the factory opened fire against the mobs outside. Most of the crowd scattered, but a few youths managed to break into the plant. They stormed up stairways and fought amid upturned desks and filing cabinets in the factory's offices. A clash inside the building destroyed the plant laboratory, and, at one point the fighters nearly touched off an explosion as they smashed the plant's fuel tanks.

The Chengdu military garrison, fearful of exposing itself to charges of supporting the wrong side, had avoided open involvement in the battle. Later documents would allege that its commanders secretly aided the Industrial Workers Combat Corps. But finally, acting on instructions from Beijing, troops intervened to restore order on the evening of May 6. By that time the recorded casualties totaled forty-five dead and nearly three thousand hospitalized with serious injuries. Countless others had been slightly hurt, and numbers were missing.[56] But the casualties were overshadowed by the fact that guns had been used heavily by civilian activists for the first time in the Cultural Revolution.

This phenomenon alarmed everyone but the most intransigent of the Maoists in Beijing. For despite their commitment to revolution, the Chinese Communist leaders could recall that civil strife had torn China apart for a century before the Communist rise to power. And they must have felt that, perhaps in different form, history might repeat itself. Moreover, the prospect of dissidence in Sichuan was an especially sensitive one, since the province's separatist tendencies had traditionally concerned China's rulers for centuries.

In late April, even before the Chengdu battle, the Beijing leaders had been trying to alter Sichuan's administrative structure. They perceived that they could no longer tolerate Li Jingquan and his Party apparatus without risking protracted turmoil. But they could not hand control over to the radicals, who lacked the experience and discipline to manage such a vital area. Hence they sought to work out a compromise arrangement and, on May 7, they announced it in a ten-point directive.

Entitled "Red Ten Articles," the directive dismissed Li Jingquan and two of his principal Army associates, and it placed Sichuan under the command of two seasoned officers—General Zhang Guohua, the boss of Tibet, and General Liang Xingzhu, deputy political commissar in south China. This reshuffle seemed peculiar, since both men had been strongly opposed by Red Guards in their former areas. But the appointments had a three-fold purpose. First, as veterans of the First and Second Field Armies that had conquered Sichuan for the Communists, the two generals had old ties with officers still serving in the region and could therefore be expected to maintain a hold over the garrison. Second, they presumably carried weight with the Sichuan conservatives, whom Beijing regarded as the main source of

the trouble. And finally, they could always be relieved, in the event
of failure, much more easily than figures closer to Mao. Meanwhile,
to placate the Sichuan leftists, the directive promoted Liu Jieting and
his wife to a four-member "preparatory group," headed by General
Zhang, commissioned to establish a tripartite Revolutionary Committee to govern Sichuan.[57]

When General Zhang Guohua was summoned from Tibet to receive his new appointment, the Maoist hierarchy convened a conference. Present were Zhou Enlai, Jiang Qing, and Xiao Hua, chief
of the Army's General Political Department. They made it plain to
Zhang that they considered the Sichuan military command to have
been grievously at fault in its handling of the earlier situation. Zhang
would have to perform better.

Almost patronizingly, Jiang Qing told General Zhang that the
Army could redeem itself in Sichuan. "We have such a fine Army,
and must not jump to the conclusion that it is always wrong just
because it makes mistakes in one area or over a particular question,"
she said, explaining sweetly that troops "are boys of the people" who
must be treated "leniently" when they commit errors. The correct
role for the Army in Sichuan, she prescribed, was to "minimize internal strife" and to isolate Mao's enemies by unifying the radicals
and winning over the "masses" allied to "conservative" factions whose
"force . . . is not negligible."[58]

Xiao Hua, in contrast, bluntly denounced the Sichuan garrison.
The Army's duty was to "safeguard the gains of the Cultural Revolution and defend the people," but the Sichuan commanders had
deployed troops "to suppress the revolutionary masses" and, as a
consequence, "the Cultural Revolution has suffered a setback. How
grave this mistake is!" The Army's consistent failure to support the
Sichuan leftists had served to strengthen the "reactionaries," he said,
with the result that the "sharp and complicated class struggle" in the
region could not easily be resolved. Referring to the Chengdu armaments factories damaged the day before, he warned that the violence was especially serious since the province "is an important base
of national defense construction." Unlike Jiang Qing, he had few kind
words for Sichuan's senior officers. They must "criticize themselves,
examine their errors, mend their ways, really join Chairman Mao's
revolutionary line," and, above all, Xiao Hua insisted, they must
"resolutely back the true proletarian revolutionaries."[59]

Zhou Enlai spoke calmly. "Some comrades" considered conditions
in the province to be "chaotic," he said. But viewed "dispassionately,"

the Sichuan situation "is excellent and is taking a turn for the better."
Li Jingquan had been "unhorsed" and "the liberation of the southwest
has begun." In his practical fashion, Zhou urged General Zhang to
be prudent when he reached Sichuan. "Don't expect to change everything at one stroke," he advised, pointing out that Sichuan was so
huge and diverse that all its problems together added up to an unduly
"dark picture." A solution to the region's complex questions would
"take time." With an extraordinary eye for minutiae, Zhou concluded
his talk by settling a few details. There was the case, for example, of
two Beijing Red Guards who had been killed in Chengdu. "Why ship
their bodies when they can be cremated in Sichuan and their ashes
sent home?" Zhou asked. Someone present replied that the Chengdu
crematorium was being held by the "reactionary" Industrial Workers
Combat Corps. "Then telephone orders to the Army to capture it,"
said Zhou.[60]

General Zhang Guohua had little to say when his turn to speak
came. In good soldierly style, he vowed to fulfill his assignment "one
hundred per cent" even though he was "not acquainted" with the
Sichuan issue.[61] But in reality his mission would be almost impossible
to carry out, and he barely managed to survive it.

Several fundamental flaws marred the Sichuan compromise. In the
first place, General Zhang Guohua instinctively sympathized with
the provincial military commanders and shared their impatience with
the students. Second, faced with the task of restoring law and order,
Zhang would be compelled to seek help from Sichuan's *apparatchiks*,
whom the young militants were striving to overthrow. And finally,
because of his basically conservative inclinations, he would inevitably
clash with Liu Jieting and Zhang Xiting, now the area's foremost
radicals. In other words, jointly assigning General Zhang and Comrade Liu to the job of managing Sichuan was unrealistic. Their interests and aims were wholly incompatible and the arrangement was
bound to founder—unless one or the other prevailed. Not until ten
months later, in one of its periodic conferences on Sichuan, did the
Beijing hierarchy reveal the extent to which the attempt to reconcile
the divergent regional factions had failed.

At that conference, held in Beijing on March 15, 1968, Jiang Qing
accused General Zhang Guohua mercilessly of having encouraged
"reactionary" groups while suppressing "true revolutionaries" in Sichuan. She charged that he had failed to promote the campaign to
defame Li Jingquan and the region's Party bureaucrats, and really
favored Mao's enemies, had ignored directives from Beijing, and had

worked with his associates to create their own "independent king-dom." In the cruelest cut of all, she denounced him for "bourgeois objectivity." Referring to one of his speeches, Jiang Qing said scorn-fully: "You talked like a newspaper reporter. We don't know where your sympathies lie."

Premier Zhou Enlai was reluctant to lose Zhang Guohua, how-ever, and he came to the general's rescue. "He is familiar with the Sichuan situation, but he has a habit of muttering and mumbling," Zhou explained to the others. Turning to Zhang, he advised, "You should speak up boldly." He reminded the general that he had for-merly been regarded as one of Mao's most resolute disciples. "Why is it that you no longer have the same determination?"[62]

Underlying General Zhang's ambiguity, in part at least, was sheer bewilderment. An honest soldier with no great diplomatic skill, he had been caught in an incomprehensible political tangle. Indeed, Zhang confessed, he and his staff had been confused from the moment they assumed their posts in May. "Hardly had we arrived in Sichuan than we were attacked from all sides."[63]

The ferment that had greeted Zhang on his arrival in Sichuan dramatized the unresponsiveness of China's provinces to Beijing's decrees at the time. The so-called "Red Ten Articles," designed to revamp the provincial administrative structure, was having virtually no effect. Chengdu continued to be the scene of bloody skirmishes. On May 8, the Industrial Workers Combat Corps counterattacked radical strongholds in two factories, leaving seventy dead in an en-counter that lasted three days.[64] Over the following week, violence enveloped the city's outlying farm districts as the rural population joined in the fighting. In the suburb of Luoshan, nearly a hundred people were killed in one incident.[65] In Zhonghe, a village six miles outside Chengdu, workers and peasants captured some two thousand students who had evidently gone into the countryside in quest of support. Afterward, it was reported, the headless bodies of thirty-four youths were found in a stream near the village.[66]

According to many documents, large numbers of activists on both sides were armed—and determined to remain so. Rejecting demands by the local military garrison that it hand over its weapons, one group of Chengdu radicals declared: "We must use our guns to defend the Cultural Revolution and the proletarian dictatorship. We will not surrender them lightly."[67]

Meanwhile, the violence spread like an epidemic to other parts of Sichuan. It particularly shook Chongqing, the largest city in the

province. It had not been easy for the Beijing leaders to appraise the
political map of Chongqing. After several futile meetings devoted to
deciphering the Chongqing puzzle, they resorted to a facile expedient. They reshuffled the city's Army commanders, creating a temporary committee empowered to work out a compromise.

This approach infuriated the Chongqing University August 15th
Combat Regiment, an important student group supported by the local
military garrison. It resented the idea of sharing the spotlight with
other factions, and its activists inaugurated a resistance campaign.[68]
They plastered up posters openly denouncing Beijing and, in a re-
freshing change from the solemnity of most Red Guards, resorted to
satirical criticism of the Maoist leadership. Recalling a statement
by Lin Biao that Mao's edicts must be obeyed even if not understood, the youths formed a faction labeled the Fail-to-Understand
Combat Group and staged a burlesque rally at which speakers read
Beijing directives as the audience shouted in reply: "We fail to understand."[69]

The resistance in Chongqing was more than satirical, however.
On May 19, more than two thousand students invaded the railway
station and blocked train traffic for two days.[70] Tensions grew during
the ensuing weeks, and in early June youths were armed with rifles
and bayonets besides such improvised weapons as clubs, crowbars,
and vials of sulphuric acid. A few Army units split into competing
cliques, while peasants and apprentice workers as well as rusticated
students streamed into Chongqing to vent their grievances.

There were hints amid this ferment that Li Jingquan, Sichuan's
former Party boss, was still wielding a measure of power. Local security agents loyal to him were said to be operating in several areas.
Significantly, too, radio broadcasts attacking him originated in neighboring Guizhou, where the Maoists were strong, rather than in Sichuan.[71] By August, the province was in the throes of almost complete
civil war. The following year, Zhou Enlai would be prompted to quote
an old Chinese adage:

> Long before the world fell into chaos,
>   Sichuan was chaotic.
> Long after the world became calm,
>   Sichuan was still chaotic.

Nearly every other region of China was experiencing something
close to civil war during the late spring of 1967. Radio broadcasts

from Anhui disclosed that different factions there were fighting among themselves as well as indulging in theft, murder, and other forms of lawlessness.[72] In the Jiangxi province capital of Nanchang, production in thirty-three factories had stopped or slowed down as a result of clashes among workers, while rail service to nearby Fuzhou halted for ten days in early June following a skirmish in which twenty-nine youths were killed.[73] At the end of May, a battle in the Yunnan province capital of Kunming left close to three hundred dead and more than a thousand wounded.[74]

Exalted by this frenzied atmosphere, reckless Red Guards in a paroxysm of xenophobia even attacked foreign diplomats stationed in China. On May 24, truckloads of Red Guards broke into the British Consulate compound in Shanghai and harassed the British Consul, Peter Hewitt, his wife, and two children, who were under orders to leave China within forty-eight hours. Chinese youths tore Hewitt's clothes, spat in his face, and smeared him with glue as he ran the gantlet to his aircraft.[75] In Beijing not long afterward, two Indian diplomats were kicked, punched, and forced to their knees as they also departed the country on an expulsion order.[76] Soviet, French, Yugoslav, Indonesian, and Mongolian diplomats were also assaulted by unruly radicals. Even envoys representing China's sole ally, Albania, were mistakenly mistreated. At the same time, Chinese diplomats abroad went on rampages inside their missions to display their revolutionary zeal.

Despite efforts by moderate leaders in Beijing to keep the Cultural Revolution confined to China, the Maoist drive spilled over the borders of Guangdong province into the tiny Portuguese enclave of Macao and, somewhat later, into the British Colony of Hong Kong. While relatively restrained, the Hong Kong episode resembled the real Cultural Revolution in at least two important respects.

Though a British possession, Hong Kong was pervaded by a Communist bureaucracy of banking, commercial, and propaganda agents serving as China's representatives to the outside world. These operatives, many of whom live in "bourgeois" style in the Colony, now came under pressure from younger militants in much the same way that Party officials in China had been subjected to Red Guard assaults. As in China, moreover, the Cultural Revolution in Hong Kong gave many local Chinese workers, students, and others a chance to express valid as well as imaginary grievances. But three factors saved Hong Kong from the turmoil that convulsed China. First, British-led police and troops maintained firm control over the situation. Second, the radical activists failed to gain support from Hong Kong's population of 4 million, a large percentage of them Chinese refugees anxious to avoid political involvements. And finally, Beijing never gave the agitators more than rhetorical encouragement—for the simple reason that China relied on Hong Kong for nearly half its foreign-exchange earnings and its leaders were reluctant to slaughter the goose that laid its golden eggs.

In November 1966, Premier Zhou Enlai had issued instructions to a group of Hong Kong Communist *apparatchiks* invited to Beijing. Zhou told them that he contemplated no change in the Colony's status—unless it were turned into an "active" base for American naval vessels engaged in the Vietnam war. More significantly, he advised them that Beijing expected the Colony's Chinese population to be "patriotic" and "productive"—in other words, to pledge their allegiance to the homeland while earning hard currency for China.[77] But just as Zhou was unable to curb the excesses of the Cultural Revolution inside China, he could not prevent its disruption of Hong Kong.

Several events combined to stimulate the Hong Kong radicals in the spring of 1967. The purge of Tao Zhu, the Communist boss of adjacent Guangdong province, weakened the Colony's Party machine and correspondingly reinforced its radical fringe. The capitulation of the Portuguese authorities to leftist agitators in Macao also fired the Hong Kong radicals with ambitions to inflict the same humiliation on the Colony's British administration. In addition, a variety of legitimate labor protests persuaded the Hong Kong leftists that the Colony's "proletariat" was ripe for revolution.[78]

Under radical guidance, some workers added an ideological touch to their protests. In late April, for example, employees at a Hong Kong cement plant waved Mao's "little red book" and chanted his catechisms as they complained about labor conditions, and they were imitated by striking workers at an artificial-flower factory. These incidents led to limited clashes between strikers and police.[79] Soon afterward, the radicals organized demonstrations—in which several respectable Communist figures, compelled to keep pace with the "masses," uncomfortably participated. The Hong Kong colonial establishment handled them with characteristic British aplomb—and a dash of condescension. A typical confrontation occurred on May 18, when some five hundred Communist militants assembled at the handsome mansion of Sir David Trench, K.C.M.G., C.M.G., M.C., the Governor.

The solemn young activists all wore badges bearing Mao's profile, and they clutched the red-covered *Quotations*. Braving the intense heat of the day, the hardier among them had trudged up Garden Road, past the Hilton Hotel and the United States Consulate. Others arrived in automobiles and chartered sight-seeing buses that traffic officers politely directed to a lot marked "Petitioners' Special Car Park." Finally, lined up under the Queen's emblem E2R emblazoned on the mansion gate, the youths began waving their red books and chanting such Mao aphorisms as "Unity Is Strength" and "Patriotism Is Guiltless and Violence Is Justified."

Behaving as coolly as they looked in their crisp khaki shorts, a scattering of colonial Chinese policemen and British constables watched quietly. They were under orders not to react—or, as one of their superiors had put it, "Jolly useful to let the Communist 'glee clubs' sing off a bit of steam." And passive they remained while agile youths plastered the Governor's sentry boxes with Beijing-style wall posters denouncing "British brutality" and "Trench's atrocities."

Inside his mansion, Sir David was conferring with the Colony's military garrison commander and other advisers. He decided against receiving any Communist delegations, since "reasonable dialogue" with them was impossible. "Even when we've tried to ring up a Communist headquarters," a colonial civil servant said, "the girl at the other end simply sings Mao Zedong over the telephone."

But despite his exterior composure, Sir David was perturbed by the impact of the demonstration on his poodle, who was upset by the noise and had been taken to a kennel after staging a tantrum. A British officer later explained that "the animal was frantic with indignation."

At the gates outside, meanwhile, the crowd was warming up as a four-car motorcade appeared, led by a sleek black Mercedes-Benz. At first it seemed as if a Chinese wedding party had somehow gone astray. But when the occupants emerged, the crowd cheered. For these were Hong Kong's Communist leaders, the most distinguished among them Fei Yimin, the urbane editor of the newspaper *Da Gong Bao*. A slight, bespectacled gentleman in his fifties, Fei Yimin had been Shanghai correspondent for Agence France-Presse in his youth, before he rallied to the Communists, and he sent his children to school in Paris. He had acquired a good deal of real estate during his years in Hong Kong, and though he was not as wealthy as some other Chinese Communist sympathizers in the Colony, his fortune was considerable. Perhaps for these reasons, Fei demonstrated louder and lustier than anyone else. He demanded to see the Governor and, brandishing his volume of Mao's *Quotations*, he cried: "We want Trench."

The Governor's aide-de-camp, a slim British Army major, descended the steps of the mansion, strode across the courtyard and stopped inside the iron gate. He detailed a Chinese policeman to approach Fei Yimin with the message that Sir David was "too busy" to see him. Recovering quickly from this rebuff, Fei called to the major to step outside to receive a petition. The major agreed on condition that Fei bring it to the gate. There was a pause as the two men, twenty yards apart, stared at each other. Face was at stake. Neither budged.

Suddenly the silence was shattered as Fei Yimin held up two fingers, a signal to the Communists to open Mao's missal. With the crowd chanting slogans on cue, he read aloud a lengthy statement assailing the Governor for his "fascist attitude." It was nearing one o'clock when he finished and climbed back into his Mercedes, which needed a push to start. The other demonstrators marched back to their vehicles in the "Petitioners' Special Car Park." A British constable glanced at his watch. "They keep union hours," he observed, "it's time for tiffin."[80]

As the weeks wore on, the confrontation between the Communist militants and the British authorities in Hong Kong slid down toward violence. In early July, more than a thousand Chinese stormed a British frontier post, killing five colonial policemen and injuring twelve others.[81] The next day, a crowd attacked a police patrol, killing one officer with a cargo hook as the others, opening fire, fatally wounded two youths.[82] For weeks after, gangs roamed the Colony's downtown sections, raiding police stations with acid-filled bottles, bricks, and other objects as the police retaliated by ransacking Communist offices throughout the city.

As long as the Communists fought the police, the apolitical Hong Kong population remained largely neutral. But in mid-August, two incidents lost the Communists whatever tolerance they may have enjoyed. In the first incident, two small children were blown to pieces by a terrorist bomb.[83] A couple of days later, radical youths attacked a popular local Chinese radio performer, burning him alive.[84] Not long afterward, in a face-saving statement calculated to curb his followers, a Communist spokesman urged activists to switch to a "practical" approach by concentrating on the "political struggle."[85] In short, his statement implied, armed violence had failed.

Throughout the Hong Kong episode, Beijing's conduct was ambivalent. Mao's publicists had constantly exhorted the Colony's Chinese to overthrow the British administration and recover territory "occupied by the imperialists." Yet Chinese military units stationed along the border strenuously prevented mobs from crossing the frontier, and Beijing's repeated diplomatic protests to London were as toothless as they were vociferous. Though it had been feared that they would try to dehydrate the Colony into submission, the Chinese scrupulously resumed the water supply to Hong Kong on October 1, in accordance with their contract.

But this ambivalence on the part of Beijing's leaders was not limited to their Hong Kong policy. In many ways, it reflected their confusion as they sought to cope with the immense national problems created by the Cultural Revolution. As summer approached, the leaders in Beijing saw a country whose social and administrative fabric was being frayed by the traumatic impact of Mao's campaign. One sign of the deterioration was apparent in the rise of common crime. For the first time in years, foreign visitors were advised to lock their hotel doors and carry their valuables with them. In many cities, young people were taking advantage of the political disorder to rob, steal, and even murder. Reports from Shanghai disclosed that discharged soldiers, vagrant students, escaped prisoners, and other alienated elements were operating as outlaw gangs.[86] On June 9, the Shanghai authorities held a rally calling for "tighter public security" at which speakers warned against the recrudescence of "hoodlums and juvenile delinquents" of the kind common to that coastal metropolis prior to the establishment of the Communist regime.[87]

Equally critical was the breakdown of law and order in the countryside, as rival groups organized armed peasants to set up roadblocks, sabotage rail lines, and destroy other transport facilities. In several provinces, peasants were induced to invade urban areas to fight in factional disputes, with the result that agricultural production was suffering.[88] The strategy of mobilizing peasants had been Mao's great innovation in his struggle to attain power in China. But now, the Chairman personally decreed, that strategy was "reactionary." "Surrounding the cities" had been a "correct" doctrine in the past, but, he insisted, "circumstances have changed." Now, Mao said, "to encircle cities is to encircle the proletarian class."[89] In plainer language, this meant that peasants should be excluded from the Cultural Revolution.

On June 6, the Beijing leaders issued yet another impressive and somewhat contradictory edict. Henceforth, it declared, Red Guard organizations must not make arrests or conduct "private" trials. The directive forbade youths from stealing official files and documents, wrecking State installations, and raiding the strongholds of rival factions. In addition, "it is strictly prohibited to carry on armed struggle, to beat up people, to fight in groups . . . or to rob properties belonging to individuals." And the directive empowered military garrisons throughout the country to impose law and order.

On its face, the June 6 edict looked like the beginning of a return to normalcy—except for one crucial detail. Nothing in it suggested that the Army could employ force against unruly factions or individuals.[90] Thus commanders remained powerless to stop trouble unless they acted on their own initiative—which many were hesitant to do for fear of exposing themselves to Beijing's censure.

The dilemma confronting the Beijing leaders at that time, then, essentially resembled the problem they had faced throughout the Cultural Revolution: how to push Mao's drive forward without destroying the country. But now, the pervasive violence made the problem more acute than ever before. "Anarchy," the Maoists warned, "must be overcome without fail." Yet they refused to direct the Army to use its muscle, recommending instead that soldiers "patiently" strive to preach good conduct to the "masses."[91]

Early in the summer, the Beijing hierarchy met yet again to discuss ways to meet the challenge of continued tumult. Zhou Enlai and the senior military commanders spoke in favor of permitting the Army to suppress disorderly factions, while Jiang Qing, Chen Boda, and the other prominent radicals predictably advocated more militancy. After "heated discussions," the debate ended with a compromise decision to try a new approach. High-ranking government and Army delegations would be dispatched to investigate specific provinces in an effort to determine which local factions were "legitimate" and therefore deserved support. The touring teams were also commissioned to enjoin radical groups to stop their internecine fighting and unite in "revolutionary alliances."[92] At the head of the most prestigious of these delegations were Xie Fuzhi, Minister of Security, and Wang Li, the radical publicist. In July, they embarked on a trip that would trigger the most dramatic chapter of the Cultural Revolution.

CHAPTER 16

Explosion on the Yangzi

Some people say there is no civil war in China. But I think this is a civil war. It is not a foreign war. It is a violent struggle.
— MAO ZEDONG, *September 1967*

O N JULY 14, 1967, Xie Fuzhi and Wang Li flew into the Hubei province capital of Wuhan to negotiate an end to the turbulence that had troubled that city for months. They had every expectation that their mission would succeed. They were personal envoys of Mao Zedong. In addition, Premier Zhou Enlai had preceded them to Wuhan and had persuaded the various factions there to cease their internecine fighting—or so he believed. Moreover, Xie and Wang had just spent eleven days in Kunming, capital of Yunnan province, contriving a formula to paste over the differences between Red Guards and the Army garrison there.[1]

But their arrival in Wuhan, far from restoring peace, provoked an unprecedented mutiny on the part of workers and soldiers headed by General Chen Zaidao, the regional military commander—and the revolt would have decisive consequences for the Cultural Revolution and for the ultimate political shape of China. Indeed, among the many upheavals that disrupted communities all over China during the Cultural Revolution, none occurred in more surprising and spectacular fashion than this event. Nor did any other have so significant an impact on the eventual outcome of Mao's ambitious campaign. Until then, the Cultural Revolution had largely featured clashes between various local factions, each claiming to be faithful to Mao and his doctrines. At Wuhan, in contrast, a military commander and his supporters overtly defied Mao—challenging not only the Chairman's sanctity but the concept of central authority that the Communists had strenuously tried to secure since 1949, when they extended their control over a land that had been fragmented by internal strife and foreign invasion for more than a century.

That gesture of defiance, reminiscent as it was of the "warlordism" of a generation before, had immediate repercussions throughout China. Red Guard groups and military legions fought against each other and among themselves with unbridled ferocity. The month of anarchy that followed was so devastating that, by early September, the Beijing leaders were compelled once again to direct troops to take drastic measures to save China. This brought the Army to the fore and spelled the beginning of the end of the Cultural Revolution. Thus, while it represented the height of turmoil, the Wuhan uprising also marked a turning point, after which Mao's drive never fully recovered its momentum. In a matter of weeks, the Cultural Revolution went from a Reign of Terror to the equivalent of Brumaire.

Wuhan was a plausible scene for such high drama. Composed of Wuchang, Hankou, and Hanyang, three cities facing each other at the confluence of the Yangzi and Han rivers, the Hubei capital had long been one of China's most sensitive urban areas. During the late nineteenth century, its location on the Yangzi halfway between Shanghai and Chongqing made it a natural trading post for British, French, Russian, Japanese, and other foreign commercial firms seeking to penetrate the interior of China. Local Chinese reformers also endowed Wuhan with factories and arsenals, and its economy further burgeoned in the early twentieth century when it became a key junction on the newly constructed Beijing-Guangzhou railway. After 1949, the Communists transformed Wuhan into a major industrial complex featuring a huge iron and steel mill, heavy machine-tool plants, and metallurgical installations. One of their most impressive achievements, completed with Soviet aid in 1958, was a mile-long bridge spanning the Yangzi between Hanyang and Wuzhang that turned Wuhan into a strategic communications center—as Mao phrased it in a poem celebrating the structure, "a chasm becomes a thoroughfare."

Over the years, Wuhan's increasing economic importance was matched by its growing vitality as a political crucible. The foreign companies that opened offices in Hankou in the nineteenth century inadvertently imported Western ideas along with Western merchandise. And the railway had encouraged the growth of a proletariat receptive to the radical nationalism spreading through China during the early years of this century. In 1911, the revolution that resulted in the creation of the first Chinese Republic began in Wuzhang when elements in its garrison revolted against the Manchu authorities. The city's students and workers were frequently active in the next decade, and in the mid-1920s Wuhan was the seat of a short-lived national government that included Communists. In 1927, Chiang Kai-shek abandoned it to set up his own Nanjing regime. During that period, too, Mao based his Institute of the Peasant Movement in Wuhan. Hence the city had a tradition of dissidence that persisted even after China came under Communist rule. In 1957, three Wuhan youths were publicly executed for having staged a riot in protest against rigid university controls.[2]

Against that background, there were several new social and political stresses and strains that were crucial in Wuhan during the Cultural Revolution. For one thing, the city's early industrialization had spawned an elite labor force that was closely linked to the provincial Party apparatus. These workers, like veteran trade unionists in the United States and Western Europe, perceived that they had much to lose from the destruction of the local political bureaucracy. They therefore became stanch defenders of the *status quo* in opposition to the Red Guards and other militants striving to overthrow the Party machine.[3] Similarly, the Army garrison had become firmly implanted in Wuhan since 1949, when it had occupied the area during the Communist take-over of China. Its senior officers, intimately affiliated with the regional Party Committee, were committed to protecting the bureaucracy against Maoist assaults. Moreover, as some Western analysts have suggested, the Wuhan commanders were associated with certain figures in Beijing who had consistently resisted Mao's purge.[4] Thus, among its many causes, the Wuhan uprising in 1967 reflected a desire on the part of the provincial Party and Army hierarchy to preserve its autonomy, and so it was a rebellion for the sake of conservatism. In that respect, the Maoists accurately portrayed the Wuhan episode as "counterrevolutionary."

The Wuhan events also dramatized the importance of the human quotient in the Cultural Revolution. The Beijing leaders, scarred by the memory of "warlordism," may have overreacted to signs of regional resistance in the belief that the fragmentation of China they had worked so hard to avoid was returning to threaten national unity. Judging from their public and private statements, too, Mao and his comrades seemed to have been persuaded that their enemies had mounted an extensive and intricate conspiracy against them, and this may have prompted them to respond to the Wuhan dissidents more forcefully than was necessary. And, finally, the age-old Chinese preoccupation with "face" undoubtedly played a key role in the episode. For the Beijing leaders apparently abandoned diplomacy and confronted the Wuhan commander with an ultimatum that made graceful retreat impossible. Thus cornered, he rebelled.

To label Chen Zaidao a "warlord," as the Maoists did, was gross exaggeration. But he typified the entrenched provincial commander. Born in Hubei in 1908, he was a peasant of nineteen when he joined a Communist guerrilla band operating near his village, and he served throughout the rest of his career in central China. In 1954, he was put in charge of the Wuhan Military Region, with responsibility for Hubei and Henan provinces, and he was still in that post thirteen years later. As part of a Communist system in which political and military affairs overlapped and intertwined, Chen developed a complex web of Party and Army relationships. Starting in the mid-1930s, for example, he formed close links with Liu Bocheng, the celebrated "one-eyed dragon" later to become one of China's ten Marshals, who was an early critic of Mao's guerrilla doctrines and a foremost advocate of military professionalism.[5] Afterward, as the senior soldier in the Wuhan region, Chen also forged ties with the area's Party *apparatchiks*. These included Tao Zhu, and Wang Renzhong, the Communist boss of Hubei.

During the summer of 1966, as the Cultural Revolution was getting under way, Chen Zaidao and the other Wuhan leaders had reason to be optimistic for their future. Tao Zhu was then achieving prominence in Beijing as national propaganda chief, and he was using his influence to promote his old comrades. Wang Renzhong not only had taken over the Party's Central-South Bureau but was given a place in the Cultural Revolution Directorate. Wang's elevation, in turn, assured the authority of Chen and other key figures in Wuhan.

Like Party officials and Army officers elsewhere in China during that period, Wang and Chen went through the motions of subscribing to the Cultural Revolution in order to control the Maoist campaign and shield themselves in the process. They sent Work Teams into Wuhan's universities as a way of checking student agitation and, along with other maneuvers, directed local Red Guard attacks against convenient scapegoats. Among their targets was Li Da, one of the founders of the Chinese Communist Party, then president of Wuhan University.

Seventy-six years old and suffering from a bleeding ulcer, Li Da addressed a personal message to Mao, pleading: "Please save me." Mao eventually received the message and issued orders to the Wuhan

Red Guards not to "kill Li Da by persecution." But that order allegedly was intercepted and withheld by Wang Renzhong, and Li Da
was forced to face a kangaroo court that branded him a "black gangster" and recommended his expulsion from the Party. Other Red
Guard assaults against the old man continued until, on the morning
of August 13, he suddenly collapsed. For nine days after that, Red
Guards refused to permit his hospitalization, even though he was
spitting blood and running a high fever. On August 22, now realizing
that Li was nearing death, the youths rushed him to a clinic, registering him under a pseudonym. Li died two days later.[6]

The disappearance of Li Da compelled the Wuhan leaders to find
other victims for the Red Guards, and they arraigned several minor
functionaries in the following months. They also strove to keep pace
with the rhetoric of the Cultural Revolution. On one occasion, Hubei
Governor Zhang Tixue told a youth rally: "The more chaos the better.
Only through chaos can we cultivate and stiffen our ability."[7]

But during the fall of 1966, as they sought to curb Red Guard
excesses, the Wuhan Party leaders turned more and more to the
Army for help. General Chen Zaidao, who until then had remained
behind the scenes, appeared at the rallies. He exhorted Red Guards
and other militants to carry on the Cultural Revolution, promising
them that the Army would serve as a "defender of the people's interests."[8]

Whatever his long-range design, Chen's growing prominence put
him into a pivotal position. For Tao Zhu's collapse in December
brought with it the downfall of Wang Renzhong and his associates in
the Party's Central-South Bureau, and Chen filled the vacuum created
by their purge. In January 1967, when Mao issued the call to his
followers to "seize the bourgeois strongholds," Chen simulated obedience by organizing Red Guard groups to storm Wuhan's factories,
banks, radio stations, newspapers, and other enterprises. As became
clear later, his action was calculated to convince Beijing that he was
responding to Mao's decree directing the Army to support the radicals. In reality, like other regional commanders. Chen appeared to
believe that he could prevent the Red Guards from causing irreparable damage by controlling their destructive appetites.

At that stage, however, controlling the Red Guards was almost
impossible as the youths, once unleashed, refused to submit to discipline. On January 9, for example, a report from Wuhan disclosed
that thousands of young men and women had blockaded the Yangzi
River bridge and occupied the airport, disrupting traffic of all kinds

into and out of the city. Referring for the first time to a problem that was to become increasingly serious—and would later have critical international implications—the same report revealed that the turmoil in Wuhan was interrupting railway shipments of Soviet and Chinese military supplies to North Vietnam.[9]

Other indications of growing turbulence were to be contained in the Wuhan garrison's attempts to impose law and order. On February 3, the Army published a thirteen-point edict criticizing the city's radical factions for "sabotaging" industrial production, cutting communications, and, among other things, inciting peasants to leave the surrounding countryside to participate in the urban ferment. While paying lip service to the Cultural Revolution, the edict plainly tried to limit the campaign. Red Guards and other activists, it asserted, should pursue the Maoist drive only "in their spare time," adding that meetings and rallies must be conducted in a "rational manner" that would not impede the economy."[10] These and other admonitions were futile, however. The situation in the city gradually polarized as two rival coalitions mobilized their forces.

One of these coalitions, put together by Chen Zaidao as his instrument for preserving order, was called the Wuhan Area Proletarian Revolutionary Liaison Center of Mao Zedong Thought Million Heroic Troops—or, in familiar abbreviated form, the Million Heroes. Included in this "conservative" movement were groups of skilled workers, office employees, minor officials, militiamen, older students, and others who had most to lose from a revolutionary purge. They were backed up by the 9th Independent Division, an Army unit used for internal security purposes."[11]

The Million Heroes, which comprised about a half-million activists, outnumbered its rival coalition, the Mao Zedong Thought Fighting Team's Wuhan Workers General Headquarters—or, in shorthand, the Workers Headquarters. This movement, considered to be radical, was mainly composed of workers from the Wuhan Iron and Steel Company as well as university and school students. In its ranks, too, were Red Guards sent to Wuhan from Beijing.[12] The Workers Headquarters was also supported by certain military units loyal to Li Yingxi, a local Army political commander determined to challenge Chen Zaidao's authority.[13] The split within the Wuhan garrison had been widening since February and, like the polarization of the city's political factions, became increasingly acute as summer approached.[14]

Throughout the late spring the rival coalitions escalated their attacks against each other from verbal exchanges to physical clashes. On May 17, for instance, some two thousand members of the Workers Headquarters assaulted the Army garrison, seriously injuring ten soldiers.[15] Sporadic fighting continued after that until June 14, when skirmishes again led to the closing of the Yangzi River bridge.[16] After this, in an attempt to restore order, Chen Zaidao drastically cracked down on the city's radical youth groups. The radicals fought to defend themselves, and by the latter half of June, Wuhan had degenerated into anarchy.

Chen Zaidao began his operation against the radicals on June 17. At one o'clock in the afternoon, according to several versions of the event, the Wuhan garrison deployed a number of trucks filled with members of the Million Heroes armed with spears, axes, and pitchforks against a student hostel in Hankou. The battle raged all night and by the next morning more than a hundred were dead and some three hundred injured. On the same day, the Army sent thousands of peasants against youths gathered at the site of a suburban water-reservoir project, and the toll in that battle was nearly two hundred killed and more than a thousand injured.[17] The next morning, when a group of young people tried to visit their hospitalized comrades, they were kidnaped and beaten, and their Polish-made automobile was confiscated. In another part of the city, seven students were clubbed to death by a Million Heroes group when they tried to negotiate a truce to end the fighting at a railway office.

Wuhan's hospitals were crowded with wounded, and the water and electricity supply in several districts had broken down.[18] Yet the rioting continued. Night after night, opposing gangs fought at different places in the sprawling metropolis. On the afternoon of June 23, at the Hanyang Steel Rolling Mill, rival factions used improvised weapons, homemade incendiary bombs, and vials of acid in a clash that claimed eight dead and more than a hundred injured. About the same time, buildings of the Water Transport Engineering College were guttted by fire as opposing student groups battled for control.[19] Other skirmishes erupted daily, and reports in Beijing estimated that some two thousand factories, mines, and other enterprises in the Wuhan area either had suspended their activities entirely or were operating only part-time.[20]

Alarmed by the havoc wrought on one of China's key industrial sectors, the Beijing leaders telephoned Chen Zaidao on June 26, commanding him to halt the fighting. But Chen, apparently convinced that he had to suppress the radicals in order to protect his own authority, refused to comply. Finally, Zhou Enlai himself reportedly flew to Wuhan to examine the situation.

Precisely when Zhou went to Wuhan, how he conducted his investigation, or how he reached his conclusion has never been made clear. But on July 14, he convened a meeting at the local Army headquarters at which he decreed that Chen Zaidao had erred in backing the "conservative" Million Heroes and should shift his support to the truly revolutionary Workers Headquarters. At noon of the same day, Xie Fuzhi and Wang Li arrived in Wuhan, together with several Red Guards from Beijing and General Yu Lijin, chief political commissar of the Air Force. Zhou returned to Beijing, leaving Xie and Wang to persuade the city's assorted factions to accept his verdict.[21]*

During their first few days in Wuhan, Xie and Wang met with delegates of the various Red Guard movements. On the evening of July 15 they accepted arm bands and badges from Red Guards of the Central China Technical College, an affiliate of the Workers Headquarters, thus endorsing their organization. When they convened representatives of the Million Heroes two days later, in contrast, Xie and Wang blamed them for making trouble. This tactless approach divided the rival groups even further, and recurrent skirmishes occurred around the city despite the presence of Mao's two emissaries. One afternoon, for example, during demonstrations staged to hail the envoys, eight people were killed when a fight broke out between members of the Million Heroes and the Workers Headquarters.[23]

On the evening of July 19, the explosion came. Xie and Wang, having compiled sufficient documentation to substantiate their case, summoned Chen Zaidao and other senior military officers to a conference at Wuhan Army headquarters. Their message essentially repeated Zhou Enlai's earlier verdict. They urged Chen and his associates to support the Workers Headquarters and disband the Million Heroes, telling them, "You must only correct your mistakes and all will be well." According to Xie's own account, that decision particularly infuriated one officer, Niu Hailong, commander of the

---

* According to one account, Mao also went to Wuhan, and remained there after Zhou's departure. This account claimed that the Chairman anticipated an attempted *coup d'état* and spoke with Chen Zaidao on July 18 in an attempt to "give him a chance to rein in on the brink of the precipice." But Chen "did not listen, being a reactionary." The account claimed that Mao stayed in Wuhan until the night of July 21, narrowly escaping capture by the mutineers.[22] The authenticity of this sole version has been questioned. It may simply have been contrived to dramatize Mao's prescience.

9th Independent Division. Niu refused to believe that Zhou Enlai had issued the instructions and claimed that Wang Li had invented them.[24] After much argument, he jumped up and walked out of the conference, shouting: "I am prepared to risk my life."[25]

It was nearly midnight when Xie and Wang returned to their suite at the Dong Hu Hotel. As they were preparing for bed, trucks, fire engines, and loudspeaker vans suddenly swept into the hotel compound. According to several versions, including Xie's own, two hundred men descended from the vehicles and encircled the building while others sealed off nearby streets. Armed with rifles, spears, and knives, many were troops of Niu Hailong's 9th Division even though they wore arm bands identifying themselves as members of the Million Heroes. As they milled around in the compound, the loudspeakers broadcast slogans denouncing Xie and Wang and proclaiming loyalty to Mao.

Chen Zaidao, summoned by telephone, arrived to explain that the situation was beyond his control. His explanation was probably sincere, for a dozen agitators shortly burst into the hotel room, threw him to the floor, and began to kick him—until one of them discovered they were attacking the wrong man,[26] whereupon they turned on Xie Fuzhi and Wang Li. Leaving Xie in the room, they took Wang to the Wuhan garrison headquarters, where they tore off his clothes and beat him. At about two o'clock in the morning, meanwhile, Xie Fuzhi managed with the help of sympathetic Red Guards to escape from the hotel. He made his way to the Hydroelectric Institute, a radical stronghold. There, he learned of Wang's whereabouts and went to the garrison headquarters to rescue him—only to be placed under guard himself. By now, the episode was changing from a confused political dispute into a direct military confrontation between the Wuhan command and the Beijing authorities."[27]

Anticipating a reaction from Beijing, Chen Zaidao's military and civilian followers reinforced their defenses. They replaced the regular guards at the garrison headquarters, seized the radio station, took over vital positions along the railway, occupied the airport, and blocked the approaches to the bridges across the Yangzi and Han rivers, thus isolating their adversaries in each of Wuhan's three cities. They also staged forays against the main radical strongholds, killing and injuring those who resisted them. And, to justify their actions, they broadcast declarations asserting that their goal was to eradicate Mao's "counterrevolutionary" foes.[28]

The Beijing leaders received news of the abduction of Xie and

Wang at dawn on July 20, and they responded swiftly and forcefully. An airborne division and three infantry divisions were ordered to move toward the city from posts in the province, and five gunboats of the East Sea Fleet were sent from their Shanghai naval base up the Yangzi to Wuhan.[29] At the same time, Zhou Enlai left Beijing by airplane—convinced, apparently, that he could persuade Chen Zaidao to free Xie and Wang.

By now, however, Chen could not retreat. Apprised of Zhou's imminent arrival, he sent twenty-five truckloads of troops and civilian vigilantes to take the Premier into custody as his airplane landed. But loyal Air Force elements radioed Zhou's plane of this maneuver, and the pilot set down at an alternate field south of Wuhan.

In the meantime, Xie Fuzhi and Wang Li, incarcerated in separate rooms at the garrison headquarters, were in danger of being transferred by the mutineers to a more secure place outside Wuhan. According to some reports, Chen Zaidao planned to transport them by boat up the Yangzi to Chongqing, then also in chaos, to hold them there as hostages.[30] He could then use the two captives as bargaining counters to negotiate a compromise with Beijing—in much the same way that the Communists had imposed a settlement on Chiang Kai-shek after kidnaping him in Xi'an in 1936.

At this critical juncture, a daring officer known only as Zhang made his appearance. The chief political commissar of a regular Army division stationed near Wuhan, Zhang had been aligned against Chen Zaidao for months. On the evening of July 20, according to his own story, he led three men into the garrison headquarters, overcame the sentries, and discovered the room in which Wang Li was being held. Taking Wang with them, they fled into the Hongshan highlands outside Wuhan, eluding capture by Chen Zaidao's men. In the morning, they were able to contact other loyal troops, and finally escorted Wang to the airfield at which Zhou Enlai had landed.[31] There they found Xie Fuzhi, who had been rescued by an airborne contingent. Leaving the two men at the airfield, now under regular Army control, Zhou returned to Beijing to arrange for their reception. At two o'clock in the morning of July 22, Xie and Wang departed Wuhan, reaching the national capital at dawn.[32]

The rescue of Mao's emissaries did not bring the Wuhan mutiny immediately to an end. On July 21, as Zhou Enlai was returning to Beijing, no less a figure than Lin Biao visited Wuhan to organize the offensive against the dissidents. He appointed General Yu Lijin, the Air Force political commissar who had originally accompanied Xie and Wang, to command the operation. By July 23, the loyalist forces had gone into action. Gunboats of the East Sea Fleet, joined by additional vessels, cruised into position and trained their cannon on targets in the three Wuhan cities while airborne troops, some of them reportedly parachuted into the fray, seized the bridges, the radio station, the main telegraph office, and other strategic points. Units of the Fifteenth Army moved into the city from their base near Xiaogan.[33]

Confronted by this awesome display of military muscle, many of the dissidents capitulated without a fight and, according to one report, the weapons they surrendered filled thirty trucks.[34] Chen Zaidao and his staff were arrested and sent to Beijing, and the Wuhan Military Region was placed under the command of General Zeng Siyu, former deputy Army chief of Manchuria. Under his aegis, local officers promptly issued a series of statements admitting their errors and pledging to pursue the "correct" line in the future.[35]

But the rebellion persisted in one form or another into early August. On July 27, the Maoist leaders were still calling on the Wuhan garrison to overthrow the insurgents,[36] and the Beijing press two days later said that the struggle for the city had moved "into a new stage" as opposing factions were deployed on "battlefields along both banks of the Yangzi."[37] On July 31, the Beijing radio dislcosed that aircraft had showered Wuhan with leaflets urging radicals in the city to intensify their attacks against remnant dissidents.[38] Wuhan's hospitals were crowded with wounded soldiers and civilians, and thousands of refugees were disrupting railway service as they tried to flee south to Guangzhou.[39] Another sign that Wuhan remained unstable for weeks was that the gunboats of the East Sea Fleet did not finally return to their Shanghai base until October.[40]

On July 26, meanwhile, China's principal civilian and military leaders met in Beijing for nine hours to question Chen Zaidao and his comrades. The next morning, Red Guards invaded the hotel where Chen was being held and dragged him out for the first of a series of unofficial interrogations.[41] At one of these sessions, convened on August 4, Army representatives grilled Chen for ten hours. The disgraced general was compelled to bow to his inquisitors as the hearing began. But he stubbornly denied having engineered the mutiny—until, in the end, his exasperated interrogators forced him to repeat that he had been "the manipulator and ringleader of the incident." Thus they were able to announce that Chen had confessed.[42] Apparently anxious to avoid aggravating the dissension in the Army, however, the Chinese leaders treated Chen with surprising leniency. Some months later, Zhou Enlai quoted Mao as having said that Chen "may come forward again"—but only after he had "mended his ways in all seriousness," presumably through "labor reform."[43]

Ironically, when the Army was suppressing radicals throughout China a year later, Chen Zaidao's Wuhan rival, Li Yingxi, would be among those brought to trial. He was accused of having attempted an unauthorized seizure of power in February 1967, labeled a "typical soldier ruffian," and, like Chen, condemned to redeem himself at hard labor—once again demonstrating the tendency of the revolution to devour its most devoted activists.[44]

Inglorious though it was, the Wuhan uprising heartened the most militant advocates of the Cultural Revolution. For by dramatizing that Mao's doctrines still faced widespread opposition, they were able to clamor for intensified purges not only in the Party but in the Army as well. The extremists also urged that Red Guards and other radical activists across China be armed. But this prospect of increased violence inevitably prompted the regional Army commanders and their supporters to respond with force. From late July through early September, China seemed dangerously close to civil war.

Nobody encouraged the revival of violence more openly than did Mao's wife, Jiang Qing. She cautioned the Red Guards against disarming, and her exhortations were echoed by Chen Boda. "Prepare for protracted war," he said, insisting that the struggle will not be resolved by the exchange "of a few words."[45] Most important, Mao himself circulated various decrees authorizing the distribution of arms. "Issue weapons to the leftist masses," one read, and another declared: "Everyone should be prepared to take up bayonets." He was also quoted as saying: "We are now carrying pens, but we should be ready to carry rifles."[46]

Maoist leaders also utilized the Wuhan rebellion to initiate a series of demonstrations and rallies calculated to whip up fervor among the Red Guards, many of whom had been earlier showing signs of weariness with the Cultural Revolution. Starting on July 22 with the airport reception for Xie Fuzhi and Wang Li on their return from Wuhan, the organized excitement reached a high point three days later, when a million people were mobilized to fill Tiananmen Square. Mao was absent, but Lin Biao and nearly every other Chinese leader appeared on the balcony of the Tiananmen Gate, and the rhetoric that pervaded the rally was belligerent. Speakers called for fresh efforts to "strike down" Mao's adversaries and warned that the Cultural Revolution would be subverted unless it was defended "with blood and life."[47] The same emotional tone vibrated in the press. One *People's Daily* editorial, portraying Mao's enemies as "rats running across the street," cried out: "Kill them! Kill them!"[48]

Amid these passionate pleas for a radical resurgence emerged a new and significant theme—the demand for a thorough purge of the Chinese armed forces. Demands for the elimination of individual officers had been put forth before. But now, for the first time, the entire Beijing press and radio resonated with strident allegations that the Army was riddled with Mao's foes. Recalling the "betrayals" of Peng Dehuai and Luo Ruiqing, the commentaries contended that their sympathizers in the Army were engaged in a wider conspiracy inspired by Liu Shacqi and the "revisionist" Party machine. It was imperative "for the proletariat to keep a firm hold over the Army" in order to "destroy the bourgeois reactionary line."[49] Some radicals even favored the cancellation of Army Day, since Mao had not participated in the historic episode which it commemorated."[50]

Though the attempt to purge the Army was at the outset plainly endorsed by Mao's closest subordinates, its most dynamic advocate in Beijing was a group of ultraleftists known as the May 16th Detachment, named after the date of the important circular issued by the Chairman early in the Cultural Revolution. One of the leaders of this movement was Wang Li, who had apparently become embittered against the Army as a result of his experience in Wuhan. The May 16th Detachment also included Qi Benyou, the radical journalist, who had triggered the offensive against Liu Shaoqi in April, and Yao Dengshan, the Chinese diplomat who had been expelled from Indonesia. Several of these extremists belonged to the Cultural Revolution Directorate and, in that capacity, were intimately affiliated with Jiang Qing, Chen Boda, and other figures in charge of Mao's campaign.[51] They were probably associated as well with General Xiao Hua, the Army's chief political commissar, whose main function was to eradicate military professionalism. Thus their attacks against the Army—along with the other disruptive activities they promoted during the turbulent month of August—may have initially been tolerated if not actually approved by Mao.

Ultimately, however, the May 16th Detachment would be branded "counterrevolutionary" by the professional military commanders, who realized that the country could not withstand endless turmoil. Worried by both the growing Soviet threat on China's northern borders and the escalating American presence in Vietnam, the commanders apparently warned Mao and the other Beijing leaders that they had reached the limit of their endurance. The commanders may have also resented Lin Biao's association with the radicals who, in the wake of the Wuhan mutiny, called for a purge of the Army. And their resentment may have been at the origin of Lin's downfall four years later.

The Wuhan revolt and its aftermath, like the Cultural Revolution itself, served to bring to the surface tensions which had plagued China even before the establishment of the Communist regime. These tensions illustrated the degree to which the "souls" of the Chinese people, which Mao had sought to transform, remained unchanged.

CHAPTER 17

The Guns of August

> *As revolutionary masses, you should take up arms to defend yourselves. . . . Don't be naïve. Don't lay down your weapons when your enemies use pistols, rifles, spears, and big swords against you.*
>
> —JIANG QING, *July 22, 1967*

> *Under the dictatorship of the proletariat, there is no reason whatsoever for the working class to split into two big irreconcilable organizations.*
>
> —MAO ZEDONG, *September 1967*

THE MONTH OF AUGUST 1967 was the most dangerous period of the Cultural Revolution—indeed, perhaps of the entire Communist regime. Inspired by the Wuhan mutiny, factions throughout the country rose to the attack—their agitation further encouraged by official criticisms of the Army. And Mao's directive to "arm the leftists," published in late July, significantly contributed to the turmoil. Every faction regarded itself as truly revolutionary, and many now felt licensed to acquire weapons. In some areas, the Army mobilized armed groups to suppress them. Elsewhere, extremist organizations were given guns by military units trying to perpetuate the ferment for their own purposes. In several places where militant youths were denied arms, they broke into arsenals to steal rifles and heavier equipment, and many even ambushed soldiers in order to seize their weapons. In south China, trains transporting Soviet and Chinese military supplies to North Vietnam were looted more and more frequently, thus aggravating the already strained relations between Beijing and Hanoi and deflating China's claim to being a "reliable rear area" in the struggle against the United States.

On August 10, the Army command in Jiangxi province issued weapons to special vigilante groups directed to "protect State property and maintain revolutionary order."[1] For similar motives, the Hunan military commander armed some three thousand members of two civilian organizations formed under Army auspices.[2] In Beijing, in contrast, more than two thousand youths affiliated with the Aviation Institute's Red Flag faction, one of the most radical movements in the city, were furnished with rifles and mobilized into a paramilitary regiment that would "strengthen the morale of revolutionary groups . . . and guarantee the smooth development of the Cultural Revolution." The Jinggangshan Red Guards at the Beijing Normal College, another extremist faction, were also armed.[3] Hence the potential for violence was enlarged to a degree that Mao had never envisaged. And that potential rapidly became reality.

Shandong was one of the first regions to react directly to the events in Wuhan. There, local dissidents abducted a team of Mao's emissaries investigating the political situation in the city of Linyi. Radio broadcasts from Shandong disclosed that the dissidents had brought "large numbers of ignorant peasants" into the city, inciting them to "encircle, attack, and beat up" the visiting investigation team. Similar outbreaks also erupted at Zaozhuang, another Shandong city on the main rail line to Beijing, where rebels unsuccessfully attempted to overthrow the Municipal Revolutionary Committee loyal to Mao. In both places, the radio broadcasts claimed, the revolts were "coordinated with the recent Wuhan incident."[4]

By the middle of the month, the ferment had spread to other parts of Shandong. Rival labor factions in the port city of Qingdao were reported to be battling each other with the usual assortment of crowbars, knives, and axes. Here, the radicals' apparent objective was to topple the local Revolutionary Committee, which had evidently excluded the more militant Maoist groups when it was founded earlier in the year. In short, the Revolutionary Committee had become as entrenched and conservative in office as the former Party apparatus it had displaced. As its spokesmen declared: "Our stand is clear-cut. No matter whether it is rightist subversion or leftist attack, we must resolutely counter them."[5]

Insurgent elements also rose up in Henan province, an area under the jurisdiction of the Wuhan Military Region. Led by General He

Yunhong, the Army's deputy political commissar there, the Henan activists were reportedly joined by allies sent into the region from Sichuan. This suggested a measure of collusion among military commanders throughout the Yangzi River valley from Wuhan to Chongqing, and the nationwide implications of this frightened the Beijing leaders. A committee of Henan representatives was convened in Beijing in late July, when one of Mao's aides advised them that the "devious, complicated, and arduous" fight for control of the province had reached a critical level. He warned them against emulating the Wuhan dissidents: "The schemes and tricks of those who cooperate with the mutineers will sooner or later be brought to light."[6]

The uprising in Wuhan also ignited a fresh explosion of violence in Sichuan, where, according to several reports, weapons were being shipped down the Yangzi from Hubei province.[7] By early August, Sichuan Army units, Red Guard factions, and other groups were armed with everything from rifles to tanks and artillery. During one period of fighting in Chengdu, hundreds of buildings were leveled by artillery fire, and communications in and out of the city were cut off completely. Similar battles destroyed sections of Chongqing, Nanzhong, and other cities, and the provincial Army commander, General Zhang Guohua, narrowly escaped death when snipers fired at him in Chengdu.[8] Though casualty figures were never published, the toll in Sichuan was illustrated in Beijing on August 20 when hundreds of Red Guards, each carrying a chrysanthemum, marched silently through the city in mourning for their comrades killed in the province. "Sichuan Is Swimming in Blood," their banner pleaded, "The Central Committee Must Act."[9]

As in other provinces, the rival groups in Sichuan had inflated their ranks with peasants from nearby villages. According to one report, a half-million peasants poured into Chengdu alone during August.[10] The peasants apparently welcomed this opportunity to break out of the rigors of their "people's communes" and, in the general confusion, to loot urban shops and warehouses for merchandise that was unavailable in the rural regions.

Mao had conceived of this strategy of "surrounding the cities by the countryside" decades before during his wars against both the Japanese and the Nationalists. He had later broadened the concept to form the basis of his strategy for world revolution, arguing that the underdeveloped areas of the globe would eventually defeat the industrial nations. Now he perceived that his strategy was being used by his opponents against him, and he tried to stop it. His private secretary, Chen Boda, undertook to explain the doctrinal shift in almost scholastic style. The mobilization of peasants had been "correct" during the struggles to take over China, he said. But since the establishment of the "dictatorship of the proletariat, conditions have changed." Therefore, Mao had decreed that peasant deployments should be judged "reactionary." Speaking in Beijing on July 21, Mao said: "To mobilize peasants to flock to the cities is a crime—a crime—a crime against the proletariat, against the people, and, from the viewpoint of the peasants, against themselves."[11]

Aggravating the ferment in Sichuan were serious schisms in the military establishment. The most distinguished unit in the province was the Fifty-fourth Army, which had served in both the Korean War and the Indian border conflict. Afterward assigned to Sichuan, the Fifty-fourth Army was divided into forty smaller units by Li Jingquan, the regional Party boss who doubled as the Army's political commissar in the province. Li dispersed these units to different districts in order to integrate officers with local Party officials. In theory, this policy conformed to the Maoist dogma which favored civic action by the Army among the "masses." But in practice, close affiliations between Army officers and Party *apparatchiks* worked against Mao's goals. For the officers not only acquired a vested interest in defending the Party machine, but soon developed a concern for their own authority. In many instances, their wives were employed in local government or Party agencies and their children attended local schools. Thus, as a study of the Army's behavior in the Sichuan city of Zigong concluded, officers stationed there instinctively tended to side with the entrenched "power-holders" against the Red Guards and other radicals.[12]

Another Sichuan force, the Fiftieth Army, adopted a somewhat different posture. Based almost entirely in the region around Chengdu, the province capital, it was more responsible to General Zhang Guohua, the regional commander. Though nominally faithful to the Maoist line, Zhang regarded the imposition of law and order as his primary function. His detachments were therefore detailed to suppress various factions irrespective of their ideological leanings and, as a result, they frequently clashed with military units backing troublesome groups. As a Beijing analysis of the situation pointed out, many rival movements in Sichuan distorted Mao's old slogan "Support the Army" to suit their own purposes. "Certain people," the analysis

said, "support only the military units that back up their faction. . . . This practice of bourgeois and petty bourgeois factionalism . . . has served to split the Army."[13]

By late August, a crazy quilt of Army and Red Guard factions
were engaged in battles throughout Sichuan. Some had formed into
guerrilla bands fighting in the hills and mountains. To the delight of
the Chiang Kai-shek regime, which consistently claimed to have sympathizers within the People's Liberation Army, some of the irregulars
were described by Beijing propagandists as remnant Nationalist
troops.[14] General Zhang Guohua, unable to cope with the disorder,
was finally compelled to ask Beijing for reinforcements in the hope
that soldiers from outside the province, unfettered by links with local
factions, could restore peace.[15] The device of deploying outside troops
was used elsewhere, too—notably in Guangdong, where the turbulence during the summer became too difficult for the local Army
garrison to handle.

In mid-April, during his quick visit to the Guangdong province
capital of Guangzhou, Zhou Enlai had criticized the military command
there for having manhandled student activists. He had also exonerated
the main radical organization, which the Army garrison sought to
suppress. These moves seemed to restore calm to the city, but the
differences dividing the factions were too acute to permit more than
a temporary peace. Hardly had Zhou departed than they began to
prepare for another round. By then, two large coalitions were forming, distinguished from each other primarily by their past relationship
with the Army. Those that had been suppressed by the Army formed
a loosely knit movement known as the Red Flag. Those favored by
the Army designated themselves the East Wind, the name borrowed
from a couplet that had celebrated the period of military control in
early spring as the "March east wind."[16] The leaders of the East Wind
were said to include the son of General Huang Yongsheng, commander of the Guangzhou Military Region, as well as the sons of a
half-dozen other senior officers stationed in the Guangdong area.[17]
The rival movements mobilized forces in anticipation of a pretext to
resume fighting. That pretext was provided by the mutiny in Wuhan.

On July 21, the Guangzhou Army garrison and its civilian supporters struck first at their radical adversaries, imitating the military
dissidents in Wuhan. East Wing vigilantes, aided by troops, besieged
a hundred Red Flag activists in a Guangzhou sugar refinery. Armed
with improvised weapons, they killed four young radicals during the
skirmish. Two days later, the Red Flag organized a service to mourn

its fallen comrades, and this ignited a bigger battle. As Red Flag members marched from a local stadium to the Sun Yat-sen Memorial Hall to hold the service, East Wind activists attacked them. The two sides fought all day to gain control of the hall. By evening, thirty-three Red Flag and an undetermined number of East Wind supporters were dead. After the battle, according to one participant, the East Wind contingent retreated to safety under Army protection.[18]

If the radicals harbored grievances against the Guangzhou military authorities for that incident, they were quickly given doctrinal justification to assault the Army openly. On July 22, Jiang Qing warned Red Guards and other militants against surrendering their weapons, and the official Beijing press was calling for a purge of the Army. The Guangzhou radicals began to refer to General Huang Yongsheng, the local military chief, as "Guangzhou's Chen Zaidao." Both they and their rivals also started to raid arsenals for weapons, and the violence rapidly escalated.[19]

A new series of clashes broke out on August 13, when the Army killed eighteen young people aboard a boat transporting guns to a Red Flag stronghold on the Pearl River. The Red Flag faction retaliated two days later, by assaulting the headquarters of the Guangdong Province General Trade Union, which was occupied by East Wind members. As a participant in that skirmish later related, the defenders of the building fought from the roof, bombarding their foes with bottles and spraying them with pistol, rifle, and machine-gun fire. Using mortars to open the way, Red Flag activists stormed into the building and up the stairs as East Wind fighters shot down at them from above. In Beijing, Zhou Enlai received reports of the fracas. He immediately directed the rivals to compose their differences. But soon afterward the Red Flag took over the contested building and the fighting resumed.[20]

The brief rise of the Red Flag faction in the center of Guangzhou prompted East Wind activists to retreat to the suburbs, where they sought support from workers in the industrial sectors outside Guangzhou. Many of them also fled to nearby villages to mobilize the assistance of peasants. Pursuing their enemies, Red Flag groups attacked and occupied suburban schools, using them as strongholds. At the suburb of Gaozhong, for example, one Red Flag band took over a school, cemented up its entrance, encircled it with an electrified fence, and put up a sign reading: "If anyone dares to encroach upon our school property, his wife will be called a widow and his filial son will pay homage to his dead father."[21]

By this time, Guangzhou was in total chaos. Thousands of residents were fleeing to the countryside, disrupting suburban bus traffic. Skirmishes near the municipal airport delayed scheduled flights, and with the main railway station in the midst of the combat zone, travelers had to drive or walk to the outskirts of the city to board trains. A Hong Kong Chinese, returning from a family visit in a town north of Guangzhou, reported that he had had to make his way south by walking, hitching rides in trucks, or hiring pedicabs. Crime in Guangzhou spiraled as the police left their posts and criminals took advantage of the situation to rob and even murder. One Guangzhou resident recounted that groups of outlaws were descending from nearby hills to attack warehouses and homes for food. Such accounts, exacerbated by rumors of similar lawlessness, plunged Guangzhou deeper into apprehension and insecurity.[22]

The turmoil in Guangzhou was even visible to foreign visitors, whom the Chinese usually shield from sights that reflect unfavorably on China. In mid-August, after a two-week tour of China, Japanese Communist students were confined to their hotel for safety's sake and later reported that they had heard shooting in the streets during the night. They were prevented by the fighting from boarding the train for Hong Kong and were taken to the border by bus under Army escort. Even so, they recalled, they were stopped en route by armed Red Guards, interrogated and permitted to proceed only after their escorts explained that they were "honored guests" of the People's Republic.[23] Also in Guangzhou at that time, a group of German tourists accidentally came upon a body hanging from a lamp post. Their embarrassed guide told them, "It is a bandit who has been executed by the people."[24]

Nothing so weakened the Army's prestige and thus intensified the violence in Guangzhou as Beijing's demand that General Huang Yongsheng submit to a "self-examination" of his "mistakes." The purpose of this demand was not clear. Perhaps the Beijing leaders believed that, by holding Huang responsible for the unrest, they might appease the Red Guards and thereby calm them. Or they may have been convinced that having failed to curb the disorder, he genuinely deserved censure. In any case, Huang and his staff made ritual confessions. They admitted that their "dictatorial measures" had placed them "in a position antagonistic to the masses," and they not only pledged to vindicate the factions they had banned but promised to release numbers of young people who had been arrested for disruptive activities.[25] But far from placating the radicals, this show of weakness on the part of the Army only encouraged them, and the ferment in Guangzhou grew. Finally, in mid-August, troops from other provinces began to move into Guangzhou to restore order. They included elements of the Forty-seventh Army stationed in Hunan. By September, eleven divisions were reported to be in the Guangzhou region.[26]

In Beijing, meanwhile, the Maoist leader again turned to Liu Shaoqi and his wife, Wang Guangmei. Though nominally still China's Chief of State, Liu no longer exercised authority either in that capacity or within the national Party apparatus. Yet he remained the symbol of opposition to Mao—the personification of all evils of bureaucratic "revisionism." Moreover, Liu was conveniently located to serve as the prime target of Maoist invective, for he had been permitted to continue living in Zhongnanhai, the closely guarded residential park reserved for dignitaries of the Chinese government.

Liu had written three "confessions" since the previous October, when he produced his first formal "self-criticism" at a Central Committee meeting in Beijing. In the last of these, completed on July 9, he had reiterated his "mistakes" in having tried to dominate the Cultural Revolution in the universities a year before, apologizing to the radicals "who have been suppressed and harmed by the erroneous line which I represent." He invited his comrades to "expose and criticize freely" the "evil influence" he was accused of exerting at the outset of the Cultural Revolution.[27]

But the Maoist faction in the government could not accept Liu's *mea culpa* without conceding that his "crimes" had been less horrible than their frenetic propaganda had been claiming for months. Nor could they liquidate him without losing a valuable target for their campaign against "bourgeois revisionism." Thus their strategy was to keep up the rhetorical drive against him while protecting him against physical assault. In late July, however, with the radicals' emotions stirred by the Wuhan mutiny and their tempers shortened by the midsummer heat of Beijing, this tricky approach was not easy to manage.

Hundreds of Red Guards began to demand that Liu and his wife face a public denunciation rally on August 5, the first anniversary of Mao's initial appeal to his disciples to "bombard" the Communist Party bureaucracy. Youths streamed by the thousands to the area outside the walls of the Zhongnanhai compound. They put up tents and makeshift huts, and they constructed an ingenious plaster effigy of Liu, its cheeks pierced by a pen and its eyes consisting of blinking blue and yellow electric lights. They also draped their sprawling encampment with banners and posters asserting their determination to place Liu on public display by their August 5 deadline. One placard proclaimed: "We Will Never Retreat Until We Drag Out Liu the Bandit."[28]

Anxious to avert a direct confrontation with Liu, the Maoist leaders delegated Qi Benyou to dissuade the Red Guards from carrying out their threat. One of the most radical members of the Cultural Revolution Directorate, Qi had published a virulent diatribe against Liu in April and was presumed to enjoy the respect of the young militants. Visiting their encampment on the night of August 2, he warned them against invading the forbidden Zhongnanhai area. He also urged them to remove their huts and tents, pointing out that they could continue to denounce Liu from the headquarters of their various organizations.[29] Disappointed by this lack of support, the Red Guards countered with an alternative proposal. They would hold a huge rally without Liu's presence—on condition that their representatives be allowed to interrogate him while the demonstration went on. The Maoist leaders agreed.

On the afternoon of August 5, this singular episode began with a million people in formation in Tiananmen Square listening to orators haranguing them with speeches hostile to Liu Shaoqi and his wife. At the same time, in the garden of their Zhongnanhai residence not far away, Liu and Wang Guangmei were forced to listen to a broadcast of the rally as a group of Red Guard inquisitors grilled them with familiar accusations. Liu had praised Chiang Kai-shek, conspired to overthrow Mao, and plotted to subvert the Cultural Revolution, the young prosecutors charged. They also blamed him for favoring capitalism, betraying the proletariat, and seeking to promote himself.[30]

Though nearly seventy and undoubtedly numbed by the campaigns again him, Liu nevertheless held his ground. He had indeed praised Chiang Kai-shek, he conceded, but as a "tactic" at a time when the Communists and Nationalists were allied against the Japanese. The charge that he had planned a *coup d'état* against Mao was false. He had certainly made mistakes, Liu went on, yet his errors could not be construed to signify opposition to either Mao or the Communist Party. Finally, exasperated by the old man's intransigence, the youths turned to Wang Guangmei and insisted that she expose her husband's lies. "He and I have lived together for more than twenty years," she responded calmly. "I have never heard him tell a lie."[31]

Elsewhere in the Zhongnanhai enclosure, other Red Guard teams were questioning Deng Xiaoping, the Party Secretary General, and Tao Zhu. Here the youths fared better. With almost no prodding, Deng Xiaoping bleated that he was a "counterrevolutionary" who had eluded Mao's control for years. Tao Zhu was equally unheroic. He admitted to having pursued a "reactionary" line, but pleaded that he had been forced to obey Liu Shaoqi. "And what kind of person is Liu Shaoqi?" the Red Guards asked. To which Tao Zhu predictably replied: "He is the biggest capitalist in the Party."[32]

Their confessions notwithstanding, neither Deng Xiaoping nor Tao Zhu was spared. Deng was sent to Jiangxi province, where he worked in a tractor plant, while his oldest son, Deng Pufang, a student at Beijing University, was thrown from a window by the Red Guards, and would be confined to a wheelchair for the rest of his life. Tao's fate was worse. Suffering from cancer, he was denied medical treatment until April 1969, when it was too late. Nevertheless, Lin Biao had him evacuated to Anhui province, where he soon died. His wife and daughter were banished to a dark, dank hut in the mosquito-infested countryside of Guangdong, the southern province that had formerly been Tao's power base. They were never told where he had been sent, nor did they ever receive his ashes.[33]

Somewhat appeased by the opportunity to harass Liu Shaoqi face-to-face, the Red Guards grudgingly folded their tents and slowly went away. But hardly had this interlude faded when even more dynamic radicals inaugurated a fresh thrust. Their main objective seemed to be to gain control over China's foreign relations. This paroxysm nearly ruptured China's diplomatic ties with several nations, among them Burma and Cambodia, and it served to damage what little was left of Beijing's international reputation at the time.

Official Beijing sources later attributed the nihilistic outburst to the May 16th Detachment, headed by Wang Li and a group of ul-traleftists that included Qi Benyou and Yao Dengshan, the former Chinese *chargé d'affaires* in Indonesia who had been active in the demonstrations against the Foreign Ministry in May. Also associated with them was an improbable figure, Sydney Rittenberg, an American in his late forties who had resided in China since the end of World War II and, under the Communists, become an "adviser" to the central radio station in Beijing.

A rebel since his youth, Rittenberg was born into a distinguished

Jewish family that had emigrated from central Europe to South Carolina in the seventeenth century. His grandfather had been Speaker of the state legislature, and his father mayor of Charleston. Rittenberg left home while still young to organize cotton-mill, public-utility, and tobacco-plantation workers. A remarkable linguist, he learned Chinese in an Army training program and later made his way to Beijing as an employee of the United Nations Relief and Rehabilitation Agency. When he disappeared from sight in 1949, his name was inscribed among the war dead in Charleston's historic synagogue.[34]

But Rittenberg was very much alive. His homespun American voice soon became a feature on Beijing's English-language propaganda broadcasts, and he enjoyed prominence in that community of "foreign friends" in China known as the "Three-Hundred Percenters" because of their excessively zealous devotion to the Communist cause. Rittenberg displayed even greater zeal during the Cultural Revolution. He delivered speeches denouncing Liu Shaoqi and, according to some accounts, went as far as to mobilize a faction of Red Guards under his own leadership.[35] Along with Wang Li and other radical activists, Rittenberg was later branded a "reactionary" and "counterrevolutionary" and indicted for plotting to overthrow both Lin Biao and Zhou Enlai.[36] But in early August, he and his comrades were still riding high.

Though China's diplomacy had been gradually paralyzed by the Cultural Revolution during the preceding months, a bigger fight for command of the Foreign Ministry began on August 7. That evening, Wang Li convened Ministry employees to a meeting at which he announced that the time was ripe for authentic revolutionaries to direct China's foreign affairs.[37] Mao had personally instructed him, he subsequently intimated, to play a key role in that realm.[38] Wang's principal aim was to challenge the authority of Zhou Enlai, who had taken responsibility for the management of the Foreign Ministry in April, when Foreign Minister Chen Yi was being subjected to increasingly severe Red Guard attacks. Now, as he had before, Zhou reacted with characteristic caution. He encouraged Red Guards to renew their assaults against Chen Yi in the hope that they would cease to trouble him. But the militants only intensified their offensive.

In mid-August, Wang Li and his comrades stormed and occupied the Foreign Ministry—this time for about two weeks, installing Yao Dengshan as Foreign Minister. China's diplomatic behavior during this period became ludicrously paranoiac. On one occasion, the new

Foreign Ministry formally protested to the Danish Government against a Copenhagen newspaper cartoon of Mao. A similar complaint was sent to the Swiss Government protesting against the presence of Tibetan refugees in the Alps. After a Burmese crowd jeered Chinese diplomats in Rangoon, an official Beijing statement described the incident as an "outrage unparalleled in the annals of international relations."[39] The Foreign Ministry also incited overseas Chinese residents in Cambodia to stage Maoist demonstrations. Infuriated, Prince Norodom Sihanouk threatened to break off relations with Beijing, thus depriving the Chinese of a pivotal post in Southeast Asia. At the last minute, however, Zhou Enlai retrieved the situation with a virtual apology.[40]

In Beijing, Red Guards victimized diplomats of almost every foreign mission. They compelled a Russian to face a kangaroo court for having accidentally broken a glass in a restaurant, and they put the Italian commercial attaché through a similar ordeal in retaliation for Italy's ban on Chinese propaganda activities in Venice. The French Ambassador, Lucien Pye, was trapped and abused, and even a North Vietnamese diplomat found himself being insulted by fanatical youths.[41] This xenophobic frenzy reached a climax on August 22, when mobs of Red Guards raided the compound of the British mission in Beijing.[42] Stimulated by the suppression of their compatriots in Hong Kong, they bombarded the British Chancery with bottles of gasoline, setting it aflame. They then pounced on the British fleeing the burning building, beating and kicking both men and women. Grabbing Donald Hopson, the *chargé d'affaires*, by the hair, they forced him to bow his head and confess his "sins." Chinese troops eventually arrived to rescue the diplomats. Though reportedly appalled by the savagery, Zhou Enlai remained silent at the time. More than a year later, however, he quietly expressed his regrets for the incident to a British envoy.[43]

Even more crucial to China's political future was the outcome of the struggle between the radicals and the Army. In late July, Mao had called for a purge of the Army. But the regional commanders, assembled in Beijing for the Army Day celebrations to be held on August 1, were cool to the idea of an ideological drive that might disrupt their units. In a series of private sessions with Lin Biao, they undoubtedly argued that any move which undermined the Army's prestige or power could only incite the Red Guards to further violence.

Indeed, these senior officers could point to the turbulence already threatening provinces across the entire nation. Virtual civil war was cutting transportation and communications networks as well as obstructing the flow of military supplies to Hanoi. The interruptions in rail traffic were also slowing down China's nuclear and missile development program, and disorder menaced the border defenses against the Soviet Union. Equally worrisome was the damage being inflicted on industry in general and on military industries in particular. In Sichuan, for example, an aircraft factory had reportedly been gutted, and production at defense plants elsewhere throughout the provinces was slipping.[44]

On the afternoon of August 9, Lin Biao called a conference in Beijing that would prove to be one of the watersheds of the Cultural Revolution. Among those present, in addition to Zhou Enlai, were prominent Maoists like Jiang Qing and Chen Boda as well as such ultraleftists as Wang Li and Qi Benyou. The key regional commanders there included Huang Yongsheng, military chief of south China, and Chen Xilian, Army boss of Manchuria. Also present was Zeng Siyu, who had taken over Wuhan after the dismissal of General Chen Zaidao and his dissident comrades. The divergent attitudes of these figures underlined the dilemma that Lin Biao faced. He was sensitive to Mao's determination to purge the Army. But he also appreciated the apprehensions of the commanders. He therefore sought to appease both the radicals and the military professionals—and satisfied neither.

In typical Maoist fashion, Lin Biao stressed that the "educational significance" of the Wuhan mutiny had been "tremendous," since the incident had revealed "the acuteness and complexity of the class struggle." Such episodes were really welcome, he went on, for they made it possible to expose "bad people and bad things."

> The victory of the present great Cultural Revolution is very great. The price we paid is the smallest, smallest, and smallest, but the victory we gained is the greatest, greatest, and greatest. On the surface, everything seems so chaotic, but the chaos is the result of having upset the reactionary line. . . . This upheaval is necessary and normal. Had there been no upheaval, reactionary elements would not have been exposed.[45]

Having thus spouted Mao's doctrine, Lin turned to the soldiers. Beseeching the commanders to avoid another Wuhan revolt, he advised them against taking sudden initiatives that cause trouble. "Let us not have another Chen Zaidao," he pleaded, adding in peculiarly persuasive language:

We must not have the idea that we needn't report to the Central Committee because we ourselves understand the situation. Nor should we think it unnecessary to seek instructions because the matter is small and we are intelligent enough to handle it. We must not hesitate to disturb the Central Committee. . . .

Send a telegram or make a telephone call, or take an airplane and you'll be here in an hour or two. Don't act on your own because you think your ideas are right or you are clever.[46]

In contrast to the radical statements of only a week earlier, demanding that the Army be cleansed of "counterrevolutionaries," this was unusually mild. Officers had inevitably made "mistakes," he said, because their intervention in the Cultural Revolution had been "rather hasty," and he recommended instead that "we should solve problems slowly and step-by-step."

Evidently hoping to win the favor of the professional officers, Lin Biao castigated the Army political commissars whose position he himself had strengthened. The commissars had been initially successful, he explained, but had "performed badly and failed to keep abreast of the situation" during the Cultural Revolution. In particular, he blamed Xiao Hua, the head of the Army's General Political Department, who had "made one mistake after another." Now, Lin asserted, the country could only rely on "the various military districts, armies, divisions, regiments, battalions, and companies." In short, the commanders would become the principal repository of power. "The old leadership group fell, and it has been supplanted by the military," he proclaimed.[47] But despite his recognition of their authority, the regional commanders never forgave Lin for having encouraged the radicals against the Army. Four years later, in tandem with Zhou Enlai, they would move to eliminate him.

Lin Biao's statement heralded the rise of military influence in China. In the following weeks, a series of measures was initiated to reassure the regional Army commanders. The Beijing authorities publicly condemned more than fifty Army political commissars who had actively promoted the Cultural Revolution to the detriment of the military professionals.[48] At the same time they refrained from punishing Chen Zaidao publicly, and Mao was even quoted as saying that the rebel officer might win redemption if he "mended his ways."[49]

Simultaneously, a nationwide campaign was launched to "support the Army and cherish the people," with rallies throughout the country thumping the theme of solidarity and mutual trust between soldiers and civilians.[50]

This major reversal of policy must have irritated the left-wing members of the Cultural Revolution Directorate like Jiang Qing and Chen Boda, who were insisting only a few weeks earlier that the Army be purified. But they prudently remained silent and delegated radical subordinates like Wang Li to voice protests. Whether or not they realized they were being used as lightning rods, Wang and his comrades of the May 16th Detachment spoke out boldly for a purge in the Army. One of them, a radical writer named Guan Feng, reportedly sent a student group from Beijing to Guangzhou with instructions to abduct Huang Yongsheng.[51] Wang Li himself assailed Xu Shiyou, commander of the Nanjing Military Region, for "opposing Mao's leadership."[52] The futility of radical efforts to topple these and other officers was later reflected in the fact that Huang Yongsheng was elevated to the post of Chief of General Staff, and both he and Xu Shiyou were promoted to the Communist Party's revamped Politburo.

During August, then, China was buffeted by two conflicting winds. On one hand, the regional commanders were determined to resist radical onslaughts. At the same time, persistent criticism of the Army on the part of Wang Li and other members of the Cultural Revolution Directorate stimulated the Red Guards and other activists to new heights of violence. By late August, armed factions were raiding arsenals for weapons and fighting pitched battles in nearly every province.

Finally acknowledging the gravity of the situation, Mao and his colleagues were compelled to concede that the restoration of order was imperative. This prompted them to initiate two related measures. The first was to disassociate Mao himself from blame by finding scapegoats on whom to pin responsibility. Thus the Beijing leaders singled out Wang Li and the May 16th Detachment. These radicals had only advocated policies that Mao himself originally favored. But since Mao's policies could not be criticized, it was necessary to sacrifice his more expendable subordinates. In late August, therefore, the May 16th Detachment came under fire, and some of the accusations directed against members of the movement were characteristically exaggerated. Simultaneously describing them as "ultraleftists" and "reactionaries," Beijing publicists not only linked Wang Li and his comrades to Liu Shaoqi and the Party bureaucracy but charged them with "working closely with United States and Chiang Kai-shek secret agents and Soviet revisionists."[53] The fate of Yao Dengshan was typical. He had been given a warm airport welcome after his expulsion from Indonesia, and even accorded an audience with Mao. Now he was branded as a "schemer of the Khrushchev type" who was "mad with ambition and blinded by the lust for gain."[54] Yao faded from public sight until June 11, 1971, when he was brought to trial before a crowd of four thousand at a Beijing stadium[55] and sentenced to a jail term.

In addition to jettisoning these radicals, Mao made a far more significant move. On September 5, for the first time in the Cultural Revolution, he agreed to authorize the Army to shoot at unruly "mass organizations or individuals." Though this directive was specifically designed to discourage the seizure of weapons, ammunition, vehicles, and other military supplies, it gave troops the latitude to open fire on any elements they deemed beyond their control. The test of the directive, however, seemed to betray Mao's extreme reluctance to take this step. As the operative passage read:

> Local garrison forces must first patiently carry out political and ideological work, carefully reason with offenders in order to dissuade or stop them from committing offenses. When such dissuasion or prevention proves ineffective, shots should be fired in the air as a warning, and they should be ordered to withdraw. When such warnings prove ineffective, their behavior may be declared counterrevolutionary, and action should be taken to arrest the few bad ringleaders and trouble-making murderers so that they may be dealt with according to law.
>
> When such persons resist arrest or fight back, the Army may act and retaliate in self-defense.[56]

Jiang Qing began to publicize the new line to Red Guard groups, and it was no accident that she had been selected for this task. As Mao's wife and a confirmed extremist since the start of the Cultural Revolution, she carried enormous weight with the radicals. Her credibility was bound to be enhanced by the fact that she had formerly been a most outspoken opponent of moderation.

Zhou Enlai may well have prodded Jiang Qing into undertaking this assignment. For she indicated in one of her speeches that the role she was performing had not been her idea. She had been "unexpectedly" summoned to utter "a few words," she explained, apologizing that she had "not prepared herself for this" and inviting criticism "if what I say is wrong." But, old actress that she was, Jiang Qing played her part—with feeling.[57]

Emphasizing the new plea for temperance, she blithely contradicted the very slogans she had earlier promoted. On July 22, she had urged the Red Guards to "take up arms" to defend the Maoist cause "by force," but now she denounced "armed struggle" that would "ruin the nation." Six weeks before, in the wake of the Wuhan mutiny, she had clamored for a purge of the Army. Now, she declared, the Army was the inviolable "cornerstone of proletarian dictatorship," and chaos would follow were it "thrown into disorder." Moreover, she pointed out to the young radicals, the Army's "deadly" directive meant business. Troops would indeed shoot at Red Guards and other youths who abashed them. "The penalty for stealing weapons is death," she said, adding: "If I were a soldier and someone tried to grab my rifle, I would certainly retaliate."

Jiang Qing further backtracked by repudiating radical attempts to topple all authority as a dangerous "left wind." Absent from her speeches, too, were emotional exhortations to the Red Guards to defeat Mao's adversaries. "It is mistaken to run through the streets," she said. "This is the time to sit down, mobilize your brains, and study documents, however difficult and painful that may be." She told the radicals to "criticize and reform themselves," and she advised rival Red Guard organizations to hold "dispassionate" discussions in order to "seek agreement on major issues while tolerating differences over minor issues." In contrast to her previous declarations, which consistently boasted of triumphant progress, Jiang Qing now conceded that the Cultural Revolution was losing momentum. The Beijing leaders were now striving to solve the problems of "one province at a time and one city at a time." In that way, she concluded, regional Revolutionary Committees that had failed to develop in the spring would be "set up gradually" in an atmosphere of peace and unity.

Jiang Qing was not alone in her appeal for temperance. Chen Boda, another fierce Maoist, now assailed "extreme leftists" who were spreading anarchy. "We must not allow factionalism to dominate everything. . . . Ransacking does not constitute a revolutionary act." And Xie Fuzhi, the Minister of Security who had been abducted at Wuhan, echoed the same theme. Calling for an end to "civil war" and "violent struggle," he cautioned the Red Guards, "Do not let your minds become overheated."[58]

In early 1966, Mao had advanced the argument that "destruction must precede construction." By the fall of 1967, the Communist Party bureaucracy that once ruled China had been shattered from top to bottom. The Politburo was decimated. Of the ninety-three full members of the Central Committee, only thirty-six were still active. The Party's six Regional Bureaus had virtually ceased to exist. Among the twenty-eight provincial Party bosses functioning at the start of Mao's campaign, only five were still in office.[59] Equally devastated were the trade unions, youth associations, women's movements, and other organizations that had underpinned the Party apparatus. Many officials who disappeared later surfaced, either at their old jobs or in different positions. For the Cultural Revolution, with all its tumult, was not a Stalinist terror. But in late 1967, it remained for the Army to pick up the pieces of a country in disarray. Thus from early September onward, military commanders sought to fill the vast power vacuum throughout China.

Conspicuously eclipsed in the new power structures that painfully evolved during the next two years were the Red Guards. Mao had conceived of his cataclysmic drive largely as a training exercise for "revolutionary successors." The more he observed the Red Guards, however, the more he was convinced that they had failed to pass the test. In the summer of 1968, after a brief period of renewed violence, he would disavow them in a poignant scene. But even now, he could not conceal his disappointment with them—and perhaps, too, with the course taken by the Cultural Revolution.

In mid-August, just one year after the great Beijing rallies had introduced the Red Guards to China and the world, Mao was asked by an aide if the militant youths might some day be able to take over the provincial Party committees. "In my opinion," Mao replied sourly, "they won't even be fit to take over county committees."[60]

PART FIVE

THE PENDULUM
SWINGS

Some comrades have come to regard them-
selves as "most revolutionary and most ad-
vanced" because they had made some
contributions during the Great Proletarian
Cultural Revolution. This shows that they
fail to view themselves correctly, and lack
the spirit to remold themselves. Others have
desperately exaggerated the role of the for-
mer mass organizations, incorrectly han-
dled relations between mass organizations
and the Party, and tried to put themselves
above the Party in an attempt to challenge
its leadership. This is an expression of re-
actionary anarchism.

—Red Flag, *January 5, 1970*

CHAPTER 18

Dialectics in Action

⟱

> *Under the dictatorship of the proletariat,*
> *there is no reason whatsoever for the work-*
> *ing class to split into two big irreconcilable*
> *organizations.*
> —MAO ZEDONG, *September 1967*

> *Chaos is another expression of the eruption*
> *of class contradiction, and the culmination*
> *of the struggle between the two lines in vio-*
> *lence. There is nothing wrong with sowing*
> *chaos in the enemy ranks.*
> —*Shanghai Radio, June 11, 1968*

ON APRIL 14, 1969, addressing the Chinese Communist Party's Ninth Congress midway through its deliberations, Lin Biao announced that the Cultural Revolution had achieved a "great victory" despite its chaotic "twists and reversals."[1] That claim, though debatable, was significant, for it signaled that Mao Zedong's tumultuous campaign was officially finished. But in reality the Cultural Revolution had begun to die in the fall of 1967, when the Army embarked upon its vigorous drive to stamp its rule on China. And years later, the repercussions of the period would still be felt.

China's high military officers, as their behavior demonstrated, had never fully subscribed to the Cultural Revolution. As soldiers, they were instinctively conservative men suspicious of grandiose schemes. As veterans who had fought for decades to unify their country, they were dedicated to national cohesion, and their sense of nationalism also dictated a desire for political stability, social equilibrium, and vital economic development. In short, they favored the construction of a strong China whose domestic solidity would serve as a defense against external enemies.

Mao shared this objective. Yet he and his commanders differed in one important respect. They advocated pragmatic policies while he, in contrast, was convinced that China's avenue to greatness lay in permanent revolution that would release the energies of the "masses."

Though Mao's propensity for episodic upheavals may have dismayed them, most senior Chinese commanders at least acknowledged his leadership. They were mesmerized by his charisma and captivated by his immense prestige. They undoubtedly felt as well that he personified the national cohesion they cherished, and they seemed to believe that any overt action against him might jeopardize China's unity.

By August 1967, however, the Army's tolerance was exhausted. In their view, the foreign threat was present again. The United States was within striking distance of their southern borders. Russia's military build-up along the northern and western frontiers was reaching alarming proportions. And Japan, the old enemy, had become the most powerful nation in Asia. On September 1, at a meeting of the Beijing Revolutionary Committee, one Chinese leader reflected the apprehensions of his comrades at what he described as the growing "encirclement" of China by its foes. The Soviet "revisionists" and their Mongolian satellite, he said, were now colluding openly with American "imperialism" and the Japanese "militarists." To assure China's security, the imposition of internal order under Army auspices was imperative.[2]

This concern on the part of China's military officers was fully appreciated by Zhou Enlai and, to a certain extent, by Lin Biao. But the job of imposing order on China would not be easy. To tame the millions of Red Guards and other militants was a gigantic challenge. Equally difficult was the task of disciplining workers and peasants who in the past years had tasted real freedom for the first time since the Communists established their regime. Also, in a society where conciliation is an alien concept, months of bloody clashes between rival clans and factions had left a residue of feuds and vendettas that promised to persist, making a return to social peace extremely difficult.

Moreover, there was no guarantee that Mao would continue to cooperate. He had oscillated throughout the past year between encouraging ferment and calling for order. Now, he had acquiesced in the Army's assertion of power, but he was capable of reviving the "masses" at any moment.

Despite these obstacles, Zhou Enlai and the Army commanders managed in the next few years to put China back on the road to recovery. Their success was partly due to their ability to exercise authority. They were also helped by the extraordinary resilience of the Chinese people, whose capacity to survive cataclysms had shown itself throughout history.

Late in 1958, when the Great Leap Forward was devastating the Chinese economy, Mao had gone on one of his rare inspection tours of the provinces, and he concluded from his observations that the program required "tidying up." In September 1967, under somewhat comparable circumstances, he took a similar trip. He traveled to Shanghai and around to Henan, Hubei, Hunan, Jiangxi, and Zhejiang, the particularly troubled areas along the Yangzi River, talking with local officials and regional commanders. His conclusion, he candidly admitted, was that the turmoil plaguing the country was serious. Summing up the situation in Hubei, for instance, he said: "Some people say there is no civil war in China. But I think this is a civil war. It is not a foreign war. It is a violent struggle."[3]

His first-hand impressions evidently persuaded Mao of the urgent need for moderation, at least for the present. His alarm was reflected in a new set of "supreme instructions" handed down after his return to Beijing.

One of these was essentially a repetition of the edict, issued in the spring, which had urged the Red Guards and other activists to stop their wanton attacks against Party and government officials and collaborate in creating unity. The "ferocious" and "inexperienced" Red Guards would have to stop their practice of "beating up cadres, making them kneel, hanging signboards from their necks, and forcing them to wear dunce's caps." Officials "as a rule" should not be condemned, Mao said, and even the "most stubborn" among them "must be given a bowl of rice." Loyal to his concept of "thought reform," he emphasized that careful indoctrination rather than brutality was the only technique for transforming attitudes. "Cadres should not be punished without being educated, nor should they be punished by way of education."[4]

This call for leniency toward officials reflected the Army's need for experienced cadres to help manage the country, and it touched off an extensive campaign publicizing the cases of veteran Party workers who were "rehabilitated" after recognizing their "errors." Some of these accounts, however, inadvertently explained why many officials whom the Red Guards had denounced and mistreated were reluctant to undertake their duties again. One Shanghai Party cadre was said to have been handled "a bit excessively" by the Red Guards, who had refused to exonerate him even after he had admitted his mistakes.[5] The report had a happy ending, but it suggested that many officials must have declined to resume their former jobs for fear that they might again become targets for the radicals.

Mao also urged rival groups to compose their differences amicably. "Really promising men are those who think, not those who show off," he said, explaining that "people who are now making trouble and noises are merely flashing across the stage of history." With that, he uttered a quotation that would become the slogan of the movement:

There is no fundamental clash of interests within the working class. Under the dictatorship of the proletariat, there is no reason whatsoever for the working class to split into two big irreconcilable organizations.[6]

Along with this plea for unity, Mao underlined the pre-eminence of the Army, a key instrument for the restoration of order. "The chief danger at the moment is that some people want to crush the Army," he warned, asserting that "the Army's prestige must be resolutely safeguarded." Problems nagging military units should be negotiated "within the scope of each individual province," he said—in effect conceding to the regional commanders' demand for autonomy by telling them to resolve their own difficulties rather than responding automatically to Beijing's directives.[7] On September 26, back in Beijing, Mao expressed his renewed faith in the Army by holding a reception for a number of provincial officers.[8] About the same time, the press initiated a supportive campaign. "Without a people's Army, the people have nothing," proclaimed the *People's Daily*. "The Army is the chief component of State power. Whoever wants to seize and retain State power must have a strong Army."[9]

Zhou Enlai echoed the same theme in a series of talks with different youth groups. On September 17, he scolded Red Guards for having continued to attack military units even after the "erroneous" call to purge the Army had been retracted. "You did not listen," he told them, "but instead went on attacking the Army until, by the end of August, the situation had become impossible." Describing the present time as a "transitional period," he said that "we need the Army" to serve as "the Great Wall that protects our frontiers." In a further effort to discipline the young radicals, he ordered them to return to school within a month. Those who disobeyed, he warned, would be expelled and refused jobs by the State, the country's sole employer.[10] That order, like others before and after it, went largely unheeded—since most of China's schools, closed in the spring of 1966, had not reopened.

Zhou delivered a similar speech at an all-night meeting of Red Guard representatives from Guangzhou. "There is no need to divide people into the Red Flag faction and the East Wind faction," he said. Such factions were "man-made" and could be dissolved. Their rivalry mainly represented "petty bourgeois" egotistical ambitions, he said, urging the youths to forge an alliance with their adversaries. Zhou also told the Red Guards to refrain from interfering with workers, while he stressed that workers must remain in their factories and stop political agitation. Finally, on the question of relations between the Army and the radicals, Zhou underlined the new policy he had undoubtedly helped to shape.

During his visit to Guangzhou in April, Zhou had sided with the radicals. But now, attuning himself to the new trend, he reproved them for having followed the line he had then favored. He denounced their assaults against Huang Yongsheng, the Guangzhou commander, and ordered them instead to acknowledge the General's leadership. Conditions in Guangzhou and elsewhere had so deteriorated that military rule had become imperative, he disclosed. Police authority had collapsed, ports were paralyzed, and lawlessness was rampant. The Army was therefore taking control of internal security agencies, airports, railways, warehouses, and wharves. "Revolutionary order should be improved," he went on. Communciations and transportation must be guaranteed so that "coal is delivered and electricity generated." To maintain order in the cities, squads of soldiers would take on police duties and patrol the streets. He called on the Red Guards to cooperate with the local commanders and reiterated that the appeal to purge the Army, issued after the Wuhan mutiny, had been "a wrong slogan." To emphasize this point, Zhou resorted to a familiar device. Knowing that the young radicals admired Jiang Qing, he claimed that she had been the first person to oppose the "ultra-leftist" plot against the Army.[11]

Nothing dramatized the new influence of the People's Liberation Army more vividly than the positions occupied by senior Chinese officers during National Day celebrations on October 1. Though they had been bitterly denounced by Red Guards, the old Marshals like

Zhu De, Chen Yi, Xu Xiangqian, Nie Rongzhen, and Ye Jianying were to be seen in prominent places along with such military professionals as General Su Yu. Six regional commanders were also placed favorably, among them Huang Yongsheng of Guangzhou; Xu Shiyou, the top officer in central China; Chen Xilian, military chief of Manchuria; and Han Xianchu, Army boss in Fujian. All of these Army men had been targets of the Red Guards in the preceding year, as were a number of other figures on the Tiananmen Gate. The appearance of You Qiuli, Minister of Petroleum Industry, along with that of other protégés who had been defended by Zhou Enlai against severe Red Guard attacks, testified to the Premier's success in protecting his subordinates.[12] Their re-emergence also mirrored the attempt to return to stability.

Most of the rhetoric that now resonated in official press and radio statements bluntly contradicted the earlier slogans of the Cultural Revolution. In July, Jiang Qing had been urging the Red Guards to "take up arms" to defend Mao's cause "by force." Now, as a provincial radio commentary put it, "to stress 'defending by force' deviates from the general orientation of the struggle and this is extremely wrong."[13] Earlier declarations had affirmed that those who emphasized economic output were traitors to the Cultural Revolution. Now *Red Flag* intoned that to ignore production was to "undermine the mass revolutionary alliance and . . . cause unnecessary damage" to the economy."[14] With the same passion once directed against "reactionaries," demonstrations and rallies now denounced "ultraleftists." At one rally held in Changsha in mid-October, the Hunan Army commander, General Li Yuan, used language that would have been heretical eight months before. He criticized the radicals for their attacks on "middle-of-the-roaders" and their resistance to the Army and, rephrasing one of Mao's celebrated exhortations, he reproached them for "bombarding the proletarian headquarters." Soon afterward, the Hunan military authorities singled out a typical "ultraleftist" in much the same way that the Red Guards had once humiliated alleged "bourgeois revisionists." Put on display before a crowd of sixty thousand, an obscure figure by the name of Cai was charged with crimes ranging from "making rebellion" and "striking down everyone" to seizing weapons and promoting violence.[15] His mistake, of course, had been his overzealous allegiance to the Maoist cause.

In several places, the suppression of radicals took a harsher form. On September 12, for instance, a crowd of ten thousand assembled under Army auspices at a Beijing stadium as speakers pronounced the death sentence on four "counterrevolutionary murderers" who had been convicted by the Beijing Municipal People's Court of having "hoodwinked the masses, incited struggle by force, sabotaged production, and even committed murder." They were summarily executed at the end of the rally.[16] Other trials and executions took place during September in Shanghai, Qingdao, Hangzhou, and Harbin. Variously described as "enemy agents," "looters," "thieves and hooligans," and "counterrevolutionaries," many were presumably Red Guards or other militants whose criminal activities had once been an accepted part of the turmoil of the Cultural Revolution.[17] Years later, large numbers of former Red Guards were still being punished. Ironically, many of these young radicals in south China fled for safety in Hong Kong.

As part of the drive to impose law and order, meanwhile, the Beijing leaders inaugurated a major offensive against the May 16th Detachment. The case of the May 16th Detachment was a significant example of the process by which the Beijing leaders sought to absolve Mao and themselves of responsibility for the excesses of the Cultural Revolution by pinning the blame on convenient scapegoats.

That the May 16th Detachment had existed was undeniable. But in September 1967, Zhou Enlai advised against "exaggerating its importance," since the movement consisted of "only a few hotheads who cannot do much harm."[18] A lesser Chinese official later described it as a radical "state of mind" rather than a real movement. By the end of 1970, however, Beijing publicists were portraying the May 16th Detachment as a vast network of military and civilian conspirators whose objective had been to overthrow Lin Biao and Zhou Enlai and govern China with Mao as their figurehead.[19] The basic pattern underlying this change was simple. The campaign had apparently been mounted to shield Mao from criticism for the radical strategies he had initiated. In later years, as Beijing's policies became more moderate, the need to explain the wild turbulence of the Cultural Revolution became greater and the importance of the May 16th Detachment was proportionately inflated. By mid-1971, in still another reverse, Lin Biao himself would be assailed as the "black hand" behind the "ultraleftist" conspiracy.

In September 1967, however, it was Jiang Qing who fired the opening salvo against the May 16th Detachment. In a rather unconvincing polemical display, she accused the movement of having attempted to topple Zhou Enlai and described it as an "ultraleftist" faction that was serving American "imperialism" and Soviet "revisionism."[20] Her charges were amplified by Yao Wenyuan, the radical Shanghai writer who had been Mao's charter publicist in the Cultural Revolution. He accused the May 16th Detachment of "creating dissension and exploiting confusion," alleging that it was linked to Tao Zhu.[21] By December, the movement's most prominent members had disappeared: Wang Li, the Maoist troubleshooter who had been abducted in Wuhan; Qi Benyou and Guan Feng, *Red Flag* editors and deputies to Chen Boda; and Mu Xin, a radical Beijing propagandist. All had belonged to the Cultural Revolution Directorate which, by the end of 1967, was down as a result of purges to six of its original thirteen members.[22]

The purge of the radicals in late 1967 also took a devastating toll on Mao's seven-man "brain trust" of theoreticians in the Department of Philosophy and Social Sciences at the Chinese Academy of Sciences. The entire group—including its head, Zhang Jichun—was dismissed and, presumably, sent to "labor reform" camps. Purged as well were Jiang Qing's literary and artistic advisers on the staff of the Cultural Revolution Directorate. The most influential among them was Zheng Gongdun, head of the literary and art department of *Red Flag*, who was arrested in November and charged with a familiar assortment of crimes, ranging from "ultraleftism" to operating as a "secret agent" for Chiang Kai-shek. With him fell a number of his comrades who had been associated with Jiang Qing's programs to "purify" Chinese literature and art.[23] Jiang Qing herself dropped from public view for nearly two months, inspiring speculation that her star had waned. Zhou Enlai fueled this speculation. "Arduous struggle" had impaired her health, he explained, adding ominously that "spiritual consolation and inspiration will certainly make up for the loss."[24] Whether real or diplomatic, her illness was brief, and she was to resurface with a vengeance in the spring.

Throughout the Cultural Revolution, Mao periodically revived the idea of a Chinese version of the Paris Commune. This notion, which had been frequently suggested by Chen Boda in his ideological essays over the years, had commended itself to the most visionary Maoists as a free-flow political system "spontaneously" responsive to the "masses." In mid-January 1967, Chen Boda and Jiang Qing had actually proposed that Beijing be governed by a People's Commune composed of a constituent assembly whose leaders could be elected or recalled at any time by the "masses." Soon after, radicals in the Shanxi province capital of Taiyuan had announced that they had formed a Commune to replace the Party Committee they had overthrown, and the Shanghai radicals did the same. But the Commune concept, so attractive in theory, was subverted in practice by the very principles it sought to promote. Licensed to reject their leaders or assail their rivals as they chose, innumerable worker, student, and other factions tore apart the Commune even before it could be built. For that reason, the new prototype structure was declared to be the tripartite Revolutionary Committee. And the Commune concept was quietly buried, perhaps to be resurrected at some future date, when Mao's doctrines had "purified" the people.

Coinciding as it did with Mao's directive to the Army to intervene in the Cultural Revolution, endorsement of the Revolutionary Committees rather than the Commune may have been the price exacted by China's military commanders for their assumption of a political role that threatened to be both difficult and risky. In any case, the Revolutionary Committees were patently a device to permit soldiers and veteran cadres to discipline the fractious radicals. Thus the formation of Revolutionary Committees proceeded mainly during periods in which the Army had the upper hand and when, as the topical slogan held, the "consolidation of revolutionary order" was imperative. Revolutionary Committees were created in Heilongjiang, Shandong, Guizhou, Shanghai, Shanxi, and Beijing in early 1967, when the Army was pre-eminent. To the radicals, however, those months represented a "counterrevolutionary adverse current," and when they returned to the fore in late spring and summer, the program to set up Revolutionary Committees foundered as the Army's authority foundered. The only Committee formed during the summer was in Qinghai, a huge, arid, sparsely populated province in western China that was virtually a military domain.

In the fall, as the Army regained power, one of its priorities was to regenerate the drive to implant the Revolutionary Committees in the provinces. This priority fit into a longer-range plan. Charting the future, the leaders in Beijing hoped to convene a Party Congress, out of which would emerge a new Politburo and Central Committee that would, in turn, appoint new provincial Party Committees. In this way, the national Party structure shattered during the Cultural Revolution could be rebuilt.

Mao himself was undoubtedly suspicious that the Army might become a substitute for the Party—and might even, indeed, try to subvert his own authority. During the first half of 1967, when he had purged and reorganized nearly half the regional and district commands in the country, he was constantly grumbling that officers lacked "education" and "experience" and needed "training classes" to correct their deficiencies.[25] Even so, as Zhou Enlai observed, Chinese military commanders had effectively assumed the "monistic leadership" of China.[26] Thus Mao saw the Revolutionary Committees as instruments by which he would shape a new Party apparatus more submissive to him than the old bureaucracy headed by Liu Shaoqi and Deng Ziaoping. He therefore insisted that Revolutionary Committees be set up throughout the provinces before the end of January 1968 so that he could proceed to convene the Party Congress. By that deadline, as he put it, the "whole situation" should be "put onto the normal track."[27]

Xie Fuzhi, the Minister of Public Security, reflected Mao's sense of urgency. In a speech delivered in late October, he anticipated that the Ninth Party Congress might be held by the spring of 1968, or at the latest before October 1, China's National Day. The prerequisite to assembling the Congress was the formation of provincial Revolutionary Committees throughout the country, he stressed. For one thing, as the basic organs of power, the Committees would select the delegates to attend the Party Congress. For another, they were the only bodies capable of governing China until a renovated Party machine could be installed.[28]

The Chinese Communists normally had the capacity to make remarkably rapid institutional changes. During the Great Leap Forward, they had organized twenty-four thousand People's Communes within months. But forging the Revolutionary Committees for China's twenty-nine provinces and special municipalities was a slow process, and Mao's timetable would be stretched by eight months.

Only two Revolutionary Committees were created from August until the end of 1967. One of these, set up on November 1 to rule Inner Mongolia, was headed by General Deng Haiqing, who had been sent to pacify the region in the spring and only succeeded by bringing several fresh Army divisions into the province. The other Committee, formed in Tianjin on December 6, came under the chairmanship of Xie Xuegong, a former member of the Party's North China Bureau. He, too, required at least two additional Army divisions to restore order.[29]

After the turn of the year, Revolutionary Committees were organized at a faster pace, with nine new Committees created by the end of March. Most of them shared the predictable characteristic that they were headed by generals, some of whom had only recently arrived into the provinces to quell disturbances. The Jiangxi Committee, for instance, was inaugurated on January 5 under the chairmanship of General Cheng Shiqing, a tank commander and political commissar who had brought two Army units into the province in mid-August. The Hubei Revolutionary Committee, established on February 5, was headed by General Zeng Siyu, who had been transferred from Manchuria to replace General Chen Zaidao, the instigator of the Wuhan mutiny. In other areas, the new Revolutionary Committees were simply taken over by entrenched local commanders. General Huang Yongsheng took charge of the Guangdong Committee, General Xu Shiyou became Chairman in Jiangsu, and General Nan Ping, the Army commander in Fujian, broadened his powers there. One of the few civilians designated to direct a Revolutionary Committee during this period was Li Xuefeng, the former Secretary of the Party's North China Bureau, who became Chairman in Hebei, the province surrounding Beijing. However, four of his seven senior deputies were officers.[30] Not long before the Hebei Committee was inaugurated on February 3, the Thirty-eighth Army was moved into the province to put down an attempt by local radicals to challenge military rule.[31]

Part of the delay in forming the Revolutionary Committees stemmed from the reluctance of veteran Party officials to cooperate. China's official press and radio urged cadres to contribute their services, saying that their "richer experience, better organizing and working ability, and higher understanding of policy" would make them the "backbone of the revolutionary provisional organs of power."[32] These exhortations were matched in Beijing propaganda by moralistic tales of old functionaries who mended their "errors" and were once again playing important roles. But the frequency of these pleas suggested that many local officials who had survived the worst excesses of the Cultural Revolution were still in no mood to expose themselves again.

The reluctance of experienced officials to become involved also contributed to the breakdown of administrative controls, thereby eroding the entire national economy. Humiliated by repeated criticism, many cadres simply refused to perform their duties on the grounds that they could no longer command the respect of workers and peasants. In the farming areas around Shanghai, regional radio broadcasts disclosed, rural production was "abandoned" and "the collective economy disrupted" as agriculture officials shunned the countryside, contending that they "cannot firmly wield power."[33] Similarly, an account from Henan province revealed, spring planting was "going very slowly" because rural cadres formerly victimized by Red Guards were "afraid to make mistakes and thus do not dare to lead boldly." Many of these cadres, the Henan report added, "even lie down and do nothing. None of them cares about collective production."[34]

Meanwhile, as they had the year before, urban workers were taking advantage of the unrest and confusion to reassert demands for higher salaries, improved welfare benefits, and better labor conditions. In the Anhui province capital of Hefei, according to an official report, a special congress was convened in January to demand that workers return "extra wages, incentive money, subsidies, overtime pay, public funds, and welfare benefits that they were accorded or acquired illegally."[35] An account from Inner Mongolia warned that "economism is again rearing its head" and that the "demons and monsters" were reaping financial gains.

Some of them have scooped up fat profits through speculative business ventures. Some created rumors to create a rush on the market for daily commodities. Some have set up factories and stores without permission, upsetting the system. Some have acted as contractors and middlemen. Some have even opened gambling houses in broad daylight. . . .[36]

Work stoppages, transport difficulties, and other problems combined to cause shortages of food, fuel, and other necessities. Reports from Beijing and Shanghai disclosed that private homes in both cities were suffering from a lack of coal. The dearth of coal was also impairing the electricity supply, compelling factories to slow down. According to one account, peasants in Guangdong province intercepted a freight train and looted large quantities of grain. In December, another account revealed, peasants near Guangzhou staged a demonstration to protest against a decision to ship five thousand tons of rice to Chinese radicals then still struggling against the British authorities in Hong Kong.[37]

Predictably, no Beijing leader was more outraged by the damage being inflicted on the economy than Zhou Enlai. At a gathering of Red Guards in Beijing on January 17, he flayed the youths mercilessly for having obstructed production in various sectors and blamed them outright for industry's failure to meet the quotas for 1967. He deplored the conflicts then disrupting the Seventh Ministry of Machine Building, a defense agency, where the employees "often turn to fighting among themselves" because "they have nothing else to do after meals." He also demanded a halt in the disputes nagging the Scientific and Technological Commission, the department responsible for China's nuclear and advanced military development. He angrily divulged that Red Guards had seized rifles, cannons, ammunition, and other equipment destined for Hanoi and, in a factional clash, "fired into the air thousands of shells that should have been sent to Vietnam." Uncharacteristically, he concluded his remarks in a burst of temper, exploding: "I am indeed very much upset, very very upset."[38]

In addition to impeding production, the discord among rival Red Guard and other groups was subverting the Army's efforts to recruit representatives of the "masses" to serve as window dressing on the Revolutionary Committees. One aspect of the factionalism fragmenting the multitude of Red Guard movements was described in a Shanghai newspaper article written to urge militant youths to cease their squabbling and merge into alliances.

> Some say, "Since our organization was the earliest to rise up, we should be the nucleus." Others say, "But we made the greatest contribution, so we should be the nucleus." Still others say, "We should be the nucleus since our group is the largest." And so on and so forth. . . .
>
> Thus nobody serves as the nucleus, and each unit occupies a mountain peak, claiming to be heroic master of its own territory. The result of this is disintegration.[39]

As the drive to restore order accelerated throughout the fall and into early 1968, the strident campaign to curb factionalism grew in intensity. An Anhui province account depicted factionalism as "a malignant political epidemic" whose most visible symptom was the determination of rival groups to defend only their own interests.[40] Employing a different image, a Shanghai journal called factionalism "a huge poisonous snake . . . that has already encoiled some comrades and is drawing tighter and tighter around them."[41] In another denunciation of unruly Red Guards, a Henan radio broadcast described them as "imperial inspectors" who "give directives on this and that and monopolize everything, assuming that they alone are revolutionaries." Underlining the change that had occurred since the start of the Cultural Revolution, the Henan broadcast conceded that the Red Guards had once been justified in "whipping up the wind and kindling the fires," but now their agitation was "splitting our ranks and causing great disturbances."[42]

Far more dramatic—and, in some ways, rather poignant—was the disillusionment of many Red Guards with what they considered to be a betrayal of the Maoist revolution. Only a year before they had been extolled as "little red generals" and encouraged by Mao himself to believe that they represented the most dynamic force in China. But now, they perceived, the revolution that was supposed to have transformed the "very souls" of the people had altered the appearance rather than the reality of China's political structure. They had only to examine the composition of the Revolutionary Committees to appreciate this bitter truth. Among the eighty-nine Vice-Chairmen of the Committees, only twenty-nine could be classified as "revolutionary rebels," Mao's label for his young acolytes.[43] The rest were either officers or old *apparatchiks*, and these bureaucrats were to become even stronger in the years ahead.

No document to emerge from the Cultural Revolution more vividly illustrated the frustrations of the disappointed radicals than a rambling essay published on January 6, 1968, by the *Shengwulian,* the Proletarian Revolutionaries Great Alliance, an admittedly "ultraleftist" movement in Hunan. Composed in October 1967 of about twenty factions, most of them secondary-school student groups, the Alliance also included at least one civil-service organization and counted two former Army officers among its leaders.[44] The essay, "Whither China?," sounded an anguished cry of protest against the conservative trend then gathering momentum. Essentially, the Alliance concluded to its dismay that *le plus ça change, le plus c'est la même chose*.

> The form of political power has only superficially changed. The old Party Committee and the old Military District have become the Revolutionary Committee [and] old bureaucrats continue to play the leading role. Thus, as the masses say, everything remains the same after so much ado.

When the radicals were riding high at the beginning of 1967 and again during the summer, the Alliance asserted, "the whole country had a sense of vigorous growth," and it was believed that the Cultural Revolution would be "carried through to the end," smashing "all traditional ideas that had fettered the minds of people." But in the autumn, with the rise of Army officers and veteran Party cadres to positions of authority, an "adverse current of counterrevolutionary reformism" appeared to create "an atmosphere of class compromise." This was first felt by "extrasensitive" young intellectuals and students, the Alliance said, and its members drafted their essay in an attempt to explain the development.

In a rare swipe at Mao, the Alliance argued that his guidelines for the Cultural Revolution had merely been an "abstract prediction." He had initially recommended the establishment of a Commune, for instance, inspiring the hope that China was headed toward "utopia." But in fact China had drifted away from the Commune concept and was edging closer to the "revisionist" Soviet model. To "expose" this "deception of the masses," the essay reached back to analyze events in 1967.

During the stormy month of January, the Alliance's analysis pointed out, almost the entire Party and government apparatus was overthrown, leaving the management of the country in the hands of the "masses." Despite warnings by the bureaucrats that "production would collapse and the society would fall into chaos," the essay claimed, "productivity was greatly liberated. . . . Workers for the first time felt that it was not the State that directed them, but they who directed the State." But then Mao "suddenly" reversed his line. He abandoned his plan to set up a Commune, and he called for Army intervention, which inevitably brought back the Party *apparatchiks*.

In February and March, the bureaucrats returned to power, suppressing the "masses" by the "most urgent and savage means." The chief engineer of this "counterrevolutionary" thrust was Premier Zhou Enlai, excoriated by the Alliance as the "general representative of China's red capitalist class." His ally in this drive was the Army.

The Alliance analysis argued that the radicals had originally harbored "very childish ideas" about the Army, believing as they did that military commanders would join with them to crush the Party machine. But in reality, Army bureaucrats would always side with Party bureaucrats, for one clear-cut reason: the Army had undergone a process of *embourgeoisement* since the days when it was a guerrilla force. Living in barracks and enjoying special privileges, soldiers "have not only changed their blood-and-flesh relations with the people . . . but they have become tools for suppressing revolution." This was evident, the Alliance contended, in the turmoil that ravaged China in August. By attacking troops and seizing their weapons, the essay continued, the "masses" were displaying their hostility toward an Army that had lost its revolutionary fervor. The Alliance therefore suggested that only a purge "from the lower level upward" could free the Army of its domination by the bureaucrats and restore its good relations with the population.

But since September, the Party bureaucrats and their military cohorts had come back stronger than ever. They had authorized the Army to shoot at radicals. They had revived the program to establish Revolutionary Committees—a device for imposing a "new bourgeois dictatorship" on China. And they were planning a national Party Congress in order to legitimize their "bourgeois reformism." Consequently, the Alliance charged, the "contradictions" in the society "remain fundamentally unresolved."

> The overthrow of the new bureaucratic bourgeoisie, changes in the armed forces, the establishment of communes and other basic social changes that were supposed to be fulfilled by the Cultural Revolution have not been fulfilled. . . . The fruit of victory has been usurped by the bourgeoisie.[45]

With all their frustrated indignation, however, the Hunanese extremists offered little in the way of a positive strategy beyond advocating that the dynamism originally released in the Cultural Revolution be prolonged. In that sense, they seemed more akin to student activists in the United States, Western Europe, and Japan than to the orthodox Red Guards first mobilized by Mao. Moreover, their "ultraleftism" contravened Maoist doctrine. For Mao, despite his exhortations to youths to rebel against authority, had never favored anarchy. The Hunan Alliance was therefore too revolutionary even for the Beijing radicals, and it was denounced by Jiang Qing as a "hodgepodge of rubbish" operating on behalf of the American "imperialists" and the Soviet "revisionists."[46] Curiously, though, the movement was not disbanded. By early 1968, the disenchantment with the course taken by the Cultural Revolution was shared by more distinguished radicals, including Jiang Qing herself. To have banned the Alliance, they apparently believed, would have been to play into the hands of their adversaries.

⚓

Though they had criticized the Hunan students for their "ultraleftism," the Maoist leaders themselves began to show concern at some aspects of the conservative trend developing in early 1968. Like the young Hunanese, they were troubled by the predominance of military commanders and old *apparatchiks* in the Revolutionary Committees, and they were alarmed by the Army's efforts to exclude Red Guards from positions of responsibility. Equally worrisome was the Army's frequent mobilization of labor vigilante groups, militia units, and special security teams charged with suppressing Red Guards and other agitators in the name of enforcing law and order. In another device calculated to discipline Red Guards while strengthening the country's defenses, regional commanders had been stepping up a program to conscript youths into the Army. Starting in February, registrations and examinations of draftees met with little overt opposition, and this testified to the progress made by the Army since September in imposing routine administrative procedures.[47]

Hints of dissatisfaction with these developments first emerged from Shanghai, where the Cultural Revolution had received its initial impulse in the fall of 1965. In late December, a newspaper there published a plea for workers, peasants, students, and "advanced elements" who had "distinguished themselves during the revolutionary struggle" to be given places in the future Party apparatus and that officials "devoid of revolutionary zeal" be expelled.[48] By March, this relatively mild request had escalated into a major counteroffensive aimed at regaining prominence for the radicals.

As the radicals perceived it, the country was then going through a repetition of the so-called "adverse current" that had subverted their revolutionary push in early 1967, and they were determined to block it. Only a few months earlier, one of the main themes in Beijing's propaganda had been leniency for reformed Party officials. Now, in contrast, the radicals inveighed against the exoneration of "black cadres" who had been ousted during the Cultural Revolution. Not long before, there had been proposals that Red Guard groups had fulfilled their "historic task" and should be dissolved as the new Revolutionary Committees assumed power. "This view is completely wrong," the radicals now asserted, demanding instead that their organizations "be further strengthened" and given "effective roles in the class and produciton struggle."[49] And in response to the Beijing publicists' strenuous campaign discouraging factional disputes and urging rival movements to resolve their differences, the radicals contended that "the factionalism of the proletarian revolutionaries is very good, very good indeed. There is no room whatsoever for reconciliation" with the "bourgeoisie.[50]

Challenging the entire effort by the Army and its allies to pacify

China during the previous months, the radicals also revived their appeals for a recrudescence of violent conflict. As one of their spokesmen put it:

> Chaos is another expression of the eruption of class contradiction, and the culmination of the struggle between the two lines in violence. There is nothing wrong with sowing chaos in the enemy ranks by attacking and purging the handful who have burrowed deep among them. These hidden enemies cannot be uprooted without creating chaos.[51]

This crescendo of appeals for radical resurgence could not possibly have occurred without the approval of Mao and Lin Biao. By early spring, apparently persuaded that the pendulum had swung too far in the direction of stability, they were convinced that a radical push was necessary—even if its costs might be high. Loyal to the Maoist dialectic, Lin cautioned against fearing disruption: "the situation will improve when disorder has reached its extreme." "Even if heaven collapses," he went on, Mao and his "invincible thought" could "prop it up and mend the cracks."[52] Mao himself, meanwhile, gave his blessing to the radicals in one of those ambiguous yet pregnant pronouncements favored by charismatic leaders: "To protect or oppress the masses—that is the fundamental difference between the Chinese Communist Party and the Kuomintang, between the proletariat and the bourgeoisie, and between the dictatorship of the proletariat and the dictatorship of the bourgeoisie."[53]

Now back in the limelight after a winter's absence, Jiang Qing also stepped forth with a series of speeches in mid-March, warning that the "main danger all over the country" was coming from the conservatives. This tendency "has not just sprouted" but had been emerging for "several months," she said. And in a tortuous attempt to justify her diatribes against the "ultraleftists" only a few months earlier, she argued that they had really been "rightist in essence" and appealed for a fresh attack against the "class enemy."[54]

That summons to action was echoed by the entire Beijing leadership, including Zhou Enlai. Chen Boda, head of the Cultural Revolution Directorate, especially welcomed the new line with the announcement that the Maoist campaign was now entering its fifth "major round." The first round, he said, had been the dismissal in early 1966 of Peng Chen and the Beijing Party machine. The second had been the denunciation of Liu Shaoqi, Deng Xiaoping, and their "revisionist" colleagues. The third was the defeat of the "counterrevolutionary adverse current" in the spring of 1967, and the fourth round had been the ouster of Wang Li and the "ultraleftists' who were really "rightists."[55]

On March 22, the fifth round officially opened with the purge of three senior Army officers—General Yang Chengwu, Acting Chief of General Staff; General Yu Lijin, political commissar of the Air Force; and General Fu Chongbi, commander of the Beijing garrison. All were formally indicted for having committed "extremely serious mistakes." General Huang Yongsheng, controversial military boss of south China, was appointed to succeed Yang as Chief of Staff.[56]

A native of Fujian province, then in his mid-fifties, Yang Chengwu was one of the most experienced field commanders in the Chinese Army. After fighting in several critical battles during the Long March, he had played a prominent role in both the Sino-Japanese war and the conflict against the Nationalists, and was probably engaged as well in the Korean War. By 1959, he was Deputy Chief of General Staff and, six years later, he filled the post vacated by the dismissal of Luo Ruiqing.

Running true to form, Red Guard publicists now charged Yang, once his indictment was announced, with every imaginable crime. They linked him with elements as diverse as the "ultraleftist" May 16th Detachment, the Soviet "revisionists," and the American "imperialists," claiming that he had even gone so far as to install bugging devices in Mao's residence and office in his plot to overthrow the Chairman.[57] Lin Biao, however, offered a more authoritative if not necessarily accurate account of the circumstances surrounding Yang's ouster in a talk with Army officers in Beijing on March 25.[58]

Among other maneuvers, Lin said, Yang and his comrades had conspired against both Zhou Enlai and Jiang Qing, employing "secret police methods" to compile a dossier of "black materials" with which to incriminate them. In addition, Yang had jockeyed to eliminate a number of key field commanders as well as the chief of the Air Force so as to put his own protégés into their positions. Lin portrayed Yang as an overweeningly ambitious man who "believed only in himself and his tiny group of men" and therefore violated the basic premise of communism—"devotion to public interest." And in the same moralistic vein, Lin added a piquant anecdote. As part of his plot to gain control of the Air Force, Lin related, Yang had delegated his own daughter to have "illicit sexual relations" with a high-ranking officer in that service whose marriage was then in trouble. This only became known, Lin divulged, when the jealous wife reported the love affair to her husband's superiors—who promptly transferred him to another post "to protect his honor."

Judging from Lin's speech and other documents, the purge of Yang Chengwu and his two colleagues was prompted by an assortment of factors—some related to events of the moment and others reflecting deeper stresses and strains within the Chinese leadership.

Contrary to allegations linking them to the "ultraleftists," Yang and his comrades had clearly been in the forefront of the Army's efforts to subdue the Red Guards. For one thing, Yang had been closely associated throughout his career with Marshal Nie Rongzhen, the director of China's nuclear development program and one of the most conservative officers in the Chinese Army.[59] Months later, in fact, the Red Guards denounced Nie for having tried to protect Yang.[60] Yang Chengwu's concern for law and order was also mirrored in his behavior immediately after the Wuhan mutiny. While Beijing's entire propaganda machine was appealing for a purge of the Army, Yang pursued a significantly different line, declaring that the purported "counterrevolutionary" plot to "usurp control of the Army" had been "discerned in good time and smashed," and that "all the commanders and fighters . . . are boundlessly loyal" to Mao. And, at a moment when events within China were of the utmost importance, Yang deliberately diverted to foreign affairs, even digressing so far afield as to discuss the "Afro-American struggle in Detroit."[61]

Yang's concern for internal "peace" inevitably inspired his hostility toward Jiang Qing and the radicals, and there was undoubtedly a large measure of truth in Lin Biao's charge that he strove to neutralize them. On one occasion, Yang reportedly sent two truckloads of armed troops to the headquarters of the Cultural Revolution Directorate in Beijing in an attempt to arrest some of its minor functionaries. He evidently tried as well to curb the Red Guards at Beijing University, who in the late winter of 1968 were seeking Jiang Qing's support for a resurgence.

Like establishments everywhere in the world, the Chinese military hierarchy was riddled with personal, professional, and regional rivalries. Hence Yang Chengwu may well have maneuvered to displace several senior officers in favor of his own protégés, as Lin Biao charged. Or he could have fallen victim to the ambitions of his opponents within the Army. In any case, two of the men Yang had allegedly tried to eradicate went on to become members of the Politburo. One was General Xu Shiyou, commander of central China.

The other, Yang's replacement as Chief of Staff, was Huang Yongsheng. Their later promotions contained important clues to the motives underlying the dismissal of Yang and his colleagues.[62]

Men like Huang Yongsheng and Xu Shiyou were no more sympathetic to the radicals than Yang. Indeed, Huang had persistently suppressed Red Guards in Guangzhou, and Xu had repeatedly come under fire from extremists in his area. Thus Yang's purge, whatever its later effect would be, was not intended to encourage the radicals to initiate fresh rampages. Instead, it seemed to represent a compromise worked out by Lin Biao to placate both the Maoists and the commanders. While they accepted the compromise at the time, the commanders may have later held the purge of Yang, one of their kind, against Lin.

Lin made it clear that the decision to oust Yang had involved a good deal of intricate negotiating. The subject had been discussed at four separate meetings held at Mao's private residence before those present—presumably selected Maoist leaders and Army officers—finally agreed to dump Yang. Philosophizing somewhat sadly on the move, Lin later explained that "the objective situation changes independently of man's will" and so, faced by the necessity for perpetual "struggle," they had "no choice but to expose and resolve the conflict. . . . The abscess must be punctured, and fire cannot be wrapped up in a piece of paper."[63]

At the same time, Lin took pains to stress that Yang's dismissal by no means signified a wholesale purge of the Army. Just because Yang had been wrong was no reason to eliminate his past supporters, subordinates, and acquaintances. Lin generously allowed that these relationships may have been dictated by "historical conditions," or that Yang had perhaps "deceived people." At any rate, "we must continue to trust those comrades," and Lin assured them that "they shall have our full confidence" as long as they repudiate Yang and "stand under Chairman Mao's banner."[64]

One effect of this compromise was to give the radicals larger representation in the Revolutionary Committees formed thereafter. Radicals had accounted for about 20 per cent of the leading members of the Revolutionary Committees created from August 1967 through March 1968. In contrast, the proportion of Red Guards and other activists jumped to more than 30 per cent between April and September 1968. Still, the Committees essentially remained under Army control And the roles played by the field commanders showed the reinforcement of the power of the regional military authorities. This was to become even more dramatically apparent with the emergence of the new Party Politburo a year later.[65]

The other consequence of Yang's ouster was a fresh explosion of violence throughout the provinces. In part at least, simmering factional tensions had never eased. But there was no doubt that Jiang Qing and her radical comrades in Beijing and Shanghai helped to ignite the new outburst. As usual, they interpreted the willingness of regional commanders to strike a compromise as weakness, and this prompted them to push ahead. As faithful Maoists, they believed as well in the Chairman's dialectical thesis that "the situation will improve when disorder has reached its extreme."

CHAPTER 19

The Storm Before the Calm

♨

*You have let me down and, moreover, you
have disappointed the workers, peasants,
and soldiers of China.*

— MAO ZEDONG
to Red Guard leaders, July 27, 1968

EMPOWERED SINCE SEPTEMBER to shoot at fanatical agitators, the Army had managed to make some progress toward the restoration of order during the fall and winter of 1967–1968. Many local commanders formed special vigilante groups to help troops maintain peace. One such group in Shanghai—called the Attack By Reason Defend By Force Great Column, its name ironically borrowed from one of Jiang Qing's bellicose slogans—was composed of thousands of armed workers, and it claimed to have staged seven major actions against "renegades, secret enemy agents, counterrevolutionaries, and incorrigible hooligans" during the month of December.[1] Similar teams were mobilized under military auspices in Guangzhou, Nanjing, and other cities.

Nevertheless, the Army encountered enormous difficulties in its efforts to impose discipline, and even Beijing, patrolled by soldiers day and night, was not immune to violence. In mid-January, four people were killed and eighteen injured in a village near Beijing when Red Guards wielding knives and clubs attacked peasants in an attempt to steal food.[2] A clash broke out in the heart of the city itself between textile workers and laborers engaged in constructing the capital's new subway.[3] By late March, factions of every stripe were again skirmishing openly.

One major scene of conflict in the national capital was Beijing University, which had been recurrently torn by discord ever since the Cultural Revolution erupted there two years before. Underlying the new outburst was a disagreement between the institution's two main student movements, both of which had originally been regarded as radical. One, the Jinggangshan, had taken its title from Mao's celebrated mountain stronghold of the late 1920s. The other was called New Beida—"Beida" being the familiar name for Beijing University. Their dispute had arisen out of the Jinggangshan's opposition to Nie Yuanzi, the radical woman activist who had risen during the Cultural Revolution to become a Deputy Chairman of the Beijing Revolutionary Committee. During the last week of March, Jinggangshan activists raided their rivals' offices, wrecked a radio station, abducted several New Beida leaders, and invited students from other Beijing schools and colleges to participate in demonstrations denouncing Nie Yuanzi and demanding her resignation.

On March 25, the Minister of Public Security, Xie Fuzhi, visited the university in his capacity as Chairman of the Beijing Revolutionary Committee in an effort to halt the tumult. He ordered the students to stop fighting and unite behind Nie Yuanzi. But the students ignored him. Finally, on the morning of March 29, a senior Army officer arrived at the campus, flanked by soldiers and accompanied by Nie Yuanzi. As they entered one of the buildings, students armed with daggers ambushed them. They stabbed Nie Yuanzi in the back of the head, and escaped in the ensuing melee.[4] Nie Yuanzi survived. The daring students, however, were apparently never found, despite pleas by the authorities that they surrender or be handed over by their comrades.

Troops deployed to control Beijing University were unable to prevent continued skirmishing there throughout April. One of the few foreigners to observe the actual fighting, Jean Vincent, Beijing correspondent for Agence France-Presse, witnessed on the afternoon of April 28 a battle in which competing students fought each other from fortified buildings on the university campus. Barricading smashed windows with mattresses, radiators, and furniture, the rival factions conducted an "artillery" duel from the rooftops—the artillery consisting of improvised catapults with which they hurled bricks, tiles, and other projectiles at their foes as loudspeakers on both sides kept up a fusillade of propaganda.[5]

Radical zealots were also reported to be killing suspected "bourgeois" and "revisionist" elements or driving them to suicide in a new wave of terror. At a session of the Beijing Revolutionary Committee on May 15, Xie Fuzhi revealed that activists in one suburb had rounded up and slaughtered a number of alleged "counterrevolutionaries" and their families, children included. He disclosed as well that suicides were proliferating as a result of Red Guard harassment of Mao's purported adversaries. Acknowledging that many people had committed suicide "out of fear of punishment for their crimes," Xie nevertheless urged the Red Guards to restrain themselves, explaining that "even counterrevolutionaries must be given a chance" to redeem their sins. Touching on a point that would increasingly preoccupy the Beijing leaders, Xie warned that continued violence would complicate the country's future social and political problems. "Feudal" family and clan relations in China were still strong, and bloodshed now would create vendettas for years to come. Or as he put it: "When the father is killed, it is difficult to remold his children. This is a serious question."[6]

If Beijing was in ferment, turbulence in the provinces was even more acute. In several areas, the establishment of Revolutionary Committees had merely exacerbated the frustrations of the radicals. Two other factors combined to heighten the level of violence: Thousands of young militants were now armed with weapons they had stolen or been issued the previous summer. And troops were still authorized to shoot at agitators. Thus the provincial clashes that broke out in the middle of 1968 were especially bloody, particularly in south China.

Reports during the spring indicated that frontier regions like Xinjiang, Tibet, and Inner Mongolia were being plagued by persistent turmoil. In Sichuan, despite the introduction of outside troops, local conflicts reached critical proportions as rival Red Guard and Army factions fought each other with modern antiaircraft guns and artillery pieces presumably manufactured for shipment to Vietnam.[7] But the worst violence of that period gripped the volatile provinces of Guangdong and Guangxi.

On September 27 of the previous year, Zhou Enlai had convened a meeting in Beijing at which he exhorted delegates of competing Guangdong factions to resolve their differences and rally behind General Huang Yongsheng, the regional military commander.[8] A few weeks later, the delegates returned to Guangzhou with a set of agreements to merge their organizations and respect the authority of the local Army garrison.[9] But the settlement quickly collapsed as rival groups asserted themselves anew. In mid-December, student gangs fought to occupy a school in the town of Jiangmen, about fifty miles south of Guangzhou.[10] Soon after, Red Guards in a Guangzhou suburb abducted a student in a rival gang and, according to one grisly account, smashed his kneecaps and finally murdered him by driving nails into his forehead.[11]

The conflicts in Guangdong inevitably intensified. On February 18, after one youth movement tried to prevent another from pasting up wall posters, a battle erupted that spread through Guangzhou.[12] Three days later, the provincial Revolutionary Committee was established under General Huang Yongsheng, who bluntly emphasized in his inaugural address that he would "resolutely punish all class enemies" in a determined drive to restore order in the province.[13] Even as he spoke, rival Red Guards attending the inauguration ceremony at a Guangzhou stadium began fighting among themselves, and hundreds were reportedly injured.[14]

In the spring, the increasing number of Red Guard clashes in Guangzhou seemed to be simply a confused assortment of local struggles for power. A typical explosion of passions flared up on May 25 in the five-story office building of the state-owned Guangzhou Electric Company, located in Sea Pearl Square, not far from the exhibition hall where China's biennial international trade fair is held. Like workers, students, officials, and nearly everyone else in Guangzhou, the employees of the company belonged to factions affiliated with either the East Wind or the Red Flag. Complying with the numerous directives to resolve their differences, their delegates were meeting that day to choose representatives to a joint committee to be set up in the Electric Company. By noon, the debate had degenerated into emotional name-calling and table-thumping, and the delegates agreed to adjourn for lunch.

The East Wind group was conferring in its second-floor office when a band of thirty Red Flag activists swept down the stairs in an attack. Flinging rice bowls, flasks, and light bulbs, the East Wind drove them back. Then both factions barricaded their offices and sent out for reinforcements.

At about four o'clock in the afternoon, some three hundred Red Flag fighters arrived on the scene, armed with improvised weapons. They cordoned off the streets around the building and occupied its ground floor. Soon afterward, three truckloads of East Wind youths appeared, many of them wearing steel helmets. Greeted by a hail of stones, the East Wind responded by throwing vials of sulphuric acid and homemade incendiary bombs at their opponents, forcing them to retreat into the building. From the third floor, meanwhile, members of the Red Flag bombarded their foes with bricks, tiles, and even a few grenades.

An hour later, a battalion of troops encircled the area in an attempt to prevent more youths from pouring in. The soldiers, restrained by their officers from shooting, instead attempted to cool the mob by chanting Mao's dictum to "struggle with reason, not with force." But they were ignored. At one point, a group of East Wind youths broke through the Army line in a stolen bus containing ten barrels of gasoline and set the Electric Company building aflame. Eventually, their patience exhausted, the troops opened fire, killing three young activists and wounding several others.[15]

But the fighting continued all night, spreading in the weeks that followed into other parts of the city and suburbs. On June 3, armed Red Flag students stormed the Physics Building on the Sun Yat-sen University campus , then serving as an East Wind stronghold. After nearly three days of battle, the Red Flag had killed ten students and abducted sixty others. One captive was said to have been drenched with gasoline and burned alive.[16] Students and workers were reported to be fighting in shipyards, steel mills, and other industrial enterprises.[17] By the middle of June, the Army had imposed a dusk-to-dawn curfew on the city, and troops were patrolling its streets in armored cars.[18]

The situation was aggravated, meanwhile, by severe monsoon floods which not only threatened to inundate Guangzhou, but were forcing thousands of peasants to seek asylum in the city. These peasants, suffering from food shortages, reportedly took advantage of the disorder to loot and pillage. In addition, rural youths joined disparate Red Guard factions in Guangzhou, further contributing to the ferment.

At the same time, the floods brought grim evidence to view of the troubles in south China. Swept down to the sea by swollen rivers, more than a hundred corpses washed onto the shores of Hong Kong and Macao. The bodies, despite their various degrees of decomposition, all appeared to have been murdered. A few were headless, some showed traces of gunshot wounds, many were mutilated, and most had their hands trussed behind them, suggesting that they might have been executed in Oriental style by decapitation or by a bullet in the back of the neck as they knelt. One, believed to be a girl of thirteen or fourteen, bore strands of a rope around her throat.[19] They had evidently come from the Guangxi-Zhuang Autonomous Region, bordering on Vietnam, a region that was perhaps most devastated by the upheavals of the Cultural Revolution.[20]

Over the centuries, the Han Chinese had emigrated into the Guangxi region until, by the time of the Communist victory in 1949, the native Zhuangs comprised only about a third of Guangxi's population of 20 million. The Han Chinese became urban merchants, workers, and officials, leaving the Zhuangs to cultivate their hillsides as they had for millennia by their slash-and-burn farming methods. But the Communists initiated a special program to bring Guangxi deeper into the national fold by Sinicizing the Zhuangs. This led to ethnic frictions that undoubtedly were exacerbated during the Cultural Revolution.

Guangxi had been ruled almost single-handedly since 1954 by Wei Guoqing, veteran Army officer and Party *apparatchik* who served simultaneously as the region's military commissar, political boss, and administrative governor. A Zhuang by birth, he was one of the few members of an ethnic minority to have risen to the Central Committee. Wei had joined the Communist movement as an adolescent and became a general by the time he was in his early thirties. As a senior officer in Chen Yi's Third Field Army during the war against the Nationalists, he participated in the capture of Fuzhou and remained in that sensitive coastal sector opposite Taiwan until his assignment to Guangxi five years later.

Despite his stature and skill, Wei Guoqing had apparently lagged behind in carrying out Beijing's *mission civilisatrice* among the Zhuang aborigines of Guangxi. For in 1957, an outside official by the name of Wu Jinnan had been sent into the region to speed up the assimilation process. A veteran of the Long March with impressive credentials as a Party cadre, Wu had served most of his career in his native Guangdong province. Wei Guoqing may have resented Wu's intrusion, and there could have been some tension between the two men even before the Cultural Revolution. In any case, a sharp dispute divided them in January 1967.[21]

That month, Wu Jinnan had mobilized some forty thousand Red Guards in Nanning, the Guangxi capital, in an attempt to oust Wei Guoqing and his associates. Like many other provincial Party leaders at the time, Wei defended his apparatus while seeming to obey Mao's directive. He dissolved his old Party machine and proclaimed himself the head of a new Maoist-style committee to govern the province.

But Wu Jinnan and his Red Guards, perceiving the maneuver, accelerated their offensive, and the various Guangxi organizations soon polarized into two broad coalitions. Wu's group of five large youth factions was formally mobilized on April 22, 1967, and hence called itself the April 22 Revolutionary Rebel Grand Army. Its supporters included a few senior officers, among them General Sun Feng-zhang, commander of the Fifty-fifth Army, and its main strength lay in the city of Guilin, the United States military headquarters in China during World War II. Wei Guoqing's movement, composed largely of workers and backed by most of the Army in the region, was the Guangxi Proletarian Revolutionaries Alliance Command. Its sympathizers included General Ou Zhifu, the Guangxi Military District chief and, like Wei, a Zhuang, and the local Air Force and public security commanders.[22]

The rival Guangxi factions attacked and counterattacked each other during most of 1967, their battles ending inconclusively and blending into fresh turmoil. At one point, possibly seeking to win over some of his adversaries with a ritualistic display of contrition, Wei Guoqing appeared at a public rally in Nanning to confess his "sins." But this did nothing to halt the fighting and finally, in late 1967, Beijing intervened.

Guangxi's location adjacent to Vietnam gave special cause for concern. Several new airfields had been constructed in the province, both for China's defense and also to service North Vietnamese fighter aircraft engaged in the Vietnam war. Equally important, the railway that transported Soviet and Chinese military supplies to Hanoi ran through Guangxi, and China's leaders could not afford disruptions that would impair their relations with North Vietnam and make them vulnerable to Russian criticism. With these considerations in mind, they summoned Wei Guoqing and Wu Jinnan to Beijing to negotiate a settlement.

On November 8 the Guangxi rivals signed an accord pledging to cease their conflict "immediately" and to disarm their respective factions.[23] Ten days later, the Beijing leadership issued a document approving the accord and expressing the "hope" that the opposing movements would honor the agreement "in earnest." The document bore Mao's personal endorsement as an indication that he was troubled by the unrest in Guangxi.[24]

But hardly had the truce been signed than fighting again began to convulse the province. On November 26, members of Wu Jinnan's Grand Army attacked a cotton mill and a bus depot in Guilin, killing three of their foes in the melee.[25] At the same time, Grand Army partisans were reported to be bracing for a major battle in Wuzhou, a sprawling city on the West River. They had moved large quantities of guns, ammunition, grenades, bombs, and land mines into the People's Hospital, their stronghold, and they were constructing trenches and pillboxes in the vicinity of the Municipal Council Building, the headquarters of the Alliance Command.[26] On December 6, the first of several Wuzhou skirmishes began as a gang of youths assaulted troops patrolling the city and seized their weapons. By evening, nine soldiers had been wounded, and sporadic fighting continued for weeks, gradually intensifying into what would be, in the spring, a full-scale battle.[27]

During the following month, the rival factions signed new cease-fire agreements and promptly violated them. Meanwhile, anticipating an eventual showdown, Wei Guoqing rapidly deployed his forces throughout Guangxi. In February, for instance, he reportedly dispatched five thousand troops and irregulars to take over positions held by the Grand Army in Rongan county.[28] He also placed members of his Alliance Command in charge of all the new county committees then being set up around the region. To establish the committee in Gui county, for example, he sent more than three thousand militia into the area, imposed martial law, and proceeded to round up Grand Army activists who showed signs of resistance. By late April, he controlled seventy-three of the region's eighty-six county committees, and one of his spokesmen proclaimed that "the situation is excellent."[29] On April 26, apparently ready for the showdown, Wei Guoqing virtually declared war against the Grand Army. He said: "We must not be soft or hesitant in dealing with the enemy. We must mount a fierce attack against the class enemy, and not give him breathing space. We shall not rest until complete victory is won."[30]

With that, a round of battles erupted in Guangxi's principal cities. The first—in Liuzhou, in the center of the region—lasted a month. Starting on April 28, Wei Guoqing's troops assaulted the city with rockets and incendiary bombs that demolished more than a thousand buildings, among them a steam turbine plant, a hospital, and two schools. Led by his Alliance Command, thousands of peasants poured into the city, and the fighting was savage. More than a hundred participants and countless innocent civilians were killed, and finally, outnumbered and outgunned, the decimated Grand Army forces retreated to the outskirts of the city.[31]

The Liuzhou battle was overshadowed by a simultaneous and even bigger clash in Wuzhou. As they had in Liuzhou, Wei Guoqing's forces in Wuzhou strengthened their ranks with armed peasants and some seven hundred recently demobilized soldiers, and they could count on further support from the local Army garrison. They installed loudspeakers in different districts of Wuzhou and, on April 13, they proclaimed their adversaries to be "counterrevolutionaries," and that the struggle between themselves and the Grand Army was "between Communists and the Kuomintang." Four days later, Alliance Command activists opened their offensive. Using high explosives, they blew up the offices of the State Sugar, Tobacco, and Alcohol Corporation, a Grand Army stronghold, and seized the city's Central Post and Telegraph Bureau. They then encircled the Zaofan Building, the headquarters of the Grand Army, ordering residents of the neighborhood to leave the area within twenty-one hours or "face the consequences." That night, evidently equipped by the Army, the Alliance Command wheeled light howitzers, antiaircraft guns, mortars, and machine guns into range of the Zaofan Building. On April 18, the attack began.

The Zaofan Building collapsed under the first artillery barrage, and the Grand Army forces streamed into the streets, seeking protection elsewhere. But Alliance Command vigilantes pursued them. The two factions skirmished in alleys and lanes, public buildings and private homes. On the night of April 19, when a band of Grand Army youths took refuge inside a compound, the Alliance Command hurled napalm bombs over the walls to flush them out. The next day, surrounding some fifty Grand Army activists inside the offices of a government trading company, Alliance Command cadres appealed to them to surrender, explaining that they had been "hoodwinked" and would be shown leniency. But when they emerged, the Grand Army youths were bound and taken to the local Culture Hall, now a temporary Alliance Command prison.[32]

By May 3, according to one version of the episode, more than two thousand Wuzhou buildings were in ruins and some forty thousand inhabitants of the city had been rendered homeless. With the Grand Army routed, Alliance Command vigilantes began mopping up. Assisted by local troops and police, they conducted a house-to-house manhunt, arresting hundreds of their rivals. Finally, with more than three thousand captives crowded into the Culture Hall and other makeshift jails, the Alliance Command leaders proceeded systematically to interrogate, torture, and execute their prisoners. They staged at least three mass executions, evidently by firing squad, and three hundred seventeen bodies were reported to have been dumped into shallow graves at the Balongli cemetery. Other bodies were thrown into the West River and some of these corpses later washed ashore in Hong Kong and Macao.[33]

In a post-mortem report, the defeated Grand Army described the "fascist atrocities" committed in Wuzhou as "even worse than those of the Kuomintang and the Japanese devils." The report estimated that fifty thousand Grand Army members had been massacred throughout the region, and that twenty thousand others fled to the neighboring provinces of Yunnan, Guizhou, and Guangdong.[34] Whatever the reliability of those statistics, the devastation in Guangxi was dramatic—and the fighting did not cease with the victory of Wei Guoqing's Alliance Command.

Members of Grand Army remnants, seeking asylum in Guangdong, were arrested by troops there and shipped by river boat back to the Wuzhou military authorities.[35] Calling themselves an "accusation mission," several members of the Grand Army even made their way to Beijing in hopes of expressing their grievances to China's top leaders. Neglected, they wandered aimlessly around the capital for weeks, searching for an audience to hear their protests. Their money soon ran out and some, caught stealing, were branded "bandits and hooligans" and imprisoned.[36] In contrast, Wei Guoqing and his comrades were summoned to Beijing in grand style and, on July 3, they were photographed with Mao to illustrate that they enjoyed the Chairman's "greatest support." Wei's visit to Beijing was marred, however, when frustrated activists in the Grand Army "accusation mission" broke into his hotel, denounced him as a "capitalist" and, according to one account, "made a great hullabaloo." Soldiers intervened to restore order and the rioters were "arrested on the spot."[37]

Mao's accolade for Wei Guoqing came as a hint that, perceiving anew that China could not sustain continued turmoil, he was once again swinging to the side of moderation. His shift may well have been a measure of the growing influence of Zhou Enlai and the regional commanders, who were alarmed by the chaos sweeping through south China.

Though their comrades in Beijing had been subdued, frustrated Grand Army agitators in Guangxi could not be easily checked. Following their defeat in Wuzhou, they again struck out in passionate and often indiscriminate attempts to retrieve their momentum. Other local factions emulated them, and Guangxi was soon slipping toward fresh turbulence. With no apparent motive, for example, Red Guards stormed Hanoi's consulate in Nanning on June 2, forcing the puzzled North Vietnamese diplomats out of the building and assailing them as they emerged.[38] Desperate for weapons, youths also ambushed, derailed, and raided trains carrying military supplies to Vietnam.

The extraordinary amplitude of these raids was first revealed on June 13 by the Beijing leaders in a stern directive calling for a halt to the tumult obstructing the Guangxi railway system. The directive said that rival factions had "looted our country's aid-Vietnam supplies . . . carried out armed attacks against trains and damaged railways, completely disrupting traffic" in the vicinity of Liuzhou. The document insisted that "no time be lost in restoring communications and transport," and it decreed that all stolen weapons and equipment be surrendered to the Guangxi military authorities.[39] Some idea of the magnitude of the pillage was contained in other disclosures by the Beijing leaders that one Guangxi faction had seized more than eleven thousand cases of ammunition while another had stolen six thousand rifles.[40]

The June 13 directive was ignored. A week later, Zhou Enlai telephoned the Guangxi military headquarters to demand that law and order be imposed in Guilin and Nanning, and he issued an ultimatum insisting that rail traffic in the Liuzhou area be returned to normal within three days.[41] But the Guangxi factions went on running rampant. Beijing issued another directive along the same lines on July 3, and this edict was stronger in two respects. It bore Mao's personal imprimatur and it warned that prolonged resistance would be "severely punished."[42] Again, there was no sign of compliance from Guangxi. Indeed, three weeks after the directive was issued, rail service near Liuzhou remained paralyzed as youths continued to attack and pillage trains.[43]

On July 24, the Beijing leaders put out yet another appeal for order to the entire nation. The edict disclosed the extent to which China's social fabric was torn. For it revealed that "counterrevolutionaries" in several regions were robbing banks and warehouses, burning or blowing up public buildings and private homes, stealing automobiles and trucks, disrupting rail traffic, killing soldiers and seizing their weapons—and refusing to obey Beijing directives. While again threatening the guilty with "severe punishment," it added a sweetening promise that those who had been "coerced" or "hoodwinked" into committing crimes would be pardoned.[44]

The lengths to which the Beijing leaders were compelled to go in their efforts to restore order illustrated not only the extent of anarchy within China but the degree to which central authority had collapsed. This critical state of affairs resonated as well in the exasperation of the Chinese leaders with the Red Guards and other young militants. Gone were lavish phrases extolling the "little red generals" and hailing them as "revolutionary heirs." Now they upbraided the youths like old-fashioned cops scolding juvenile delinquents.

Kang Sheng, China's security chief, was the most archetypical exemplar of the new line. In a talk with a group of Guangxi militants in Beijing on July 25, Kang bluntly warned that they had not been convened to "submit a lawsuit" and were in no position to "discuss terms." They were there to listen and obey. "Do you know who you're making happy?" Kang asked them. "The American imperialists, the Soviet revisionists, the traitors, and special agents—that's who you're making happy. You shout about wanting revolution, but you oppose revolution. I want no more double-dealing. Some of you have reached the edge of the cliff. One more step and you'll go over." And though himself a university graduate, Kang infused the meeting with an air of Maoist anti-intellectualism: "You students never fought the Kuomintang or the Americans in Korea. Yet you think you're superior just because you've been educated."[45]

Two days later, in an attempt to destroy the monster he had invented, Mao himself repudiated the Red Guards. Speaking to five radical leaders, among them Beijing University's Nie Yuanzi and Kuai Dafu of Qinghua, he catalogued their blunders. They had failed to unite, and their persistent fighting was ruining the country. Besides, they had not even begun to transform their inner selves in the process that was supposed to shape them into truly "Communist men." Then, reportedly with tears in his eyes, Mao disavowed them: "You have let me down and, moreover, you have disappointed the workers, peasants, and soldiers of China."[46]

Even before that scene was played, regional commanders had been taking steps to suppress the Red Guards. In Guangzhou, Army officers staged a rally on July 11 to endorse the authority of the Workers Provost Corps, a labor vigilante force. The next day, the local Revolutionary Committee published a ten-point decree on "stopping armed struggle," enfranchising the Army and the Workers Provost Corps to "take compulsory action against those who refuse to comply" with the directive. A week later, the Committee announced a new program to transfer thousands of students to rural areas, and soon after that the first batch was reported to have "joyfully" entrained for Army-run farms, repudiating the bourgeois notion that "it is better to go to college first."[47] At the end of the month, the Revolutionary Committee indicted Wu Zuanbin, the dynamic Red Guard who had done most to promote the Cultural Revolution in Guangzhou during the spring of 1966.

A year before, when Wu had come under fire from the military authorities in Guangzhou, Zhou Enlai had personally exonerated him, praising his "political prescience" and devotion to "revolutionary truth," and that plaudit won the student activist a prominent place in the Guangdong Revolutionary Committee.[48] Now Zhou stigmatized him as a "black character."[49] At a meeting held in Guangzhou on July 31, Wu was further denounced as an "overbearing and arrogant scoundrel" whose crimes included espionage and violence. He was blamed as well for sexual promiscuity with young girl Red Guards and this, speakers at the meeting said, had "left a big stain on his moral reputation."[50] The Revolutionary Committee also arrested a number of radical professors who had been active during the early stages of the Cultural Revolution in Guangzhou, predictably charging them with being American or Kuomintang agents, or both.[51]

Army-dominated Revolutionary Committees in several provinces now began to dissolve the large coalitions that had held sway at the peak of the Cultural Revolution. In Changchun, a major Manchurian industrial city, a movement known as the August 10 Commune proclaimed on July 23 that it had "voluntarily" disbanded, quoting Mao to the effect that "an organizational form that no longer conforms to the needs of the struggle must be abolished."[52] Other Red Guard factions that ceased functioning included Henan's troublesome February 7 Commune. The public rationale for this move held that the revolutionary cause would be "strengthened and consolidated" by replacing the big Red Guard movements with smaller occupational and school groups. In reality, smaller groups were easier to control. County and other local administrative bodies were also directed to "streamline" by reducing staff—advice that authorized them to oust their disruptive elements.[53]

By the middle of summer, the trend toward moderation was firmly established, and it was publicized by a lexicon of mirror-language phrases. What had formerly been justifiable "rebellion" now became "counterrevolution." Red Guards were now "anarchists" poisoned by "bourgeois factionalism" and "leftist opportunism." The restoration of law and order by the Army and its auxiliaries was no longer a "reactionary adverse current," but the imposition of "revolutionary discipline" designed to defend the "dictatorship of the proletariat" against its "class enemies." And the rationale for the new line, like the rationale for the exhortations that had launched the Cultural Revolution, would be found in Mao's immense body of doctrine.

CHAPTER 20

The Road to Recovery

❧

The People's Liberation Army is the mighty pillar of the dictatorship of the proletariat . . . the main component of the State.
— LIN BIAO, *April 14, 1969*

IN LATE JULY, immediately after Mao Zedong's tearful disavowal of the Red Guards, troops surrounded Beijing's Qinghua University, and a veil of silence fell over the campus. It was broken ten days afterward by a bizarre announcement.

On August 6, the *People's Daily* covered its entire front page with the news that, the day before, Mao had sent a basket of mangoes to workers and peasants engaged in promoting his doctrine among Qinghua University students. The mangoes had been a gift to Mao from Pakistan's Foreign Minister Arshad Husain, who had just ended a visit to China and, the *People's Daily* related, their delivery to the Qinghua campus was greeted with "seething jubilation." The recipients of the fruit were reported to have cheered, wept, and chanted Mao's slogans, describing his generous gesture as the "greatest inspiration" to proletarian militants. The mangoes then sat on the red table in the middle of the Qinghua campus for several days, until they began to rot. Thereupon, according to one official account, experts placed them in a glass jar of formalin, to be preserved for posterity like hair from the beard of the Prophet.[1]

This extravagant fuss over a basket of fruit was enormously significant. For Mao's presentation of the mangoes to workers and peasants—rather than to students—symbolized in exquisitely esoteric style a totally new tactic: the introduction of so-called Mao Zedong Thought Propaganda Teams into universities and schools throughout the nation. While nominally composed of workers and peasants, the real backbone of these teams were soldiers. Their essential purpose

] 408 [

was to impose military control over the Red Guards and other young activists—though the sinister connotation of Army rule was camouflaged by rhetoric claiming that the "working class" would henceforth play the "leading role" in the Cultural Revolution.[2]

The Army's real power was visible, however, in the final Revolutionary Committees created during August and September in Yunnan, Fujian, Guangxi, Xinjiang, and Tibet. All were headed by generals, and each featured a high percentage of officers among its leading members.[3] The renewed importance of the Chinese military establishment was also apparent in the Army Day celebrations held on August 1 in Beijing, heralded by the issuance of a special set of postage stamps which celebrated the Army as an "invincible force."[4] The keynote speaker, General Huang Yongsheng, emphasized that the Army's "glorious" function was, among other things, to exercise "military control" of the country.[5]

Though it comprised some five thousand workers and peasants, the Mao Zedong Thought Propaganda Team that entered Qinghua University in mid-July was under the direction of an Army unit. The Team's first task, according to an order issued by Xie Fuzhi, Chairman of the Beijing Revolutionary Committee, was to separate the rival university factions "until their hostility has disappeared" and then, through persuasion rather than force, disarm the students and urge them to resume their studies.[6] But in several areas, aware that their heyday was over, the youths put up resistance.

In Shanghai, where some ten thousand soldiers and workers moved into universities, colleges, and other educational institutions in August, resentment among student activists ran high. They complained that China's younger generation had been "discredited" and had "fallen out of favor" and, in some parts of the city, the youths physically fought against the intruders.[7] On August 6, students beat up six members of a Mao Thought Team who had entered the Shanghai Foreign Language Vocational School to conduct an investigation.[8] Students in Sichuan reportedly opposed similar teams on the grounds that soldiers and workers "do not understand education" and would create "an awful mess if they try to lead the schools."[9] In the Shaanxi province capital of Xi'an, tensions between youths and workers were reflected in the remark of a speaker at a meeting held to endorse a newly formed disciplinary Mao Thought Team. "We will never," he said, "allow young students and intellectuals to wave their hands and feet and interfere with the workers' movement."[10]

Clashes between Red Guards and the Army-run Mao Thought

Teams were especially severe in the southern parts of Zhejiang province. In mid-September, a serious skirmish broke out in Wenzhou when workers and soldiers intervened to stop a fight between rival youth factions. But instead of quelling the disturbance, the workers and soldiers reportedly sided with one faction while the police came to the aid of the other, and the fight spread through the city. A Wenzhou resident wrote to his sister in Hong Kong that "several hundred" people had been killed and "the sound of gun shots can be heard every night."[11] A clue to the degree of turbulence was contained in news of a series of mass trials held in Zhejiang's cities from early August through late September. The defendants were variously portrayed as murderers, hooligans, corrupt officials, thieves, and speculators, and one group was accused of "attempting to wreck our steel wall—the People's Liberation Army."[12] Two of the trials ended in executions.[18]

Mao's most massive effort to restore order, meanwhile, was conducted through a revival of the *Xiafang*, or "Down to the Countryside," program. Variations of this program had been initiated and abandoned on several occasions. But now, undertaken with almost desperate urgency, it became the biggest and most intensive migration scheme in human history, as an estimated 20 million people were moved from China's cities to rural and remote border regions during the winter of 1968–1969.

One reason for the effectiveness of the movement was its acceptance, for different motives, by assorted groups within the ruling Chinese hierarchy. Moderate leaders in Beijing viewed the scheme as a tactic for ridding urban areas of disruptive Red Guards and other youths. They also saw the program as an opportunity to alleviate the congestion of China's crowded cities, solve the problem of unemployment caused by sluggish economic development, and streamline and rationalize factories, commercial firms, offices, and other enterprises that had become clogged with superfluous employees. At the same time, the Army welcomed the population shift as a chance to decentralize China and strengthen the self-sufficiency of its provinces, thereby reinforcing their capacity to resist an enemy invasion. Concerned mainly with the growing Soviet threat, senior Chinese military strategists particularly emphasized the importance of populating the frontier areas of Xinjiang, Inner Mongolia, and Manchuria.[14] Later, when much of the country's defense system had been restructured around the network of "people's communes" created earlier during the Great Leap Forward, the Chinese boasted that an invader would be confronted "not by one China but by twenty-four thousand Chinas."[15]

Significantly, the *Xiafang* program had Mao's overwhelming support. For it promised to fulfill his lifelong vision of eradicating what his publicists termed the "three disparities" that had traditionally separated workers from peasants, intellectuals from manual laborers, and urban from rural sectors. Until these barriers were obliterated, Mao believed, China could not advance. And, consistent with his faith in peasant revolution, he further held that it was the duty of teachers, students, doctors, engineers, scientists, office employees, officials, and similar "mandarins" to acquire a "proletarian" outlook by soiling their hands in the good earth of China. On December 22, therefore, Mao gave fresh impetus to the *Xiafang* movement by proclaiming that city youths should be "re-educated" by the peasantry. Urging urban residents to send their children to the countryside—and appealing to peasants to accept them—Mao intoned: "Let us mobilize."[16]

Hardly a day passed without the Beijing and provincial press and radio reporting migrations. By February 1969, official Chinese sources claimed, more than two hundred thousand youths had been transferred out of Beijing and, by the end of the year, nearly a half-million "young intellectuals" had migrated from Shanghai to Jiangxi villages, Yunnan labor camps, and Manchurian forestry projects.[17]

The Chinese authorities resorted to all kinds of publicity devices to whip up enthusiasm for the program. An Academy of Sciences employee told an interviewer that she had persuaded her daughter to "live in the countryside until the last day of your life" by describing the sufferings of peasants before the Communists took power.[18] A female engineer from Shenyang was quoted as saying that the rigors of farm life had taught her the futility of her "bourgeois" education.[19] Inevitably, publicists glorified model heroes like Jin Xunhua, a Shanghai student who drowned in an attempt to save "state property" while working on a project in Heilongjiang.[20] Official press agents even resurrected Mao's son Anying, who had died in the Korean War. Returning from school in the Soviet Union in 1946, he volunteered to work as a peasant and, as the story went, proudly announced afterward that he had graduated from a genuine "agricultural college."[21]

In many cities the need to send young people "down to the countryside" was largely dictated by the disruption of the educational system during the Cultural Revolution. The suspension of classes for three and even four years in some places had created a backlog of thousands of students who could no longer make up for lost time since the schools had to make way for new candidates, and for whom there were no jobs. Except for certain specialized defense research-and-development institutes, almost all of China's universities, colleges, primary and secondary schools had ceased to function in the spring of 1966. The lower-level schools began to resume classes in late 1967, but higher institutions only started to operate again in mid-1970—and even then, many still remained paralyzed.[22] The repeated delays in reactivating the universities and colleges were in part due to recurrent ferment in the cities. In part, too, the Chinese leaders encountered difficulties as they sought to implement Mao's reform program, which called for shortened schooling periods, formal studies integrated with physical labor, the elimination of examinations, and other changes designed to destroy the remnants of the rigid, narrow, elitist educational system that had produced the mandarins of ancient China.

In any case, during the Cultural Revolution, China's educational institutions had served primarily as headquarters, dormitories, and fortresses for Red Guard factions. Classes, such as they were, featured little more than genuflection to Maoist doctrine and adoration of the Mao cult. At Dongshi Engineering University in Shanghai, for example, the day began at six in the morning with loudspeakers broadcasting revolutionary songs, after which students devoted most of their classroom hours to chanting Mao's slogans and confessing their "failure" to apply the Chairman's wisdom to their daily life. A visitor to Dongshi in early 1968 was told by students that scholarship was "bourgeois" and "revisionist," since high achievement in examinations represented surrender to "vulgar self-interest."[28] A second-grade Shanghai pupil later recalled that her school day included reciting Mao's proverbs, singing his aphorisms, and dancing to music composed as settings for Mao's quotations. Younger children in her school were assigned to such tasks as counting pills manufactured at a nearby pharmaceutical plant while the older boys and girls were given the privilege of working on farms in the Shanghai suburbs.[24]

For all their excited rhetorical allegiance to the Cultural Revolution, students were not generally enthused by the prospect of rural labor. In Guangzhou, for instance, the local authorities had to take measures to induce—or coerce—young people to leave the city. School committees set up daily indoctrination sessions at which cadres outlined numerous reasons for students to volunteer for farm work.

Among their other arguments, the cadres appealed to patriotism, explaining that the resettlement scheme was of "vital strategic significance" in stiffening China's defenses. In November, Mao Zedong Thought Propaganda Teams conducted a house-to-house campaign, striving to persuade students and their parents that voluntary enlistment was advantageous. Volunteers could select rural areas near Guangzhou, and thus visit their families on holidays. Those who lagged behind or refused soon felt pressure from Army representatives and, virtually forced to comply, they were usually sent to difficult spots like Hainan Island or to distant regions such as Xinjiang or Inner Mongolia. Students reputed to be troublemakers could also expect faraway assignments—and these youths, ironically, included many Red Guards who had been most active during the early stages of the Cultural Revolution in Guangzhou.

Two devices were employed by the municipal authorities to discourage students from attempting to flee back to Guangzhou. Their identity cards, revised to show their new rural address, now prevented them from claiming the city to be their legal residence. And their urban ration cards were canceled, thus precluding them from rice and other food staples if they returned home.[25] Strong resistance to the resettlement program nevertheless came from students and their families as well as from peasants in the regions to which the youths were assigned. In a Gansu province commune, according to an official account, peasants rejected a contingent of city youths on the grounds that they were difficult to manage, lacked farming experience, demanded more food than they deserved and, in sum, represented a "burden."[26] When a trainload of students arrived in one Guangdong commune, peasants simply sent them home. Elsewhere in Guangdong, peasants arrested four students who had accidentally broken farm equipment while working, and charged them with "counterrevolutionary" sabotage.[27] To many youths, the program represented a form of punishment that fit no discernible crime. Reporting on the resettlement of thirty-four thousand city teachers and students in an area of Jiangxi province, a Beijing commentator denounced them for floundering in lethargy, squabbling with peasants, and criticizing rural life as "monotonous and distasteful."[28]

Faced with the prospect of rural exile, several doctors, professors, and professional men in Guangzhou reportedly committed suicide. In a few places, rusticated students were said to have escaped from their assigned communes into mountainous areas to form guerrilla bands, raiding Army posts for weapons and villages for food. More of a problem, however, were youths who made their way back to the cities, where they had no choice but to go underground as virtual outlaws. It was to these youths that newspaper articles and radio broadcasts often referred in their periodic attacks against "juvenile delinquents and hooligans." In the spring of 1970, the Guangzhou authorities would initiate a severe crackdown against them, publicly judging and executing more than a hundred within a one-month period.[29]

Despite its shortcomings and difficulties, the *Xiafang* movement nevertheless scored notable achievements. Among these was the extension of public health services to the countryside by the transfer of thousands of so-called "barefoot doctors" to rural areas. Given a few months of rudimentary medical training, these "doctors" were commissioned to treat common ailments and practice preventive medicine—and one of their key functions was to promote birth-control information and techniques in an effort to curb the growth of China's huge population.[30] The *Xiafang* movement also contributed to the decentralization of China's resources—and this would be especially crucial as the threat of a war with the Soviet Union loomed.

The massive migration was matched during the winter of 1968–1969 by a number of economic experiments somewhat reminiscent of the years during and after the Great Leap Forward. Peasants in a few provinces were deprived of the private gardens they had been granted as a means of stimulating food production after the Great Leap. Several areas also introduced a radical "free supply" system, under which peasant families would receive a large portion of income in the form of food, medical care, education, and essential services.[31] On one hand, these experiments may have reflected an effort on the Army's part to restore the rural controls that had broken down in the course of the Cultural Revolution. At the same time, the ideologues appeared to believe that the moment was ripe for a fresh campaign along the lines of the Great Leap Forward. But the caution with which these innovations were introduced—and the fact that they were limited to only a few regions of the country—indicated that the Beijing leaders were trying to test new policies rather than initiate sweeping changes. Their prudence, then, suggested that they were locked in a debate over economic strategy.

Expressions of an eagerness for grandiose Maoist schemes could be seen in statements by Yao Wenyuan, the radical Shanghai publicist, calling for the unleashing of "social productive forces" in a "vigorous technical revolution."[32] And signs of a revived Great Leap

Forward mentality were also contained in a rash of patently fraudulent production statistics and output targets.[33] In contrast, the moderates publicized their views by reprinting an old essay by Mao, originally published in March 1949, that stressed the virtues of temperance, warned against "blind and haphazard" programs, and insisted that economic growth should proceed "step-by-step." And in strange contrast to the rhetoric of the Cultural Revolution, it urged that the "positive qualities of urban and rural capitalism" be mobilized "as far as possible in the interests of developing the national economy."[34] Mao's essay was significant for another reason. It had been written at the end of the civil war against the Nationalists—and it was now being reprinted at the end of another civil war.

The economic debate was paralleled by a similar political debate. Mao and his associates held a full-scale Central Committee Plenum during late October—their first such session since the hectic days of August 1966—at which they summarily expelled Liu Shaoqi from both his Party and government posts, declaring that he had been thrown "onto the garbage heap of history." They also stated that the Ninth Party Congress, which Mao had hoped to convene much earlier, would be assembled "at an appropriate time" in the near future.[35] Both the dismissal of Liu and the persistent ambiguity shrouding the date of the forthcoming Congress were indicative of differences within the Beijing leadership.

Though they usually adhered strictly to legal form, Mao and his comrades had acted unconstitutionally in their expulsion of Liu from his positions. For under the Party Constitution, he should have been arraigned before a Congress of the Party. Nor could he be officially removed as Chief of State except by the National People's Congress, the rubber-stamp Chinese legislature. Thus it appeared that Mao had moved hastily against Liu out of fear that a trial of his adversary would turn into a protracted, messy spectacle that might exacerbate divisions within the hierarchy.[36]

But legalities made no difference. Following the "struggle sessions" against him in August 1968, Liu Shaoqi was placed under house arrest in Zhongnanhai, the residential district of Beijing reserved for China's leaders, where his health steadily declined. He could barely dress himself, much less walk to the dining room, and his guards flinched at assisting him out of fear that they might be accused of aiding a "renegade, hidden traitor, and scab," as Mao's propagandists called him. Suffering from diabetes and denied medicine, he grew worse. His teeth fell out and his hands trembled, and, unable to get out of bed, he lay in the stench of his own excrement. Doctors summoned to treat him suggested that he be hospitalized, but their proposal was rejected. Nevertheless, he was kept alive, fed through a tube in his nose, until the Central Committee formally expelled him from the Communist Party in November 1968. Nearly a year afterward, still living, he was flown to a prison in the city of Kaifeng, where, lying on a concrete floor, he succumbed to pneumonia. His body was secretly taken to a nearby crematorium and registered under the pseudonym of Liu Weihuang, the cause of death listed as "illness." Not for three years was his family told of his fate; five years later, his children were given a shabby box containing ashes that may not have been his. Thus disappeared one of the founders of the Chinese Communist Party, the nation's Chief of State, and its most conscientious bureaucrat.[37]

Liu's wife, Wang Guangmei, somehow survived. In September 1968, after defying the Red Guards, she was placed in solitary confinement in a prison near Beijing, where she spent the next twelve years under a suspended sentence of death. When her children were finally permitted to visit her, they found her bent and emaciated. At first she looked at them blankly. Then, like numbers of Chinese mothers who had feared for their children during the Cultural Revolution, she said: "I never dreamed you would live."[38]

In October 1967, discussing plans for the Ninth Congress, Xie Fuzhi had candidly stated that delegates would be appointed by the central authorities in Beijing in order to "guarantee" that the radicals would "be in the majority" and hence assure a Maoist success.[39] Now, however, the Army-dominated Provincial Revolutionary Committees were determined to designate the delegates, making it almost certain that representatives dedicated to moderation would be pre-eminent. That the Provincial Committees intended to control the radicals was apparent in various statements demanding that "intellectuals"—a term synonymous with Red Guards and other student activists—must accept the leadership of workers, peasants, and, of course, soldiers. Replying to Red Guards in Henan province who were seeking representation, for example, the local Revolutionary Committee asserted:

Can you represent the working class? No! Absolutely not! You vainly attempt to vie for leadership power with the working class. This shows that you do not resemble the working class in the slightest. On the contrary, by resisting the leadership of the working class, you are representing the

interests of the bourgeoisie, the extremely reactionary bourgeois authorities and the landlords, rich peasants, bad elements, counterrevolutionaries
and rightists. . . . Improperly reformed intellectuals and scholars belong
to the petty bourgeoisie. They can by no means become the leading force
of the proletarian revolution.[40]

The dispossessed radicals, in the meantime, were protesting with
increasing vehemence against their exclusion. In many places, they
inveighed against what they called "the restoration of the old"—
implying that veteran Army commanders and Party bureaucrats supposed to have been purged in the Cultural Revolution had instead
regained power or never lost it.[41] As usual, the loudest complaints
came from Shanghai. In one editorial, the city's foremost newspaper
pointed out that many Revolutionary Committees were "composed
entirely of former personnel," while the Red Guards and other "new
proletarians" had been "squeezed out like toothpaste from a tube."[42]
Another article criticized officials who were concerned only with "production" and "labor discipline," warning that such attitudes threatened to sabotage the drive to convert the Party into "a militant,
vigorous and vital organization of vanguards."[43] Therefore, the Shanghai radicals insisted, the new Party should be built on a "crash priority
basis," with its ranks open to "outstanding revolutionary rebel fighters
who have been tested in the fires of the Cultural Revolution."[44]

Much of the debate over representation in the future Party re-
volved around a declaration that Mao had issued not long before.
Comparing the Party to a human being, he had warned that it
would lack vigor unless "it eliminated waste and absorbed fresh
blood."[45] To the radicals, "fresh blood" signified the Red Guards.[46]
To the military commanders and old *apparatchiks*, the Party's "fresh
blood" would be "primarily the advanced elements among industrial
workers."[47]

By the spring of 1969, the debate had been more or less resolved
in favor of cohesion and stability. Beijing directives urged that "class
struggle" be dampened, emphasizing that "the target of attack must
be narrowed and more people must be helped through education."[48]
Key editorials stressed the importance of pragmatic economic and
social policies, quoting Mao's latest instruction that planning and
production be pursued with "enough leeway" to permit flexibility.[49]
And still another epitaph was written for the Red Guards. They had
made "tremendous contributions" but, as "intellectuals," they "often
vacillate and lack a thoroughgoing revolutionary spirit." Therefore,

said the *People's Daily*, they must "overcome their weaknesses" by "integrating themselves with the masses of workers and peasants."[50]

The Ninth National Congress of the Chinese Communist Party, which finally did open on April 1, 1969, eight months later than Mao had anticipated, was unique in many ways. In violation of the Party Constitution, which called for a new Congress every five years, it was the first such conference to be held in more than a decade. In contrast to past Party conclaves, it was closed to foreign Communist observers. And unlike previous Party Congresses, which merely ratified decisions reached beforehand, the April meeting seemed to have been organized without careful preparation—as if the Beijing leaders, impatient after repeated delays, felt that they could wait no longer.

Various indications testified to hasty preparation. The unusually large size of the Congress—more than fifteen hundred delegates were present—suggested that the selection process had not been easy. The fact that the Congress dragged on for twenty-four days reflected the difficulties encountered by delegates as they worked to choose the new Central Committee. In addition, the Central Committee was greatly expanded, perhaps as a result of compromises.

The principal speeches at the Congress and at the Central Committee Plenum that followed were less than inspiring. Mao's address to the Central Committee seemed defensive, and Lin Biao's Political Report failed to have an immediate impact. Delivered on April 1, it underwent two weeks of discussion before its adoption and was not finally published until April 27.

As one perceptive observer has noted, Lin Biao's performance was essentially an attempt to reconcile what happened in the Cultural Revolution with what should have happened.[51] In short, it sought to provide a rationale for Mao's campaign, whose origin Lin traced back to the mid-1950s. At that time, he said, Mao had observed two disturbing trends: one was the growth of a Chinese Party bureaucracy that was increasingly "divorced from the masses," and threatening to stifle their "revolutionary initiative." The other was Khrushchev's abrupt doctrinal switch at the Soviet Union's Twentieth Party Congress, which revealed the "rampancy of revisionism in the international Communist movement," convincing Mao that the struggle between capitalism and socialism was "still not really solved."

The relationship between these two trends, in Mao's view, was that China would degenerate into Soviet-style "revisionism" unless he intervened. Thus, Lin Biao recalled, Mao delivered his celebrated speech in 1956 on "contradictions among the people," in which he tried to define the nature of the real enemy. Implicit in this thesis was the assumption that the people would rally to his cause if liberated from bureaucratic restraint. That assumption prompted him to initiate a series of nationwide campaigns designed to revitalize the different sectors of Chinese society. But each effort ended in disappointment.

Lin Biao described how Mao had pitted the intellectuals against the Party in the "Hundred Flowers" episode, only to find that the intellectuals themselves were tainted with "bourgeois rightism." He launched the Great Leap Forward in an attempt to release peasant energies, only to discover that peasants responded more enthusiastically to free enterprise than to his appeals for self-sacrifice. He initiated the Socialist Education campaign in 1962 in an effort to purify low-level Party officials, only to be confronted by their determination to preserve their ossified, corrupt bureaucracy.

Still clinging to his faith in the "masses," Mao concluded that the real culprits were entrenched in the upper echelons of the Party apparatus. His final strategy, then, was to mobilize the "masses" against Liu Shaoqi and the *apparatchiks*—which he did by unleashing the Red Guards. In a hitherto unknown speech delivered in February 1967, Lin Biao disclosed, Mao had outlined the process that led him to launch the Cultural Revolution:

> In the past, we waged struggles in the rural areas, in factories, in the cultural field, and we carried out the Socialist Education movement. But all this failed to solve the problem because we did not find a form, a method, to arouse the broad masses to expose our dark aspect openly, in an all-round way and from below. The answer was the Great Proletarian Cultural Revolution.

When Lin Biao turned to the events of the Cultural Revolution itself, however, he was less precise. Mao had been almost as confused as everyone else by the turmoil, he concluded, explaining that intractable heretics became "mixed up" with misguided sinners, and it was "hard to sort them out." Amid the chaotic "twists and reversals" of the Cultural Revolution, Lin implied, the opposition to Mao had changed. The Red Guards who had represented Mao's "revolutionary successors" in the summer of 1966 became a "reactionary evil wind" a year later, when they went on uncontrollable rampages. As a consequence, Lin said, Mao switched his trust to the "working class," saying it with mangoes.

That switch had taken place eight months earlier, yet Lin closed his account without suggesting whether the "working class" had yet fulfilled Mao's trust. His assertion that the Cultural Revolution had resulted in a "great victory" indicated that the upheavals of the past four years were formally finished. Yet, Lin hinted, Mao's optimism in the power of the "masses" remained unquenched. When he had asked Mao what to do "if bad people go wild again," the Chairman had replied that he would "just arouse the masses and strike them down."

Though his Report had been advertised in advance as a "great program" to guide China's "production," Lin devoted only two paragraphs to the economy, and these offered little more than vague generalities. He appealed for "new leaps forward" in economic output. But stressing that "production would not be replaced by revolution," he made it clear that there would not be another Great Leap Forward of the kind that had disrupted China in 1958. He emphasized the importance of economic moderation, reiterating that agriculture would take precedence over industrial development. The guarantor of temperance was, of course, the Army, which Lin again described as "the mighty pillar of the dictatorship of the proletariat." As for the Communist Party, it still required major reform—and that task would be a key challenge in the years ahead.[52]

The deliberately muted tone of Lin Biao's Report was matched by Mao's equally sober statement. Speaking to the new Central Committee at its first Plenum on April 28, he focused on the need for unity and, though justifying the Cultural Revolution, he almost apologized for its excesses. "You must operate with discretion," he told the new Party leaders, pointing out that brutality and indiscriminate arrests compounded rather than rectified "mistakes." There were conflicts between and within groups, between the Army and civilian organization, and inside military units. But most of these were "internal contradictions among the people" rather than "antagonistic" differences between the people and their implacable enemies, Mao said, therefore they could be resolved. The Party was large and flexible enough to tolerate divergent opinions as long as "people of all circles unite," Mao concluded, again underlining that "our goal is solidarity that will strengthen the dictatorship of the proletariat."[53]

One of the principal documents to emerge from the Ninth Congress was a new Party Constitution. The document had been drafted either in late 1967 or early 1968 by a ten-man commission headed by Zhang Chunqiao and Yao Wenyuan, the radical Shanghai leaders, and it was afterward circulated in Beijing and throughout the provinces for comments before its adoption by the Congress. Predictably, it contrasted drastically with the 1956 Constitution, which had been the product of a highly structured Party apparatus. Influenced by de-Stalinization in the Soviet Union, the 1956 document had been careful to avoid any hint of devotion to the "cult of personality," emphasizing instead the Party's collective leadership. The new Constitution changed all that. It equated Mao's doctrine with Marxism-Leninism as the "theoretical basis" of China's political, social, economic, and military policies.* Moreover, it confirmed Lin Biao's status as Mao's "close comrade-in-arms and successor." Conforming to Mao's preoccupation with "spiritual" renovation, the new Constitution also dropped the passage in the 1956 document that had called for the "gradual and continuous improvement of the living conditions of the people," stressing instead the necessity for protracted "class struggle." Absent from the new Constitution as well was the Party's table of organization, such as had been detailed at length in the 1956 charter. And among its other contents, the new Constitution denounced Russian "revisionism"—a notable switch from the 1956 reference to the Soviet Union as the leader of international communism.[54]

In essence, then, the new Constitution was more an impressionistic political platform than a durable code of laws, and its amorphousness seemed to have been intended to negate the existence of a Party bureaucracy. But its very fuzziness appeared to suit the Army commanders controlling most of China. For they would not be restricted by sharp definitions of their authority and could, consequently, exercise their power with considerable flexibility. Thus the Politburo and Central Committee elected by the Ninth Party Congress simply ratified the Army's predominance, while it elevated several regional commanders who had been the targets of Red Guard attacks during the Cultural Revolution.

Mao, of course, remained Chairman of the Central Committee, with Lin Biao as his deputy. And they, along with Zhou Enlai, Chen Boda, and Kang Sheng, comprised the Politburo Standing Committee. The new Politburo also featured prominent Maoists like Jiang Qing and the two Shanghai radicals Zhang Chunqiao and Yao Wenyuan, as well as Lin Biao's wife, Ye Qun, and Mao's former bodyguard,

* Mao's elevation to the Communist pantheon was marked by the omission of the hyphen in the English transliteration of his name, which now became Mao Zedong in official documents. This permitted the slogan Marxism-Leninism—Mao Zedong Thought. In Chinese, however, the characters Ze and Dong remained distinct.

Wang Dongxing. Most significant, however, was the rise of Army representation in the ruling body. Three old Marshals—Zhu De, Liu Bocheng, and Ye Jianying—regained their former places on the Politburo, but among the new military faces were such men as Huang Yongsheng, Chief of General Staff; Chen Xilian, commander of Manchuria; Xu Shiyou, senior officer in central China; Li Zuopeng, Navy political commissar; Wu Faxian, the Air Force commander; Li Desheng, Army chief of Anhui province; and Qiu Huizuo, head of the Army's Logistics Department. The Politburo also included one old Party official, Li Xuefeng, now Chairman of the Hebei Revolutionary Committee.[55]

Almost twice the size of its predecessor, the new Central Committee contained two hundred seventy-nine full and alternate members, and, like the provincial Revolutionary Committees, it was overwhelmingly weighted in favor of Army officers and Party cadres who had survived the Cultural Revolution. Indeed, the Red Guards ended up with derisory treatment. Two of Jiang Qing's female firebrands, the Beijing University activist Nie Yuanzi and Zhang Xiting of Sichuan, were elected only as alternates. In contrast, figures like You Qiuli, the Minister of Petroleum Industry who had been desperately defended against radical assaults by Zhou Enlai, rose to full membership. Another sign that very few drops of "fresh blood" had been infused was that the average age of its full members was fifty-nine, and most had been affiliated with the Party before the Communists attained power in 1949.[56]

But the new central hierarchy would not endure for long. In the summer of 1970, apparently seeking to eliminate the radicals who had become prominent during the Cultural Revolution, the Beijing leaders were to purge Chen Boda, who had guided the Maoist campaign. A year after that, no less a figure than Lin Biao was dismissed. With him fell Huang Yongsheng, Wu Faxian, Li Zuopeng, and Qiu Huizuo, all generals and members of the Politburo. Unlike Liu Shaoqi and the Party *apparatchiks*, whose lives were spared during the Cultural Revolution, these men were reportedly liquidated in a short but bitter power struggle that reached its climax in the autumn of 1971.

Nor did the establishment of a new leadership structure at the top automatically bring stability to the Chinese provinces. Though nothing in the period following the Ninth Party Congress resembled the turmoil of the two preceding years, a number of incidents nevertheless erupted in various parts of the country, most of them the result of resistance by Red Guards and other youths to military efforts to impose law and order. In Fujian province, for example, students clashed with soldiers striving to deport them to the countryside and, on one occasion in August, several participants were killed in a skirmish.[57] The biggest outbreak during the summer occurred in the Shanxi province capital of Taiyuan, where Liu Geping, Chairman of the Revolutionary Committee, was challenged by General Zhang Riqing, a local Army political commissar. Their rivalry ignited factional fighting of the kind that had nagged the province before and, on July 20, troops surrounded the city, issuing an ultimatum to its opposing groups to cease their conflict. Liu and Zhang were then invited to Beijing to resolve their differences, but their compromise settlement remained tenuous.[58]

Apparently convinced that the Ninth Party Congress had spelled the end of the Cultural Revolution, the Revolutionary Committees showed confidence as they initiated measures to restore or maintain discipline around the country. In Shaanxi province, they mobilized "command groups" to scour factories, schools, and rural communes for cases of disobedience and, in the Hunan capital of Changsha, they organized mass meetings to denounce "class enemies" suspected of fomenting trouble. The civilian vigilante movement in Guangzhou known as the Workers' Provost Corps was reinforced by other amateur police outfits, among them the Little Red Sentinels, schoolchildren assigned to spy on citizens and perform other minor security jobs.[59] A new wave of public trials and executions also began, with most of those singled out for punishment accused of "ultraleftism." More than forty persons were sentenced to death in Guangzhou on March 10, and similar trials were held about the same time in Beijing and other cities.[60] In a few instances, those convicted seemed to be the victims of old clan feuds, family vendettas, and personal grudges. In Fujian province, for example, an aged dentist and his son were executed for having raped a local woman twenty years before.[61] That incident, underlining as it did the length of the Chinese memory, suggested that the social tensions generated by the Cultural Revolution might remain fresh long after a surface appearance of calm had returned to China.

The authorities in many areas also now began to compel Red Guards and other agitators to compensate for the damage they caused at the outset of the Cultural Revolution, when they had responded to Mao's exhortations to smash "feudal" and "bourgeois" vestiges throughout China. A Guangzhou schoolteacher whose five sons and daughters had been Red Guards was required to pay the equivalent of a year's salary to cover the cost of "feudal" antiques and "reactionary" books destroyed by his children. A former Red Guard from Guandong recounted that he had been billed by the provincial apparatus for 600 *yuan* in expenses he had incurred in Beijing, Shanghai, and Chongqing while "exchanging revolutionary experiences" during the fall of 1966. The itemized bill included the precise costs of food, lodging, and travel, and the youth, who fled to Hong Kong to escape his creditors, expressed amazement that the Chinese accounting system had functioned so efficiently during that chaotic period.[62]

Further evidence of moderation was seen on October 1, 1969, in the Beijing celebrations marking the twentieth anniversary of the Chinese People's Republic. Striving to publicize their preoccupation with unity, the Beijing leaders displayed several figures who had been denounced during the Cultural Revolution, among them the liberal economist Chen Yun, Marshals Xu Xiangqian and Nie Rongzhen, Foreign Minister Chen Yi, and Madame Sun Yat-sen.[63] Conspicuously absent from the list of twenty-nine official slogans was the familiar exhortation to "carry the Cultural Revolution to the end." The accent was on "socialist revolution" and, in his keynote speech, Zhou Enlai modestly praised China's "rudimentary prosperity" and called for a "new high tide in industrial and agricultural production, culture, and art."[64]

The new sobriety was especially pronounced in efforts to recuperate the lost economic momentum of the mid-1960s. An important *People's Daily* editorial published in November, for example, offered an assortment of pragmatic recommendations for improving working methods. Among other proposals, it urged economic officials to plan carefully, reminding them that "experience gained in selected units cannot be spread to the whole area at once." The editorial also insisted that labor be given time to relax, and it advised cadres to cease wasting days in marathon political rallies and preparing long reports, saying that "meetings, documents, and forms should be drastically cut down and simplified."[65] Matching this revival of pragmatism, *Red Flag* even went so far as to suggest that China might accept foreign aid and learn from "good foreign experience," provided it could "keep the initiative in its own hands."[66] Later directives would also stress the importance of technical skills and even material incentives, once considered to be "revisionist."

This changed attitude was illustrated as well at Guangzhou's International Trade Fair held in the fall of 1969. Before, foreign trade representatives visiting the biennial fair had been nagged constantly by songs, speeches, and meetings extolling Mao and the Cultural Revolution, and several had even joined in the ferment in hopes of pleasing the Chinese. But now, when a Swedish importer tried to engage a Chinese commercial specialist in an ideological discussion, the official cut him short, saying: "We're here to talk business, not politics."[67]

Amid all these shifts, however, China's leaders still faced the gigantic task of rebuilding the decimated Chinese Communist Party. One problem complicating this effort was the reluctance of former officials to participate in the renovated Party apparatus. In many areas, officials continued to be harassed by remnant radicals who claimed prominent places in the new Party machine. At the same time, persistent struggles for power by rival factions impeded the establishment of Party Committees, even at the lowest echelons. This struggle for power was paralleled at the highest level by a growing dispute between groups headed by Zhou Enlai on the one hand, and Lin Biao on the other. Not until September 19, 1969—nearly five months after the end of the Ninth Congress—did the first regional Party Committee materialize, and it was merely at the level of a commune in Hunan province, Mao's birthplace.[68] More than a year would pass before the first provincial Committee emerged, again in Hunan. Even by then, fewer than a hundred of China's two thousand counties had succeeded in forming Committees.[69]

In December 1969, endeavoring to speed up the process of Party reconstruction, Beijing publicized the ideal procedure recommended for emulation throughout China, selecting as its model the Committee set up in the printing plant of the New China News Agency in the national capital. At the start, former cadres, "outstanding" workers, and soldiers at the plant created a Revolutionary Committee whose function was to unify the employees, then divided by "bourgeois factionalism, sectarianism, mountain-stronghold mentality, and anarchism." Unity was largely achieved, the report claimed, by an intensive campaign to persuade the plant officials and staff to confess their "errors" and pledge to mend their ways. But the key role in this operation was played by an Army unit that had apparently assumed the direction of the plant in the summer of 1968. Moreover, the report divulged, Army officers would continue to exercise authority in the plant as members of both the Revolutionary Committee and the new Party Committee.[70]

This pattern of military predominance was dutifully applied to the

Party Committees germinating in the provinces. A Party-building conference held in the Henan province capital of Zhengzhou proclaimed: "The Army is the chief component of the State, and its strength determines the degree of consolidation of political power."[71] Fresh directives made it clear that the Red Guards and other radical activists would be given minimal functions, if any, in the new Party Committees. An official announcement from Guangdong province stated that "revolutionary mass representatives" were being barred from working sessions of an embryonic county Committee in order to curb their "unnecessary upper-level activities."[72] In early January, the Beijing leadership dealt a severe blow to the radicals with a decision denying them any real position in the new Party apparatus. The decision, contained in a *Red Flag* editorial, was couched as a reply to elements claiming to be "most revolutionary and most advanced" and demanding pre-eminence in the reformed Party:

> This idea is extremely wrong. . . . Some comrades have come to regard themselves as "most revolutionary and most advanced" because they had made some contributions during the Great Proletarian Cultural Revolution. This shows that they fail to view themselves correctly, and lack the spirit to remold themselves. Others have desperately exaggerated the role of the former organizations, incorrectly handled relations between the mass organizations and the Party, and tried to put themselves above the Party in an attempt to challenge its leadership. This is an expression of reactionary anarchism.[73]

Most significantly, the *Red Flag* editorial went on to negate a fundamental tenet of Mao's doctrine. To rely on the Red Guards and other radicals as the "foundation" of the new Party, it said, would be to "reduce" the Communist apparatus from a "vanguard" movement to simply "the level of a mass organization." This portrayal of the Party as the "vanguard" effectively sounded the death knell of Mao's ideological aspirations. For, by returning to the Leninist concept of the Party as an "elitist" hierarchy, it subverted his dream of perpetual revolution in a society free of bureaucratic routine. In short, if Mao's misty vision of a Chinese equivalent of the Paris Commune had died during the Cultural Revolution, it was now being unceremoniously buried.

The last of the new Party Committees were finally established in late August 1971, twenty-one months after the first new provincial apparatus had been set up in Hunan, and the Army's predominance throughout the country was dramatic. Twenty of the twenty-nine First

Secretaries were military officers, and all but one of the nine civilian Committee heads concurrently assumed positions as political commissars of provincial military commands. Of the one hundred fifty-eight Committee leaders down to the rank of Deputy Secretary, nearly 60 per cent were soldiers, 25 per cent civilian *apparatchiks,* and only about 5 per cent radicals who had emerged during the Cultural Revolution. The exception to this pattern was Shanghai, where the new Party Committee was headed by Zhang Chunqiao and his deputy, Yao Wenyuan. But as Politburo members, these men spent most of their time in Beijing, leaving the administration of Shanghai to two subordinates—an Army officer and a veteran Party cadre.[74]

Another indication of the Army's pre-eminence was to be found in the slowness of Party reconstruction, which was largely due to the refusal of radicals to submit to military domination. In Tibet, one of the last areas to form a Committee, a serious dispute had developed between General Ren Rong, the Army commissar, and General Zeng Yongya, the military commander and Chairman of Tibet's Revolutionary Committee. Zeng had apparently shifted to the left, and he was ousted three months before the Party Committee emerged under General Ren's leadership. Another late-forming Committee, in Heilongjiang, was delayed by a fight in which General Wang Zhaidao, the local Army commander, ousted Pan Fusheng, the former province boss. In contrast, the areas that established Committees most rapidly were those where military authority had been preponderant from the start—such as Jiangsu, Anhui, and Zhejiang, all of them under the jurisdiction of the Nanjing Military Region commanded by General Xu Shiyou, a Politburo member and one of China's senior officers. Similarly, the early formation of Party Committees in Hunan and Guangdong testified to the power of the Guangzhou Military Region and its former boss, General Huang Yongsheng.

Along with being a vehicle for the Army's authority, the new Committees also featured veteran Party figures who had dropped from public view during the Cultural Revolution and no doubt underwent "thought reform" before staging a comeback. One such figure was Zhuo Ziyang, former First Secretary of the old Guangdong province Party Committee. Initially denounced by Red Guards in Guangzhou in January 1967, he was purged the next month and disappeared not long afterward. By mid-1971, however, he had been resurrected in a senior capacity on the Inner Mongolia Party Committee. Similarly, the former First Secretary in Hunan, Zheng Binghua, reappeared on the Shanxi Party Committee, and Tan Qilong, who had been dismissed as Communist boss of Shandong, surfaced four years later in a key post in Fujian province.[75]

Nothing vindicated these "bourgeois revisionists" more vividly, however, than the eventual humiliation of one of the Cultural Revolution's foremost activists, Chen Boda. Mao's private secretary and chief ideological counselor since Yenan days, Chen had managed the Cultural Revolution Directorate from its inception, capping his rise in influence with membership in the Politburo's supreme Standing Committee. But if his record was pure by Maoist standards, it evidently appeared spotty to the Army commanders and Party officials who now had assumed control over China. Like so many of those he had helped to eliminate, Chen fell from public sight in the summer of 1970 and, ten months later, hints emerged to indicate that he was in serious trouble. On May 25, 1971, for example, a Beijing journal reached back into history to assail the author of an essay written nearly forty years before as a "sham Marxist." The journal did not identify the author by name, but it was Chen Boda.[76] Not long afterward, in an editorial marking the fiftieth anniversary of the Chinese Communist Party, *Red Flag* denounced "the type of person who claims to be a 'humble little commoner' but is actually a big careerist."[77] The reference, though esoteric, was plain to Beijing insiders. In a speech delivered on April 13, 1967, Jiang Qing had described Chen as a "humble little commoner"—and she depicted herself as an "even smaller one."[78]

A more dramatic—and still largely mysterious—episode unfolded late in the summer of 1971. On the night of September 12, a British-built Trident jet airliner belonging to the Chinese Air Force crashed about a hundred miles inside the People's Republic of Mongolia, a satellite of the Soviet Union. The seven men and two women aboard were killed, their bodies charred beyond recognition. At the same time, a helicopter that had taken off from Beijing's Qinghua University campus in an apparently desperate attempt to reach the Mongolian border was forced down. All but one of its occupants committed suicide.

The Beijing authorities immediately grounded all air traffic throughout China. They also let it be known that the National Day celebrations marking the twenty-second anniversary of the Communist rise to power, scheduled to be held on October 1, would be canceled. Soon afterward, almost unbelievable tales of intrigue and conspiracy began to be heard inside China.

Confidential documents circulated among Party officials related that Lin Biao, his wife, Ye Zhun, and their son Lin Liguo, an Air Force officer, had been killed in the crash of the Trident along with General Huang Yongsheng, Chief of General Staff; General Wu Faxian, the Air Force commander; and General Li Zuopeng, chief commissar of the Navy. The documents alleged that Lin Biao had attempted unsuccessfully on three occasions to assassinate Mao—the last time in early September by ordering a senior officer in central China to bomb a train carrying the Chairman from Nanjing to Beijing. The officer refused and, according to the account, informed the Beijing leadership of Lin's plot. As the story went, Lin was also betrayed by his daughter, whose nickname "Doudou," meaning "beans," stood for her father's favorite dish. Fearing arrest, the documents continued, Lin and his fellow conspirators commandeered the Trident in an effort to escape to the Soviet Union. But the aircraft crashed, either for lack of fuel or because of bad weather.

Though fascinating, those details of Lin's attempted escape and death were probably fabricated. Both Soviet and Mongolian investigation teams examined the remains of the crashed Trident, reporting that its occupants all seemed to have been below the age of fifty. The teams further reported that some of the bodies contained bullet holes, and speculated that a fight could have taken place aboard the aircraft. This suggested that the Trident, one of four such airplanes purchased by China from Pakistan and used exclusively by high-ranking Chinese officers, may have been the scene of a clash between rivals—some trying to flee the country and others striving to prevent their flight. The helicopter that attempted to take off from Qinghua University no doubt carried other potential defectors.

But whether or not Lin Biao and his comrades were victims of the crash, the fact that the Beijing authorities asserted that they were killed was significant. For it indicated that they were dead—perhaps from other causes. They may have been shot in an abortive bid for power.[79]

One of the earliest hints that Lin Biao was slipping into disfavor with Mao was communicated in a strangely esoteric form. During the summer, Jiang Qing distributed a collection of photographs that she had purportedly taken. A portrait of Lin showed him hatless and almost completely bald—a condition about which he was known to be extremely sensitive.[80] By autumn, it was clear that Lin and his associates had been defeated in some kind of power play. Lin dropped out of sight after having last been seen publicly at a Beijing reception for Rumanian President Nicolae Ceaucescu on June 3, and foreign embassies in the capital were later instructed by Chinese protocol officials to cease mentioning his name in toasts and congratulatory messages.[81] Veiled attacks against him also became apparent in official Chinese newspaper articles and radio broadcasts.

On October 20, for instance, Beijing Radio quoted a passage by the writer Lu Xun, who died in the 1930s, that seemed to mirror Mao's chagrin toward the man he had designated as his "close comrade-in-arms" and heir. "The enemy is nothing to fear," it said. "What hurt and disappointed me most was the sinister arrow fired by my ally, and his smiling face after I was wounded."[82] An analogous theme was featured in another broadcast that appeared to equate Lin's alleged opposition to Mao with Khrushchev's betrayal of Stalin. Khrushchev had "pretentiously praised" Stalin while the Soviet dictator was alive but "viciously denounced" him after his death, the broadcast said. It warned against those who "pretend to be good people but actually commit evil deeds," and, describing them as "sham Marxists," it called them the "most dangerous, ferocious, and wicked enemies of the dictatorship of the proletariat."[83] A spate of other articles and broadcasts also assailed Lin obliquely by harking back to his portrayal of Mao as the "genius of the world revolution." The implication here was that Lin, as Mao's successor, was claiming to have inherited the right to be considered as infallible as the Chairman. Or as a *People's Daily* editorial put it: "By pretending to acclaim someone else as a genius, renegades from the Communist movement present themselves as 'geniuses.'"[84]

If one pieces together the available evidence, the dispute between Lin Biao's group and the faction headed by Mao and Zhou Enlai was apparently confined to Beijing, and did not, therefore, augur another nationwide upheaval of the kind that erupted during the Cultural Revolution. It was, in short, essentially a limited power struggle at the leadership level—even though its outcome would determine the future course of China as a whole.

Some analysts have contended that the quarrel represented a continuation of the conflict between professional soldiers and political commissars that had long plagued the Chinese Communist Army. This conflict reached a peak during the Cultural Revolution, when the commissars tended to side with the radicals against the professionals, who sought to maintain law and order. According to this thesis, Lin Biao tried to perpetuate the authority of the commissars in the provincial Party committees being reconstructed after the Cultural Revolution. His objective was to reinforce his own power, which he had built up since his emergence as Defense Minister in 1959. But he was opposed by Zhou Enlai and the regional commanders, who worked to put the new Party machine under the control of an alliance of civilians and professional soldiers. Their aim was to prevent another Cultural Revolution, which they believed would cause irreparable damage to China.

Lin Biao apparently reached the height of his power in April 1969, when he managed to have himself appointed Mao's official successor in the new Party Constitution. After that, however, his position was slowly undermined by Zhou and his supporters among the professional officers. In late 1969, for example, the Army's General Political Department, which had traditionally been headed by a commissar, came under the tutelage of General Li Desheng, a veteran commander. During the following year, almost all the commissars in charge of provincial Revolutionary Committees were removed.[85] And in August 1970, the radicals were further weakened with the purge of Chen Boda.

By the middle of 1971, the renovated Party was strenuously working to impose its authority over the Army elements inspired by Lin Biao that still sought to exercise power. Time and again, reflecting this effort, the official Beijing media asserted that placing the Army "under the absolute leadership of the Party" was imperative. Propaganda also publicized a song entitled "Three Main Rules of Discipline and Eight Points for Attention," which stressed the need for soldiers to obey the Party. Lin Biao and his comrades presumably tried to resist, and the showdown between them and Zhou Enlai's faction apparently arose as the Chinese leaders approached the convocation of a National People's Congress to select a new Chief of State to replace the dismissed Liu Shaoqi. Fearing that Lin would attempt to grab that post, Zhou evidently moved to block him.

The quarrel was probably complicated by a dispute over the allocation of China's meager resources. Judging from the evidence, Zhou and the regional commanders favored investment in industry and agriculture. They also sought to concentrate on support for the Chinese Army's ground forces. Lin Biao and his comrades, among them the heads of the Air Force and Navy, apparently advocated a larger focus on the development of sophisticated weapons.

Underlying this debate over budgetary questions was the issue of China's foreign policy at the outset of the 1970s. Zhou and his group were plainly partial to a *rapprochement* with the United States as a way of countering the growing Soviet threat to China. Lin and his colleagues were not entirely opposed to that strategy. But they must have argued that a reconciliation with the United States might provoke the Russians, and thus they contended that the Chinese armed forces be fortified for the possibility of a pre-emptive Soviet attack. When their views were rejected, they may well have attempted to balance Zhou's move toward the United States by seeking a *détente* with the Kremlin. After their purge, official propaganda excoriated them as "bourgeois careerists and conspirators having illicit relations with foreign countries."[86] The phrase had been used in 1959 to describe Peng Dehuai. Now, ironically, it was being used against Lin Biao, who had succeeded Peng as Defense Minister.

How this conflict reached its climax may one day be elucidated. By early 1972, it was only clear that Zhou and his group had won.

Mao undoubtedly watched the squabble from the sidelines, finally swinging over to the victor. But his own prestige could not have gone unscathed. Just as he had earlier extolled Liu Shaoqi and afterward found him to be a traitor, now he had been betrayed by Lin Biao, the man he had hand-picked as his heir. The omniscient deity had proved to be fallible.

By 1971, then, Mao's second revolution had devoured its most prestigious offspring, and China was moving in a direction that would have been considered unthinkable only a few years before. The direction was toward *rapprochement* with the United States, and Beijing was steering a triangulated course.

CHAPTER 21

Rejoining the World

❦

How to give "tit for tat" depends on the situation. Sometimes, not going to negotiations is tit for tat; and sometimes, going to negotiations is tit for tat.
— MAO ZEDONG, *October 17, 1945*

ON THE NIGHT OF July 15, 1971, in a brief television address, President Richard Nixon revealed that he had accepted an invitation from Premier Zhou Enlai to visit Beijing at an "appropriate date" within the next ten months. The purpose of his "journey for peace," as the President termed it, was not only "to seek the normalization of relations" between the United States and China, but "also to exchange views on questions of concern" to both countries. He expressed his "profound conviction" that "all nations will gain from a reduction of tensions and a better relationship between the United States and the People's Republic of China."[1] Less than seven months later, Nixon arrived in Beijing, and his week of discussions there put Sino-American relations on a totally new course.

That sensational sequence of events would have been impossible four years earlier, when Mao Zedong and his comrades were encouraging Red Guards to storm foreign embassies and assault foreign diplomats in Beijing, and China appeared to be receding into the xenophobic isolation that had characterized its attitudes toward the world in centuries past. The willingness of China's rulers to negotiate with the "ugly imperialist chieftain," as their publicists had portrayed Nixon, illustrated the degree to which the fanaticism of the Cultural Revolution had evaporated. It also dramatized the rise of Zhou Enlai and the Army commanders, who had long advocated sobriety in the interests of China's foreign relations.

Yet this stunning switch did not signify any fundamental reversal of the Chinese leaders' long-range aspirations and ambitions. As dynamic Communists, they still clung to their faith in the inevitability of world revolution. As Chinese, they were still determined to defend their nation's security, retrieve its lost territories, and win it international recognition as a major power. What had essentially changed was their tactics. Diplomatic tractability now promised to be more effective than intransigence. As usual, they found the ideological rationale for the new approach in one of Mao's apothegms: "Our principles must be firm. We must also employ all permissible and necessary flexibility to serve our principles."[2]

The Chinese leaders saw this tactical flexibility working to their advantage on a number of foreign-policy issues. For one, a thaw in their frozen relations with the United States would dilute American support for Chiang Kai-shek's regime on Taiwan, thereby inducing elements among the Nationalists to concede to an accommodation with Beijing. They estimated as well that a Sino-American *détente* might prevent the rearmament of Japan and, in particular, forestall the development of a Japanese nuclear arsenal. Motivating their effort to achieve a modus vivendi with the United States, too, was their hope of playing a role in Southeast Asia following the withdrawal of American forces from Indochina. And finally, they viewed a *rapprochement* with Washington as a unique opportunity to counter the Kremlin. They had come close to war with the Russians in 1969, and even though a full-scale conflict was averted, the Chinese were by no means certain that the Soviet threat had abated.

All these foreign-policy issues were crucial to the Chinese, but the most urgent concerned their dispute with the Soviet Union—a quarrel that had its origins in a wide range of ideological, national, economic, and even racial differences. An important ingredient in Beijing's fear of the Soviet Union was the primacy of Inner Asia in traditional Chinese strategic thinking. Rebels and pirates had chronically marauded China's maritime provinces, but no major enemy had ever penetrated the country from the sea. In contrast, China had been invaded time and again over the centuries by the "barbarians" of the interior, many of whom were absorbed into Chinese civilization. Indeed, half the emperors who reigned during the last thousand years of imperial China were not Chinese.[3] Starting with the Khitan Mongols, who established the Liao dynasty in the tenth century, the "barbarian" cavalry thrusts grew more powerful until, in the seventeenth century, the Manchus swept into Beijing to found the Qing dynasty.

As they built an empire that stretched from Tibet and Xinjiang through Mongolia and Manchuria down into Southeast Asia, the Manchus themselves became obsessed by the strategic significance of Inner Asia. Even after the British demonstrated China's coastal vulnerability in the Opium War, the Manchu rulers still continued to be preoccupied with the menace of continental aggression. In 1875, faced by the choice of constructing a navy to resist Japan's rising influence in Korea or sending an expedition three thousand miles to block Russian advances into Xinjiang, the Manchus opted in favor of protecting their western frontier.

The Chinese Communists inherited this inward focus. Just as the Manchus had banished dissidents and criminals to remote border areas, the Communists shipped contingents of demobilized troops, students, and refractory intellectuals out to populate and cultivate Xinjiang, Tibet, and Inner Mongolia, and to convert their indigenous peoples to Han Chinese culture. One of the Communists' top military priorities after coming to power, for example, was to restore Chinese hegemony over Tibet—an objective that met with Chiang Kai-shek's envious approval. And in their earliest negotiations in Moscow, the Beijing leaders sought to curb Soviet influence in Xinjiang by setting up "joint-stock companies" with the Russians to develop the region's resources. These companies were transferred to Beijing's exclusive ownership in 1952. But the Chinese continued to be worried by the Soviet shadow hovering over them from the north and west. In 1954 and again in 1957, both Mao and Zhou Enlai raised the question of borders with Khrushchev. On each occasion, the Chinese disclosed, the Soviet Premier had either declined to discuss the subject or refused to give them a "satisfactory answer."[4]

From the seventeenth century onward, Beijing claimed, Tsarist Russia had annexed a half-billion square kilometers of Chinese territory reaching from the vicinity of the Amur River adjoining Manchuria to the Pamir mountains adjacent to the southern corner of Xinjiang. Much of this territory was acquired by the Soviet Union under what Beijing termed "unequal treaties" forced by Tsarist Russia on the decaying Qing dynasty in the mid-nineteenth century, when China had fallen prey to foreign imperialists. The Chinese insisted that Moscow acknowledge these treaties to have been "unequal" even though, they said, they were prepared to "respect them . . . as the basis for a reasonable settlement."[5] To bolster their case, Beijing recalled Lenin's pledge in 1920 to return "gratis and forever everything the Tsarist regime and the Russian bourgeoisie rapaciously stole" from China.

Against these arguments, the Russians contended that Lenin's statement had been a "declaration of principles" rather than a promise.[6] They flatly rejected Beijing's demands that the old treaties be qualified as "unequal," asserting instead that the boundaries had been "fixed by life itself, and treaties concerning the border cannot be disregarded."[7] Kremlin spokesmen pointed out that the Chinese emperors had taken over Xinjiang and other parts of Central Asia by "aggression" and, in one area, had slaughtered more than 2 million local inhabitants in an unparalleled instance of "mass brutality."[8]

By 1964, the Sino-Soviet boundary problem had begun to escalate, and Russian statements charged for the first time that the Chinese had been "systematically violating the Soviet frontier" since 1960.[9] In reply, Beijing alleged that the Kremlin had carried out "large-scale subversive activities" in Xinjiang in the spring of 1962 by "enticing and coercing" tens of thousands of Uighurs, Kazakhs, and other indigenous Muslims to go over the border into the Soviet Union.[10] As other accusations and counteraccusations flew back and forth between Beijing and Moscow, Mao himself weighed into the dispute with a blunt complaint against the Russians. To a group of Japanese visitors to Beijing in mid-1964, he declared that "there are too many places occupied by the Soviet Union." And, he added ominously: "We have not yet presented our account for this list."[11]

Aggravating the border issue were ideological and political differences between the Russian and Chinese Communists that dated back decades. Either through errors of judgment or efforts to promote Soviet interests, Stalin had repeatedly sought to subordinate Mao and Qu Qiubai, Li Lisan, Wang Ming, and other Chinese Communist rivals who were more responsive to Moscow's dictates. In the late 1920s, Stalin had tried to compel them to preserve a "united front" with the Nationalists even after they had been decimated by Chiang Kai-shek. Twenty years later, apprehensive lest the United States intervene in the Chinese civil war and thus involve the Soviet Union, he attempted to restrain the Communists from pushing on to victory and, according to one source, proposed that China be partitioned along the line of the Yangzi River. Years afterward, disclosing Stalin's pressures on him, Mao said: "But we did not obey, and the revolution succeeded."[12] The trouble with Stalin persisted after the Chinese Communist triumph. Increasingly paranoiac, Stalin stalled signing an alliance with them for two months in 1950 because, as Mao himself recollected, he "feared that China might degenerate into another Yugoslavia, and that I might become a second Tito."[13] About the same time, Stalin was said to have conspired to extend his control over Manchuria through its Chinese leader, Gao Gang, whom Mao purged soon after the Soviet dictator's death in 1953.[14]

But in the minds of the Chinese, the memory of Stalin's maneuvers was pale in contrast to their experience with Khrushchev. The three years from Stalin's death until the Soviet Communist Party's Twentieth Congress in February 1956 was the only real period of friendship between the Russians and Chinese. The new Soviet leaders, less secure than Stalin had been, were eager to have Beijing's support, and therefore endowed China with economic and military aid and assistance. Now committed to industrialization and military modernization along Russian lines, the Chinese were reliant on Moscow and willing to pay tribute to Soviet leadership of the Communist bloc. But the seeds of discord were germinating beneath this apparently harmonious relationship. Among other things, Chinese pretensions to big-power status rankled the Russians. Chinese self-confidence had also been boosted by economic and social progress at home and successes abroad. They had fought the United Nations to a stalemate in Korea, and they had played a key role at the Geneva Conference of 1954 and at Bandung the following year. Now, they felt, they were surpassing the Soviet Union in prestige and influence, particularly in Asia and Africa. "When we speak," asserted Madame Sun Yat-sen, "we speak not only for ourselves, but for all of Asia."[15]

According to an official Chinese recapitulation, the Sino-Soviet honeymoon ended with Khrushchev's revelations of Stalin's "crimes" at the Russian Party's Twentieth Congress. The Chinese were not surprised by the catalogue of Stalin's excesses, but in their view, Khrushchev's denunciation signified that he aspired to replace his former boss as the uncontested ruler of world communism. This represented a challenge to their own ambitions. In addition, Mao perceived that Khrushchev's policies, especially his efforts to ease tensions with the United States, threatened to weaken international Communist unity. As Mao analyzed the world situation at that point, Soviet technological advances had swung the balance of power in favor of the Communist camp—in his celebrated phrase, "the East wind is prevailing over the West wind." Thus he argued for a rougher rather than a moderate stance toward the United States, even if such a strategy provoked nuclear war. "If worse came to worse and half of mankind died," he said, "the other half would remain while imperialism would be razed to the ground, and the whole world would become socialist."[16]

This logic sounded to Khrushchev like the rantings of a madman, and he behaved accordingly. During the Middle East crisis of 1958, in which American and British troops landed in Lebanon and Jordan, he proposed a summit meeting of the major world powers, including India but pointedly excluding China. Soon afterward, when the Chinese Communist leaders began preparations for a military offensive to "liberate" Taiwan from Chiang Kai-shek's control, Khrushchev rushed to Beijing in an attempt to dissuade them from an adventure that he feared might ignite a wider war. In the course of that visit, he reportedly rejected a Chinese request for Soviet nuclear warheads to deploy in the offensive. Less than a year later, the Kremlin retracted its 1957 agreement to provide China with a "sample" atomic bomb and "technical data concerning its manufacture." That decision, the Russians explained, stemmed from their "serious doubts regarding the aims" of Chinese foreign policy.[17]

At the end of September 1959, Khrushchev infuriated the Chinese even more. After completing a visit to the United States, he flew directly to Beijing for the tenth anniversary of the Chinese Communist regime, and there, in a banquet speech, he publicly extolled President Eisenhower as a sincere advocate of peace.[18] The Chinese replied by describing Eisenhower's conduct as a "smoke screen" designed to camouflage his intensification of the Cold War.[19]

Now the dispute between Russia and China was plainly visible, and it was escalating at a rapid pace. Khrushchev and the other Soviet leaders openly denounced the Great Leap Forward and backed Marshal Peng Dehuai, the Defense Minister, in his assault against Mao. And in the summer of 1960, in his most dramatic gesture of hostility, Khrushchev abruptly withdrew more than a thousand Russian technicians then in China under Soviet assistance agreements, and canceled the Soviet aid program. This move hit the Chinese during the dismal aftermath of the Great Leap Forward and, they conceded, "caused our construction to suffer heavy losses, thereby upsetting our original plan for the development of our national economy and greatly aggravating our difficulties."[20]

By 1962, the rupture between the two countries seemed beyond repair. Late in that year, when Chinese and Indian forces clashed in the Himalayas, the Russians effectively sided with India. While adopting a posture of neutrality, they continued to deliver military aircraft to the Indians to be used against the Chinese and in addition supplied

India with twelve MIG-21 fighter airplanes—an advanced model they had refused to give the Chinese.[21] Not long afterward, in the summer of 1963, Beijing stressed a theme that was to dominate its propaganda against Moscow in the coming years. Excoriating the Russians for signing the Nuclear Test-Ban Treaty, the Chinese accused them of "colluding" with the United States against China and other Communist countries. "The real aim of the Soviet leaders is to compromise with the United States in order to . . . maintain a monopoly of nuclear weapons and lord it over the socialist camp."[22]

Beijing's charges of Soviet-American collaboration became more vociferous after the United States dispatched combat troops to South Vietnam and began bombing North Vietnam in early 1965. For the Vietnam war was intensifying a complex triangular relationship involving China, the Soviet Union, and the United States. This relationship was further tangled by stresses and strains within China as Mao launched his Cultural Revolution. And it was significantly influenced by changing policies in Hanoi.

⬥

During the first years following the 1954 Geneva Conference, which concluded their war against the French, the North Vietnamese tended to emulate the Chinese. Among other things, they slavishly imitated Beijing's land-reform program—and with disastrous consequences. But in 1957, beset by severe economic problems largely caused by their inability to rely on traditional rice supplies from South Vietnam, the Hanoi leaders turned to the Soviet Union for assistance. Within a year, Moscow had replaced Beijing as Hanoi's principal source of aid, and the North Vietnamese, now subscribing to Khrushchev's pleas for "peaceful coexistence," toned down their talk of "liberating" South Vietnam by force and urged instead that priority be given to economic development in their zone. The neutralization of Laos in 1962 strengthened the partisans of restraint in Hanoi. They argued that the Laotian settlement could serve as a model for South Vietnam, and thus eventual unification could be achieved through diplomatic rather than military means, an approach favored by the Russians. But when it became clear that the United States had no intention of accepting a neutral South Vietnam, the Hanoi hierarchy veered away from the Soviet Union and began heeding Chinese advice to pursue a tough line.[23]

By 1964, the North Vietnamese were firmly lodged in the Chinese camp—even to the extent of denouncing Soviet "modern revision-ism."[24] Khrushchev's impetuous reaction to this switch was to dis-engage completely from Indochina. But after his ouster in October 1964, the new Kremlin leaders tried to rebuild Soviet influence in Hanoi. First, with the United States plainly escalating the war, they could not abandon North Vietnam without courting the risk of losing prestige in the eyes of Communist countries and movements for whom Hanoi's struggle symbolized the fight against "imperialism." Second, worried by the danger of a wider war, the Russian leaders were anxious to persuade the North Vietnamese to come to terms with the United States. Early in February 1965, Premier Alexei Ko-sygin went to Hanoi with a dual proposal. He would increase Russian military and economic aid to North Vietnam, but he counseled the Hanoi leadership to help the United States to "find a way out" of the conflict through negotiations.[25] In the middle of Kosygin's visit, how-ever, the United States raided targets north of the seventeenth par-allel in retaliation for Vietcong assaults against American installations in the South. Kosygin had no choice but to accelerate Russian aid to Hanoi, perhaps hoping that he might temper the North Vietnamese in the future.

The Chinese view of the Vietnam situation at that stage was com-plicated by the rivalries then dividing Mao and his adversaries in the Communist Party and Army. Mao's primary concern was the forth-coming Cultural Revolution, in which he would require the services of the Army. He was therefore determined to avoid Chinese involve-ment in Vietnam. His opponents, in contrast, favored a direct military commitment to Vietnam as a way of depriving Mao of the Army for domestic political purposes. Thus the debate that arose in Beijing over the question of Chinese help for Vietnam was intimately tied to the growing tensions then building up between Mao and his foes. In this debate, Liu Shaoqi and the Chief of General Staff, Luo Ruiqing, favored intervention, while Mao stood for caution. In short, they were "hawks" and he was a "dove."

The Vietnam issue was in turn intricately linked to China's dispute with Moscow. Consistent with their willingness to risk intervention, Mao's opponents called for a *rapprochement* with the Soviet Union that would discourage the United States from counterattacking China. But Mao rejected any arrangements that might restore Soviet influ-ence in China. He rebuffed several Soviet proposals for "united ac-tion" on Vietnam, contending that they were "designed to meet the needs of American imperialism."[26] He also denied the Russians the use of Chinese airfields and the right to fly supplies over China to North Vietnam. His motives were simple, he told them:

> Frankly speaking, we do not trust you. We and other fraternal countries have learned bitter lessons in the past from Khrushchev's evil practice of control under the cover of aid. . . . China is not one of your provinces. We cannot accept your control. Nor will we help you to control others.[27]

For all his criticism of the Kremlin for colluding with American "imperialism," however, Mao made it clear that he would do nothing to deter United States escalation in Vietnam so long as China was not directly threatened. To be sure, he briefly deployed a squadron of Chinese aircraft in Hanoi in August 1964 to help defend North Vietnam against the possibility of American raids, and he constructed airfields in south China as alternate bases for North Vietnamese fighter aircraft. Beginning in the fall of 1965, he also sent some fifty thousand labor troops into North Vietnam primarily to maintain railway communications between Hanoi and China.[28] But he indicated plainly on several occasions and through different channels that he was as anxious to avert a clash with the United States as President Lyndon Johnson was to avert a clash with China.

Throughout late 1964 and early 1965, for example, there were no Chinese troop movements toward the Vietnam border of the kind that preceded the entry of China's "volunteers" into the Korean War. And Chinese representatives at the Sino-American ambassadorial talks in Warsaw signaled to United States diplomats that Beijing was striving to avoid involvement in Vietnam. Mao's prudence was also reflected in the fact that he barred North Vietnamese aircraft from using Chinese bases for operational purposes lest the United States invoke the right of "hot pursuit."[29] And he further transmitted his desire to keep out of Vietnam through the medium of Lin Biao's famous essay, "Long Live the Victory of People's War!" Though labeled Mao's *Mein Kampf* by facile analysts in Washington and elsewhere, Lin Biao's essay was really an announcement that China had no plans to intercede militarily in Vietnam. "Revolution or people's war in any country is the business of the masses in that country," it said, "and should be carried out primarily by their own efforts."[30]

Even American bombing flights near or over their borders evoked essentially cautious reactions from the Chinese. When American aircraft attacked a North Vietnamese target ten miles from their frontier on August 13, 1967, for example, Beijing's spokesmen waited nine days before warning, rather lamely, that "if you impose war on the Chinese people, we will accommodate you to the end."[31]

Hence there was little evidence to substantiate such alarmist statements as the observation of Secretary of State Dean Rusk that China was poised to "overrun" Southeast Asia.[32] On the contrary, Mao's Vietnam strategy was founded on the principle of nonintervention, for several reasons. Not only did he believe that "people's war in any country is the business of the masses in that country," but he viewed the Vietnam conflict as his "war by proxy" against "imperialism," in which the United States would be drained and ultimately defeated at virtually no cost to China. And finally, as his exhortations to the Vietnamese Communists to continue fighting revealed, he favored a protracted struggle that would eventually leave Vietnam exhausted, weak, and in no position to resist Chinese influence.

The North Vietnamese were fully aware that the Chinese, despite their protestations of friendship, were mainly concerned with advancing their own interests. As a consequence, relations between Hanoi and Beijing were often tense, particularly in 1967 and 1968. Appalled by the excesses of the Cultural Revolution, the North Vietnamese criticized Mao for shattering the Chinese Communist Party, calling him a "Don Quixote tilting against windmills."[33] And they were outraged by Red Guard attacks against trains transporting Soviet and Chinese military supplies to Hanoi, even though Zhou Enlai repeatedly tried to reassure them of China's devotion to their cause. They were also irritated in early 1968 by Beijing's awkward attempts to dissuade them from entering into talks with the United States in Paris. With these and other differences, relations between Hanoi and Beijing reached a low point in the fall of 1968, and the two Vietnamese Communist officials chosen to attend the Chinese National Day celebration on October 1 were so obscure that they were ranked behind a Maoist from Auckland, New Zealand.[34]

Zhou Enlai did much to improve China's relations with North Vietnam when he rushed to Hanoi to pay his condolences on the death of Ho Chi Minh in September 1969. He also went to considerable lengths to cultivate the Vietnamese Communists following the allied invasion of Cambodia in the spring of 1970. But by the summer of 1971, the Chinese appeared to have downgraded the importance of Vietnam. For the chances of a *rapprochement* with the United States now seemed to offer a broader spectrum of gains more tempting than their narrow commitment to Hanoi.

In contrast to the dispute between Beijing and Moscow, which was rooted in deep historical, national, and ideological animosities, the tensions that separated China and the United States for two decades after 1950 were largely the result of mutual distrust and misunderstanding that might have been overcome. And indeed, the Chinese were able to alter their attitude toward the United States in 1971 with remarkable rapidity and ease. Official reassessments in Washington at that time, similarly, were quick to argue that, after all, the Chinese menace had perhaps been exaggerated.

During World War II, the leaders of the Chinese Communist Party had been fairly cordial toward the United States as they sought American support for their resistance against Japan. In 1944, for instance, Mao praised the United States and expressed the hope that Americans might play a more active role in China. His senior military leader, Zhu De, even proposed that an American officer be appointed to command the Communist and Nationalist forces.[35] But this cordiality soured after General Marshall's failure to arrange a political compromise between the rival Chinese movements. With the revival of the civil war against the Nationalists, the Communists publicly aligned themselves behind the Soviet Union in the "international struggle against imperialism" and proclaimed their mission to foment revolution throughout the world. Coinciding as it did with the emerging Cold War in Europe and elsewhere, this stance prompted the United States to view the Chinese Communists as an instrument of aggressive and expansionist Soviet policy. When they took power in 1949, Washington refused to recognize them immediately and unsuccessfully attempted to dissuade allies such as Great Britain from establishing diplomatic relations with the new Beijing leadership. The United States also opposed the Communist claim to represent China at the United Nations.

At the same time, however, the United States was cautiously receptive to the idea of an eventual accommodation with Mao. When the Communists were capturing China's major urban areas in the last days of the civil war, for example, American diplomats stationed in those cities were instructed to stay at their posts and make contact with new local regimes. Significantly, the American Ambassador, John Leighton Stuart, remained in Nanjing when the Communists seized Chiang Kai-shek's capital—while the Soviet envoy accompanied the Nationalists as they fled south. But the Communists, flushed by victory, showed few signs of conciliation toward the United States, mistreated several American diplomatic representatives, and arbitrarily grabbed U.S. consular property in a move that finally prompted Washington to withdraw all its officials from China.[36]

Despite these indications of Communist hostility, the United States disengaged from the Chinese civil war. In January 1950, the Truman Administration declared that it would cease to aid the Nationalists on the grounds that the civil war was, as Secretary of State Dean Acheson put it, "the product of internal Chinese forces" that were "beyond the control" of the United States.[37] Though the rapid establishment of formal relations between the United States and the Communists seemed to be precluded, the logic of the situation suggested that Washington's recognition of the Beijing regime was probably only a matter of time. In June 1950, however, the North Korean Communists invaded South Korea, and the consequences of that event were to set back any *rapprochement* between the United States and Communist China for years to come.

The North Korean invasion was primarily instigated by the Soviet Union, perhaps in the expectation of a quick victory. For in the spring of 1949 and again in early 1950, both General Douglas MacArthur and Secretary Acheson had publicly excluded Korea from the American defense perimeter in the Pacific, and their statements constituted a virtual invitation to Communist aggression.[38] But in June 1950, when the North Koreans initiated their thrust, President Truman reversed American policy. Along with sending American forces to Korea under the banner of the United Nations, he ordered the Seventh Fleet to "neutralize" the Taiwan Strait and subsequently revived military aid to the Nationalists—thereby engaging the United States anew in the Chinese civil war. In October, ignoring warnings from Beijing that its troops would intervene, Washington directed American units to cross the thirty-eighth parallel into North Korea. The result was a military collision between the United States and the Chinese Communists. The accumulation of these moves had profound political effects.

The most crucial of these, in Beijing's view, was the American commitment to the Nationalists on Taiwan. Formerly controlled by Japan, the island had been returned to China at the end of World War II. But now it was occupied by the Nationalists, who relied for their survival on United States assistance. There were American troops on the island, and American warships patrolled its waters. The United States supplied Chiang Kai-shek with vast amounts of military aid, and all this support was given a legal rationale in a 1954 treaty pledging to protect the Nationalist regime against a Communist assault. Moreover, Washington backed Chiang Kai-shek's claim to speak for China at the United Nations, and exerted pressure on its allies to do the same. To the Communists, then, these actions represented intolerable interference in China's internal affairs, and the Taiwan question became the key obstacle to establishment of relations between the United States and the Chinese Communists.

Curiously, though, the sharp differences separating Washington and Beijing did not prevent them from carrying on official, if irregular, diplomatic conversations. Formally termed Ambassadorial Talks, these conversations started in Geneva in 1955 and continued in Warsaw, and they produced one tangible achievement—an agreement by the Chinese to release a number of American military and civilian prisoners who had been held captive in China.[39] But the meetings also served as a kind of "hot line" between the United States and the Chinese Communists that was occasionally effective. When the Communists feared an invasion by Chiang Kai-shek in the spring of 1962, for example, President Kennedy used the Warsaw channel to allay their apprehensions. During the Vietnam war, the Warsaw conversations again helped to avoid a miscalculation that might have pushed the United States and China into a conflict that neither wanted.

Over the years, however, the United States and the Chinese Communists were unable to reach a real modus vivendi, often because of ill-timed or uncoordinated shifts in their respective foreign policies. In the mid-1950s, shelving the knotty Taiwan problem temporarily, Zhou Enlai offered to permit American newsmen to visit China and proposed other measures designed to ease tensions with the United States. But his overtures were rejected by Secretary of State John Foster Dulles, who decried them as "propaganda" maneuvers. Dulles's hostility toward the Communists was such, in fact, that he refused to shake hands with Zhou when the two men met at the 1954 Geneva Conference on Indochina. Beginning in the early 1960s, the United States contrastingly undertook gradual steps aimed at breaking down the barriers with Beijing. But the Chinese, now striving to demonstrate their revolutionary purity to the Soviet Union, adamantly rebuffed any *détente* with Washington so long as the Taiwan question had not been resolved on their terms.

To a large extent, the rigid American attitude toward Communist

China during the 1950s stemmed from Senator Joseph McCarthy's purge of the State Department. McCarthy had compelled the Truman and Eisenhower Administrations to dismiss or transfer a number of American officials with valuable experience in China, alleging that they had contributed to the Communists' victory there. Among those fired were John Stewart Service, John Carter Vincent, and John Paton Davies, whose purported "crimes" as foreign-service officers in China during World War II had been to report objectively on the ineptitude of the Chiang Kai-shek regime. Other victims of the McCarthy era included Robert Barnett, who was born in China and had served there as an adviser to General Claire Chennault. Slated to become Director of Chinese Affairs in the State Department, Barnett appeared on one of McCarthy's "lists" in 1951 and, though there was no evidence against him, he was "advised" to accept a post in Europe. The departure of these and other specialists like them deprived Washington of men with imaginative ideas on China and created an atmosphere of "knee-jerk anti-Communism" that discouraged any innovations that might relax tensions between the United States and Beijing.[40]

The evangelical anti-Communism personified by Senator McCarthy persisted after his death in the spirit infused into the State Department by Secretary of State Dulles, who considered initiatives toward Beijing to be heretical. In December 1961, however, President Kennedy appointed W. Averell Harriman as Assistant Secretary of State for Far Eastern Affairs. Though Harriman's principal assignment was to reach a peace settlement in Laos, then threatened by war, he brought back some of the China specialists who had been eclipsed earlier and commissioned them to chart a new American policy toward Beijing. They outlined a series of steps that included the revision of the total United States embargo on trade with China that had been decreed at the outset of the Korean War, a modification of the ban on travel to China by Americans, and, among other things, a proposal to invite Beijing to join in disarmament talks. These specialists were not optimistic at that stage that Beijing would reply to their initiatives, provided they were actually taken. Underlying their strategy, instead, was the idea that a fresh "climate" might, over the long term, evoke a Chinese Communist response. It was this strategy, under different circumstances, that later proved successful for President Nixon.

The trend set by Harriman was continued and amplified by his successor, Roger Hilsman. He broadened his staff to include such younger China experts as Lindsey Grant, Allen S. Whiting, and James C. Thomson, Jr., and they promoted the first official public United States overture to Beijing. Speaking in San Francisco on December 13, 1963, Hilsman expressed the hope that "evolutionary forces" inside Communist China might eventually contribute to a Sino-American *rapprochement*, adding that Washington intended to "keep the door open" to the possibility of a negotiated settlement of its differences with Beijing.[41]

Mild as it looked in retrospect, that overture was daring for its time. Indeed, members of Hilsman's staff were doubtful, as they drafted his speech, that it would gain prior acceptance from the Secretary of State, Dean Rusk, who regarded attempts at a thaw with Beijing to be detrimental to United States interests. Preparing to depart for a conference abroad, Rusk hastily approved the Hilsman statement, but soon afterward apparently regretting his decision, he countered Hilsman's initiative with a tough address of his own. Speaking in Tokyo on January 28, 1964, he asserted that the Chinese Communists scorned peace and warned that "free nations must not reward the militancy of Beijing."[42] Predictably, the Communists denounced Hilsman, calling his hope of "peaceful evolution" in China a case of "self-delusion."[43] Judging from the evidence that emerged during the Cultural Revolution, however, the American overture may have left an impression on some Chinese minds.

The legacy of the McCarthy era was still so strong in Washington in the mid-1960s that State Department officials were reluctant to consort with China specialists who had been criticized by the Senator. On one occasion, when Hilsman and his staff invited the eminent Harvard expert John Fairbank to address a group of government employees concerned with China, they held their meeting at the Washington home of John D. Rockefeller IV rather than at the State Department building. As one of the organizers recalled later: "We figured that they couldn't accuse Rockefeller of being a Communist."[44]

With the Johnson Administration immersed in the Vietnam war, there were no significant gestures made toward China until December 1965. At that time, acting at the behest of the celebrated heart specialist Dr. Paul Dudley White and others, President Johnson amended travel restrictions to allow American doctors and health experts to visit China. Soon after that, he also eased the limitations on travel to China for teachers, athletes, businessmen, and, among others, members of Congress. In speeches, too, Johnson defined "reconciliation" with Beijing as an ultimate American policy goal.[45]

Against that background, then, President Nixon's dramatic move in July 1971 was less a "turning of the tide" than the logical continuation of a trend that had begun a decade earlier.

In Beijing, meanwhile, the conduct of foreign policy had been paralyzed by the Cultural Revolution throughout most of 1967. All of China's forty-six ambassadors abroad except Huang Hua, the envoy to Cairo, had been recalled home for "re-education." On more than one occasion, radicals had physically occupied the Foreign Ministry, destroyed documents, manhandled officials, and harassed Foreign Minister Chen Yi. Chen was said to have lost twenty-seven pounds during his ordeals and Mao, deploring his mistreatment, reportedly commented: "I cannot show him to foreign guests in this condition."

But as the Army accelerated its drive to impose order in China during early 1968, there were indications that Zhou Enlai and his moderate colleagues were edging toward the resumption of normal diplomatic activity. They signed a trade agreement with Ceylon, played host to Nepalese dignitaries, apologized for their earlier troubles with Cambodia, started to repair their damaged ties with Burma, and, in July 1968, granted exit visas to several British diplomats who had been refused permission to return home.[46] Counterpointing these signs of flexibility, however, prominent Beijing radicals like Chen Boda and Jiang Qing sought to subvert the movement toward moderation in China's foreign affairs. They seemed particularly eager to block efforts aimed at reaching a *détente* with the United States, and their obstruction would make contacts between Beijing and Washington extremely difficult at times.

Two major developments in 1968 evidently convinced Zhou Enlai and his associates that some kind of *rapprochement* with the United States might be in China's interest. The first of these was the widespread domestic revulsion in the United States against the Vietnam war. This suggested to the Beijing leaders that American forces would sooner or later be withdrawn from Southeast Asia. China could play a role in a peace settlement covering the region. Even more significant to the Chinese was the Soviet invasion of Czechoslovakia and the enunciation of the "Brezhnev doctrine," which asserted Moscow's right to intervene in Communist countries whose policies deviated from Kremlin standards. The Soviet action persuaded the Beijing leaders that the Russians were quite capable of attacking China. The Chinese apparently calculated, therefore, that their defenses could be reinforced by a closer diplomatic relationship with the United States.

In the Chinese view, the Americans had sustained a decisive setback in Vietnam by the middle of 1968. Beijing perceived evidence of this defeat in the antiwar demonstrations then occurring with increasing frequency in the United States, in the popularity of such "doves" as Senators Robert Kennedy and Eugene McCarthy, and in the announcement by President Johnson on March 31 that he would not run for re-election. They were also impressed by Johnson's decision to call a total halt to American air raids north of the seventeenth parallel, an event Beijing noted without its usual adverse comment.[47] The American writer Edgar Snow, who visited China somewhat later, reported being told by a senior Beijing official: "Nixon is getting out of Vietnam."[48]

The same estimate of American policy was indirectly expressed in an authoritative Chinese assessment of the current situation in the Far East. Reviewing the history of the previous two decades, a Beijing analysis accused the United States of having repeatedly tried to "strangle" the Chinese Communist regime. But now, the analysis concluded, the "heavy defeat" suffered by the United States in Vietnam had "seriously upset its deployments for a war of aggression against China and Asia."[49] In short, the Beijing statement implied, the American threat had receded. Now, it was clear, the Russians represented the new danger.

Mao himself was reported to have put his personal imprimatur on the shift in Beijing's foreign policy at a Plenary Session of the Chinese Communist Party Central Committee held in October 1969. Declaring that the Soviet Union had become China's "greatest enemy," he proposed that Beijing seek to establish relations with Western nations that agreed to recognize the Communist claim to sovereignty over Taiwan.[50] As usual, however, Mao's public pronouncement merely served to endorse a strategy that Zhou Enlai and his civilian and military colleagues had already been pursuing for nearly a year.

By 1969, the Soviet build-up along the Chinese frontier had reached huge proportions. Roughly two hundred thousand Soviet troops were deployed in the area facing Manchuria, and an equal number had been transferred to the region adjacent to Xinjiang. Beginning in early 1966, the Kremlin also moved nearly a hundred thousand men into the People's Republic of Mongolia.[51] Outfitted with the latest tanks, aircraft, and nuclear-tipped missiles, the Soviet units were superior in firepower to anything the Chinese could muster. Beijing's forces, stretched from Manchuria through Xinjiang, numbered more than a million men. But in contrast to the Russians, whose contingency plans probably called for strikes against China's nuclear installations and industrial cities, the Chinese were relying on a "defense-in-depth." In the event of war, they hoped to take advantage of their large population to drown an invader in an "ocean of people." Or, as their statement said, making a virtue of necessity: "The outcome of war is decided by the people, not by one or two new types of weapons."[52]

Matching their troop deployments, the Russians escalated their propaganda campaigns against Beijing. Authoritative Soviet commentaries vilified Mao as a "nationalistic anti-Marxist" who had come to dominate China "through the use of violence and unbridled demagogy."[53] A series of Moscow broadcasts beamed to China and manifestly designed to demoralize the Chinese Army stressed the superiority of Soviet weaponry, asserting that "a powerful modern arsenal" rather than Maoist doctrine was the "crucial criteria for victory."[54] The Kremlin also instructed its operatives abroad to contact Chinese Nationalist diplomats and journalists. One Soviet agent, the colorful journalist Victor Louis, even visited Taiwan, where he talked with high Nationalist officials and later wrote accounts of his trip for the American press.[55]

At the same time, the Russians accelerated an ambitious program to strengthen their influence from Japan through the states of Southeast Asia to India and Pakistan. They sent cultural delegations to the Philippines, signed trade accords with Singapore and Malaysia, reinforced their naval fleet in the Pacific and Indian Oceans, and not long afterward, the Soviet Communist Party Secretary General, Leonid Brezhnev, proposed an Asian "collective security" system that, Moscow spokesmen indicated, would be designed to "contain" Communist China's "hegemonistic pretensions."[56] That proposal, redolent of Dulles's geopolitical pacts, appeared to have been primarily contrived to create pyschological havoc in Beijing. For it failed to go far beyond the rhetorical stage.

But the Chinese leaders did register a visible jolt on August 20, 1968, when Soviet and Warsaw Pact troops invaded Czechoslovakia. Until then, the confrontation between Moscow and the Dubček regime had been a real dilemma for the Chinese. They were inclined to sympathize with Dubček as a victim of Soviet "big-power chauvinism," but their fierce hostility to "revisionism" prevented them from openly supporting the Czechoslovak reformers. As a result, they adopted the rather tortuous expedient of assailing the Kremlin for having encouraged the Prague liberals to deviate from orthodox Marxism.[57] Now, however, Moscow's invasion of Czechoslovakia simplified the issue. The Kremlin's "naked armed intervention" highlighted the "grisly fascist features" of the Soviet "renegade clique," Beijing publicists asserted as they compared the Russian action to Hitler's occupation of the Czechoslovak Sudetenland prior to World War II and the American "aggression" in Vietnam.[58]

This response by the Chinese partly reflected their consistent view of themselves as the defenders of small nations against the "super-powers." More profound, though, was Beijing's new fear that the Russians were not above invading China as they had Czechoslovakia. Zhou Enlai openly voiced this fear in a speech on September 30, when he claimed that the Kremlin was "stepping up armed provocations against China while intensifying its aggression and threats against Eastern Europe." He accused the Russians of stationing "massive" troop concentrations in Mongolia and along the border, and added that their aircraft were violating Chinese airspace with increasing frequency.[59] Beijing backed up Zhou's accusation with statistics alleging that Soviet military aircraft flew twenty-nine sorties for purposes of "reconnaissance, harassment, and provocation" over Heilongjiang during a period of twenty-one days in August, and that the Russians had violated the Chinese border more than a hundred times during the previous seven months. Linking these alleged forays to the Soviet thrust into Czechoslovakia, Beijing asserted that these intrusions had been "in no way accidental."[60] Flatly denying the charges, Moscow described them as Beijing's "feeble contribution to the anti-Soviet hysteria unleashed in the imperialist reaction to the events in Czechoslovakia."[61]

In the face of this growing Soviet threat, the Chinese made a move that was to be the start of a wholly new direction in their foreign policy. On November 26, they issued a formal Foreign Ministry statement proposing that the Sino-American Ambassadorial Talks in Warsaw, which had been repeatedly postponed over the past year, be resumed on February 20, 1969—at a time when the newly elected President, Richard Nixon, "will have been in office for a month" and his Administration had been "able to make up its mind" about China.[62]

The Chinese Foreign Ministry statement was extraordinarily subdued in style and substance compared to the fiery utterances of the

Cultural Revolution. At a Warsaw meeting in September 1966, for example, the Chinese spokesman had demanded that the United States "get out of Asia" and dismissed American desires for "peaceful cooperation" with China as "high-sounding words" that were "not worth a penny."[63] Now, in contrast, Beijing recommended soberly that the United States and China could improve their ties by adhering to the "five principles of peaceful coexistence."[64] Similarly, Liu Shaoqi had been denounced in October 1967 for "advocating national egoism and betraying proletarian internationalism" by suggesting that China could "develop friendly relations" with the United States once American troops were out of Taiwan.[65] Now Beijing put forth that very line, declaring that the United States and China could reach an agreement if Washington merely withdrew its military and naval forces from Taiwan and the Taiwan Strait.[66] Underscoring this policy switch, the Beijing press publicized a 1949 Mao essay which had hailed the value of negotiations and emphasized the advantages of making "temporary concessions" to enemies in order to "win them over to our side or neutralize them politically."[67]

Beijing's policy shift predictably nettled the Kremlin, and Russian commentators were quick to claim that China was "colluding" with the United States against the Soviet Union. Indeed, many of these indictments were minor versions of China's anti-Soviet propaganda. One Moscow broadcast, for example, contended that the "Maoist clique" was "kowtowing to the imperialists and sabotaging national liberation movements" around the world.[68] And others accused the Chinese of servicing American warships in Hong Kong or selling military equipment to the United States for use in Vietnam.[69] Particularly galling to the Kremlin was Beijing's decision to inaugurate contacts with a president whose career had been built on his anti-communism. But Nixon's record may have been precisely what appealed to the Chinese at that point in time.

As they looked back on their own experience, Chinese Communists perceived that they had fared better with Republicans than with Democrats. After all, they had gone to war in Korea against the Truman Administration, but had signed a truce with President Eisenhower. Kennedy and Johnson had escalated the Vietnam conflict, while Nixon was basing his election campaign on a pledge to wind down the war. Ideology also colored the Chinese analysis of the American political dynamic. Republicans, they believed, were closer to "monopoly capital," the real source of power in the United States, and they were convinced that Nixon, as a representative of the capitalist "ruling class," could operate with an authority that the Democrats lacked. Finally, the Chinese were perhaps gratified to see Nixon's past hostility to the Soviet Union. From their viewpoint, there was a certain reality in the old adage that "the enemy of my enemy is my friend"—or at least an expedient ally.

During his election campaign, Nixon had shown signs of a new attitude toward Beijing. In August 1968, at the Republican National Convention in Miami Beach, he voiced the view that the United States must eventually negotiate with China, which he described as "the next super-power,"[70] and expressed the hope that he might visit Beijing "if they would give me a visa." Soon after assuming office, he made known that breaking the twenty-year deadlock in Sino-American relations was one of his priorities. In the course of a discussion with a group of American specialists on China at the White House, a conservative scholar warned Nixon against any switch in United States policy. The President replied: "I used to share your opinion, but I've changed."[71]

The shaping of a new foreign policy was as intricate, difficult, and perilous a process for Nixon as it was for Zhou Enlai. Both had to take into account their domestic opposition as well as the potential reactions of their allies. Nixon, for example, could not afford to incur the wrath of the conservative American politicians who had contributed to his election. He was also wary of alienating the Chinese Nationalist, South Vietnamese, South Korean, Thai, and other Asian regimes that had committed themselves to America's anti-Communist strategy in the past. Similarly, Zhou Enlai and his colleagues faced the resistance of the prominent radicals in the Party regime, and they were sensitive to pressures coming from the North Vietnamese, North Korean, and other Communist movements whose positions would be weakened by a Sino-American *rapprochement*. Above all, Nixon and Zhou had to overcome the deep mutual hostility and mistrust that had characterized relations between the United States and China for decades. Thus they proceeded slowly, cautiously, and with extreme secrecy. And neither could run the risk of being rebuffed by the other.

Nixon was particularly anxious to avoid any advances that might provoke a rejection from Beijing. In effect, his design was based on the judgment that the pragmatic Chinese leaders would respond on their own initiative to his overtures if he could create a climate that encouraged them to realize that a *détente* with the United States served their own vital interests. Only twelve days after his inauguration, then, Nixon took the first step in the long march that would, he hoped, ultimately bring him to Beijing.

On February 1, 1969, he instructed Dr. Henry Kissinger, his chief foreign-policy adviser, to begin exploring avenues that might open the way to Beijing. Kissinger thereupon initiated two related tactics. On one hand, he signaled the President's general plan to French, East European, and other diplomats with contacts in the Chinese capital in the expectation that they would pass on the word to the Communist leadership. At the same time, he ordered his own staff to review America's China policy and to offer recommendations that might induce a nod from the Communists.[72] Within three months, hints from Washington indicated that the Nixon plan was in operation.

In a speech on April 22, for instance, Secretary of State William Rogers referred to China for the first time as the "People's Republic."[73] Soon afterward, in the first of a series of gestures aimed at revising the United States embargo on trade with Beijing, the President authorized Americans to purchase a hundred dollars' worth of Communist merchandise. Meanwhile, Nixon sought the assistance of key European leaders who might help to clear the path to Beijing. On a visit to Paris in March 1969, he discussed the China question with Charles de Gaulle, apparently obtaining the French President's pledge to help his effort.[74] Five months later, Nixon traveled to Rumania and there enlisted the even more important cooperation of President Nicolae Ceausescu, whose independence from Moscow had given him unusual leverage with the Chinese.[75] Nixon's visit to Bucharest came at the end of a round-the-world trip during which he enunciated the so-called "Guam Doctrine," his policy for a "lower profile" in Asia.

A measure of Beijing's receptivity to the Nixon overtures was reflected in several esoteric and often negative ways. Chinese propagandists greeted the President's modification of the trade embargo with significant silence, and they conspicuously refrained from denouncing Secretary of State Rogers when he visited Hong Kong during the summer of 1969. At the same time, however, evidence suggested that the radicals in Beijing could still muster enough influence to hinder moves designed to break the deadlock with the United States. When a minor Chinese diplomat in the Netherlands defected to Washington in February, for example, the radicals apparently seized on the incident to compel the Beijing moderates to cancel the session of the Sino-American Ambassadorial Talks to be held in Warsaw that month.[76] But these problems merely delayed rather than stopped the trend toward reconciliation between the United States and China. For Beijing was still confronted by the overwhelming challenge of the Soviet Union, which made its need for a *détente* with the United States imperative. The Russian challenge in fact turned into an urgent threat when an actual battle between Chinese and Soviet troops erupted.

The scene of the clash was an uninhabited island—called Damansky by the Russians and Zhenbao by the Chinese—situated in the frozen Ussuri River separating Manchuria from the Soviet Union's easternmost Maritime Provinces. Only Soviet sources have given a detailed account of the event, gleaned from survivors and from a special investigation team. As they told the story, on the morning of March 2, 1969, about three hundred Chinese troops dressed in white camouflage crossed the ice to the island the night before, dug foxholes, and laid telephone wire back to their command post in an apparent plan to provoke an incident. At about eleven o'clock the next morning, the Russians observed twenty or thirty armed Chinese moving toward the island, shouting Maoist slogans as they approached. A Soviet platoon drove out in military vehicles to warn them to halt. According to the Kremlin's version, the Russians dismounted and locked arms in an attempt to block the Chinese. At that point, the advancing Chinese scattered to the side, exposing a second line of Chinese troops who opened fire with submachine guns, killing seven Russians outright. Simultaneously, the Soviet account claimed, the entrenched Chinese also opened fire with mortars, machine guns, and antitank artillery. The Chinese then charged the remaining Russians, and the skirmish ended two hours later with thirty-one Soviet soldiers dead. The number of Chinese casualties was never reported by Beijing.[77]

In an exchange of angry protests, the Chinese and Russians immediately accused each other of having triggered the incident. But even though the local Chinese commander probably took the initiative, as the evidence appeared to indicate, a clash along the volatile frontier was almost certain to have occurred sooner or later.

After studying most of the available documents, one American scholar[78] has concluded that the Beijing leaders had decided on a "tough" line toward the Soviet Union. According to his theory, Zhou Enlai and the Chinese Army commanders may have sought a diversion from the domestic tensions then arising from their efforts to curb the Cultural Revolution, and needed a war scare to justify their calls for national unity. Consistent with this approach, they may also have felt compelled to discourage the increasingly menacing Soviet build-up along the border and ordered Chinese patrols to intensify their activities, even to the point of countering the Russians with force if necessary. As a result, the Chinese commander in the vicinity of the disputed Ussuri River island could well have sparked the incident in the belief that he was obeying Beijing's directives—or simply from an excess of zeal.

Another theory has been advanced suggesting that Lin Biao personally gave the order to provoke the attack in the belief that the clash would reinforce his authority in Beijing. The Soviet civilian and military leaders, meanwhile, appeared to be pushing as well for a showdown with China, and they had undoubtedly instructed Russian officers in the frontier region to check Chinese provocations. Thus it was likely that the Soviet unit involved in the March 2 incident would have shot first had it not been pre-empted by the Chinese.

On March 15, indeed, the Russians evidently did strike the first blow. This time, there was no element of surprise. Both sides were prepared for a second round, and the engagement resembled a set-piece battle. According to a plausible reconstruction of the event, the Chinese and Russians began exchanging mortar and artillery fire at about ten o'clock in the morning. Soon afterward, a regiment of some two thousand Chinese charged across the ice to gain possession of part of the island. Outnumbered, the Russians retreated and, adopting the tactic employed by American troops during the Korean War, allowed the Chinese "human wave" to advance. Then they counterattacked with large numbers of tanks, armored cars, and infantry in armored personnel carriers, covering their action with a fierce artillery barrage on Chinese positions as far inland as four miles. The battle ended after nine hours. The Russians lost about sixty men, while Chinese casualties were said to have run as high as eight hundred killed and wounded.[79] Following the battle, the Soviet forces systematically defoliated large tracts of forest on their side of the Ussuri River in order to open a clear field to the Chinese border. Fearful of being trapped in a bigger engagement yet to come, thousands of Russian civilians who had been resettled in the frontier zone abandoned their farms and fled back to the European parts of the Soviet Union.[80]

The Soviet initiative in the second Ussuri River battle had apparently been prompted by three principal motives. First, the Russians simply wanted to wreak revenge on the Chinese for the first attack. Second, they had evidently calculated that a failure on their part to react forcefully would have marked them as weaklings and hence damaged their prestige. And finally, they seemed to believe that military pressure would persuade Beijing to concede to a boundary settlement on their terms. The Russians pursued this tough strategy throughout the spring and summer.

In mid-June, focusing on a sparsely populated and ill-defended sector of the Chinese frontier, they thrust into Xinjiang province.[81] Following that raid, Soviet forces reportedly constructed fortifications inside the Chinese area in order to secure their own communications in the frontier zone.[82] Xinjiang inevitably erupted in another clash in August, with the Russians deploying tanks, aircraft, and other sophisticated equipment in a brief but large-scale battle.[83] Meanwhile, Moscow continued to strengthen its forces along the Ussuri River sector, where Khabarovsk and Vladivostok were particularly vulnerable to a Chinese assault. Matching these actions, the Kremlin offered Beijing the chance to resolve the disputed border question—on Soviet conditions.

On March 29, two weeks after the second Ussuri River clash, the Russians proposed that boundary negotiations begin "in the nearest future." They made it clear, however, that they could not accept Beijing's demand that the past border treaties be acknowledged as "unequal." The boundaries were not only "natural" but, the Soviet note insisted, they had been given "legal status" in the nineteenth-century accords signed by the Tsarist regime and the Qing dynasty administration. The Chinese were warned to expect further blows if the dispute dragged on. The statement pointedly recalled that "the Japanese aggressors [in the 1930s] were administered a crushing rebuff."[84]

The Chinese predictably rejected the Soviet proposal, reasserting that talks would be fruitless unless Moscow agreed in advance to recognize the nineteenth-century boundary treaties as "unequal."[85] By now, the question of the "unequal treaties" had become more crucial to the Chinese than the boundary itself. They had made it plain time and again that they were not calling for the return of all the territory lost by China throughout history. Yet they could not retreat from the principle they had enunciated, for several reasons. In part, their national pride was at stake. Nor could they capitulate on the border issue without jeopardizing their claims to Hong Kong,

Macao, sectors of their contested frontier with India, and other areas, the most important of which was, of course, Taiwan. If they dropped their demand that Moscow aknowledge the invalidity of the old treaties, the Beijing leaders felt, their claim to sovereignty over Taiwan would collapse and their crusade to unseat the rival Chiang Kai-shek regime be subverted.

Somewhat comparable considerations prompted Soviet intransigence. The Russians could not recognize the illegitimacy of their boundaries with China without courting the risk of inciting Poland, Rumania, Turkey, and other states adjacent to the Soviet Union to dun them with territorial claims. Nor could the Kremlin plausibly accept the principle of "unequal treaties" without facing the potential danger of protests from the Lithuanians, Latvians, Estonians, Ukrainians, Kazakhs, and other nationalities inside the Soviet Union, many of whom resented Moscow's domination. Distrusting Beijing as they did, the Russians also feared that even a theoretical concession on their part would provide the Chinese with a pretext to overrun areas of Siberia that, as a Kremlin statement put it, had been acquired "by the Soviet people only at the price of immense efforts and sacrifices."[86] Thus Russian attitudes were governed by a chauvinistic emotion at least equal to the nationalism of the Chinese.

Atavistic Russian passions were vividly personified in Yevgeny Yevtushenko, the liberal Soviet poet. After the first border clash in March, he composed a poem entitled "On the Red Snows of the Ussuri," warning that the Russians were prepared to crush the Chinese just as the knights of old Muscovy had defeated the Mongol hordes at the battle of Kulikovo in 1380.

> Vladimir and Kiev, observe in the murky dusk
> The bombs in the new Mongol quivers.
> But warning bells will peal should they come,
> And there will be enough warrior knights
> For many more Kulikovos.[87]

Chinese nationalist sentiment was expressed in a succession of rallies around the country attended, according to Beijing statistics, by more than 400 million people. Terming them "new Tsars," speakers at these rallies denounced the Kremlin leaders for striving to "turn the Soviet Union into a larger Russian Empire" than that controlled by the old Moscow rulers.[88] This theme was obviously contrived to unify the population, and its effectiveness could be discerned in Chinese communities outside China. In Hong Kong, for example, the anti-Communist newspaper *Daily Light* was stirred to a pitch of patriotic fervor. Despite the "many changes" wrought by the Communists, it said in a front-page editorial, "the national spirit of the Chinese people still flourishes."[89] Hong Kong's Chinese, many of them refugees from communism, also displayed their patriotism by crowding into local cinemas to see "Anti-China Atrocities of the New Tsars," a propaganda film produced in Beijing. Documenting China's case against Moscow, the film portrayed Chinese troops finally overcoming the Russians as the narrator warned that the Soviet "revisionists" would be "wiped out thoroughly, wholly, and completely" if they "dare to continue their intrusions into the sacred territory of our great motherland."[90] This rhetoric was paralleled, meanwhile, by urgent and extensive Soviet and Chinese defense efforts in the frontier areas.

In addition to accelerating troop deployments in the region, the Russians initiated measures aimed at mobilizing the populations near the border. A campaign to sharpen military preparedness was begun in the Central Asian republics of Kazakhstan, Tadzhikistan, and Kirgiz with a program to train youths as artillerymen, tank drivers, radio operators, and border guards. On March 10, a similar program was inaugurated under military auspices in the Maritime Province adjacent to Manchuria.[91] The Kremlin also attempted to encourage the movement of settlers from western parts of the Soviet Union to the border zones from which thousands of frightened Russian farmers had fled during the first frontier clashes. Moscow offered land grants and attractive loans to volunteers, but the migration scheme failed to generate much enthusiasm.[92] The Soviet defense effort was thus primarily a military deployment of troops and equipment.

The Beijing defense plan, on the other hand, was essentially predicated on the mobilization of people—and the program was designed to serve economic, social, and political as well as military purposes. It afforded Beijing the chance to decentralize the economy by transferring industries that were formerly concentrated in coastal cities and vulnerable regions like Manchuria. It was also a device to shift fractious Red Guards and other youths to the countryside. And it provided local Army commanders and government officials with the opportunity to restore and in some cases stiffen the controls that had broken down during the Cultural Revolution.

Following the border battles in March, the Beijing authorities issued a series of directives aimed at increasing the country's grain reserves, for both economic and military reasons. Peasants in Guangdong province were reportedly compelled to contribute 10 per cent of their monthly rice ration to collective granaries.[93] In the Shanghai area, told that China might face a protracted war, farm families were instructed to store a six months' supply of food.[94] State agents in several other regions also used the defense drive to extract larger percentages of rice, wheat, and other cereals from peasants than were required by procurement quotas. According to official accounts published in August, about 20 per cent of China's production brigades had overfulfilled their annual grain procurement targets ahead of schedule. At the same time, some provincial regimes curbed private cultivation and marketing by peasants. In late July, for instance, the Guangzhou Revolutionary Committee put the city's "free" markets under State control and ordered peasants to sell their private produce only to government purchasing depots at fixed prices.[95]

Beijing also accelerated a campaign to disperse urban factories and workshops throughout the hinterlands. *Red Flag* called this a "strategic redeployment" destined to create "reliable industrial bases" around the country and thus increase China's "maneuverability" in the event of an enemy attack. "Each locality could conduct the war autonomously, wipe out the enemy, and win the conflict."[96]

This ambitious decentralization program probably began in the fall of 1968. A sampling of published evidence disclosed that a boiler factory and a welding-rod plant were transferred from Guangzhou to towns deeper in Guangdong province, and a shipyard situated on the Pearl River east of the city was relocated farther into the interior. The Shanghai authorities moved a large textile mill into the suburbs, advising its employees that the installation would now be safe from "possible air raids." In line with this "strategic redeployment," communes were also exhorted to develop small nitrogenous-fertilizer plants, electric-power stations, iron and steel works, tool factories, and other small enterprises that could be constructed with little investment.[97] To a significant degree, then, the Chinese leaders seemed to be taking advantage of the war scare to promote projects similar to those pushed during the Great Leap Forward.

During the summer, as the danger of war appeared to be growing, a vast drive was initiated to build air-raid shelters in China's major cities. In Guangzhou, a tremendous tunnel complex was laid out, with underground passages leading from the center of the city to

White Cloud Hill, near the airport. Striving to keep the city's residents alert, the Guangzhou military garrison conducted frequent air-raid drills, often with Chinese aircraft flying overhead in simulated attacks.[98] Ships entering Shanghai and other Chinese ports, meanwhile, were being given instructions on harbor positions to adopt in the event of air raids.[99] And even Beijing was digging bomb shelters in what a Hungarian correspondent there described as a "frenzy of activity."[100]

Loyal to their conviction that an invader would be "drowned in an ocean of people," Chinese strategists mounted a rigorous program of military training for civilians rather than intensive troop deployments. A key feature of this program was the reactivation of the People's Militia, whose estimated 7 million recruits consisted mainly of peasants and students who had been transferred to the countryside.[101] Thousands of members of the militia were reportedly incorporated into a paramilitary organization known as the Production and Construction Corps. The corps had originally been formed by the Army to serve as a labor force in Xinjiang province. Now, however, similar contingents were being established throughout the country. They were also being moved into areas close to the border with the Soviet Union, apparently to bear the brunt of an initial enemy assault while regular Army troops stood at distances of about two hundred miles from the frontier in counterattacking formations.[102] Confronted by enormous of Soviet military power, many professional Chinese officers must have taken a skeptical view of the militia's ability to stop the Russian juggernaut. An attempt to dispel this skepticism was mirrored in an official rationale of the militia's role:

Is the Militia now outdated? No, absolutely not! It is true that modern arms have some impact on war, but no modern weapon changes the objective laws of war nor the great truth that "the Army and the people are the foundation of victory." On the contrary, the larger the scale of war and the more complicated the war situation, the more necessary it is to bring the masses into full play and to turn the whole nation into soldiers.[103]

Doubt about the efficacy of the militia was only one of the problems facing the Beijing leaders as they tried to mobilize for war. In several places, troops and civilian officials questioned the reality of the Soviet threat, claiming that the Russians "would not dare to invade."[104] Members of the militia were blamed for "taking the enemy lightly" or arguing that a war, if it came, would only affect the border areas.[105] Apathy even extended into regions adjacent to the Soviet Union. A Heilongjiang province broadcast complained of "the lethargy of people who have little or no awareness" of the danger of war.[106] And, as it had in 1965, when the threat of an American attack loomed large, the possibility of war again revived the long-standing strategic debate that divided professional Chinese officers and Maoist ideologues—with the ideologues repeating that the Army required more political indoctrination, and the professionals emphasizing the need for "practical training." Against the ideologues' insistence on continual political meetings and indoctrination sessions, the *Liberation Army Daily* stated: "It will not do to rely solely on lectures. More time must be given to training."[107]

By the middle of the summer, reports from China revealed that special teams were advising Army officers and government officials throughout the country to expect an "inevitable" Soviet assault against such targets as the Chinese gaseous-diffusion plant at Lanzhou, in the northern province of Gansu, and the atomic test site at Lop Nor, in Xinjiang. One document distributed at these briefings was a new Beijing directive authorizing troops to intensify their suppression of "anarchists," "counterrevolutionaries," and "subversive elements" who might "obstruct war preparedness."[108] And a Communist spokesman in Hong Kong took pains to tell a Western journalist that the war preparations were "not just a gimmick to rally a disunited people behind the Mao regime" but were being made "in deadly earnest because of the continued danger of a Soviet attack."[109]

The Kremlin's increasingly belligerent rhetoric was largely responsible for these Chinese fears. In one statement, Soviet Deputy Defense Minister Matvey V. Zakharov bluntly warned Beijing that the Russians had the capability to launch a "blitzkrieg" against China.[110] Even more threatening was an article by Victor Louis, the Soviet publicist. Plainly calculated to shock Beijing, his article disclosed that Soviet missiles were already zeroed in on Chinese nuclear installations and other targets, adding that the Kremlin would not hesitate to act against China as it did against Czechoslovakia. Louis pointed out that China's most vulnerable region was Xinjiang, and suggested that Muslim dissidents in that area might well form a cohesive movement that would call on the Soviet Union for "fraternal help." Implicit in the Louis scenario, then, was the possibility that the Russians might stir up a Muslim revolt as they did in 1962—but use it this time as a pretext to invade Xinjiang in much the same way that they intervened in Czechoslovakia.

The Soviet Union is adhering to the doctrine that socialist countries have the right to interfere in each other's affairs in their own interests or those of others who are threatened. The fact that China is many times larger than Czechoslovakia and might offer active resistance is, according to Marxist theoreticians, no reason for not applying this doctrine.[111]

At the same time, changes in Soviet military personnel in the areas bordering China indicated that there was a reality to Russian rhetoric. The Kremlin promoted several younger officers to command posts in the region and, significantly, they placed a missile expert, General Vladimir F. Tolubko, in charge of the frontier zone adjacent to Manchuria.[112] The Russians had earlier set up missile sites at two places in Mongolia, both within easy range of Beijing and Manchuria's industrial cities.[118]

In line with their carrot-and-stick strategy, the Kremlin leaders continued to parallel their menacing gestures with offers to negotiate with the Chinese. An opportunity for Sino-Soviet talks finally emerged with the death of Ho Chi Minh in early September. The North Vietnamese President's funeral presented an occasion for prominent Communists from around the world to assemble in Hanoi and, while there, the most autonomous among them maneuvered to mediate the dispute. Rumanian Premier Ion Gheorghe Maurer, for example, reportedly urged Zhou Enlai to open discussions with Soviet Premier Kosygin.[114] And Kosygin, who arrived in Hanoi after Zhou's departure, asked the North Vietnamese to help arrange a meeting with the Chinese.[115]

The North Vietnamese were desperately anxious to avert a war between Moscow and Beijing. A conflict, they realized, would force them to choose sides and deprive them of their profitably neutral position, and it would totally cut them off from Russian military supplies that traversed China. Thus they stressed the necessity for "solidarity within the socialist camp" and, following Ho Chi Minh's death, publicized a document quoting him as deploring "the dissensions that are dividing the fraternal parties" and calling for "the restoration of unity."[116] In addition, the North Vietnamese leaders actively pressed the Chinese to accept the Soviet invitation to discuss the border issue. The result, on September 11, was a brief yet decisive encounter between Zhou and Kosygin in Beijing that at least took the Chinese and Russians off their collision course.

A terse Chinese report revealed rather casually that the encounter took place as Kosygin "was passing through Beijing on his way home."[117] Actually, the Soviet Premier's journey was far more complicated. After requesting a meeting with Zhou Enlai, he had left Hanoi without a reply. He then stopped at Calcutta and proceeded to Dyushambe, the capital of Soviet Tadzhikistan in Central Asia. Zhou's affirmative answer probably reached him somewhere en route, and he doubled back to Beijing, where his reception was frosty. The Chinese refused to permit him to enter the city, insisting instead that their meeting be held in an airport lounge. Though infuriated by this lack of courtesy, Kosygin nevertheless did most of the talking during the four-hour encounter and his statements essentially reflected the Kremlin's sweet-and-sour strategy.

He reminded Zhou Enlai that the Soviet Union had the military muscle to bomb China back to the Han dynasty, and further warned him that a war between the two Communist giants would be a world conflict. He therefore proposed that the two countries seek to avoid such a catastrophe by opening negotiations to resolve their specific boundary problems and also to discuss the resumption of trade. In that way, Moscow and Beijing could at least return to normal diplomatic relations even if their ideological schism remained unhealed.[118] Zhou, however, asserted that an over-all boundary accord was not possible until Moscow acknowledged that Tsarist Russia had illegally seized Chinese territory. He agreed to Kosygin's proposal to open talks—but he recommended that both sides pull back their troops from the frontier in order to "avert armed conflicts" that might impede even a limited settlement.[119]

Quite plainly, then, the Russians had frightened Beijing into conceding to some kind of modus vivendi, and the Chinese virtually admitted that they had been driven by fear to negotiate. Alleging that there were "a handful of war maniacs" in the Kremlin who would "dare to raid China's strategic sites," they declared: "There is no reason whatsoever for China and the Soviet Union to fight a war over the boundary questions."[120]

On October 19, a thirty-man Soviet delegation arrived in Beijing to begin the border negotiations. The Russian group was headed by First Deputy Foreign Minister Vasili V. Kuznetsov, a former Soviet Ambassador to China who had, in his youth, worked in a Pittsburgh steel mill. Representing the Chinese was Deputy Foreign Minister Giau Quanhua, an experienced and sophisticated official who had the rare distinction of having obtained a doctorate in philosophy in Germany.

The talks between the two delegations were to drag on for more than a year, their only visible result being that they arrested what appeared to be a slide toward war in late 1969. But they did nothing to halt the exchanges of vitriolic propaganda between Beijing and Moscow. Nor did they discourage either the Chinese or the Russians from continuing to reinforce their respective frontier zones. In 1971, the Kremlin was still building up its troop strength in Siberia and Central Asia while the Chinese were stiffening their air defenses with new radar networks, surface-to-air missiles, and other modern equipment.[121]

But the persistent Soviet threat indirectly stimulated Beijing's increased diplomatic flexibility and, as the decade of the 1970s opened, the Chinese were engaged in an assortment of different maneuvers designed to win recognition abroad. Diluting their pretensions to ideological purity, they made overtures to "revisionist" Yugoslavia. They repaired their frayed ties with Burma and began wooing such anti-Communist Asian states as the Philippines and Malaysia, and they supported Pakistan's military regime despite its slaughter of thousands of East Pakistan peasants whose struggle for independence would, under different circumstances, have been hailed by Beijing as a "national liberation movement." Their rice-for-rubber trade accord with Ceylon also prompted the Chinese to ignore a revolutionary peasant revolt in that country.[122]

A striking example of Beijing's new pragmatism was its agreement on October 13, 1970, to establish diplomatic relations with Canada. Twenty months earlier, when the negotiations on this issue began, the Chinese had stubbornly demanded that the Canadians recognize the Communist regime as the "sole legal Government" for all China, including Taiwan. The Canadians refused, asserting that they would neither endorse nor oppose Beijing's position on the status of the island. After repeated delays, the Chinese finally yielded to a compromise formula that acquiesced to Canada's decision merely to "note" their claim to sovereignty over Taiwan.[123] That major concession, dramatizing as it did Beijing's desire to play a role in world politics, had an immediate impact. On November 20, for the first time in twenty years, a majority of General Assembly members voted to seat the Communists in the United Nations as the representative of China. Beijing was barred from actual representation by a two-thirds majority rule that had been contrived by the United States.[124] A year later, however, the Nixon Administration agreed to scrap that rule and support. Beijing's claim to United Nations representation—on condition that the Chiang Kai-shek regime retained a place in the General Assembly.[125]

The change in relations between the United States and the Chinese Communists began to become perceptible toward the end of 1969. In a significant address aimed at reassuring the Beijing leadership, a member of President Nixon's cabinet declared that the United States "did not seek to exploit" the Sino-Soviet dispute for its own advantages, and would refrain from associating "with either side against the other."[126] At the same time, Nixon also continued his gradual efforts to reach an accommodation with the Communists. His speeches stressed that "no stable and enduring international order is conceivable" without China's "contribution."[127] And he carried on his program of revising discriminatory American trade and travel restrictions toward China. In early 1970, by way of a reply, the Chinese resumed the formal diplomatic talks in Warsaw after a two-year suspension.

The first outright indication that the Communists were actually embarking on a new policy toward the United States was visible in Beijing on October 1, 1970, the twenty-first anniversary of the founding of the People's Republic of China. On that day, Mao invited his old American biographer Edgar Snow to stand beside him on the rostrum of the Tiananmen Gate. When their photograph was published in the *People's Daily* nearly three months later, it was accompanied by one of Mao's quotations stating that "peoples of the world, including the American people, are all our friends."[128] That esoteric signal, hardly noticed at the time, augured a fresh Chinese approach to the United States called "people's diplomacy."

Beijing's next step in that direction came on April 7, 1971, when a Chinese table-tennis team in Japan officially invited a group of fifteen American Ping-Pong players to tour China.[129] Accompanied by the representatives of four American news media, the athletes created a sensation in China and around the world. Soon afterward, Edgar Snow was authorized by the Chinese to publish an article revealing that Mao had told him that Nixon would be welcomed in Beijing "either as a tourist or as President" because "at present the problems between the United States and China would have to be solved" with him.[130]

Until April, the President had been in secret contact with the Chinese through various intermediaries, the most prominent among them Pakistani President Yahya Khan and Rumanian President Nicolae Ceaucescu. So by the time Edgar Snow published Mao's invitation Nixon already knew that the Chinese had endorsed the idea of his visiting Beijing. But to put an affirmative response on the record, the President went out of his way in a speech on April 29 to say that he expected to visit China "in some capacity."[131]

The next step was to begin making practical arrangements for the trip. On July 9, concocting a story that he was ill with stomach trouble en route home from Vietnam, Kissinger flew from Pakistan to Beijing for two days of conversations with Zhou Enlai. He returned to Beijing in October, and preparations for the President's visit were completed by late 1971.

Speaking to a group of Cairo newsmen in Beijing in November, Vice-Premier Li Xiannian sardonically pointed out that "a visit by the chief of a state that regards itself as one of the two super-powers" required vast planning—while, in contrast, visits between "friends" like the Chinese and Egyptians could be organized "in ten minutes."[132] But despite that comment, the Chinese authorities were amazingly cooperative in the huge operation that the President's trip entailed. One indication was their willingness to permit American television networks, which function with an enormous superstructure of technicians and electronic paraphernalia, to install themselves in Beijing for the duration of Nixon's visit.

The President's week-long trip to China, which began on February 21, 1972, was a spectacular event. Nixon, his wife, the White House party, and the newsmen accompanying them were feted in lavish style, and some members of the United States group were almost speechless when, after years of Sino-American distrust and hostility, a Chinese military orchestra played "Turkey in the Straw" at a banquet in Beijing. The President was received by Mao, and the edition of the *People's Daily* featuring a front-page photograph of the two men shaking hands was sold out on the streets of Beijing within three hours of its appearance.

Nixon and Zhou Enlai also discussed bilateral questions, such as the establishment of scientific, cultural, sports, journalistic, and trade exchanges between the United States and China. They talked at great length as well about problems ranging from Vietnam and Japan to Korea, the Soviet Union, and the conflict between India and Pakistan. Perhaps the most consequential result of the meeting, evidently reached after hard bargaining, was a pledge by the President that the United States would "progressively" withdraw its forces and military installations from Taiwan "as the tension in the area diminishes." That pledge, combined with an acknowledgment that Taiwan is a province of China, was designed to set in motion a political process that would encourage the Communists and the Nationalists to resolve their differences without outside interference. This essentially conformed to the demands that the Beijing regime had set forth since its foundation in 1949.

Though the issues dividing the United States and China were not easily resolved—and would not be for some time to come—the summit meeting had inaugurated a new dialogue between the two nations, and that was significant in itself. For the United States, it spelled the end of more than twenty years of striving to "contain" the Chinese Communists, a policy that had proved to be as costly as it was fruitless. For the Beijing regime, it meant the attainment of big-power status.

Beijing's position as a big power had been given international recognition in the autumn, when the People's Republic of China won the right to occupy the Chinese seat at the United Nations and Chiang Kai-shek's Nationalists were expelled from the world organization. Though the Nixon Administration seemingly had made an attempt to prevent that result, it was really unruffled by the outcome of the United Nations vote. For in President Nixon's view, the main priority was the establishment of a relationship between the United States and Beijing. He was ready to pay a price for that achievement.

The initial contact between the United States and Communist China appeared at first to play in Beijing's favor. Even though Nixon sought to reassure them that his "new relationship" with the Communists would "not be made at the expense of old friends," Chiang Kai-shek's Nationalists were immediately demoralized by the loss of the American support they had enjoyed for two decades. The Japanese, whom Nixon had circumvented in pursuing his overtures in Beijing, also felt that they had been outmaneuvered. And the Kremlin reacted with predictable hostility, asserting that "those who advocate a United States *rapprochement* with China are rabid haters of the Soviet Union."[133]

Exalting his voyage to Beijing in a toast to his Chinese hosts, Nixon had described it as "the week that changed the world." His language sounded exaggerated, yet the breakthrough journey did indeed alter international relationships drastically. Moscow propagandists at first reacted angrily, but Soviet leader Leonid Brezhnev met with Nixon at a scheduled summit in May 1972 to discuss arms control and other issues. So Nixon's visit to China, instead of alienating the Russians, dramatized to them the importance of maintaining their ties with America lest they be isolated in the new diplomatic balance. The North Vietnamese, who until then had been juggling the rival Communist giants for their own benefit, now felt abandoned—and, following a final offensive to improve their negotiating posture, they agreed to a cease-fire with the United States in January 1973. The fragile peace gradually eroded, and they swept into Saigon two years afterward. Three years later, however, they were at war with China, their former ally—whose purported threat to Southeast Asia had originally been America's motive for intervening in the region.

The United States and China established formal diplomatic ties at the end of 1978, and their reconciliation further spurred the momentum that Nixon and Mao had set in motion. Within a decade, Asia was unrecognizable compared with what it had been a generation earlier. Gone was the bipolarity of the 1950s. The triangular competition involving Washington, Moscow, and Beijing, which had characterized the latter half of the 1960s, had also ended. The transition continued through the 1970s and 1980s, stimulating the emergence of a complicated array of fresh forces. The Soviet Union and China largely buried their differences, thus contributing to peace in the area, and that development basically served America's interests. But Japan's extraordinary dynamism, coupled with the phenomenal success of South Korea, Hong Kong, Taiwan, and Singapore, confronted the United States with new and complex challenges as the Pacific, once a cockpit of military tensions, became an arena of economic rivalries.

Amid these changes, a pivotal question was whether China's domestic stability and consequent foreign alignments could be preserved. For the cataclysmic Cultural Revolution had lacerated the country's social and psychological texture, and the traumatic experience was to have an impact on its leaders and people far into the future.

CHAPTER 22

Continuing Turmoil

❧

> A revolutionary party must worry about its
> inability to hear the voice of the people.
> What is to be feared most is silence.
> — DENG XIAOPING, 1978

> Don't be afraid to spill blood.
> — DENG XIAOPING, 1989

SHORTLY after midnight on September 9, 1976, Mao Zedong died
in Beijing at the age of eighty-two. China's authorities decreed
ten days of formal mourning as radio stations and loudspeakers intoned somber music and official newspapers, bordered in black,
praised him as the "greatest Marxist of the contemporary era," whose
contributions to worldwide revolution had been "immortal." The period of bereavement ended nine days later with a memorial rally in
Tiananmem Square attended by a million people.[1] But the organized
expressions of grief concealed the real feelings of the Chinese, who,
as far as Western correspondents could judge at the time, seemed to
be apprehensive rather than distraught.[2] Though Mao was gone, they
could not be sure that the upheavals he had sparked were truly
finished. Their anxieties would be justified during the years ahead,
as contending factions battled to fill the vacuum left by his death.

Mao had been tormented by the fear that his Communist Party
comrades would subvert his utopian vision and personal authority by
creating a Soviet-style bureaucracy. So he had celebrated the virtues
of volatility—and, typically borrowing from Chinese mythology, portrayed himself as the Golden Monkey, wrathfully wielding the "massive cudgel" of "class struggle" as he preached perpetual revolution.[3]
A maniacal, almost nihilistic streak thus characterized his apocalyptic
campaigns, the last of them the destructive Cultural Revolution.

Though he typically blamed others for the anarchy, he belatedly conceded during his final years to the necessity to restore order. By then, however, the devastation had been too profound and pervasive, and his heirs would be saddled with the gigantic burden of rebuilding the shattered society.

But they were to be nagged by bitter internecine disputes. For Mao, despite his rhetorical reverence for its supremacy, had prevented the Communist Party from becoming an effective, durable institution—and instead, promoting the cult of his infallible personality, refused to relinquish or even dilute his absolute rule. Similarly convinced that his doctrines would be betrayed after his disappearance, he had also recoiled from preparing for a smooth transition of authority. So fresh conflicts inevitably erupted as rival groups jockeyed for power in an atmosphere that resembled the arcane struggles for the throne that had followed the deaths of China's ancient emperors.

Claiming his mantle, his widow, Jiang Qing, and three of her close associates, Zhang Chunqiao, Wang Hongwen, and Yao Wenyuan, later vilified as the ultraleftist "Gang of Four," initially moved to seize control. They were crushed by Hua Guofeng, a colorless hack whom Mao had vaguely named as his heir, presumably to avert posthumous clashes. Deng Xiaoping and a group of Party veterans eventually ousted him, and introduced an impressive array of economic innovations. But they rapidly began to squabble among themselves as the reforms, though hugely successful at first, dislocated the country. Their reluctance to sponsor liberal political changes meanwhile alienated numbers of teachers, students, and other intellectuals, whose demands for democracy escalated into a series of massive protests in Beijing during the spring of 1989. On the evening of June 3, alarmed by what they perceived to be a threat to their regime, Deng and his comrades brought loyal elements of the Army into the capital to quell the demonstration. The soldiers fired into the crowd, and the massacre again plunged China into turmoil.

So Mao's dream of permanent revolution had bequeathed the nation a legacy of permanent instability and uncertainty from which it would not easily recover.

The convulsions of the Cultural Revolution appeared to the outside world to have subsided during the early 1970s, after Mao ended

China's self-imposed isolation by inviting President Nixon to Beijing. Soon Western businessmen, scholars, journalists, and tourists were discovering a country that had been closed to them for more than twenty years. Americans, whose missionaries and educators had originally sought to convert the Chinese to Western ways a century before, were particularly elated. Many had felt spurned when China embraced communism, and their admiration for their protégés had degenerated into hatred. But now, it seemed, the Chinese had redeemed themselves. The aggressive "Red" China of the Korean conflict and the Cold War, which had threatened its neighbors and enslaved its own people, suddenly became the China of acupuncture, priceless art treasures, and delicious cuisine. Celebrities as diverse as Shirley MacLaine and John Kenneth Galbraith applauded China's progress, and even usually skeptical journalists were ecstatic. A decade earlier, James Reston of *The New York Times* had dismissed the Chinese revolution as a "ghastly mess." Reporting from Beijing in 1971, by contrast, he compared Mao's mass mobilization schemes to an old-fashioned "cooperative barn-raising" that ought to make Americans "outrageously nostalgic and even sentimental." Another *Times* correspondent, Harrison Salisbury, exalted the new "Maoist man" as a spiritual model for Americans: "When would the New American Man and the New American Woman walk the earth, proud and confident, making the oceans boil and the continents shake?"[4]

Not even Mao painted so rosy a picture. Indeed, he had acknowledged to Edgar Snow, his American biographer, that the Cultural Revolution had caused "great chaos."[5] But certain sectors, carefully protected from the tumult, had registered remarkable accomplishments.

China's first artificial satellite, launched in April 1970, indirectly revealed that its scientists had perfect computers and other sophisticated electronic equipment. The successful space shot also testified to advances in the metallurgical, chemical, and machine-tool industries. Experimental tests of thermonuclear devices, conducted during the late 1960s, further indicated that the defense establishment was shielded. Nor had the turbulence crippled the nation's capacity to produce modern fighter and bomber aircraft as well as naval vessels.[6]

Essentially an urban phenomenon, the Cultural Revolution had largely spared the economy. Natural calamities and misguided policies notwithstanding, China's economic growth rates during the previous twenty years had outstripped those of India and Indonesia, the other populous nations of Asia.[7] Grain production had reached more than 240 million tons in 1970—an increase of 25 per cent over 1957, until then the peak year. And, through rationing, the rigorous procurement of crops from peasants, and massive wheat imports from Canada, Australia, and elsewhere, grain reserves had risen to 40 million tons by 1971.[8] A respectable industrial foundation had been laid, as mirrored by the output of iron, steel, cement, and electrical energy. Compared with other developing countries, moreover, China ranked high in literacy and life expectancy.[9] But many of its remote rural areas were still abysmally poor and, by the early 1970s, becoming even poorer. The economy was also extremely fragile, which meant that another catastrophe could cause widespread misery, including starvation. At the same time, the growth rates of the past were beginning to show signs of slipping.

The Red Guards had vanished, numbers of them suppressed by the Army with the same brutality they had inflicted on others. Also gone were Mao's fiercest slogans, supplanted by appeals for realism, diligence, and discipline. In August 1971, for example, a *Red Flag* editorial warned against "rejecting the experts" and "denying or neglecting the role of specialists."[10] Primary and secondary schools, which along with the universities had been ravaged by the Cultural Revolution, had returned to conventional curricula. A Western visitor to a Beijing middle school in the spring of 1971 found the students engrossed in such courses as mathematics, chemistry, physics, history, and geography—the lessons flavored, apparently as protocol, with platitudes from Mao's book of quotations. A French class, for instance, was reciting by rote, *"Unissons-nous pour remporter des victoires encore plus grandes!"* as an English class intoned its equivalent, "Let us unite to achieve even greater victories!" Many teachers, banished to manual labor in distant villages, had been brought back, and, to allay their worries of renewed trouble, soldiers were stationed in the schools to protect them.[11]

Official publicists continued to praise the "victory" of the Cultural Revolution. But such propaganda recalled the days when senior Communist figures, in deference to Mao's godlike status, had deviously bowed to him while circumventing his authority. Some of the same men were now playing a similar charade as they awaited his death in hopes of unraveling his policies. Foremost among them was Deng Xiaoping, who had been humiliated by Mao's acolytes for having championed flexibility rather than mindless ideology. An incurable chain-smoker, barely five feet tall, he was then close to seventy, and as tough and resilient as bamboo. His old comrades respected his organizational talent, his network of contacts, and his political experience. A veteran of the Long March and an Army commissar during the civil war against the Nationalists, he was closely linked to the Chinese military establishment. He had intimate connections as well within the Party, having served as its Secretary General two decades before. Zhou Enlai, who by 1972 was being treated for cancer, had chosen him to be his successor as Prime Minister—and thus supervise China's recovery. Despite their differences, Mao begrudgingly admired Deng and, at the time, endorsed Zhou's proposal to rescue him from disgrace.

Soon Zhou had steered Deng into the position of First Deputy Prime Minister and later engineered his promotion to Party Vice-Chairman and Chief of Staff of the People's Liberation Army. As Zhou's health declined, Deng gradually took over, and drafted a comprehensive program called the "four modernizations," aimed at overhauling China's agriculture and industry, system of higher education, scientific and technological research, and national defense. He envisioned more latitude for local officials and factory managers to make decisions. Peasants and workers, rather than harnessed and exhorted to produce, would be offered profits, bonuses, and other incentives to increase output. Teachers and students would be permitted to go to Japan, the United States, and other Western countries in order to acquire the latest knowledge. Conversely, Western and Japanese advisers were to be admitted to China, and foreign investors would be invited to put their capital into joint ventures.

To attain these objectives, Deng realized, would entail a two-pronged strategy. His first step was to smash the residual ultraleftists unleashed by Mao during the Cultural Revolution, who still aspired to preserve their waning influence. Thus he contemplated a vigorous offensive against them by reasserting the Communist Party's political controls.[12] After that, he would have to persuade the old Party *apparatchiks* to give up their orthodox Marxist belief in central planning, and to support his reforms. Both tasks were to prove daunting.

The Party machine, which Deng hoped to direct against the radicals, was in ruins. Seven of the seventeen members of the Politburo had been dismissed during the Cultural Revolution. Of the ninety-seven members of the Central Committee, fifty-three had been purged, along with four of the Party's six regional first secretaries and twenty-three of its twenty-nine provincial first secretaries. With them had gone their aides and other employees, so that, from top to bottom, the nationwide administration was scarcely more than a skeleton. The psychological impact of the upheaval on the bureaucracy was equally disastrous. Surviving officials, unable to predict whether the political pendulum might swing again and expose them to new assaults, prudently avoided responsibilities. Years of zigzagging ideological campaigns had taught them that yesterday's revolutionaries might be suddenly derided as today's counterrevolutionaries, and vice versa.[13]

Another obstacle to the restoration of stability was the inclination of Chinese to nurse grievances—a tendency that left little scope for reconciliation. Their sensitivity to real or imagined slights and insults, as epitomized in the traditional notion of "face," had long been apparent in the family and clan vendettas that persisted as generation after generation recalled old grudges and sought to settle old scores.[14] So the murders, tortures, and other savagery of the Cultural Revolution were often the manifestations of longstanding feuds rather than ideological clashes, and they left a legacy of acrimonious memories that made the return to national unity difficult.

The principal foe of moderation was Mao's wife, Jiang Qing, whose inner circle of comrades represented the intransigent ultraleftists. Operating from their base in Shanghai, they had initially been active in propelling the Cultural Revolution across China. The campaign had thrust them into unprecedented prominence, and they still retained a countrywide web of loyal supporters, many of them in key positions. So they plainly had a stake in preventing Zhou, Deng, and the Party veterans from consolidating their authority. During 1974 and 1975, therefore, they maneuvered strenuously to secure their own power.

Though a cloak of secrecy then shrouded Mao's health, he was widely assumed to be near death. Stories circulated that he owed the flickering spark of life still in him to the virgins procured to share his bed—an ancient Chinese practice that supposedly revived dying men. Whatever his actual condition, Jiang Qing signaled her intention to succeed him and, either because he was feeble or because he chose to indulge her, he said nothing to the contrary. She received foreign dignitaries on his behalf, and the press, under her control, increasingly evoked the auspicious reigns of female rulers, like Empress Lu of the Han dynasty and Tang dynasty Empress Wu, who had ascended the throne after their husbands died. Her publicists also attacked Zhou obliquely through allegorical denunciations of Confucius, professing that his conservative ethic had opposed the interests of the people.[15] In a similar ploy, they attacked a documentary film by the noted Italian movie director Michelangelo Antonioni which portrayed

China as poor and backward. It seemed like an absurd tactic, since the film was not being shown in China. But the Chinese, with their skill at reading oracle bones and other esoterica, were expected to infer from the assault that Zhou and Deng, who had invited Antonioni to China, shared his "reactionary" views. Assailing Zhou further, Jiang Qing's spokesmen denounced his decision to restore Deng to office as a "rightist wind."[16]

The first of several crises broke in January 1976, when Zhou died after his long bout with cancer. A devoted Communist since his youth, he had participated in the Party's bloodiest episodes. But he was an urbane figure who, like a character in Chinese legend, personified the sagacious courtier who had restrained the despotic emperor. Intellectuals respected him for his attempts to protect them, and even peasants in remote areas revered him as a species rare in China—an honest official. And though he had been careful not to defy Mao directly, he had done his utmost to keep the government on an even keel during the worst of the Cultural Revolution. A million people, many of them sobbing, lined up in the bitter winter cold of Beijing to pay him homage as a funeral cortege carried his body through the city to a crematorium. The unusual display of emotion implicitly symbolized their resistance to the ultraleftists. Reacting to the sentiment, which she knew to be directed against her, Jiang Qing refused to bare her head as she approached Zhou's bier. Her tactless gesture, seen on national television, exacerbated tensions.

On March 8, exactly two months following Zhou's death, the largest meteorite ever to hit the earth fell in northeastern China. To numbers of superstitious Chinese, the event evoked the memory of Zhuge Liang, the dazzling hero of the classic epic *Romance of the Three Kingdoms,* who had died nearly two thousand years before as a meteorite had also blazed across the sky. The coincidence suggested that Zhou, like Zhuge, was destined for immortality.[17] Then, in early April, came the annual Qingming festival, at which Chinese customarily pray at the tombs of their ancestors. Aware that Zhou had been childless, hundreds of thousands undertook to serve as his surrogate family. They marched to the Monument of Revolutionary Heroes, in the heart of Beijing's Tiananmen Square, which they piled high with wreaths in his honor. Among them were students, teachers, workers, and peasants, many carrying infants, and several recited poems or pasted up wall posters praising him, or took oaths of allegiance to his memory. More and more people poured in, swelling into the largest spontaneous demonstration in Chinese history.

As news of the processions spread throughout the country, provincial sympathizers sent flowers to the city aboard trains that were covered with crude slogans and caricatures hostile to Jiang Qing. Salacious stories about her quickly spread. One, ignoring the fact that she was in her fifties, alleged that she had borne a child by her deputy Zhang Chunqiao. Such tales were indirectly aimed at Mao, since they pictured him as a helpless old cuckold. He soon became a transparent target of criticism as intellectuals repeated his claim to have been the equal of Qin Shi Huang, the unifier of China in the third century B.C., who had boasted of having "burned the books and buried the scholars."

What happened in Tiananmen Square at that stage ironically prefigured the tragic events, orchestrated by different leaders, that were to occur in the same spot thirteen years later.

On the morning of April 5, 1976, vanloads of police drove into the square, presumably on Jiang Qing's instructions. They ordered the crowds to disperse, then removed the wreaths and wall posters honoring Zhou. The protesters objected, fighting broke out, and the violence escalated. At dusk, platoons of troops moved in, wielding guns and truncheons. After systematically cordoning off the area, they began to shoot and club the unarmed demonstrators, killing or wounding thousands. Numbers of others were rounded up, branded "counterrevolutionaries," and summarily executed. The radicals had prevailed and, during the following days, they organized rallies at which some 2 million people, many of whom had earlier paid their condolences to Zhou, were brought by truck or bus to Tiananmen Square to shout their support for Mao's "proletarian revolutionary line."[18]

Mao evidently swallowed Jiang Qing's allegation that Deng Xiaoping had instigated the protests as a way of discrediting him and repudiating the Cultural Revolution. He hastily ousted Deng from all his positions, thus blocking him from succeeding Zhou as Prime Minister. Jiang Qing sought the job for Zhang Chunqiao, her reputed lover. But Mao was still lucid enough to realize that Deng's old Party comrades, who hated her, might plunge the country into civil strife if he complied. Accordingly, he compromised by naming Hua Guofeng, an obscure figure, to be Prime Minister and First Deputy Chairman of the Central Committee.

Hua, at the time in his fifties, had been a minor official in Mao's native Hunan province. He survived the purges of the Cultural Revolution to gain the vacant position of Provincial Party Secretary, and was subsequently summoned by Mao to Beijing. Though he later claimed that Mao had anointed him his successor, Mao never clarified the point. In any case, Hua's appointment fulfilled its purpose as an interim measure. The Party stalwarts seemed to be satisfied, since Hua posed no threat to them. Nor could the radicals complain, since he was Mao's choice. Both sides knew, however, that the lull created by Hua's promotion was only temporary—and that the power struggles would resume after Mao's disappearance.[19]

Just as the fall of a meteorite had dramatized Zhou Enlai's death, so another event portended ominous change. In the early hours of July 28, 1976, an earthquake suddenly struck Tangshan, almost completely annihilating the northern industrial city and killing an estimated million people in the worst natural calamity in human history. The stupendous death toll was largely due to the negligence of the authorities, who were either incompetent or too embroiled in ideological disputes to mobilize an effective rescue operation. Rumors meanwhile spread that new tremors were about to hit Beijing and other cities, and millions scrambled for safety into improvised underground shelters, where they huddled for weeks and, in some places, for months. Officials issued optimistic reports, deliberately concealing the magnitude of the devastation out of fear that numbers of Chinese would interpret the catastrophe to signify that Mao, like an ancient emperor forsaken by the gods, no longer enjoyed the mandate of heaven. They were prescient. Mao died on September 9, six weeks after the earthquake.[20]

During the preceding months, Jiang Qing and her comrades had been inciting demonstrations and fomenting strikes in hopes of grabbing power once Mao had died. And, in a desperate gamble after his death, they forged documents contrived to prove that he had appointed her as his successor, and they called for attacks against anyone who tried to "tamper" with his sacred testament. Their move furnished Hua Guofeng and the top Party leaders with the pretext they needed. They conceived a scheme to seize Jiang Qing and her three close associates at a session of the Politburo on the night of October 6. Her confederates were arrested as they arrived—but, sensing trouble, she boycotted the meeting. An Army unit thereupon drove to Zhongnanhai, the Beijing district where the Chinese leaders resided, and at gunpoint hauled her off to jail. The operation was commanded by Mao's former bodyguard, General Wang Dongxing, once a member of her inner circle, who personally handcuffed her—an action for which he was acclaimed a hero. The countrywide dragnet that followed snared hundreds of other ultraleftists.

Jiang Qing and her clique were sentenced to long prison terms amid campaigns blaming them for the worst horrors of the Cultural Revolution and nearly everything else that had gone wrong in China. At her trial, claiming that she had only obeyed her husband's orders, she pleaded: "I was Chairman Mao's dog. Whoever he told me to bite, I bit."[21] Many Chinese, assuming that Mao was really responsible, had long been raising five fingers at mention of the Gang of Four.

So ended the Maoist era, which was supposed to have cleansed China of its feudal past, with an episode as gaudy as a Chinese opera. But if the Chinese were relieved, they were also worried. Mao was gone, yet he would continue to haunt the future.

A day after Jiang Qing's collapse, the Politburo endorsed Hua Guofeng as Chairman of the Communist Party and head of its Military Affairs Commission as well as Prime Minister—the three most important positions in China. No Chinese leader, including Mao, had ever held such a panoply of power. But the impressive titles rapidly proved to be tinsel.

Hua began by stressing his loyalty to Mao's memory in an effort to certify his own legitimacy. He concocted a slavish slogan, subsequently derided as the "two whatevers," declaring that the nation should "resolutely defend whatever policies Chairman Mao has formulated, and unswervingly adhere to whatever instructions Chairman Mao has issued." Though he purged some egregious ultraleftists, he declined to disavow the Cultural Revolution or to reinstate its most notable victims—among them Deng Xiaoping. Similarly, he initiated a few modest economic reforms, like allowing limited free markets for agricultural products, but he pledged to "deal blows to capitalism" and clung to centralized planning. The old political and military bosses, who respected strength, swiftly judged him to be indecisive and ineffectual. In any case, they had only supported him as a way of buying time to settle the succession problem.[22]

They leaned on him until, in March 1977, he agreed to Deng's second return from disgrace and reappointment to his previous positions—Party Vice-Chairman, Chief of Staff of the People's Liberation Army, and Deputy Prime Minister. Deng, however, saw Hua's concessions as a sign of weakness, and he patiently pushed ahead toward total power. He reminded the Party veterans that Hua was an opportunist who had advanced his career during the Cultural

Revolution while they and their families had suffered. The only "true theory" was "objective reality," he said, warning that Hua had not reconciled himself to Mao's failures and might drive the country back into chaos. He resorted as well to a Maoist tactic. Just as Mao had used the Red Guards to voice his views, so Deng urged young intellectuals to demand greater freedom. "A revolutionary party," he cautioned, "must worry about its inability to hear the voice of the people. What is to be feared most is silence." Toward the end of 1978, inspired by his appeals, professors and students improvised the Democracy Wall, a brick barrier near Beijing University, on which they pasted up posters expressing their opinions. Some called for a more flexible political structure, others denounced corruption and favoritism—but most described, often in poignant detail, the personal tragedies of the past decade.

Deng scored a major victory at a Central Committee Plenum in December 1978, when the top Party bosses discarded Mao's theory of perpetual "class struggle" in favor of his modernization plan. In addition, they supported his motion to scuttle Hua Guofeng's doctrine of Mao's infallibility. The decisions represented a setback for Hua, who was slowly reduced to little more than a figurehead until his retirement three years later.[23] Shortly afterward, Deng closed down the Democracy Wall and imprisoned a few vocal dissidents—among them Wei Jingsheng, the son of a senior official, who was to languish in jail for years. He also banned wall posters, which even Mao had tolerated, and issued a set of "principles" restricting criticism of the Party line as he defined it. His subsequent drives against "bourgeois liberalism" and "spiritual pollution" made it clear that, like his old Party comrades, he did not equate economic and political flexibility.

His curbs on political freedom reflected his own creed. As a convinced Communist, he subscribed to the Leninist thesis of "democratic centralism," which confined debate to the Party leadership. But his firmness also reflected his realism. He was aware that he could not govern, much less sponsor innovations, without the cooperation of the elderly Party cadres, among them Chen Yun, Peng Zhen, Wang Zhen, Bo Yibo, Yang Shangkun, and Li Xiannian. Though they had resisted Mao for years, they were hardly liberals. On the contrary, they were diehard Communists dedicated to the supremacy of the Party. Deng reassured them that he shared their views and, with that, they reinforced his coalition. He then proceeded to strip his rivals of authority. By 1980, he had dismissed Hua Guofeng's closest supporters from the Politburo, and a year later eased

Hua himself out as Party Chairman. He then maneuvered to promote his protégés to crucial jobs. One was Hu Yaobang, the former head of the Communist Youth League, whom he raised to the rank of Party Secretary General—a position that effectively put him in day-to-day control of the Party's activities. Another, whom Deng later appointed Prime Minister, was Zhao Ziyang, who had survived the ravages of the Red Guards in Guangdong province, and subsequently became Party chief of Sichuan, where his reforms saved the region from famine. Shrewdly avoiding the limelight, Deng chose instead to rule from behind the scenes under the unofficial title of "paramount leader." However, he arrogated for himself the powerful chairmanship of the Military Affairs Commission, which put him in charge of the armed forces.

His modernization plan, Deng realized, depended on foreign loans and investments. Thus he sought to stress that China had regained its sanity following the Maoist madness, and deserved the world's confidence. He dramatized his point on a visit to America in early 1979, soon after the Carter Administration established official diplomatic ties with China, portraying himself to be as cuddly as a panda bear. At the Kennedy Center in Washington, he clowned onstage with the Harlem Globetrotters, who towered over him like giants over a midget. He postured in a ten-gallon hat in Texas and hobnobbed with Hollywood movie stars. It was a dazzling public-relations performance that, in different form, he repeated in Japan— and it paid off handsomely.

Over the next decade, China was to sign accords for nearly $40 billion in foreign loans, and contract for more than ten thousand joint ventures, valued at some $30 billion, with foreign firms.[24] Among them were big Japanese corporations like Sony, Hitachi, and Toshiba and such giant U.S. companies as Pepsi-Cola, Beatrice, and the plumbing manufacturer American Standard, as well as the makers of products ranging from toys, tennis shoes, and clothing to electronic equipment and pharmaceutical products. Deng and his planners encouraged foreigners to build industrial and technological plants in four special economic zones situated in selected coastal regions, where they could employ cheap yet skilled Chinese labor. The largest of these zones, Shenzhen, was located across the frontier from Hong Kong, to lure capital from the affluent British colony. At the same time, China opened to Western, Japanese, and overseas Chinese tourists, and hundreds of thousands flowed in. To accommodate them, chains like Hilton and Sheraton were invited to construct hotels in

Beijing, Shanghai, and other cities. Beijing soon boasted a Kentucky Fried Chicken outlet and a *succursale* of Maxim's, the fancy Paris restaurant. Thousands of young Chinese went to the United States and Western Europe to study, and numbers of Western teachers and technicians invaded China.

Deng knew, however, that the fate of the economy hinged on peasants, who had been repeatedly alienated by Mao's collectivist schemes. As a first priority, therefore, he initiated incentives that would enable them to benefit from their labor and thus boost production. He began by allowing them to keep a portion of their harvests once they had fulfilled their official quotas. Spurring them further, the government raised the prices it paid for grain and other staples. State procurement agencies were permitted to retain a share of the output on condition that they met their quotas, and both their surpluses and those of the peasants could be sold for profit at free markets. Soon mandatory quotas were completely abolished, virtually unshackling the peasants from all constraints. The last vestiges of collectivism were eventually erased by the inauguration of a "household" system, under which rural families could lease land and set their own work schedules. The results were phenomenal. In 1984, defying the predictions of most experts, China produced 400 million tons of grain.[25]

The countryside went through an astonishing transformation in another respect as peasants, aside from growing food, branched out into manufacturing firecrackers, transistor radios, and other simple items. In Sichuan province, for example, an American correspondent visited a village whose income had soared from the equivalent of $70,000 in 1977 to $1.5 million in 1984. "The village," he wrote, "looked like one big construction site, with new houses crowding out the rice fields." One family, flush with profits from the production of rice liquor, had gone on a spending spree to purchase a color television set, a washing machine, and an electric fan—a far cry from the day when a wristwatch and a bicycle were the most a Chinese peasant could hope to acquire. Besides improving rural living standards, the sideline activities absorbed the excess labor that would have otherwise clogged the cities and increased unemployment.[26]

But Chinese industry was unequipped to meet the skyrocketing demand for consumer goods, which had to be imported, primarily from Japan. Nor could China export enough to balance the trade. Accordingly, its trade deficit climbed from nearly $4 billion in 1980 to more than $15 billion in 1985.[27] Though astronomic debts strapped other developing countries, the elderly Chinese leaders were appalled to discover that the nation had mortgaged itself to foreigners. Worse lay ahead, however, as Deng and his brain trust tried to extend their reforms into the urban areas.

Apart from purging its ultraleftists, Deng had flinched at streamlining the Communist Party, the source of his authority. So China's industrial sector remained under the domination of an entrenched, antiquated, inefficient Party apparatus that saw his economic reforms as a danger to its power and prerogatives. He had insinuated reformers like Hu Yaobang and Zhao Ziyang into the top levels of the Party as a way of outflanking its conservative wing. Nevertheless, he was constantly compelled to compromise. His programs degenerated into a hybrid of free-market forces and state controls, continually contradicting each other. It was a formula for trouble.

The Party purists deplored the alien decadence that economic liberalization had brought to China. Women had abandoned their drab tunics for colored skirts and blouses, and some even dared to snuggle with their boyfriends on park benches. Young Chinese, frequenting the discotheques that spread around the country, grew addicted to Western music, which they also heard on the Voice of America. Foreign tastes were starkly visible in coastal cities like Guangzhou, where local officials became accustomed to Chivas Regal whiskey and Marlboro cigarettes, and entrepreneurs screened pornographic videos smuggled in from Hong Kong. Perhaps nothing mirrored the new freedom more than the prostitutes who accepted American Express traveler's checks.

But the Party hacks who scorned these evil influences also took advantage of them to adopt what one observer termed "feudal socialism"—the kind of nepotism and corruption that had been endemic in China for centuries. The traditional "squeeze" system had returned, as bureaucrats insisted on bribes and kickbacks for services rendered. Their children were frequently given berths in government enterprises, where they earned handsome profits by selling price-controlled merchandise on the open market. Not even the reformers were clean. Advertising his filial ties, one of Zhao Ziyang's sons went into the consulting business in Hong Kong, and Deng's crippled son, Deng Pufang, was implicated in dubious deals that included the illegal transfer of funds to Swiss banks.[28] Family ties also pervaded the Chinese military establishment. General Chi Haotian, the Army Chief of Staff, owed his position to his father-in-law, Yang Shangkun, an elderly retired general and head of state. The Army's senior political commissar was Yang's younger brother, Yang Baibing, whose son, Yang Jianhua, commanded the unit that suppressed the students in Beijing in June 1989.

⬇

It was clear by the late 1980s that, while Deng's innovations had altered China beyond recognition, they had gravely disrupted the society. But no solution could be applied to the complicated assortment of problems without taking into account its possible political repercussions. So, whatever the prescription for the ailing economy, it would inevitably inflame the struggles for authority within the country's ruling hierarchy.

Unfettering agriculture, one of Deng's fundamental reforms, had at first stimulated record increases in production. But it had largely been predicated on generous payments to the peasants for their crops. Thus, by the late 1980s, the state treasury was bereft of funds, and peasants were being offered dubious bonds instead of cash. They reacted by hoarding grain, edible oils, cotton, tea, and raw silk, or selling those commodities at free markets for high prices. Scarcities of food and raw materials developed, confronting Deng with a dilemma. Unable to impose pressures on the peasants, who would have slowed down—or even ceased to work, as they did during Mao's collectivist campaigns—he continued to coddle them, thus driving the regime deeper into debt. Even so, the agricultural sector slid into stagnation.

The food shortages dismayed the urban population at the end of 1987, when the government reimposed the rationing of sugar, pork, and eggs in Beijing, Shanghai, and other big cities. The lack of raw materials was meanwhile crippling factories, many of whose operations had dwindled to a tiny fraction of capacity. As unemployment in some industries had climbed to 50 per cent, many plant managers elsewhere refused to lay off workers and deny them housing, medical, and child-care allowances, thereby saddling their enterprises with stupendous expenditures. The scarcities also encouraged rampant inflation, which was being aggravated as well by the promiscuous spending on consumer goods of privileged officials and affluent peasants. As the government printed money to maintain the momentum, banks were loaning at an unprecedented rate out of fear of imminent controls, and unbridled borrowing by speculators intensified the inflation. The situation was further blurred by a split-level system under which the state subsidized hundreds of products to keep their price low, while the same items sold for three or four times more on the free market. All this was a bonanza for the corrupt bureaucrats, who could wheel and deal through *guanxi*, inside connections.[29]

In June 1988, the senior Chinese leaders assembled at the beach resort of Beidaihe, on Bo Hai Gulf, where they usually vacationed. This time, however, they were not on holiday. They knew that the economy was in disarray and that discontent was spreading, with potentially severe consequences for their own authority. Hence they had gathered to ponder the crisis and to discuss possible remedies. But they were split among themselves, just as they had been for a decade, over whether to continue with reforms or return to rigid policies.

A year before, under pressure from the Party conservatives, Deng had ousted the liberal Hu Yaobang as Secretary General and replaced him with Zhao Ziyang. But Zhao, who was also liberal, presented the Beidaihe conference with a sweeping program that sounded almost capitalistic. To reduce government expenditures, he favored a gradual end to subsidies and price controls, coupled with a major currency devaluation that would boost exports and replenish the empty state treasury. He recommended more open competition for money, labor, and raw materials, as well as salary increases for teachers, technicians, and other intellectuals, who earned less than manual workers. In addition, he proposed sharp cuts in the bloated bureaucracy while raising the wages of the remaining employees as a deterrent to corruption. Implicit in his suggestions was the necessity for political reform. Without denying the supremacy of the Communist Party, he favored a larger degree of democracy, including a free press, that would serve to keep officials honest.

The Party elders, as a counterweight to Zhao, had earlier elevated Li Peng to the position of Prime Minister. Li, whose father was executed by the Nationalists, had been adopted by Zhou Enlai and sent to study engineering in the Soviet Union, where he acquired the concept of orthodox Marxist central planning. Now, at the Beidaihe meeting, he spoke for the hard-liners by blaming Zhao for China's current problems and warning that aggressive reforms would only make matters worse. The reforms until then had indeed overheated the economy. But Li's arguments largely reflected the political concerns of the Party veterans, who feared that Zhao's proposed decontrols would jeopardize their authority. Their alternatives were unrealistic, however. For the Communist regime would probably face widespread disaffection if, as some suggested, it sought to regulate the peasants, close the free markets, reverse the consumer revolution, and generally clamp down on the population.[30]

Thus, after much wrangling, the conference at Beidaihe ended inconclusively. Nevertheless, the Party machine had seized the initiative from Zhao and the liberals as Deng typically remained aloof, waiting to see which side would triumph. But the changes that had transformed China had already gone too far for them to turn back the clock. So the failure of the rival factions to reach a consensus heightened the tensions that were to grow during the year ahead.

Throughout this period, China's intellectuals were becoming increasingly disillusioned by the stymied reforms. They included scientists, technicians, teachers, students, artists, writers, and journalists, whose talents were vital to the modernization of the country. Numbers had returned from the United States, where the atmosphere of freedom had intoxicated them, and they argued that economic change could not proceed without democracy. Many, who regarded themselves to be true Marxists, felt that the principles of communism were being traduced by the corruption and nepotism that contaminated Chinese society. Some were also distressed by the fact that, despite their education, they were at the bottom of the pay scale. One of their most eloquent spokesmen was Fang Lizhi, a distinguished astrophysicist and vice-president of the University of Science and Technology in Hefei, the capital of Anhui province. He had long been ventilating his views around the country and, in late 1986, his speeches touched off a series of student demonstrations at several campuses.

The old Party cadres, who had been rankled by Hu Yaobang's liberalism, forced Deng to drop him as Secretary General on the grounds that he had failed to check the protests. They also ousted Fang from the Party along with dissidents like Liu Binyan, a literary critic for the *People's Daily*, and Wang Ruowang, a Shanghai writer. Approving the hard line, Deng decried dissent, and reintroduced ideological indoctrination courses into schools, and prohibited student demonstrations. But he refrained from imposing more severe measures, perhaps out of fear of provoking new disorders. Nevertheless, numbers of young Chinese still felt restive, and their dissatisfaction was to spread and deepen.[31]

The student militants remained relatively quiet until April 15, 1989, when Hu Yaobang suddenly died of a heart attack. They had counted him among their supporters and, disregarding the ban on demonstrations, thousands filled Tiananmen Square, where they posed wreaths, read poetry, and pasted up posters as an expression of their sorrow. It was a replay of the homage to Zhou Enlai of thirteen years earlier—except that now the government exercised restraint by allowing the youths to manifest their grief. Soon the students were insisting on the ouster of Li Peng and other political changes, and their demands resonated through campuses across the country. The *People's Daily*, echoing a private speech by Deng, called their protests a "conspiracy" to "create national turmoil and sabotage stability." The students reacted by staging new marches in Beijing as the authorities, perplexed and divided among themselves, continued to show caution.

Their passions aflame, the students organized still another demonstration for May 4, 1989. The date marked the seventieth anniversary of the May 4th Movement, which had started as a protest against the cession of Chinese territory to Japan after World War I, and later became a symbol of nationalism. Knowing that the commemoration coincided with a conference in Beijing of the Asian Development Bank, student activists figured that the regime would recoil from a crackdown that might shock the delegates and blemish its image. Their calculations were correct, and the government did nothing to obstruct the crowds flooding back into Tiananmen Square. Zhao Ziyang was largely responsible, having instructed the police to avoid violence. Speaking to a group of foreign visitors, he stressed the need for conciliation, saying: "Reasonable student demands should be met through democratic and legal means." But several of his comrades in the Communist Party hierarchy took a different view. Nor did the student militants feel that they had made much headway.[32]

They prepared to reassert themselves on May 15, when Mikhail Gorbachev, the Russian leader, was scheduled to land in Beijing for a three-day visit. The first Sino-Soviet summit in thirty years, it was to be an historic occasion that would finally end the dispute between the Communist giants, which dated back to the 1960s. The students intended to impress Gorbachev, whose reforms they admired, in the expectation that he might sway the Chinese Communist Party conservatives in their behalf. Days before his arrival, they began to pack Tiananmen Square, and soon a million people filled the area. Student activists, by now skilled at public relations, faced foreign television crews with banners in English proclaiming such familiar Western slogans as "I Have a Dream" and "We Shall Overcome." Some three thousand also started a hunger strike that was to drag on for more than a week as doctors and nurses tried to save them. None died.

The demonstrations, as intended, spoiled Gorbachev's visit, and embarrassed the Chinese hierarchy. On May 18, as a Beijing television team filmed the scene, Li Peng convened a group of student representatives to caution them that the capital was "on the brink of anarchy." Implicit in his warning was a hint he might declare martial law, and bring in soldiers to quell the protests. One of the youths curtly interrupted him to say that he was wasting their time, adding that they should be recognized as patriots rather than denounced as rebels. His impudence was unprecedented in a country where people seldom challenged their superiors, at least directly. But his televised display of disrespect for Li earned him the admiration of many Chinese, who had lost faith in their leaders.

Neglecting Gorbachev, members of the Politburo urgently gathered to discuss the crisis. Zhao Ziyang proposed that they placate the students, but Deng objected that "one retreat will lead to another." Zhao offered to step down, but his comrades refused to accept his resignation out of fear that it would make him a hero in the eyes of the students. He confided to Gorbachev following the session that he was helpless, explaining that Deng "is still our main helmsman." Infuriated by his disclosure, the old Party bosses charged him with shifting to Deng the responsibility for whatever might go wrong. Before dawn on May 19, Zhao drove to Tiananmen Square to apologize to the students for not having adequately supported their cause or having visited them earlier. "I came too late," he said. "I am sorry."[33]

The students ought to have concluded from Zhao's emotional confession that he could no longer defend them. They should have also sensed the danger that faced them when, a day later, Li Peng imposed martial law in parts of Beijing. Instead, they erected a large plaster statue called the Goddess of Democracy in Tiananmen Square. But, in the carnival atmosphere that pervaded the city, their gesture seemed to be more jocular than defiant. Deng was most amused. Like Mao, he believed that "political power grows out of the barrel of a gun." Thus he had decided that force was his only option. Or, as he subsequently put it, the "storm was bound to happen sooner or later."[34] Uppermost in his mind was dread of disorder. Like most Chinese of his generation, he recalled the civil strife that had ripped

China apart during his youth. Even more vivid in his memory were the ravages of the Red Guards, whom he equated with the students now camped in Beijing. During the last week of May and first days of June, he planned a military strategy at meetings with loyal Army figures at the city of Wuhan and again at the seaside resort of Beidaihe. Concerned that some officers might balk at attacking unarmed civilians, he entrusted the spearhead assault to the Twenty-seventh Army, which was commanded by Yang Jianhua, the nephew of his elderly comrade Yang Shangkun. "Don't be afraid to spill blood," Deng said as the sessions ended.[35]

The operation unfolded sporadically on the afternoon of June 3, a Saturday, as troops dispersed students in areas of Beijing. But the real offensive started that night, as trucks and personnel carriers filled with soldiers of the Twenty-seventh Army rumbled toward the center of the city from the west. After crushing the makeshift obstacles that had been thrown up to block them, they launched canisters of tear gas. Then, to the amazement of the crowds in the streets, they opened fire. Two students were shot as they tried to rescue another, who had been bayoneted. Others were killed by grenades and machine-gun volleys, or clubbed to death with truncheons and rifle butts. Soon youths were fighting back with rocks and bottles. They hurled Molotov cocktails at Army vehicles, setting some ablaze. The battle intensified after midnight, as troops began to enter Tiananmen Square. Ignoring pleas to withdraw in peace, they fired indiscriminately into the crowds. Hospitals, unable to handle the hundreds of casualties, became a battleground as soldiers invaded their wards in search of wounded students. An American physician in Beijing at the time learned from medical colleagues that at least nine Chinese doctors were killed as they sought to protect their patients. Though the government never published the death toll, Amnesty International later estimated that at least thirteen hundred civilians died and thousands more were injured.[36]

Their passions inflamed by the massacre, mobs had castrated and disemboweled several soldiers. They burned the corpses or threw them into canals, and in one instance displayed the mutilated body of an officer with a crude sign attached: "The people will be victorious." The authorities later showed these atrocities on television in an effort to inculpate the students as criminals. The world, however, saw a more credible picture in the footage of the slaughter in Tiananmen Square filmed by foreign television crews. Nothing dramatized the tragic episode more poignantly than the televised scene of a solitary youth in a white shirt, shouting as he confronted a column of tanks: "Why are you here? You have done nothing but create misery. My city is in chaos because of you."[37]

Addressing a group of Army commanders shortly afterward, Deng praised them for having crushed a "counterrevolutionary rebellion" perpetrated by the "dregs of society." Perhaps now, he said, China could "go ahead with reform . . . at a more steady, better, even faster pace." He emphasized the need for balance between "a planned economy and a market economy," adding that it would be a grave error to close the door to the international community.[38] But it was plain both then and later that China would neither regain its domestic stability rapidly nor continue during the foreseeable future to attract the foreign loans, trade, and investment crucial to its modernization.

The regime followed its repression in Tiananmen Square with nationwide arrests of real and suspected dissidents. Many youths managed to escape to Hong Kong, the United States, and Western Europe. Aided by an American friend, Fang Lizhi and his wife found asylum in the U.S. embassy in Beijing. But numbers of others were detained as they tried to flee the country or hide in remote rural areas. Some were turned in by neighbors or even relatives, who feared being denounced for concealing criminals. Justice was harsh. One student went to jail for nine years for telephoning a Western correspondent, and a teacher who splashed paint on Mao's portrait was given a life sentence. Worse was reserved, however, for several peasants and workers convicted of attacking soldiers or burning Army vehicles. Their heads shaved and eyes cast downward, they were tried before television cameras as a warning to the public, and afterward executed in traditional Chinese fashion with a bullet in the back of the head—for which their families were taxed the equivalent of two cents. As the roundup accelerated, it became clear that peasants and workers were being punished more brutally than students, whose family connections may have earned them relatively lenient treatment.[39]

A high-level culprit was also needed, and the obvious choice was Zhao Ziyang, who had openly sided with the students. Though his rivals had been preparing a case against him since late May, it was only after the events in Tiananmen Square that they had the votes to act. On June 23, at a secret Central Committee session, they formally condemned him for "supporting the turmoil and splitting the Party." Troops had been deployed to "protect" the delegates, one of whom later disclosed that they "used guns to force us to put up our hands in approval." Deng thereupon removed Zhao from the position of Secretary General, but allowed him to retain his Party membership—presumably because he might prove useful at another time. Zhao was also permitted to live, lightly guarded, in Zhongnanhai.[40]

The problem now confronting the senior Chinese bosses was to name a Secretary General to replace Zhao. The appointment was pivotal, since the new Party chief would be seen as the potential heir to Deng, who was then eighty-five and reported to be sick. Various factions promoted different candidates, but Deng made the final decision. He gave the job to Jiang Zemin, the mayor of Shanghai, a stocky, affable functionary in his early sixties who had climbed his way up through the bureaucracy. Jiang had kept the students in his city under control, which commended him to the conservatives. And he spoke English, Japanese, and Russian, which suggested to the few remaining economic reformers that he could deal with foreign investors. An internal Party document circulated in October referred to him as the "core" of the next generation of Chinese leaders, a hint that Deng had selected him as his heir. But Jiang had plainly been chosen as a compromise to appease the rival Party groups. So, like his predecessors, he was likely to be a transitional figure.[41]

He immediately articulated a tough line. "Not an iota of forgiveness" would be shown the "counterrevolutionaries," he said, warning that intellectuals in particular would be subjected to "ideological education" designed to cleanse them of their "bourgeois liberalism."[42] Speaking even more stridently shortly afterward, he declared that China was gripped in a "serious class struggle" as "hostile forces" sought to reimpose the "capitalist system" on the country.[43] Universities became the targets of a new campaign. Students were compelled to confess their "errors" at indoctrination sessions, and courses in history, philosophy, and international relations, considered too liberal, were closed to freshmen. Resurrecting a Maoist concept, the regime required graduates to work on farms or in factories before qualifying for advanced studies. Many students, their spirit sapped, cynically went through the motions of regurgitating slogans they read in the official press.[44] At the same time, the Party initiated a drive to investigate its members, cautioning that those who had displayed insufficient zeal during the events in Tiananmen Square would be purged.[45] But the rigid measures dismayed several senior Communist officials, who asserted that a retreat into the blind alley of the Maoist past would damage China's chances for growth and prosperity. Thus, at the end of 1989, the Chinese leaders were locked in still another debate over future policies.

By then, Deng's modernization program had been stalled by the Party's orthodox bosses. Claiming that reforms had caused crippling inflation, shortages, and deficits, they had already introduced programs designed to discourage independent managers, private entrepreneurs, and free markets. Now, further seeking to promote their gospel of rigorous central planning, they moved to tighten controls over the coastal zones, notably in the south, which had been carved out as havens for joint business ventures with Western, Japanese, and overseas Chinese investors. Guangdong province, adjacent to Hong Kong, had been especially successful, accounting for one-third of China's foreign-currency earnings. Nevertheless, the Party conservatives in Beijing maneuvered to dismiss several of its top bureaucrats on grounds of corruption. The charge was probably justified, since local authorities were conspicuously involved in everything from property speculation and the import of consumer goods to accepting bribes. The real aim of the purge, however, was to reduce the region's autonomy. But it frightened away outside capital, which recoiled from the prospect of a return to heavy-handed Communist regulation.[46]

Though Deng and his comrades reiterated their intention to keep China open to the world, the world abruptly soured on China in tribute to the Chinese students slain in Tiananmen Square. At universities across America, graduates at commencement ceremonies wore white armbands on their gowns. A group of young Chinese was chosen to head the procession in Paris marking the bicentennial of the French Revolution, and even Communist officials in the Soviet Union and Eastern Europe openly expressed disapproval of the Beijing massacre. The Chinese leaders brushed aside the criticism, assuming that it would pass. But they had cause to be concerned by the reaction that had been bullish on China—and now realized that they had been investing in a precarious country.

The tourist traffic, which was expected to earn China some $2 billion in 1989, fell sharply as potential foreign visitors canceled their trips, either out of fear or for moral reasons. Japan, the largest of China's foreign donors, postponed $5.6 billion in loans, and other sources of assistance, like the World Bank and the Asian Development Bank, shelved their aid projects. Several Western companies that had long been frustrated by the red tape, corruption, and other obstacles to operating in China, also began to reconsider their commitments. A major casualty was Hong Kong, scheduled to change from British to Chinese rule in 1997. Deng had promised that China would respect its capitalist system for the following fifty years. But the crackdown in Beijing shattered the confidence of its skilled, sophisticated Chinese residents, many of them refugees from communism. Thousands who had earlier contemplated departure accelerated their plans to leave. So the colony, whose extraordinary prosperity has been a boon to China for years, will probably be an empty shell when it reverts to Chinese sovereignty.

Reflecting public American revulsion against the events in Beijing, the U.S. Congress voted overwhelmingly to impose sanctions on trade with China. President George Bush, who had headed the so-called liaison mission in Beijing in 1974 and 1975, suspended $500 million in arms contracts with China, saying: "It's not going to be business as usual." He also announced that "all high-level exchanges" of U.S. officials with senior members of the Chinese regime would be suspended. Arguing that America's relations with China were too vital to jeopardize, however, he warned against stronger measures. He was supported by several U.S. companies, like the Boeing Company, which were reluctant to lose their sales to China, while other American enterprises awaited the opportunity to return to "business as usual." The same position was adopted by former President Nixon, who visited China in October 1989. Former Secretary of State Henry Kissinger, whose consulting firm advised companies doing business with China, not only concurred in but defended the suppression of the students in Beijing. "No government in the world," Kissinger wrote, "would have tolerated having the main square of its capital occupied for eight weeks."[47]

Toward the end of 1989, America's interest in China seemed to be flagging. Dissident Chinese students in the United States no longer drew crowds, and their protest movements were divided by factional rivalries. In December, however, China suddenly returned to the news as President Bush disclosed that he had just sent Brent Scowcroft, his National Security Adviser, and Lawrence Eagleburger, the Deputy Secretary of State, on a covert mission to Beijing. The trip, in addition to violating Bush's pledge to suspend "high-level exchanges" with China, featured televised scenes of Scowcroft enthusiastically toasting the Chinese leaders and decrying the "negative forces" in both countries that were hindering improved relations. A White House spokesman further aggravated matters by revealing that Scowcroft and Eagleburger had secretly traveled to Beijing in July. Worse yet, Secretary of State James A. Baker III conceded that he "may have misled" the public when he said that the voyage had been the first journey to Beijing by senior U.S. officials since the massacre in Tiananmen Square. In short, the Bush Administration had lied.

The renewed contacts with China, coinciding as they did with appeals from progressives in Eastern Europe for U.S. support, alarmed American liberals and conservatives alike. "This a fresh insult to the memory of those who died in Tiananmen Square," said Senator Albert Gore, Jr., a Tennessee Democrat. He was echoed by Representative Mickey Edwards of Oklahoma, chairman of the House Republican Policy Committee, who called the two visits to Beijing "an outrage"—adding that Bush "has lost his moral compass." Bush defended himself by claiming that he did not want to isolate China, but the U.S. press almost unanimously termed his explanation lamentable. What, then, had prompted his move? He had clearly heeded Nixon and Kissinger, who consistently subordinated human rights to big-power relationships, and also clung to the outmoded idea that links with China would counterbalance the Soviet Union. At the same time, however, Bush had based the decision on his own experience in Beijing, which had left him with the dangerous illusion that he was a China expert.[48] But whatever Bush's motives, the euphoria over China that enthralled America since Nixon's journey to Beijing in 1972 had evaporated. Or, as *The Economist* wrote: "America has had to recognize that its romance with China . . . was an infatuation."[49]

Though the outside world had helped China with capital and technological assistance, the Chinese would have to resolve their immense problems by themselves. But their leaders had not yet found a system capable of governing one-quarter of humankind. Instead, they had experimented for forty years with different and often divergent Communist doctrines—and rival factions among them were still struggling to promote their formulas.

Mao, more than anyone, was responsible. To his credit, he had steered the Chinese people toward a rediscovery of their grandeur, instilling in them a spirit of national identity, a sense of purpose, and a dedication to self-reliance. But he had also displayed the most egregious traits of an imperial despot, playing off his courtiers against each other, crushing his foes, encouraging terror, suppressing dissent. Above all, unwilling to adjust to the prose of stable administration, he unrealistically sought to sustain the poetry of revolution. So he had bequeathed China a legacy of turmoil.

ACKNOWLEDGMENTS

REFERENCE NOTES

INDEX

ACKNOWLEDGMENTS

E XCEPT for my journalistic experience and instincts, I was unprepared to cover China when, in May 1959, I arrived in Hong Kong as chief Asia correspondent for *Time* and *Life* magazines. I had previously worked in Western Europe, North Africa, and the Middle East, and I began my assignment with little knowledge of China's history and customs, much less the Chinese language. My task was further complicated by the fact that both the U.S. and Chinese governments then prohibited Americans from visiting China. So, like my Hong Kong colleagues, I had to observe China from a distance. We were known as "China watchers."

I finally went to China in February 1972, when, as *The Washington Post* diplomatic correspondent, I accompanied President Richard Nixon on his dramatic voyage to Beijing. For the first time, I saw China and its people first-hand. By then, I had become familiar enough with the country to claim a measure of expertise. I have continued to write on China and Asia, so that now, in late 1989, my ties to the region reach back thirty years. But the more I learn, the less I know. As the old aphorism goes, Asia is a university in which nobody ever earns a degree.

This is not a plea for the virtues of ignorance. But as Professor John K. Fairbank of Harvard, *doyen* of America's China scholars, observed in the introduction to the original edition of this book, I had perhaps brought a fresh approach to the subject. As a journalist, he suggested, I wrote in "intelligible English for the intelligent layman, avoiding the quagmire of definitions and frames of reference in which social scientists sometimes bog down." Whatever the validity of his perception, I have endeavored to tell the story as clearly, concisely, and impartially as possible. My audience has always been the general reader.

I depended heavily on specialists more qualified than myself. But if I was frequently perplexed by the Chinese puzzle, they were often no better informed. None of us, to cite one example, fully grasped the disastrous consequences of the Great Leap Forward of 1958, which devastated China economically, caused widespread famine, and nearly sparked a mutiny in the Army. Nor did we wholly perceive the splits that Mao Zedong's frenetic campaign subsequently created within the Chinese Communist Party. The conventional wisdom about China at the time was that its Communist rulers, in contrast to their squabbling Soviet counterparts, were extraordinarily cohesive. Not even Mao's biographer Edgar Snow, the American most welcome in China, discerned the truth. After a visit during the early 1960s, when the Communist leadership was bitterly divided by internecine tensions, he pointed to its "impressive record of unity," purportedly the result of Mao's refusal to impose his will on his comrades. This was just as Mao was contemplating the Cultural Revolution, which he later launched to purge his opponents inside the Communist Party.

The Cultural Revolution touched off an avalanche of newspapers, tracts, handbills, pamphlets, and wall posters, most of them put out by the Red Guards and other activists in Beijing and throughout China's provinces. Their style was frequently florid and their accounts exaggerated, but they contained descriptions of skirmishes between rival factions, transcripts of secret speeches, confidential directives, and other material not contained in official Chinese publications. Thousands of these documents flowed into Hong Kong, where they were compiled and translated by the U.S. Consulate General in its *Survey of the China Mainland Press*. As the reference notes in this book indicate, I have used them extensively in the preparation of *Mao and China*. My other primary sources included the official New China News Agency and provincial China radio broadcasts as monitored by the British Broadcasting Corporation and the Foreign Broadcast Information Service, a U.S. government agency. I was also able to interview numbers of refugees who had fled to Hong Kong from China, and I counted as well for details on many foreign diplomats and journalists based in Beijing.

Gathering information on China was only the prelude to a more difficult challenge—its analysis. In this respect I was assisted by journalistic, academic, and diplomatic colleagues and friends. I wish to acknowledge the help of Morton Abramowitz, Anthony Ashworth, A. Doak Barnett, Gordon A. Bennett, John Gittings, William Gleysteen, Merle Goldman, Jean-Yves Gory, Charles Hill, Neale Hunter, Ellis Joffe, Donald W. Klein, Paul Kriesberg, Burton Levin, Simon Leys, Sydney Liu, Ronald N. Montaperto, Harald Munthe-Kaas, Charles Neuhauser, Nicholas Platt, C. V. Ranganathan, Thomas Robinson, Alan Romberg, Franz Schurmann, Benjamin I. Schwartz, Stein Seeberg, Richard Solomon, Ross Terrill, James C. Thomson, Jr., Ting

Wang, William W. Wells, Allen S. Whiting, William Whitson, and Edward K. Wu. My warm thanks to Nien Cheng for her introduction to this edition. I owe a particular debt of gratitude to Kwoh Yu-pei, who provided me with invaluable insights into Chinese life and behavior.

Nancy Evans and Priscilla Rope, my assistants in Hong Kong, were tireless researchers. Kate M. Simpson performed the job of changing the Wade-Giles system of transliteration to pinyin, thereby bringing this edition up to date. I am also grateful to Christine Pevitt of Viking Penguin for her encouragement and cooperation in the publication of this edition. My special thanks to Elisabeth Sifton, formerly of Viking Penguin, for editing the original version.

This book owes its genesis to John K. Fairbank, who as director of Harvard's East Asian Research Center in 1970 furnished me with inspiration, guidance, and financial aid. My thanks as well to Ezra Vogel, then deputy director of the Center, which has since been justly named for Professor Fairbank. I was simultaneously a Fellow of the Institute of Politics of the John F. Kennedy School of Government at Harvard. I am thus indebted to Richard E. Neustadt, then director, and Alvin J. Bronstein, then associate director. I also owe thanks to my colleagues at *The Washington Post*—Benjamin C. Bradlee, executive editor, and Philip Foisie, formerly assistant managing editor.

Finally, I must express my gratitude to my wife, Annette, and to my children, Curtis, Catherine, and Michael, who displayed patience, understanding, and solicitude beyond the call of familial duty, and who have been true "comrades in arms" on the Long March of authorship.

REFERENCE NOTES

In these notes, documents that originally bore titles in the Wade-Giles system of transliteration have been left as such, and all other names have been modernized to pinyin. The Joint Publications Research Service is abbreviated JPRS; Selections from China Mainland Magazines, SCMM; Selections from China Mainland Magazines (Supplement), SCMM (Supp.); Survey of China Mainland Press, SCMP; and Survey of China Mainland Press (Supplement), SCMP (Supp.). The Supplements were originally classified confidential to protect sources, but have since been declassified.

Chapter 1. The Vision and the Challenge

1. Mao Zedong, "Speech at the Chengtu Conference," March 22, 1958, *JPRS*, No. 90 (February 12, 1970), p. 49; "Talk at the Hangchow Conference," December 21, 1965, *ibid.*, p. 3.
2. Mao Zedong, "Speech at a Central Committee Work Conference," October 25, 1966, *ibid.*, pp. 58–59.
3. New China News Agency, April 27, 1969.
4. See *JPRS*, No. 90, p. 57.
5. Mao Zedong, "The Foolish Old Man Who Removed the Mountains," June 11, 1945, *Selected Works* (Beijing, 1965), III, 322.
6. See Richard Lowenthal, "Unreason and Revolution," Irving Howe, ed., *Beyond the New Left* (New York, 1970), pp. 55–84; Benjamin I. Schwartz, "China and the West in the 'Thought of Mao Tse-tung,'" Ping-ti Ho and Tang Tsou, eds., *China in Crisis* (Chicago, 1968), pp. 365–79.
7. Charles B. McLane, *Soviet Strategies in Southeast Asia* (Princeton, N.J., 1966), pp. 4–5.
8. See Ping-ti Ho, "Salient Aspects of China's Heritage," *China in Crisis*, pp. 15ff.

9. *Ibid.*, pp. 30ff.
10. Mao Zedong, "Rectify the Party's Style of Work," February 1, 1942, *Selected Works*, III, 50.
11. André Malraux, *Anti-Memoirs* (London, 1968), pp. 392–94.

Chapter 2. The Ailing Giant

1. See Ping-ti Ho, "Salient Aspects of China's Heritage," and Kwang-ching Liu, "Nineteenth Century China," Ping-ti Ho and Tang Tsou, eds., *China in Crisis* (Chicago, 1968), pp. 19ff, 95ff; also John Fairbank, Edwin O. Reischauer, and Albert M. Craig, *East Asia, The Modern Transformation* (Boston, 1965), p. 89.
2. See Fairbank *et al.*, *op. cit.*, pp. 99ff.
3. See Ping-ti Ho, *The Ladder of Success in Imperial China: Aspects of Social Mobility, 1368–1911* (New York, 1962), pp. 48–49.
4. See Stuart Schram, "Mao Tse-tung and Secret Societies," *China Quarterly*, No. 27 (July–September 1966), pp. 1ff.
5. See Harold Isaacs, *The Tragedy of the Chinese Revolution* (Stanford, Calif., 1961), p. 175.
6. Cited in Robert Payne, *Mao Tse-tung* (New York, 1969), p. 7.
7. Cited *ibid.*, p. 12.
8. Kwang-ching Liu, *op. cit.*; Fairbank *et al.*, *op. cit.*
9. Mao Zedong, "On Tactics Against Japanese Imperialism," *Selected Works* (Beijing, 1965), I, 178.
10. Quoted in Franz Schurmann and Orville Schell, *Imperial China* (New York, 1967), pp. 108, 109. The translation is by Harley Farnsworth MacNair.
11. Cited in Fairbank *et al.*, *op. cit.*, p. 177.
12. Cited *ibid.*, p. 382.
13. *Ibid.*, p. 320.
14. Cited *ibid.*, p. 392.
15. Qi Benyou, "Patriotism or National Betrayal?" *Peking Review*, April 7, 1967, pp. 10–12.

Chapter 3. The Making of a Rebel

1. Quoted in Jerome Ch'en, *Mao* (Englewood Cliffs, N.J., 1969), p. 2.
2. Edgar Snow, *Red Star Over China* (New York, 1961), p. 125.
3. *Ibid.*, p. 126.
4. Jerome Ch'en, *Mao and the Chinese Revolution* (London, 1965), p. 19.
5. Snow, *op. cit.*, p. 130.
6. *Loc. cit.*
7. *Loc. cit.*
8. *Ibid.*, p. 131.
9. See Stuart Schram, *Mao Tse-tung* (London, 1966), p. 25.
10. Cited *ibid.*, p. 41.

11. Snow, *op. cit.*, p. 138.
12. Schram, *op. cit.*, p. 43.
13. "A Conversation between Mao Tse-tung and his Niece, Wang Haijung," Beijing wall poster, February 1967.
14. Mao Zedong, "Talk at the Hangchow Conference," December 21, 1965, *JPRS*, No. 90 (February 12, 1970), p. 3.
15. Mao Zedong, speech delivered at the School for Military Affairs, February 20, 1967, quoted in wall poster of the 5th Middle School, Beijing, February 21, 1967.
16. Mao Zedong, conversation with Comrades Chen Boda and Kang Sheng (1965), in *JPRS*, No. 90, p. 26.
17. Ch'en, *Mao and the Chinese Revolution*, pp. 63ff.
18. Snow, *op. cit.*, pp. 155ff.
19. Mao Zedong, "The Immortals" (trans. Michael Bullock and Jerome Ch'en), in Ch'en, *Mao and the Chinese Revolution*, p. 347.
20. See Schram, *op. cit.*, p. 56.
21. Cited in Benjamin I. Schwartz, *Chinese Communism and the Rise of Mao* (Cambridge, Mass., 1951), p. 37.
22. Cited in John Fairbank, Edwin O. Reischauer, and Albert M. Craig, *East Asia, The Modern Transformation* (Boston, 1965), p. 678.
23. Mao Zedong, "Report on an Investigation of the Peasant Movement in Hunan," *Selected Works* (Beijing, 1965), I, 23ff.
24. Robert Payne, *Mao Tse-tung* (New York, 1969), p. 145.
25. Snow, *op. cit.*, pp. 72ff; Agnes Smedley, *Battle Hymn of China* (New York, 1943), pp. 168–69.
26. Mao Zedong, "Recruit Large Numbers of Intellectuals," *Selected Works*, II, 302.
27. Cited in Schram, *op. cit.*, pp. 220–21.
28. Benjamin I. Schwartz, "The Evolution of the Chinese Communist Party and Its Impact on Chinese Communist Policy since 1949," speech delivered at University of Michigan, March 1958.
29. See Ch'en, *Mao*, p. 22.
30. *Chingkangshan News*, Qinghua University, Beijing, March 15, 1967, translated by Union Research Institute, Hong Kong, April 14, 1967.
31. Liu Shaoqi, "On the Party," *Collected Works 1945–57* (Hong Kong, 1969), pp. 29–30.
32. See Edgar Snow, *Random Notes on Red China* (Cambridge, Mass., 1968), p. 3.
33. See Chalmers Johnson, *Peasant Nationalism and Communist Power* (Stanford, Calif., 1962), p. 73.
34. Mao Zedong, conversation with French delegation at Hangzhou, September 1964, unpublished.
35. Ch'en, *Mao and the Chinese Revolution*, p. 240.
36. Theodore H. White and Annalee Jacoby, *Thunder Out of China* (New York, 1946), p. 132.
37. Evans Carlson, *Twin Stars of China* (New York, 1940), p. 80.
38. William Whitson, "The Concept of Military Generation: The Chinese Communist Case," unpublished manuscript, July 1968, p. 8.

39. Ch'en, *Mao and the Chinese Revolution,* p. 374.
40. Mao Zedong, "The Momentous Change in China's Military Situation," *Selected Works,* IV, 288.
41. John Gittings, *The Role of the Chinese Army* (London, 1967), pp. 3ff; Ch'en, *Mao and the Chinese Revolution,* pp. 281ff.
42. Schram, *op. cit.,* p. 244.

Chapter 4. Cracks in the Monolith

1. I am indebted to Edward Behr of *Newsweek,* who was present at the evening with Mao, for providing me with a description of the encounter. Details of the conversation are contained in an unpublished record made available by informed sources.
2. Edgar Snow, "Interview with Mao," *The New Republic,* February 27, 1965, p. 23.
3. André Malraux, *Anti-Memoirs* (London, 1968), pp. 383–84.
4. Mao Zedong, "Reply to Comrade Kuo Mo-jo," reprinted in *China Pictorial,* April 1967, p. 49 (inset).
5. William Whitson, "The Concept of Military Generation: The Chinese Communist Case," unpublished manuscript, July 1968.
6. *Ibid.*
7. Xu Gaiyou, *Chou En-lai: China's Gray Eminence* (New York, 1968), p. 109; see also Whitson, *op. cit.*
8. Mao Zedong, "Problems of War and Strategy," November 6, 1938, *Selected Works* (Beijing, 1965), II, 224.
9. Mao Zedong, "On Coalition Government," April 24, 1945, *Selected Works,* III, 296.
10. See Stuart Schram, "The Party in Chinese Communist Ideology," *China Quarterly,* No. 38 (April–June 1969), pp, 2–3.
11. Quoted *ibid.,* p. 3.
12. Variations of this anecdote have been related by many refugees interviewed in Hong Kong. One form of the anecdote is contained in Mao's speech at the Eighth Plenary Session of the Communist Party Eighth Central Committee, July 1959, reprinted in *The Case of P'eng Teh-huai* (Hong Kong, 1968), p. 21.
13. Malraux, *op. cit.,* p. 394.
14. Zhang Guotao, Introduction to *Collected Works of Liu Shao-chi* (Hong Kong, 1969), p. i.
15. *Ibid.,* pp. vi–vii.
16. Quoted in Schram, *op. cit.,* p. 6.
17. Liu Shaoqi, "On Self-Cultivation of Communists," *Collected Works,* p. 162.
18. Liu Shaoqi, "On Inner-Party Struggle," *ibid.,* p. 343.
19. Liu Shaoqi, "Liquidate the Menshevik Ideology," *ibid.,* p. 446.
20. Liu Shaoqi, "On the Party," *ibid.,* pp. 29–30.
21. Liu Shaoqi, "Concluding Report at the National Land Conference," July 13, 1947, *SCMM,* No. 651, April 22, 1969, p. 20.
22. Tibor Mende, *China and Her Shadow* (New York, 1962).

23. See William Whitson, "The Field Army in Chinese Communist Military Politics," *China Quarterly*, No. 37 (January–March 1969), p. 11. I am also indebted, for much of this material, to Whitson's "The Concept of Military Generation."

24. John Gittings, *The Role of the Chinese Army* (London, 1967), pp. 294–99.

25. Alexander L. George, *The Chinese Communist Army in Action* (New York, 1967), p. 170.

26. Frank E. Armbruster, "China's Conventional Military Capability," Ping-ti Ho and Tang Tsou, eds., *China in Crisis* (Chicago, 1968), p. 171.

27. Gittings, *op. cit.*, p. 126.

28. Quoted in Ellis Joffe, *Party and Army: Professionalism and Political Control in the Chinese Officer Corps, 1949–64* (Cambridge, Mass., 1967), p. 2.

29. For material and quotations in this and the following paragraphs, I am indebted to Joffe's *Party and Army;* see esp. pp. 30, 39–42, 49.

30. Mao Zedong, "Speech at Symposium of Group Leaders of the Enlarged Meeting of the Military Commission," June 28, 1958, *SCMM (Supp.)*, No. 21 (April 2, 1968), p. 6.

31. Quoted in Gittings, *op. cit.*, p. 162.

32. Luo Ronghuan, "Continue to Promote the Glorious Tradition of the Chinese People's Liberation Army," *People's Daily* (Beijing), August 1, 1955, cited in Joffe, *op. cit.*, p. 74.

33. Dong Jing, "An Evaluation of the Passé Concept," *Liberation Army Daily* (Beijing), August 29, 1958, cited *ibid.*, p. 79.

34. Cited in Gittings, *op. cit.*, p. 173.

35. Cited in Joffe, *op. cit.*, p. 82.

36. "Opinions of Non-Military Comrades on the Army," *Liberation Army Daily* (Beijing), May 23, 1957, cited *ibid.*, p. 82.

37. On this and the next paragraphs, see *ibid.*, pp. 87–89.

38. Cited in Alice Langley Hsieh, *Communist China's Strategy in the Nuclear Era* (Englewood Cliffs, N.J., 1962), p. 1.

39. Su Yu, "Strengthen National Defense, Consolidate the Fruits of Victory of the Revolution!" *People's Daily* (Beijing), August 1, 1957, cited *ibid.*, p. 67.

40. Cited in John Gittings, *Survey of the Sino-Soviet Dispute* (London, 1968), p. 83.

41. John Foster Dulles, "Report from Asia," *The Department of State Bulletin*, XXXII, No. 821 (March 21, 1955), 459–60.

42. Schram, *op. cit.*, p. 12.

43. Mao Zedong, "Socialist Upsurge in China's Countryside," cited in Stuart Schram, *Mao Tse-tung* (London, 1966), p. 281.

44. Cheng Chu-yuan, *Scientific and Engineering Manpower in Communist China, 1949–1963* (Washington, D.C., 1965), p. 237.

45. Liu Shaoqi, "Speech at the 1951 National Propaganda Work Conference," and "Speech to Forum of Chinese People's Political Consultative Conference," May 13, 1951, *SCMM*, No. 652 (April 21, 1969), pp. 1, 11.

46. Liu Shaoqi, "Work Directive for Tientsin," April 24, 1949, *ibid.*, p. 12.

47. *Ibid.*, p. 11.

48. Mao Zedong, "On the People's Democratic Dictatorship," *Selected Works*, IV, 421.

49. Mao Zedong, "Instruction Given at the Spring Festival Conference Concerning Educational Work," February 14, 1964, *Current Background*, No. 891 (October 8, 1969), p. 42.

50. Mao Zedong, "Speech at the Chinese Communist Party's National Conference on Propaganda Work" (Beijing, 1966), p. 26.

51. Liu Shaoqi, "Political Report of the Central Committee of the Communist Party of China to the Eighth National Congress of the Party," September 15, 1956, *Eighth National Congress of the Communist Party of China* (Beijing), I, 37.

52. *Ibid.*, p. 74.

53. Deng Xiaoping, "Report on the Revision of the Constitution of the Communist Party of China," September 16, 1956, *ibid.*, pp. 213–14.

54. Lu Dingyi, "Let a Hundred Flowers Bloom, a Hundred Schools of Thought Contend," quoted in Richard H. Solomon, "One Party and One Hundred Schools: Leadership, Lethargy, or *Luan*," *Current Scene*, October 1, 1969, p. 10.

55. Kenneth R. Walker, "Collectivization in Retrospect: The Socialist High Tide of August 1955–Spring 1956," *China Quarterly*, No. 26 (April–June 1966), pp. 22–25.

56. Quoted *ibid.*, p. 22n.

57. *Ibid.*, pp. 7ff.

58. Mao Zedong, "The Question of Agricultural Cooperatives," July 31, 1955, *Communist China, 1955–1959: Policy Documents with Analysis*, with a Foreword by Robert R. Bowie and John K. Fairbank (Cambridge, Mass., 1962), p. 94.

59. Liu Shaoqi, "Speech at the 1951 National Propaganda Work Conference," *SCMM*, No. 652, p. 3.

60. Liu Shaoqi, "Political Report . . . to the Eighth National Congress," pp. 19, 20.

61. Mao Zedong, "Socialist Upsurge in China's Countryside," *Communist China, 1955–1959: Policy Documents*, p. 118.

62. Li Zhouming, "Economic Development," *China Quarterly*, No. 1 (January–March 1960), p. 42.

63. In *Communist China, 1955–1959: Policy Documents*, p. 7.

64. *Ibid.*, pp. 7–8.

65. Mao Zedong, "Speech to the Central Work Conference," October 1966, *JPRS*, No. 90; see also *Yomiuri* (Tokyo), January 7, 1967.

66. Liu Shaoqi, "Political Report . . . to the Eighth National Congress," pp. 19–20, 65, 96, 103.

67. Deng Xiaoping, "Report on the Revision of the Constitution of the Communist Party of China," *Eighth National Congress of the Communist Party of China*, I, 200.

68. "The Criminal History of the Big Conspirator, Big Ambitionist, Big Warlord P'eng Teh-huai," published by Beijing Red Guard Congress, Qinghua University, Jinggangshan Corps, August 1967, *The Case of P'eng Teh-Huai* (Hong Kong, 1968), p. 201.

69. *The New York Times*, October 26, 1970.

70. Richard H. Solomon, "One Party and 'One Hundred Schools,'" *Current Scene*, October 1, 1969, pp. 36–37.
71. "More on the Historical Experience of the Dictatorship of the Proletariat," December 29, 1956, *Communist China, 1955–1959: Policy Documents,* pp. 257ff.
72. Mao Zedong, "On the Correct Handling of Contradictions Among the People," *ibid.*, p. 273.
73. See Roderick MacFarquhar, *The Hundred Flowers* (London, 1960), pp. 45, 51.
74. Cited in *ibid.*, pp. 87–88.
75. *Ibid.*, p. 52.
76. Mao Zedong, "Twenty Manifestations of Bureaucracy," January 1967, *JPRS*, No. 90, pp. 40–43.
77. Cited in MacFarquhar, *op. cit.*, p. 261.
78. Cited in Solomon, *op. cit.*, pp. 32–33.
79. See Frederick C. Teiwes, "The Purge of Provincial Leaders 1957–1958," *China Quarterly*, No. 27 (July–September 1966), p. 14.

Chapter 5. The Leap That Failed

1. "Resolution of the Central Committee of the Chinese Communist Party on the Establishment of People's Communes in Rural Areas," August 29, 1958, *Communist China, 1955–1959: Policy Documents with Analysis,* with a Foreword by Robert R. Bowie and John K. Fairbank (Cambridge, Mass., 1962), p. 456.
2. "Hold High the Red Flag of People's Communes and March On," *People's Daily* (Beijing), September 3, 1958, *ibid.*, p. 460.
3. Stuart Schram, "Mao Tse-tung and Secret Societies," *China Quarterly*, No. 27 (July–September, 1966), p. 16.
4. Mao Zedong, "Speech at the Supreme State Conference," January 28, 1958, *SCMM (Supp.)*, No. 21 (April 2, 1968), pp. 2–5.
5. Quoted in Richard Hughes, *The Chinese People's Communes* (London, 1960), p. 38.
6. Quoted in Li Zhouming, "Economic Development," *China Quarterly*, No. 1 (January–March, 1960), p. 46.
7. Tibor Mende, *China and Her Shadow* (New York, 1962), p. 71.
8. Li, *op. cit.*, p. 44.
9. Liu Shaoqi, "Report on the Work of the Central Committee of the Communist Party of China to the Second Session of the Eighth National Congress," *Collected Works* (Hong Kong, 1969), p. 10.
10. Quoted in Schram, *Mao Tse-tung* (London, 1966), p. 271.
11. New China News Agency, August 12, 1958.
12. "Peking Scientists Plan Higher Goals," New China News Agency, June 6, 1958, *Communist China, 1955–1959: Policy Documents,* p. 17.
13. The following material is based on extensive interviews by the author with Albert Belhomme in Hong Kong in 1963. Portions of the interview appeared in Stanley Karnow, "The G.I. Who Chose Communism," *Saturday Evening Post*, November 16, 1963.

14. Mao Zedong, "Speech at the Supreme State Conference," p. 2.
15. Based on an interview in Hong Kong by the author.
16. "Letter of the Chinese Communist Party to the Communist Party of the Soviet Union," February 29, 1964, in John Gittings, *Survey of the Sino-Soviet Dispute* (London, 1968), p. 139.
17. Zhou Enlai, "Report on Adjusting the Major Targets of China's 1959 National Plan," August 26, 1959, *Communist China, 1955–1959: Policy Documents*, pp. 540ff.
18. Lord Montgomery, *The Sunday Times* (London).
19. Conversation between Chen Yi and Walton A. Cole, general manager of Reuters News Agency, January 18, 1960.
20. Interview by author with Hong Kong government officials, 1961.
21. Communicated to author by Bernard Ullmann, Agence France-Presse.
22. Stanley Karnow, "Why They Fled: Refugee Accounts," *Current Scene*, October 15, 1963, p. 3.
23. Interview with a refugee by author.
24. Karnow, "Why They Fled," p. 12.
25. See C. S. Chen and Charles P. Ridley, eds., *Rural People's Communes in Lien Chiang* (Stanford, Calif., 1969).
26. *Ibid.*, pp. 101, 102.
27. *Ibid.*, pp. 109, 140.
28. These documents, obtained by the Central Intelligence Agency, can be consulted in J. Chester Cheng, ed., *The Politics of the Chinese Red Army* (Stanford, Calif., 1964). See pp. 279–80.
29. *Ibid.*, p. 284.
30. *Ibid.*, pp. 284, 584, 281.
31. *Ibid.*, p. 43.
32. *Ibid.*, p. 287.

Chapter 6. The Marshal vs. Mao

1. Mao Zedong, "A Letter to Production Team Leaders," November 29, 1959, *Current Background*, No. 891 (October 8, 1969), pp. 34–35.
2. Lord Montgomery, *The Sunday Times* (London).
3. *People's Daily* (Beijing), November 4 and May 13, 1958.
4. James T. Myers, "The Fall of Chairman Mao," *Current Scene*, June 15, 1968, p. 3.
5. "Resolution on Some Questions Concerning the People's Communes," December 10, 1958, *Communist China, 1955–1959: Policy Documents with Analysis*, with Foreword by Robert R. Bowie and John K. Fairbank (Cambridge, Mass., 1962), pp. 492–95.
6. "Decisions Approving Comrade Mao Tse-tung's Proposal That He Will Not Stand as Candidate for Chairman of the People's Republic of China for the Next Term of Office," December 10, 1958, *ibid.*, pp. 487–88.
7. Red Guard wall posters, quoted in *Mainichi Shimbun* (Tokyo), January 5, 1967.
8. "Decision Approving Comrade Mao Tse-tung's Proposal That He Will

Not Stand . . . ," *Communist China, 1955–1959: Policy Documents with Analysis*, pp. 487–88.

9. General Gong Zhu, Introduction, *The Case of P'eng Teh-Huai* (Hong Kong, 1968), pp. i–iii; also private notes of Zhang Guotao.

10. Quoted in Gong, *op. cit.*, p. xiii.

11. "P'eng Teh-huai's Crimes in the 'Resist-U.S. and Aid-Korea War,'" published by *Mass Criticism and Repudiation Bulletin* (Guangzhou), October 5, 1967, cited *ibid.*, p. 153.

12. "The Criminal History of the Big Conspirator, Big Ambitionist, Big Warlord P'eng Teh-huai," published in August 1967 by Beijing Red Guard Congress, Qinghua University, Jinggangshan Corps, cited *ibid.*, p. 201.

13. "Principal Crimes of P'eng Teh-huai, Big Ambitionist and Schemer," in *Chingkang Mountains* (Guangzhou), September 5, 1967, cited *ibid.*, p. 176.

14. Mao Zedong, "Speech at a Meeting," October 24, 1966, *JPRS*, No. 90 (February 12, 1970), p. 10.

15. Soviet government statement, September 21, 1963, quoted in John Gittings, *Survey of the Sino-Soviet Dispute* (London, 1968), p. 98.

16. *Life*, June 12, 1959.

17. "Statement by the Spokesman of the Chinese Government," August 15, 1963, in Gittings, *op. cit.*, p. 105.

18. *People's Daily* (Beijing), November 2, 1957.

19. David A. Charles, "The Dismissal of Marshal P'eng Teh-huai," *China Quarterly*, No. 8 (October–December 1961), pp. 63–76.

20. "Letter of the Chinese Communist Party Central Committee to the Central Committee of the Communist Party of the Soviet Union," February 27, 1964, *People's Daily* (Beijing), May 9, 1964.

21. Mao Zedong, "Speech at the Enlarged Meeting of the Military Commission of the Chinese Communist Party Central Committee . . . ," September 11, 1959, *SCMM (Supp.)*, No. 21 (April 2, 1968), p. 37.

22. Cited in Stuart Schram, *Mao Tse-tung* (London, 1966), pp. 276–77.

23. Private source.

24. Peng Dehuai, "Excerpts from Talks at the Meeting of the Northwest Group of the Lushan Meeting," July 3–10, 1959, *The Case of P'eng Teh-huai*, pp. 1–5.

25. Peng Dehuai, "Letter of Opinion," *ibid.*, pp. 7–13.

26. Mao Zedong, "Comment on the Article 'How Should the Revolutionary Mass Movement Be Handled by Marxists,'" August 15, 1959, *SCMM (Supp.)*, No. 21, p. 31.

27. Mao Zedong, "Talk on July 10," *ibid.*, p. 10.

28. Mao Zedong, "Speech at the Eighth Plenary Session of the Chinese Communist Party Eighth Central Committee," July 23, 1959, *ibid.*, pp. 11–18; see also *The Case of P'eng Teh-huai*, pp. 15–26. The various versions of this speech differ only slightly in wording. I have therefore taken the liberty of using those parts of different versions which best seemed to convey Mao's intentions.

29. Charles, *op. cit.*, p. 68.

30. "The Criminal History of . . . P'eng Teh-huai," *The Case of P'eng Teh-huai*, p. 205.
31. Mao Zedong, "Letter to Chang Wen-t'ien," August 2, 1959, *SCMM (Supp.)*, No. 21, p. 24.
32. Mao Zedong, "Comment on a Letter," July 26, 1959, *ibid.*, p. 19.
33. Mao Zedong, "The Origin of Machine Guns and Trench Mortars and Other Things," August 16, 1959, *ibid.*, p. 33.
34. Mao Zedong, "Speech at the Enlarged Meeting of the Military Commission," September 11, 1959, *ibid.*, p. 35.
35. Mao Zedong, "Talk at the Eighth Plenary Session of the Chinese Communist Party Eighth Central Committee," August 2, 1959, *The Case of P'eng Teh-huai*, pp. 27–30.
36. Peng Dehuai, "Speech at the Eighth Plenary Session of the Eighth Central Committee," August 1959, *ibid.*, pp. 31–38.
37. "Resolution of the Eighth Plenary Session of the Eighth Central Committee Concerning the Anti-Party Clique Headed by P'eng Teh-huai," August 16, 1959, *ibid.*, pp. 34–44.
38. Peng Dehuai, "Letter to Mao Tse-tung," September 9, 1959, *ibid.*, pp. 45–46.
39. Order of the Chairman of the People's Republic of China, September 17, 1959, *ibid.*, p. 47.
40. Peng Dehuai, Record of Interrogation, December 28, 1966–January 5, 1967, *ibid.*, pp. 119–22.

Chapter 7. The Party Takes Command

1. "Comment on Liu Shao-chi's 1961 Visit to Hunan," *SCMM (Supp.)*, No. 26 (June 27, 1968), pp. 1–18.
2. "The Whole Party and the Whole People Go In for Agriculture in a Big Way," *Red Flag*, No. 17, reprinted in *Peking Review*, September 14, 1960, pp. 32–36.
3. Liu Shaoqi, "Speech at Party Work Conference," 1962, and "Speech at Meeting of Office of Finance and Trade," October 1960, cited in "Forty Instances of the Reactionary Statements of the Top Party Person in Authority," *The Rural Youth* (Shanghai), May 10, 1967.
4. "Struggle in China's Countryside Between Two Roads," *People's Daily* (Beijing), November 23, 1967.
5. Quoted in *Current Background*, No. 878 (April 28, 1969), p. 8.
6. *Ibid.*, pp. 7, 13.
7. *Ibid.*
8. "Stand Firm on the Policy of Letting a Hundred Flowers Bloom and a Hundred Schools of Thought Contend in Academic Research," *Red Flag*, No. 5 (February 28, 1961), *SCMP*, No. 2451 (March 8, 1961), p. 2.
9. *China Youth*, September 2, 1961, *SCMP*, No. 2581 (September 19, 1961), pp. 1–7.
10. Sven Lindquist, *China in Crisis* (London, 1963), pp. 44–48.
11. Liu Shaoqi, "Speech Made on January 27, 1962," *Current Background*, No. 652, p. 30.

12. See Merle Goldman, "The Unique 'Blooming and Contending' of 1961–62," *China Quarterly*, No. 37 (January–March 1969).

13. *Ibid.*, pp. 70–73.

14. Liu Mianjin (pseudo. Wu Han), "Hai Jui Upbraids the Emperor," *People's Daily* (Beijing), June 16, 1959, quoted in James R. Pusey, *Wu Han: Attacking the Present Through the Past* (Cambridge, Mass., 1969), pp. 15–16.

15. *People's Daily* (Beijing), May 29, 1967, p. 3.

16. See Goldman, *op. cit.*, pp. 76–83.

17. Charles Neuhauser, "The Chinese Communist Party in the 1960's: Prelude to the Cultural Revolution," *China Quarterly*, No. 32 (October–December 1967), pp. 14–16.

18. *Kwangming Daily* (Beijing), August 9, 1967, quoted in *South China Morning Post* (Hong Kong), October 6, 1967.

19. Liu Shaoqi, "How to Be a Good Communist," *Collected Works* (Hong Kong, 1969), pp. 219ff.

20. See Stanley Karnow, "Sinkiang: Soviet Rustlers in China's Wild West," *The Reporter*, June 18, 1964.

21. Interviews with Zhang Guotao by the author.

22. Quoted in Philip Bridgham, "Mao's Cultural Revolution: Origin and Development," *China Quarterly*, No. 90 (January–March 1967), p. 4.

23. New China News Agency, March 6, 1954.

24. "The Whole Country Must Learn from the PLA," *People's Daily* (Beijing), February 1, 1964.

25. See Richard H. Solomon, "One Party and 'One Hundred Schools': Leadership, Lethargy or *Luan*," *Current Scene*, October 1, 1969.

26. *Ibid.*

27. Quoted in Ellis Joffe, "The Chinese Army on the Eve of the Cultural Revolution," a paper prepared for the Conference on Government in China, August 18–23, 1969.

28. Stanley Karnow, *The Washington Post*, September 17, 1967; also interviews in Hong Kong.

29. Fred L. Karpin, *The Washington Post*, April 29, 1967.

30. Bridgham, *op. cit.*, pp. 8–9.

31. New China News Agency, June 6, 1966.

32. *People's Daily* (Beijing), July 14, 1964.

33. "Draft Resolution of the Central Committee of the Chinese Communist Party on Some Problems in Current Rural Work," May 20, 1963, cited in Richard Baum and Frederick C. Tiewes, *Szu-Ching: The Socialist Education Campaign of 1962–66* (Berkeley, Calif., 1968), pp. 60–61.

34. *Ibid.*

35. See Ting Wang, "Profile of Wang Kuang-mei," *Far Eastern Economic Review*, June 22, 1967, p. 654.

36. Quoted in Baum and Tiewes, *op. cit.*, p. 120.

37. Liu Shaoqi, "Self-Criticism," *Collected Works* (Hong Kong), p. 362.

38. *Liberation Daily*, Beijing Domestic Service, November 13, 1964.

39. "Resolutely Boycott Bourgeois Thoughts and Modes of Living," *Liberation Daily* (Shanghai), October 11, 1964.

40. Shanghai *Evening Post*, December 15, 1964.

41. "The Basic Difference Between Us and Comrade Feng Ting," *People's Liberation Army Journal*, December 1964.

42. Interview in Hong Kong by author.

43. Mao Zedong, "Spring Festival Day in Education," February 13, 1964; "Talk with the Nepalese Delegation on Education Problems, 1964," *Current Background*, No. 891, p. 46.

44. Edgar Snow, "Interview with Mao," *The New Republic*, February 27, 1965, p. 23.

45. Mao Zedong, "On Khrushchev's Phoney Communism and Its Historical Lessons for the World," *Red Flag*, July 14, 1964, cited in A. Doak Barnett, *China After Mao* (Princeton, N.J., 1967), pp. 148–49, 183.

46. *Ibid.*, pp. 178, 183–192 *passim*.

47. *Ibid.*, p. 192.

48. Danish News Agency, May 24, 1966, quoted in John Gittings, *Survey of the Sino-Soviet Dispute* (London, 1968), p. 160.

49. Snow, *op. cit.*, pp. 22–23.

50. Quoted in Uri Ra'anan, "Peking's Foreign Policy Debate 1965–1966," Ping-ti Ho and Tang Tsou, eds., *China in Crisis* (Chicago, 1968), pp. 36–37.

51. *People's Daily* (Beijing), February 9, 1965.

52. Li Zuopeng "Strategically Pitting One Against Ten, Tactically Pitting Ten Against One," *Red Flag*, December 22, 1964.

53. Quoted in Ra'anan, *op. cit.*, p. 44.

54. Quoted *ibid.*, p. 44.

55. Quoted *ibid.*, p. 45.

56. Quoted *ibid.*, p. 53.

57. Snow, *op. cit.*, p. 18.

58. *Peking Review*, September 3, 1965.

59. Lin Biao, "Long Live the Victory of People's War," September 3, 1965, quoted in Ra'anan, *op. cit.*, pp. 54ff.

60. Quoted in Donald Zagoria, "The Strategic Debate in Peking," *China in Crisis*, p. 267.

61. "Manifold Crimes of the Counter-Revolutionary Revisionist Element Lo Jui-ch'ing," *Struggle* (Beijing), January 30, 1967.

Chapter 8. The Opening Salvos

1. Mao Zedong, "A Talk to Foreign Visitors," August 31, 1967, *SCMP*, No. 4200 (June 18, 1968), p. 2.

2. See Neale Hunter, *Shanghai Journal* (New York, 1969), p. 5.

3. See Philip Bridgham, "Mao's Cultural Revolution: Origin and Development," *China Quarterly*, No. 29 (January–March, 1967), p. 16.

4. *Peking Review*, October 1, 1965, pp. 8–12.

5. Quoted in Richard H. Solomon, "One Party and 'One Hundred Schools': Leadership, Lethargy, or *Luan*," *Current Scene*, October 1, 1969.

6. See Joan Robinson, *The Cultural Revolution in China* (London, 1969), p. 51.

7. Cited in Hunter, *op. cit.*, p. 20.

8. Yao Wenyuan, "On the New Historical Play *Dismissal of Hai Jui*," *People's Daily* (Beijing), November 30, 1965.
9. Quoted in Hunter, *op. cit.*, p. 18.
10. Peng Chen, "Talk at the Festival of Peking Opera on Contemporary Themes," July 1, 1964, in *Red Flag*, No. 14, July 14, 1964.
11. Peng Chen, "Speech at China's National Day Celebration in Peking," New China News Agency, October 1, 1965.
12. *People's Daily* (Beijing), November 30, 1965.
13. Wu Han, "Self-Criticism on *Dismissal of Hai Jui*," *People's Daily*, (Beijing), December 30, 1965.
14. Bridgham, *op. cit.*, p. 19.
15. Solomon, *op. cit.*
16. "The February Outline Report," *Peking Chingkangshan*, May 27, 1967.
17. *Ibid.*
18. *Peking Review*, June 2, 1967, pp. 10–16.
19. *People's Daily* (Beijing), June 19, 1966.
20. *Peking Chingkangshan*, May 27, 1967.
21. *Ibid.*
22. *Red Flag*, No. 9, July 3, 1966, quoted in Bridgham, *op. cit.*, p. 22.
23. "Circular of the Central Committee of the Communist Party of China, May 16, 1966," New China News Agency, May 16, 1967.
24. Cuo Muorou, "Learn from the Masses of Workers, Peasants, and Soldiers and Serve Them," *Kwangming Daily* (Beijing), April 28, 1966.
25. Yao Wenyuan, "Destroy the 'Gangster Inn' Run by Teng T'o, Wu Han, and Liao Mo-sha," Shanghai *Wen Hui Pao*, May 10, 1966.
26. "Chronology of Important Events in the Struggle Between the Two Lines in the Field of Higher Education," *SCMM (Supp.)*, No. 18 (February 26, 1968), p. 30.
27. Roderick MacFarquhar, *The Hundred Flowers* (London, 1960), p. 264.
28. See Victor Nee, *The Cultural Revolution at Peking University* (New York, 1969), pp. 28–29.
29. New China News Agency, June 1, 1967.
30. See Nee, *op. cit.*, pp. 53–56.
31. See *People's Daily* (Beijing), June 2, 1966.
32. Mao Zedong, "Talks to Central Committee Leaders," July 21, 1966, *Current Background*, No. 891 (October 8, 1969), p. 58.
33. See V. I. Lenin, *Writings on the Commune* (New York, 1968), pp. 91, 116–17.
34. *People's Daily* (Beijing), June 2, 1966.
35. *The New York Times*, June 6, 1966.
36. New China News Agency, June 5, 1966.
37. Nee, *op. cit.*, p. 60.
38. Stanley Karnow, *The Washington Post*, July 18, 1966.
39. Cited in Louis Barcata, *China in the Throes of the Cultural Revolution* (New York, 1968), p. 53.
40. *People's Daily* (Beijing), June 1, 1966.
41. Jack Gray and Patrick Cavendish, *Chinese Communism in Crisis* (New York, 1968), pp. 118–19.
42. See Nee, *op. cit.*, pp. 42–43.

43. Mao Zedong, "On Khrushchev's Phoney Communism and Its Historical Lessons for the World," July 14, 1964, in A. Doak Barnett, *China After Mao* (Princeton, N.J., 1967), p. 193.

44. See Solomon, *op. cit.*

45. Mao Zedong, "Talks to Central Committee Leaders," July 21, 1966, *Current Background*, No. 891, pp. 58–59.

46. *Ibid.*

47. Liu Shaoqi, "Self Criticism," October 23, 1966, *Collected Works* (Hong Kong, 1969), p. 358.

48. Liu Shaoqi, "Self Examination," July 9, 1967, *Collected Works*, pp. 372–73.

49. Nee, *op. cit.*, pp. 61–62.

50. *Ibid.*, pp. 62–63.

51. *Ibid.*, p. 64.

52. *People's Daily* (Beijing), December 20, 1966.

53. Chu-Yuan Cheng, *Scientific and Engineering Manpower in Communist China, 1949–1953* (Washington, D.C., 1965), pp. 45–47.

54. New China News Agency, March 31, 1967.

55. Ding Wang, "Profile of Wang Kuang-mei," *Far Eastern Economic Review*, June 22, 1967, p. 654; "Dossiers of Wang Kuang-mei," *Supplement to Worker-Peasant-Soldier*, September 1967, *Current Background* (supplement), No. 27 (June 8, 1968), pp. 6off.

56. New China News Agency, March 31, 1967; Jean Esmein, *La Révolution Culturelle* (Paris, 1970), p. 11.

57. Kuai Dafu, "A Big-Character Poster Entitled 'Let's Think,' " June 21, 1966, *Current Background* (supplement), No. 20 (March 18, 1968), p. 6.

58. Kuai Dafu, "Speeches at the June 27th Debate," *ibid.*, p. 25.

59. Kuai Dafu, "Statement Concerning the June 27th Meeting," *ibid.*, p. 16.

60. Kuai Dafu, "Two Letters to Comrade Yeh Lin," *ibid.*, pp. 46–47.

61. Kuai Dafu, "To Admit and Examine Mistakes in the Presence of the Party and All Revolutionary Teachers and Students of the University," *ibid.*, pp. 53–55.

62. Kuai Dafu, "An Open Letter to the Premier," *ibid.*, pp. 57–58.

63. See Stanley Karnow, *The Washington Post*, December 28, 1966.

64. See Andrew Watson, "Revolution in Sian," *Far Eastern Economic Review*, April 20, 1967.

65. Using the pseudonym Dai, the young Chinese recounted his experiences to two American scholars in Hong Kong. See Gordon A. Bennett and Ronald N. Montaperto, *Red Guard* (New York, 1971), pp. 33–49.

66. Hunter, *op. cit.*, pp. 29–30.

67. *Ibid.*, pp. 39–40.

68. *Ibid.*

69. *Ibid.*, pp. 44, 48.

70. *Ibid.*, pp. 58–60.

71. New China News Agency, July 25, 1966.

72. Mao Zedong, "Swimming," quoted *ibid.*

73. *Ibid.*

74. Mao Zedong, "Speech at a Certain Conference, July 21, 1966," *Current Background,* No. 892, pp. 35–37.

Chapter 9. The Children's Revolt

1. *Red Flag,* August 6, 1967.
2. Mao Zedong, "A Letter to the Red Guards of the Middle School Attached to Tsinghua University," August 1, 1966, *Current Background,* No. 981 (October 8, 1969), p. 63.
3. Mao Zedong, "Bombard the Headquarters—My First Big-Character Poster," August 5, 1966, *ibid.,* p. 63.
4. Liu Shaoqi, "Talk at a Debate at the Peking College of Construction Engineering," August 2, 1966, *Collected Works* (Hong Kong, 1969), pp. 331–33.
5. Liu Shaoqi, "Talk to the Great Proletarian Cultural Revolution Corps," August 3, 1966, *ibid.,* p. 351.
6. Liu Shaoqi, "Talk to the Work Team of the Peking College of Construction Engineering," August 4, 1966, *ibid.,* p. 351.
7. Mao Zedong, "Talk to Foreign Visitors," August 31, 1967, *SCMP,* No. 4200, p. 2.
8. Lin Biao, "Speech at the Eleventh Plenary Session of the Eighth Central Committee of the Chinese Communist Party," *SCMP (Supp.),* No. 159 (December 16, 1966), pp. 38–40.
9. Lee Pat-po, "Unleashing the Youth," *Far Eastern Economic Review,* August 17, 1967, p. 327.
10. Thomas Robinson, "Chou En-lai and the Cultural Revolution in China," unpublished manuscript, the Rand Corporation (Santa Monica, Calif.).
11. "Decision of the Chinese Communist Party Central Committee Concerning the Great Proletarian Cultural Revolution," New China News Agency, August 8, 1966.
12. Chen Boda, "Speech at Peking University," July 23, 1966, *JPRS,* No. 394 (May 10, 1967), p. 2.
13. Kang Sheng, "Speech at Peking Normal University," July 1966[?], *JPRS,* No. 398 (June 8, 1967), p. 5.
14. Chen Boda, *op. cit.*
15. Lin Biao, "Speech at Peking's Mass Rally Celebrating the Great Proletarian Cultural Revolution," *Peking Review,* No. 35 (August 26, 1966), pp. 8–9.
16. From an official film of the August 18, 1966, rally shown in Hong Kong.
17. Beijing Radio, August 23, 1966.
18. "The Factions in Canton," a privately prepared study obtained in Hong Kong.
19. From an interview conducted by the author in Hong Kong.
20. Neale Hunter, *Shanghai Journal* (New York, 1969), p. 65.
21. *Ibid.,* p. 68.
22. Gordon A. Bennett and Ronald N. Montaperto, *Red Guard* (New York, 1971).
23. New China News Agency, August 23, 1966.

24. *Yang-chen Wan-pao* (Guangzhou), August 24, 1966.
25. "Hundred Rules for Destroying the Old and Establishing the New," Red Guards of the Beijing Municipal No. 26 Middle School, September 1, 1966. Pamphlet obtained by author in Hong Kong.
26. From an interview by the author with Branko Bogunivic, Tanjug correspondent in Beijing.
27. See Bennett and Montaperto, *op. cit.*, for the following material from Dai's account.
28. *Asahi* (Tokyo), January 8, 1967.
29. *Yomiuri* (Tokyo), January 8, 1967.
30. Reuters, August 26, 1966.
31. *Hong Kong Standard*, September 1, 1966.
32. Private sources and interviews in Hong Kong.
33. *China News Summary* (Hong Kong), July 24, 1967.
34. Zhou Enlai, "Speech to Red Guard Representatives," September 1, 1966, *Current Background*, No. 819 (March 10, 1967), p. 19.
35. Stanley Karnow, *The Washington Post*, September 25, 1966.
36. Anne F. Thurston, *Enemies of the People* (New York, 1987), pp. 133ff.
37. *Ibid.*, pp. 228–29.
38. Robert Tung, "The Sins of the Capitalists," *Far Eastern Economic Review*, September 8, 1966, pp. 441ff.
39. Nien Cheng, *Life and Death in Shanghai* (New York, 1986), p. 6.
40. *Peking Review*, No. 37 (September 23, 1966), p. 10.
41. *Ibid.*
42. Changchun Radio, September 2, 1966.
43. Henan Radio, September 21, 1966.
44. Chengdu Radio, November 11, 1967.
45. Stanley Karnow, *The Washington Post*, August 6, 1967.
46. Chengdu Radio, November 11, 1967.
47. *Ibid.*, September 13, 1966.
48. Guizhou Radio, June 23, 1967.
49. See *China News Summary* (Hong Kong), September 22, 1966.
50. *Current Background*, No. 855, June 17, 1968.
51. *People's Daily* (Beijing), September 11, 1966.
52. Bennett and Montaperto, *op. cit.*, pp. 91–111.
53. From an interview conducted in Hong Kong by the author.
54. Bennett and Montaperto, *op. cit.*
55. See Stanley Karnow, *The Washington Post*, May 21, 1970.
56. Zhou Enlai, "Speech on September 25, 1966," in *Collection of Leaders' Speeches* published by Qinghua University Defend-the-East Corps, November 1966, cited in Robinson, *op. cit.*
57. See Robinson, *op. cit.*
58. Zhou Enlai, "Speech to Red Guard Representatives," pp. 16–17.
59. Zhou Enlai, "Speech on September 25, 1966."
60. *Ibid.*
61. Zhou Enlai, "Speech to Red Guard Representatives," p. 19.
62. Zhou Enlai, "Speech on September 25, 1966."
63. Zhou Enlai, "Speech at Altar of Agriculture Park on September 13, 1966," *Current Background*, No. 819 (March 10, 1967), p. 41.

64. Zhou Enlai, "Speech on September 9, 1961," *JPRS*, No. 394 (May 10, 1967), p. 1.

65. Zhou Enlai, "Urgent Instructions by Telephone," October 24, 1966, *SCMM (Supp.)*, No. 15 (May 8, 1967), pp. 22–23.

66. Zhou Enlai, "Speech on September 25, 1966," and "Speech to Red Guard Representatives," p. 18.

67. Chen Yi, "To Red Guards on Welcoming Foreign Guests and Overseas Chinese," *Collection of Materials Pertaining to the Great Proletarian Cultural Revolution* (Guangzhou), October 28, 1966.

68. "Regulations of the Chinese Communist Party Central Committee and the State Council Concerning the Protection of the Security of Party and State Secrets during the Great Cultural Revolution Movement," September 8, 1966. Document obtained by author in Hong Kong.

69. New China News Agency, September 19, 1966.

70. *Ibid.*, September 23, 1966.

71. *Red Guard Daily* (Guangzhou), No. 15 (December 22, 1966), *JPRS*, No. 383 (March 13, 1967), p. 1.

72. See his remarks in "Speech on September 25, 1966."

73. *Yomiuri Shimbun* (Tokyo), September 26, 1966, cited in Robinson, *op. cit.*

74. *Ibid.*

75. See Mao Zedong, "Speeches at Central Committee Work Conference," October 24–25, 1966, *Current Background*, No. 891 (October 8, 1969), pp. 70–75; see also *JPRS*, No. 90 (February 12, 1970), pp. 8–16.

76. Liu Shaoqi, "Self-Criticism," *Collected Works*, pp. 375ff.

77. Cited in *Nihon Keizai* (Tokyo), January 5, 1967; *Yomiuri* (Tokyo), January 10, 1967.

78. Chen Boda, "Speech on October 25, 1966 at Central Committee Conference," obtained from private sources.

79. New China News Agency, October 31, 1966.

80. Stanley Karnow, *The Washington Post*, November 12, 1966.

81. New China News Agency, December 3, 1966; see also *Peking Review*, November 9, 1966, p. 5.

82. New China News Agency, November 3, 1966.

83. Hunter, *op. cit.*, pp. 138–40.

84. From an interview conducted by the author in Hong Kong.

85. Bennett and Montaperto, *op. cit.*

86. See *Far Eastern Economic Review*, December 1, 1966, p. 477.

87. "Tao Chu Is the Khrushchev of Central-South China," in publication of the Revolutionary Rebel Liaison Center of Red Guards of Metropolitan Universities and Colleges, February 22, 1967, *Current Background*, No. 824 (April 27, 1967), p. 2.

88. From private sources in Beijing.

89. "Remove the Mask of Tao Chu as a 'Proletarian Revolutionary,'" *Peking Chingkangshan*, January 11, 1967, *Current Background*, No. 824 (April 27, 1967), p. 26.

90. *South China Morning Post* (Hong Kong), January 6, 1967.

91. *Yomiuri* (Tokyo), December 29, 1966.

92. *People's Daily* (Beijing), December 25, 1966.

93. *Yomiuri* (Tokyo), January 4, 1967.
94. *Red Flag*, December 31, 1966.

Chapter 10. The January Tempest

1. Mao Zedong, "Talk to Foreign Visitors," August 31, 1967, *SCMP*, No. 4200 (June 18, 1968), p. 3.
2. Wall poster, March 4, 1967, *China Topics* (Hong Kong), March 10, 1967.
3. This and the following quotations from Mao Zedong, "Talk to Foreign Visitors," *op. cit.*, pp. 2–4.
4. New China News Agency, December 31, 1966.
5. Tanjug News Agency, December 7, 1966; *Izvestia* (Moscow), December 11, 1966.
6. "Comment of the Chinese Communist Party Central Committee on the Transmission of the Report of the Work Group Concerning the Problem of Lo Jui-ch'ing's Mistakes," May 16, 1966, *Chinese Communist Party Documents of the Great Proletarian Cultural Revolution* (Hong Kong, 1968), pp. 31–32.
7. "Struggle Meeting Against P'eng Chen *et al.*," January 5, 1967, *SCMP* (*Supp.*), No. 165 (March 10, 1967), pp. 1–5.
8. Zhou Enlai, speech to a Red Guard conference, reported in *Tokyo Shimbun*, January 11, 1967; quoted in Thomas Robinson, "Chou En-lai and the Cultural Revolution in China," unpublished manuscript, the Rand Corporation (Santa Monica, Calif.), August 1971.
9. See *Current Scene*, May 31, 1967, pp. 11–12.
10. *Sankei* (Tokyo), January 9, 1967.
11. For the details of this incident, see *Current Scene*, May 31, 1967, pp. 7–11.
12. *Sankei* (Tokyo), January 16, 1967.
13. Agence France-Presse, March 28, 1968.
14. Neale Hunter, *Shanghai Journal* (New York, 1969), pp. 141ff.
15. *Ibid.*, pp. 153ff.
16. *Wen Hui Pao* (Shanghai), January 11, 1967.
17. Hunter, *op. cit.*, p. 213.
18. "Message of Greetings from Chinese Communist Party Central Committee, the State Council, the Military Commission and the Cultural Revolution Group to the Revolutionary Rebel Organizations in Shanghai," January 11, 1967, *Current Background*, No. 852 (May 6, 1968), p. 38.
19. Mao Zedong, "Speech at a Meeting of the Cultural Revolution Group," January 9, 1967, *Current Background*, No. 892 (October 21, 1969), p. 47.
20. *People's Daily* (Beijing), January 22, 1967.
21. *Sankei* (Tokyo), January 21, 1967.
22. New China News Agency, February 1, 1967.
23. *China News Summary* (Hong Kong), January 19, 1967.
24. See Andrew Watson, "Showdown in Sian," *Far Eastern Economic Review*, May 18, 1967, pp. 404–406.

25. *Asahi* (Tokyo), January 24, 1967; also *The Washington Post*, January 23, 1967.
26. *Asahi* (Tokyo) and *Tokyo Shimbun*, January 8, 1967.
27. Urumchi Radio, September 14 and 16, 1966.
28. *Ibid.*, November 30, 1966.
29. Donald W. Klein and Anne B. Clark, *Biographic Dictionary of Chinese Communism 1921–1965* (Cambridge, Mass., 1971), p. 904.
30. William Whitson, "The Concept of Military Generation: The Chinese Communist Case," unpublished manuscript, July 1968.
31. "The January 26 Counter-Revolutionary Sanguinary Incident at Shih-ho-tzu Sinkiang," mimeographed handbill by Xinjiang rebel groups, January 20, 1967, *SCMP (Supp.)*, No. 185 (May 27, 1967), pp. 1–4.
32. *Nihon Keizai* (Tokyo), January 26, 1967; *Mainichi* (Tokyo), January 28, 1967.
33. "Accusation by a Comrade-in-Arms Saved from the Mouth of a Tiger," *Tienshan Beacon Fire*, January 15, 1968, *Current Background*, No. 855 (June 17, 1968), pp. 5–8.
34. *Mainichi* (Tokyo), January 29, 1967.
35. *China Topics*, February 20, 1969; *Nihon Keizai* (Tokyo), February 1, 1967.
36. "Regulations of the Chinese Communist Party Central Committee, the State Council and the Military Commission of the Central Committee," February 11, 1967, *Current Background*, No. 852 (May 6, 1968), pp. 68–71.
37. Gordon A. Bennett and Ronald N. Montaperto, *Red Guard* (New York, 1971), p. 153.
38. Guangzhou Radio, January 11, 1967.
39. *South China Morning Post* (Hong Kong), January 14, 1967.
40. Bennett and Montaperto, *op. cit.*, p. 154.
41. "Some Views on Present Situation of the Great Proletarian Cultural Revolution in the Canton Area," Kwangtung *Red Guard*, February 10, 1967, *SCMP*, No. 3929 (May 1, 1967), p. 3.
42. "Facts of the January 22 Seizure of Power," *ibid.*, p. 8.
43. "Message from the Chinese Communist Party Kwangtung Provincial Committee to all Party Members, Cadres, and the People of the Province," *ibid.*, p. 12.
44. "Facts of the January 22 Seizure of Power," *ibid.*, p. 7.
45. New China News Agency, January 28, 1967.
46. "News in Brief," *Red Banner* (Beijing), January 30, 1967, *SCMP (Supp.)*, No. 176 (April 14, 1967), p. 28.
47. "Drag Out the Handful of Counter-Revolutionaries in the 'Hui Nationality Rebel Regiment' to Face the Public," *Pei-ching Jih-pao* (Beijing), February 12, 1967, *SCMP (Supp.)*, No. 177 (April 19, 1967), pp. 29–32.
48. *Asahi* (Tokyo), January 10, 1967.
49. These and following quotations from Jiang Qing, "Revolutionary Rebels Should Form a Great Alliance and Seize Power after the Pattern of the Paris Commune," *New Peking University*, January 28, 1967, *SCMP (Supp.)*, No. 174 (April 10, 1967), p. 14.

50. Jiang Qing, "Speech on January 17, 1967," *Railway Red Banner*, January 20, 1967, *SCMP (Supp.)*, No. 171 (March 30, 1967), p. 11.

51. *Nihon Keizai* (Tokyo), January 7, 1967.

52. "News in Brief," *Red Banner* (Beijing), January 30, 1967.

53. *Red Banner News*, published by the South China Technical College, September 10, 1967.

54. "Whom Are Such Schools Meant For?" *Criticism and Reform in Middle Schools* (Beijing), June 19, 1967, *SCMP (Supp.)*, No. 200 (August 31, 1967), p. 33.

55. *Ibid.*, p. 30.

56. Bennett and Montaperto, *op. cit.*, pp. 137–41.

57. *Sankei* (Tokyo), October 7, 1967.

58. "See What Kind of Goods the 'United Action Committee' Is," *Chingkangshan* (Beijing), January 23, 1967, *SCMP*, No. 3905 (March 23, 1967), p. 16.

59. *Sankei* (Tokyo), October 7, 1967.

60. "What the Commotion of the 'United Action Committee' Has Explained," *Peking Middle School Cultural Revolution Paper*, February 10, 1967, *SCMP (Supp.)*, No. 183 (May 16, 1967), pp. 18–19.

61. *Life*, April 30, 1971.

62. See Philip Bridgham, "Mao's Cultural Revolution in 1967: The Struggle to Seize Power," *China Quarterly*, No. 34 (April–June 1968), p. 10.

63. "Ch'en Po-ta and Chiang Ch'ing Talk to Students," January 26, 1967, *The East Is Red* (Beijing), February 4, 1967.

Chapter 11. The Revolt of the Proletariat

1. *Red Flag*, January 12, 1967.

2. *Current Scene*, VI, No. 5 (March 15, 1968), p. 18.

3. "Three Years of Blood and Tears," *Canton Aid-Agriculture Red Flag* (Guangzhou), No. 7, (January 1968), *China Topics* (Hong Kong), May 27, 1968.

4. *Revolutionary Youth* (Guangzhou), November 10, 1967.

5. See *Current Scene*, VI, No. 5, p. 21.

6. *Ibid.*, pp. 4–6.

7. See Philip Bridgham, "Mao's Cultural Revolution in 1967: The Struggle to Seize Power," in *China Quarterly*, No. 34 (April–June 1968), pp. 8–9.

8. See Neale Hunter, "Port in a Storm," *Far Eastern Economic Review*, June 22, 1967, pp. 663–67.

9. See *ibid.*

10. *Mainichi* (Tokyo), February 28, 1967.

11. *China News Analysis* (Hong Kong), No. 65 (March 10, 1967), p. 5.

12. New China News Agency, January 11, 1967.

13. *Current Scene*, V, No. 8 (May 19, 1967), p. 3.

14. *People's Daily* (Beijing), January 20, 1967.

15. *Current Scene*, V, No. 8, p. 4.

16. *Asahi* (Tokyo), February 11, 1967.

17. "News for Reference," *Revolutionary Workers' Paper* (Beijing), January 20, 1967, *SCMP (Supp.)*, No. 169 (March 20, 1967), p. 10.

18. New China News Agency, March 3, 1967.

19. *Asahi* (Tokyo), January 12, 1967.

20. *Kwangming Daily* (Beijing), January 20, 1967.

21. *Nihon Keizai* (Tokyo), January 16, 1967.

22. *Current Scene,* V, No. 8, p. 13.

23. "News for Reference," p. 10.

24. Li Xin, "Denounce Hsiao Wang-tung's Crimes of Practicing Economism," *Marching Journal* (Beijing), January 28, 1967, *SCMP (Supp.)*, No. 174 (April 10, 1967), pp. 10–11.

25. "Smash Anti-Revolutionary Economism," in *ibid.*, pp. 8–9.

26. *Nihon Keizai* (Tokyo), January 12, 1967.

27. Mainichi (Tokyo), February 18, 1967.

28. *Sankei* (Tokyo), January 19, 1967.

29. *Yomiuri* (Tokyo), February 4, 1967.

30. Jiangxi Radio, January 30, January 23, 1967; Jiangsu Radio, January 24, 1967; Guangzhou Radio, January 17, 1967; New China News Agency, January 15, 1967; *Wen Hui Pao* (Shanghai), January 20, 1967; Fujian Radio, January 24, 1967; *People's Daily* (Beijing), January 23, 1967; New China News Agency, January 26, 1967.

31. "An Appeal to All Revolutionary Commune Members and Poor, Middle and Lower Peasants," Shanghai wall poster, January 14, 1967.

32. *Wen Hui Pao* (Shanghai), February 12, 1967.

33. *Liberation Daily* (Shanghai), February 16, 1967; see also *Current Scene*, V, No. 16 (October 2, 1967), p. 7.

34. *Wen Hui Pao* (Shanghai), January 5, 1967.

35. *Ibid.*, January 9, 1967.

36. See Neale Hunter. *Shanghai Journal* (New York, 1969), p. 215.

37. *Ibid.*

38. *Ibid.*, p. 218.

39. "Document of the Chinese Communist Party Central Committee, the State Council and the Military Commission," January 11, 1967, *Current Background*, No. 852 (May 6, 1968), p. 39.

40. *Yomiuri* (Tokyo), January 19, 1967.

41. "Notification by the Chinese Communist Party Central Committee on Opposition to Economism," January 11, 1967, *Current Background*, No. 852, pp. 40–41.

42. "Notification by the Chinese Communist Party Central Committee Concerning Broadcasting Stations," January 11, 1967, *ibid.*, p. 43.

43. *People's Daily* (Beijing), January 30, 1967.

44. Hunter, *Shanghai Journal*, p. 220.

45. Zhou Enlai, speech of January 17, 1967, in *Railway Red Banner*, *SCMP (Supp.)*, No. 171 (March 30, 1967), p. 12.

46. *Asahi* (Tokyo), January 12, 1967.

47. Zhou Enlai, "Directive to the Proletarian Revolutionary Rebels," *Red Staff Members and Workers* (Beijing), January 29, 1967, *JPRS*, No. 396 (May 22, 1967), p. 4.

Chapter 12. Out of the Barrel of a Gun

1. "Decision of the Chinese Communist Party Central Committee, the State Council, the Military Commission of the Central Committee and the Cultural Revolution Group on Resolute Support for the Revolutionary Masses of the Left," January 23, 1967, *Current Background*, No. 852 (May 6, 1968), p. 49.

2. Mao Zedong, "A Talk to Foreign Visitors," August 31, 1967, *SCMP*, No. 4200 (June 18, 1968), p. 3.

3. Mao Zedong, "Speech at the Enlarged Meeting of the Military Commission" (as relayed by Premier Zhou Enlai on January 27, 1967), *Current Background*, No. 892 (October 21, 1969), p. 49.

4. *Peking Review*, October 14, 1966, p. 3.

5. William W. Whitson, *The Political Dynamics of the Chinese Communist Military Elite* (privately printed, Hong Kong, 1969), p. 15.

6. "Urgent Directive of the Military Commission and the General Political Department on the Great Proletarian Cultural Revolution in Military Academies and Schools," October 5, 1966, *Current Background*, No. 852, pp. 19–20.

7. Whitson, *op. cit.*, p. 14.

8. He Long, "Speech at Meeting of Revolutionary Teachers, Students and Staffs of Various Military Colleges and Schools of the Whole People's Liberation Army Who Have Come to Establish Revolutionary Experiences in Peking," November 13, 1966, *SCMM (Supp.)*, No. 16 (June 5, 1967), pp. 34–35.

9. Ye Jianying, "Speech at the Cultural Revolution Rally of All Army Academies," October 5, 1966, *Current Background*, No. 819 (March 10, 1967), pp. 63–64.

10. Xu Xiangchen, "Speech at Meeting of Revolutionary Teachers, Students and Staffs . . . in Peking," November 13, 1966, *SCMM (Supp.)*, No. 16 (June 5, 1967), pp. 34–35.

11. *Liberation Army Daily* (Beijing), January 14, 1967.

12. "Down with Ho Lung, Conspirator Seeking to Usurp Power in the Party, the Government and the Army," *New Peking University*, January 20, 1967; "Down with Ho Lung," pamphlet compiled by the Jinggang Mountain Corps, Qinghua University, November 1967, *Current Background*, No. 859 (August 8, 1968), pp. 2, 15, 24–25.

13. "Black Line of Ho Lung's Clique," *Physical Culture Combat Bulletin*, November 14, 1967, cited in *Current Background*, No. 859, p. 27.

14. *Asahi* (Tokyo), May 8, 1967.

15. *Sankei* (Tokyo), May 9, 1967.

16. *Mainichi* (Tokyo), February 7, 1967.

17. "Down with the Old Swine Chu Teh," *The East Is Red* (Beijing), February 11, 1967, *SCMP (Supp.)*, No. 172 (April 3, 1967), p. 21.

18. *Ashai* (Tokyo), January 24, 1967; Whitson, *op. cit.*, p. 18.

19. *Sankei* (Tokyo), February 2, 1967.

20. *China Topics* (Hong Kong), January 19, 1967.

21. "Directive of the Military Commission of the Central Committee Reiterating the Implementation of the Cultural Revolution Stage by Stage

and Group by Group in Military Regions," January 28, 1967, *Current Background*, No. 852 (May 18, 1968), p. 56.

22. "Instruction to the People's Liberation Army" (as relayed by Vice-Chairman Ye Jianying on January 27, 1967), *Current Background*, No. 892 (October 21, 1969), p. 50.

23. "Order of the Military Commission of the Central Committee," January 28, 1967, *Current Background*, No. 852, p. 54.

24. "Notification by the Chinese Communist Party Central Committee and the State Council Concerning the Question of Exchange of Revolutionary Experiences on Foot by Revolutionary Teachers, Students and Red Guards," February 3, 1967, *ibid.*, p. 59.

25. "Supplementary Notice of the Chinese Communist Party Central Committee Concerning the Question of Broadcasting Stations," January 23, 1967; "Order of the State Council and the Military Commission of the Central Committee Concerning the Takeover of the Civil Aviation System by the Army," January 26, 1967, in *ibid.*, pp. 51, 53.

26. Thomas W. Robinson, "Chou En-lai and the Cultural Revolution in China" (unpublished manuscript), p. 80.

27. Lin Biao, "Speech on March 30, 1967," obtained from a private source.

28. "Document of the Chinese Communist Party Central Committee, the State Council and the Military Commission," January 11, 1967, *Current Background*, No. 852, p. 39.

29. "Document of the Chinese Communist Party Central Committee," January 19, 1967, *ibid.*, p. 48.

30. "Notification by the Chinese Communist Party Central Committee Ordering That the Spearhead of Struggle May Not Be Directed Against the Armed Forces," January 14, 1967, *ibid.*, p. 46.

31. *Mainichi* (Tokyo), January 25, 1967.

32. *Yomiuri* (Tokyo), January 24, 1967.

33. Neale Hunter, *Shanghai Journal* (New York, 1969), pp. 244ff.

34. *Wen Hui Pao* (Shanghai), February 6, 1967.

35. Mao Zedong, "Speech at His Third Meeting with Chang Ch'un-ch'iao and Yao Wen-yuan," February 1967, *JPRS*, No. 90 (February 12, 1970), p. 44; wall poster, March 4, 1967, *China Topics* (Hong Kong), March 10, 1967.

36. Ellis Joffe, "The Chinese Army in the Cultural Revolution: The Politics of Intervention," *Current Scene*, VIII, No. 8 (December 7, 1970), pp. 10–11.

37. New China News Agency, January 24, 1967.

38. Private source in Hong Kong.

39. New China News Agency, January 24, 1967.

40. *Kwangming Daily* (Beijing), March 23, 1967.

41. *Red Flag*, No. 4, cited on Beijing Radio, February 27, 1967.

42. *Red Flag*, February 1967, *SCMM*, No. 566 (March 6), 1967, p. 1.

43. Donald W. Klein and Anne B. Clark, *Biographic Dictionary of Chinese Communism 1921–1965* (Cambridge, Mass., 1971), pp. 708–10; and Parris H. Chang, "The Revolutionary Committee in China," *Current Scene*, VI, No. 9 (June 1, 1968), p. 8.

44. Chang, *op. cit.*, p. 4; *People's Daily* (Beijing), March 21, 1967.

45. Beijing Domestic Service, February 9, 1967.
46. New China News Agency, February 1, 1967.
47. *People's Daily* (Beijing), February 2, 1967.
48. *Red Flag*, No. 5 (March 1967), *SCMM*, No. 572 (April 17, 1967), p. 11.
49. "The People's Liberation Army Takeover of the Municipal Public Security Bureau Is Very Fine," and "The People's Liberation Army Takes Over Control of the Municipal Public Security Bureau," *Peiching Jihpao* (Beijing), February 12, 1967, *SCMP (Supp.)*, No. 174 (April 10, 1967), pp. 1–3.
50. *China News Summary* (Hong Kong), March 15, 1967.
51. "Documents of the Chinese Communist Party Central Committee," *Current Background*, No. 852, p. 96.
52. "Chinese Communist Party Central Committee's Letter to Poor and Lower-Middle Peasants and Cadres at All Levels in Rural People's Communes Throughout the Country," *ibid.*, p. 90.
53. New China News Agency, March 22, 1967.
54. This and the following data from an interview conducted by the author in Hong Kong.
55. Zhou Enlai, "Talk to Revolutionary Rebels of Industrial and Communications Departments," February 1, 1967, *Red Staff Members and Workers*, March 2, 1967, *SCMP (Supp.)*, No. 178 (April 24, 1967), p. 21ff.
56. See *The Washington Post*, February 25, 1967.
57. *Asahi* (Tokyo), February 18, 1967.
58. Philip Bridgham, "Mao's Cultural Revolution in 1967: The Struggle to Seize Power," *China Quarterly*, No. 34 (April–June, 1968), p. 13.
59. *Mainichi* (Tokyo), February 25, 1967.
60. New China News Agency, February 3, 1967.
61. *South China Morning Post* (Hong Kong), February 27, 1967.
62. New China News Agency, March 2, 1967.
63. *Ibid.*
64. *Red Flag*, February 23, 1967.
65. *People's Daily* (Beijing), February 15, 1967.
66. Kweichow Radio, March 8, 1967.
67. *People's Daily* (Beijing), February 26, 1967.
68. New China News Agency, February 27, 1967.
69. *Red Flag*, March 1967.

Chapter 13. The Army Attempts to Rule

1. Beijing Radio, January 30, 1967.
2. *China Topics* (Hong Kong), April 25, 1967.
3. Lin Biao, "Speech on March 30, 1967," from a private source.
4. *China News Summary* (Hong Kong), March 27, 1969.
5. *People's Daily* (Beijing), February 24, 1967.
6. Ellis Joffe, "The Chinese Army in the Cultural Revolution: The Politics of Intervention," *Current Scene*, VIII, No. 8 (December 7, 1970), pp. 13–14.

7. See Stanley Karnow, *The Washington Post*, May 25, 1967.
8. Lin Biao, "Report to the Ninth National Congress of the Communist Party of China," April 14, 1969, in *Current Background*, No. 880 (May 9, 1969), p. 30.
9. Lin Biao, "Speech on March 30, 1967."
10. See Victor C. Falkenheim, "The Cultural Revolution in Kwangsi, Yunnan, and Fukien," *Asian Survey*, IX, No. 8 (August 1969), pp. 582–84.
11. *Ibid.*, pp. 587–88.
12. See "Yunnan Provincial Revolutionary Committee Born in the Midst of Armed Clashes," *Facts and Features* (Taibei), I, No. 24 (September 18, 1968), pp. 11–13.
13. Falkenheim, *op. cit.*, pp. 591–93; New China News Agency (Fuzhou), February 16, 1967.
14. "Regulations of the Chinese Communist Party Central Committee, the State Council and the Military Commission of the Central Committee," February 11, 1967, *Current Background*, No. 852 (May 18, 1968), pp. 68–70.
15. Urumchi Radio, February 11, 1967.
16. Tashkent Radio, February 18 and 23, 1967.
17. From a private source in Alma Ata.
18. Paul Hayer and William Heaton, "The Cultural Revolution in Inner Mongolia," *China Quarterly*, No. 36 (October–December 1968), pp. 116–18.
19. *Ibid.*, p. 119.
20. Agence France-Presse (Beijing), January 26, 1967.
21. Hayer and Heaton, *op. cit.*, pp. 122ff.
22. See Stanley Karnow, *The Washington Post*, May 25, 1971.
23. "Chronology of the Cultural Revolution in the Tibet Region," *Red Rebel Paper* (Lhasa), August 6, 1967, *SCMP (Supp.)*, No. 216 (January 26, 1968), pp. 30–31.
24. *China Topics* (Hong Kong), August 30, 1968.
25. *Hindustan Times* (New Delhi), October 24, 1967.
26. *China Topics* (Hong Kong), August 30, 1968.
27. *Ibid.*
28. Agence France-Presse (Gangtok, Sikkim), February 16, 1967.
29. "Please See How Cruelly the Handful of Persons in the Military Region Party Committee Persecuted the Rebels," a Lhasa handbill, February 10, 1967, *SCMP (Supp.)*, No. 179 (April 26, 1967), p. 113.
30. "Chronology of Cultural Revolution in Tibet," p. 39.
31. *China Topics* (Hong Kong), August 30, 1968.
32. "Chronology of Cultural Revolution in Tibet," p. 40.
33. *Ibid.*, p. 41.
34. "Stalemate in Szechwan," *Current Scene*, VI, No. 11 (July 1, 1968), p. 6.
35. Cited in Thomas Jay Matthews, "The Cultural Revolution in Szechwan" (unpublished manuscript), June 1971.
36. See *ibid.*
37. "Stalemate in Szechwan," p. 6.
38. *Ibid.*, pp. 6–7.

39. "A Bloodstained Scrap of Paper," *Combat Corps News* (Beijing), May 30, 1967, in *SCMP (Supp.)*, No. 191 (July 14, 1967), p. 11.
40. New China News Agency, February 24, 1967.
41. *China Topics* (Hong Kong), August 18, 1967.
42. Guizhou Radio, July 13, 1967.
43. "A Bloodstained Scrap of Paper," p. 11; "Important Speeches of Central Leaders on March 15, 1968," *SCMP*, No. 4181 (May 20, 1968), p. 2.
44. Parris H. Chang, "The Revolutionary Committee in China," *Current Scene*, VI, No. 9 (June 1, 1968), p. 10.
45. "A Short Talk with Revolutionary People in the Capital on the Great Proletarian Cultural Revolution in Honan," *Honan Revolutionary Rebel General Command Post*, March 8, 1967, *SCMP (Supp.)*, No. 185 (June 22, 1967), p. 6.
46. *Ibid.*, pp. 11–12.
47. *Ibid.*
48. Premier Zhou Enlai, Directive of February 17, 1967, *SCMP (Supp.)*, No. 177 (April 19, 1967), p. 23.
49. Chang, *op. cit.*, p. 11.
50. "Order of the Military Commission of the Party Central Committee," February 8, 1967, *SCMP*, No. 3900 (March 16, 1967), p. 1.
51. Gordon A. Bennett and Ronald N. Montaperto, *Red Guard* (New York, 1971).
52. See Donald W. Klein and Anne B. Clark, *Biographic Dictionary of Chinese Communism 1921–1965* (Cambridge, Mass., 1971), pp. 405–406.
53. "Who Led the Doctrine Guards Astray?" *Red Banner News* (Guangzhou), September 10, 1967.
54. See Ezra Vogel, *Canton Under Communism* (Cambridge, Mass., 1969), pp. 329–30.
55. Bennett and Montaperto, *op. cit.*
56. *Ibid.*
57. *Ibid.*
58. "The Crimes of Wu Chuan-pin, a Counter-Revolutionary Bug," *Sun Yat-sen University Combat Bulletin* (Guangzhou), August 4, 1968, *SCMP*, No. 4257 (November 13, 1968), pp. 1–5.
59. "Supreme Directive of the Kwangtung Military District," March 1, 1967, *SCMP*, No. 3905 (March 23, 1967), pp. 1–6.
60. "Report on an Investigation into the Facts of Persecution of the August First Combat Corps," *Steel August First* (Guangzhou), October 15, 1967, *SCMP*, No. 4096 (January 10, 1968), pp. 1–8.
61. "Kwangtung Provincial Military District Command's Self-Criticism," *ibid.*, pp. 9–12.
62. Bennett and Montaperto, *op. cit.*

Chapter 14. The Radical Resurgence

1. *Asahi* (Tokyo), March 16, 1967.
2. Zhou Enlai, "Speech to Representatives of Different Parties and Differ-

ent Departments of the State Council," April 30, 1967, from a private source.

3. *Asahi* (Tokyo), March 16, 1967.
4. *Ibid.*
5. Kuai Dafu, "Analysis of the Present Situation," *Red Worker* (Nanjing), March 24, 1967, *SCMP (Supp.)*, No. 188 (June 22, 1967), pp. 1–3.
6. *Red Flag*, March 9 and 22, 1967.
7. Lin Jie, "Courageously Forging Ahead in the Teeth of Great Storms of Class Struggle," *Red Flag*, April 3, 1967.
8. Mao Zedong, "Conversation with Premier Chou En-lai on Power Struggle," Jerome Ch'en, *Mao Papers* (New York, 1970), pp. 48–49.
9. From interviews conducted by the author in Hong Kong.
10. See *South China Morning Post* (Hong Kong), April 14, 1967.
11. See *Tokyo Shimbun*, January 11, 1967.
12. See *Yomiuri* (Tokyo), April 10, 1967.
13. See *Asahi* (Tokyo), March 27, 1967.
14. *The Washington Post*, April 3, 1967.
15. Qi Benyou, "Patriotism or National Betrayal?" *Red Flag*, April 1, 1967.
16. Liu Shaoqi, "Confession," Summer 1967, *Collected Works* (Hong Kong, 1969), pp. 365–68.
17. *People's Daily* (Beijing), April 8, 1967.
18. Liu Shaoqi, "How to Be a Good Communist," *Collected Works*, 162–63.
19. "Down with Liu Shao-ch'i," pamphlet published by the Jinggangshan Fighting Corps of the Fourth Hospital, Beijing, May 1967, *Current Background*, No. 834 (August 17, 1967).
20. This quotation and the following material from "Three Trials of Pickpocket Wang Kuang-mei," pamphlet compiled by the South Sea Great Wall Fighting Detachment of the Jinggangshan Corps, Qinghua University, *Current Background*, No. 848 (February 27, 1968), pp. 1–39; also *Current Scene*, VI, No. 6 (April 15, 1968).
21. Wang Guangmei, "Letter of April 20, 1967," and "Self-Examination of June 28, 1967," *Current Background*, No. 848, pp. 40–41.
22. *Asahi* (Tokyo), April 6, 1967.
23. Robinson, *op. cit.*
24. From a private source in Beijing.
25. "What Ch'en Yi Did in Yunnan," January 23, 1967, based on information supplied to Huang Fenglin, Director of the Public Relations Department of Yunnan, *SCMM*, No. 635 (December 2, 1968), p. 6.
26. Melvin Gurtov, *The Foreign Ministry and Foreign Affairs in China's Revolution*, a Rand Corporation memorandum (Santa Monica, Calif., March 1969), p. 5.
27. "Ch'en Yi's Self-Examination," January 24, 1967, pamphlet published by the Red Guards of the Second Foreign Languages Institute, *SCMM*, No. 636 (December 9, 1968), pp. 5–6.
29. "Speeches by Ch'en Po-ta and Chou En-lai," January 24, 1967, *ibid.*, p. 7.
30. *Red Guard Combat Paper* (Guangzhou), April 8, 1967.

31. Chen Yi, "Speech of February 12, 1967," *SCMM*, No. 636 (December 9, 1968), p. 25.

32. Stanley Karnow, *The Washington Post*, May 9, 1967.

33. Gurtov, *op. cit.*, pp. 27–28; Reuters (Beijing), May 15, 1967.

34. Gurtov, *op. cit.*, p. 30.

35. New China News Agency, April 30 and May 1, 1967.

36. See "Drag Out Yao Teng-shan, Big Political Pickpocket," *Red Guard Paper* (Beijing), September 15, 1967, *SCMP (Supp.)*, No. 213 (December 13, 1967), pp. 4–5.

37. "T'an Chen-lin's Black Words," *Red Guard News*, April 5, 1967, *SCMP (Supp.)*, No. 238 (November 8, 1968), p. 8.

38. "T'an Chen-lin in the 'February Adverse Current,' " *Sun Yat-sen University Red Flag* (Guangzhou), April 4, 1968, *SCMP*, No. 4169 (May 2, 1968), p. 7.

39. "Manifestations of the 'February Adverse Current' in the Ministry of Agriculture," *Red Guard News*, April 5, 1967, *SCMP (Supp.)*, No. 238 (November 8, 1968), p. 12.

40. "T'an Chen-lin in the 'February Adverse Current,' " p. 9.

41. "Manifestations of the 'February Adverse Current' in the Ministry of Agriculture," p. 12.

42. "Look at T'an Chen-lin, Filial Scion of the Landlord Class," *New Agriculture*," p. 12.

Chapter 15. The Troubled Spring

1. "Decision of the Chinese Communist Party Central Committee on the Question of Anhwei," March 27, 1967; "Decision of the Chinese Communist Party Central Committee on the Handling of the Inner Mongolia Question," April 13, 1967; and "Decision of the Chinese Communist Party Central Committee, the State Council, the Military Commission of the Central Committee, and the Cultural Revolution Group Concerning the Question of Tsinghai," March 24, 1967; *Current Background*, No. 852 (May 6, 1968), pp. 109–19 *passim*.

2. "Document of the Chinese Communist Party Central Committee," April 1, 1967, *ibid.*, pp. 111–12.

3. "Order of the Military Commission of the Chinese Communist Party Central Committee," *ibid.*, pp. 115–16.

4. See William W. Whitson, *The Political Dynamics of the Chinese Communist Military Elite* (privately printed, Hong Kong, 1969), p. 33.

5. *Yomiuri* (Tokyo), May 27, 1967.

6. See Philip Bridgham, "Mao's Cultural Revolution in 1967: The Struggle to Seize Power," *China Quarterly*, No. 34 (April–June 1968), p. 20.

7. *Liberation Army Daily* (Beijing), April 20, 1967.

8. *Red Flag*, May 12, 1967.

9. See Bridgham, *loc. cit.*

10. "Report to the Revolutionary Masses on the Public Examination of Mistakes Made in the Work of Supporting the Left," submitted by the Shandong Provincial Revolutionary Committee and Jinan Military Dis-

trict to the Cultural Revolution Group, May 31, 1967, reprinted in *Canton Medical College Red Flag*, July 10, 1967, *SCMP*, No. 4061 (November 16, 1967), pp. 11–12; "Document of the Chinese Communist Party Central Committee," *Current Background*, No. 852, p. 13.

11. *Nihon Keizai* (Tokyo), April 7, 1967.
12. Jiang Qing, "Do New Services for the People," April 13, 1967, *The East Is Red* (Beijing), June 3, 1967, *SCMP (Supp.)*, No. 192, July 17, 1967, pp. 7–15.
13. *Wen Hui Pao* (Shanghai), April 28, 1967.
14. *People's Daily* (Beijing), May 21, 1967.
15. Xie Fuzhi, "Speech to Peking University Red Guards," May 7, 1967, from a private source in Beijing.
16. Bridgham, *op. cit.*, p. 20.
17. Xie Fuzhi, "Speech to Peking University Red Guards," May 7, 1967.
18. *Tokyo Shimbun*, May 5, 1967.
19. *Sankei* (Tokyo), May 31, 1967.
20. From a private source in Beijing.
21. See *Asahi* (Tokyo), May 1, 1967.
22. *Ibid.*, April 27, 1967.
23. *Yomiuri* (Tokyo), May 20, 1967.
24. "The Strongest Protest," Shijiazhuang wall posters, June 13, 1967, *SCMP (Supp.)*, No. 195 (July 31, 1967), pp. 18–19; *Sankei* (Tokyo), June 9, 1967.
25. *Mainichi* (Tokyo), May 31, 1967.
26. "Appalling Bloody Incident of June 6," Selected Big-Character Posters (Changsha), June 11, 1967, *SCMP (Supp.)*, No. 193 (July 21, 1967), pp. 3–6.
27. *Asahi* (Tokyo), June 9, 1967; *Mainichi* (Tokyo), June 10, 1967.
28. "A Cruel Scene," Selected Big-Character Posters (Changsha), June 11, 1967, *SCMP (Supp.)*, No. 193, p. 9.
29. "Letter of Accusation to the People of the Whole Country," untitled Red Guard newspaper, July 3, 1967, *SCMP*, No. 197 (August 14, 1967), pp. 31–35.
30. "Whither China?" January 6, 1968, *Printing System Red Flag*, March 1968, Union Research Service (Hong Kong), Vol. 51, Nos. 19 and 20, June 7, 1968. See also John Gittings, "Student Power in China," *Far Eastern Economic Review*, June 27, 1968, pp. 648–50.
31. Cited in *February Seven News* (Henan), June 5, 1967.
32. "Ho Yun-hung's Underground Twelve Black Articles," handbill distributed in Zhengzhou, April 12, 1967.
33. *February Seven News* (Henan), June 5, 1967.
34. Parris H. Chang, "The Revolutionary Committee in China," *Current Scene*, VI, No. 9 (June 1, 1968), p. 12.
35. Zhengzhou Radio, May 25, 1967.
36. "Long Premeditated Counter-Revolutionary Incident," *The East Is Red* (Beijing), June 7, 1967, *SCMP (Supp.)*, No. 192, (July 17, 1967), pp. 16–17.
37. "Fragrant Plants Thrive in Blood-Bathed Honan," *February Seven News* (Henan), June 5, 1967, in *ibid.*, pp. 22–23.

38. Zhengzhou Radio, May 26, 1967.
39. *Tokyo Shimbun,* June 2, 1967.
40. "The Hearts of Revolutionary Rebels Are Linked Together," *The East Is Red* (Beijing), June 7, 1967, *SCMP (Supp.)*, No. 192, pp. 19–21.
41. *Mainichi* (Tokyo), June 2, 1967.
42. Zhengzhou Radio, May 30, 1967.
43. *Ibid.,* June 1, 1967.
44. "Cudgels Cannot Strike Down Heroes Nor Can Spears Pierce the 'West Honan Group,'" *West Honan Combat Bulletin* (June 30, 1967), *SCMP (Supp.)*, No. 197 (August 14, 1967), pp. 6–7.
45. "Heroic and Tenacious Are the Young Revolutionary Fighters of the 'August Sixteen' Corps" *ibid.,* p. 15.
46. See *The Washington Post,* June 3, 1967.
47. Chang, *op. cit.,* p. 18.
48. "Important Speeches of Central Leaders on March 15, 1968," *SCMP,* No. 4181 (May 20, 1968), p. 2; *China Topics* (Hong Kong), August 11, 1967.
49. Thomas J. Matthews, "The Cultural Revolution in Szechwan," (unpublished manuscript.) June 1971.
50. "Speeches at the Meeting for Reading the Chinese Communist Party Central Committee's Decision on the Handling of the Szechwan Question," *August 26 Gunfire* (Beijing), May 12, 1967, *SCMP (Supp.)*, No. 190 (July 6, 1967), p. 31.
51. "Chinese Communist Party Central Committee's Notice on the Rehabilitation of Comrade Lin Chieh-ting of Ipin District Party Committee, Szechwan Province," April 4, 1967, *Special Issue of Reference Material* (Guangzhou), May 1968, *SCMP,* No. 4196 (June 12, 1968), p. 5.
52. *Asahi* (Tokyo), May 1, 1967.
53. Kyoto News Agency (Tokyo), May 8, 1967.
54. *Sankei* (Tokyo), May 18, 1967.
55. "Red Blood, Heroic Epic," *Red Flag News* (Beijing), May 22, 1967, *SCMP (Supp.)*, No. 189 (June 30, 1967), pp. 11–16.
56. "Only Sacrifice Can Show Your Strong Determination," *Red Flag News* (Beijing), May 22, 1967, *ibid.,* pp. 1–10; "Greet the New High Tide in the Cultural Revolution in Szechwan," *August 26 Gunfire* (Beijing), May 12, 1967, *SCMP (Supp.)*, No. 190, pp. 23–26.
57. "Decision of the Chinese Communist Party Central Committee on the Handling of the Szechwan Question," May 7, 1967, *August 26 Gunfire* (Beijing), May 12, 1967, *SCMP (Supp.)*, No. 190, pp. 20–23.
58. "Speeches at the Meeting . . . on the Handling of the Szechwan Question," *ibid.,* p. 27.
59. *Ibid.,* pp. 29–30.
60. *Ibid.,* pp. 31–34.
61. *Ibid.,* p. 28.
62. "Important Speeches of Central Leaders on March 15, 1968," *SCMP,* No. 4181, pp. 1–10.
63. *Ibid.,* p. 5.
64. *Yomiuri* (Tokyo), May 9, 1967.
65. *Sankei* (Tokyo), May 23, 1967.

66. *Nihon Keizai* (Tokyo), May 23, 1967; "News from Chengtu," *Corps Combat News* (Beijing), May 30, 1967, *SCMP (Supp.)*, No. 191, (July 14, 1967), p. 6.
67. "Statement of Congress of Red Guards on Surrendering of Arms and Ammunition," *ibid.*, pp. 13–14.
68. Matthews, *op. cit.*
69. Stanley Karnow, *The Washington Post*, August 6, 1967.
70. "News in Brief," *Storm Over Chungking*, June 14, 1967, *SCMP (Supp.)*, No. 192 (July 17, 1967), p. 2.
71. Matthews, *op. cit.*
72. *The New York Times*, June 16, 1967.
73. *Sankei* (Tokyo), June 23, 1967.
74. *Yomiuri* (Tokyo), June 8, 1967.
75. *The Washington Post*, May 25, 1967.
76. *South China Morning Post* (Hong Kong), June 15, 1967.
77. From an interview with Wu Shuding, former director of Zhonghua Book Company, a Communist firm, following his defection to Taiwan, August 22, 1967.
78. Anthony Dicks, "The Hong Kong Situation," an Institute of Current World Affairs Study, September 5, 1967.
79. *South China Morning Post* (Hong Kong), May 1, 8, and 28, 1967.
80. Stanley Karnow, *The Washington Post*, May 19, 1967.
81. *Ibid.*, July 9, 1967.
82. *Ibid.*, July 10, 1967.
83. *Tiger Standard* (Hong Kong), August 21, 1967.
84. *South China Morning Post* (Hong Kong), August 25, 1967.
85. Yang Kwong, "Welcome to Greater Victory," speech delivered in Hong Kong, September 30, 1967, from a private source.
86. "Why Is *Hung-wei-chun* Said to Be an Illegal Organization," *Revolutionary Tower* (Shanghai), March 10, 1967, *SCMP (Supp.)*, No. 184 (May 24, 1967), pp. 21–22.
87. Shanghai Radio, June 9, 1967.
88. *Asahi* (Tokyo), July 23, 1967.
89. *Ibid.*, July 13, 1967.
90. "Circular Order of the Chinese Communist Party Central Committee, the State Council, the Central Military Commission, and the Cultural Revolution Group Concerning the Strict Prohibition of Armed Struggle, Illegal Arrest, and Looting and Sabotage," June 6, 1967; *Chinese Communist Party Documents of the Great Proletarian Revolution, op. cit.*, pp. 463–64.
91. Bridgham, *op. cit.*, p. 22.
92. *Ibid.*, p. 23; Joffe, *op. cit.*, p. 16.

Chapter 16. Explosion on the Yangzi

1. Kunming Radio, July 3, 1967.
2. Roderick MacFarquhar, *The Hundred Flowers* (London, 1960), pp. 130ff.
3. Thomas W. Robinson, *The Wuhan Incident: Local Strife and Provincial*

Rebellion During the Cultural Revolution (The Rand Corporation, Santa Monica, Calif., December 1970), pp. 11–12.

4. William Whitson, "The Field Army in Chinese Communist Military Politics," *China Quarterly*, No. 37 (January–March 1969), pp. 1–30.
5. From an interview conducted by the author with William Whitson.
6. Deborah S. Davis, "The Cultural Revolution in Wuhan," unpublished manuscript; *Who's Who in Communist China* (Hong Kong, 1969), p. 399; "Truth of Persecution of Comrade Li Ta by T'ao Chu and Wang Jen-chung," *Outcry Combat Bulletin* (Guangzhou), January 1968, *SCMP*, No. 4141 (March 19, 1968), pp. 1–13.
7. Davis, *op. cit.*
8. Wuhan Radio, September 16, 1966.
9. *Ibid.*, January 9, 1967.
10. *Ibid.*, February 3, 1967.
11. "A Brief Introduction to the Various Organizations in the Wuhan Area," *Second Steel Headquarters Thunderstorm*, July 27, 1967, *SCMP (Supp.)*, No. 202 (September 11, 1967), pp. 9–11.
12. *Ibid.*, pp. 9–11; see also Robinson, *op. cit.*, p. 11.
13. "Speeches by Central Leaders at Reception of Tseng Ssu-yü, Liu Feng, and Other Comrades of the Wuhan Military District," June 12–13, 1968, *Hung-ssu Tung-hsin* (Guangzhou), July 12, 1968.
14. Wuhan Radio, February 18, 1967.
15. *Mainichi* (Tokyo), May 22, 1967.
16. *Yomiuri* (Tokyo), June 16, 1967.
17. "Wuhan Is in Critical Danger," *Red Rebel Headquarters* (Guangzhou), July 15, 1967; "Some Iron-clad Proof of Ch'en Tsai-tao's Engineering of Counter-Revolutionary Rioting," combined edition of *Kang-erh-szu* and *Wei Tung* (Wuhan), July 25, 1967; both in *SCMP (Supp.)*, No. 202 (September 11, 1967), pp. 17–18.
18. "Most Solemn Declaration on the Wuhan Situation," a Beijing wall poster, June 25, 1967.
19. "Some Iron-clad Proof of Ch'en Tsai-tao's Engineering of Counter-Revolutionary Rioting," pp. 18–19.
20. *Sankei* (Tokyo), September 29, 1967.
21. *Ibid.*
22. "Notes on Chairman Mao's Two Visits to Wuhan," *Cultural Revolution Bulletin* (Guangzhou), April 1968, *SCMP*, No. 4172 (May 7, 1968), pp. 11–14.
23. *Sankei* (Tokyo), September 29, 1967; Robinson, *op. cit.*, p. 16; "The Wuhan Storm—An Account of the July 20 Incident," *Red Flag of the Peking Aeronautical Institute*, July 29, 1967.
24. "Important Talks of the Central Committee Leaders," *Chingkangshan* (Beijing), July 26, 1967, *SCMP (Supp.)*, No. 199 (August 24, 1967), p. 29.
25. Robinson, *op. cit.*, p. 17.
26. "The Wuhan Storm . . ."
27. Robinson, *op. cit.*, p. 19; "Important Talks of the Central Committee Leaders," p. 29.
28. Robinson, *loc. cit.*

29. *Sankei* (Tokyo), September 29, 1967; Robinson, *loc. cit.*
30. Stanley Karnow, *The Washington Post*, July 26, 1967.
31. "How Did Comrade Wang Li Escape from Danger?" Red Guard tabloid of the Wuhan New China Technical College, Kaiping edition, September 16, 1967, published by Union Research Service (Hong Kong), Vol. 48, No. 23 (September 19, 1967).
32. "The Wuhan Storm . . ."
33. *Sankei* (Tokyo), September 29, 1967; quoted in Robinson, *op. cit.*, p. 20.
34. *Ibid.*
35. New China News Agency, July 28, 1967; *People's Daily* (Beijing), July 29, 1967.
36. Robinson, *op. cit.*, p. 24.
37. New China News Agency, July 29, 1967.
38. Stanley Karnow, *The Washington Post*, August 1, 1967.
39. Guangzhou Radio, August 4, 1967; see also Robinson, *op. cit.*, p. 26.
40. *Nihon Keizai* (Tokyo), October 15, 1967.
41. *Sankei* (Tokyo), September 29, 1967.
42. See "An Account of the Struggle Against the Counter-Revolutionary Element Ch'en Tsai-tao," *Third Headquarters Combat Bulletin* (Guangzhou), November 3, 1967, Union Research Service (Hong Kong), Vol. 49, No. 13 (November 14, 1967).
43. *Journalistic Soldiers* (Guangzhou), November 9, 1967.
44. "Speeches by Central Leaders at Reception of Tseng Ssu-yü, Liu Feng, and other Comrades of the Wuhan Military District."
45. "Attack by Reasoning, Defend by Force," undated leaflet, Lhasa, *SCMP (Supp.)*, No. 220 (March 8, 1968), p. 18.
46. See *ibid.*; *Sankei* (Tokyo), August 22, 1967; *Tokyo Shimbun*, August 31, 1967.
47. New China News Agency, July 25, 1967.
48. *People's Daily* (Beijing), July 30, 1967.
49. *Red Flag*, July 30, 1967; *People's Daily* (Beijing), *Liberation Army Daily* (Beijing), July 31, 1967.
50. *China News Summary* (Hong Kong), July 27, 1967.
51. Jian Youshen, *China's Fading Revolution* (Hong Kong, 1969), pp. 68–72.

Chapter 17. The Guns of August

1. A Beijing wall poster, August 14, 1967.
2. See *Tokyo Shimbun*, August 31, 1967.
3. *Ibid.*, and *Sankei* (Tokyo), August 22, 1967.
4. Jinan Radio, July 31, 1967; Stanley Karnow, *The Washington Post*, August 3, 1967.
5. Qingdao Radio, August 12, 1967; Jinan Radio, August 11, 1967.
6. "Important Talks of the Central Committee Leaders," *Chingnangshan* (Beijing), July 26, 1967, *SCMP (Supp.)*, No. 199, August 24, 1967, p. 24.

7. Ceteka News Agency (Prague), August 4, 1967.
8. Thomas J. Matthews, "The Cultural Revolution in Szechwan," unpublished manuscript.
9. Agence France-Presse, August 30, 1967.
10. Jian Youshen, *China's Fading Revolution* (Hong Kong, 1969), p. 27.
11. "Important Talks of Central Committee Leaders," *SCMP (Supp.)*, No. 199, p. 24.
12. New China News Agency, August 20, 1967.
13. "Stalemate in Szechwan," *Current Scene*, VI, No. 11 (July 1, 1968), p. 10.
14. Matthews, *op. cit.*
15. "Speech by Comrade Chang Ku-hua at Meeting Inaugurating and Celebrating the Szechwan Provincial Revolutionary Committee," *Szechwan Daily*, June 2, 1968, *SCMP (Supp.)*, August 19, 1968, p. 14.
16. Gordon A. Bennett and Ronald N. Montaperto, *Red Guard* (New York, 1971), p. 184.
17. "Canton Urgently Calls," *New South Uprooting Revisionism* (Guangzhou), July 28, 1967, *SCMP (Supp.)*, No. 199 (August 24, 1967), p. 7.
18. "An Eyewitness Account of the Tragic Case of Bloodshed on July 23," *The East Is Red* (Guangzhou), August 2, 1967, *SCMP (Supp.)*, No. 201, (September 5, 1967), pp. 1ff.
19. Bennett and Montaperto, *op. cit.*, p. 200.
20. "Premier Chou En-lai Receives Representatives of Canton Revolutionary Rebel Groups in Peking," *No. Three Headquarters Combat Bulletin*, August 24, 1967, *SCMP*, No. 4041 (October 13, 1967), pp. 11–13.
21. Bennett and Montaperto, *op. cit.*, p. 197.
22. *Sankei* (Tokyo), August 13, 1967; *South China Morning Post* (Hong Kong), August 14, 1967.
23. *Asahi* (Tokyo), August 23, 1967; *Sankei* (Tokyo), September 28, 1967.
24. Stanley Karnow, *The Washington Post*, August 18, 1967.
25. Bennett and Montaperto, *op. cit.*, pp. 201–202.
26. *China Topics* (Hong Kong), January 1968.
27. Liu Shaoqi, "Self-Examination," July 9, 1967, *Collected Works* (Hong Kong, 1969), pp. 369–77.
28. *Tokyo Shimbun*, August 3, 1967; *Sankei* (Tokyo), September 26, 1967.
29. *Asahi* (Tokyo), August 4, 1967.
30. See *Sankei* (Tokyo), and *Tokyo Shimbun*, August 16, 1967.
31. Stanley Karnow, *The Washington Post*, August 25, 1967.
32. *Sankei* (Tokyo), August 16, 1967.
33. Anne F. Thurston, *Enemies of the People* (New York, 1987), pp. 148ff.
34. I am indebted to Warren Unna for this information.
35. "Speech of Comrade Sydney Rittenberg, an American Friend, at an Oath-taking Rally for the Thorough Destruction of the Sinister Headquarters of Liu and Teng," *Corps Combat News* (Guangzhou), May 8, 1967.
36. "A Mysterious American," *Cultural Revolution Bulletin*, March 1968, SCMP, No. 4165 (April 26, 1968), pp. 1–3.
37. "Bring to Public Notice Wang Li's August 7 Speech," *Red Guard Paper*

(Beijing), October 18, 1967, *SCMP (Supp.)*, No. 214 (December 27, 1967), pp. 6–9.

38. Melvin Gurtov, *The Foreign Ministry and Foreign Affairs in China's Revolution*, a Rand Corporation memorandum (Santa Monica, Calif., March 1969), p. 54.

39. Stanley Karnow, *The Washington Post*, August 24, 1967.

40. Gurtov, *op. cit.*, pp. 58–61.

41. Stanley Karnow, *The Washington Post*, August 24, 1967.

42. Agence France-Presse, August 22, 1967; *Hong Kong Standard*, August 23, 1967; *Sankei* (Tokyo), October 3, 1967.

43. See Seymour Topping, *The New York Times*, June 21, 1971.

44. See William W. Whitson, *The Political Dynamics of the Chinese Communist Military Elite* (privately printed, Hong Kong, 1969), p. 35.

45. "Deputy Supreme Commander Lin's Important Directive," August 9, 1967, *Chu-ying Tung-fang-hung* (Guangzhou), *SCMP*, No. 4036.

46. *Ibid.*, p. 3.

47. *Ibid.*, pp. 5–6.

48. Whitson, *op. cit.*, p. 37.

49. *Journalistic Soldiers* (Guangzhou), November 6, 1967.

50. New China News Agency, September 2, 1967.

51. Jian, *op. cit.*, p. 70.

52. *Sankei* (Tokyo), August 12, 1967.

53. Jian Youshen, *loc. cit.*

54. "Drag Out Yao Teng-shan, Big Political Pickpocket," *Red Guard Paper* (Beijing), September 15, 1967, *SCMP (Supp.)*, No. 213 (December 13, 1967), pp. 4–5.

55. Seymour Topping, *The New York Times*, June 21, 1971.

56. "Order Issued by the Chinese Communist Party Central Committee, the State Council, Central Military Affairs Committee, the Central Cultural Revolution Group Forbidding Seizure of Arms, Equipment and Other Military Supplies from the People's Liberation Army," September 5, 1967, *SCMP*, No. 4026, September 22, 1967, pp. 1–2.

57. This and the following quotations from "Speech by Chiang Ch'ing on September 5 When the Central Leaders Received Anhwei Representatives for the Third Time," *Chingkang Mountains* (Beijing), September 20, 1967, *SCMP (Supp.)*, No. 209 (November 3, 1967), pp. 1–5; see also *China Topics* (Hong Kong), September 1967, and Stanley Karnow, *The Washington Post*, September 24, 1967.

58. *China Topics* (Hong Kong), September 1967.

59. Parris H. Chang, "The Fallen Idols," *Far Eastern Economic Review*, August 22, 1968, p. 352.

60. From a private source in Beijing.

Chapter 18. Dialectics in Action

1. Lin Biao, "Report to the Ninth National Congress of the Communist Party of China," April 14, 1969, New China News Agency, April 27, 1969.

2. Kang Sheng, "Summaries of Speeches by Members of the Central Cultural Revolution Group at an Enlarged Meeting of the Peking Revolutionary Committee," September 1, 1967, *China Topics* (Hong Kong), September 1967 (appendix).

3. "Great Supreme Commander Inspects Kiangsi Province," *Politics and Law Red Flag* (Guangzhou), October 17, 1967, *SCMP*, No. 4070 (November 30, 1967), p. 6.

4. "Chairman Mao's Latest Supreme Instructions During His Inspection Tour in Central and Southern Parts of China," *ibid.*, p. 3.

5. *Rural Youth* (Shanghai), October 25, 1967, Union Research Service (Hong Kong), Vol. 49, p. 138.

6. "Chairman Mao's Latest Instructions," *Cultural Revolution Bulletin* (Guangzhou), October 9, 1967, in *SCMP*, No. 4060 (November 15, 1967), pp. 1–2; "Chairman Mao's Latest Supreme Instructions During His Inspection Tour . . ." *SCMP*, No. 4070, p. 3.

7. "Chairman Mao's Latest Instructions," *SCMP*, No. 4060, pp. 1–2.

8. New China News Agency, September 26, 1967.

9. *People's Daily* (Beijing), September 9, 1967.

10. "Important Speeches of Central Leaders," September 17, 1967 (Guangzhou: Pearl River Movie Studio, October 1, 1967), Union Research Service (Hong Kong), Vol. 49, 91–94.

11. "Premier Chou's Speech to the Representatives of the Mass Organizations of the Canton Area," September 27, 1967, *Red Rebel Paper* (Lhasa), October 12, 1967, *SCMP (Supp.)*, No. 215 (January 19, 1968), pp. 1–12.

12. See *China Topics* (Hong Kong), October 26, 1967.

13. Zhejiang Radio, September 17, 1967.

14. Beijing Radio, September 19, 1967.

15. Hunan Radio, October 13 and 20, 1967.

16. New China News Agency, September 12, 1967.

17. *China News Summary* (Hong Kong), October 5, 1967.

18. "Important Speeches of Central Leaders," September 17, 1967, Union Research Service, Vol. 49, p. 92.

19. Jack Chen, "Treason at the Top," *Far Eastern Economic Review*, July 17, 1971, pp. 21–23.

20. *China Topics* (Hong Kong), September 1967.

21. *China News Summary* (Hong Kong), September 20, 1967.

22. See Stanley Karnow, *The Washington Post*, October 30, 1967.

23. *China News Summary* (Hong Kong), December 14, 1967; January 4, 1968.

24. Stanley Karnow, *The Washington Post*, January 11, 1968.

25. Philip Bridgham, "Mao's Cultural Revolution: The Struggle to Seize Power," *China Quarterly*, No. 41 (January–March 1970), p. 5.

26. "Speeches by Leaders of Central Committee," Guangzhou pamphlet, October 1967, quoted in *ibid.*, p. 6.

27. "Chairman Mao's Latest Supreme Instructions . . ." *SCMP*, No. 4070, p. 3.

28. "Vice-Premier Hsieh Fu-chih's Important Speech on Questions of 'Ninth Party Congress' and 'Party Organization,'" October 26, 1967, *Cultural*

Revolution Bulletin (Guangzhou), December 11, 1967, *SCMP*, No. 4097 (January 11, 1968), pp. 1–2.

29. Jurgen Domes, "The Role of the Military in the Formation of Revolutionary Committees," *China Quarterly*, No. 44 (October–December 1970), pp. 122–23.

30. *Ibid.*, pp. 126–131.

31. Private sources in Hong Kong.

32. New China News Agency, October 20, 1967.

33. Shanghai Radio, February 12, 1968.

34. Henan Radio, February 14, 1968.

35. Anhui Radio, January 16, 1968.

36. Inner Mongolia Radio, January 20, 1968.

37. *China Topics* (Hong Kong), May 21, 1968.

38. "Premier Chou's Talk at a Reception for Revolutionary Masses of X X Industrial Systems," *Cultural Revolution Storm* (Guangzhou), February 1968, *SCMP*, No. 4148 (March 28, 1968), pp. 3–9.

39. *Wen Hui Pao* (Shanghai), September 16, 1967.

40. Anhui Radio, January 19, 1968.

41. *Wei Hui Pao* (Shanghai), January 11, 1968.

42. Henan Radio, February 24, 1968.

43. William Whitson, "The Political Dynamics of the Chinese Communist Military Elite," unpublished manuscript, p. 45.

44. John Gittings, "Student Power in China," *Far Eastern Economic Review*, June 27, 1968, p. 648.

45. "Whither China?" January 6, 1968, *Printing Red Flag* (Guangzhou), March 1968, *SCMP*, No. 4190 (June 4, 1968), pp. 1–18.

46. Quoted in Gittings, *op. cit.*, p. 650.

47. Whitson, *op. cit.*, p. 39.

48. *Wen Hui Pao* (Shanghai), December 31, 1967.

49. *Ibid.*, March 29, 1968.

50. Anhui Radio, April 26, 1968.

51. Shanghai Radio, June 11, 1968.

52. "Nine-Point Instructions Given by Vice Supreme Commander Lin During His Reception of All Comrades of the Party Committee of the Air Force," *Cultural Revolution Bulletin* (Guangzhou), March 1968, *SCMP*, No. 4164 (April 25, 1968), p. 6.

53. *Wen Hui Pao* (Shanghai), June 6, 1968.

54. "Important Speeches by Central Leaders on March 15," publisher and date unknown, *SCMP*, No. 4181 (May 20, 1968), p. 9; "Important Speeches by Central Leaders on March 18," *Red Rebel Corps*, Yingde Middle School, Guangdong, *SCMP*, No. 4182 (May 21, 1968), p. 8.

55. "Speeches by Communist Leaders," *East Is Red* (Guangzhou), April 1968, *SCMP*, No. 4168 (May 1, 1968), p. 4.

56. "Important Speeches by Central Leaders at 100,000-Man Rally in Peking on March 27," *Pearl River Film Studio East Is Red* (Guangzhou), April 1968, *SCMP*, No. 4172, May 7, 1968, p. 2.

57. "Yang Cheng-wu's Eight Major Crimes," unnamed tabloid, May 1968, *SCMP*, No. 4168, May 27, 1968, pp. 1–5.

58. "An Important Speech by Vice-Chairman Lin at Reception of Army

Cadres on March 25," *Kung-lien* (Guangzhou), April 1968, *SCMP*, No. 4173 (May 8, 1968), pp. 2–4.

59. Whitson, *op. cit.*, p. 44.
60. "If Nieh Jung-chen Does Not Surrender, He Will Be Exterminated," *September 16 Bulletin* (Beijing), August 1968, *SCMP*, No. 4240 (August 16, 1968), p. 3.
61. New China News Agency, July 31, 1967.
62. Ellis Joffe, "The Chinese Army in the Cultural Revolution: The Politics of Intervention," *Current Scene*, VIII, No. 8 (December 7, 1970), pp. 20–21.
63. "An Important Speech by Vice-Chairman Lin Piao at a Reception . . . ," p. 2.
64. *Ibid.*, p. 9.
65. Domes, *op. cit.*, pp. 143–45.

Chapter 19. The Storm Before the Calm

1. *Wen Hui Pao* (Shanghai), March 26, 1968.
2. Agence France-Presse, January 31, 1968.
3. *China News Summary* (Hong Kong), January 31, 1968.
4. "Niu Hui-lin and His Like, Who Stirred Up Armed Struggle to Undermine Chairman Mao's Great Strategic Plan, Deserve a Myriad Deaths," *New Peking University* (Beijing), March 30, 1968, *SCMP (Supp.)*, No. 224 (May 6, 1968), pp. 23–27.
5. Agence France-Presse, April 28, 1968.
6. Xie Fuzhi, "Speech to 13th Plenum of the Peking Municipal Revolutionary Committee," May 15, 1968, *Cultural Revolution Bulletin* (Guangzhou), July 1968, in *China News Summary* (Hong Kong), July 8, 1968.
7. "Important Speeches by Central Leaders on March 15," publisher and date unkonwn, *SCMP*, No. 4181 (May 20, 1968), p. 2.
8. "Premier Chou's Speech to Representatives of the Mass Organizations of Canton Area," September 27, 1967, *Red Rebel Paper* (Lhasa), October 12, 1967, *SCMP (Supp.)*, No. 215 (January 19, 1968), p. 3.
9. "Summary of Second Meeting of Representatives of all Mass Organizations of Canton Area Who Have Returned to Canton from Peking," publisher and date unknown, *SCMP*, No. 4106 (January 24, 1968), pp. 1–4.
10. "Flag Faction Thugs, Abominable Deeds in No. 3 Middle School," *Red Flag Revolutionary Rebel Headquarters of Chiangmen Municipal No. 3 Middle School,* December 15, 1967, *SCMP*, No. 4108 (January 26, 1968), pp. 4–5.
11. "Record of Joint Examination of Chen Kuo-hsung," December 19, 1967, *ibid.*, p. 7.
12. "A Political Conspiracy to Sabotage the Establishment of Provincial and Municipal Revolutionary Committees," *Committee of the Municipal Automobile Repair Workshop under the Workers Revolutionary Alliance,* February 28, 1968, *SCMP*, No. 4144 (March 22, 1968), pp. 1–3.
13. *Southern Daily* (Guangzhou), February 23, 1968.

14. *South China Morning Post* (Hong Kong), February 23, 1968.

15. From interviews conducted by the author in Hong Kong.

16. Stanley Karnow, *The Washington Post*, June 30, 1968.

17. *China News Summary* (Hong Kong), June 20, 1968.

18. Reuters, June 17, 1968.

19. *South China Morning Post* (Hong Kong), June 27, 1968.

20. From Communist sources in Hong Kong.

21. Stanley Karnow, "Letter from Hong Kong," *Encounter*, April 1969, p. 89.

22. From private sources in Hong Kong.

23. "Crime of Wuchow Rebel Army in Violating the Ten-Point Agreement," *Voice of Proletarians* (Wuzhou), December 30, 1967, *SCMP*, No. 4110 (February 2, 1968), p. 1.

24. "Decision Concerning the Question of Kwangsi," *Red Rebels*, Jiangmen (Guangdong), December 4, 1967, *SCMP* No. 4157 (April 11, 1968), pp. 1-3.

25. "Urgent Dispatch from Kweilin," *Voice of Proletarians* (Wuzhou), December 30, 1967, *SCMP*, No. 4113 (February 7, 1968), p. 4.

26. *Ibid.*, p. 5.

27. Joint Investigation Group of the December 6 Incident, December 9, 1967, Union Research Service (Hong Kong), Vol. 29, No. 26 (December 29, 1967).

28. "True Story of Counter-revolutionary Incident in Jungan County, Kwangsi," *April 22 Bulletin* (Liuzhou), May 29, 1968, *SCMP*, No. 4202 (June 20, 1968), *SCMP*, No. 4223 (June 22, 1968), pp. 1-3.

29. "In Various Parts of Kwangsi," *Angry Waves of the West River* (Guangzhou), June 1968, pp. 16-18.

30. "A General Mobilization Order for Counter-revolutionary Massacre," *Angry Waves of the West River* (Guangzhou), June 1968, *SCMP*, No. 4215 (July 11, 1968), p. 1.

31. "Message to the People of the Whole Country," *Grand Army Bulletin* (Guangzhou), July 1968, *SCMP*, No. 4235 (August 9, 1968), pp. 5-7.

32. "Liuchow Revolutionary Rebel Grand Army Proposes Ten Measures for Stopping Armed Struggle," *Grand Army Bulletin* (Guangzhou), July 1968, *SCMP*, No. 4234 (August 8, 1968), pp. 7-8.

33. "Message to the People of the Country," *Angry Waves of the West River* (Guangzhou), June 1968, *SCMP*, No. 4220 (July 18, 1968), pp. 7-13.

34. See Karnow, "Letter from Hong Kong," p. 86.

35. See Stanley Karnow, *The Washington Post*, August 30, 1968.

36. *Sing Tao* Daily (Hong Kong), August 13, 1968.

37. "Dispatch from Kwangsi," *Political Department of Kwangsi Alliance Command*, July 3, 1968, *SCMP*, No. 4224 (July 24, 1968), pp. 1-2.

38. Stanley Karnow, *The Washington Post*, July 3, 1968.

39. "Chinese Communist Party Central Committee's New Directive on the Kwangsi Problem," *Revolutionary Rebel Forces* (Liuzhou), July 12, 1968, *SCMP*, No. 4226 (July 26, 1968), pp. 1-2.

40. "Important Instructions by Leaders of the Chinese Communist Party Central Committee, and Central Cultural Revolution Group at Reception of Comrades from Mass Organizations and Army Cadres from Kwangsi,"

July 1968, *Kwangsi Branch Office of Mao Tse-tung Thought Study Class*, July 26, 1968, Union Research Service (Hong Kong), Vol. 53, No. 9 (October 29, 1968).

41. "Chinese Communist Party Central Committee's New Directive on Kwangsi Problem," p. 3.

42. "Notice of the Chinese Communist Party Central Committee, State Council, Military Commission and Central Cultural Revolution Group," *Middle School Red Guards* (Guangzhou), July 1968, *SCMP*, No. 4232 (August 6, 1968), pp. 1–3.

43. "Important Instructions by Leaders . . . at a Reception of Comrades from Kwangsi."

44. "Notice by Chinese Communist Party Central Committee, State Council, Military Affairs Commission, and Central Cultural Revolution Group," *East Wind Workers* (Guangzhou), August 1, 1968, *SCMP*, No. 4258 (September 16, 1968), pp. 1–3.

45. "Important Instructions by Leaders . . . at a Reception of Comrades from Kwangsi."

46. Stanley Karnow, *The Washington Post*, August 28, 1968.

47. John Gittings, "Kwangtung: Anatomy of a Clamp-Down," *Far Eastern Economic Review*, September 5, 1968, pp. 464–65.

48. Gordon A. Bennett and Ronald N. Montaperto, *Red Guard* (New York, 1971), p. 183.

49. "Chou En-lai Refutes Wu Chuan-pin," *Sun Yat-sen University Combat News* (Guangzhou), August 7, 1968.

50. "Minutes of a Meeting Held by the Provincial Revolutionary Committee on the Afternoon of July 31," *Workers Commentaries* (Guangzhou), August 1968, SCMP, No. 4265, September 25, 1968, pp. 1–10.

51. *Ming Pao* (Hong Kong), September 2, 1968.

52. Kirin Radio, July 23, 1968.

53. Stanley Karnow, *The Washington Post*, August 13, 1968.

Chapter 20. The Road to Recovery

1. New China News Agency, August 6 and 8, 1968; Stanley Karnow, *The Washington Post*, August 10, 1968.

2. New China News Agency, August 14, 1968.

3. Jurgen Domes, "The Role of the Military in the Formation of Revolutionary Committees," *China Quarterly*, No. 44 (October–December 1970), pp. 137–42.

4. New China News Agency, July 31, 1968.

5. *Ibid.*, August 1, 1968.

6. "Vice-Premier Hsieh's Seven-Point Directive to the Mao Thought Propaganda Team at Tsinghua University," private source in Beijing.

7. "Clear Away Obstacles to Greet the Workers' Army Marching into the Institutes of Higher Learning," *Red Guard Combat Bulletin* (Shanghai), August 25, 1968, *SCMP (Supp.)*, No. 235 (September 23, 1968), pp. 1–4.

8. "No Mischievous Acts Will Be Allowed!," *Red Guard Combat Bulletin* (Shanghai), August 15, 1968, *ibid.*, p. 14.
9. Chengdu Radio, September 4, 1968.
10. Shaanxi Radio, August 8, 1968.
11. Private source in Hong Kong.
12. Zhejiang Radio, August 13, 1968.
13. *Ibid.*, August 31 and September 11, 1968.
14. Stanley Karnow, *The Washington Post*, February 21, 1969.
15. Private source in Hong Kong.
16. New China News Agency, December 23, 1968.
17. *China Reporting Service* (Hong Kong), February 6, 1969; New China News Agency, December 22, 1969.
18. New China News Agency, January 21, 1969.
19. *Ibid.*, January 22, 1969.
20. Stanley Karnow, *The Washington Post*, December 10, 1969.
21. "Chairman Mao Sends His Son to Participate in Agricultural Production," *Red Guard Combat News* (Shanghai), December 30, 1968.
22. *China Topics* (Hong Kong), August 27, 1970; *The New York Times*, September 24, 1970.
23. I am indebted to John Pattison of Melbourne, Australia, for this report.
24. Stanley Karnow, *The Washington Post*, April 13, 1969.
25. Based on interviews in Hong Kong.
26. *People's Daily* (Beijing), January 19, 1969.
27. Private sources in Hong Kong.
28. Stanley Karnow, *The Washington Post*, May 7, 1969.
29. Stanley Karnow, *The Washington Post*, June 3, 1970.
30. New China News Agency, October 10, 1969.
31. Colina MacDougall, "The Cultural Revolution in the Countryside: Back to 1958?" *Current Scene*, Vol. VII. No. 7 (April 11, 1969), pp. 7–10; Philip Bridgham, "Mao's Cultural Revolution in 1967: The Struggle to Seize Power," *China Quarterly*, No. 34 (April–June 1968), pp. 9–10.
32. *Red Flag*, August 25, 1968.
33. Bridgham, *op. cit.*, p. 10.
34. New China News Agency, November 24, 1968.
35. *Ibid.*, August 25, 1968.
36. Stanley Karnow, *The Washington Post*, October 19, 1968.
37. Anne F. Thurston, *Enemies of the People* (New York, 1987), pp. 151–53.
38. *Ibid.*, pp. 126–30.
39. "Vice-Premier Hsieh Fu-chih's Important Speech on Questions of 'Ninth Party Congress' and 'Party Organization'," October 26, 1967, *Cultural Revolution Bulletin* (Guangzhou), December 11, 1967, *SCMP*, No. 4097 (January 11, 1968), p. 2.
40. Henan Radio, November 19, 1968.
41. *Ibid.*, December 5, 1968.
42. *Wen Hui Pao* (Shanghai), October 18, 1968.
43. *Ibid.*, October 19, 1968.
44. *Ibid.*, October 8, 1968.
45. *Ibid.*, October 18, 1968.

46. *Ibid.*
47. *People's Daily* (Beijing), September 30, 1968.
48. Shanghai Radio, February 6, 1969.
49. *People's Daily* (Beijing), February 20, 1969.
50. *Ibid.*, May 3, 1969.
51. John Gittings, "Lin Piao's Gospel," *Far Eastern Economic Review,* May 8, 1969, p. 335.
52. New China News Agency, April 27, 1969; Gittings, *op. cit.*, pp. 336–37; *China Topics* (Hong Kong), May 19, 1969.
53. *Tokyo Shimbun,* October 27, 1969.
54. New China News Agency, April 28, 1968; *China Topics* (Hong Kong), January 22, 1968.
55. New China News Agency, April 28, 1968.
56. Donald W. Klein and Lois B. Hager, "The Ninth Central Committee," *China Quarterly,* No. 45 (January-March 1971), pp. 41–42.
57. *China Topics* (Hong Kong), November 18, 1969.
58. Stanley Karnow, *The Washington Post,* August 29, 1969.
59. *Ibid.*, see also *The New York Times,* September 3, 1969.
60. Moscow Radio, March 27, 1970; *Hong Kong Standard,* March 25, 1970.
61. Stanley Karnow, *The Washington Post,* June 4, 1970.
62. *Ibid.*, May 21, 1970.
63. New China News Agency, October 1, 1969.
64. *Ibid.*, September 30, 1969; *China News Summary* (Hong Kong), September 25, 1969, and October 2, 1969.
65. *People's Daily* (Beijing), November 5, 1969.
66. Stanley Karnow, *The Washington Post,* November 11, 1969.
67. *Ibid.*
68. *China News Summary* (Hong Kong), September 25, 1969.
69. Lee Lescaze, *The Washington Post,* December 16, 1970.
70. New China News Agency, December 16, 1969.
71. *China News Summary* (Hong Kong), November 21, 1969.
72. Guangdong Radio, November 23, 1969.
73. *Red Flag,* January 5, 1970.
74. Lee Lescaze, *The Washington Post,* February 18, 1971; *The New York Times,* August 26, 1971.
75. Private source.
76. *The New York Times,* August 8, 1971.
77. *Peking Review,* July 2, 1971, p. 20.
78. Jiang Qing, "Do New Services for the People," April 13, 1967, *The East Is Red* (Beijing), June 3, 1967, *SCMP (Supp.)*, No. 192 (July 17, 1967), p. 8.
79. See Stanley Karnow, *The Washington Post,* November 10 and 27, 1971.
80. *The New York Times,* October 8, 1971.
81. Private sources in Washington.
82. Beijing Radio, October 20, 1971.
83. Ningxia Radio, November 5, 1971.
84. *People's Daily* (Beijing), November 2, 1971.
85. I am indebted to Colonel William Whitson for this analysis.
86. *Peking Review,* No. 50, December 10, 1971, p. 5.

Chapter 21. Rejoining the World

1. *The New York Times*, July 16, 1971.
2. *Red Flag*, August 16, 1971.
3. See John K. Fairbank, "China's Foreign Policy in Historical Perspective," *Foreign Affairs*, April 1969, pp. 451–53.
4. *Asahi Shimbun* (Tokyo), August 1, 1964; *Sekai Shuho* (Tokyo), August 11, 1964.
5. *People's Daily* (Beijing), May 9, 1964.
6. Stanley Karnow, *The Washington Post*, March 12, 1969.
7. Cited *ibid.*, October 13, 1968.
8. V. M. Khvostov, "The Chinese 'Account' and Historical Truth," *Mezhdunarodnaya Zhizn*, October 1964, quoted in John Gittings, *Survey of Sino-Soviet Dispute* (London, 1968), pp. 165–66.
9. "Soviet Government Statement," September 21, 1963, in *ibid.*, p. 162.
10. *People's Daily* (Beijing), September 6, 1963.
11. Stanley Karnow, *The Washington Post*, March 12, 1968.
12. Vladimir Dedijer, *Tito* (New York, 1953), p. 322; see also *Mainichi* (Tokyo), March 9, 1967; *Red Flag*, January 5, 1964.
13. *Mainichi* (Tokyo), March 9, 1967.
14. Gittings, *op. cit.*, p. 14.
15. New China News Agency, October 26, 1954; Gittings, *op. cit.*, p. 19.
16. *People's Daily* (Beijing), September 1, 1963.
17. *Pravda* (Moscow), September 21, 1963.
18. Quoted in Gittings, *op. cit.*, p. 331.
19. *Red Flag*, January 5, 1960.
20. *People's Daily* (Beijing), December 4, 1963.
21. Gittings, *op. cit.*, pp. 175–76.
22. *People's Daily* (Beijing), August 15, 1963.
23. See Donald Zagoria, *Vietnam Triangle* (New York, 1967), pp. 105–111.
24. Quoted *ibid.*, p. 111.
25. *People's Daily* (Beijing), November 11, 1965.
26. Stanley Karnow, *The Washington Post*, September 10, 1969.
27. "Letter of the Chinese Communist Party Central Committee to the Central Committee of the Communist Party of the Soviet Union," July 14, 1965, Gittings, *op. cit.*, p. 263.
28. Allen Whiting, "How We Almost Went to War with China," *Look*, April 29, 1969.
29. Private sources.
30. Lin Biao, "Long Live the Victory of People's War," quoted in Uri Ra'anan, "Peking's Foreign Policy Debate 1965–1966," Ping Ti-ho and T'ang Tsou, eds. *China in Crisis* (Chicago, 1968), pp. 54ff.
31. Stanley Karnow, *The Washington Post*, August 22, 1967.
32. *The Washington Post*, October 13, 1967.
33. *Hoc Tap* (Hanoi), May 1967.
34. Stanley Karnow, *The Washington Post*, October 2, 1968.
35. A. Doak Barnett, *A New U.S. Policy Toward China* (Washington, D.C., 1971), p. 5.
36. *Ibid.*, pp. 7–8.

37. *The China White Paper*, August 1969 (Stanford, Calif.), p. xvi.
38. Allen Whiting, *China Crosses the Yalu* (New York, 1960), pp. 34–46.
39. Kenneth T. Young, *Diplomacy and Power in Washington-Peking Dealings, 1953–1967* (Chicago, 1967), p. 12.
40. Stanley Karnow, *The Washington Post*, July 25, 1971.
41. *The New York Times*, December 14, 1963.
42. *Ibid.*, January 29, 1964.
43. *People's Daily* (Beijing), February 19, 1964.
44. Stanley Karnow, *The Washington Post*, July 25, 1971.
45. *Ibid.;* Barnett, *op. cit.*, p. 16.
46. Melvin Gurtov, *The Foreign Ministry and Foreign Affairs in China's Revolution*, a Rand Corporation memorandum (Santa Monica, Calif., March 1969), pp. 66–68.
47. *People's Daily* (Beijing), November 3, 1968.
48. Edgar Snow, "A Conversation with Mao Tse-tung," *Life*, April 30, 1971.
49. Stanley Karnow, *The Washington Post*, September 30, 1969.
50. Private sources in Beijing.
51. *The New York Times*, May 24, 1969.
52. Inner Mongolia Radio, November 11, 1969.
53. *Kommunist*, Moscow, June 26, 1968.
54. Moscow Radio, December 31, 1967; Moscow Radio, May 26, 1968.
55. See Stanley Karnow, *The Washington Post*, December 2, 1968; Associated Press, February 3, 1969.
56. *The New York Times*, June 14, 1969.
57. Stanley Karnow, *The Washington Post*, August 3, 1968.
58. New China News Agency, August 22, 1968; *People's Daily* (Beijing), August 23, 1968.
59. New China News Agency, September 30, 1968.
60. *Ibid.*, September 16, 1968.
61. *Izvestia* (Moscow), November 2, 1968.
62. New China News Agency, November 26, 1968.
63. *South China Morning Post* (Hong Kong), December 1, 1968.
64. New China News Agency, November 26, 1968.
65. *People's Daily* (Beijing), October 16, 1967.
66. New China News Agency, November 26, 1968.
67. Stanley Karnow, *The Washington Post*, November 26, 1968.
68. Moscow Radio, November 29, 1968.
69. *Ibid.*, December 13, 1968.
70. Associated Press, August 6, 1968.
71. Stanley Karnow, *The Washington Post*, July 16, 1971.
72. Don Oberdorfer, *The Washington Post*, April 23, 1971; John Osborne, "Signals to Mao," *The New Republic*, May 1, 1971; Stanley Karnow, "The Meaning of Nixon's China Coup," *The Progressive*, September 1971.
73. Associated Press, April 22, 1969.
74. Edith Lenart, "U.S.–China: The Matchmakers," *Far Eastern Economic Review*, August 21, 1971, pp. 14–15.
75. Edith Lenart, "Backdoor to China," *Far Eastern Economic Review*, August 21, 1969.

76. Stanley Karnow, *The Washington Post*, February 20, 1969.
77. Moscow Radio, March 8, 1969; *New Times* (Moscow), May 18, 1969.
78. See Thomas W. Robinson, *The Sino-Soviet Border Dispute: Background, Development and the March 1969 Clash* (Rand Corporation Study, Santa Monica, Calif., August 1970), pp. 41–71.
79. *Ibid.*, pp. 38–40.
80. From interviews conducted by the author in Khabarovsk.
81. *The New York Times*, June 12, 1969.
82. Stanley Karnow, *The Washington Post*, August 20, 1969.
83. *The New York Times*, August 14, 1969.
84. Tass, March 30, 1969.
85. New China News Agency, May 24, 1969.
86. Tass, March 30, 1969.
87. Reuters, March 19, 1969.
88. Stanley Karnow, *The Washington Post*, March 6, 1969.
89. *Ming Pao* (Hong Kong), March 5, 1969.
90. Stanley Karnow, *The Washington Post*, May 16, 1969.
91. *The New York Times*, March 11, 1969.
92. *South China Morning Post* (Hong Kong), April 22, 1969.
93. Private source in Hong Kong.
94. *Sing Tao* (Hong Kong), September 12, 1969.
95. *China News Summary* (Hong Kong), August 15, 1969.
96. Stanley Karnow, *The Washington Post*, October 15, 1969.
97. *Ibid.*
98. *The New York Times*, November 21, 1969.
99. Private sources in Hong Kong.
100. Hungarian News Agency MTI, Budapest, January 16, 1970.
101. Stanley Karnow, *The Washington Post*, December 4, 1969.
102. Private sources in Hong Kong.
103. *Liberation Army Daily* (Beijing), November 27, 1969.
104. Jiangxi Radio, July 31, 1969.
105. *China News Summary* (Hong Kong), July 1, 1969.
106. Heilongjiang Radio, July 7, 1969.
107. See Stanley Karnow, *The Washington Post*, December 19, 1969.
108. *Ibid.*, September 11, 1969; *China Topics* (Hong Kong), January 28, 1970.
109. Agence France-Presse, November 16, 1969.
110. Stanley Karnow, *The Washington Post*, October 9, 1969.
111. Victor Louis, "Will Russian Rockets Czech-mate China?" *Evening News* (London), September 16, 1969.
112. Reuters, December 6, 1969.
113. *The Sunday Times* (London), October 6, 1968.
114. *The New York Times*, September 12, 1969.
115. Sanzo Nosaka, Japanese Communist Party Chairman, *Kyodo* (Tokyo), September 12, 1969.
116. *Nhan Dan* (Hanoi), September 1, 1969; *The New York Times*, September 12, 1969.
117. New China News Agency, September 11, 1969.
118. *The New York Times*, September 25, 1969.

119. Stanley Karnow, *The Washington Post*, October 10, 1969.
120. *Ibid.*, October 8, 1969.
121. Private sources in Washington.
122. Lee Lescaze, *The Washington Post*, May 21, 1971.
123. *The New York Times*, October 14, 1970.
124. *Ibid.*, November 21, 1970.
125. *Ibid.*, September 17, 1971.
126. Associated Press, September 5, 1969.
127. *Ibid.*, February 19, 1970.
128. Edgar Snow, "Aftermath of the Cultural Revolution," *The New Republic*, April 10, 1971, p. 18.
129. *The New York Times*, April 8, 1971.
130. Snow, "A Conversation with Mao Tse-tung."
131. *The New York Times*, April 30, 1971.
132. *Al-Jumhuriyah* (Cairo) November 18, 1971.
133. Tass, August 10, 1971.

Chapter 22. Continuing Turmoil

1. Harry Harding, *China's Second Revolution: Reform After Mao* (Washington, D.C., 1987), p. 11.
2. *Loc. cit.*
3. Mao Zedong, "Reply to Comrade Kuo Mo-jo," *Ten More Poems of Mao Tse-tung* (Hong Kong, 1967), p. 14.
4. As quoted in Stanley Karnow, "China Through Rose-Tinted Glasses," *The Atlantic Monthly*, October 1973.
5. Edgar Snow, "A Conversation with Mao Tse-tung," *Life*, April 30, 1971.
6. Stanley Karnow, *The Washington Post*, July 6, 1970; *The New York Times*, May 31, 1971.
7. Harding, *op. cit.*, p. 30.
8. Edgar Snow, "The Open Door," *The New Republic*, March 27, 1941.
9. Harding, *op. cit.*, p. 30.
10. *Red Flag*, August 22, 1971.
11. *The New York Times*, May 7, 1971.
12. Harding, *op. cit.*, p. 49.
13. Anne F. Thurston, *Enemies of the People* (New York, 1987), p. 108.
14. Lucian Pye, "Hostility and Authority in Chinese Politics," *Problems of Communism*, May-June 1968, pp. 10–22.
15. Nien Cheng, *Life and Death in Shanghai* (New York, 1986), p. 437.
16. *Ibid.*, pp. 458ff.
17. Thurston, *op. cit.*, pp. 5ff.
18. *Ibid.*, pp. 20ff; Cheng, *op. cit.*, pp. 470ff.
19. Harding, *op. cit.*, pp. 50–51; Cheng, *op. cit.*, p. 437.
20. Cheng, *op. cit.*, pp. 458ff.
21. Thurston, *op. cit.*, pp. 5ff; Harding, *op. cit.*, p. 52; Fox Butterfield, *China: Alive in a Biter Sea* (New York, 1982), p. 357.
22. Harding, *op. cit.*, pp. 56–57.
23. *Ibid.*, pp. 61–62.

24. Jan S. Prybyla, "China's Economic Experiment: Back from the Market," *Problems of Communism,* January–February 1989, p. 3.

25. Louise do Rosario, "Rural Reforms Outstrip Those in the Cities," *Far Eastern Economic Review,* October 5, 1989, pp. 51ff.

26. Richard Hornik, "The Road to Reform," in *Massacre in Beijing: China's Struggle for Democracy* (New York, 1989), pp. 105–6.

27. *Ibid.,* p. 108.

28. *Ibid.,* p. 113; Prybyla, *op. cit.,* p. 30; *The Wall Street Journal,* October 29, 1985.

29. Hornik, *op. cit.,* p. 109; *The Wall Street Journal,* June 16, 1989.

30. *The Wall Street Journal, op. cit.*

31. Jaime Florcruz, "Long Live the Students!" in *Massacre in Beijing,* pp. 123ff.

32. *Ibid.,* pp. 135ff.

33. *Ibid.,* pp. 150–53; *The Washington Post,* August 20, 1989.

34. *The New York Times,* June 30, 1989.

35. Fred C. Shapiro, "Letter from Beijing," *The New Yorker,* June 19, 1989.

36. *The Economist,* September 2, 1989.

37. The most dramatic American television reports of the events in Beijing were those of Dan Rather on CBS. The best newspaper accounts were those of Nicholas D. Kristof and Sheryl WuDunn in *The New York Times* and Daniel Southerland in *The Washington Post.* A valuable retrospective, filled with vivid detail, is David Aikman, "The Battle of Beijing," in *Massacre in Beijing,* pp. 31–69.

38. *The New York Times,* June 30, 1989.

39. *The Economist,* September 2, 1989; Sandra Burton, "The Crackdown," in *Massacre in Beijing,* pp. 213ff.

40. Burton, *op. cit.,* pp. 219–21; *The New York Times,* October 12, 1989.

41. Burton, *op. cit.,* p. 222; *The New York Times,* October 11, 1989.

42. *The New York Times,* June 30, 1989.

43. *Ibid.,* October 30, 1989.

44. *Ibid.,* October 20, 1989.

45. *Ibid.,* October 16, 1989.

46. *Far Eastern Economic Review,* September 28, 1989; *The Economist,* September 19, 1989.

47. Howard G. Chua-Eoan, "A Cry Heard Around the World," in *Massacre in Beijing,* p. 177; *Far Eastern Economic Review,* September 21, 1989; *The Wall Street Journal,* September 15, 1989.

48. *The New York Times,* December 19, 1989; *The Washington Post,* December 20, 1989; *The New York Times,* December 20, 1989; *The Economist,* December 16, 1989.

49. *The Economist,* October 14, 1989.

INDEX